FOUNDATION PRESS

INTELLECTUAL PROPERTY STORIES

Edited By

JANE C. GINSBURG
Professor of Law
Columbia University School of Law

ROCHELLE COOPER DREYFUSS
Professor of Law
New York University School of Law

FOUNDATION PRESS
2006

Cover Design: Keith Stout

395 Hudson Street
New York, NY 10014
Phone Toll Free 1–877–888–1330
Fax (212) 367–6799
foundation-press.com
Printed in the United States of America

ISBN–13: 978–1–58778–727–0
ISBN–10: 1–58778–727–X

INTELLECTUAL PROPERTY STORIES

FOUNDATION PRESS

INTELLECTUAL PROPERTY STORIES

*

Introduction and Overview

Jane C. Ginsburg and Rochelle Cooper Dreyfuss

For the previous generation of legal academics, intellectual property was, if not *terra nullius*, fairly underpopulated relative to other disciplines. But matters have changed significantly in recent years. The American economy has evolved into one based more on knowledge production than on manufacturing, technology has transformed the methods of distributing information, and globalization has led to greater appreciation for the cultural production of other countries. This includes not only works of authorship, such as music, films, and literature, but also trademarks and trade symbols. The shift toward an information economy has also put new emphasis on the scientific enterprise and the marketing of its output. Interest in copyrights, trademarks, and patents—in practice and among scholars, nationally and internationally—has grown apace.

This book reflects the emergence of intellectual property as an academic subject. Twenty years ago, it would have been difficult to obtain the participation of fifteen nationally-recognized full-time members of the intellectual property professorate. The cases examined here have not, by and large, been marked by the accretion of modern scholarship that characterizes many of the other topics in the STORIES series. Even the subject of the book needs explanation: while copyright, patent, trademark and unfair competition are conventionally conjoined—perhaps to give the field more heft—is the combination coherent? After all, few lawyers' practices encompass all of these.

Nonetheless, these subjects share certain characteristics. Because all these legal regimes cover intangibles that can be enjoyed "non rivalrously"—that is, without depriving other consumers of equal benefit—they require justification. And since exclusivity may not be appropriate for every intangible, each regime must articulate its threshold qualifications. Each of these fields carries the potential for conflict between the goals of protection and other social values, notably freedom of speech and of competition. In some instances, there are also conflicts internal to the field: where the justification rests on encouraging innovation, too little protection may fail to propel further development; but knowledge is cumulative, and too much protection may thwart its advance. These fields are also shaped by technology, and must continue to respond to technological change. This is most apparent in copyright, which was born in part of the printing press, and now confronts the Internet. But it is also true of the others. New developments in science impel reconsideration of the content, scope and application of patent law. In trademarks and unfair competition, new goods and services make once-distinct product lines converge, while new modes of communication generate new methods of advertising, and bring once-distant markets closer.

INTELLECTUAL PROPERTY STORIES is organized into six chapters, each drawing on cases in patents, copyrights, trademarks, or unfair competition, to illustrate the problems intellectual property law encounters. The works, inventions, and marks at issue in these cases vary widely. In Chapter 1, Justifications for Intellectual Property Protection, *International News Service v. Associated Press* discusses the right to control transmissions of World War I news bulletins from the East to the West Coasts. *Wheaton v. Peters* concerns copyright ownership of reports of decisions of the United States Supreme Court. In Chapter 2, Creativity and Inventiveness, *Bleistein v. Donaldson Lithographing Co.* raises the question of the copyrightability of commercial art (circus posters). The *Story of Graham v. John Deere Company* presents three inventions, a plow, a resealable cap for an insecticide sprayer, and a battery, and asks whether each achieves the level of inventiveness required to merit patent protection. In Chapter 3, Freedom of Ideas and of Competition, *Baker v. Selden* considers the copyrightability of a system of bookkeeping. *Diamond v. Diehr* explores the effects of patents on the production of computer software. *Kellogg Co. v. National Biscuit Co.* examines trademark protection in the context of generic and functional symbols: the name of the Shredded Wheat biscuit and its pillow shape. In Chapter 4, Scope of Protection, *Folsom v. Marsh* takes us back to the birth of the Republic to examine the scope of copyright protection for George Washington's letters. *Graver Tank and Mfg. Co. v. Linde Air Prods. Co.* looks at patent scope in the context of a welding flux. In Chapter 5, Responses to Technological Change, *Sony v. Universal Studios* takes up the question of facilitating and encouraging copyright infringement through the sale of mass market copying equipment, the videotape recorder. *Diamond v. Chakrabarty* examines the patentability of genetically modified microorganisms. Finally, in Chapter 6, International Dimensions of Protection, *Steele v. Bulova* deals with the extraterritorial application of US trademark law to watches manufactured and sold in Mexico.

Many of the Stories illustrate more than the issue identified in the chapter title. Thus, it is possible to confine one's reading to an individual intellectual property regime, and still encounter most of the issues common to the whole field. However, we believe that each of the Stories is written in a manner that will interest and instruct intellectual property students and scholars across the breadth of the field, without requiring particular knowledge of any of its specialized branches. For example, we believe students of patent law would learn from and enjoy the copyright *Story of Baker v. Selden*, just as students of any field would appreciate the international implications of the trademarks *Story of Steele v. Bulova.*

Each Story may be viewed from several perspectives. They chronicle a variety of creative endeavors, but often tell broader tales as well. Several Stories offer considerable human interest, deriving from the historically notable or simply curious character of the parties, their lawyers, or the judges in the case. *Wheaton* and *Folsom* provide insights into the Framers' intellectual goals, as well as into the close-knit society of writers, publishers, statesmen and judges in the early Republic. Indeed, a subplot emerges from these two Stories: the Story of Justice Story. *Kellogg* glimpses into a very different world, an "odd mix of evangelists armed with even odder theories of nutrition and health." But this Story, especially viewed together with *INS*, includes a subplot of its own: the Story of Justice Brandeis' intellectual property and antitrust jurisprudence. Similarly, *Bleistein* reveals the artistic yearnings of the young Oliver Wendell Holmes, Jr.

Some Stories tell compelling socio-economic tales. They provide a glimpse of americana, and they are best appreciated in light of the particular place and time in which the disputes emerged. For example, *Bleistein* recounts the significance of circuses as rural entertainment in 19th-century America, and the efforts of German immigrants to succeed in the market for advertising these spectacles, using lithography techniques developed in the old country. It also confronts high and low art, through the ostentatiously ecumenical perspective of one of our more highbrow jurists. *Graham v. John Deere* addresses an invention inspired by adversity, "the Plow to Save the Plains," farm machinery designed to spare Dust Bowl farmers the effects of severe wind erosion. If *Deere* celebrates overcoming natural forces, by contrast, lurking in *Diamond v. Chakrabarty* is public fear of intervening to correct or improve nature's course.

Several of these are "war" stories. Some involve war in the literal sense, with subject matter devised or popularized in response to wartime needs, such as the welds at issue in *Graver Tank*, and the watches counterfeited in *Bulova*. Wartime supplied the backdrop for *INS*, which concerned the transmission of news bulletins reporting from the World War I Western Front. In other instances, the "war" is metaphorical. For example, *Sony* pits modes of exploitation against each other, and in *INS*, the parties were vying for control of new media of communication. *Diehr* illustrates the tensions between hardware manufacturers and software designers over the kind of legal protection that best would serve the computer industry.

The Stories also illustrate problems at the boundaries between legal regimes. *Wheaton* implicates the relationship of statutory law to common law or natural law. *Baker* addresses the dangers of overlap between copyright and patent. It shows why the copyright law, to which the Constitution assigns the role of promoting the progress of "science" by encouraging the dissemination of learning, should not be interpreted to do so at the expense of science's counterpart in promotion, the useful arts. *Kellogg* offers a similar moral, though this time trademark, rather than copyright, law threatened the encroachment into the realm of patent law. *Baker*, *Diehr* and *Kellogg*, along with the broader dispute between INS and AP, touch on the tensions between monopoly rights and competition, incentives to create and public access.

In other Stories legal institutions conflict. In both *Diehr* and *Chakrabarty*, patent courts battled the Patent Office. More significantly, as told here, *Chakrabarty* marks an institutional watershed, a shift in the "burden of inertia." While once it may have fallen to Congress to declare the inclusion of a category of inventions within the ambit of statutory protection, after *Chakrabarty* courts have taken on that role; it seems that Congress' function now is to exclude categories of inventions from patentability. Sovereign authorities also come into contact in these Stories: Mexico and the United States in *Bulova*, federal and state law in *Kellogg* and, indirectly, in *INS*.

We chose these cases for the long shadow they have cast over intellectual property law. As the Stories demonstrate, however, sometimes the shape of the shadow does not match that of its progenitor. For example, neither scholars nor courts appear aware that the parties concocted the dispute in *INS* in order to establish a property right in the transmission of the news. *Baker* has meant different things at different times, as each generation of litigants and judges have construed the case through the prism of their technological concerns. The meaning of the Supreme Court's decision in *Sony* has developed most dramatically: initially viewed as a case about fair use, it evolved for a time into a charter for copyright-free technological development. After the Supreme Court's decision in *Grokster* (whose grant of certiorari postdates our selection of *Sony* for IP STORIES), it would now seem that *Sony* does not condone the promotion of technologically-assisted piracy. But *Grokster* declined to resolve whether the *Sony* standard should be understood to favor technological advancement over the protection of creators' rights, and has doubtless introduced ambiguities of its own.

* * *

When we read the collected Stories, we were pleasantly surprised to see that, without intent aforethought, we had selected cases whose outcomes divided fairly evenly between upholding protection (*INS, Bleistein, Diehr, Folsom, Graver Tank, Chakrabarty, Bulova*), and denying it (*Wheaton, Graham, Baker, Kellogg, Sony*). Even those decisions that afforded protection were sensitive to countervailing considerations, or elicited strong dissents, including by a Justice who was later vindicated (*INS, Kellogg*). Perhaps our cases are not fully representative of the 175 years of intellectual property litigation from which they were drawn because they posed difficult issues, often at the limits of the law as it was at their times. The golden glow of even-handedness that the Stories' assembly nonetheless imparts contrasts with today's widespread perception that intellectual property law leans too heavily in favor of rightholders. Certainly one can point to federal statutory developments in all three fields that provoke this view. For example, the copyright term has been extended, the Digital Millennium Copyright Act (DMCA) has created new violations; in trademarks the anti dilution act and Anti-cybersquatting Consumer Protection Act (ACPA) expand the scope of protection; with the establishment of the Federal Circuit, patents are now often found to be valid and infringed. Similarly, the entry of the United States into the Berne Convention and US implementation of the TRIPs Agreement have increased the availability and level of protection abroad. These international developments have also required that the United States provide greater protection at home, at least for foreign works.

Why this apparent disjunction between past cases and current developments? One answer may be that the perception of expansion is ill-founded. In fact, looking only at the statutes leaves three important elements out of the picture. First, for copyright and trademarks, technological changes largely subsequent to the cases recounted here have shifted the practical balance of power away from rightholders toward users and new exploiters. Provisions such as the DMCA and the ACPA may be restoring the alignment. Taking the pre-DMCA and pre-ACPA balance as somehow normatively compelled ignores the reality that intellectual property "balances" are highly contingent and contextual. Second, judicial decisions have occasionally limited the reach of statutory expansions, most notably in the area of dilution. Third, in some cases, federal protection has merely supplemented or replaced other law. Examples include the additions to federal copyright law to protect sound recordings and certain live performances, and trademark dilution, both of which mirror state laws. In addition, international protection for well-known marks would lead to the kind of outcome the plaintiff sought in *Bulova*.

Even if the perception of expansion is correct, and there is indeed, overall, more protection today than in the past, perhaps this development should be celebrated rather than deplored. It may be that, before, the level of legal protection was inadequate. For example, Congress may have created the Federal Circuit because regional federal appellate courts were overly skeptical of patent protection. On the international copyright scene, before it joined the Berne Convention, the United States was an outlier, virtually alone among nations in imposing formalities that divested authors of protection. Furthermore, the importance of knowledge-based products may call for more protection now, regardless of the adequacy of the old regime in its time. Because advances in computer software enhance productivity, perhaps they deserve the protection they are now receiving under the patent and copyright laws. Similarly, biotechnological products are contributing in new and important ways to medical research; therefore it may be desirable to encourage their creation through the patent system. Regarding the baseline of any one era as enduringly right and good misses the dynamic nature of innovation.

To the extent that intellectual property rights have expanded, several of the cases foreshadow that growth. Seeds were planted in *Bleistein* and *Folsom*, where courts strove to broaden the subject matter and scope of copyright protection, perhaps because the authors of the opinions were also authors of books. But some seeds may have sprung weeds. As its Story shows, *Diehr* proposed an unworkable solution; the PTO and the Federal Circuit proved unable to remain within the boundaries the court tried to set. Business method patents may be the most noxious of the nettles thus cultivated. In *Graham* the failure to articulate the policies underlying the test for non obviousness has led to the inability of the doctrine to identify inventions unworthy of protection. The horticultural characterization of *INS* remains uncertain; the decision's own agricultural metaphor suggests potential for doctrinal overrun, but courts routinely prune back its tendrils.

Of course, the legislature could impose more control over the development of intellectual property law. If Congress' tendency has been more often to lead the advance than to retreat, the political economy may be responsible. Intellectual Property owners have long been effective lobbyists, and now have an increasing population of lawyers to draw upon. But the public is becoming more aware of intellectual property through technological developments such as peer-to-peer file copying, books aimed at general audiences, and articles in the popular press. With a swelling cadre of commentators, among them those committed to cutting back, we may come to see a wider range of solutions proposed and adopted.

* * *

This volume benefited immensely from the discussions held in May 2004 at the Samuelson/Glushko Center, sponsored by the Berkeley Center for Law and Technology and by the Engelberg Center on Innovation Law and Policy at New York University School of Law. We are most grateful to Pam Samuelson and Bob Glushko for their hospitality. Not only did the conference create an opportunity to discuss the cases and identify their common themes and points of difference, it also provided a chance for the contributors to discuss the field as a whole and to contemplate its trajectory.

We would also like to thank Deborah Katz, NYU Class of 2007, for her editorial assistance. Finally, we wish to acknowledge our great debt to Nicole Arzt for a superb job organizing the conference held at Samuelson/Glushko Center, and for providing the administrative assistance that made it possible to complete this book.

*

1

Justifications for Intellectual Property Protection

The Story of *INS v. AP*: Property, Natural Monopoly, and the Uneasy Legacy of a Concocted Controversy

Douglas G. Baird*

International News Service v. Associated Press[1] has long occupied a prominent place in American legal education. As recounted in law school classrooms countless times, Associated Press and International News Service were rival wire services that spent millions gathering news, both in the United States and abroad, and disseminating it across the country. In 1916, INS began to copy AP bulletins as they appeared in East Coast papers and then wire them to the West Coast. INS newspapers there carried AP stories without attribution, even before their AP rivals. AP sued to stop this practice. It won in the Supreme Court on the ground that it enjoyed a "quasi-property" interest in the news it gathered and was entitled to the fruits of its labor.[2]

The case has appeared in many contexts. It was prominently featured in Henry Hart and Albert Sacks's *Legal Process*[3] materials, a

* I am grateful to Rochelle Dreyfuss, Jane Ginsburg, William Landes, Douglas Lichtman, Richard Posner, and Jonathan Silberstein–Loeb for helpful comments on an earlier draft. I owe the inspiration and many of the ideas for this essay to two extraordinary mentors in intellectual property—Paul Goldstein and Gerry Gunther.

1 248 U.S. 215 (1918).

2 Deciding the case in AP's favor required establishing a new legal principle. Copyright protects only expression, not underlying facts. Trade secret law protects news services from theft, but such protection disappears upon publication. Conventional unfair competition focuses on "passing off." As applied in this context, unfair competition law prevented INS from presenting its own news as that of AP, but INS was doing the opposite. It was presenting AP's news as its own.

3 Henry M. Hart & Albert M. Sacks, The Legal Process (2001).

mainstay of the first-year curriculum at Harvard and other law schools for decades. Hart and Sacks used the case to spark a classroom debate on the relative competence of judges and legislatures. Believers in the incremental power of common law reasoning argue against those who hold that the legislature is better equipped to balance competing public policies.

The case also serves to launch a general discussion on the nature of property rights. In the first-year property class, Lockeans who believe that property comes into being as a result of labor pit themselves against utilitarians who insist on weighing the costs and benefits of bestowing rights and denying them. The survey course on intellectual property uses *INS v. AP* to explore the tension dominating so much of intellectual property law: how to motivate creators to do their work while ensuring public access to the work once created.

INS v. AP, however, is not what it appears to be. In fact, the case has more to do with the regulation of a natural monopoly than with property rights. In the first part of the twentieth century, a wire service consisted primarily of a large network of leased telegraph lines. The expense of creating and maintaining such a network dwarfed the costs of actually gathering the information. These large fixed costs created a natural monopoly; how best to regulate it cannot be easily deduced from the principles that preoccupied the Justices who decided the case or the legal academics who have taught it.

Making matters more complicated, AP magnified its own market position through its membership in an international cartel that gave it exclusive rights to bulletins of foreign news services and exclusive access to official government communiqués. No one else could provide foreign news of comparable quality. In addition, under AP's by-laws, a newspaper entering the market of an existing AP member that wanted access to AP's wire service was subject to a veto from that member. AP members thereby protected their own market positions from competition from outsiders and from one another.

The litigation that generated *INS v. AP* was part of AP's larger program of navigating technological and economic change. AP's goals had little to do with INS. Indeed, contrary to the traditional account, there was no evidence that INS was copying bulletins on the East Coast and transmitting them to papers on the West Coast. The injunction AP sought (and eventually obtained) did not require INS to change its practices in any meaningful way—or indeed at all.

General principles can be tested and tempered only when they are squarely contested. Hence, it should come as no surprise that the "quasi-property" right in news that the Court discovered in *INS v. AP* came without any metes and bounds and proved nearly impossible to apply in later cases. Even as applied to AP, the contours of the right were unclear. Indeed, only a decade and a half before this litigation, AP had argued that a property right in news did not prevent exactly the sort of copying that, by its account, INS was doing.

Understanding how AP came to promote the idea of news as property as part of a strategy to deal with technological and economic change is the focus of the first part of this essay. The essay then turns to the peculiar relationship between INS and AP. It concludes with a brief examination of the reception the case received in the lower courts. That the Supreme Court saw only high principle is perfectly understandable: the Justices assumed, reasonably but wrongly, that the litigants before them were genuine adversaries. The hold that the case has had over legal academics, however, is much more troubling and shows starkly how using canonical cases to understand first principles is a hazardous business.

The McCullen Brothers Steal from Melville Stone

Melville Stone is the person most responsible for developing the idea of a property right in news and initiating the litigation in *INS v. AP.* He was preoccupied with the idea of a property right in news throughout his fifty-year career in journalism. The idea that news should be treated as property took hold while Stone was running the *Chicago Daily News* in the 1870s. Stone thought a set of norms should govern all newspaper editors. Among other things, they should not copy from one another. Papers ought to use their own resources to report on local as well as distant events.

In Stone's eyes, the McMullen brothers, who owned the rival *Post and Mail* in Chicago, were shameless pirates who epitomized everything that was wrong with journalism. Stone acquired stories at great expense, only to see them appear in the *Post and Mail* a few hours later. Stone's battle with the McMullens came to a head when Stone published the following story in the noon edition of his paper on December 2, 1876:

Sad Story of Distress in Servia

> London, Dec. 2—A correspondent of the *Times* writing from Servia, where he has spent many weeks, says that the country presents a gloomy picture to the traveler. The land is devastated and the people are starving.
>
> Everywhere he found men and women crying for food. He could see in any large village hundreds of young women in a state of semi-nudity. It has been a hard matter for the priests to keep the populace under their control. Children are starving by thousands throughout the country.

> The men, young and old, go through the streets shouting for bread, cursing the rich for not coming to their aid. A few days ago the mayor of the provincial town of Sovik issued a proclamation ending with the ominous words: "*Er us siht la Etsll iws nel lum cmeht*" (the municipality cannot aid).
>
> Upon reading this, the people, led by the women of the town, organized a riot, in the course of which a dozen houses were pillaged and over twenty persons were brutally murdered.[4]

The McMullens bought a copy of the *Chicago Daily News* a few minutes after it hit the streets, and by three o'clock they were running the same story in the *Post and Mail*. Apart from a new headline, "Horrid Starvation in Servia," the story copied the one in the *Daily News* word for word, including the mayor's formulaic confession of helplessness.

Stone had no avenue of legal redress. Common law copyright disappeared upon publication, and to enjoy federal copyright protection one needed to deposit a copy with the Registrar of Copyrights before publication. A daily newspaper in Chicago had no way of doing this. If Stone wanted to prevent the McMullens from copying the news, he had to take matters into his own hands. The McMullens soon discovered that self-help was a time-honored and often effective weapon. As it happened, the mayor of Sovik did not utter the ominous words, "*Er us siht la Etsll iws nel lum cmeht.*" Nor did any other Serbian official. The pronouncement is not even in Serbian, but rather in English—backward. The mayor is saying, "The McMullens will steal this sure."

Stone made up the story out of whole cloth in the expectation that the McMullens would steal it from him and, once exposed, become laughingstocks. He was right on both counts. However much the public might tolerate pirates, it had no fondness for ones so gullible. The McMullens' paper lost circulation and ceased publication within two years. Stone purchased the assets in a liquidation sale. These included a membership in AP, and thus began an affiliation that was to last for more than four decades.

When Stone became a member of AP, it was little more than a diverse set of regional newspapers willing to share the information each gathered. The impetus behind the organization is easy to understand. If two nearby towns have separate newspapers, residents will read only their own town's paper, but they still have some interest in what happens elsewhere. Circulation for each paper increases when they share news with one another. The only additional cost is that of transmitting the news from one town to the next.

---

[4] *See* MELVILLE E. STONE, FIFTY YEARS A JOURNALIST 63 (1921).

The benefits become greater when a number of newspapers in a region join. News coverage expands. Soon people expect regional as well as local news, and newspapers must belong to the service to remain competitive. The network becomes larger, and the quality of the information improves still more. But a way must be found to prevent a paying member from entering into side deals with nonmember papers that want access to the same news on the cheap. The news organization must lay down rules. At this point, however, the agreement can also facilitate collusion. Take, for example, a provision that prevents any member from using the news service for any new paper they begin in a town already served by an existing member. Such a provision is only a step short (if that) of an explicit agreement in which all the papers agree to stay out of one another's markets.

News services such as AP took shape in such a fashion during the second half of the nineteenth century. Limiting membership and reserving the right to expel those who violated the rules were essential features of the organization from the start. AP's contracts committed the newspapers to sharing their local news only with AP. Moreover, members enjoyed "franchise rights" that enabled them to blackball any new paper from becoming a member of AP within a given circulation area of the member's own paper.

As national news became increasingly important, the principal advantage of belonging to a news service lay in the economies of scale that existed in transmitting information across long distances. Getting national news to a small town in the Midwest required a large network of telegraph wires and many telegraph operators. Each dispatch had to be retransmitted as it went from one node on the network to another. Maintaining this infrastructure—leasing the telegraph lines and hiring telegraph operators—was expensive. This was AP's principal activity, not the gathering of information. Once such a network was created, there was no need for a second network. For this reason, AP fit the classic definition of a natural monopolist.[5]

Melville Stone became the head of AP in the early 1890s. At this time, the infrastructure was well established and what it needed most was someone to police its members more effectively and ensure they abided by its rules. Stone was the obvious choice. He was not much of a businessperson, but his convictions aligned perfectly with AP's self-interest. These included a hatred of pirates and a belief that AP's by-laws, far from being anticompetitive, were founded on high principle.

---

5 *See* Kenneth E. Train, Optimal Regulation: The Economic Theory of Natural Monopoly 1 (1991) ("a natural monopoly exists when the costs of production are such that it is less expensive for market demand to be met with one firm than with more than one").

Stone had an appetite for agreements that had the effect of preserving the competitive edge that AP papers enjoyed in the marketplace. Shortly after becoming the head of AP, Stone entered into an agreement with Reuters and other European news services in which AP acquired exclusive access to their news. This agreement gave AP a lead over any rivals in publishing foreign news, one that persisted for decades. The close affiliation between these foreign news services and the governments of their respective home countries also ensured that AP had exclusive access to government communiqués.

Among his contemporaries, Stone was the person most associated with the idea that the law should protect news as property.[6] Moreover, Stone did not limit his preaching to fellow journalists. Those in his social circle with any connection to law were subjected to lengthy lectures on Maine, Blackstone, Roman law, and rights in property.[7] The nature of the property in news that Stone wanted was distinctly tied to the characteristics of a wire service at the time. The story Stone fabricated to fool the McCullens underscores this point. In it, Stone's own paper is paraphrasing the *London Times*. Stone could have easily claimed to have a correspondent in Serbia (as opposed to one in London who merely read the newspapers there), yet it never occurred to him to do this. For Stone in 1876, copying from the *London Times* was entirely unobjectionable.

Stone took the same view when it came to actual controversies. During the Boer War, Stone had AP's London correspondent buy the *London Times*, copy its war news, and then cable it back to this country. The *Chicago Tribune*, which had paid the *London Times* for the exclusive right to carry its war news in the United States, sued on the ground that such copying was theft. Stone and AP took the opposite view and prevailed.[8]

Stone saw no inconsistency. In 1900, the heavy lifting in reporting distant events came from the cost of transporting information. Indeed, this is what made a wire service a natural monopoly. AP was primarily a transportation system, a network of wires and telegraph operators. It

---

[6] Among Stone's papers, for example, is a letter from a fellow journalist in 1883:

> I am anxious and curious to know how you are progressing with your plans to test ownership in news. It is growing more and more important.

STONE, *supra* note 4, at 358.

[7] *See id.* at 355–59.

[8] *See* Tribune Co. v. Associated Press, 116 F. 126, 127 (C.C.N.D. Ill. 1900). The court found that this controversy between "the rights of the Tribune Company to the fruits of its enterprise and expenditure under its contract arrangement with the Times, and, on the other hand, the rights of the public to the news matter thus published in the leading English newspaper" ultimately turned on copyright law. The case does not discuss misappropriation as an independent theory.

spent little time or effort in gathering information. The value of what it put into the wires was trivial compared to its value when it came out thousands of miles away. The "news" that came over AP wires during this period was a stream of raw facts and figures for local editors to shape into stories. It consisted of facts about shipping, markets, and sporting events, congressional reports, and whatever bits of ordinary information that found their way to the telegrapher.[9] Telegraph operators had little education. Their skill lay in quickly transmitting large amounts of information in a highly compressed form.

If one were in Washington, D.C., there was no magic in learning the outcome of a Supreme Court case. It was not important that the telegraph operator in Washington read about the decision in a local newspaper or learned about it by some other means. The trick was transmitting the information at low cost. A typical AP cable of the time read this way:

t scetus tdy dodd 5 pw f potus dz n xtd to t pips, ogt all pst cgsl xgn q sj is uxl.

The operator receiving the cable unpacked it and it became this:

> The Supreme Court of the United States today decided that the power of the President of the United States does not extend to the Philippines, on the ground that all past Congressional legislation on the subject is unconstitutional.[10]

The editor then took this story and expanded it further, drawing on existing information (such as the name of the case, the facts behind it, and likely fallout from the decision). When published, the story did not carry any attribution to AP and might look entirely different from the dispatch itself or from a story in another paper that used the same cable. The value of the information lay entirely in its transmission across great distances.

This notion was reinforced in *National Telegraph News Company v. Western Union Telegraph Company,* another case from the Seventh Circuit decided at about the same time as Stone's dispute with the *Chicago Tribune.*[11] One of the great technological marvels of the late nineteenth century was the telegraph ticker. It converted a telegraph signal into printed letters on long, narrow paper tapes. These "ticker tapes" made stock quotes available to brokers and banks. As the cost of telegraphy fell, tickers become more widespread. By 1900, hotels and saloons, for a modest monthly fee, leased tickers from Western Union so

---

[9] *See* STONE, *supra* note 4, at 210.

[10] *See* STONE, *supra* note 4, at 237–38.

[11] 119 F. 294 (7th Cir. 1902).

that patrons could learn baseball scores and racing results from other cities in close to real time. Western Union, however, soon faced a problem similar to the one Stone had with the McMullens. A company that distributed news only in Chicago bribed someone to gain access to a ticker and thereby acquired on the cheap whatever information Western Union brought to the city.

When Western Union brought an action to stop the practice, it had the good fortune to appear before Circuit Judge Peter Grosscup. Grosscup recognized the need for an injunction that prevented third parties from gaining unauthorized access to the information. To be sure, the immediate business of Western Union, one that catered to gamblers and grain speculators, did "not arouse any great solicitude," but this service was merely a manifestation of a great technological change, one that allowed events across the world to come, "almost instantly, into the consciousness of mankind." By this technological achievement, "the world [was] made to face itself unceasingly in the glass."[12] But all this was possible only if those who provided the service could enjoy a large enough return to justify their investment. The matter before Judge Grosscup could be reduced to a simple, almost rhetorical question:

> Is service like this to be outlawed? Is the enterprise of the great news agencies, or the independent enterprise of the great newspapers, or of the great telegraph and cable lines, to be denied appeal to the courts, against the inroads of the parasite . . . ?[13]

Judge Grosscup saw that Western Union was no different from a news service such as AP. Information—be it a sports score or an account of starvation in a foreign country—is itself free for anyone to gather. No one can claim an ownership interest in it at the source. But the news can be conveyed quickly across great distances only if a large infrastructure is in place. No one will build and maintain this infrastructure if the information cannot be protected at the other end. Western Union had a right to enjoin people who sought unauthorized access to the information sent out over its lines. Other courts, including the Supreme Court, were quick to follow Judge Grosscup.[14]

Peter Grosscup saw things in much the same way as Melville Stone. This was no accident. Grosscup and Stone were neighbors. Long before

---

[12] *Id.* at 300.

[13] *Id.* at 300–301.

[14] The Supreme Court adopted his position in *Board of Trade v. Christie Grain & Stock Co.*, 198 U.S. 236, 250–51 (1905):

> The plaintiff does not lose its rights by communicating the result to persons, even if many, in confidential relations to itself, under a contract not to make it public, and strangers to the trust will be restrained from getting at the knowledge by inducing a breach of trust and using knowledge obtained by such a breach.

the litigation, Grosscup had endured long winter evenings in which Stone lectured him on how property rights in the news ought to be recognized, and they continued to talk about the idea while the Western Union case was being litigated.[15]

In Stone's view, however, Judge Grosscup's opinion did not go far enough. It did not explicitly recognize a property right in news. An analogy helps to explain what Stone had in mind. Suppose a town is many miles from a large lake. The water in the lake is inexhaustible and free for anyone to take. An entrepreneur builds an aqueduct to bring water to the distant town and then sells it to the local residents. Water is protected once it is put into the aqueduct. If others tap into the aqueduct or bribe residents to redirect water intended for their own personal use to others, the entrepreneur can bring a conversion action. The stream of quotidian facts that coursed through AP's wires should be treated the same way.

While he lauded the result in cases such as *National Telegraph*, Stone wanted courts to do more than fit the cause of action awkwardly into the pigeonhole of tortious interference. Courts should treat information sent over a telegraph network as they would treat water sent through an aqueduct. Both should become the property of the person that transported them.

Stone did not understand the conflict between his notion of a property right in news and his belief that it was perfectly appropriate for AP to relay stories carried in London newspapers. This tension grew greater as the cost of transmitting information declined. Returning to the analogy, Stone's idea makes sense in a world in which aqueducts are expensive and water is plentiful at the source. It is perfectly coherent to talk about recognizing a property interest in water coming out of an aqueduct but not water going in. When the cost of transporting the water declines dramatically, however, everything changes. One must protect water as property everywhere or nowhere. So too when the cost of transmitting information falls.

Innovations in telegraphy did not stop with the ticker. Thomas Edison, Elisha Gray, and the other great inventors of the nineteenth century brought a host of other improvements. It became dramatically cheaper to transport information. As the cost of transporting information fell, it became hard to distinguish between reprinting news stories that appeared in a distant city (a practice Stone firmly thought unobjectionable) and taking stories from a local paper (a practice Stone believed morally repugnant).

---

15 *See* STONE, *supra* note 4, at 359–60.

Obtaining a property right in news that advanced AP's interests (or at least did not run counter to them) was tricky. Stone's quixotic and relatively unfocused belief that a court should find a property right in news would likely go nowhere without help. Fortunately, one of AP's rising stars, the man who would succeed Stone at the helm, was at hand. He understood far better than Stone the forces of technological change and how to reshape Stone's notion of a property right in news that would work to AP's advantage.

Kent Cooper Joins AP

By 1910, Stone had led AP for almost two decades, and he changed nothing. Everything from the furniture in his office to the contracts he signed was trapped in the nineteenth century. By one firsthand account, "[t]he place was not even pleasantly antique—it reeked with old age."[16] The board of AP was becoming frustrated with Stone.[17] His operation was losing money, and he did nothing about it. Only when his board pushed him did Stone hire someone to reduce the cost of AP's telegraph operations, something that was still consuming 75 percent of its expenses. This man was Kent Cooper.

Stone did little to help Cooper. On one trip, Cooper found that he could lease telephone wires and telegraph stories at one-fourth the price that AP was paying Western Union. But he had no authority to enter into such transactions on his own. When he wrote Stone for permission, Stone never bothered to respond. Exasperated, Cooper closed the deal anyway, half expecting Stone to fire him. Stone, however, received the news of the new contract with complete indifference. When Cooper asked why his letters went unanswered, Stone merely said, "I've always said that a lot of things will answer themselves in three weeks if no attention is paid to them."[18]

From this point onward, Cooper started taking action first and worrying about Stone's permission later. Cooper renegotiated contracts to take account of reduced transmission costs. In the space of a year, he reduced AP's costs by $100,000. Cooper also replaced telegraph operators with teletypes and improved the network. In October 1916, Cooper was able to have a single operator transmit a play-by-play account of the World Series directly to 700 newspapers throughout the country. This event was a milestone. Previously, messages had to be sent and resent a number of times to reach everyone. For the first time, there was a true countrywide network, and information spread at the speed of light. As

---

16 Kent Cooper, *Kent Cooper and the Associated Press: An Autobiography* 36 (1959).

17 *See id.* at 46.

18 *Id.* at 47.

Thomas Edison told Cooper at the time, AP had given the country "a real arterial system and it is never going to harden."[19]

Cooper knew that AP could not stand still. Reductions in costs for AP meant that they would decline for others as well. Rivals would replace telegraphs with teletypes too. Creating a network was becoming progressively cheaper. Providing an infrastructure for transmitting information was becoming too easy. To flourish, AP's business model had to change.

Only a month after the 1916 World Series, Cooper orchestrated a precinct-by-precinct tally of the presidential election. With it, AP became the first to establish that Woodrow Wilson had been reelected. Collating precinct-by-precinct vote counts was qualitatively different from sending whatever information was available over a network. Cooper understood that AP could assemble information and repackage it better than anyone else. Its existing network (and the various by-laws) gave it better access to domestic information, and its cartel agreement with foreign news services gave it an advantage with news from abroad. But these packages of information, once assembled and published, are easy for others to retransmit. Cases such as *National Telegraph* no longer provided sufficient protection.

To extend the reach of existing law, Cooper needed to go to court. But first he needed to find a suitable defendant. No one remotely resembling the McCullen brothers was on the scene. No one was lifting AP's stories and reproducing them wholesale. After AP carried a story, rival news services often ran ones that conveyed the same facts. But it was hard to show that they were copying rather than providing their own independent account of the same events. For example,[20] on December 11, 1916, AP received the following cable from its correspondent in London:

> British official report intermittent enemy shelling Ancre area nothing report night.

From this, AP created the following dispatch:

> Following is the official report of today from the Franco–Belgian front: "Aside from intermittent enemy shelling in the Ancre area, there was nothing to report last night."

The *New York Evening Journal*, which was not a member of AP, ran the following story some hours later:

---

[19] *Id.* at 72.

[20] *See* Supporting Affidavit of Melville E. Stone at 28, Associated Press v. International News Service, 240 F. 983 (S.D.N.Y. 1917) [hereinafter Stone Affidavit].

> Aside from intermittent shelling in the Ancre sector of the Somme Front, there is nothing to report, British War Office announced today.

The *Journal*'s story is similar and could have been lifted from the AP dispatch, but it does not bear any telltale signs of copying. Nothing prevented the *Evening Journal* from insisting that it had an independent source. Among other things, the *Journal*'s story had details (such as references to the Somme Front and the British War Office) not in the AP account.

Cooper did find a handful of instances in which the evidence of copying was stronger. In several cases, AP ran a story that omitted an eminent person's title or committed some other faux pas, and a rival newspaper soon carried a similar story that made the same mistake. The strongest example came when AP carried a story that mistook one person for another. One day AP sent the following story out on its wires with a Paris dateline:[21]

> President Poincare has awarded a gold medal to Mrs. Harry Duryea of New York for her services during the last two years as head of the American Aid Committee for War Victims.

The next day the *Washington Herald*, not an AP member, ran the following story, again with a Paris dateline.

> Mrs. Harry Duryea of New York was awarded a gold medal by President Poincare for her services in war relief work. Mrs. Duryea has been president of the American Aid Committee for two years. She returns to America tomorrow.

As it happened, Poincaré gave the award to New York socialite Nina Duryea, not her sister-in-law, Mrs. Harry Duryea. But even here, the case for copying is not watertight. Both papers might have been given the same misinformation from a common source. Indeed, the *Herald*'s story contained a detail—Duryea's return the next day to the United States—that AP's account did not. How could the *Herald* have known about Duryea's impending departure unless it had a correspondent on the scene? How could such a correspondent know about her departure but not about the medal? And if the *Herald* had such a correspondent, why would it have copied from AP?

Cooper did find one issue of a Georgia newspaper that copied a translation that AP made of an official French government report. The same issue had several other instances of copying of foreign government reports to which AP's agreements gave it exclusive access. But such isolated instances of copying, not of stories it wrote but of government reports, might not be sufficient to persuade a court that AP was entitled

[21] Stone Affidavit at 28–29.

to extraordinary relief. Among other things, AP would be asking for exclusive rights to government communiqués that it acquired not through hard work but through a cartel agreement. To establish a property right in news above and beyond what already existed, Cooper needed something more than stray instances of copying of government documents. He found such a case—in Cleveland.

Kent Cooper Goes to Cleveland

Late in the day on October 3, 1916, two streetcars collided on the West Third Bridge in Cleveland, killing two and injuring thirty others. The timing of the accident was particularly unfortunate for Fred Agnew, who ran the INS bureau in Cleveland. Part of his job was to report such stories to INS's main office in New York. Instead of doing his own reporting, Agnew bribed a telegraph operator who worked at the *Cleveland News* $5 a week to keep him abreast of such stories. But this telegraph operator left work each day at 3 o'clock and was not in the office when the news of the accident came to the newsroom. As a result, Agnew missed the story and so too did every INS paper in the country.

The *Cleveland News* was bound by contract to AP and could not share its news with anyone else. Cases such as *National Telegraph* flatly prohibited Agnew from getting his news by paying off one of its employees. Agnew's secret arrangement did not trouble INS's general manager in New York, however. Indeed, INS's central office had known about and explicitly encouraged it for years.[22] But the general manager was displeased nevertheless. If bribing one employee at the Cleveland press was not enough, two should have been bribed. In his eyes, Agnew was a telegraph operator who had been overpromoted. He lacked initiative and judgment. The general manager demoted Agnew and appointed someone else to run the office.[23]

Agnew returned to his job as a telegraph operator embittered. He started complaining—both about the way he had been treated and the way INS did business. The world of telegraph operators was small, and Cooper kept close tabs on it. Agnew's stories about INS's practices in Cleveland found their way back to Cooper, and Cooper soon found himself on a train to Cleveland.[24] Cooper met with Agnew, and Agnew provided specific instances in which INS's Cleveland bureau had taken facts from the AP wire and repeated them in its own dispatches.

Agnew also turned over to Cooper written evidence that the Cleveland office was acting with the blessing of INS headquarters. For

---

[22] *See id.* at 23.

[23] *See* Affidavit of Fred J. Wilson at 79.

[24] *See* OLIVER GRAMLING, AP: THE STORY OF NEWS 285 (1940).

example, the New York office had sent Agnew's successor a letter containing the following passage:

> Agnew had an arrangement somewhere in the Cleveland office whereby he could tip us off on big news stories that the A.P. was carrying. I wish you would find out from him just what this connection was and if you could make use of it. It proves very valuable to receive a tip what the A.P. is carrying as soon as it puts it out on the wire.[25]

The letter added:

> Don't mention the A.P. in any messages of that kind but simply say: "Ansonia carrying fifty dead Pennsylvania wreck Pittsburgh," or whatever it may be.

INS copied comparatively little of the Cleveland material. More often it was interested merely in confirming facts it already had.[26] INS also took Cleveland material and double checked it against other sources, sometimes correcting what AP had reported.[27] Actual copying of material outside of Cleveland, published or otherwise, was equally modest.[28] INS

---

25 Stone Affidavit at 23.

26 For example, the New York office knew from other sources that Lloyd George was about to resign as War Secretary and asked the Cleveland office whether AP was reporting that he had actually done so. *See* Affidavit of Fred W. Agnew at 37.

27 For example, when Cleveland told New York that AP was reporting that the trawler *Narzal* was missing, reporters in New York did enough of their own work to learn that AP had misspelled the ship's name, and in their account they corrected it to read *Narval*. Affidavit of Fred W. Agnew at 35–36.

28 The only other evidence of using nonpublic material involved INS's use of the AP wire of a Hearst-owned New York paper, the office of which was in the same building as INS headquarters. This evidence, however, was circumstantial and to some extent undercut by the Cleveland evidence. The New York office should not have needed to rely on people in Cleveland if it already had unfettered access to an AP wire in New York.

In the end, AP found only minor paraphrasing here and there and occasional copying of government documents to which AP had exclusive access. In its supporting affidavits, AP alleged only ten instances of misappropriation (not counting the Cleveland material):

- paraphrase of a fifty-word summary of an official statement of British officials on a Zeppelin raid;
- copy of a twenty-word quote of a captain whose boat the Germans torpedoed;
- paraphrase of the eleven-word report of shelling on the Somme Front (discussed above);
- paraphrase of the thirty-two-word account of the Duryea medal (discussed above);
- reference to the Secretary of Scotland by only his last name and reference to the Lord Chancellor for Ireland as "Ignatius J. O'Brien" rather than "Sir Ignatius J. O'Brien," after AP did the same thing;

rarely did more than take an AP bulletin that ran fifty words or fewer, paraphrase it, and then embellish it with a few details of its own, and it did not appear to do this often.

Cooper, however, did not need to show much copying to bring the case. INS had overstepped the bounds by bribing a reporter in Cleveland. With the Cleveland affidavits in hand, AP would invoke *National Telegraph* and demand an injunction against INS. In defending its actions, INS would claim that it had not obtained the information by bribery but had merely used AP bulletins that had already been made public. Once INS admitted to copying bulletins, AP would claim that copying public material also violated its rights. A court then would have to rule on this question as well. It would have to decide whether copying of published material was permissible, even though little or no copying of it could be proven.

William Randolph Hearst Defends Himself

The litigation in the district court consisted of a one-day hearing on a preliminary injunction. At the hearing, AP's lawyer spent several hours reviewing the Cleveland evidence, both to put INS in a bad light and to smooth the way for its principal claim. But Cleveland was a sideshow, and everyone understood this. INS's lawyer cut to the chase:

> [T]his controversy comes down to the question of law, as to whether we have the right to use material that had already been published . . . and all this other matter is a pretext, ballast and evasion, and it is all put in for the purpose of being a makeweight, on which to carry the other legal propositions.[29]

- paraphrase of AP's translation of French press comments on a German peace proposal;
- statement of the Emperor Charles to his army and navy previously carried on AP wires;
- paraphrase of a report on the reaction of the Tokyo stock market to the German peace proposal;
- one-sentence quote from the *London Globe* contained in an extract that AP had run earlier; and
- several verbatim extracts of AP's summary of a speech made in the House of Commons.

If AP detected large-scale copying, it would not need to rely on such things as a paraphrase of an eleven-word dispatch. The four last instances of appropriation are from two issues of the *Atlanta Georgian* that ran on successive days. What is most striking is how much of the alleged appropriation is of public statements and material AP itself had taken from the foreign press. Very little is of AP's own work, as opposed to work to which cartel agreements gave it exclusive access.

[29] Hearing Transcript at 205.

As there was little evidence of outright copying, AP's lawyer had to rely on hypotheticals:

> Suppose some man, by some modern process, could duplicate and reproduce the *Evening Post* entirely, within half or three-quarters of an hour of the time when the first copy was available.... Now someone ... decides that he will establish a paper called, we will say, the *Evening Call*. He makes a business of taking the first copy of the *Evening Post* that comes out, and ... reproduces it entire ... and then sells that at one cent instead of three cents, in competition with the *Evening Post*.[30]

The conduct of INS employees, AP's lawyer claimed, was different only in degree, and "by these methods they have reaped where they have not sown."[31]

District Judge Augustus Hand was openly skeptical that the injunction should extend to published material. After all, AP did not yet require papers to identify AP as a source when it used its materials:

> I don't get your point. I get the words of course that you use, but I don't see anything immoral at all, when a thing has been put out on a bulletin board, whatever the source may be, when the source is not disclosed, in one's copying it and giving it to anyone else, either as a matter of business or as a matter of pleasure.[32]

When AP's lawyer started talking about the realities of the news business, the judge again cut him off:

> Aren't these people supposed to be getting news from any source they can, so long as they don't commit fraud or break a contract or deceive the public?[33]

Hand forced AP to confront a second issue as well. AP routinely monitored the bulletins of other wire services and used them as a starting point for its own stories.[34] If pressed, AP would have difficulty explaining why this use of bulletins of rival services ought to be permissible, while the use INS allegedly made should not be.[35] Anyone familiar with the different wire services could see that drawing a line between copying with independent confirmation and copying without greatly

---

30 *Id.* at 158.

31 *Id.* at 160.

32 *Id.* at 161.

33 *Id.*

34 Affidavit of Edward R. Sartwell at 125–26.

35 Affidavit of Kent Cooper at 261–63.

favored AP. Most obviously, AP's competitive advantage came in large measure from its cartel agreement with foreign news services. AP could report on a government communiqué, and other news services had no way of confirming the story. No one else had access to it. Because of the cartel agreement, the only way to learn about the report was by reading about it in a paper that belonged to AP. The problem did not run the other way. Other wire services did not belong to any cartels or otherwise publish information to which they alone had access.

Moreover, it was much easier for AP to confirm facts. AP's membership agreements required newspapers to share their news with AP and with no one else. A paper such as the *Cleveland News* itself subscribed to both INS and AP,[36] but AP's by-laws ensured that the two services did not stand on equal footing. AP could count on reporters at the *Cleveland News* to confirm stories that INS carried, while INS could not use the same reporters to confirm AP stories.

In addition, a legal rule that required double-checking merely required AP to do what it was already doing. AP occupied a market niche in which it emphasized the accuracy of its news. AP made much of the fact that a rumor of the death of a pope or the end of a war did not become credible until it was carried on the AP wire.[37] By contrast, rival news services catered to a clientele that was not so punctilious. Their subscribers cared less about accuracy, and hence they did not engage in much double-checking of any of their sources. A legal rule requiring wire services to confirm facts would impose new burdens on them but not on AP.

In short, AP had exclusive access to more information, a greater ability to check facts, and greater reason to do so in the absence of a legal rule. The distinction between using tips and copying was hardly a neutral one that affected everyone equally. Hand found the distinction unpersuasive for a different reason. The idea that confirmation privileged copying could not be reconciled with the principle AP was trying to establish. Using bulletins as leads and copying them directly were both inconsistent with treating news as property:

> [T]he only way to afford full protection to the news gatherer is to prevent the use of news by a rival, either in the form of tips, or otherwise, for a sufficient time to enable the daily newspapers throughout the country to receive and publish the news.

---

36 *See* Affidavit of E. A. Smiley at 96.

37 A rival wire service prematurely reported the end of World War I. When the armistice was actually signed a few days later, a hagiographic history of AP recounts, people were not satisfied even with a statement from the State Department. What mattered was whether AP carried the story. *See* GRAMLING *supra* note 24, at 283.

In addition, the idea of confirming facts was inherently wasteful. As Hand put it, "[t]here is something rather grotesque in going through the form of verifying a tip, no matter how authentic it may be."[38]

INS, however, failed to convince Hand that the idea of a property right in news was fundamentally unsound. Nor did Hand understand that AP and INS occupied fundamentally different places in the market. Hand believed that, because an injunction would apply to both AP and INS,[39] the problem of crafting one that applied evenhandedly was one that the parties could resolve.

Hand shared AP's suspicion that more copying was going on than it could prove. The Cleveland evidence put INS in a bad light, and INS was already held in low repute. Most INS subscribers were newspapers that, like INS itself, were owned by William Randolph Hearst. Hearst's papers were tabloids filled with sensational headlines, human-interest stories, and Hearst's own idiosyncratic view of the world.[40] One would expect him to copy without compunction if he needed to, and it appeared he did.

The British and the French governments had banned INS from sending cables from their countries. If INS could not use AP bulletins, it seemed it had no way to provide war news. In the end, Hand was willing to believe that there had been substantial copying, and he refrained from granting a property right in news only because he thought the responsibility for establishing a new doctrine belonged to the court of appeals.

For the appeal, AP brought on a new lawyer, one whose credentials regarding common law intellectual property were impeccable. He was Peter Grosscup, the former judge and longtime friend of Stone's who had handed down the decision in *National Telegraph*.[41] He continued to make the same argument. INS should not be able to reap what AP had sown. By the time the case reached the court of appeals, the Cleveland issue disappeared. INS had no interest in litigating a question when the law was clear and the facts cast it in a bad light. All that was left was an abstract question about news as property, not connected to particular facts or indeed much contested by opposing counsel.

INS could have advanced a number of arguments in its defense. It might have been expected to argue that recognizing a property right in

---

38 Associated Press v. International News Service, 240 F. 983, 991, 992 (S.D.N.Y. 1917).

39 AP's lawyer conceded this point in the hearing in the district court. *See* Hearing Transcript at 197–98.

40 For an account of how Hearst advanced his own, decidedly anti-establishment, view of World War I in his papers, *see* W.A. SWANBERG, CITIZEN HEARST: A BIOGRAPHY OF WILLIAM RANDOLPH HEARST 301–06 (1961).

41 When the case reached the Supreme Court, Frederick Lehmann joined the AP team. Lehmann had served as Solicitor General under William Howard Taft.

news would limit what people learned about the war raging in Europe. Those living in cities that lacked an AP paper would be left in the dark, given the bans imposed on INS. INS chose not to make this argument and with some reason. It was hard for INS to argue copying war news was justified without appearing to admit that it had done so. Hearst refused to admit either that INS copied or that British and French censors affected INS's ability to report on the war. Even if pointing to censorship would enhance INS's chance of winning (and it is not obvious it would[42]), Hearst did not care much about the outcome of the case. Losing the case would have a trivial impact on INS's operations. Against a man utterly without scruples (such as Hearst), an injunction prevents only copying that can be proven, and, as the record in the case makes plain, AP could prove little.

Hearst did not engage in word-for-word copying from AP in the style of the McCullens. He was quite content to take the essential facts of an AP story and make up the rest. Many of INS's overseas correspondents were and had always been fictitious. Their reporting could continue unimpeded no matter what the British and the French did.[43] In such an environment, Hearst needed only to refrain from outright bribery (or do more to ensure the loyalty of those doing the bribing) and to avoid traps such as the one the McCullens fell into.[44] In any event, INS's need for a source of war news had disappeared by the time the case came to the Supreme Court, as the censorship ban had been lifted well before then.

---

[42] Complaining about British and French censors might have done little good. INS's activities in Cleveland showed that it took advantage of AP for both domestic and foreign news and had been doing long before the British and French bans. Moreover, the bans would not have gained INS much sympathy, as they arose from INS's entirely casual commitment to accurate reporting. One story that purported to come from London described a Zeppelin raid with the headline, "London in Flames." The details that gave the story its power (especially the headline) did not come from London at all, but were invented in New York. An account of the battle of Jutland began, "The British Admiralty to-night admits an overwhelming defeat by a portion of the German High Sea Fleet in the first great naval engagement of the war." The British Admiralty never admitted to an overwhelming defeat or indeed a defeat of any kind. Compounding the problem, to publish such a story with a London dateline falsely implied the seal of approval from British censors.

[43] *See* Oliver Carlson & Ernest Sutherland Bates, Hearst: Lord of San Simeon 186 (1936).

[44] In this, Hearst was not entirely successful. After AP brought its case, another news service ran a story from Russia about "Foreign Undersecretary Nelotsky," and several INS newspapers ran a story with a London byline covering the same facts and referring explicitly to Nelotsky's involvement. *See United Press Explains the Identity of Secretary Nelotsky*, N.Y. Times, January 25, 1918, at 3. As the New York Times eagerly pointed out, no Russian minister existed whose name was "stolen" spelled backwards, with a "ky" added for Russian flavor.

INS's lawyer still might have focused on the anticompetitive features of AP's operations. He could have attacked both the by-laws that protected the markets of individual AP members[45] and AP's cartel agreement with foreign news services. INS could have maintained that the "franchise rights" were an illegal restraint of trade in violation of the antitrust laws. Even if they were not, INS could have argued that a wire service was like a common carrier obliged to accommodate all comers. Hence, a court of equity should not protect a news service that refused to provide its news to papers willing to pay for it. Similarly, INS could have argued that a court of equity should not step in to prevent one wire service from copying official government documents—especially when the party asking for the injunction had acquired the documents in question through a cartel agreement. But INS's lawyer did none of these things.

It was not that INS's lawyer was blind to such issues. To the contrary, his special expertise was in antitrust.[46] He declined to make such arguments because he was following the wishes of his client. William Randolph Hearst was the most important member of AP. He owned more newspapers than any other member of AP and contributed millions to its coffers. Hearst had long lived in the strange world in which he could use AP's wire service for only some of his papers. Hearst recognized the value of his own franchise rights. He had no interest in an outcome that undercut his own ability to prevent rival newspapers from competing with his AP papers.[47] He had no desire for a legal rule that would force AP to sell its news to anyone willing to pay for it.[48]

Because Hearst did not care much about the principle that AP was advancing, he had little reason to have his lawyer question its soundness or scope, especially as doing so would call into question AP practices that inured to his benefit. On appeal, as before the district court, INS's lawyer did nothing to test the limits of such a principle or shape its contours.

The court of appeals took the step that Augustus Hand did not to take on his own. It concluded that AP was entitled to "an injunction

---

[45] When the anticompetitive nature of the by-laws was ultimately presented to the Supreme Court, it struck them down. *See* Associated Press v. United States, 326 U.S. 1 (1945).

[46] INS's lawyer, Samuel Untermyer, was one of the leading lawyers of his time. He gained fame as the lawyer for the Pujo Committee's investigation of the money trusts. His brilliant cross-examination of J. P. Morgan made headlines and led both to the creation of the Federal Reserve and to the Clayton Antitrust Act.

[47] *See* Cooper, *supra* note 16, at 198–99.

[48] Indeed, during this period, Hearst fought inside AP to maintain franchise rights while Kent Cooper wanted to limit them. *See id.* at 74–75, 198–99.

against any bodily taking of the words or substance of [its] news.''[49] The court did so without recognizing that nothing in the record showed INS had in fact engaged in the ''bodily taking'' of AP stories.[50] On appeal, the property right in news that AP sought was completely abstracted from the facts.

In the Supreme Court, Justice Pitney assumed that AP and INS were two competitors doing business in much the same way on a more or less level playing field. He then confused hypotheticals about copying news on the East Coast and publishing on the West with facts of the actual case:

> [T]he distribution of news matter throughout the country is principally from east to west; and, since in speed the telegraph and telephone easily outstrip the rotation of the earth, it is a simple matter for [the INS] to take complainant's news from bulletin or early editions of [AP]'s members in the eastern cities and at the mere cost of telegraphic transmission cause it to be published in western papers issued at least as early as those served by [AP].[51]

Justice Pitney immediately adopted exactly the principle that Cooper wanted without any effort to qualify it:

> [INS], by its very act, admits that it is taking material that has been acquired by [AP] as the result of organization and the expenditure of labor, skill, and money, and which is salable by [AP] for money, and [INS] in appropriating it and selling it as its own is endeavoring to reap where it has not sown. . . .[52]

News services were entitled to the fruits of their own labors, and others therefore could not appropriate their work. Justice Pitney dismissed INS's argument that AP's use of INS's wire service for tips gave it unclean hands. He was oblivious to the ways in which the distinction between using tips and copying favored AP.

Justice Brandeis dissented, largely on the ground that judges are ill equipped to resolve such disputes. His instincts served him well. He may not have recognized what was going on, but at least he knew not to enter

---

49 Associated Press v. International News Service, 245 F. 244, 253 (2d Cir. 1917).

50 Stone and Cooper seem to have thought that the censorship ban effectively prevented INS from getting any news from abroad. From this, they thought that one could infer that any news INS published was likely taken from AP or some other wire service. But some war news came from elsewhere, and, given INS's penchant for embellishment and outright fabrication, one could not infer copying merely from that fact that INS continued to report on the war.

51 International News Service v. Associated Press, 248 U.S. 215, 238 (1918).

52 *Id.* at 239.

deep waters he did not understand.[53] He recognized that some limits needed to be put on Justice Pitney's new principle.

After the decision, AP and INS soon settled. This was to be expected. Each party had much to lose if the relationship fell apart. Hearst wanted the benefits of AP service wherever he could get them. For their part, other AP members had no wish to exclude him or for him to leave the fold.[54] As much as they disliked him, they were too dependent on his financial support. Genuine disputes between AP and Hearst had to be resolved outside the courtroom.[55]

In their settlement, AP and INS agreed that neither would engage in "bodily taking" the words or substance of the other's wire services. If Kent Cooper had brought the litigation on the assumption that such an injunction would change INS's practices, he would have been terribly naive. Because AP had not been able to prove INS had engaged in such activities, an injunction had little effect on the way INS did business. Cooper was many things, but he was not naive.

Cooper understood that the victory had little to do with INS and everything to do with his vision of AP's future. The case reversed the outcome of cases such as *Tribune Co. v. Associated Press,* which blessed AP's earlier practice of copying news first published elsewhere. Nevertheless, the doctrine was completely consistent with a future in which

---

53 Justice Brandeis' take on the relationship between competition and exclusive rights is further explored in Graeme B. Dinwoodie, The Story of *Kellogg Co. v. National Biscuit Co.*: Breakfast with Brandeis, elsewhere in this Volume.

54 Only one director said as much publicly. *See* FERDINAND LUNCHBERG, IMPERIAL HEARST: A SOCIAL BIOGRAPHY 209 (1936). Oswald Garrison Villard, the publisher of the Evening Post, complained that "the Board of Directors lacked either the moral or business courage to rid their service of the Hearst connection." As he put it,

> [I]t certainly seems incomprehensible that the Associated Press should have permitted a man to remain a member who had struck at its very integrity and had not hesitated at the use of any means to gain his end. It is the simple truth that a small newspaper doing these things would have been expelled; the Associated Press was afraid of Mr. Hearst's power, and the growing number of news papers brought into his chain of dailies.

OSWALD GARRISON VILLARD, THE PRESS TODAY, 13–14 (1930).

55 When AP decided several years later to control Hearst's copying, it relied on private negotiation rather than litigation. Potentially anticompetitive practices could be kept out of the spotlight and the remedy could be crafted to ensure Hearst's compliance. In this deal, Hearst, rather than promising not to copy published AP reports, agreed to limit the distribution of Universal Service, the morning news division of INS, only to papers that Hearst owned. Universal Service sent its wires close to the time that most of AP's papers were published, and hence it was the entity most likely to take its facts from the AP wire. The solution worked for all concerned. Hearst distributed the morning news to the papers he cared most about (his own), and AP found a way to limit the use of its own material in a way that it could police. *See* LUNCHBERG *supra* note 54, at 209.

AP spent fewer resources on transporting information and more on fashioning it in the first instance.

Immediately after the case was decided, AP required that member newspapers tag each of the reports they ran with either the words "Associated Press" or the symbol "AP." Cooper also used the opinion to justify a legend all member papers were required to run in every issue:

> The Associated Press is entitled exclusively to the use for republication of all news dispatches credited to it or not otherwise credited in this newspaper and all the local news published herein. Rights of republication of all other matter herein are also reserved.[56]

Under Cooper's leadership, AP introduced feature stories and allowed the names of its reporters to appear in the bylines. Its reports became less dry accounts of facts and government reports that local editors could embellish and more news accounts with bylines that included local color. This change did not meet with universal approval. As one former AP board member complained:

> Mr. Kent Cooper ... represents an entirely new school from that of Melville E. Stone ... He has broken with tradition after tradition of the service—comic strips are his latest venture. So the Associated Press has long since abandoned its original conception of being a service devoted exclusively to the gathering of news ...[57]

The decision in *INS v. AP* allowed AP to make claims of ownership when the occasion demanded. Because of this decision, AP was able to sell its service to radio stations—and pursue vigorously radio stations that used its news without its permission.[58] But one should not overstate the importance of the case. AP usually turned to the legal doctrine only after more familiar and more distinctly anticompetitive tactics failed. In the case of radio, for example, AP tried to form a cartel with large radio stations and other news services (including INS) to impose strong limits on the news that radio stations could transmit.[59]

---

56 *See* COOPER *supra* note 16, at 198.

57 VILLARD *supra* note 54, at 22.

58 *See*, e.g., Associated Press v. KVOS, Inc., 80 F.2d 575 (9th Cir. 1935), *rev'd on jurisdictional grounds*, 299 U.S. 269 (1936).

59 At the outset, newspapers welcomed radio and raised no objections when stations repeated items in newspapers. *See* ERIK BARNOUW, A TOWER IN BABEL: A HISTORY OF BROADCASTING IN THE UNITED STATES, VOLUME I, TO 1933, at 138 (1966). Their own circulations increased because fans of radio relied on the broadcast schedules in their local newspapers. By 1933, the value of the radio market for radio news was too large to ignore. AP, INS, and United Press banded together and negotiated a deal with network broadcasters that would,

The Reception of *INS*

Justice Pitney's opinion lacked the essential quality that justifies common law adjudication. Its reasoning was entirely ungrounded. Instead of resolving an actual dispute between two opposing litigants, it merely gave an abstract pronouncement of a grand principle that has no obvious boundaries. The justice overlooked problems—in particular AP's various anticompetitive practices—that complicated the application of the principle in the case before him. If forced to consider that AP shared features with other natural monopolies, such as a telephone network, Justice Pitney would likely have considered alternative approaches, such as one that would have conditioned AP's right to prevent unauthorized copying on its willingness to sell its news to any paper willing to pay for it. Solving these problems is hard, but had the natural monopoly, the cartel, and the anticompetitive provisions of the by-laws been recognized, Justice Pitney would not have been able to stop with the observation that a wire service was entitled to prevent others from reaping what it had sown.

Nor is the principle Justice Pitney sets out of much use in environments in which the intellectual property questions can be treated in isolation. If the issue had been contested, he would likely have realized that the principle he was advancing needed to have discernible boundaries. News and indeed other forms of intellectual property generate benefits far beyond what the persons who brought them into being can or should be entitled to enjoy. We want to recognize the right of the creator to some reward, if only to ensure that others have the incentive to gather news in the future. But the right must be limited. As Benjamin Kaplan famously observed, "if man has any 'natural' rights, not the least must be a right to imitate his fellows, and thus to reap where he has not sown. Education, after all, proceeds from a kind of mimicry, and 'progress,' if not entirely an illusion, depends on generous indulgence of copying."[60]

Had Justice Pitney faced litigants who cared about the outcome of the case in an environment stripped of all but questions of intellectual property, he might, as Richard Epstein has shown, have drawn upon customs or common practices to draw limits on the right he was recognizing.[61] But he neither did this nor suggested it was even appropri-

---

among other things, prevent radio from using news less than twelve hours old. This cartel, the Press–Radio Bureau, however, had the predictable consequence of encouraging stations to start their own independent news services and fell apart. *See* Erik Barnouw, The Golden Web: A History of Broadcasting in the United States, Volume II, to 1933–1953, at 20–22 (1968).

[60] Benjamin Kaplan, An Unhurried View of Copyright 2 (1966).

[61] Richard Epstein recasts Justice Pitney's principle using a theory of natural rights anchored in customary practice. Epstein provides the best modern rationalization of *INS v.*

ate. Because they set precedent that lower courts are obliged to follow, Supreme Court cases that put forward such unbounded propositions are nightmares. A succession of cases in the Second Circuit illustrates the problems that arise.

Cheney Bros. made silk cloth and each season developed a number of new patterns. Only one in five proved successful, but the profit made from the one successful pattern each year outweighed the losses from the four that failed, or at least until competitors such as Doris Silk came along. Once Doris discovered which patterns caught the public's fancy, it would copy the pattern and rush it into production. Neither having to pay to come up with a design nor having to bear the cost of producing unsuccessful ones, Doris was able to undercut Cheney.[62]

Judge Learned Hand's instincts told him that Cheney must lose as a matter of first principle. But *INS*, unqualified as it was, seemed to compel a decision in Cheney's favor. As Hand confided to the other members of the panel, "the *Associated Press Case* is somewhat of a stumbling block." It did not make sense to him:

> I do not believe that the five justices who united in Pitney, J's opinion meant to lay down a general rule that a man is entitled to "property" in the form of whatever he makes with his labor and money, so as to prevent others from copying it. To do so would be to short-circuit the Patent Office and throw upon courts the winnowing out of all such designs that might be presented. While I agree that on principle it is hard to distinguish, and that the language applies, I cannot suppose that any principle of such far-reaching consequence was intended. It will make patent cases an exception; it will give to State courts jurisdiction over inventions; it will overthrow the practice of centuries.[63]

Hand concluded that *INS* had to be understood as a case that dealt with the narrow and peculiar problems of a news service. As he confided in deciding another case:

> It is absurd to say a man has "property" in all the product of his brains; the law has never said that or anything like that . . .

AP. *See* Richard A. Epstein, *International News Service v. Associated Press: Custom and Law as Sources of Property Rights in News*, 78 VA. L. REV. 85 (1992).

62 As in *INS v. AP* itself, common law principles of intellectual property governed. The cost of obtaining a design patent on all the patterns to protect the few that proved successful (and then only for a season) was too onerous, even if the patterns qualified for protection. Copyright law was equally unavailable. *See* Cheney Bros. v. Doris Silk Corporation, 35 F.2d 279 (2d Cir. 1929).

63 Memorandum from Learned Hand to Martin T. Manton & Thomas W. Swann (Oct. 8, 1929) (Learned Hand Papers, Harvard Law School Library).

> We should be making an entirely new right never known before. . . .
>
> That ends the case . . .[64]

But, of course, it did not end the case.[65] Hand still had to contend with *INS v. AP*. He continued to insist that it had to be confined to its facts:

> Probably Holmes and Brandeis were right in holding that there was no real property there, but right or wrong it was a very narrow decision; all it did was to forbid copying news for the four hours that it takes the sun to move from New York to Seattle. You can't blow that up into a doctrine that a man has power to prevent everyone from copying what he has put together with his own brains and skill.

Another judge was more direct:

> In principle, this case is entirely indistinguishable from [*INS v. AP*], and we might as well admit it. But we have conquered the *News* case before; it can be done again.[66]

Starting with these cases in the Second Circuit, *INS v. AP* has come to be read narrowly.[67]

Intellectual property disputes, like all legal disputes, cannot be decided merely by invoking an idea as vague as the right to reap what one sows. Thanks to judges such as Learned Hand and the preemptive sweep of federal patent and copyright law, *INS* has become a doctrine that lives at the margins of intellectual property law.[68] There are oddball cases now and then. There was, for example, a recent dispute between the Chicago Cubs baseball team and the owners of buildings behind Wrigley Field.

For years, those who lived in these buildings took lawn chairs to their rooftops with binoculars and beer to enjoy the game. Over time, the rooftops changed from being places where the building owners and their friends watched the games to a small cottage industry. As the neighbors became more entrepreneurial, the Cubs became increasingly unhappy.

---

64 Memorandum from Learned Hand to Charles E. Clark & Robert P. Patterson (June 20, 1940) (Learned Hand Papers, Harvard Law School Library).

65 The case in question was *RCA Mfg. Co. v. Whiteman*, 114 F.2d 86 (2d Cir. 1940).

66 Memorandum from Charles E. Clark to Learned Hand & Robert P. Patterson (June 21, 1940), *supra* note 64.

67 The doctrine of misappropriation lives on, but wherever it appears, it is read narrowly. *See*, e.g., National Basketball Association v. Motorola, Inc., 105 F.3d 841 (2d Cir. 1997).

68 For a forceful articulation of this view, *see* Richard A. Posner, *Misappropriation: A Dirge*, 40 HOUS. L. REV. 621 (2003).

When the neighbors began to install stadium seats and sell season tickets to the general public, the team sued and sought to stop them. The outcome turned on *INS*.[69]

But the legal doctrine is only one part of the story. To maintain its stadium and make even modest renovations, the Cubs needed to obtain variances from the city. In Chicago, obtaining such variances requires the local alderman's blessing, and aldermen pay attention to homeowners. A negotiated outcome is inevitable. The reception that *INS* might enjoy in court affects the dynamics of these negotiations, but it is only one of the many forces at work.

A similar account can be given of a recent matter involving AP itself. An agreement among college football teams selects (in ways that are often controversial) what are supposed to be the best teams to compete against each other in bowl games. AP asserted that it had the right to prevent the use of its own ranking of college football teams in the selection process. One may doubt that *INS* grants AP rights that extend so far. Nevertheless, property-rights talk added strength to AP's claim, and the bowl organizers immediately acquiesced.

Principles that emerge from a case that is not moored to an actual dispute between two genuine adversaries are suspect. Ironically, *INS v. AP* may have earned its central place in the law school curriculum because of its failings rather than in spite of them. If Justice Pitney had grasped the anticompetitive features of AP's structure or sensed how the market for news was in transition, he would have resisted the impulse toward vague abstraction. If he had kept the controversy in tighter focus, however, his opinion would become more time-bound and much more complicated. Most cases arise from the facts and circumstances of a particular time and place. They usually cross subject matter areas. Intellectual property, industrial regulation, and antitrust issues arise simultaneously. These do not end up in casebooks. The iconic cases tend to have easy facts and straightforward principles. We need to worry more that they seem to have these desirable traits only because the judges are in the dark. In law, as in life, matters are rarely as simple as they appear.

---

69 The facts of this case were anticipated in Justice Brandeis's dissent in *INS*, in which he cites an English case involving a dog show where the court specifically addresses the rights of a person (in that case a photographer) viewing a dog show from the top of a nearby house. *See* 248 U.S. at 255 (citing Sports & General Press Agency, Ltd. v. "Our Dogs" Publishing Co., [1916] 2 K.B. 880).

The Story of *Wheaton v. Peters*: A Curious Chapter in the History of Judicature

Craig Joyce*

Overview

In the wake of the American Revolution, a new nation arose on the western shores of the Atlantic Ocean, in conception distinct from any other that had gone before. Lacking a sovereign or a strong central government, it was in many ways a curious society, both culturally and politically. Literature and discoveries, the foundations of progress, existed without protection under any single law embracing all thirteen former colonies that had become, in name if not yet in fact, these "United States." America, in due course to be the greatest engine of expression and invention in the history of the globe, was unable to protect either effectively.

A fledgling Supreme Court, of no significance to the world at large but ultimately to be transformed into the most powerful judicial tribunal ever created, struggled into being. The decisions of that body were, however, at first almost entirely unknown to the people whose future they would govern, because there was no systematic or reliable reporting of the Court's opinions. The Early Republic's most eminent jurists were uncertain even as to the ownership of the text of their decisions. Who—the judges themselves, the lawyers who reported the decisions, or the people of the United States—owned the Justices' accounts of the law?

Such was the state of law, and of law reporting, in America in the aftermath of the Revolution and during the half century that followed, culminating in the Supreme Court's great decision in *Wheaton v. Peters*[1] in 1834.

The main participants in *Wheaton* include many of the giants of early American law. But there were others, too, unremembered today,

---

* I am deeply grateful to Peter Egler, Head of Reference, at the Law Center's O'Quinn Law Library, and Helen Boyce, Head of Document Services, to Spencer Simons, Director of the O'Quinn Library, Mon Yin Lung, Associate Director, Marek Waterstone, Head of Technical Services, and to Andrew Wolf, University of Houston Law Center Class of 2004, Laura Rees, UHLC Class of 2005, and the editors of *Houston Law Review*.

[1] 33 U.S. (8 Pet.) 591 (1834).

whose ambition and investment in the future of the country would preserve the first stirrings of our national jurisprudence, and the great constitutional decisions of the Marshall Court, for generations to come.

The list begins, in order of importance as history has remembered those involved, with Chief Justice John Marshall and Joseph Story, Marshall's colleague on the Supreme Court for a quarter century and the greatest legal scholar of the age. The other Justices include Bushrod Washington, nephew of George Washington and inheritor of both Mount Vernon and the papers of the first American president,[2] but also lesser lights whose infirmities of mind and body, though important to the story that follows, now are long forgotten.

The lawyers, too, are distinguished: Daniel Webster, noted orator, powerful politician, and admired advocate; William Pinkney, leading member of the Supreme Court bar; Richard Rush, Attorney General of the United States; and a host of others.

Making an appearance, as well, are various patriots and presidents, a future Secretary of the Treasury, and a judge whose uncle, Washington's successor as president, saved him from financial ruin by appointment to a Washington, D.C., court where he would serve for 54 years.

But the main figures, notwithstanding the historic renown of others, are the true antagonists. Henry Wheaton was a protégé, friend and roommate of Story during their Washington winters, savior of the Reports of the Supreme Court of the United States, distinguished diplomat, and preeminent expounder of international law in nineteenth century America. All the same, Richard Peters Jr., fortunate offspring of a well-placed father, second-rate lawyer but brilliant entrepreneur, would emerge the victor in the Supreme Court decision that bears his, and Wheaton's, names.

The saga of *Wheaton v. Peters* is a tale of inherent dramatic structure and significance. Wheaton himself, writing years later, put the point succinctly: "The incidents attending this case, should they ever be given to the world, would form a curious chapter in the history of judicature & indeed of human nature."[3] This "Story" explores that chapter in all its curiosity.

---

2 Justices Story and Washington would play important roles in another early copyright controversy. *See* R. Anthony Reese, The Story of *Folsom v. Marsh*: Distinguishing Between Infringing and Legitimate Uses, elsewhere in this Volume.

3 Henry Wheaton to Levi Wheaton (Apr. 15, 1840), Wheaton Papers, The Pierpont Morgan Library, New York City. All materials from the Morgan Library are used with permission. Due to the large number of letters in this Story, citations to all correspondence, regardless of repository, appear in abbreviated form.

Law Reporting in the New Republic

The First Reporters

Until 1776, the American colonies were England's "Plantations." In 1781, despite a successful war for independence and ratification of the Articles of Confederation, there was still, for practical purposes, little (verging on no) national law in America. In 1787, when Washington, Madison, Hamilton, Franklin, and others assembled in Philadelphia to draft the Constitution, there was, as yet, no national government. And in 1790, when the newly appointed Supreme Court gathered for the first time in New York City, while there was (finally) a national judicial tribunal, no Reporter of Decisions stood ready to record its decisions for lower courts, the bar, or posterity.

Indeed, with one exception, there were in 1790 *no* judicial reports, federal, state or colonial, anywhere in America.[4] The necessary prerequisite to the preeminence of the Nation's Court as we know it today—the Court of Marshall, Story, and their descendants on the Supreme Bench—was a system of reporting the Justices' decisions that had yet to be devised.[5]

What followed, almost by happenstance, was the creation of the series of volumes known now as *United States Reports*, but known then by the names of the first four Reporters (through the decision in the *Wheaton* case): Dallas, Cranch, Wheaton, and Peters.[6]

---

[4] English law reports, from Littleton and Coke forward, were not unknown in colonial America. *See generally* Edwin C. Surrency, *Law Reports in the United States*, 25 Am. J. Legal Hist. 48 (1981). The first comprehensive volume of native reports after independence was Ephraim Kirby's Reports of Cases Adjudged in the Superior Court of the State of Connecticut From the Year 1785 to May 1788 With Some Determinations in the Supreme Court of Errors (1789). Kirby's reports preceded Dallas's Reports, *see infra*, by barely a year.

[5] For further discussion of the Reporter of Decisions' role in American law, see Craig Joyce, *The Torch Is Passed: In–Chambers Opinions and the Reporter of Decisions in Historical Perspective*, *in* III In-Chambers Opinions by the Justices of the Supreme Court of the United States vii-xxiii (Cynthia Rapp ed., 2004), a principal source in the narrative that follows. A complete list of the Reporters and their terms of service appears at vii. The volumes of the first seven Reporters, who with their publishers financed their own *Reports*, bear their names. They are known, collectively, as the "nominative" Reporters. From 1875 on, Congress financed the *Reports*, and the names of the Reporters themselves ceased to appear on the spines. *Id.* at xx. The last decision in the last volume of the last nominative Reporter, John W. Wallace, *American Wood–Paper Co. v. Fibre Disintegrating Co.*, commonly would be cited today as 90 U.S. (23 Wall.) 566 (1874). The successor volume, William T. Otto's first, reporting the October 1875 Term, begins with *McComb v. Commissioners of Knox County, Ohio*, and is cited as 91 U.S. 1 (1875).

[6] The story of the early Reporters is told in much greater detail in Craig Joyce, *The Rise of the Supreme Court Reporter: An Institutional Perspective on Marshall Court Ascendancy*, 83 Mich. L. Rev. 1291 (1985), from which this Story is adapted. Primary

The breakthrough came when the Supreme Court, and the Federal Government generally, moved to Philadelphia in 1791. There, a young lawyer named Alexander J. Dallas became, unofficially and by self-appointment, the Supreme Court's first Reporter. Born in Jamaica, Dallas had migrated to the United States after the Revolution. In due course, he would achieve success at the Philadelphia bar and serve as Secretary of the Treasury (and, briefly, of War) during Madison's presidency.

Early on, however, Dallas endured lean years of practice. To supplement his income, he began publishing reports of local judicial decisions for use by fellow attorneys. The venture was entirely private, the reporter acting without salary or commission from the relevant courts. His first volume, *Reports of cases ruled and adjudged in the courts of Pennsylvania, before and since the Revolution*, appeared in 1790. Three more volumes followed.

Volume 1 of Dallas's *Reports*, however, is unique. In the succeeding three volumes, Dallas included, for the convenience of his practitioner purchasers, the decisions of those "local" federal courts—including the District Courts, the Circuit Court (what today is the Third Circuit Court of Appeals), and the Supreme Court—by then resident in Pennsylvania. The new nation's highest court did not become resident, however, until the year after Dallas began publishing. Thus, alone in the entire series of *U.S. Reports*, 1 U.S. (1 Dall.) contains *not one* decision by the Supreme Court of the United States!

Dallas faced no easy task in reporting the work of that Court.[7] Except in the most important cases, the Justices often delivered opinions extemporaneously from only the most rudimentary of jottings. Dallas had to rely on his own notes from those sittings he could attend and on the notes of fellow attorneys (and, very occasionally, Justices) for the many he could not, making the accuracy and completeness of his *Reports* problematic. Thanks to high printing expense, they were costly as well.

The most serious complaint against Dallas's *Reports*, however, was their chronic tardiness. Five years elapsed between the last Supreme Court decision recorded in 2 *Dallas* and publication of that volume; between Dallas's retirement as Reporter and publication of 4 *Dallas*, his last volume, seven years passed. That delay so unnerved bench and bar as to prompt a plea by Dallas's successor that he be allowed to publish

sources are cited where appropriate. For entertaining biographies of Dallas, Cranch, Wheaton and Peters, see MORRIS L. COHEN & SHARON HAMBY O'CONNOR, A GUIDE TO THE EARLY REPORTS OF THE SUPREME COURT OF THE UNITED STATES (1995).

[7] For details of the Court's work during its first decade of existence, the authoritative source is THE DOCUMENTARY HISTORY OF THE SUPREME COURT OF THE UNITED STATES, 1789–1800 (Maeva Marcus ed., 1985 to date).

the missing cases in the first volume of his own *Reports*: "It would certainly be interesting to the profession, and important to the stability of our national jurisprudence, that the chain of cases should be complete."[8]

Although Dallas eventually did his duty, by 1800, when the Court and the Government decamped for Washington City,[9] his patience, and hopes for financial gain, were at an end. "I have found such miserable encouragement for my Reports," he wrote to a friend, "that I have determined to call them all in, and devote them to the rats in the State–House."[10]

William Cranch, the Court's second Reporter, was, like Dallas, a volunteer. Born in Massachusetts, he had relocated to the new federal capital to make his fortune as legal agent for a real estate speculation syndicate. Happily for Cranch, son of Abigail Adams's sister and Harvard classmate of John Quincy Adams, he survived the syndicate's spectacular collapse through appointment to public office by his well-placed uncle, Quincy's father, on the eve of the latter's forced retirement from the presidency. In turn, Cranch's court survived extinction in the purge of Federalist judges engineered by John Adams's successor, Thomas Jefferson. In 1805, Cranch became Chief Judge of the District of Columbia Circuit Court, serving until his death in 1855.

Precisely how Cranch came to be Reporter is not known. The older histories occasionally refer to him as the first "regularly appointed" Reporter of the Court's decisions.[11] But no such entry appears in the minutes of the Court, nor had Congress or the Court provided for such an appointment by statute or rule.[12] Without doubt, the reports published by Cranch, like the volumes of his predecessor, remained at all times a private venture.[13] Thus, it seems most likely that Cranch, like Dallas, appointed himself to report the decisions of the Court.

Despite high hopes and laudable intentions, however, Cranch and his readers found Supreme Court reporting an exercise in disappoint-

---

[8] William Cranch to Alexander J. Dallas (July 25, 1803), George M. Dallas Papers, Historical Society of Pennsylvania, Philadelphia.

[9] *See* Act of July 16, 1790, ch. 28, §§ 1, 5, 1 Stat. 130 (known as the "Residence Act," under which the Government relocated permanently to the District of Columbia in 1800).

[10] Alexander J. Dallas to Jonathan Dayton (Oct. 18, 1802), Dallas Papers, *supra* note 8.

[11] *See, e.g.,* HAMPTON L. CARSON, THE HISTORY OF THE SUPREME COURT OF THE UNITED STATES, WITH BIOGRAPHIES OF ALL THE CHIEF AND ASSOCIATE JUSTICES 619 (1891).

[12] Alexander B. Hagner, *William Cranch, 1769–1855, in* 3 GREAT AMERICAN LAWYERS 93 (William Draper Lewis ed., 1907).

[13] *See* text at notes 54–57 *infra* (protests of Cranch and Wheaton regarding impact of Peters's *Condensed Reports* on income of Peters's predecessors).

ment. True, Cranch managed, as he had urged Dallas, to keep the chain of cases complete. And certainly he made every effort to please the profession by improving on the standard of his predecessor's volumes. While retaining the case tables, indices and rudimentary notes introduced by Dallas, the new Reporter also pledged to provide "faithful summar[ies] of the arguments of counsel."[14] The result, as described by William Pinkney of Baltimore, the Supreme Court bar's leading advocate, was merely "unprofitable and expensive prolixity."[15] The greater length of Cranch's *Reports* also worked against their success as a commercial venture by contributing to their cost. Eventually, the combined expense of a full set of Cranch's volumes approached the then-exorbitant amount of fifty dollars.[16]

In other respects, Cranch's deficiencies resembled his predecessor's, especially "painfully erroneous" reports of decisions[17] and repeated delays in the publication of his volumes.[18] Year after year, cases lay unreported, to the great dismay of the Court. Justice Story, newly appointed in 1811 and greatly concerned with the development of its jurisprudence as a tool of national power, complained of Cranch's "extraordinary delay."[19] Even Chief Justice John Marshall, upon receiving prepublication copies of Cranch's final volumes after his departure as Reporter, directed his thanks to Cranch's successor, apparently believing that Cranch himself had abandoned them.[20]

Wheaton's Reportership

By 1815, what Story termed the Court's "disrelish" with Cranch's work had reached the breaking point.[21] The bar concurred. Cranch had failed to place in print a single case decided since 1810. Richard Rush, Attorney General of the United States, whose many appearances before the Court required frequent reference to its precedents, despaired of

---

14 5 U.S. (1 Cranch) at iv.

15 William Pinkney to Henry Wheaton (Sept. 3, 1818), Wheaton Papers, *supra* note 3.

16 Justice Smith Thompson's purchase of Volumes 7–9 alone cost him $16 in 1818. W. Gould to Smith Thompson (Feb. 3, 1818), Gilbert Livingston Papers, New York Public Library, New York City.

17 Joseph Story to Richard Peters Jr. (Dec. 10, 1829), Peters Papers, Historical Society of Philadelphia, Pennsylvania.

18 When published in 1816, Volume 7 of Cranch's *Reports* included cases decided as early as 1810.

19 Joseph Story to Richard Rush (June 26, 1814), Rush Family Papers, Princeton University Library, Princeton, N.J.

20 John Marshall to Henry Wheaton (Oct. 27, 1816), Wheaton Papers, *supra* note 3.

21 Joseph Story to Henry Wheaton (Sept. 15, 1816), Wheaton Papers, *supra* note 3.

seeing them and lamented that the Reporter "ought to be supplanted as some penalty for his inexcusable delays."[22] But by whom?

Story and Rush already knew the answer: an ambitious young New York lawyer and scholar named Henry Wheaton.[23] Wheaton had come to prominence during the War of 1812 owing to his ardent support of the Madison Administration and his early writings, particularly in admiralty matters and comparative law. His *Digest of the Law of Maritime Captures and Prizes*, published in 1815, not only summarized, but also provided a full analysis of, the prize decisions of the tribunals of the United States and England and included a general exposition of the law of nations.

The selection of the Court's third Reporter seems to have occurred by informal agreement among the Justices themselves. As an inducement to procure his appointment, which he hoped might lead to greater fame in the profession and increased income through the production of his reports, Wheaton had submitted a plan proposing "regular annual publication" of the Justices' opinions, "with good type, and to be neatly printed."[24] Anxious to improve the accuracy and promptitude of the reports, the Justices apparently agreed to furnish to Wheaton any written opinions they might prepare, or notes they might make, in connection with their oral opinions.[25]

Wheaton immediately set about industriously discharging his new responsibilities through daily attendance at the Court's sittings. The demands of the Reportership, and conditions in the Federal City itself, drew him close to the tight circle of people with whom he worked most regularly: the Justices of the Court, all of whom lived and took their meals together in the same boarding house on Capitol Hill.[26] There, Wheaton joined them, quickly becoming Story's roommate (or "chum").[27]

---

22 Richard Rush to Henry Wheaton (Apr. 6, 1815), Wheaton Papers, *supra* note 3.

23 Born Providence, R.I., Nov. 27, 1785; died Dorchester, Mass., Mar. 11, 1848.

24 REPORT OF THE COPYRIGHT CASE OF WHEATON VS. PETERS 6 (1834) (on file with Columbia University Library, New York City), *cited in* ELIZABETH FEASTER BAKER, HENRY WHEATON 1785–1848 at 27 n.5 (1937).

25 4 THE RECORDS AND BRIEFS OF THE SUPREME COURT OF THE UNITED STATES 2 (microfilm: Scholarly Resources, Inc., Wilmington, Del.) [hereinafter RECORD] (Wheaton's bill in equity); *see also* Wheaton v. Peters, 33 U.S. (8 Pet.) 591, 614–15 (1834) (noting assertion by Wheaton's counsel that the Justices "invited [Wheaton] to attend at his own expense and report the cases; and there was at least a tacit engagement on their part to furnish him with such notes or written opinions as they might draw up").

26 JAMES S. YOUNG, THE WASHINGTON COMMUNITY 1800–1828, at 76–77 (1966). For an enjoyable re-creation of a typical term at the Court, see G. Edward White, *Imagining the Marshall Court,* 1986 Y.B SUP. CT. HIST. SOC'Y 77.

27 *See, e.g.,* Joseph Story to Henry Wheaton (Dec. 23, 1816), Wheaton Papers, *supra* note 3 (responding to Wheaton's suggestion of the arrangement that "[n]othing could be

Close both personally and professionally, they assembled a common library for use while in Washington.[28] Wheaton's relationships with the other Justices, while not nearly as familiar as with Story, seem in most instances to have been professionally cordial.[29]

The results of Wheaton's efforts to justify his appointment as Reporter were immediate and impressive. Within two months after the 1816 Term ended, he had completed his work in preparing the opinions, abstracts, and arguments of counsel for the press. Seven months elapsed before he could locate a bookseller who would publish the reports, albeit on terms barely palatable to Wheaton, and see them into print.[30] But by the time the Court arrived in Washington for its 1817 Term, the bench and the bar of the Supreme Court had in hand, for the first time in history, a published set of cases from the preceding Term. "The promptitude, with which the Reports follow the decisions," wrote William Pinkney, "greatly enhances their value to us all.... The Profession [is] infinitely indebted to you ... "[31] Later volumes appeared even more promptly, at worst within six months of the conclusion of the term in which the last case had been decided.

---

more pleasant to me than to chum with you this winter; & we will so arrange it at all events").

28 *See, e.g.*, Henry Wheaton to Joseph Story (Dec. 25, 1817), Wheaton Papers, *supra* note 3 (indicating which volumes Wheaton would carry with him for the 1818 Term and requesting Story to extract cases from others that "Lord knows ... will not be found in Washington").

29 For example, in entrusting an opinion to the Reporter for the press, Bushrod Washington enjoined Wheaton warmly "to correct with freedom all errors in language." Bushrod Washington to Henry Wheaton (May 24, 1817), Wheaton Papers, *supra* note 3.

30 As Peter Du Ponceau, Wheaton's agent in Philadelphia, succinctly advised him: "Bookselling is at present a very bad business, & Booksellers are all out of spirits, & unwilling to undertake any original work." Peter Du Ponceau to Henry Wheaton (June 13, 1816), Wheaton Papers, *supra* note 3. After difficult negotiations, Wheaton accepted $1200 in notes from Mathew Carey, a publisher not normally engaged in the law trade, actually selling to Carey the copyright in the volume—the only occasion on which he parted with the copyright in his *Reports*. *See* Joyce, *The Rise of the Supreme Court Reporter*, *supra* note 6, at 1325–26, 1339–40. Volume 1 sold slowly. In 1821, five years after printing 1000 copies with high hopes, Carey still had 200 of them lying about. Evidence of H.C. Carey, reprinted in Record, *supra* note 25, at 23–24. Carey sold the remaining copies, and assigned all of his interest under the contract, to Robert Donaldson of New York, Wheaton's publisher for Volumes 2 through 12. Assignment by Carey to Donaldson (Sept. 7, 1821), reprinted in Record, *supra* note 25, at 23. Wheaton retained his copyrights in the latter volumes only by giving his publisher an exclusive license to print a set number of copies. *See, e.g.*, the Memorandum of Agreement between Cornelius S. Van Winkle and Charles Wiley, two New York printers, and Wheaton (Apr. 28, 1817), *reprinted in* Record, *supra* note 25, at 28 (license for 1000 copies, subsequently conveyed to Donaldson). Donaldson eventually would become Wheaton's co-complainant in *Wheaton v. Peters*.

31 William Pinkney to Henry Wheaton (Sept. 3, 1818), Wheaton Papers, *supra* note 3.

Such promptitude was not without reward, albeit a paltry one. At the urging of the Court itself,[32] Congress consented to recognize the Reporter's office and to appropriate a salary of $1000, but only on condition that eighty copies of each volume of reports be donated for government use.[33] Wheaton thus became the first official Reporter in the history of the Court, but with financial encouragement wholly insufficient to overcome his dependence on sales to the profession.

Wheaton pressed on, producing over the course of the twelve terms he served what has been called "the golden book of American law."[34] In *Wheaton's Reports* appear many of the greatest cases of the Marshall Court, including *Martin v. Hunter's Lessee*,[35] *McCulloch v. Maryland*,[36] *Dartmouth College v. Woodward*,[37] *Sturges v. Crowninshield*,[38] *Gibbons v. Ogden*,[39] *Osborn v. Bank of the United States*,[40] and *Ogden v. Saunders*.[41] But there was more.

Under Wheaton, the fidelity of the reports was paramount. Accuracy and completeness, like timeliness of publication, improved dramatically. In addition, Wheaton provided to purchasers a resource unimagined by his predecessors: extensive scholarly annotations intended to furnish readers a comprehensive view of entire areas of law, apropos the decisions of each term.[42] Many of the annotations were prepared anonymously for Wheaton by Story, his Washington "chum."

---

[32] John Marshall to the Senate Judiciary Committee (Feb. 7, 1817), *reprinted in* 2 WILLIAM CROSSKEY, POLITICS AND THE CONSTITUTION IN THE HISTORY OF THE UNITED STATES, app. G, at 1246 (1953).

[33] Act of Mar. 3, 1817, ch. 63, § 1, 3 Stat. 376. The present statute is 28 U.S.C. § 672.

[34] German obituary (source unknown), Wheaton Papers, *supra* note 3.

[35] 14 U.S. (1 Wheat.) 304 (1816).

[36] 17 U.S. (4 Wheat.) 316 (1819).

[37] 17 U.S. (4 Wheat.) 518 (1819).

[38] 17 U.S. (4 Wheat.) 122 (1819).

[39] 22 U.S. (9 Wheat.) 1 (1824).

[40] 22 U.S. (9 Wheat.) 738 (1824).

[41] 25 U.S. (12 Wheat.) 213 (1827).

[42] Wheaton's aim, as he explained in the preface to Volume 1, was "to collect the rules and grounds dispersed throughout the body of the same laws, in order to see more profoundly into the reason of such judgments and ruled cases," with the expected result "that the uncertainty of law, which is the principal and most just challenge that is made to the laws of our nation at this time, will, by this new strength laid to the foundation, be somewhat the more settled and corrected." 14 U.S. (1 Wheat.) at v-vi (1816) (quoting Lord Bacon). In all, the annotations (or appendix notes) to Wheaton's twelve volumes run to 516 pages.

Unfortunately for Wheaton, his otherwise admirable scholarship, combined with such factors as generous margins and handsome bindings, contributed greatly to the expense of his reports—and, accordingly, to the same slow sales that had afflicted Dallas and Cranch before him. Sporadic retainers to argue cases before the Court alone or with others (including Daniel Webster in *Ogden v. Saunders*),[43] and occasional but unsuccessful runs at appointment to the Court himself (in 1823 and 1826),[44] provided additional frustrations. In 1827, Wheaton resigned as Reporter to accept a diplomatic posting to Denmark (thereby quadrupling his salary)—and to hope for better things to come.[45]

In accepting Wheaton's resignation, Chief Justice Marshall wrote: "I can assure you of my real wish that the place you have resigned had been more eligible [i.e., remunerative], and had possessed sufficient attractions to retain you in it. I part with you with regret . . . "[46] Sadly for Wheaton, whose plans for a happy retirement from the Court's employment contemplated continued income from sales of his *Reports*, the greater sorrow would soon be his.

Peters's Reportership and Wheaton's Peril

Wheaton's successor was Richard Peters Jr.[47] The new Reporter's father, Richard Peters Sr., had been a member of the Continental Congress and become U.S. District Judge for the District of Pennsylvania in 1792, remaining on the bench until his death in 1828. As District Judge, Peters Sr. served on the Circuit Court with Justice Bushrod Washington, whose decisions on that court Peters Jr. had edited. With Washington's support, Peters the Younger apparently secured appointment to the Reportership by unanimous vote of the Justices.[48]

---

43 25 U.S. (12 Wheat.) 213 (1827). Webster and Wheaton's arguments were rejected by the Court on a 4–3 vote. Regarding Wheaton's other cases, *see* Joyce, *The Rise of the Supreme Court Reporter*, *supra* note 6, at 1340–42, 1348–49.

44 *See* Joyce, *The Rise of the Supreme Court Reporter*, *supra* note 6, at 1348–49.

45 Joseph Story to Sarah Story (Mar. 8, 1827), Story Papers, University of Texas Library, Austin, Texas. The post paid $4500 a year, plus expenses.

46 John Marshall to Henry Wheaton (June 21, 1827), Wheaton Papers, *supra* note 3. All told, Wheaton's twelve years of labor as Reporter earned him $9900. For further details, *see* Joyce, *The Rise of the Supreme Court Reporter*, *supra* note 6, at 1338–40. Any hope for further income from his [could be "Reports"] depended on continued demand for those copies already in print and available for sale by his publisher, Donaldson. If that supply could be exhausted before Wheaton's copyrights expired, new sales—and income—might follow.

47 Born Belmont, Pa., Aug. 4, 1779 (sometimes reported as Aug. 17, 1780); died Belmont, Pa., May 2, 1848.

48 *See* C.C. Biddle to Richard Peters Jr. (Dec. 15, 1827), Peters Papers, *supra* note 17 (congratulating Peters on his appointment).

While not pretending to the intellectual stature of Dallas, Cranch and Wheaton, nor destined to rival their accomplishments in other offices, Peters possessed one attribute his illustrious predecessors all notably had lacked: a keen business sense. He believed that the *Reports* could be made to pay. His plan for publishing them resembled the man himself: brisk, practical, and determined to avoid unremunerative detours into esoteric scholarship.

Peters's publication plan had two components. The first concerned the traditional annual volumes of reports. In terms of the Court's opinions, the accuracy and completeness of Peters's *Reports* proved to be comparable to Wheaton's; and the new Reporter's Act of 1827,[49] requiring publication at a price not exceeding five dollars per volume within six months of the close of each sitting of the Court, assured timeliness and affordability. With respect to presentation and the Reporter's own contributions, however, Peters's *Reports* became the subject of much criticism.[50]

The second, more ambitious component of Peters's plan to make the reports pay is described aptly by the title of the project: *Condensed Reports of Cases in the Supreme Court of the United States, Containing the Whole Series of the Decisions of the Court From Its Organization to the Commencement of Peters's Reports at January Term 1827*. Both the need for such a publication and Peters's gift for exploiting it shine from the pages of his self-confident *Proposals* for the work, issued less than six months after assuming the Reporter's office:

> The [decisions of the] Supreme Court of the United States . . . should be universally known. That there should be found but few copies of the reports of the cases decided in the Supreme Court of the United States in many large districts of our country . . . is asserted to be a frequent fact. . . . These things should not be.

[49] Act of Feb. 22, 1827, ch. 18, §§ 1–3, 4 Stat. 205.

[50] Upon receiving his copy of Volume 1, Justice Story wrote immediately to the new Reporter to express his regret "that the text is so compact & small," a measure he supposed "unavoidable to bring the work into a moderate compass" but nonetheless a respect in which he "greatly . . . preferred . . . the 12th of Wheaton." Joseph Story to Richard Peters Jr. (June 26, 1828), Peters Papers, *supra* note 17. In place of Wheaton's expansive scholarship explicating the jurisprudence of the Term, moreover, Peters offered only compressed abstracts (or headnotes) of the cases decided. This innovation received similarly unflattering reviews. Boston's *American Jurist and Law Magazine* wrote: "After studying a page or two of fine type, [the reader's] mind is in a painful state of uncertainty as to the points actually decided by the court, and can only be relieved by examining the body of the decision." In at least one instance, Peters had stated as the holding of a case a rule "directly the reverse of the opinion" handed down by Marshall. "Indeed there is scarcely a single abstract in the volume which states the points in the case definitely and tersely, and which is not open to serious objections." *Peters's Reports*, 3 AM. JURIST & L. MAG. 101–03, 108–09 (1830).

It will not be denied that these circumstances are the consequences of the heavy expense which must be incurred by the purchase of the two [sic] volumes of the Reports of Mr. Dallas, the nine volumes of Mr. Cranch, and the twelve of Mr. Wheaton's Reports; together twenty-three [sic] volumes—the cost of which exceeds one hundred and thirty dollars.

It is proposed to publish all the cases adjudged in the Supreme Court of the United States from 1790 to 1827, inclusive, in a form which will make the work authority in all judicial tribunals, and to complete the publication in not more than six volumes, the price of which shall not exceed thirty-six dollars.[51]

There were trade-offs, to be sure. The type employed would be smaller than in the original volumes. The arguments of counsel that had appeared in the earlier reports were to be omitted entirely, as well as the scholarly notes contained in Wheaton's twelve volumes. Most significantly, in his zeal to present the cases in "abbreviated form," Peters intended to pare away concurring and dissenting opinions. The means might be draconian, but the aim was brilliantly appealing: at one stroke, Peters's *Condensed Reports* would supplant the entire market for all of his predecessors' volumes through slashing both bulk and expense by 75%.

Two sorts of reactions followed predictably. First, those deeply concerned with, but not financially interested in, disseminating broadly the reports of the Supreme Court (like the Justices themselves) rejoiced. Justice Story thought the "compressed Edition" contemplated by Peters "a most valuable present to the Profession."[52] Justice Washington lauded it as "a treasure" that would "liberally reward" the Reporter.[53]

What, on the other hand, of Dallas, Cranch and Wheaton, Peters's predecessors in production of the Court's reports? Dallas had died in 1817, and the copyright in his volumes had expired. Cranch, still a sitting judge in the District of Columbia and still out of pocket $1000 on the expenses of his final volumes, objected strongly.[54] Peters riposted that his project "will [not] injure the sale[s] of your or Mr. Wheaton's

---

51 *Proposals For publishing, by subscription, The Cases Decided in the Supreme Court of the United States, From its organization to the close of January term, 1827* (1828), *in* RECORD, *supra* note 25, at 9–11. Clearly, owning a full set of the reports of Dallas, Cranch, and Wheaton at $130 was beyond the means of all but the most successful lawyers in major commercial centers.

52 Joseph Story to Richard Peters Jr. (June 26, 1828), Peters Papers, *supra* note 17.

53 Bushrod Washington to Richard Peters Jr. (July 21, 1828), Peters Papers, *supra* note 17.

54 William Cranch to Richard Peters Jr. (July 18, 1828), Peters Papers, *supra* note 17.

Reports," but on the contrary would render them "more in demand . . . " More to the point, Peters averred, his reports "will not be obnoxious to the law protecting literary property," for he planned to take from Cranch's volumes nothing written by his predecessor himself: "My work will be a 'Digest' of the facts of the case and the opinions of the Court—no more."[55] Seeing the handwriting on the wall, Cranch ultimately settled with Peters in return for fifty copies of the *Condensed Reports*.[56]

That left only Peters's immediate predecessor, Henry Wheaton. Wheaton had counted on future sales of his *Reports* to realize the fruit of his labors. Unfortunately for him, Peters's "Digest" was anything but a digest. By reproducing the Court's opinions in full, it might, if it proved popular with the practicing bar, eliminate entirely the need to consult Wheaton's volumes.

Happily occupied with diplomacy in faraway Denmark, Wheaton seems not to have appreciated, at first, the gravity of his peril. Surely, he wrote to Daniel Webster in late 1828 following the publication of Peters's *Proposals*, "amicable remonstrances" would dissuade his successor from proceeding?[57] Nothing, however, would budge Peters from his chosen path. The first volume of the *Condensed Reports* went to press late in 1829. Having just lost his principal patron, Bushrod Washington, to death, Peters wasted no time in shoring up his support on the Court against any eventuality. He promised to dispatch a copy of his newest work immediately when printed to Justice Story,[58] and dedicated the work itself, "most respectfully and affectionately," to Chief Justice Marshall.[59]

Peters's *Condensed Reports* quickly became an enormous success. In February of 1831, Volume 3 appeared in an edition of 1500, with more than 900 copies sold by subscription in advance.[60] In addition to Cranch's last two volumes, this latest installment of the *Condensed Reports* contained the first volume of Wheaton's *Reports*.

---

55 Richard Peters Jr. to William Cranch (Aug. 14, 1828), Peters Papers, *supra* note 17.

56 Richard Peters Jr. to Richard S. Coxe (Dec. 13, 1829), Peters Papers, *supra* note 17.

57 Henry Wheaton to Daniel Webster (Nov. 25, 1828), Wheaton Papers, Library of Congress, Washington, D.C. (noting that his expectations for future printings of his *Reports* "in order to realize the fruits of my labor . . . will be entirely defeated should Mr. Peters persist in his design.").

58 Richard Peters Jr. to Joseph Story (Nov. 26, 1829), Story Papers, Massachusetts Historical Society, Boston.

59 Richard Peters Jr., 1 CONDENSED REPORTS OF CASES IN THE SUPREME COURT OF THE UNITED STATES, CONTAINING THE WHOLE SERIES OF THE DECISIONS OF THE COURT FROM ITS ORGANIZATION TO THE COMMENCEMENT OF PETERS'S REPORTS AT JANUARY TERM 1827, at iii (1830).

60 FREDERICK C. HICKS, MEN AND BOOKS FAMOUS IN THE LAW 208 (1921).

In May of 1831, on behalf of Wheaton and himself, Wheaton's publisher, Robert Donaldson,[61] filed suit in the Circuit Court for the Eastern District of Pennsylvania against Peters and his publisher, John Grigg of Philadelphia.[62] Donaldson wrote to Wheaton, in demanding that the latter immediately engage counsel to protect their mutual interests: "[U]ntil an example is made of these literary Pirates there can be no security for the labours of authors and Publishers."[63] For two years, however, the matter remained mired in the Circuit Court, until ultimately it ruled in favor of Peters and Grigg.

In April of 1833, Wheaton and Donaldson appealed.[64] But was it too late? Wheaton, absent on diplomatic missions abroad since the conclusion of his Reportership, already had lost the first round. The matter now would proceed to Wheaton's former employers at the Supreme Court, where Peters served by the Justices' side in Wheaton's former place. "Peters is on the spot," wrote Wheaton's former New York law partner, Elijah Paine, "& alas, the face of a party does often turn a doubtful balance held by human judges."[65]

Wheaton now had no choice. His continued income from his *Reports*, his legacy to his family, and perhaps all remembrance of his name in the annals of American law, hung in the balance. The time for "amicable remonstrances" was past. His own presence "on the spot" was required. And so, in the middle of October,[66] Wheaton set sail from Liverpool to New York City on a boisterous late-season passage across the Atlantic to take charge of his own case—and to help write the first great chapter in the jurisprudence of American intellectual property law.

Introducing the Issues

The protection of literary property in England and America had enjoyed a checkered history in the several centuries before *Wheaton v.*

---

61 As recited earlier, *see supra* note 30, Donaldson held both the copyright in Wheaton's first volume and the rights to first printings of Volumes 2 through 12. The complainants thus held closely related interests: if Peters's project destroyed the market for Wheaton's *Reports*, Donaldson would be unable to sell his remaining copies of the first printings; if Donaldson's supply of copies of the first printings could not be exhausted, Wheaton's right to print further copies of the volumes to which he had retained the copyrights would be without value.

62 For a discussion of the claims themselves, *see* "*Wheaton v. Peters* in the Courts," *infra*.

63 Robert Donaldson to Henry Wheaton (Aug. 11, 1828), Wheaton Papers, *supra* note 3.

64 RECORD, *supra* note 25, at 61.

65 Elijah Paine to Henry Wheaton (Aug. 28, 1833), Wheaton Papers, *supra* note 3.

66 BAKER, *supra* note 24, at 127.

Peters.[67] In England, following a regime of private rights created by the booksellers' (or stationers') guild and supported for its own purposes by the Crown, Parliament had adopted the Statute of Anne,[68] the world's first copyright act, in 1710. In 1774, the House of Lords had held definitively, as to published works, that the *only* protection available to authors and their assignees was statutory.[69] In America, the Framers had acted swiftly in 1787, following the failure of the Articles of Confederation, to empower the new national government created by the Constitution to act forcefully on intellectual property law,[70] as on many other fronts. In 1790, Congress duly enacted a national copyright statute[71] (and acted again with further legislation in 1802,[72] 1819[73] and 1831[74]).

---

[67] For a detailed recounting of the history summarized above, *see* L. Ray Patterson & Craig Joyce, *Copyright in 1791: An Essay Concerning the Founders' View of the Copyright Power Granted to Congress in Article I, Section 8, Clause 8 of the U.S. Constitution*, 52 EMORY L.J. 909 (2003).

[68] An Act for the Encouragement of Learning, by Vesting the Copies of Printed Books in the Authors or Purchasers of such Copies, during the Times therein mentioned, 1710, 8 Anne, c. 19 (Eng.).

[69] *Donaldson v. Beckett*, 4 Burr. (4th ed.) 2408, 2417, 98 Eng. Rep. 257 (H.L. 1774).

[70] Under the Copyright and Patent Clause, art. I, § 8, cl. 8, the Constitution empowered Congress "[t]o Promote the Progress of Science and useful Arts, by securing for limited Times, to Authors and Inventors, the exclusive Right to their respective Writings and Discoveries."

[71] An Act for the Encouragement of Learning, by Securing the Copies of Maps, Charts, and Books, to the Authors and Proprietors of Such Copies, during the Times Therein Mentioned, Act of May 31, 1790, 1st Cong., 2d Sess., 1 Stat. 124. Following the Statute of Anne, the 1790 Act provided the copyright holder an exclusive right to print and vend copies of a protected work for a term of fourteen years, with possible renewal for fourteen years more (if the author lived out the first term), but subject to specified conditions to qualify for protection. Congress made eligible for copyright both works already printed in the United States (thereby avoiding problems that might otherwise have arisen from formulating the grant as a term extension only for works then subject to state copyrights) and those afterwards published in America (thereby establishing the uniform schema that would obtain throughout the nation once all pre–1790 copyrights had expired).

The first Congress also drafted the Bill of Rights, including the Free Press and Speech Clauses, and forwarded them to the states, which then ratified them in 1791. Some (but not all) commentators infer that the Founding Generation envisaged the Copyright Clause and the First Amendment as complementary parts of a coherent and consistent system of law capable of promoting and protecting creativity by encouraging the protection of new works, ensuring freedom of expression, strengthening trade in the marketplace of ideas, and securing the public domain. *See generally* Patterson & Joyce, *Copyright in 1791*, *supra* note 67, and the selected list of authorities cited there; *and see* "*Wheaton* and Its Legacies," *infra*.

[72] Act of Apr. 29, 1802, 7th Cong., 1st Sess., 2 Stat. 171.

[73] Act of Feb. 15, 1819, 15th Cong., 2d Sess., 3 Stat. 481.

[74] Act of Feb. 3, 1831, ch. 16, 21st Cong., 2d Sess., 4 Stat. 436.

Thus, by 1834, the stage was set for the great contest over the protection of law reports, and of literary property generally, that would culminate in the Supreme Court's decision in *Wheaton v. Peters*. *Wheaton* would react with this history principally on the three issues previewed below.

Statutory Right vs. Natural Law

In England, the nature of copyright in books had been settled in 1774 by the House of Lords' great decision in *Donaldson v. Beckett*.[75] The principal question there was whether, after the Statute of Anne, copyright law, at least as to manuscripts subjected to publication, had become solely a creature of statute, all rights existing subject to constraints enacted by the legislature, or whether a common law entitlement, arising by virtue of an author's natural right in the product of her creations, had preexisted adoption of the Statute and then survived its enactment unfettered by the Statute's limitations (including as to duration). In *Donaldson*, the House of Lords had adopted the statutory right (or positive law) theory of copyright, and thus assured that published books which did not qualify for copyright or exceeded the statutory term of protection would escape the claims of would-be proprietors and fall forever into the public domain, there to be enjoyed freely by all.

In the United States, no such authoritative judicial determination as to the basis of copyright holders' rights—including Wheaton and his publisher's rights, if any, in Wheaton's *Reports*—had yet been made.

The Importance of Statutory Formalities

The Statute of Anne, the model for all early American copyright legislation, had prescribed certain statutory formalities,[76] including registration of the title of the book and deposit of a copy thereof with the Stationers' Company, in order to perfect copyright protection. Similarly, the Copyright Act of 1790 prescribed registration of a copyright claim with the local federal district court clerk and deposit of a copy of the work, within six months of publication, in the office of the Secretary of State. The 1802 Act added a new formality: the placement of a notice of copyright on every publicly distributed copy of the work. Finally, the 1831 Act revised the details of all of three of the by-then established formalities, namely, registration, deposit, and notice.[77]

---

75 *See supra* note 69.

76 For a detailed description of the Statute of Anne's provisions, *see* Patterson & Joyce, *Copyright in 1791*, *supra* note 67, at 916–23.

77 In addition to the summary of these Acts provided earlier in the Story, fuller descriptions are available in 1 William F. Patry, Copyright Law and Practice 25–39 (1994).

In seeking to protect his volumes of *Reports*, had Wheaton and his publisher complied scrupulously with the statutory formalities? If not, what became of their claimed copyrights in the contents of those volumes?

Owning the Reports of Opinions[78]

Neither the Statute of Anne nor any American enactment had spoken directly to one remaining question that would prove pivotal in *Wheaton v. Peters*. Even if, in the United States, copyright for published works was a creature solely of statute, and even if all of the formalities provided by such statutes had been observed punctiliously in the publication of Wheaton's *Reports*, that question remained. Peters had asserted (in his reply to Cranch's objections, later copied also to Wheaton) that Peters's republication of opinions and underlying facts from his predecessors' volumes was "not obnoxious to the law protecting literary property" because the matter taken from the reports of Dallas, Cranch and Wheaton was *incapable* of protection.

How could that be? Assuming, for the sake of argument, that Wheaton had satisfied all requirements prescribed by law for obtaining the protection afforded by statute, how could Peters's taking *not* offend the law of copyright? How could anyone *other* than Wheaton, who had obtained by gift from the Justices, in return for faithful service, such written opinions as they possessed, and created all of the remaining opinions himself from notes laboriously taken in the courtroom, not possess the exclusive right, promised by Constitution and statute alike, to print and vend the heart and soul of his *Reports*? In short, who owned the Justices' official accounts of American law?

Wheaton v. Peters in the Courts

The Proceedings Below

Henry Wheaton arrived in Washington, D.C., in mid-January 1834 looking, in the words of his opponent, Richard Peters Jr., "very mad,"[79]

---

[78] Neither Henry Wheaton nor any of his predecessors claimed explicitly to own "the law" itself, if by "the law" is meant the holdings and rationales of the Justices' opinions. *See infra* text accompanying notes 87–95 for Wheaton's own precise specification to his counsel of those aspects of the *Reports* (head notes, etc.) in which he claimed personal authorship. His analysis, however, leveraged that authorship, plus his reconstruction of opinions delivered from the bench with no written text by the Justices, into a claim of copyright that protected the contents of his twelve volumes of *Reports* in their entirety. If Wheaton's monopoly rights under copyright extended, as he claimed, so far as to preclude his successor, Richard Peters Jr., from copying any part of those volumes, in practice no one could obtain access to the Justices' accounts of "the law" except by the purchase of books, published or licensed by Wheaton, in which those accounts were to be found.

[79] Richard Peters Jr. to Thomas Sergeant (Jan. 15, 183[4]), Sergeant Papers, Historical Society of Pennsylvania, Philadelphia.

and threw himself immediately into preparations for the argument of his case before the Supreme Court. The case had gotten there by a curious route.[80]

Wheaton and Donaldson's bill in equity, filed against Peters and Grigg in the Circuit Court for the Eastern District of Pennsylvania, had sought an injunction to prevent the defendants from further printing or disseminating copies of Volume 3 of Peters's *Condensed Reports*, plus an accounting of profits. The bill alleged that Peters's volume contained, "without any material abbreviation or alteration, all the reports of cases" in Volume 1 of Wheaton's *Reports*.[81] In his answer, Peters denied that he had violated the complainants' rights, contending that the statutory requirements for securing a federal copyright had not been met, that no right to common law copyright existed in the United States, and that, in any event, the contents of Wheaton's *Reports*, insofar as they had been republished in the *Condensed Reports*, were incapable of supporting a copyright either under statute or at common law.[82]

Initially, the court issued the preliminary injunction sought by Wheaton and Donaldson.[83] In early 1832, Peters and Grigg moved to dissolve the injunction. The two judges constituting the court—Henry Baldwin (who had succeeded Bushrod Washington on the Supreme Court) and Joseph Hopkinson (who had succeeded Peters's father on the District Court)—found themselves unable to agree on a disposition. Hopkinson favored dissolving the injunction; Baldwin, dismissing the motion. Accordingly, the injunction remained in force. Circumstances had changed, however, by the time the action came before the court for final hearing in December of 1832. Baldwin, incapacitated by a "derangement of the mind" of progressive severity, could not or would not sit. Hopkinson, refusing to defer the hearing "for a day," proceeded with the arguments. His opinion, dismissing the bill and dissolving the injunction, was entered on January 9, 1833.[84] In essence, Hopkinson agreed with Peters and Grigg that the complainants had failed to accomplish the prerequisites for statutory copyright under the laws of

[80] The proceedings in the Circuit Court, as well as the Supreme Court, are discussed also in Howard B. Abrams, *The Historic Foundation of American Copyright Law: Exploding the Myth of Common Law Copyright*, 29 WAYNE L. REV. 1119, 1178–85 (1983).

[81] RECORD, *supra* note 25, at 6–7.

[82] *Id.*, at 14–18. Grigg's separate answer contained substantially the same allegations. *Id.* at 18–21.

[83] The following account relies primarily on Paine's report to Wheaton on the progress of the litigation. Elijah Paine to Henry Wheaton (Jan. 16, 1833), Wheaton Papers, *supra* note 3.

[84] Wheaton v. Peters, 29 F. Cas. 862 (C.C.E.D. Pa. 1832) (No. 17,486), *reprinted in* Wheaton v. Peters, 33 U.S. (8 Pet.) 591 app. at 725 (1834).

the United States and that any claim to common law copyright, state or federal, had been precluded by the pertinent enactments of Congress.[85] The opinion did not address the issue of the copyrightability of the opinions and other matter taken by Peters from earlier reports. Wheaton and Donaldson's appeal to the Supreme Court followed quickly.[86]

The Issues from Wheaton's Perspective

Ultimately, the outcome of the controversy, once Hopkinson rendered his judgment in Peters's favor, lay in the viability of Peters's predecessor's justifications for the protection he always had assumed attached to his *Reports*. We pause briefly, therefore, to review from Wheaton's perspective the critical issues of the case, as reflected in two extraordinary memoranda in Wheaton's own hand, written for the benefit of his counsel, Daniel Webster and Elijah Paine, upon Wheaton's arrival in Washington.[87]

In their efforts to predict and influence the resolution of the dispute by the Justices, Wheaton (and counsel on both sides) could draw on relatively little American case law, and certainly no precedents of the Court itself. Of the handful of lower court cases on the law of copyright decided in the four decades since the founding of the national government, only two were directly relevant. One, decided by a state court,[88] had displayed a liberal attitude toward authorship by excusing certain prerequisites to statutory copyright as merely "directory," while the other, a Circuit Court decision by Justice Washington,[89] had held any departure from the strict requirements of the Acts of 1790 and 1802

---

85 Act of May 31, 1790, ch. 15, 1 Stat. 124, and Act of Apr. 29, 1802, ch. 36, 2 Stat. 171.

86 RECORD, *supra* note 25, at 61. Peters, for his part, proceeded with publication of the remaining three volumes of the *Condensed Reports*. Volume 6 appeared in January of 1834, two months prior to argument of the appeal in the Supreme Court.

87 Wheaton had sought to enlist Webster (cousin of Noah Webster of dictionary fame) in July 1831. Wheaton to Webster (July 22, 1831) ("consider yourself as retained for me"), quoted in BAKER, *supra* note 24, at 126. Paine, Wheaton's long-time friend and former partner from New York City days, reinforced the invitation that December. Paine to Webster (Dec. 6, 1831) ("[t]his suit . . . will without any doubt be carried to Washington"), Webster Papers, New Hampshire Historical Society, Concord, N.H., quoted in BAKER at 347 n.5. The documents prepared by Wheaton for counsel, located in Wheaton's Papers, *supra* note 3, are cited hereinafter as *Wheaton's Pre–Argument Memorandum A* and *Wheaton's Pre–Argument Memorandum B*.

88 *Nichols v. Ruggles*, 3 Day 145, 158 (Conn. 1808) (publishing title of book in newspaper and delivering copy to Secretary of State "constitute no part of the essential requisites for securing the copyright").

89 *Ewer v. Coxe*, 8 F. Cas. 917 (C.C.E.D. Pa. 1824) (No. 4584) (holding all statutory requirements under 1790 and 1802 Acts, by virtue of latter enactment, to be mandatory).

fatal to the author's rights. Neither case spoke to the question of Wheaton's unique circumstances as Reporter.

Unquestionably, in Wheaton's view, "a Reporter is an *Author*," his "exclusive right to the Copy" in his *Reports* unaltered by either his appointment by the Justices or receipt of a paltry salary from Congress under the Reporter's Act of 1817. The true reward for Wheaton's twelve years of labor was his expectation of continuing revenue from purchases of the *Reports* themselves, which in turn rested on the promise of continuing protection of the Reporter's copyrights under the laws of the United States.[90]

Wheaton's point—that the decisions of the Court as rendered in the *Reports* always had been regarded as subject to copyright by the Reporter—rested on well-recognized practical and theoretical foundations. English court reporters of the day were assumed to own the copyrights in their reports.[91] Moreover, historically, copyright law in America has served (in the words of the Copyright Clause itself) "[t]o promote the Progress of Science" by incentivizing authors financially.[92] Prior to publication of the *Condensed Reports*, scarcely anyone had questioned the wisdom of according to Wheaton and his predecessors the exclusive right to multiply copies of their volumes as a key incentive to their labors.[93] That assumption simply had not had occasion to be examined with a critical eye until challenged by Peters.

Wheaton faltered slightly, however, in describing for counsel precisely which aspects of his works constituted copyrightable authorship. "Mr. W. is unquestionably author," he wrote, "of the Summaries of Points decided—of the Statements of the Cases prefixed—of the analytical

---

90 *Wheaton's Pre-Argument Memorandum A, supra* note 87.

91 *See, e.g.,* Butterworth v. Robinson, [1801] 31 E.R. 817 (assuming copyright in reports in action for injunction); Saunders v. Smith, [1838] 40 E.R. 1100 (same). *See* also Sweet v. Benning, [1855] 16 C.B. 459 (holding, in a case involving the piracy of abstracts of cases from the plaintiffs' "weekly paper called 'The Jurist,' . . . consist[ing] principally of reports of decisions in the various superior courts of law and equity," that the reports were copyrighted and, in the absence of a fair abridgment, had been infringed).

92 *See, e.g.,* Harper & Row, Publishers, Inc. v. Nation Enters., 471 U.S. 539, 606 (1985) (copyright law "supplies the economic incentive to create and disseminate" nonprotectible ideas and facts clothed in protectible expression).

93 "Who would have undertaken the expense & risk of publishing an edition of [judicial reports]," Wheaton would later cry, if they "might be encountered the next day by a piratical edition?" *Wheaton's Pre-Argument Memorandum A, supra* note 87. Certainly Justice Story, Wheaton's mentor and friend, had harbored no doubts concerning the copyrightability of such reports. In response to Wheaton's plea for assistance in finding a publisher for his first volume in 1816, Story had written: "I am fearful that at present there is not a bookseller in Boston who is able to print them, *or give anything for the copy right.*" Joseph Story to Henry Wheaton (May 25, 1816), Wheaton Papers, *supra* note 3 (emphasis added).

Indexes at the end of each vol. All these Mr. P. has pirated." But what of the opinions themselves, the principal component of the *Condensed Reports*' commercial appeal? Wheaton noted that "there [were] in every volume several Opinions delivered orally from the Bench, & taken down by Mr. W." Even so, it might be argued that the rationale for according such opinions copyright protection did not extend to the Court's more significant opinions, actually prepared by the Justices themselves. To this objection, Wheaton suggested the following reply:

> Supposing then Mr. W. has no Copy Right in the written opinions of the Judges—for argument's sake,—it is enough if he has such Right in any substantial portion of his 12 vols., which Mr. Peters has copied, no matter how little mind it may have required to compose that portion, or how piddling the labour may have been.[94]

In effect, Wheaton found himself reduced to arguing that the *Reports*, because they included parts individually susceptible to copyright, constituted compilations entitled to protection in their entirety.[95]

Similar difficulties confronted Wheaton in attempting to dispose of Peters's remaining defenses to his claims. On the issue of his compliance with the statutory formalities imposed by the Copyright Acts of 1790 and 1802,[96] Wheaton assured his attorneys that each and every requirement had been fulfilled. He failed, however, to note or suggest solutions to chronic and potentially fatal evidentiary deficiencies concerning publication of the copyright claims in the public press (a requirement deleted by the 1831 Act but too late to help Wheaton in protecting volumes published earlier); and he attempted feebly to explain away his own inattention to depositing a copy of each volume of the *Reports* with the Secretary of State, pursuant to the Copyright Acts, with the argument that he considered furnishing eighty copies, as required under the Reporter's Act, sufficient for both purposes.[97] In sum, Wheaton believed

---

[94] *Wheaton's Pre-Argument Memorandum A, supra* note 87.

[95] Cf. the Copyright Act of 1976, which specifically approves the copyrightability of compilations, but provides that "[t]he copyright in a compilation . . . extends only to the material contributed by the author of such a work [i.e., by the compiler], as distinguished from the preexisting material employed in the [compilation] . . . " 17 U.S.C. § 103 (2000).

[96] Taken together, the Acts prescribed four steps to be accomplished by an author seeking to obtain a federal statutory copyright: (1) record the title of the work in the office of the clerk of the federal judicial district in which the author resided; (2) print a copy of the record thus procured on the title page, or following page, of the work; (3) within two months of recording the title, cause a copy of the record to appear in the public press for a period of four weeks; and (4) within six months of publication of the work itself, deliver a copy thereof for deposit at the Department of State. Specifically, Peters claimed that Wheaton had failed to perform the third and fourth steps.

[97] Carey, Donaldson's predecessor as proprietor of the initial term of the copyright to Wheaton's first volume, had attended to compliance with the statutory formalities concern-

he had achieved substantial compliance with all of the statutory requirements; and, in those instances when his observance had been less than punctilious, the requirements were "directory merely" and "not a condition, the non-compliance with which forfeits the right."[98]

On the issue of a possible common law copyright subsisting apart from the right claimed under statute, Wheaton declined "to be drawn into the field of controversy whether the federal Courts have a common law jurisdiction, although it would be easy to show that they have." Instead, he considered it sufficient to "assume that the Acts of Congress were intended to secure my right of property existing independent of the Acts themselves." Being "remedial & protective" only, they should be given a "liberal construction." Thus, Wheaton considered himself entitled to an injunction to secure the enjoyment of "sacred rights," whose origin (apart from statute) he was unwilling or unable to describe.[99]

Would such responses suffice to overturn Hopkinson's ruling in the court below?

The Arguments

In the actual argument of the case on March 11, 12, 13 and 14, 1834, before six of the seven members of the Court[100] (Marshall, Story, Duvall, McLean, Thompson and Baldwin, now partially recovered from his apparent breakdown during the Circuit Court proceedings), the propositions propounded in Wheaton's memoranda metamorphosed significantly in the hands of Webster and Paine. Paine assumed, without really arguing, that proper notice of Wheaton's copyright claims had been given in the press, and asserted, without really proving, that in actuality eighty-one copies of the *Reports* (not simply the eighty copies required to obtain the Reporter's salary) had been transmitted annually to the Department of State.[101] Wheaton was thus within the letter of the law,

ing that volume. RECORD, *supra* note 25, at 23–24 (evidence of Henry C. Carey). With respect to succeeding volumes, Wheaton himself had exercised considerable care to assure proper delivery of the 80 copies required to obtain payment of his salary. *Id.* at 40–48 (deposition of Daniel Brent and certificates of receipt by Department of State). None of the available evidence, however, suggests that Wheaton ever sought to insure a separate deposit of one copy of each of his volumes (making a total of 81) for purpose of securing his copyrights.

98 *Wheaton's Pre-Argument Memorandum B*, *supra* note 87.

99 *Id.*

100 "Mr. Justice Johnson was absent, from indisposition, during the whole term." 33 U.S. (8 Pet.) iii (1834).

101 "The fact is, that eighty-one copies were sent, but the law giving the salary, not requiring more than eighty, the papers in the department under these acts speak of but

and most certainly within its spirit. The statutes at issue must not be construed in such a way as to impair an author's right of property in copies of his works by loading down that right "with burthensome and needless regulations" making the preservation of the right "wholly dependent on accidental mistake or omission."[102] For the Framers of the Constitution had "adopted it with a particular view to preserve the common law right to copyrights untouched."[103]

Unlike Wheaton, however, Paine located the origin of an author's "acknowledged pre-existing right" to profits derived from the multiplication of copies of his work not in federal common law, but in the common law of Pennsylvania. Merely by adopting the Constitution, the states "ha[d] not surrendered to the Union their whole power over copyrights, but [had] retain[ed] a power concurrent with the power of congress."[104] For any violation of his common law right, Paine declared, an author might obtain "the ordinary remedies by an action on the case and bill in equity,"[105] either in state court or "in the circuit court of the United States ... independently of the provisions of the act of congress."[106] Thus, the federal copyright acts neither conferred the natural property right sued upon by Wheaton nor diminished in any way the ordinary remedies available to him to vindicate it. Instead, the Acts of 1790 and 1802 operated only to "secure" the author's rights by adding to his remedies under state law the possibility of "penalties and forfeitures" to be enforced against infringing parties upon compliance by the author with the statutory formalities.[107] Wheaton had sought no such penalty or forfeiture. Hence, any non-compliance with the Acts, even if conceded, could hardly deprive him of his right to obtain justice in the federal courts.

Paine reserved his greatest ingenuity, however, for the coda to his argument. Of the four supposed objects of Peters's piracy,[108] only one really mattered: unless Wheaton had somehow obtained copyrights in

---

eighty; and all being sent to the department together, is the reason why there was no minute, or memorandum, or certificate.... " 33 U.S. (8 Pet.) at 612.

[102] *Id.* at 605–06.

[103] *Id.* at 601.

[104] *Id.* at 597–98.

[105] *Id.* at 607.

[106] *Id.* at 606.

[107] *Id.* at 609–10.

[108] "[F]irst, ... the abstracts made by Mr. Wheaton; secondly, ... the statements of the cases ...; thirdly, ... points and authorities, and, in some instances, the arguments, and in all cases oral opinions ...; [and] fourthly, ... the whole of the [written] opinions" prepared by the Justices. *Id.* at 617.

the manuscript opinions of the Justices in every significant decision handed down during his tenure as Reporter, the *Condensed Reports* had infringed no interest of any real value in the marketplace. Paine thought the matter transcendently clear. Wheaton had acquired a copyrightable interest in all such opinions, he averred, "by judges' gift":[109]

> The copy[right] in the opinions, as they were new, original and unpublished, must have belonged to some one. If to the judges, they gave it to Mr. Wheaton. That it did belong to them is evident; because they are bound by no law or custom to write out such elaborate opinions. They would have discharged their duty by delivering oral opinions. What right, then, can the public claim to the manuscript? The reporter's duty is to write or take down the opinions. If the court choose to aid him by giving him theirs, can anyone complain?[110]

All this, the Court had known in appointing Wheaton its Reporter and furnishing him the Justices' opinions. Reporters always had been assumed to acquire copyrightable interests in this, the single most valuable component of their works. To rule otherwise now would be to deprive not only Wheaton, but all other reporters as well, of their familiar

---

109 *Id.* at 614–15. Peters seems to have anticipated, and in some measure feared, this argument, at least in the period following the publication of his first volumes of *Condensed Reports* and prior to the filing of Wheaton's action. Unable to know in advance the disposition of the issues that would be decided finally by the Court in 1834, he hedged his bets regarding what he supposed to be the nonprotectibility of the Justices' opinions. Writing to Justice McLean in early 1830, Peters observed that the *Condensed Reports* had excited among booksellers holding unsold copies of his predecessors' volumes "no small degree of hostility," which he apprehended might lead to "an attempt to *injure*" his own *Reports*. Therefore, Peters wrote, "as I am under some doubt whether by the mere circumstance of my being *Reporter* I obtain a *property in the opinions* of the Court I have thought it a measure of prudence to obtain from each member of the Court a special assignment [of] the right to each opinion delivered by him." Richard Peters Jr. to John McLean (May 24, 1830), Miscellaneous Papers, New York State Library, Albany, New York. McLean, author of the Court's opinion in *Wheaton v. Peters* four years later, responded with notable care: "A faithful report of the decisions of the Supreme Court of the United States, is of great importance to the public, & I should exceedingly regret, any interference with your rights as Reporter. *So far as I have any right in the opinions delivered by me*, at the late session of the Court, I hereby, freely and fully, transfer it to you." John McLean to Richard Peters Jr. (June 3, 1830), Peters Papers, *supra* note 17 (emphasis added). Other members of the Court exercised similar caution. *E.g.*, Joseph Story to Richard Peters Jr. (June 1, 1830), Peters Papers, *supra* note 17 (assigning the copyright in his opinions "in as ample a manner as I now hold the same," while reserving the right of Congress to authorize future publications by others); and Henry Baldwin to Richard Peters Jr. (June 8, 1830), Peters Papers, *supra* note 17 (same). The prickly William Johnson, however, rejected Peters's request *in toto*, on grounds that "our opinions I have never doubted were public property & not assignable by us." William Johnson to Richard Peters Jr. (June 5, 1830), Peters Papers, *supra* note 17.

110 33 U.S. (8 Pet.) at 615.

rights.[111] Such a result, as Paine foresaw clearly, would alter fundamentally the entrepreneurial underpinnings of court reporting throughout the country.

J. R. Ingersoll and Thomas Sergeant, on behalf of Peters, contradicted Paine's argument on every point. Each recognized, however, that Wheaton's case would stand or fall according to the Court's disposition of Paine's claim that the opinions of the Justices constituted copyrightable matter, the rights to which they had transferred to the Reporter. Sergeant foreshadowed one rationale for the exclusion of protection for what we now call "work[s] of the United States Government"[112]:

> The court appointed [Wheaton] under the authority of a law of the United States, and furnished him the materials for the volumes; not for his own sake, but for the benefit and use of the public: not for his own exclusive property, but for the free and unrestrained use of the citizens of the United States.[113]

Ingersoll put the matter on an even higher plane, evoking a "due process" basis for that same exclusion, and according equal dignity, and an equal necessity of diffusion, to enactments of Congress and decisions of the Court:

> Reports are the means by which judicial determinations are disseminated, or rather they constitute the very dissemination itself.... The matter which they disseminate is, without a figure, the *law of the land*. Not indeed the actual productions of the legislature. Those are the rules which govern the action of the citizen. But they are constantly in want of interpretation, and that is afforded by the judge. He is the "*lex loquens*." His explanations of what is written are often more important than the mere naked written law itself. His expressions of the *customary law*, of that which finds no place upon the statute book, and is correctly known only through the medium of reports, are indispensable to the proper regulation of conduct in many of the most important transactions of civilized life. Accordingly, in all countries that are subject to the sovereignty of the laws, it is held that their promulgation is as essential as their existence.... It is therefore the true policy, influenced by the essential spirit of the government, that laws of every description should be universally diffused. To fetter or restrain their dissemination, must be to counteract this policy. To limit, or even to regulate it, would, in fact, produce the same effect. Nothing can be done,

---

[111] *Id.* at 616–17.

[112] *See* 17 U.S.C. § 105.

[113] 33 U.S. (8 Pet.) 591 at 638.

consistently with our free institutions, except to encourage and promote it.[114]

Webster's speech to the Court, concluding the arguments, briefly engaged the doctrinal points discussed by other counsel but sought primarily to reduce the case to its essential human dimension. There had come a point late in the reportership of Wheaton's predecessor, Webster said, when the very continuance of the *Reports* had hung in the balance. But for Wheaton's appearance on the scene, with the promise of "a regular annual publication of the decisions" of the Court, there might have been no dissemination whatsoever of future reports. In order to supplement his income for the copyright to his *Reports*, "[i]t was found necessary that there should be some patronage from the legislature," i.e., a salary for the Reporter. The Reporter's Act had been renewed regularly, and "[t]he successor of Mr. Wheaton has had the full benefit of the grant obtained by the personal exertions of Mr. Wheaton." Lately, although "well advised" of Wheaton's rights, Peters had "materially injured" those interests by publication of the *Condensed Reports*. In short, he had made "an indefensible use of [his predecessor's] labours," which the Court must now remedy by construing Wheaton's rights "liberally."[115]

The Decision (and the Opinions)

The reluctance of the Court in deciding so bitter a controversy between two of its own officers, past and present, with whom the Justices had lived and worked on intimate terms, readily can be imagined. That discomfort is reflected vividly in a series of extraordinary occurrences preceding and accompanying the announcement of the decision itself.

On the morning of March 18, 1834, Justice Story, acting, in what the messenger assured Wheaton were the Justice's own words, "entirely on his own hook," summoned the Court's past and present Reporters to meet with him personally, in succession, in his chambers.[116] Upon arriving, Wheaton was greeted by Story "in his usual cordial manner" and handed a memorandum which Story had been "authorized by the Court to communicate to" each of the litigants.[117] The memorandum, which

114 *Id.* at 619–20.

115 *Id.* at 651–52.

116 *Wheaton's Post-Argument Memorandum* (Mar. 18, 1834), Wheaton Papers, *supra* note 3 [hereinafter *Wheaton's Post-Argument Memorandum*]; Joseph Story to Henry Wheaton (Mar. 17, 1834), Wheaton Papers, *supra* note 3.

117 *Wheaton's Post-Argument Memorandum*, *supra* note 116. Apparently, Story's particular contribution to the Court's design to force a resolution of the controversy short of

Story likewise furnished to Peters, advised the parties that the decision of the Court, if handed down, would hold unanimously that no right of property did or could exist in the Justices' opinions, and that they were without power to confer upon the Court's Reporters any copyright thereto. As to the marginal notes and indices prepared by Wheaton, however, the Court had touched upon but not finally determined the litigants' rights, believing that matter to be "a fit subject for honourable compromise between the parties . . . "[118]

Wheaton reacted angrily. Three weeks earlier, Peters had rejected his offer that "the whole Cause" be referred to arbitrators. Story suggested that Wheaton might be operating under a supposition regarding the remaining issues in the case "that my rights were more extensive than they might turn out to be."[119] Wheaton then asked for and received leave to confer with Webster, who "unhesitatingly advised" him to reject the suggested compromise. Wheaton's formal reply to the Court after consultation with Webster, while restrained in tone, firmly insisted that "the merits of the Cause so fully & ably discussed" now be finally resolved.[120] Left with no choice, the Court proceeded to do as Wheaton had demanded at its conference later in the same day.

The necessity of resolving the difficult and highly charged issues presented by the case brought to a head many stresses already present among the Justices. The death of Bushrod Washington five years before, as Peters then observed to Story, had destroyed "[t]he triple column [Marshall, Story and Washington] on which the Court ha[d] rested for many years in balance."[121] In the White House sat a President hostile to many of the doctrines theretofore promulgated by the Court, now busily installing new men in the old Justices' places.[122] By 1832, Story lamented to Peters that the "dignity, character, & courtesy" of the Court had declined noticeably.[123]

---

final decision was his plan to broker the compromise personally in meetings with the parties.

[118] *Id.*; *Story's Post–Argument Memorandum* (undated copy furnished by Story to Wheaton with letter of Mar. 25, 1834), Wheaton Papers, *supra* note 3.

[119] *Wheaton's Post–Argument Memorandum*, *supra* note 116.

[120] *Id.*; Wheaton's letter to the Court (Mar. 18, 1834), Wheaton Papers, *supra* note 3. Wheaton's reply also specifically noted his claims, which he supposed the Court had "omitted by accident to mention," to his abstracts and statements of the facts and cases.

[121] Richard Peters Jr. to Joseph Story (Nov. 26, 1829), Story Papers, Boston, *supra* note 58.

[122] Interestingly, Andrew Jackson's first two appointees, McLean (1829) and Baldwin (1830), split in *Wheaton v. Peters*, McLean writing for the majority (with Marshall, Story and Duvall, holdovers from the Court's "glory days") and Baldwin dissenting (along with Thompson, a Monroe appointee).

[123] Joseph Story to Richard Peters Jr. (Mar. 31, 1832), Peters Papers, *supra* note 17.

The atmosphere at the Justices' conference late on March 18 no doubt was made more painful by the reopening of old wounds inflicted in prior discussions of the case at hand. In recounting the conference to Wheaton on the day following the Court's announcement of its decision,[124] Baldwin recalled that Story had accused him, at an earlier date, "of having granted an Injunction [on circuit] to prevent the publication of the Decisions of the Court."[125] Perhaps to reduce the likelihood of such exchanges recurring, the conference decided without discussion (and adversely to the complainants) the question of the validity of Wheaton's supposed copyright under federal or state common law. On the statutory issues (also decided against Wheaton and Donaldson), discussion was allowed but kept so brief that the Justices left the conference unclear, as they would discover the next morning, as to precisely what the majority had concluded regarding the requisite formalities. Finally, while all of the conferees departed with an understanding that the matter must be remanded to the Circuit Court for further evidentiary proceedings, the majority was unwilling or unable to instruct Baldwin, who, with Hopkinson, would have to preside over the trial, concerning matters of law certain to arise there.[126]

Confusion at the conference presaged disaster on the day of decision. Just how deeply the matter had divided the Court became startlingly clear on the morning of March 19, 1834, when the Justices convened to announce their opinions.[127] Story, the member of the Court previously closest to the two main litigants, missed the melee altogether. He had departed Washington on the 8 a.m. stage, leaving Justice McLean, in Wheaton's words, "to fire off the blunderbuss [Story] had loaded, but had not courage to discharge."[128]

---

124 All information in this paragraph, unless otherwise stated, is taken from *Wheaton's Post-Decision Memorandum* (Mar. 20, 1834, the day after the decision), Wheaton Papers, *supra* note 3.

125 Story's attitude toward the case may be conjectured further from his remark to Peters that he had been "surpri[s]ed at the appeal." Joseph Story to Richard Peters Jr. (Nov. 13, 1833), Peters Papers, *supra* note 17.

126 In particular, Baldwin sought direction regarding how to instruct the jury as to the effect of lapse of time on Wheaton's assertions of actual, albeit unprovable, compliance with the statutory formalities.

127 All information in the next three paragraphs, unless otherwise stated, is taken from Charles Sumner's account to Story, written in the courtroom itself on March 19, 1834, immediately after the incidents he describes, and Sumner's supplementary letter to Story on the same subject, dated March 20, 1834. Story Papers, Library of Congress, Washington, D.C.

128 Henry Wheaton to Catherine Wheaton (Mar. 21, 1834), Wheaton Papers, *supra* note 3. Story would later confide to his friend Chancellor Kent of New York: "I am sorry for the

The unfortunate McLean, on behalf of himself, Marshall, Story and Duvall, began by reading his opinion for the Court.[129] It denied any claim by the complainants to copyright at common law, leaving their rights in published works—at least, with respect to matter other than the opinions of the Justices—entirely dependent upon compliance with the 1790 and 1802 Acts of Congress. While remanding for certain factual determinations on that question, the opinion also reflected considerable doubt (and apparently straddled considerable internal confusion within the majority) concerning which of the statutory formalities had to be, and might have been, satisfied. Wheaton appeared "strongly excited during its reading," while Peters was "anxious but perfectly calm." Immediately upon McLean's conclusion, Thompson delivered the "purport" of his own opinion[130]—which (in a tradition dating back to the Court's first sessions forty years before) he had not yet written out in full but which adopted the main points of Paine and Webster's argument—"with much feeling." On the question of common law copyright, Thompson would have recognized Wheaton and Donaldson's claims under the law of Pennsylvania; as to protection under the applicable federal statutes, he asserted that "the Ct. were *equally* divided, so far as the operation of the St[atute] of 1802 went."[131] Baldwin followed,[132] agreeing with Thompson on the statutory question and also dissenting "from another point of the

---

controversy . . . [and] wish Congress would make some additional provisions on the subject, to protect authors, of whom I think no one more meritorious than Mr. Wheaton. You, as a Judge, have frequently had occasion to know how may bitter cups we are not at liberty to pass by." Joseph Story to James Kent (May 17, 1834), *reprinted in* 2 JOSEPH STORY, LIFE AND LETTERS OF JOSEPH STORY 182 (William W. Story ed., 1851).

129 33 U.S. (8 Pet.) at 654–68. The scene that followed no doubt owed its origin in part to the Court's failure during this period to circulate opinions among the Justices prior to reading them in the courtroom. *See* G. Edward White, *The Marshall Court and Cultural Change, 1815–1835, in* 3–4 THE OLIVER WENDELL HOLMES DEVISE HISTORY OF THE SUPREME COURT OF THE UNITED STATES 181–82 (1991), for a description of contemporary practices in this regard. The problem may have been compounded by the breathtaking speed with which the Court routinely handed down its decisions. *Id.* at 181.

130 33 U.S. (8 Pet.) at 668–98.

131 Charles Sumner to Joseph Story (Mar. 19, 1834), *supra* note 127. In William Johnson's absence from the bench, there were only six members of the Court sitting. Thompson did not disclose which majority Justice he believed disagreed with McLean on the point at issue. In any event, an equally divided vote would have resulted in letting stand Hopkinson's decision that the 1802 Act made the performance of all four of the statutory requirements mandatory.

132 33 U.S. (8 Pet.) at 698–98*bb* (F. Brightly ed., 1883). Baldwin apparently delivered a copy of his lengthy dissent to Peters too late for inclusion in the first edition of the *Reports* for the 1834 Term, thereby necessitating the unusual pagination of the opinion in later editions. The three opinions in the case are discussed at length, with helpful background concerning the doctrinal development of copyright law in America, in chs. 9 and 10 of L. RAY PATTERSON, COPYRIGHT IN HISTORICAL PERSPECTIVE (1968).

opinion of the Ct.—viz. that the U. States *qua* U.S. had no common law" under which Wheaton might claim copyright.

McLean then attempted an explanation of the Court's holding on the statutory issues, claiming that his analysis "was based on the St[atute] of 1790"[133] and that the matter "was all clearly stated in the opinion he had read." Thompson, "with intemperate warmth," replied that "if [the analysis] had been clearly stated there w[ou]ld have been no need for explanation." At this juncture, Marshall "made a statement of the opinion of the Ct. on the debated point [i.e., statutory construction] which was listened to with gr[ea]t attention." McLean, "with mingled pride & feeling checked by the proprieties of the place,"[134] at once "read the very words of the opinion & added that *this dialogue across from one to another* was very unpleasant."[135] Thompson rejoined "in a perfect boil,"[136] while Baldwin, "by looks & motions & whispers" evidenced a "strong passion at his back."[137] The Chief Justice "then s[ai]d that unless he had thought that the opinion as read needed explanation, he sh[ou]ld not have made it." Looking "like the good man whom Virgil has described as able to still the tumult of a crowd, by his very appearance,"[138] Marshall then "stated in full" the holding of the majority on the point of statutory construction. Through it all, Duvall sat "in utter unconsciousness of the strife around him," thereby "add[ing] to the grotesqueness of the scene," while "a large number of the bar" looked on "in anxiety & grief."[139]

At length, calm prevailed, and the Justices concluded their business for the Term. Word of the unusual "altercation" in court quickly spread to "*all Congress*," where it was "magnified . . . ten times over."[140] The profession at large, however, was not to be similarly titillated. Before quitting Washington late the same afternoon, Marshall admonished Peters that he "did not wish [him] to make any mention of the *differences* in his report of the case."[141] Peters did as bidden.

---

133 Charles Sumner to Joseph Story (Mar. 19, 1834), *supra* note 127.

134 Charles Sumner to Joseph Story (Mar. 20, 1834), *supra* note 127.

135 Charles Sumner to Joseph Story (Mar. 19, 1834), *supra* note 127.

136 Charles Sumner to Joseph Story (Mar. 20, 1834), *supra* note 127.

137 *Id.*

138 *Id.*

139 *Id.*

140 *Id.*

141 *Id.*

Apart from the colorful events of the day, what, exactly, had the Court ruled? It is difficult, exactly, to say. The opinions in *Wheaton* are, to put the matter in modern terminology, a mess. Neither of the Court's leading Justices, Marshall and Story, wrote a word (nor should that fact surprise, given their prior relationships with the Reporters). McLean's opinion for the majority, and Thompson's dissent, ramble, reflecting powerfully what McLean described as "[t]he limited time allowed for . . . preparation"[142]—five days following the close of argument! Baldwin's own ponderous dissent, apparently prepared after the event,[143] received no comment in the two opinions contemporaneously filed and remains almost unknown, even to scholars, today.[144]

On the question of an *author's right at common law*, the opposing philosophies do, indeed, receive clear statement. For McLean and the majority, Wheaton's claim to a copyright at common law, of unlimited duration, raised the specter of a monopoly on printed works that was inimical to the public interest:

> That an author, at common law, has a property in his manuscript, and may obtain redress against any one who deprives him of it, or by improperly obtaining a copy endeavors to realize a profit by its publication, cannot be doubted; but this is a very different right from that which asserts a perpetual and exclusive right in the future publication of the work, after the author shall have published it to the world.[145]

Thus, while an author no doubt "is as much entitled to the product of his labor as any other member of society, . . . he realizes this product by the transfer of his manuscript, or in the sale of his works, when first published."[146] Thereafter, no copyright monopoly can exist beyond the limits of statutory law as enacted by Congress.

The dissenters, on the other hand, saw no objection to a claim of perpetual copyright on printed matter. As Thompson's opinion asserted:

> The great principle on which the author's right rests, is, that it is the fruit or production of his own labour, and which may, by the labour of the faculties of the mind, establish a right of property, as well as by the faculties of the body; and it is difficult to perceive any

---

142 33 U.S. (8 Pet.) at 654.

143 *See supra* note 132.

144 Quite apart from its omission from *U.S. Reports*, Baldwin's opinion currently is unavailable at such on-line reports as Lexis or Westlaw.

145 33 U.S. (8 Pet.) at 657.

146 *Id.*

> well founded objection to such a claim of right. It is founded upon the soundest principles of justice, equity and public policy.[147]

Therefore, "[i]f there be a common-law right," as Thompson deemed certain, "there certainly must be a common-law remedy" underlying the merely "cumulative security or protection" afforded statutorily by Congress.[148] For Thompson and for Baldwin, because the author's fundamental right rested upon his creative act rather than any grant by Congress, no limitation on term applied.

While the philosophical distinction between the majority and the dissenters on the issue of author's rights was sharp, the "remembered holding" of *Wheaton* as a wholesale rejection of that principle with respect to published works overstates the clarity of the detailed analysis provided in the remainder of the opinions. The dissenters, Thompson and Baldwin, would have recognized such a right in favor of the complainants, although on different bases: Thompson, under the common law of Pennsylvania; Baldwin, under federal common law. McLean for the majority, however, recognized neither, at least on the facts presented in the case at bar. The applicable state law, if any, was the law of the state where the complainants' bill in equity had been filed. But no common law right of the sort claimed "had [t]heretofore been asserted," or by "custom or usage established," or by "judicial decision . . . given," in Pennsylvania. Nor could such a right be recognized federally, because there was "no common law of the United States." The Copyright Act of 1790, "instead of sanctioning an existing right, . . . [had] created it."[149]

McLean's analysis of Pennsylvania law is a classic bootstrap argument. A natural right in favor of an entire class of persons would not cease to exist, always and everywhere, simply because no person had yet asserted the right in a Pennsylvania courtroom. Likewise, McLean's federal common law analysis is, at best, suspect. It seems doubtful that Story, who eight years later recognized federal common law in *Swift v.*

---

147 *Id.* at 669–70.

148 *Id.* at 692, 696. The late L. Ray Patterson of the University of Georgia, leading copyright historian of our era, once observed:

> The striking point about the premises of the majority and the dissenters is that they are polar, the one proceeding from the interest of the public, the other from the interest of the individual creator. . . . [T]heir premises brought the justices to different conclusions as to how best to resolve the conflict between the public's interest in learning and the author's interest in his property. The majority, viewing copyright as a monopoly, was content to protect the author's property for a limited period under the conditions prescribed by the statute. To do otherwise would be contrary to the public interest. The dissenters, on the other hand, seemed to think that the best way to protect the public interest would be to give unlimited protection to the author's property.

PATTERSON, *supra* note 132, at 211.

149 33 U.S. (8 Pet.) at 658–61.

Tyson,[150] or for that matter Marshall, would have denied unequivocally the existence of such law, in an opinion of their own, in 1834. Nor is McLean's reading of the language of the 1790 Act compelling. Congress could well have "secure[d]" existing rights (a clearly plausible meaning to attribute to that term in both the Constitution and the Act) at the same time as it created new ones.

No matter, practically speaking. On the question of common law rights, the complainants in *Wheaton* had lost 4–2. Once the author has published the work, the right must exist, if at all, by virtue of compliance with applicable statutory law.

The vote count as to the proper application of the *statutory formalities* is less clear. McLean's own view concerning the mandatory character of such formalities as a prerequisite to copyright protection[151] was, he said, "principally founded" on his reading of the 1790 Act. But "if doubts could be entertained"—McLean did not say by whom, although presumably their number did not include others in the majority—whether that enactment's requirements of notice and State Department deposit "were essential to the title," there was, "in the opinion of three of the judges"—apparently not including McLean himself—"*no* ground for doubt" as to the mandatory character of the newspaper publication commanded by the 1802 Act, in its own terms, "in addition to the requisitions enjoined" by the 1790 Act.[152] Thompson was astonished. McLean's construction of the 1790 Act itself "c[ould] not be sustained" under any rule of statutory interpretation; and "as to the effect of the act of 1802 upon the act of 1790, the court is *equally* divided."[153] "Upon the whole," he declared, "and in whatever light this case is viewed,"[154] the judgment below should be reversed. Baldwin, believing the congressional acts to be "merely directory, explanatory, or constructive"[155] in support of Wheaton's preexisting common law copyright, concluded that Wheaton and Donaldson, while unable (absent further proof at trial) to avail themselves of any legal benefits added by statute, nonetheless were

---

[150] 41 U.S. (16 Pet.) 1 (1842) (bill of lading).

[151] "No one can deny that when the legislature are about to vest an exclusive right in an author or inventor, they have the power to prescribe the conditions on which such right shall be enjoyed; and that no one can avail himself of such right who does not substantially comply with the requisitions of the law." 33 U.S. (8 Pet.) at 663–64.

[152] *Id.* at 665 (emphasis added), *quoting* An Act for the Encouragement of Learning, by Securing the Copies of Maps, Charts, and Books, to the Authors and Proprietors of Such Copies, during the Times Therein Mentioned, Act of May 31, 1790, 1st Cong., 2d Sess., 1 Stat. 124.

[153] 33 U.S. (8 Pet.) at 694 (emphasis added).

[154] *Id.* at 698.

[155] 33 U.S. (8 Pet.) at 698*aa* (F. Brightly ed., 1883).

entitled to all remedies afforded them by equity, including injunctive relief and an accounting.

Again, no matter. A majority of the Court seemingly had held the 1790 Act's (and only the 1790 Act's) formality requirements to be conditions precedent to protection.[156] "The construction of the acts of congress being settled," wrote McLean, "in the further investigation of the case it would become necessary to look into the evidence" to ascertain whether Wheaton and Donaldson had shown "a substantial compliance with every legal requisite."[157] The judgment and decree of the Circuit Court, accordingly, were reversed and remanded, subject to a mandate to try the case on those issues.[158] Only if the complainants could demonstrate their compliance with the statutory formalities at trial would they establish any rights as to Wheaton's *Reports*.

As to what aspects of the *Reports*, however? McLean, for the majority, did not say. Nor did Thompson. Only Baldwin, in the single opinion in the case most favorable to the complainants, was explicit. Wheaton's marginal notes, etc., "are as much literary property as any productions of the mind," he observed, and capable of protection under Wheaton's copyrights, if any. But "the opinions of the court are clearly not so."[159]

And there lay the rub. As Peters's *Condensed Reports* by their very nature attested, the entire commercial value of Wheaton's volumes resided in *owning the opinions*,[160] whatever other rights he might possess in such peripheral matter as syllabi of cases or scholarly annotations. Whether anything regarding the latter remained to be tried below, and whether the principles involved meant enough to Wheaton to pursue

---

156 The contretemps on the bench on the day of decision, and even Marshall's explanation that day of the Court's holding on the debated point of statutory construction, seem not to have settled the matter sufficiently for McLean to reduce it clearly to writing. Thompson could only sputter in dissent: "[S]uch I understand to be the opinion of a majority of this court, . . . that . . . the decision of the cause rests upon the act of 1790." *Id.* at 694. Dissenting from Thompson's dissent, however, the relevant volume of the Holmes Devise declares: "On the mandatory nature . . . of the 1790 Act's provisions . . ., [McLean] did not have a majority . . . " WHITE, *supra* note 129, at 421.

157 33 U.S. (8 Pet.) at 667.

158 *Id.* at 698.

159 33 U.S. (8 Pet.) at 698*g* (F. Brightly ed., 1883).

160 In *Gray v. Russell*, 10 F. Cas. 1035, 1039 (No. 5,728) (C.C. Mass. 1839), Justice Story observed: "In the case of Wheaton v. Peters, . . . [i]t was not doubted by the court that Mr. Peters' Condensed Reports would have been an infringement of Mr. Wheaton's copyright, supposing that copyright properly secured under the act, if the opinions of the court had been or could be the proper subject of the private copyright by Mr. Wheaton."

them,[161] the case was irretrievably lost when, in the concluding paragraph of his opinion, McLean announced:

> It may be proper to remark that the court are unanimously of opinion, that no reporter has or can have any copyright in the written opinions delivered by this court; and that the judges thereof cannot confer on any reporter any such right.[162]

On that point, there was no dispute by any Justice in any opinion.

---

[161] Emotionally, if not financially, they did, to the respondents' great dismay. The parties, at the time, regarded this disposition as a matter of considerable consequence. Peters sought vigorously, but unsuccessfully, to have the mandate amended and thereby avoid the inconvenience of a trial of the remaining factual questions, however trivial. *See, e.g.*, John Marshall to Richard Peters Jr. (May 15, 1834), Peters Papers, *supra* note 17 (one of several letters by various members of the Court rejecting Peters's argument that the mandate did not accurately reflect McLean's opinion). Wheaton returned to Denmark in June, BAKER, *supra* note 24 at 132–33, but not before setting in progress through his Philadelphia attorneys the necessary work of gathering the evidence to be adduced at trial. *See, e.g.,* Charles Chauncey to Henry Wheaton (Apr. 11, 1834), John Cadwalader to Henry Wheaton (Apr. 24, 1834), Charles Chauncey to Henry Wheaton (Apr. 29, 1834), and John Cadwalader to Henry Wheaton (June 10, 1834), all in Wheaton Papers, *supra* note 3.

[162] 33 U.S. (8 Pet.) at 668. In so holding, the Court, of course, broke from its own prior assumptions regarding the ownership of judicial opinions. It appears also to have departed from the contemporary English understanding concerning such ownership. *See supra* text accompanying note 91. Clearly, insofar as the English cases reflect a view that *actual opinions of judges* as contained in reports of decisions are capable of protection, the *Wheaton* Court was of a different mind.

But why? Several explanations suggest themselves. First, the English cases seem to assume, as to the courts being reported, a predominance of oral opinions, with reporters assembling, from notes by gentlemen of the bar, approximations of the opinions actually delivered by the judges. Such practice, arguably, bespoke greater "authorship" by English reporters than occurred in the Supreme Court of the United States between 1816 and 1827. In earlier days, the Court had provided little written matter for the Reporters' guidance in reconstruction oral opinions. During Wheaton's tenure, however, written opinions prepared by the Justices themselves (albeit often after their announcement from the bench) had become more common practice and were furnished as a matter of course to the Reporter. *See supra* text accompanying notes 24–25. In addition, Wheaton's personal attendance at the Court's sessions produced reports markedly more faithful to the Justices' own utterances and writings, *see supra* text accompanying notes 26–42, than in the days of Dallas and Cranch—reports, in short, much less subject to claims of "authorship" by the Reporter than were the volumes described in the nineteenth century English cases cited above. For further comparative reflections on authorship and ownership in nineteenth century law reports, see EATON S. DRONE, A TREATISE ON THE LAW OF PROPERTY IN INTELLECTUAL PRODUCTIONS IN GREAT BRITAIN AND THE UNITED STATES 159–63 (1879).

That said, the practical excellences of Henry Wheaton's *Reports* can account only in part for the disparate treatment given law reports in nineteenth century English and American courts. McLean's opinion for a unanimous bench in *Wheaton* applied to *all* "written opinions delivered by this court," a rubric that embraced not only Wheaton's volumes but also those of Dallas and Cranch, the "volunteers" who had preceded him, as well as his successor, Peters—and all the Reporters of Decisions to come.

Thus, one further explanation for the separate path taken by American courts, beginning with *Wheaton v. Peters*, suggests itself. Perhaps the true key to a fuller

In sum, on all the issues of law, Peters had triumphed. A tiny portion of the matter claimed by Wheaton as author might indeed be subject to copyright, protected by compliance with the applicable enactments of Congress, and infringed by Peters, pending further proof.[163] But the Court had made clear that copyright in the United States, at least as to published works, was a creature of federal statute only. It had ruled that obedience to the formalities required by such statutes was a *sine qua non* of protection. And it had established, emphatically, that the opinions of the Court's members could not be owned by them or by any Reporter.

Wheaton v. Peters thus obliterated a presumption of intellectual property ownership long shared by Wheaton, his predecessors and the Justices themselves which, if given the force of law, would have bestowed upon the Reporters exclusive title to those classic expressions of American law that constitute the Court's essential legacy to the nation. No doubt, Wheaton and Peters saw the matter in more narrow, immediate, and personal terms. The Court, however, saw further than they. In a case that saddened and pained the Justices themselves even as they rendered a decision indispensable to the progress of a national jurisprudence, the Court assured that henceforth American law should be owned by no one—and thus be owned by all, for the benefit of all. In retrospect, in a nation dedicated to free speech, free press, and the widest possible dissemination and debate of facts and ideas, the outcome could not have been otherwise.

---

understanding of *Wheaton*'s determination that law reports of decisions of the federal courts cannot be owned by anyone—not the judges, and not the reporters—lies in a recognition of the New Republic's comparatively robust commitment to free speech and press values and in an accompanying commitment (as yet more instinctive than doctrinal) to protecting and enhancing the public domain so as to provide ready access to the laws that governed its citizens' lives. For more on these matters, see text accompanying notes 182–88 *infra*; Patterson & Joyce, *Copyright in 1791*, *supra* note 67, at 942–45, 949–50.

163 Who, however, would continue to buy copies of Wheaton's *Reports* with Peters's compendium of their truly valuable components—the opinions—available at a fraction of the cost? "Justice will never be done me," Wheaton wrote. Had the Court not upheld Peters's duplicity in offering to the marketplace his *Condensed Reports* as a cheaper alternative to Wheaton's own, "I might have published new editions of each volume as the [copy]right successively expired, and should have been in the possession of a regular and annual income of at least 2,000 dollars from this source for many years to come. Such is the extent of the mischief done by the reckless partiality of prevaricating judges." Henry Wheaton to Eliza Lyman (May 22, 1837), *quoted in* BAKER, *supra* note 24, at 130.

The Aftermath

The Litigation and the Participants

The decision in *Wheaton v. Peters* on March 19, 1834 (and subsequent issuance of the mandate) marked the end of the Supreme Court's involvement in the case, but not the end of the saga (or the proceedings) for the litigants themselves.

In terms of reporting at the Court, the Justices, stung by the results of lax prior practices concerning opinions, began to regularize their procedures. Already, on the last day of argument in *Wheaton*, they had adopted an order providing that, upon publication of each volume of the *Reports*, the originals of such written opinions as had been prepared should be filed by the Reporter with the Clerk and preserved for posterity.[164] By a subsequent order, the Court required that opinions be first delivered to the Clerk for recording and then sent to the Reporter.[165] Under prior practice, physical copies of the opinions had been treated as the Reporters' personal property. Henceforth, both the copies of, and the law contained in, the Justices' opinions would be, unquestionably, public property.

Richard Peters Jr. had the pleasure of memorializing *Wheaton v. Peters* in Volume 8 of his own *Reports*. For many in the bar, however, Peters's efforts, particularly his garbled abstracts of the main points of cases, always had provided a benchmark for mediocrity.[166] In time, relations with the Court likewise became strained by perceptions of inaccuracy in the *Reports*.[167] The Court summarily dismissed Peters in 1843.

Henry Wheaton returned to diplomatic service and to scholarship. Serving abroad under six presidents, he rose to U.S. minister plenipotentiary to Prussia and membership in elite academic societies throughout Europe. In addition, his *Elements of International Law*[168] earned him acclaim among contemporaries as the "chief modern expounder of the science of international law."[169]

The case itself, owing to the Court's remand, did not end for all purposes in 1834. The majority's disposition—although it had ruled for Peters on all key points of law—returned the matter to the Circuit Court

---

164 33 U.S. (8 Pet.) vii (1834), *reprinted in* 42 U.S. (1 How.) xxxv (1843) (Rule No. 41).

165 42 U.S. (1 How.) xxxv (1843) (Rule No. 42).

166 *See supra* note 50 (critical reviews of Peters's early volumes).

167 *See* COHEN & O'CONNOR, *supra* note 6, at 71–74.

168 HENRY WHEATON, ELEMENTS OF INTERNATIONAL LAW (1836).

169 HICKS, *supra* note 60, at 215 (1921).

for a trial by jury to determine whether, in fact, Wheaton had published proper newspaper notice of his claim and delivered the requisite copy of the work to the Secretary of State for each volume of his *Reports*.[170] The jury returned a verdict in Wheaton's favor in 1838.[171] The matter then dragged on interminably on its way back to the Supreme Court.[172] Before the appeal could be heard there, however, both of the principal protagonists died: Wheaton, on March 11, 1848, and Peters, less than two months later, on May 2, 1848. Ultimately, their estates settled the litigation, Peters's paying Wheaton's $400, in 1850.[173]

Wheaton and Its Legacies

In the end, *Wheaton v. Peters* is a "great case"[174] (indeed, the last great case decided by the Marshall Court) for none of the reasons usually associated with Marshall Court opinions. Its focus is not predominately constitutional, nor can it claim authorship by the Chief Justice himself or even by Justice Story. Rather, the "greatness" of the case lies in what it tells us about the Court itself—and in the critical doctrines of intellectual property law that it propounded or has come to represent.

Statutory Right vs. Natural Law

We know from the dissents in *Wheaton* that the question of the existence of common law copyright in Wheaton's *Reports* was decided negatively on a 4–2 vote. But the reasoning of the members of the majority appears, from a reading of Justice McLean's opinion, to have been an unstable mix at best.

That said, U.S. law since *Wheaton,* at least until the 1976 Act, has proceeded on the assumption that copyright for published works arises only by virtue of federal statute, and that authors (and their transferees) are accorded copyright for their works only instrumentally, i.e., to encourage creativity in aid of the common welfare.[175] Congress does, from

---

170 33 U.S. (8 Pet.) at 698–99.

171 John Cadwalader to Henry Wheaton (May 23, 1838), Wheaton Papers, *supra* note 3 (verdict advisory only, however, to equity court).

172 The appeal in the case was finally perfected in 1846. John Cadwalader to William Lawrence (Wheaton's friend, and later executor) (Sept. 24, 1846), Cadwalader Papers, Historical Society of Pennsylvania, Philadelphia.

173 William Lawrence to Robert Wheaton (Henry's son) (Feb. 18, 1850), Wheaton Papers, *supra* note 3.

174 White, *supra* note 129, at 421.

175 *See, e.g.,* Mazer v. Stein, 347 U.S. 201, 219 (1954): "The economic philosophy behind the clause empowering Congress to grant patents and copyrights is the conviction that encouragement of individual effort by personal gain is the best way to advance public welfare through the talents of authors and inventors in 'Science and useful Arts.' "

time to time, enact statutes creating new rights for authors under U.S. law.[176] But however just may be the case for such rights existing apart from statutory law, the reality in America is that today they do not exist until recognized in Title 17 of the *United States Code*.[177]

The Importance of Statutory Formalities

While Justice McLean's own rendering of the vote count is no model of lucidity, he appears to have enjoyed a bare numerical majority in *Wheaton* for a reading that at least substantial compliance with the statutory formalities prescribed by applicable Acts of Congress (in the case at bar, the 1790 Act) was essential to perfecting title in copyrightable works.

Nonetheless, owing if nothing else to the posture of the matter as it had arrived at the Court, the case was remanded to the court below to determine whether the copyright claimants could demonstrate compliance with "every legal requisite."[178] Arguably from this modest beginning,[179] U.S. copyright law embarked on a long national obsession with what became the "unholy trinity" of statutory formalities—notice, deposit, and registration—complete with often draconian penalties for failure to comply.[180] Not until the United States fully joined the world

---

[176] The watershed event was U.S. adherence to the Berne Convention of the Protection of Literary and Artistic Works, effective March 1, 1989 by virtue of the Berne Convention Implementation Act of 1988 ("BCIA"), Pub. L. 100–568, 102 Stat. 2853 (1988). The leading illustration of such authors' rights legislation, enacting what in Europe would be regarded as the *natural rights* of authors, is the Visual Artists Rights Act of 1990, Pub. L. No. 101–650, tit. VI, 104 Stat. 5089, 5128–33 (effective June 1, 1991).

[177] The rights are stated broadly in §§ 106, 106A and 602 but are limited by §§ 107–122.

[178] 33 U.S. (8 Pet.) at 667.

[179] In fairness to the Court, instead one might plausibly lay the (credit or) blame at the feet of Congress, which passed both the 1790 and 1802 Acts at issue in *Wheaton* and subsequent legislation which it then became the duty of U.S. courts to construe. Of the 1831 Act (not material in *Wheaton* because Wheaton's final volume had been published in 1827), for example, the Supreme Court would later rule: "Undoubtedly, the [formalities] prescribed by the statute . . . are conditions precedent to the perfection of the copyright." Callaghan v. Myers, 128 U.S. 617, 652 (1888).

[180] The tale is told elsewhere in painful detail. *See generally, e.g.*, CRAIG JOYCE ET AL., COPYRIGHT LAW ch. 6 (6th ed. 2003) (detailing both the history of the formalities themselves and their relationship to the doctrines of limited and general publication), and the following three studies (including the decisions and legislative revisions cited therein) prepared for the Subcommittee on Patents, Trademarks, and Copyrights of the Committee on the Judiciary, United States Senate (86th Cong., 1st Sess.) in anticipation of passage of the Copyright Act of 1976: VINCENT A. DOYLE ET AL., STUDY NO. 7: NOTICE OF COPYRIGHT (1957); BENJAMIN KAPLAN, STUDY NO. 17: THE REGISTRATION OF COPYRIGHT (1958); and ELIZABETH K. DUNNE, STUDY NO. 20: DEPOSIT OF COPYRIGHTED WORKS (1960).

copyright community in the waning years of the twentieth century would the statutory formalities beast assume the role of largely toothless tiger that it occupies today.[181]

Owning the Reports of Opinions

No one who knew Henry Wheaton as Reporter, least of all the Justices with whom he served, could doubt his devotion to the advancement of the Supreme Court as an institution and the progress of national law in early America. All the same, Wheaton as Reporter (like Dallas and Cranch before him) had been motivated, too, by hope for at least a modest financial reward. The decision in the great case that bears his name dashed that hope forever. For all the words spilt in *Wheaton*, the truly critical question in the case was distilled in a single sentence at the end of McLean's opinion that reads almost as an afterthought: Was copyright protection for the Justices' opinions available under any U.S. law, federal or state, under any circumstances? McLean's answer, for *all* of the Justices, unequivocally was no.

The afterlife of this pronouncement is clear, as indeed it had to be if public documents constituting the "law of the land"—opinions authored by judges; statutes authored by legislators; addresses, messages, regulations, and the like authored by Executive Department officials—are to be, as Ingersoll put the matter in his argument on behalf of Peters, "universally diffused."[182] The principle now has been codified for U.S. Government works[183] and received general acceptance in the states as well.[184]

Of course, many questions concerning the law of copyright (and of intellectual property law generally) remained unanswered in 1834. During the remainder of the nineteenth century, for example, and consistent with the pro-public domain values signaled in *Wheaton* (the denial of

---

181 *See* §§ 7–9 of the BCIA, *supra* note 176. Even today, however, a few teeth remain. Registration is a prerequisite to suit for United States works and a precondition for awards of statutory damages and of attorney's fees. *See* 17 U.S.C. §§ 101 (definition of "United States work"), 411(a) (registration and infringement actions), 412 (registration and availability of certain remedies for infringement), 504(c) (statutory damages), 505 (costs and attorney's fees).

182 33 U.S. (8 Pet.) at 620.

183 17 U.S.C. § 105.

184 *See generally* L. Ray Patterson & Craig Joyce, *Monopolizing the Law: The Scope of Copyright Protection for Law Reports and Statutory Compilations*, 36 UCLA L. Rev. 719 (1989), and the cases cited there. While there appear to be limits on the general principle as applied in the states with respect to documents created or adopted by state or local governments that are not "the law," there is no doubt as to copyright protection for statutes, ordinances, judicial opinions and the like even below the federal level: There *is* no protection.

copyright protection for judicial opinions; the embrace of statutory copyright, to the exclusion of common law perpetual rights, for published works; and the beginnings of rigorous enforcement of formalities requirements that would place all non-compliant works in the public domain),[185] U.S. law would adopt other critical doctrines promoting the marketplace of ideas in America. Notable among these were the so-called idea/expression dichotomy[186] and the fair use defense,[187] which together are described in a leading recent Supreme Court decision as now constituting part of the "traditional contours of . . . protection" representing "copyright's built-in First Amendment accommodations."[188]

Those developments and others, however, lay in the future. *Wheaton v. Peters* marked the beginning, not the end, of the Supreme Court's major decisions in the law of copyright. But what a beginning it was! In engaging Daniel Webster to argue the case before the Supreme Court, Wheaton's friend Elijah Paine long ago observed: "This suit . . . will be more interesting than any reported case on copyrights, and . . . the future interest of all authors in this country will be greatly affected by its decision."[189] In the long view of copyright history, he could not have been more right.

185 *Wheaton* makes no pronouncement regarding the "public domain" by name. The term itself would not appear in an opinion of the Court concerning intellectual property law until *Singer Mfg. Co. v. June Mfg. Co.*, 163 U.S. 169, in 1896 (or in statutory law until the 1909 Act). *See generally* Tyler T. Ochoa, *Origins and Meanings of the Public Domain*, 28 U. Dayton L. Rev. 215, 239–46 (2003). *Wheaton* represents a point in time when underlying public domain values were in place as part of the judicial consciousness, but when the Court behaved only instinctively concerning such matters. We should remember that the case constituted the Court's first encounter with copyright and that its entire discussion of the copyrightability of opinions is contained in a single sentence at the end of McLean's opinion. If the Court had, in 1834, possessed a coherent *theory* of the public domain, it would have stated that theory in *Wheaton*. Instead, the Court's collective thoughts, if any, regarding the "public domain" in intellectual property were, at best, inchoate at that date. Thus, the case provides intimations of what was to come, but *only* that.

186 Copyright law protects expressions of ideas, as a means of incentivizing their elaboration and dissemination, but not the underlying ideas themselves, which remain in the public domain for use by others. *See* Baker v. Selden, 101 U.S. 99 (1880); 17 U.S.C. § 102(a). *See also* Pamela Samuelson, The Story of *Baker v. Selden*: Sharpening the Distinction Between Authorship and Invention, elsewhere in this Volume.

187 Copyright law provides limited opportunities for subsequent authors and the public itself to enjoy the use of others' copyrighted works, in what would otherwise be infringing activity, to advance the general welfare. *See* Folsom v. Marsh, 9 F. Cas. 342, 13 Copr. Dec. 991 (1841); 17 U.S.C. § 107. *See also* R. Anthony Reese, The Story of *Folsom v Marsh*: Distinguishing Between Infringing and Legitimate Uses, elsewhere in this Volume.

188 Eldred v. Ashcroft, 537 U.S. 186, 219–21 (2003).

189 Elijah Paine to Daniel Webster (Dec. 6, 1831), Webster Papers, New Hampshire Historical Society, Concord, N.H., *quoted in* Baker, *supra* note 24, at 347 n.5.

2

Creativity and Inventiveness

The Story of *Bleistein v. Donaldson Lithographing Company*: Originality as a Vehicle for Copyright Inclusivity

Diane Leenheer Zimmerman[1]

On February 2, 1903, with the wife of the President of the United States seated as his guest in the audience,[2] Oliver Wendell Holmes, Jr., newly appointed to the United States Supreme Court,[3] delivered the opinion of the Court in *Bleistein v. Donaldson Lithographing Company*.[4] The reverberations set off by that succinct and elegant little opinion continue to echo in the copyright case law more than a century later.

Bleistein at its inception was, from the viewpoint of a modern reader, an unprepossessing case, involving a garden-variety claim of copyright infringement. The plaintiffs' company had designed and printed advertising posters for a traveling circus, and when the circus ran short of them, it asked the defendant to make some more. Donaldson Lithographing did so, using the plaintiffs' designs as its models. For this,

---

1 The author would like to thank her research assistants, Alma Asay and Lana Maier, for their creative and energetic contributions to this chapter as well as Gretchen Feltes who was of inestimable assistance in finding even the most obscure sources. The support of the Filomen and Max D'Agostino Research Fund at New York University is also greatly appreciated.

2 Sheldon M. Novick, Honorable Justice: the Life of Oliver Wendell Holmes 254 (1989).

3 Oliver Wendell Holmes Jr. was nominated to the Court by President Theodore Roosevelt in the summer of 1902, and joined the Court in December of that same year. Sheldon M. Novick, *Holmes, Oliver Wendell, in* Oxford Companion to the Supreme Court of the United States 407 (Kermit L. Hall ed., 1992).

4 188 U.S. 239 (1903).

the plaintiffs sought damages of one dollar per illicitly copied sheet.[5]

But as the litigation progressed from district to circuit to Supreme Court, an aspect of the case, one not hinted at in the complaint, answer, or the questions and answers during testimony at the trial, emerged that gave the dispute its legal gravitas and rendered it memorable.

There are many ways to characterize what the *Bleistein* case was "about" by the time it reached the Supreme Court. Perhaps the simplest thing to say is that the case had morphed by that stage into a debate over the kind of a contribution to "science and useful arts"[6] a claimant had to make to be eligible, as a constitutional matter, for protection by copyright. Although the problem is sometimes said to be deciding how high the threshold of originality should be set to qualify for a copyright, this description does not entirely capture the issue that either the lower courts or the Justices of the Supreme Court understood themselves to be facing when they endeavored to resolve the *Bleistein* dispute. What separated the majority opinion of the Supreme Court from the decisions below—and from Justices Harlan and McKenna in dissent—was Holmes's profound skepticism about the propriety of any attempt by judges to engage in qualitative line-drawing to decide which sorts of contributions were or were not copyrightable.

The Background to the Litigation

In April, 1898, the Courier Lithographing Company shipped three boxes of circus posters—in a range of sizes—from its plant in Buffalo, New York, to Peru, Indiana. The boxes contained 1,760 pounds of printed paper, including depictions of a wide range of subjects, from trapeze artists to elephant and camel races. Some posters were big enough to use on billboards; others were small enough to be pasted on walls or windows. Included in the lot were three images that subsequently became the source of the dispute in this case. One depicted a bicycle act, another a group of ballerinas, and a third something called a "statuary act." All of the posters were ordered by the Great Wallace Shows, a traveling circus based in Indiana, and were due to arrive there by April 15, 1898. The posters were then turned over to the circus's advance men who went ahead of the traveling show and advertised the fact, along its intended route, that the circus was on its way.[7] Each poster included a picture of the owner, Ben Wallace, in a circle at the upper left, and a legend indicating that the act depicted would be part of what people would see if they came to a performance of his circus.

---

[5] Bleistein v. Donaldson Lithographing Co., 98 F. 608, 613 (D.Ky. 1899) (noting that the plaintiffs were seeking this sum in damages).

[6] United States Constitution, Art. I, § 8, cl. 8.

[7] Record at 54–55 (testimony of George A. Scheffler and Exhibit D).

Wallace was a typically colorful showman who got into the circus business by a circuitous route. After serving as a Union soldier in the Civil War, he at first took up work as a hostler in a livery stable. In his new position, he frequently helped take care of animals belonging to the circuses that came through town. Increasingly intrigued by what he saw and learned, in 1884, Wallace found some partners, and they joined to found what was called, in the typically grandiose terms of the Victorian era, "Wallace & Co.'s Great World Menagerie, International Circus, Museum, Alliance of Novelties, and Mardi–Gras Street Carnival."[8] By 1891, the Wallace circus had grown to become one of the seven largest traveling circuses in the country, requiring twenty railroad cars to transport it.[9] Later renamed the Hagenbeck–Wallace circus,[10] the circus continued to belong to Wallace until 1913. It continued in operation under the same name, however, until the late 1930s, during which time it became part of the Ringling Brothers operation and, for a brief while, counted as the second largest circus in the United States.[11]

Traveling circuses for decades were the major form of public entertainment for rural Americans and traveled from town to town from the eighteenth[12] into the twentieth century. Advertising posters—or "paper" as it was known in circus jargon—were central to their success. Like any traveling circus of its era, the Wallace Shows had an insatiable need for "paper." Circuses moved from place to place, typically for a succession of one-day stands. To build the necessary audience interest and awareness, the circus proper would be preceded by an advance team of "billers"[13]

---

8 C. G. Sturtevant, *Little Biographies of Famous Circus Men*, White Tops, May 1930, at 3. A later report gives the name as Wallace & Co.'s Great World Menagerie, Grand International Mardi Gras, Highway Holiday Hidalgo, and Alliance of Novelties. Hal Lancaster, *Circus Fever Struck Peru, Ind., Long Ago and Has Never Left*, Wall St. J., Aug. 30, 1982, at 1. (Unless otherwise noted, the newspaper articles cited in this chapter were found in the Proquest Historical Newspapers database.) At one point in the 1890s, the circus operated under the name "Cook & Whitby Circus" but soon turned back into the Wallace Shows again. Sturtevant, *supra*; Tom Ogden, Two Hundred Years of the American Circus: from Aba-daba to the Zoppe-zavatta Troupe 113 (1993).

9 John Durrant & Alice Durrant, Pictorial History of the American Circus 79 (1957).

10 *Id.*; C. E. Duble, *They Have Come and Gone*, White Tops, Nov.-Dec. 1954, at 8.

11 *Hagenbach Circus To Return to Road*, Christian Science Monitor, Jan. 29, 1937, at 3. In 1886, when the Wallace circus first began to move by train, it occupied 15 railway cars. Sturtevant, *supra* note 8, at 3; in 1934, the circus's greatest year, it required 50 cars. Joseph T. Bradbury, *The Hagenbeck–Wallace Circus, Season of 1937*, White Tops, Nov.-Dec. 1968, at 4.

12 The first circus in the United States is said to have been started in Philadelphia in 1793. Neil C. Cockerline, *Ethical Considerations for the Conservation of Circus Posters*, 17 Waac Newsletter, May 1995, at 1, *at* http://palimpsest.stanford.edu/waac/wn/wn17/wn17–2/wn17–205.html (last visited October 26, 2004).

13 Posters were also called "bills," hence the term "biller" for someone whose job it was to put them up. The posters were also, once the technology came into widespread use, often referred to simply as "lithos." *Id.* at 1.

and "tackers"[14] whose job it was to plaster practically every flat surface in the general vicinity of the target town or city with chromolithographs in sizes great and small, advertising the show. A skilled biller could cover up to 7,000 square feet in a day with circus ads;[15] five to ten thousand lithographs might be put up by the advance men in a single day.[16] Advertising, and posters in particular, were the lifeblood of the traveling circus, and occasioned their single greatest outlay of money. According to one scholar, "The circus spent more for advertising than any other component of its operation, and for most of show history, the poster was the single most important element. Because of this, show posters constituted one of the principle products of the commercial printing industry throughout the 19th century."[17] One can easily understand why the great showman, P. T. Barnum, once said that he put his faith in "printers' ink" and would never have been able to make a success of himself without the help of this sort of advertising.[18] The early history of advertising, in fact, is largely the history of circus advertising,[19] and hence was a matter of major economic importance to the firms that engaged in producing it.

Courier and Donaldson were but two of several companies that made a profitable business of producing color lithographs in the latter part of the nineteenth century to advertise circuses, traveling theater companies and other kinds of itinerant entertainments. Donaldson, established in 1863, was headed by William M. Donaldson, a prominent local businessman who was also involved in banking, and helped found the Ohio National Life Insurance Company.[20] The firm described itself

---

[14] Billers put up posters with a mixture of flour and water, blasted with steam to make it creamy; tackers mounted huge billboard-sized printed canvas advertisements. GENE PLOWDEN, CIRCUS PRESS AGENT 49–50 (1984); OGDEN, *supra* note 8, at 234–36.

[15] Cockerline, *supra* note 12, at 10.

[16] OGDEN, *supra* note 8, at 234.

[17] Cockerline, *supra* note 12, at 2.

[18] Chalmers L. Pancoast, *Ballyhoo and Hullabaloo of Old Days*, THE BILLBOARD, Sept. 5, 1931, at 45.

[19] *See generally* Cockerline, *supra* note 12; JOHN CULHANE, THE AMERICAN CIRCUS: AN ILLUSTRATED HISTORY 370 (1990) (circuses began the development of outdoor advertising); *The Emergence of Color in Lithographic Printing: The Development of Circus Posters as an Advertising Medium*, http://www.wisc.sit.edu/?schawla/CircusPosterWebSite/CircusHomepage.html (last visited Oct. 26, 2004) (attributing the invention of the poster industry to circuses).

[20] William M. Donaldson, *Lithographer of Cincinnati, 92, Founded Insurance Company,* N.Y. TIMES, Oct. 23, 1931, at 23. Donaldson's brother, W. H. Donaldson, was the founder of Billboard Magazine. *Discusses Suicide, Then Ends His Life*, N.Y. TIMES, Mar. 16, 1932, at 15.

on its letterhead as "Show Printers & Fine Art Publishers;" over the years, it produced posters and other material for such clients as the Harmount Company (which mounted a traveling production of "Uncle Tom's Cabin"), magicians, Wild West spectaculars, and when they became popular, the movies. The company was highly successful so that, by the early part of the twentieth century, it had expanded its operations to include not just Newport, Kentucky, but New York and London as well.[21]

Although the Courier Company also designed theatrical posters and even baseball cards, it was particularly heavily invested in the business of producing circus posters and is commonly identified by scholars of the genre as one of the most notable sources of this form of advertising.[22] In addition to the Wallace Show, the company also produced posters for the Ringling Brothers, Buffalo Bill, and the Adam Forepaugh & Sells Brothers' circuses, as well as for individual circus acts.

Designing and printing posters was initially a sideline of a Buffalo newspaper. The Courier Company, a job printer, was as an offshoot of the influential Democratic newspaper, the Buffalo Courier. By 1884, however, an article in the New York Times observed that the newspaper had become "less important than the job printing part of the concern,"[23] and the newspaper and the printing division seem ultimately to have gone their separate ways. Nevertheless, several of the partners who ran the Courier Company were also involved with the paper. George Bleistein, the president of the Courier Company, owned the Buffalo Courier in the 1890s, although he appears to have sold out by the time of the litigation.[24] Edwin Fleming, another partner, was the newspaper's Associate Editor until his death in 1923.[25]

One interesting insight into the importance of the business of making posters can be gleaned from the prominence, both social and

---

[21] A copy of the firm's letterhead can be found at http://jefferson.village.virginia.edu/utc/onstage/imagesosu/dropshp.html (last visited Oct. 26, 2004). Examples of Donaldson's work can be accessed by searching for entries under that name in the Library of Congress's on-line catalogue of prints and photographs, http://lcweb2.loc.gov/pp/varquery.html#Creator (last visited November 8, 2004).

[22] *See, e.g.*, OGDEN, *supra* note 8, at 236; CULHANE, *supra* note 19, at 164; Cockerline, *supra* note 12, at 3. Examples of Courier posters can be found in the Library of Congress collection in the Prints and Photographs Online Catalogue. By entering "circus posters" as the search term, 186 posters are retrieved. Among the many works by Courier included in the list are items 18, 30, 48, 80 and 91. http://www.loc.gov/rr/print/catalog.html (last visited November 8, 2004).

[23] *Sole Owner of the Courier*, N.Y. TIMES, Jan. 20, 1884, at 7.

[24] An article in the Washington Post in 1901 describes him as "former proprietor" of the paper, *Men Met in the Hotel Lobbies,* WASH. POST, June 27, 1901, at 16, and he describes himself in his testimony at the trial merely as a "printer and lithographer." Record at 23.

[25] *Edwin Fleming Dead,* N.Y. TIMES, Aug. 14, 1923, at 15.

political, of several of the Courier partners. George Bleistein, the named plaintiff, in addition to owning an influential Democratic newspaper for several years, was a personal friend of President Grover Cleveland,[26] and a leading organizer of the great Pan–American Exposition of 1901.[27] Several of the others partners were similarly men of influence. Gerrit B. Lansing was a prominent stockbroker who went on to become a First Deputy State Controller of New York.[28] Ansley Wilcox studied at Yale and Oxford, and became a lawyer, author, and personal friend of three presidents—Cleveland, Teddy Roosevelt, and Taft. Another indication of the significance of this kind of business is the salaries it paid. In the course of the trial, testimony revealed that an artist who originally designed one or more of the posters at issue was paid the remarkable sum, for the 1890s, of $5000 a year for his efforts.[29]

One important reason the Courier Company developed a speciality in chromolithograph show posters was that Buffalo in the nineteenth century became home to a large population of German immigrants. The technique of lithography—a method for making prints by drawing on a stone with greasy inks or crayons and then pressing the images onto paper or fabric[30]—was developed in Germany late in the eighteenth century,[31] although it did not become cheap enough to move into widespread commercial use for several more decades.[32] Germans printers became expert at the technique,[33] and as a result, when the potential of

---

26 *Mr. Cleveland in Buffalo: The Ex–President Welcomed to His Old Home*, N.Y. Times, May 12, 1891, at 1. He was rumored to have been used by President Cleveland on occasion as a political emissary. *Mr. Bleistein Denies It: A Baseless Story about a Conversation with Mr. Whitney*, N.Y. Times, Apr. 16, 1893, at 1.

27 Bleistein was on the Board of Directors, *The Pan Am's Who's Who: 1901 Buffalo, New York, Pan–American Exposition List*, *at* http://ah.bfn.org/h/panam/panwho/panwho.html (last visited on Oct. 26, 2004), and was in charge of publicity for the fair, *Men Met in the Hotel Lobbies*, *supra* note 24, at 16.

28 Gerrit B. Lansing, *Broker, Dies in Albany*, N.Y. Times, Mar. 13, 1932, at N7; *To Defer Appointments: None Likely Before Next Week, the Governor States*, N.Y. Times, Jan. 4, 1927, at 6.

29 His weekly salary was $100. Transcript at 36.

30 Paul Goldman, Looking at Prints, Drawings and Watercolours: A Guide to Technical Terms 37–38 (1988); University of Delaware Library, *Color Printing in the Nineteenth Century: Lithography*, at http://www.lib.udel.edu/ud/spec/exhibits/color/lithogr.htm (last visited on Oct. 26, 2004).

31 The originator of the technique was Alois Senefelder, a musician and playwright, who lived in Munich. Michael Twyman, Lithography 1800–1850 at 3–17 (1970).

32 Michael Twyman, Breaking the Mould: The First Hundred Years of Lithography 97–99 (2001).

33 *Id.* at 16–24.

chromolithography (the making of colored lithographs) as an advertising tool was recognized,[34] the printing establishments in the United States best situated to take advantage of it were those located in areas of extensive German immigration.[35]

German settlers began moving to Buffalo in the first half of the nineteenth century, and, by the 1840s, were setting up breweries and other businesses.[36] It appears that some members of that immigrant community were skilled printers and lithographers who found employment with the Courier Company and its lithographing division. Although little is known about him except that he designed some or all of the posters involved in the *Bleistein* litigation, the artist August Bandlow may well be the same man who is described by a descendant as having been born in Mecklenberg, Germany in 1853.[37] The most surprising thing about Bandlow is that we know his name at all; typically, designers of posters of this sort did not sign their work, and, as a result, their identities and histories are largely a blank.

Although Courier's staff artists designed and printed a variety of posters for Wallace, the order from Wallace to Donaldson Lithographing Co. of Newport, Kentucky, seems to have been limited, as best one can tell from extant records, to posters for the "Spectacular Ballet Design," the "Stirk Family Design" (the bicyclists) and the "Statuary Act Design"[38]—three subjects also depicted in Courier's posters. The owner of Donaldson Lithographing seemed to be quite conscious of the potential legal pitfalls that could attend reproducing the work in question. He apparently had the originals, and knew they bore a prominent copyright

---

34 According to Twyman, chromolithography, although known earlier, did not come into widespread use until the late 1830s. *Id.* at 102–04.

35 The completion of the Erie Canal was an important factor in jump-starting the economy of Buffalo and in attracting immigrants. During the War of 1812, about 1500 inhabitants lived there; the numbers swelled by 1832 to 10,000. Encyclopedia Britannica, *Buffalo, at* http://search.eb.com/eb/article?tocId=9017935 (last visited Oct. 26, 2004).

36 University of Buffalo Libraries, *The Immigrant Experience and the Pan-American Exposition, at* http://ublib.buffalo.edu/libraries/exhibits/panam/immigrants/germans.html (last visited Oct. 26, 2004).

37 If it is the same person, Bandlow eventually moved to another center of German immigration, Milwaukee, where he died in 1928. This information is drawn from an entry found on a genealogy bulletin board, http://www.ancestry.com. The dates of his birth and death, and the unusual name are all consistent with the hypothesis that this is the August Bandlow who, according to the testimony in the *Bleistein* trial, designed the Courier posters. *See* http://boards.ancestry.com/mbexec/message/an/surnames.bandlow/29 (last visited Oct. 26, 2004).

38 These were the titles under which the prints were registered with the Copyright Office. Courier Lithographing Co. v. Donaldson Lithographing Co., 104 F. 993, 993 (6th Cir. 1900).

notice in Courier's name. When John Rudolph, the partner who was the secretary and manager of Courier, went to Donaldson's offices, accompanied a federal marshal, to seize the ostensibly offending materials, Mr. Donaldson reportedly tried to reassure him that his version of the ballet poster did not infringe Courier's, and that he had specifically given his artists the Courier posters to ensure that they would make their own designs and not copy the earlier versions.[39]

The Donaldson posters did differ in some regards: they were smaller in size, and done in black-and-white rather than color. But they were nonetheless, as the Sixth Circuit conceded, substantially identical to Courier's. Indeed, during the litigation, counsel for the defendant never seriously tried to argue that the Donaldson prints were other than copies of Courier's work. All told, 23,795 copies of the three posters were seized from the Donaldson offices by the marshal, along with five metal electrotype plates.[40]

That Courier was upset by having its work for Wallace copied by a competitor is not surprising. The problem, however, was not merely the loss of Wallace's business. Although the posters in question were designed at the request of, and for the exclusive use of the Wallace circus, that was not their sole potential use. Lithographers turned out so-called "special paper" for a particular circus, but when the circus finished using them, the same designs could be recycled, with a simple substitution of a new identifying logo, and sold to subsequent customers.[41] Courier claimed, therefore, that it routinely kept copyright ownership of its poster designs, which (as was true here) often portrayed an artist's conception of circus acts rather than identifiable performers, because they expected to continue selling versions of them long after Wallace's demands were satisfied.

---

[39] A similar report was given by the deputy marshal who executed the order of claim and recovery against Donaldson. According to J.D. Compton, William Donaldson was present at the time, and, he added, "I believe he said to me . . . that they [his versions of the posters] were not infringements." Record at 47.

[40] *Courier*, 104 F. at 993.

[41] Cockerline, *supra* note 12, at 5–6; Transcript at 34. In this case, Wallace's picture would have to be removed, as well as the text referring to his circus, but the underlying illustration could be reutilized.

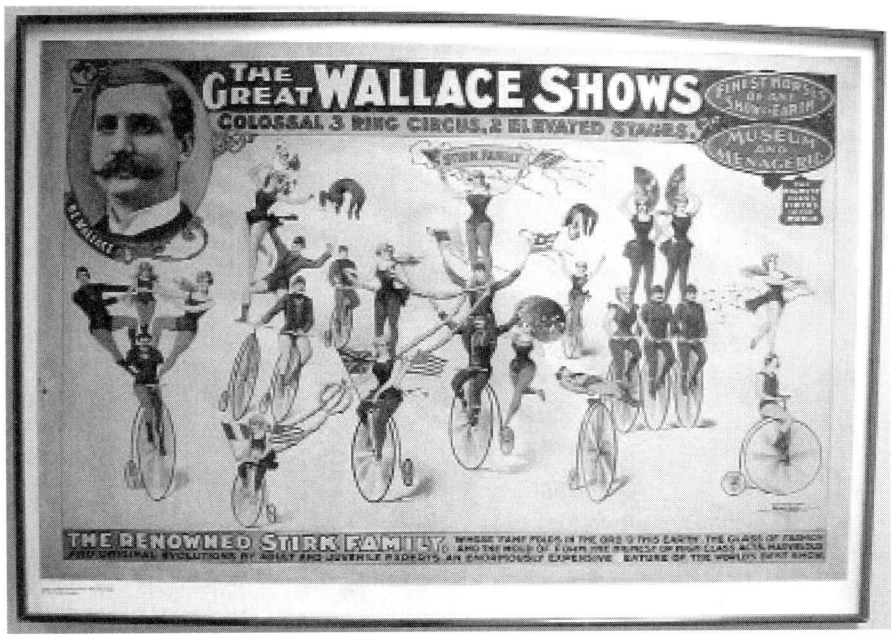

The Litigation

The law suit commenced in June, 1899, with the filing of a complaint and the issuance of a writ authorizing the U.S. Marshal to seize "all plates or stones, and copies of all prints, cuts or engravings, found in the possession of the defendant."[42] The six partners who owned Courier[43] alleged that Donaldson had infringed valid copyrights in the three posters and, invoking Section 4965 of the Revised Statutes of the United States, sought a penalty of $1 per illicit copy, an amount that would go in part to the plaintiffs and in part to the United States. The answer, when filed, gave little detail about the nature of the defenses Donaldson intended to mount. Other than admitting that it was an Ohio corporation, the defendant put in a general denial and asked that the suit be dismissed.[44] Early in December of the same year, a jury was selected, and the case went to trial in the Federal Court Hall in Covington, Kentucky. The presiding judge was the Hon.Walter Evans, a former Republican Congressman who had been appointed the previous spring to the district court bench by his close friend, President McKinley.[45]

---

[42] Transcript at 13.

[43] In addition to Bleistein, Fleming, Lansing, Rudolf and Wilcox, the sixth partner was someone named John W. Bridgman.

[44] Transcript at 14–15.

[45] *Evans, Walter*, in 6 DICTIONARY OF AMERICAN BIOGRAPHY 212–13 (Allen Johnson & Dumas Malone eds., 1931).

Donaldson was represented at the trial, and through the subsequent appeals, by Edmund Kittredge[46] of Cincinnati. Kittredge,[47] a transplanted New Englander, had done his undergraduate work at Dartmouth and later attended Harvard Law School. Once in Cincinnati, he rose to prominence in his profession, serving for several years as the president of the Cincinnati Bar Association and as chairman of the Board of Trustees of the Cincinnati Law School.[48] Courier was represented at the trial by Buffalo lawyers Ansley Wilcox (one of the plaintiff partners) and George T. Hogg, and by two local lawyers, former Kentucky state judge Charles J. Helm and W. W. Helm (most likely, Charles's brother William).

If one knew nothing about the case other than what could be gleaned from the trial transcript, it would seem to be entirely a dispute over compliance with the technical intricacies of perfecting a copyright under the existing law, and the exact nature of the agreement between Courier and Mr. Wallace about the rights to reproduce the posters. The plaintiffs offered no witnesses to prove, or in any way address, the issue of whether or not the posters were subject to copyright. They simply asserted in their complaint that they had rights in three works that fell within the statutory category of "print, cut, or engraving." No effort was made to show affirmatively that the posters had special merits, artistic or otherwise. Nor was an attempt made in either the proffered testimony or questioning by the defense attorneys to address whether or not what Donaldson had done infringed Courier's work.

The entire day was spent on efforts by the plaintiffs to establish, and the defense to disprove, that the formal requirements for obtaining a copyright had been satisfied. Since an artist, and not Courier, created each of the works, how, the defense asked, could Courier support its claim to be the proprietor of them? But, even assuming Courier was entitled to be treated as the proprietor, had it nonetheless failed to meet the requirements of the copyright statute by using an improper name in some of its copyright notices? (The company, it seems, interchangeably referred to itself by its official name, the Courier Company, and by the

---

46 As far as can be ascertained, this is the correct spelling of his last name. He does however appear in some sources as Edmund Kittridge.

47 Biographical data on Kittredge comes largely from EDMUND W. KITTREDGE, CINCINNATI IN BENCH AND BAR OF OHIO: A COMPENDIUM OF HISTORY AND BIOGRAPHY at 127–28 (George Irving Reed ed., 1897).

48 Irwin C. Rutter & Samuel S. Wilson, *The College of Law: An Overview 1833–1983*, 52 U. CIN. L. REV. 311, 316 (1983).

name "Courier Lithographing Company;" it used the latter title in at least some of the notices.) Did the plaintiff meet the requirement of deposit of copies of the works with the Library of Congress prior to publication? Although not completely clear from the transcript, the defendant also claimed that either ownership of the poster designs, or at least an exclusive license to use and reproduce them, was transferred to Wallace, expressly or by implication as part of the underlying agreement between him and Courier authorizing their creation. It was to rebut this argument that Courier put in its testimony on the custom of the trade (and its own customary practices) with regard to a publisher's retention of the right to reuse "special paper."

The technical problems with Courier's copyrights are discussed in the district court opinion, and are alluded to by the Supreme Court. But when plaintiffs rested their case after one day of testimony, defendant's counsel moved for a directed verdict—not only on the grounds already discussed, but also on the ground that the posters were not copyrightable because copyright was unavailable for "mere" advertising.[49] Unfortunately, a transcript of the argument on the motion was not a part of the record sent to the Supreme Court, but Judge Evans was clearly convinced by Kittredge's position because he ruled in favor of the defendant and issued his opinion the following day.

The promptness with which the judge acted may be explained in part from his comment that he had faced almost the same issue in a case the previous term, and was already well-versed on the applicable law. In any event, he quickly determined that the applicable statute did not mean to, and indeed could not, protect illustrations designed for advertising purposes. According to the statute, "engravings," "cuts" and "prints" could be protected only if they were "pictorial illustrations or works connected with the fine arts."[50] Whether "pictorial illustrations" and "works connected with the fine arts" were independent clauses, or whether instead both "pictorial illustrations" and "works" were modified by the phrase "connected with the fine arts" was unclear. The court concluded, however, that a resolution of this interpretive conundrum was unnecessary because the posters could not be covered under either interpretation.

The posters were not pictorial illustrations, Evans wrote, because "I think that Congress meant ... a pictorial representation placed in a

---

49 Kittredge also objected to copyright for the ballet poster on the grounds that it was "an immoral picture."

50 Act of July 8, 1870, ch. 230, 86, 16 Stat. 198 (codified at Rev. Stat. § 4952), *amended by* Act of Mar. 3, 1891, ch. 565, 8, 26 Stat. 1106, and Act of Mar. 2, 1895, ch. 194, 28 Stat. 965.

book or other publication to elucidate the text."[51] And they certainly were not connected "with the fine arts." Although Evans conceded that it was difficult, and perhaps even undesirable, to decide in close cases whether or not something was fine art, the posters before him did not pose a hard case. All of them, he said, were "merely frivolous" and, in the case of the ballet poster, "to some extent immoral in tendency, though the court by no means intends to intimate that the nude is not perfectly admissible in the fine arts."[52]

But what clearly seemed to appall Judge Evans was the idea that a ruling for the plaintiff would require the court to impose a statutory penalty of $1 per infringing item. The amount of damages estimated by the plaintiffs in their complaint and cited by the court was $12,000, which, under the existing law, was to be divided between the plaintiff and the United States government.[53] "The court cannot bring its mind to yield to the conclusion," Evans wrote, "that such tawdry pictures as these were ever meant to be given the enormous protection of not only the exclusive right to print them, but the additional penalty of a dollar each for reprints from them."[54]

Interestingly, the court cited to no external authority for its interpretation of Congress's intent either as to the meaning of the phrase "pictorial illustrations" or "connected with the fine arts." It did not matter, however, because the Sixth Circuit affirmed Judge Evan's ruling on constitutional, rather than statutory, grounds. The appellate court, in an opinion by Judge Horace H. Lurton (who was subsequently to serve with Holmes for five years as a Justice of the Supreme Court)[55] took the view that, even if the chromolithographs in question fell within the ambit of the statute as drafted, Congress had no power to protect them.

The court relied on a considerable body of precedent for the proposition that copyright was available only for works that met some basic standard of worthiness. The preamble of the Constitution specified that copyright was intended solely "to promote the progress of science and useful arts," and the power Congress obtained under that clause could not therefore be used to protect "writings" that did not further that end.

---

[51] 98 F. at 610.

[52] *Id.* at 611.

[53] In fact, the number of infringing copies seized was close to 24,000, suggesting that the award might properly have been almost double the figure mentioned in Judge Evans' opinion.

[54] 98 F. at 613.

[55] Lurton was nominated for the Court by President William H. Taft, was confirmed in 1909, and served until his death in 1914. Federal Judicial Center, *Lurton, Horace Harmon, at* http://air.fjc.gov/servlet/tGetInfo?jid=1441 (last visited Oct. 26, 2004).

Prominent among the sorts of materials deemed by prior courts to be ineligible for copyright had been various sorts of promotional or product-related writings and pictorial representations.[56] Indeed, only nine years earlier, the Supreme Court in *Higgins v. Keuffel*[57] had concluded that the labels on bottles of "disappearing ink" were not the proper subject matter of copyright. Some question existed whether labels such as these fell even nominally within copyright or were instead something assigned to trademark law,[58] but assuming that copyright was pertinent, said the Justices in *Higgins,* the labels failed to meet a basic test of protectability. Although the text on the labels was useful insofar as it served to "designate or describe the articles to which [the labels] are attached,"[59] a work that is copyrightable, they said, "must have by itself some value as a composition, at least to the extent of serving some purpose other than as a mere advertisement or designation of the subject to which it is attached."[60] Furthermore, the Court added, copyrightable works also needed to exhibit originality and be "founded in the creative powers of the mind."[61]

In addition to advertising copy, sales catalogues and product labels, other sorts of works were deemed not to meet the constitutional test because they were too "ephemeral" to be of more than fleeting use. This included newspapers and "daily price currents" (or market price listings). Furthermore, a work might be found not to promote science and the useful arts on the ground that it was indecent or immoral, or that constituted mere "spectacular pieces or exhibitions."[62] Although *Higgins* relied mostly on precedent relating to labels, a broad range of cases denying copyright to works on the ground that they did not meet the test of the preamble had previously been cited with approval by the Supreme Court in *Baker v. Selden.*[63]

Thus, the Sixth Circuit had every reason to believe that it was on solid ground in holding that Courier's posters fell outside the reach of

56 EATON S. DRONE, A TREATISE ON THE LAW OF PROPERTY IN INTELLECTUAL PRODUCTIONS IN GREAT BRITAIN AND THE UNITED STATES 209 (1879).

57 140 U.S. 428 (1891).

58 *Id.* at 432–33.

59 *Id.* at 431.

60 *Id.*

61 *Id.*

62 Barnes v. Miner, 122 F. 480, 490 (S.D.N.Y. 1903).

63 101 U.S. 99, 105–06 (1879). For a full discussion of *Baker v. Selden* and its implications for another line of cases, see Pamela Samuelson, The Story of *Baker v. Selden*: Sharpening the Distinction Between Authorship and Invention, elsewhere in this Volume.

copyright. Furthermore, the court pointed out that the plaintiffs had introduced no evidence "aside from the deductions which are to be drawn from the prints themselves" to support their claim that the posters exhibited originality in the form of "arrangement, pose, color, grouping, or expression."[64] Without more, the court concluded, no reasonable jury could be expected to find the existence of the requisite quality. Therefore, the district court had been right to enter judgment in favor of the defendant. The posters had "no use other than that of a mere advertisement, and no value aside from this function," the court of appeals reasoned, and therefore "it would not be promotive of the useful arts, within the meaning of the constitutional provision, to protect the 'author' in the exclusive use thereof, and the copyright statute should not be construed as including such a publication, if any other construction is admissible."[65]

Although a reasonable modern observer may initially have been surprised that a case about pirated circus posters would have seemed important enough to pursue all the way to the Supreme Court, the history of the case makes clear that making the graphics to advertise circuses and other traveling performances was a very big business in its own right, but also had broader significance. As the sale of consumer goods grew in economic importance, advertising that relied on arresting and colorful chromolithographic images was quickly evolving from primarily a show business phenomenon into a widely used device by manufacturers and retailers trying to build public demand for their products. The vast majority of the posters promoting circuses and traveling players were designed and executed by anonymous artists who probably conceived of themselves simply as skilled and well-paid craftspeople (as noted earlier, we know that an artist named August Bandlow designed one or more of the circus posters this case only because the *Bleistein* litigation occurred). But by the 1890s, the opportunities and challenges of graphic advertising also began to attract famous artists into the business of designing (and signing) advertising posters. The plaintiffs pointed out in their brief to the Supreme Court, for example, that the painter Sir John Millais was paid $10,000 to produce "The Boy and the Soap Bubble" to be used on posters for Pear's, a soap manufacturer.[66] Hence, the issue of whether or not these images could be copyrighted had economic significance well beyond recovery of the costs associated with creating, reproducing and distributing the images themselves; by obtaining protection for advertising imagery, commercial ac-

[64] 104 F. at 994, 997.

[65] *Id.* at 996.

[66] Brief on Behalf of Plaintiffs in Error at 39–40.

tors gained leverage in their struggle to enhance the value of their products and services in an increasingly competitive marketplace.

Before the Supreme Court

The case came to the Supreme Court on a writ of error, a procedure under which, until its abolition in 1928, parties could seek a form of appellate review limited to questions of law.[67] Ansley Wilcox continued to represent his partners, as he had throughout the earlier stages of the case, but was joined in the Supreme Court proceedings by Arthur Von Briesen, a prominent New York City attorney. Kittredge remained as attorney for the defendant, but he, too, joined forces in the Supreme Court with another lawyer, fellow Ohioan Joseph Wilby (with whom he was to appear before the highest court on at least four other occasions in his career).

Two questions were raised. The first was whether or not the trial court acted properly in taking from the jury the question of whether the posters had sufficient value to be fit subjects for copyright. The second was whether, even if copyright were available to such works, the ones for these posters had been perfected in compliance with applicable law.

The second set of questions, dealing with the technical validity of the copyrights, although they loomed large at trial, attracted only slight attention in the Supreme Court. Justice Holmes did find, as a matter of law, that it was proper for Courier to use a "variant" of its formal name in some of its copyright notices. But he concluded that whether the copyright in the posters was owned by Courier, whether it was perfected before publication, and whether the agreement between Wallace and Courier was one that permitted Wallace to obtain extra copies of the posters from another printer were not susceptible of resolution on purely legal grounds, but should go to the jury when the case was retried.

The most interesting part of the technical discussion, in retrospect, was Holmes's suggestion that, should the jury find that the posters were designed by "persons employed and paid by the plaintiffs in their establishment to make those very things,"[68] that fact alone would permit an inference that Courier owned the designs. Although the concept of works made for hire was not formally introduced into American copyright law until 1909,[69] modern commentators treat this language in

---

67 *General History of Supreme Court's Appellate Jurisdiction: History of Procedure for Direct Appeal to Supreme Court, in* 22 JAMES WM. MOORE, ET AL., MOORE'S FEDERAL PRACTICE, § 403App.01[9] (3rd ed. 2004).

68 188 U.S. at 248–49.

69 Sec. 26 of the 1909 Copyright Act introduced the work for hire doctrine into the statute. Ch. 320, 35 Stat. 1075 (1909), repealed by Copyright Act of 1976, Pub. L. No. 94–553, 90 Stat. 2541.

Bleistein as the origin of the doctrine, in that it marks the Court's acceptance of the idea that an employer could be treated as the "author" of its employee's creations.[70]

But the issue for which the case has come to stand, and the one that chiefly occupied the majority and the dissenting Justices, was whether circus posters were an acceptable subject of copyright. Although, in their brief, Kittredge and Wilby again urged the Court to accept the statutory argument that had been passed over with relatively little regard by the trial judge—to wit, that posters of this sort were excluded from the statute because it covered only those pictorial illustrations that were "connected with the fine arts," the line between their statutory argument and their constitutional claim that Congress lacked power to protect advertising posters was a blurry one, with one argument quickly shading into the other.

Wilcox and Von Briesen, for their part, vigorously defended the fit of these posters within the purview and purposes of the copyright and patent clause. The plaintiffs' attorneys were careful to show that the works in question fully met the test for originality first set out in *The Trade-Mark Cases*,[71] and later amplified in *Burrows-Giles Lithographing Co. v. Sarony*.[72] Because the artist here, unlike the photographer in *Sarony*, had made up the images, rather than copying real performers, the case for saying that these works were copyrightable because they evinced an "original mental conception" was far easier to make.

As for the question of intrinsic merit, the lawyers took two tacks. First they carefully positioned posters as a recognized art form. In this regard, plaintiffs were the beneficiaries of recent changes in critical and aesthetic tastes. In the 1890s, posters began to be perceived as a respectable art form, and several books and articles on their importance were published.[73] These works were heavily cited in the plaintiffs' brief and portions of one of them was attached in the appendices.[74] The lawyers argued, however, that a court could decide on the merit of the

---

[70] Robert Penchina, Note, *The Creative Commissioner: Commissioned Works under the Copyright Act of 1976*, 62 N.Y.U.L.REV. 373, 378 (1987); Anne Marie Hill, Note, *The "Work for Hire" Definition in the Copyright Act of 1976: Conflict over Specially Ordered or Commissioned Works*, 74 CORNELL L. REV. 559, 561–62 & nn. 14–18 (1989).

[71] 100 U.S. 82 (1879).

[72] 111 U.S. 53 (1884).

[73] *See, e.g.*, CHARLES HIATT, PICTURE POSTERS (1895); *Art in Advertising: Notes of a Lecture, by Mr. Louis J. Rhead, on the Pictorial Placard, or Poster, Delivered Before the Brooklyn Art Institute*, THE ART AMATEUR, Jan.1897, at 117; Pierre N. Boeringer, *The Advertiser and the Poster*, OVERLAND MONTHLY AND OUT WEST MAGAZINE, July 1896, at 41.

[74] In Appendix A to Brief on Behalf of Plaintiffs in Error, the attorneys attached excerpts from the first two chapters of Hiatt's book. HIATT, *supra* note 73.

posters at issue in the current case without needing to indulge in subjective aesthetic judgments about their qualities as "art." The intrinsic appeal of these depictions of the circus, according to Wilcox and Von Briesen, was proved by the incontrovertible fact that they captured the imagination of the public sufficiently well to bring audiences to the box office. In truth, the lawyers added wryly, the defendants, who had found it quite worthwhile to appropriate and copy the posters, were ill-placed to argue after the fact that the posters they purloined were wholly without intrinsic value.

On the other hand, counsel for the plaintiffs also carefully distinguished the posters in *Bleistein* from the ordinary run of commercial material, whether pictorial or otherwise, that were "*mere catalogues or price lists* . . . of articles intended for sale, but which obviously have no artistic merit or originality."[75] They chose not to contest the idea that such writings or illustrations fell outside the constitutional purposes of copyright, but they argued that the reason was not because they were intended as advertising. The constitutional distinction between what was and what was not properly protected turned, counsel argued, not on the purpose for which the work was created but on whether or not it exhibited imaginative and artistic qualities. To decide this case in plaintiffs' favor would require the Court to do no more than apply the same legal test for protectable works of authorship that was applied by it in *Sarony*.

Prior to *Bleistein*, there had been a few decisions that pointed in the same general direction suggested by plaintiffs' counsel. A federal circuit court in New York, for example, had agreed that copyright was available to a painting, lithographic copies of which were used as labels for cigar boxes. The court said that the character of the painting needed to be judged independent of the uses made of it. Otherwise, works of the quality of those produced by Rafael might end up being denied protection simply because someone decided to use them in advertising.[76] Similarly, in another case from New York, *Yuengling, Jr. v. Schile*,[77] a court upheld copyright in the plaintiff's chromolithograph of King Gambrinus holding up a glass of beer (the illustration was used to advertise beer) because it was not merely a representation of the product the plaintiff was selling, but rather was "a work of the imagination"[78] with "obvious artistic qualities."[79]

---

75 Brief of the Plaintiffs in Error at 32–33.

76 Schumacher v. Schwencke, Jr., 25 F. 466, 467–68 (C.C.S.D.N.Y. 1885).

77 12 F. 97 (C.C. S.D.N.Y. 1882).

78 *Id.* at 100.

79 *Id.*

The task of writing the majority opinion fell to the Court's most junior Justice. Oliver Wendell Holmes, Jr., at that point had been on the Supreme Court for only a few months.[80] He was an appointee of Theodore Roosevelt,[81] who recently moved from the vice presidency to the presidency when William McKinley was assassinated in Buffalo, New York, in 1901. (By an odd quirk of fate, Roosevelt took his oath of office on McKinley's death in the home of plaintiff, and counsel for the plaintiffs, Ansley Wilcox, in Buffalo.)[82] The issues posed by *Bleistein* were ones that touched Holmes at a personal level. From his earliest youth, the new Justice had an artistic bent. He himself sketched and made prints.[83] As an undergraduate, he wrote essays on the Pre–Raphaelites, and on Durer (the latter of which included a comparison of Durer's techniques for woodcut prints with those of modern artists) for Harvard Magazine.[84] He also began as a very young man to collect prints, building up a collection that included woodcuts and engravings by such luminaries as Durer, Rembrandt and Van Dyke.[85] His correspondence with friends like Sir Frederick Pollock frequently made mention of the pleasure he took in collecting prints and in reading about and looking at art.[86]

Holmes also had personal reasons to understand the value of copyright. Three-and-a-half years before coming onto the Supreme Court himself, Holmes tried unsuccessfully to get the Justices to stop the unauthorized reprinting of his father's famous book of essays, *The Autocrat of the Breakfast Table*.[87] The elder Holmes was now dead, and

---

80 He was sworn in on December 2, 1902. GARY J. AICHELE, OLIVER WENDELL HOLMES, JR.: SOLDIER, SCHOLAR, JUDGE at 132. The case was argued in mid-January, 1903 and decision in *Bleistein* issued on February 2 of that year.

81 *Id.* at 128.

82 *Mr. Roosevelt Is Now the President; Will Continue Unbroken the Policy of Mr. McKinley*, N.Y. TIMES, Sept. 15, 1901, at 1. Wilcox's house, as a result, is now a national historic site. *See* National Park Service, *Theodore Roosevelt Inaugural: Ansley Wilcox, at* http://www.nps.gov/thri/awilcox.html (last visited Oct. 30, 2004).

83 AICHELE, *supra* note 80, at 23. Holmes's artistic interests are well recognized. *See also, e.g.*, NOVICK, HONORABLE JUSTICE, *supra* note 2, at 12, 24, 27, 36, 108; G. EDWARD WHITE, JUSTICE OLIVER WENDELL HOLMES: LAW AND THE INNER SELF 33–39 (1993).

84 AICHELE, *supra* note 80, at 29; WHITE, *supra* note 83, at 39. Holmes's essays are reprinted in THE COLLECTED WORKS OF JUSTICE HOLMES: COMPLETE PUBLIC WRITINGS AND SELECTED JUDICIAL OPINIONS OF OLIVER WENDELL HOLMES 153–57 (Durer), & 167–69 (Pre–Raphaelites) (Sheldon M. Novick ed.1995). *See also*, NOVICK, HONORABLE JUSTICE, *supra* note 2, at 24; WHITE, *supra* note 83, at 33.

85 HOLMES-POLLOCK LETTERS 251, 255 (Mark DeWolf Howe ed., 2nd ed., 1961).

86 *Id.*

87 Holmes v. Hurst, 174 U.S. 82 (1899).

his son was acting in the role of his father's executor. The effort failed because, the Court pointed out, the essays in the book had originally been published in *The Atlantic*, where they appeared without the statutorily required copyright notice. The error could not be cured by collecting the individual essays into one book and issuing the book with a notice attached.[88]

Finally, Holmes was particularly unlikely to sympathize with the argument that use in advertising was enough to render pictorial illustrations unfit for copyright. He himself had created designs for advertising cards used to publicize productions of the Hasty Pudding Club at Harvard. One of his great artistic successes as a college student was a quite elaborate engraving promoting a show entitled "Mrs. Jarley's Waxworks."[89]

That Holmes found the opinion in the case both easy and fun to write is suggested in his somewhat facetious subsequent comment on it:

> I fired off a decision upholding the cause of law and art and deciding that a poster for a circus representing decolletes and fat legged ballet girls could be copyrighted. Harlan, that stout old Kentuckian, not exactly an esthete, dissented for high art.[90]

The majority opinion, no surprise from a man who admired Ruskin and was fond, whenever possible, of visiting art museums, showed off Holmes's knowledge with extensive references to the works of such famous artists as Rembrandt, Valesquez, Goya, Whistler and Degas. And Holmes could not resist a snipe at Judge Evans for even suggesting in passing, that "the curious might moot the question of the power to legislate to give exclusive privileges respecting the fine arts, unless in cases where they are also useful arts."[91]

Holmes's background and interests allowed him to see clearly what the more conventional aesthetics of Justice Harlan, author of the dissent, could not: that these posters were, on their face, skilled, vibrant, eye-catching works of visual art without regard to the purposes that gave rise to them. In this, history has vindicated Holmes. The same circus posters that Harlan deemed void of intrinsic merit in 1902 are today avidly collected both by museums and private individuals. But in a real sense, Justice Holmes's very sophistication on the subject of art may well

---

88 *Id.* at 87–88.

89 NOVICK, HONORABLE JUSTICE, *supra* note 2, at 27.

90 Quoted in *id.* at 254.

91 188 U.S. at 249 (referring without direct citation to Judge Evan's opinion below, 98 F. at 611).

have been the thing that led him to write the *Bleistein* opinion in terms that led to consequences that were in some senses quite problematic.

Holmes was unwilling simply to say that the three posters were copyrightable because they were skillfully done and, in the words of the *Sarony* case, evinced an "original mental conception."[92] In one of the most famous passages in copyright jurisprudence, Justice Holmes denounced reliance on aesthetic sensibility to distinguish between what was and was not fit subject matter for copyright. "It would be a dangerous undertaking," he wrote,

> [F]or persons trained only to the law to constitute themselves final judges of the worth of pictorial illustrations, outside of the narrowest and most obvious limits. At the one extreme, some works of genius would be sure to miss appreciation.... At the other end, copyright would be denied to pictures which appealed to a public less educated than the judge. Yet if they command the interest of any public ... it would be bold to say that they have not an aesthetic and educational value—and the taste of any public is not to be treated with contempt.[93]

What a court should look for, according to Holmes, was not some elusive definition of what did or did not further science and the useful arts (ignoring the fact that in *Higgins v. Keuffel*, eleven years before, the Court found this distinction to be crucial). Nor should judges (or by implication, juries) attempt to identify or apply a metric by which the "merit" of a work could be evaluated. Rather, the only relevant question should be, said Holmes, does the work exhibit the requisite originality to qualify as a work of authorship?

Originality as a constitutional requirement for copyright was not born in *Bleistein*. It appears to have been long recognized that copyright could not be granted to someone for something he or she had merely copied from someone else.[94] Originality's status as a constitutional requirement was actually acknowledged for the first time by the Supreme Court, however, only some two decades previously in *The Trade-Mark Cases*.[95] Justice Field, for the Court, was explaining why the copyright clause could not be used by Congress as legislative authority for passing trademark protection. He explained that something could become a trademark by mere continuous use, whereas the only writings that could be protected by copyright were those which were "original, and ...

---

[92] 111 U.S. at 60.

[93] 188 U.S. at 251–52.

[94] DRONE, *supra* note 56, at 110.

[95] 100 U.S. 82 (1879).

founded in the creative powers of the mind.''[96] By contrast, wrote Field, a trademark in no way depends "upon novelty, invention, discovery, or any work of the brain. It requires no fancy or imagination, no genius, no laborious thought."

Five years later, when the Court, in *Burrows-Giles Lithographing Co. v. Sarony,*[97] had to decide if a photograph—a mechanical recordation of external reality (in that instance, the appearance of the writer Oscar Wilde)—could qualify for copyright as a "writing" by an "author," Justice Miller reached back into *The Trade-Mark Cases* and utilized its language distinguishing copyrights from trademarks to explain why at least some (if not all) photographs could be copyrighted. Miller turned first to a dictionary definition of an author as "he to whom anything owes its origin; originator; maker; one who completes a work of science or literature."[98] He then amplified this definition to provide a somewhat more complex view of what an "originator" must do for copyright purposes. It might well be that a photograph that merely transfers "to the plate the visible representation of some existing object, the accuracy of this representation being its highest merit,"[99] would not meet the constitutional standard of originality, Miller wrote. By this, Justice Miller seemed intentionally to leave in doubt whether the average snapshot of a pretty scene or a tourist spot or a candid shot at a family gathering would qualify. But the photograph of Wilde was more complex. Napoleon Sarony did not simply produce an accurate representation of Wilde; rather, he posed him, selected his costume and the background against which he was shot, and "arrang[ed] and dispos[ed] the light and shade,"[100] among other contributions. These rearrangements of his raw material were enough, the Court concluded, to "show this photograph to be an original work of art, the product of plaintiff's intellectual invention."[101]

Holmes, picking up on this precedent, began his discussion of originality with the wholly uncontroversial observation that, if a photographic copy of something or someone in actual existence could, under certain circumstances evince enough originality to be copyrightable, then three lithographs made up wholly from the imagination of an artist certainly must qualify. The artist or artists involved, he added, had done at least as much as Napoleon Sarony in that they had chosen how to

96 *Id.* at 94.

97 111 U.S. 53 (1884).

98 *Id.* at 58.

99 *Id.* at 59.

100 *Id.* at 60.

101 *Id.*

arrange the figures, which ones to include, and how to color the whole. If Holmes had stopped at that point, as the plaintiffs'[102] brief had suggested, the decision to reverse the court below would have been fully explicated and adequately defended, but would have left for another day the task of delineating the division between sufficient and insufficient originality.

But Holmes, the art lover, clearly understood that, in hewing closely to *Sarony*'s reasoning, the opinion would leave the question open in a way that had negative implications for an entire class of important artists whose work he valued. He did not want to be interpreted as suggesting that the entitlement to copyright of representational artists, whose aim is to transfer to canvas the realistic appearance of persons, objects or scenes should be deemed in jeopardy.

To ward off this reading, Justice Holmes added two embellishments to his definition of constitutionally required originality. First, he suggested that the requirement might be satisfied simply by the level of skill evinced in producing the work. Holmes quoted from one of his favorite authors, Ruskin, to the effect that:

> If any young person, after being taught what is, in polite circles, called "drawing," will try to copy the commonest piece of real *work*,—suppose a lithograph on the title page of a new opera air, or a woodcut in the cheapest illustrated newspaper of the day—they will find themselves entirely beaten.[103]

Second, he said that even works that are intended to replicate the appearance of actual things, places, persons or events can meet the test of originality because the result exhibits "the personal reaction of an individual" to the material at issue. "Personality," Holmes wrote, " . . . expresses its singularity even in handwriting, and a very modest grade of art has in it something irreducible, which is one man's alone. That something he may copyright unless there is a restriction in the words of the act."[104]

Holmes saw the attack on the originality and inherent worth of circus posters both as a threat to great art that had as its subject matter the appearance of the real world or that might, by its very novelty and experimental qualities, seem to the uninitiated to be ugly and worthless. Holmes could find no element—be it drawing on life versus the imagination, or the subject matter depicted, or the purpose for which the work was to be used—that would exclude circus posters from copyright with-

---

102 The term actually used at the time to designate the party in question was not Plaintiffs (or as might be the case today, Appellants), but Plaintiffs in Error.

103 188 U.S. at 250 quoting from John Ruskin, Elements of Drawing 3 (1st ed., 1857).

104 *Id.*

out threatening in a similar way to exclude a Degas or Whistler, Velasquez or Goya. But what he may not have focused on as clearly was that his unwillingness to make sharp distinctions also meant that no instance of "authorship," however trivial, could be excluded. For example, his test would seem to reject the kind of distinction made in a case like *Yuengling* between a colorful and imaginative drawing and simple illustrations in catalogues of articles intended for sale. Nor did it leave much scope for distinguishing between an "artistic" photograph of the sort at issue in *Sarony* and the kinds of pedestrian snapshots millions of twentieth century camera owners would snap incessantly on family vacations. If all that was required for copyright to attach to a writing was that it exhibit something "which is one man's alone," then little but works produced by gross piracy would fail the test.

This point is underscored by an additional source of support—ironic in retrospect—that was relied upon by Holmes in support of his contention that the posters must be copyrightable. Holmes noted that one could scarcely quarrel with copyrighting these posters in light of the long tradition—apparently acceptable in his eyes—of protecting things like directories.[105] This point was picked up by courts subsequently, and was taken, as it seemed indeed to do, as sanctioning copyright protection for even the dreariest compilations of data, including telephone directories.[106]

The end result was to remand the case for a new trial. Since Holmes had disposed of the technical objections to the copyrights, and found the requisite degree of originality to exist as a matter of law, the only remaining issues were ownership and the proper interpretation of the contract or course of dealing between Wallace and Courier, so that it could be determined whether Wallace had the right to order more copies from Donaldson. It appears that the case then settled; in any event, all mention of it disappears from the minutes or docket books of both the Sixth Circuit and the courthouse in Covington, Kentucky.[107] One factor that may have influenced the parties to pursue the litigation no farther were the terrible events that transpired a few months later. In August,

105 Holmes wrote that "The least pretentious picture has more originality in it than directories and the like, which may be copyrighted." *Id.*

106 Two important appellate cases that helped establish the "sweat-of-the-brow" justification in the first decades of the twentieth century for protecting factual compilations under copyright both relied on this passage for support. *See* Leon v. Pacific Telephone & Telegraph Co., 91 F.2d 484, 486 (9th Cir. 1937) (telephone directories); Jeweler's Circular Pub. Co. v. Keystone Pub. Co., 281 F. 83, 85 (2d Cir. 1922) (index of jewelry trademarks).

107 A search for indications of what occurred on remand was conducted for the author by federal court archivist, Suzanne Dewberry. Nothing appears in either the court of appeals or the trial court records except the Supreme Court mandate of Feb. 3, 1903, reversing and remanding.

1903, in Durand, Michigan, the second of two trains that carried the Wallace Show from place to place rammed into the rear of the first train, killing 30 people and many of the circus animals.[108]

Originality after *Bleistein*

Bleistein may have disappeared from the court records, but it did not disappear from the annals of the law. Rather, it remained the Court's "final word" on originality until 1991 when the subject was revisited by the Justices in *Feist Publications, Inc. v. Rural Telephone Service Company, Inc.*[109] The effect of *Bleistein* on copyright law was dramatic.

For one thing, reliance on the preamble of the intellectual property clause to limit Congressional copyright power quickly and essentially dried up. Although courts routinely treated the preamble as bearing substantively on the extent of Congress's copyright powers prior to *Bleistein*, after it originality became a key issue, and other doctrines substituted for resort to the preamble when courts wanted to deny protection. For example, obscene or sexually explicit works were once denied copyright because they were held not to promote science and the useful arts.[110] After *Bleistein*, courts that wanted to reach the same result largely switched instead to such equitable doctrines as "unclean hands."[111] In the early 1970s, Justice Douglas in a well-known dissent to a denial of certiorari, warned that, by "judicial gloss," the preamble was at risk of becoming irrelevant in the analysis of copyright . . . cases.[112] A

---

108 *23 Killed in a Wreck*, N.Y. Times, Aug. 8, 1903, at 5. The full list of the dead, including indications of some who were never identified, can be found in Michigan Railroad History Museum and Archives, *Circuswreck, at* http://www.sdl.lib.mi.us/mrhma/circuswreck/brochure5–8.htm (last visited Oct. 30, 2004).

109 499 U.S. 340 (1991).

110 Barnes v. Miner, 122 F. 480 (C.C.S.D.N.Y. 1903) (immoral works do not promote science and the useful arts); Martinetti v. Maguire, 16 F.Cas. 920 (No. 9173) (C.C.Cal.1867) (same). Analogies to the copyright doctrine denying coverage to immoral works can be found in patent cases from the same period. *See, e.g.,* Reliance Novelty Corp. v. Dworzek, 80 F. 902 (N.D. Cal. 1897) (a patent may not issue for something that is detrimental to "the morals, health or good order of society").

111 Devils Films, Inc. v. Nectar Video, 29 F. Supp.2d 174 (S.D.N.Y. 1998) (refusing to protect legally obscene works against infringement on public policy grounds); Bullard v. Esper, 72 F. Supp. 548 (N.D. Tex. 1947) (after referring to preamble, court goes on to deny relief because neither party comes to court with clean hands). Some courts, however, have refused, relying in part on *Bleistein*, to distinguish between obscene and non-obscene or indecent and decent works for copyright purposes. *See, e.g.,* Mitchell Bros. Film Group v. Cinema Adult Theater, 604 F.2d 852 (5th Cir. 1979), *cert. denied sub nom.* Bora v. Mitchell Bros. Film Group, 445 U.S. 917 (1980).

112 Lee v. Runge, 404 U.S. 887, 890–91 (1971) (Douglas, J., dissenting from denial of certiorari).

decade later, at least one court of appeals made clear that Douglas's concern was well-founded by concluding definitively that the preamble has no substantive bearing on Congress's copyright powers.[113] This position was reiterated by that same court in its recent opinion in *Eldred v. Reno,*[114] upholding a twenty-year extension of the term of copyright for both new and existing works. In that case, the plaintiffs had argued that extending the term for existing works was impermissible because it did not promote progress in science or the useful arts.

With the preamble for practical purposes done away with as a limit, and with the failure to give *Sarony*'s originality standard the restrictive reading that it plausibly invited, *Bleistein* seemed to leave no other qualitative filter in place. This had certain advantages, of course. As Justice Holmes so cogently noted, qualitative standards as a means to rule works in or out of copyright are difficult to state and hard to apply in a principled way. Whereas patents protect "inventions" and have historically looked for novelty and nonobviousness as the distinguishing characteristics of inventions, demanding novelty as a prerequisite for copyright presents numerous problems. Although it would greatly reduce the numbers of works that could qualify, that result might be undesirable. Unlike products, which require facilities, materials and technical skills to reproduce successfully, writings are comparatively easy and cheap to copy. To limit protection only to the genuinely new or unusual works might therefore have a perverse effect on the willingness of authors and publishers to provide us with the vast number of works that, despite being derivative, are nonetheless convenient, useful and informative. Defining "newness" in the context of writings would also be harder than to do so for inventions. Nothing in the history of copyright, the copyright clause, or the earliest federal statute protecting maps, charts and books, indicated that the Framers or Congress had such a radically limited form of protection for writings in mind.

Lower court judges both understood the case as setting the threshold for copyrightability at a very low level, and appreciated the pragmatic virtues of adopting this approach. In the next decade, such pedestrian works as illustrations of clothes for sale[115] and straightforward photographs of scenery[116] were held to be copyrightable under the authority of Holmes's opinion. And within thirty years, an appellate court could list dozens of decisions and cite to major treatises[117] all agreeing that

---

113 Schnapper v. Foley, 667 F.2d 102, 112 (D.C.Cir. 1981).

114 239 F.3d 372, 377–80 (D.C.Cir. 2001), *aff'd on other grounds sub nom.* Eldred v. Ashcroft, 537 U.S. 186 (2003).

115 National Cloak & Suit Co. v. Kaufman, 189 F. 215 (C.C.M.D. Pa. 1911).

116 Cleland v. Thayer, 121 F. 71 (8th Cir. 1903) (photograph of Colorado scenery).

117 Ansehl v. Puritan Pharmaceutical Co., 61 F.2d 131, 135–36 (8th Cir. 1932).

Bleistein required only "a low degree of originality and artistic or literary merit"[118] to obtain copyright. Any remaining hesitancy about protecting textual advertising was by then largely evaporating as well.[119]

The most dramatic restatement of the meaning of *Bleistein* came from Jerome Frank in 1951. Judge Frank was asked by defendants in a case before him to deny copyright to mezzotints that reproduced famous public domain paintings. The argument was that, by their very nature, derivative works produced by carefully mimicking the appearance of pre-existing art could not satisfy the originality standard because they were "copies" and in no sense "new" works. Judge Frank disagreed, moved, it would seem, by the amount of skill that a fine reproduction required of its maker. " 'Original' in reference to a copyrighted work," he wrote, "means that the particular work 'owes its origin' to the 'author.' No large measure of novelty is necessary."[120] The reason that any quantum of novelty was required was that, because the mezzotints were derivative works that were concededly "copies," Frank felt he could not sustain the copyright without identifying some things in the work that were not attributable to imitation. What he proposed was a "distinguishable variation" standard,[121] the scope of which could be ascertained from what followed. "Originality in this context," the judge said, " 'means little more than a prohibition of actual copying.' No matter how poor artistically the 'author's addition, it is enough if it be his own.' "[122] He then went on to add that even an inadvertent variation, resulting from poor eyesight or an involuntary movement might supply the necessary "contribution" that would render a derivative work of the sort at issue in that case eligible for its own copyright.[123]

Not surprisingly, cases that failed this standard were indeed rare. A copyright was found to be proper for a miniaturized, but otherwise exact, copy of Rodin's sculpture, The Hand of God.[124] An answer sheet used to take a standardized test was similarly found original enough to obtain a copyright, even though many of its elements were dictated by the optical scanning equipment used to read it (and, arguably, by the test with

---

118 *Id.* at 136.

119 *Ansehl,* for example, protected the text in an advertisement for toiletries. *See also,* Fargo Merchantile Co. v. Brechet & Richter Co., 295 F. 823 (8th Cir. 1924) (protecting "fanciful emblem" and recipes printed on labels for food and drink).

120 Alfred Bell & Co. Ltd. v. Catalda Fine Arts, Inc., 191 F.2d 99, 102 (2d Cir. 1951) (footnote omitted).

121 *Id.* at 103.

122 *Id.* (quoting in part from *Bleistein)* (footnote omitted).

123 *Id.* at 105.

124 Alva Studios, Inc. v. Winninger, 177 F. Supp. 265 (S.D.N.Y. 1959).

which it was designed to be used).[125] Although courts occasionally made gestures toward a more demanding standard, particularly in cases involving copyrights for derivative works,[126] the vast number of works that were either "original to the author" in the sense of not copied or original in the sense of exhibiting some nontrivial variation from an original continued to enjoy copyright.

The general effect of *Bleistein* was to expand the potential subject matter of copyright enormously, and Congress followed that lead in its next statutory revision. Starting with the Copyright Act of 1790 which covered only maps, charts and books,[127] successive revisions of the copyright statute had designated only reasonably discrete categories of works as eligible for protection. Paintings, for example, were not eligible for statutory copyright until the 1870 revision.[128] By contrast, when the first post-*Bleistein* revision occurred in 1909, the scope of statutory copyright coverage was changed dramatically to encompass "all the writings of an author."[129] Similarly, the next major revision, passed in 1976, said that copyright was available for all "original works of authorship fixed in any tangible medium of expression."[130] As a result of the interplay between *Bleistein* and Congress, categories of writings were no longer deemed to be excluded because the statute failed to reach them, and they could virtually never be filtered out by a demand for novelty, creativity or social value. Although the Copyright Office did on occasion find that a writing was too trite and insignificant to qualify for protection,[131] the rarity of these determinations made them seem almost quixotic.

This coarsening of the filter for copyrightability made the differences in the originality requirement that applied to copyrights and to patents one of kind rather than of degree. In Justice Douglas's famous dissent in *Lee v. Runge*, he argued that both patents and copyrights were

---

125 *Harcourt,* Brace & World, Inc. v. Graphic Controls Corp., 329 F. Supp. 517, 523–24 (S.D.N.Y. 1971).

126 *See, e.g.,* Gracen v. Bradford Exch., 698 F.2d 300 (7th Cir. 1983) (requiring substantial variation from the original); L. Batlin & Son, Inc. v. Snyder, 536 F.2d 486 (2d Cir. 1976) (en banc) (requiring a "significant" alteration).

127 Act of May 31, 1790, ch. 15, 1, 1 Stat. 124.

128 Act of July 8, 1870, ch. 230, § 86, 16 Stat. 198.

129 Act of Mar. 4, 1909, c. 320, 4, 35 Stat. 1075.

130 17 U.S.C. § 102(a).

131 *See, e.g.,* Atari Games Corp. v. Oman, 888 F.2d 878 (D.C. Cir. 1989) (criticizing the decision of the Copyright Office to deny registration for computer screen display); Nova Stylings, Inc. v. Ladd, 695 F.2d 1179 (9th Cir. 1983) (upholding denial of registration of jewelry designs).

required by the Constitution to meet a test of novelty, albeit of different degrees of stringency.[132] Works embodying "information available to all men" should not be eligible for protection, he wrote, even in cases where the author has put it into words that were the author's own, if nothing new is added to the sum of knowledge.[133] But his was pretty much a lone voice. Few others had any quarrel to find with proposition that, in distinction to the case with patents, an effort by the Copyright Office or by judges to screen out and render uncopyrightable writings that neither contributed something new, added something of substantial usefulness, nor had special value to the public would be inappropriate.

And so matters continued until March of 1991, when the Supreme Court dropped something of a legal bombshell in the form of *Feist Publications, Inc. v. Rural Telephone Service Co., Inc.*[134] *Feist* was brought as a challenge to the practice of awarding copyrights that extended protections to the labor involved in compiling factual material. Under the "sweat-of-the-brow" theory, a copyright owner was entitled to protection not merely for the selection and arrangement of what he included, but also in a real sense for the content of the compilation itself. A competitor could compile the same facts, but only if she expended the labor to recollect them; she could not "free-ride" by copying them from the first publisher. In contrast to Holmes's tacit acceptance of it in *Bleistein*, the Court in *Feist* put an end to "sweat-based" protection. And, in the course of doing so, it also gave the concept of originality articulated by Holmes, as it applied to the copyrightable elements of selection and arrangement in a compilation, a sharp tweak. Returning to the subject in a direct way for the first time in nine decades, the Court began by noting that, "[t]he *sine qua non* of copyright is originality,"[135] and then went on to add that it was not enough merely that the author had "originated" a work in the sense of not copying it from elsewhere. The work, to be original, must also exhibit "at least some minimal degree of creativity."[136]

Although Justice O'Connor, who wrote the opinion, took pains to explain that this test was not rigorous, nonetheless, she reverted back to *The Trade-Mark Cases* and to *Sarony* to emphasize that a work must exhibit evidence of the "creative powers of the mind" to be constitutionally eligible for protection. *Bleistein*, significantly, is cited only once in the entire decision, and then only to support the proposition—mentioned

---

132 Lee v. Runge, 404 U.S. 887, 891–92 (1971).

133 *Id.* at 890–91.

134 499 U.S. 340 (1991).

135 *Id.* at 345.

136 *Id.*

in *Bleistein* only in passing—that some independently created works can be too trivial or lacking in "creative spark" to cross the threshold of copyrightability.[137]

In *Feist*, then, the plaintiffs were not only refused protection against having the names and telephone numbers copied from their compilation, but more important for the purposes of this story, they were also denied protection for their selection and arrangement of the data. According to Justice O'Connor, although Rural chose the mode of presentation itself and—because the material to be organized was unique—could not in any ordinary sense be said to have copied the selection and arrangement of the data from elsewhere, it nevertheless enjoyed no copyright. As she put it, "there is nothing remotely creative about arranging names alphabetically in a white pages directory. It is an age-old practice, firmly rooted in tradition and so commonplace that it has come to be expected as a matter of course."[138]

Exactly why the *Feist* Court chose to tamper when it did with a standard that was both time-honored and had the virtue of ease of application may never be known. But the dramatic changes that occurred in the context of copyright by the time *Feist* was decided provide one possible explanation. When Justice Holmes decided *Bleistein* as he did, copyright was still limited to defined categories of works, and nothing like the modern broad protection for so-called derivative works had yet emerged.[139] Also, a potential copyright claimant had to cross numerous hurdles successfully to obtain and then retain protection for the maximum time the law allowed. Several examples of such requirements were raised and discussed at length in the course of the *Bleistein* litigation itself. Furthermore, the copyright term was bifurcated, and half-way through the maximum time allotted for copyright, a claimant who wanted to keep the interest alive would need to file a proper notice of renewal.[140] As a result, many writings never received copyright in the first place, and of the ones that did, many more fell into the public domain half-way through the maximum permissible term of protection.

Under these conditions, it was reasonable to assume that the majority of works that took on protected status were ones that the author or owner reasonably expected to have some commercial or public impor-

---

137 *Id.* at 359.

138 *Id.* at 363.

139 Justice Holmes, however, went on several years later, to help extend rights to control derivative works. In Kalem Co. v. Harper Brothers, 222 U.S. 55 (1911), Holmes wrote an opinion for the Court finding the making of a motion picture based on the novel Ben Hur to constitute copyright infringement.

140 Act of Mar. 4, 1909, ch. 320, § 24, 35 Stat. 1075.

tance. In other words, even if the courts eschewed any attempt to devise qualitative or evaluative criteria for copyrightability, other filters then in place would nonetheless sift out much of the trivia that theoretically could be protected.

All of this changed under the 1976 Act. Beginning in 1978 when the revised statute became effective, all original writings were automatically copyrighted as soon as they were fixed in tangible form, and enjoyed protection, not merely against literal copying, but against most recognizable transformations into new works. Furthermore, once copyrighted, a work would, with rare exceptions, enjoy that status for the lifetime of its author plus an additional five decades.[141] If a work (or in the case of a derivative work, the elements added to the original) would obtain copyright merely by being created without copying, the sheer volume of protected works would increase exponentially, and their average quality would, by necessity, decrease. This changed set of circumstances could well account for the renewed interest taken by the Justices in interjecting a new filter by reformulating the originality requirement into a more stringent form.

Admittedly, the precise nature of the requirement the *Feist* Court adopted remains elusive to lower courts and commentators alike. The Court was not required to define the term definitively to reach its result, and, perhaps aware of the pitfalls inherent in the attempt, it hedged in a number of ways. Justice O'Connor said that the Court was not setting a standard that was intended to be "particularly stringent" or one that requires "novelty."[142] But some "creative spark"—however we are to understand that term—was necessary, and without it, a work could not obtain a copyright.[143] The opinion even contained a suggestion that, in close cases, authors ought not assume that they will receive the benefit of doubt on the issue of originality; they could lose their cases based solely on failure to meet their burden of proof. The Justices made a point of reminding their readers of the requirement set out in *The Trade-Mark Cases* (and largely passed over in *Bleistein*) that "an author who accuses another of infringement ... prove 'the existence of those facts of originality, of intellectual production, of thought, and conception.' "[144]

[141] The 1976 Act lengthened the term from 28 years with the possibility of another 28 upon renewal to the life of the author plus 50 years. 1976 Copyright Act, 17 U.S.C. § 302(a). Today, the period in gross has been lengthened from 50 to 70 years. Copyright Term Extension Act, § 102 (b), amending 17 U.S.C. § 302.

[142] 499 U.S. at 358.

[143] *Id.* at 359.

[144] *Id.* at 346–47. The Copyright Act, by contrast, currently grants a rebuttable presumption of copyrightability to authors or owners who register in a timely fashion. 17 U.S.C. § 410(c).

Perceptive critics have subsequently pointed out a number of the confusions inherent in *Feist*, including whether the creativity element of the originality test is directed toward something about the mental operations of the author or something objectively residing in the end product.[145] Does sufficient "creativity" inhere in the fact that a photographer like Sarony went through a mental process of deciding such elements as setting, lighting and costume? Or must the result—the photograph—itself exhibit a quality of "creativity" when measured against other works of its kind? Judges have certainly arrived at no shared understanding of this or other puzzling aspects of the test. In some cases, a careful reader might think that *Feist* changed nothing in how originality is measured,[146] whereas in other instances, works that might well have unquestionably been accepted as copyrightable in the past have been deemed not to measure up to the new test for originality.[147] The one thing, however, that should be clear from the decision is that it was intended to repudiate Justice Holmes's claim that any work, so long as it "originates" with an author and falls within the coverage of the statute, will bear enough of a distinguishing mark of personality to satisfy the Constitution's originality requirement.

Feist, therefore, has succeeded in resurrecting the debate that *Bleistein,* whether intentionally or inadvertently, had put to rest. What should be the measure of a work that entitles it to receive the rewards of copyright? Justice Holmes chose to abjure the task of making judgments other than the most basic: was the work copied or not? Did Congress intend to include works of this class in the statute? This minimalistic standard is both easy to apply and generates predictable results.

Little wonder, therefore, that as eminent a judge as Richard Posner has continued to act as if *Bleistein* and *Alfred Bell* were left intact by *Feist.* In *Bucklew v. Hawkins, Ash, Baptie & Co.*[148] Judge Posner found that, although the plaintiff's display and formatting choices for computerized forms were based on public domain sources and were not especially innovative, they were nonetheless original for purposes of obtaining copyright. The work was not copied, he said, and contained just

---

145 *See, e.g.,* Leo J. Raskind, *Assessing the Impact of Feist,* 17 U. Dayton L. Rev. 331, 334–35 (1992).

146 *See, e.g.,* Mason v. Montgomery Data, Inc., 967 F.2d 135 (5th Cir. 1992) (plat maps copyrightable).

147 *See, e.g.,* Lamps Plus, Inc. v. Seattle Lighting Fixture Co., 345 F.3d 1140 (9th Cir. 2003) (a lamp design that is a compilation of pre-existing parts does not rise to a sufficient level of originality to be copyrightable); Satava v. Lowry, 323 F.3d 805 (9th Cir. 2003) (glass-in-glass sculpture of jellyfish, although beautiful and demanding of much skill, does not meet standard for copyrightability).

148 329 F.3d 923 (7th Cir. 2003).

enough variation to render it distinguishable from its public domain model. "[A]ny more demanding requirement," he wrote, "would be burdensome to enforce and would involve judges in making aesthetic judgments, which few judges are competent to make."[149]

This standard, if it is a fair interpretation of *Feist*, would continue to treat copyright as a catch-all body of law that approaches the most trivial and the most sublime with exactly the same degree of legal seriousness. On the other hand, if *Feist* does not mean to continue this practice, some clear way to distinguish what copyright is and is not meant to cover will have to evolve, and that evolution undoubtedly will be neither painless or smooth. What the process would not be, however, is, as some have claimed, "inappropriate."

One reason that Justice Holmes's argument that it would be "a dangerous undertaking" for courts to make judgments about which works are and are not worthy of copyright has continued to exert rhetorical power is its resonance with free speech traditions. Government agents of all kinds are prohibited by the First Amendment from disfavoring speech based on its content or point of view.[150] But the analogy between free speech and copyright actually does not work as neatly as it first seems. The First Amendment prohibits government from disfavoring speech because it disapproves of its content. In creating or affirming the existence of intellectual property rights, legislators and courts are, first of all, acting to promote rather than deter works of authorship, and, second, are conferring those rights to further certain some specific set of social goals. Complete even-handedness in furthering speech activities is not required even by the First Amendment,[151] and certainly not by copyright. On the contrary, before *Bleistein*, courts would have considered it constitutionally suspect to protect writings simply because they were not copied (or if copied, at least contain a distinguishable variation from the original); the governing consideration was whether the writing in question yielded some benefit to the advancement of science and the useful arts. Perhaps *Feist* will be seen in fifty years as the first step in reviving some version of that older tradition.

---

149 *Id.* at 929. Interestingly, Posner imposed a much higher standard of copyrightability for a derivative work in an earlier opinion. In Gracen v. Bradford Exchange, 698 F.2d 300 (7th Cir. 1983), he required that the claimant show a "substantial variation" from the original.

150 *See, e.g.*, American Booksellers Ass'n v. Hudnut, 771 F.2d 323 (7th Cir. 1985), *aff'd*, 475 U.S. 1001 (1986).

151 *See, e.g.*, National Endowment for the Arts v. Finley, 524 U.S. 569 (1998) (permitting selection criteria to be used in awarding grants in the arts); Board of Educ. v. Pico, 457 U.S. 853 (1982) (acknowledging the necessity for selection criteria in determining which books to acquire for a school library).

The Story of *Graham v. John Deere Company*: Patent Law's Evolving Standard of Creativity

John F. Duffy and Robert P. Merges*

The central goal of the U.S. patent and copyright systems is to harness human creativity for socially desirable ends. The Constitution authorizes Congress to create exclusive rights not for all work or effort that may happen to promote "the Progress of Science and useful Arts," but only for the creative efforts undertaken by "Authors" in "Writing[]" and "Inventors" in "Discover[ing]."[1] Thus, for example, an archeologist who, through great effort and expense, uncovers tablets containing an ancient story or a long forgotten invention is entitled to no copyright or patent to protect the find. This result is meant not to denigrate the hard work of the archeologist but merely to recognize that the intellectual property system of patents and copyrights is directed to a particular kind of human activity: intellectual creativity.

Because of this focus on creativity, an important question in both copyright and patent law is the extent of creativity necessary for obtaining a right. In copyright law, the necessary level of creativity has been set "extremely low."[2] Copyrights are generally available for "original works of authorship."[3] While this standard requires some "spark" of creativity, "[t]he vast majority of works make the grade quite easily, as they possess some creative spark, 'no matter how crude, humble or obvious' it might be."[4] A ten-year-old who completes her creative writing homework is entitled to a copyright even if she spent only an hour writing a trite story and even if her teacher thought the effort worth no more than a "C." The student's story does not even have to be new:

---

* The authors thank Rochelle Dreyfuss, Jane Ginsburg and Marty Adelman for comments on earlier drafts.

1 U.S. Const., art. I, § 8, cl. 8.

2 Feist Publication, Inc. v. Rural Telephone Service Co., 499 U.S. 340, 345 (1991).

3 17 U.S.C. § 102(a).

4 *Feist*, 499 U.S. at 345 (quoting 1 Melvin B. Nimmer & David Nimmer, Copyright § 1.08[C][1] (1990)).

provided that she did not copy the story from another, she has a valid copyright even if every word and punctuation mark happens to be identical to something previously written by someone else.

As explained in the preceding chapter by Professor Zimmerman, the threshold of creativity needed for a copyright, though low, is not non-existent. In the recent case of *Feist Publications, Inc. v. Rural Telephone Service Co.*,[5] the Supreme Court held that a phonebook is not entitled to a copyright because the names, addresses and phone numbers are themselves not attributable to the creative efforts of the phonebook maker, and the alphabetical arrangement of names is so mechanical as to exhibit not even the modicum of creativity needed to support a copyright. The work of the phonebook maker might involve much "sweat of the brow," but that work is still more akin to the labors of the archeologist than the creative expressions of an author. Yet even with its recent revival at the Supreme Court, the creativity requirement in copyright law remains important only in a limited category of cases, outside of which the copyrightability of a creative work—a book, a song, a story, etc.—can usually be presumed provided that the work has not been plagiarized or otherwise derived from another's work.

The law is vastly different for patents. As with copyrights, no one is entitled to a patent on work copied from another (*see* 35 U.S.C. § 102(f)), but inventors must also be able to show both that their work is new (§ 102 generally) and that it is inventive—that it is not "obvious" to a person having ordinary skill in the relevant art (§ 103). In contrast to copyright, the patent standard would rarely if ever by met by a ten-year-old's homework assignment. Even people with advanced degrees in science and engineering typically fail to meet this standard in their day-to-day labors. Because the standard of creativity is so much higher for patents than for copyrights, the question whether it has been met is litigated in almost every patent case, and the precise level creativity needed to support a patent—the precise scope of what is now known as the nonobviousness requirement—is one of the most important policy issues in all of patent law.

The most famous and important case on the nonobviousness doctrine is the Supreme Court's decision in *Graham v. John Deere Co.*[6] It is the most cited of all cases concerning a creativity standard in intellectual property, and it is one of the leading precedents stating that the issue has a constitutional dimension. Yet a close examination of *Graham* shows that, while the case demonstrates the immense importance of the creativity standard necessary to support a patent, it also shows that the constitutional constraints on the standard can be easily overstated, for

[5] 499 U.S. 340 (1991).

[6] 383 U.S. 1 (1966).

the Court has allowed Congress reasonable latitude in crafting the law in the area. The standard has evolved over the past two centuries, and both the Court and the Congress have contributed to its development.

The complete story of *Graham* includes a quartet of tales. The Supreme Court litigation includes three consolidated cases; the history and function of the nonobviousness doctrine provides the fourth story. We will recount all four of those stories here, though we will stress two—the historical development of the doctrine and the *Graham* case itself. The history has a central importance, for the doctrine in this area was evolving for more than a century prior to *Graham* and the Supreme Court's decision in that case can be understood only as a step in that evolution.

Our emphasis on the facts of William Graham's case has a two justifications. First, the prevailing view among patent practitioners and scholars is that the Supreme Court in *Graham* acquiesced in the somewhat less demanding standard of creativity that Congress had codified in the nonobviousness requirement of the 1952 Patent Act. The result in *Graham*—the invalidation of the patent—is the most difficult to reconcile with this view. Second, the background story in *Graham* is rich in its own right. It shows not only how one particular patent was litigated but also how a family of patents were acquired to support an innovative business that was highly important to American agriculture. A detailed examination of the Graham's business also reveals that, while Graham was an innovator, the Supreme Court was right to invalidate that particular patent at issue in the *Graham* case. Before we turn to Graham's story, however, we begin with the function and history of the creativity standard in patent law.

The Demanding Creativity Standard in Patent Law

The dramatic difference between the standard of creativity needed to obtain a copyright and that required for a patent could be tied back to the text of the Constitution. It is simply easier, one might think, to be an "Author[]" who produces a "Writing" than it is to be an "Inventor[]" who makes a "Discover[y]." But this explanation is not wholly satisfactory for two reasons. First, the Supreme Court has not interpreted (nor should it interpret) the constitutional language to impose severe restrictions on Congress's power to set the appropriate standards of creativity for intellectual property rights. Second, even if the differing standards of creativity for copyrights and patents were set by the Constitution, we would still need a justification for the differing constitutional policy. Below we examine the policy justification for a high standard of creativity in patent law and then discuss how this standard has evolved in the last two centuries of U.S. patent law.

Scope of Rights and the Standard for Obtaining Rights

Two fundamental differences in the scope of rights protected by copyrights and patents explain the difference between the standards of creativity needed to support the rights. First, unlike a patent, a copyright prevents only copying of the protected work. It grants no rights over independent creations of similar or even identical works, nor does it preclude use of any previously available work. Granting copyrights for the trivial efforts of a ten-year-old does not necessarily stifle the creative work of others because, if other ten-year-olds can also produce the triviality, the copyright system allows them to do so. A copyright on a triviality will thus have a limited economic impact. Even if people are willing to pay for the triviality, each creator will be in competition with others, and none may be able to charge much for the trivial work.

Second, copyrights protect only the particular expressions of ideas, but patent rights can protect much more. Thus, the first writer to describe a telephone in an engineering treatise, or the first fiction writer to use a telephone as a crucial element in a story, cannot prevent other writers from describing the function of a telephone or from using the telephone as an important element in advancing a plot. A patent on the telephone, however, can—and in fact did—grant rights covering all practical uses of telephone technology during the term of the patent.[7]

The differences in the scope of patents and copyrights have long been thought to justify a very different level of creativity to obtain the rights. Because patents preclude more than just copying, patent law has always required novelty as one substantial element of the creative standard that must be met. Thus, no valid patent can be obtained by an inventor who independently creates something previously available in the prior art. This rule is easily justified, because it prevents already existing matter from falling under a new set of the exclusive rights.

In addition to the novelty requirement, patent law has long imposed an additional requirement, which has been known either as the "invention" or "nonobviousness" requirement. The policy underlying this requirement is a bit more difficult to explain. After all, if an inventor has created something completely new and valuable to society, why should she not be rewarded with a patent? Answering this question requires focusing on two points: (1) Patents confer exclusive rights over an invention even against someone who has independently invented; and (2) valuable novelties—i.e., a valuable development capable of passing patent law's novelty test—sometimes arise due to changes in needs, conditions or technology that are not fairly attributable to the creativity of the first person to make the novelty.

---

[7] *See The Telephone Cases*, 126 U.S. 1 (1888) (sustaining Alexander Graham Bell's very broad patent on basic telephone technology).

To see why these two points justify the nonobviousness doctrine, let us consider a hypothetical, which is based on a real case.[8] Suppose buttons for clothes have always been made of bone. Bone serves well as a material for making buttons and it is cheap and plentiful. Now assume that the price of bone suddenly rises. Button makers realize the problem caused by rising bone prices, and many of them, independently, make what seems to them to be an obvious switch from bone to wood as the base for making buttons. Wooden buttons are thus novel. Without the nonobviousness requirement, the first button maker to switch from bone to wood would be entitled to a patent, and that patent could be defined very broadly: it could cover not merely the particular style of buttons produced by that button maker, but all buttons of any style made of wood. Yet what function would such a patent serve? If the switch is really obvious—i.e., if other button makers could have, and did, think of the substitution independently without any great effort—then the grant of the patent will confer some market power without any corresponding benefit of producing a novelty that otherwise would not have been developed. Note that the bad effects of granting obvious patents arise only because patent law does not permit independent creation as a defense. If it did allow that defense (as copyright does), then the patent would have far fewer adverse consequences because the other button makers who independently thought of the wooden button could continue making their buttons. The patentee would remain in competition with those button makers and the patent would confer little or no market power.

This justification for patent law's relatively stringent standard of creativity suggests that, if patent law allowed independent creation as a defense, the standard of creativity could sensibly be set lower. In fact, this approach is sometimes taken in this and other countries by permitting a special class of patent-like rights that operate more like copyright. Independent creation is a defense to infringement, and correspondingly, the level of creativity needed to obtain the patent-like right is lower than the level for ordinary patents: nonobviousness is not required; sometimes not even novelty need be shown.[9] Such mini-patent rights are not,

---

8 This hypothetical is a slightly simplified version of a case recounted by Justice Nelson in the majority opinion for the Supreme Court case *Hotchkiss v. Greenwood*, 52 U.S. 248, 266 (1851).

9 The example in the United States is the Semiconductor Chip Protection Act, 17 U.S.C. § 901 et seq, which protects semiconductor chip designs only against copying and requires neither novelty nor nonobviousness to obtain rights. Similarly, German utility design right (known as Geschmacksmuster) has a lower standard of creativity required to obtain the right, but provides protection only against copying. *See* 1 DONALD S. CHISUM, CHISUM ON PATENTS § 3.06[2] (2004) (noting that the Geschmacksmuster protects "against copying or imitation of the design and does not protect against innocent duplication"); Jerome H. Reichman, *Toward a Third Intellectual Property Paradigm: Legal Hybrids*

however, necessarily wise policy.[10] While such limited rights avoid the difficulties of having to define a stringent standard of creativity, they require courts to determine whether an accused infringer has copied or independently arrived at the relevant advance. That task may be very difficult where the protected subject matter is not an idiosyncratic creation (like a story) but a conceptual advance that, even if independently created, is likely to be highly similar or identical to the first creation. Thus, society may have good reasons to permit intellectual property rights that do not allow a defense of independent creation, and where such rights do exist, we can expect a relatively high standard of creativity to obtain them.

This analysis also suggests that the important issue in applying the patentability standard should be the ex ante degree of difficulty of creating the novelty, and that the timing and circumstances surrounding the arrival of a new development can provide good proxies of difficulty: where the problem and the tools for solving it have long existed, then the advent of a new solution strongly indicates that the problem was difficult. Conversely, where the novel idea occurs to multiple people soon after a problem arises, or soon after tools for solving the problem become available, then the novelty probably should not be eligible for a patent right with its stringent rights against independent creation.

The Rise of the Nonobviousness or "Invention" Doctrine

Since its justification rests in part on the existence of change in social needs, conditions and technology, the nonobviousness doctrine should be less important in a static society or one experiencing only very gradual change: where social needs and the tools for addressing those needs are constant, the appearance of a valuable novelty might be fairly attributable to the insight of the novelty's creator. In such a society, a patent system might function reasonably well even if it required only that an invention be new. This point helps to explain a striking feature of the nonobviousness doctrine: its relative youth as a major patent doctrine. The doctrine gradually emerged during the nineteenth century and was not codified until 1952. This history is consistent with the overarching justification for the doctrine, for the doctrine emerged as society began to change more rapidly—precisely when theory would predict that the doctrine would be more important. In a real sense, the quickening pace of invention triggered the invention of nonobviousness.

Between the Patent and Copyright Paradigms, 94 Colum. L. Rev. 2432, 2458 (1994) (noting the "weaker standard than nonobviousness" needed to support the German Geschmacksmuster).

[10] *See generally* Mark D. Janis, *Second Tier Patent Protection*, 40 Harv. Int'l L.J. 151 (1999) (detailing the difficulties encountered by minor or "second tier" patent systems).

The patent law of the United States has always required that an invention must be 1) *new* and 2) *useful* to be patentable. The country's first patent statute expressly included these two requirements, though it perhaps also hinted of a third. The 1790 Patent Act conferred discretion on the members of a patent board (consisting of the Secretary of State, the Secretary of War and the Attorney General) to grant a patent "if they shall deem the invention or discovery *sufficiently* useful *and important*."[11] Though that requirement is semantically quite different from the modern nonobviousness requirement, it can be viewed as similar if "sufficiently . . . important" is construed as referring to *technical* importance. The 1790 statute was, however, short-lived and no judicial decisions ever interpreted the requirement.

The first patent act was soon replaced with the 1793 Patent Act, which contained no requirement that inventions be sufficiently important but did state that "simply changing the form or the proportions of any machine, or composition of matter, in any degree, shall not be deemed a discovery."[12] This provision was a very primitive predecessor to the modern nonobviousness requirement; it was interpreted in a line of precedents that began moving toward a more general doctrine. As early as 1816, a trial court interpreted the provision to mean that a patentable improvement must involve a change in the "principle of the machine," not "a mere change in the form or proportions."[13] This interpretation was expressly approved by the Supreme Court in 1822,[14] and later cases made clear that the change in "principle" was the key to patentability. Thus, as Chief Justice Marshall stressed, "it is not every change of form and proportion which is declared to be no discovery, but that which is simply a change of form or proportion, and nothing more. If, by changing the form and proportion, a new effect is produced, there is not simply a change of form and proportion, but a change of principle also."[15]

In determining whether a novel creation was patentable, the courts emphasized the concept of a "change in principle" to such an extent that the concept continued to thrive even after the 1836 Patent Act eliminated the statutory language barring patents on mere changes in "form" or "proportions." Indeed, the elimination of that statutory language seemed merely to have liberated the doctrine; it became free to grow into

---

[11] Act of April 10, 1790, § 1, 1 Stat. 109, 110 (emphasis added).

[12] Act of Feb. 21, 1793, § 2, 1 Stat. 318, 321.

[13] Evans v. Eaton, 8 F. Cas. 846, 852 (C.C.D. Pa. 1816) (No. 4559) (Washington, J., charging the jury), *rev'd on other grounds*, 16 U.S. (3 Wheat.) 454 (1818).

[14] Evans v. Eaton, 20 U.S. 356, 431 (1822).

[15] Davis v. Palmer, 7 F. Cas. 154, 159 (C.C.D. Va. 1827) (No. 3645) (Marshall, C.J., Circuit Justice).

a much more complex and general rule. For example, the 1846 circuit court decision in *Hovey v. Stevens* continued to apply the old rule that patentable development must be not only "new in form" but "also new in principle"[16] But the *Hovey* court also added a new feature to the doctrine: in deciding whether the invention contained a change in "principle," the court considered testimony that the change was "a very obvious change to any mechanic."[17] Thus, even before the middle of the nineteenth century, courts began to look to obviousness as at least one element in defining the concept of a "change in principle" that had become a precondition for patentability.

Hotchkiss v. Greenwood, the Supreme Court's first major opinion in this area, replaced the early requirement of inventive "principle" with a more general doctrine that demanded a sufficient "degree of skill and ingenuity" as a condition for patentability.[18] The alleged invention in *Hotchkiss* was an doorknob made of clay or porcelain; the prior art included identical knobs except made of wood or metal. *Hotchkiss* would have been an easy case under the old statute prohibiting mere changes in form. But, as previously mentioned, the repeal of that statute had not deterred the courts from requiring something more than mere novelty to sustain a patent. Consistent with this trend, the trial court instructed the jury that the patent was invalid if "the knob of clay was simply the substitution of one material for another . . . and no more ingenuity or skill required to construct the knob in this way than that possessed by an ordinary mechanic acquainted with the business."[19] The jury returned a verdict for the defendant, and on appeal, the Supreme Court affirmed.

Parts of the Supreme Court's opinion harked back to the pre-existing law. For example, the Court stressed that the change at issue was a mere "formal" change,[20] echoing the old statutory rule barring patents on mere changes in "form." But *Hotchkiss* was much more than a recapitulation of the old statutory prohibition against formal changes. The Court broadly held that "*every* invention" must be the product of "more ingenuity and skill . . . than were possessed by an ordinary mechanic acquainted with the business."[21] If that condition was not met, as the Court held it was not in *Hotchkiss*, then the "the improvement is

---

[16] Hovey v. Stevens, 12 F. Cas. 609, 612 (C.C.D. Mass. 1846) (No. 6745) (Woodbury, J., Circuit Justice).

[17] *Id.*

[18] 52 U.S. 248, 267 (1851).

[19] *Id.* at 265.

[20] *Id.* at 266.

[21] *Id.* at 267 (emphasis added).

the work of the skilful mechanic, not that of the inventor,"[22] and it could not be patented.

The holding in *Hotchkiss* can be viewed as including two parts, one of which is salutary and survives to this day; the other would lead to nearly catastrophic results for the patent system. The salutary feature is that *Hotchkiss* oriented the inquiry toward what the Court called the "ordinary mechanic acquainted with the business." This feature survives today; the statutory obviousness analysis must take place using the perspective of "a person having ordinary skill in the art to which said subject matter pertains."[23]

The troubling part of *Hotchkiss* required that an invention show "more ingenuity and skill" than is possessed by the ordinary mechanic. The difference between this and the modern standard can best be understood by considering a technical problem that is solved after a few months of modestly ingenious effort by someone skilled in the art. Under the *Hotchkiss* standard, it is not at all clear—clarity was not one of *Hotchkiss*'s strengths—that the resulting solution could be patented. Even if significant "ingenuity and skill" were involved in producing the solution, *Hotchkiss* demanded that, to be patentable, the solution had to be the product of *more* ingenuity and skill than possessed by the ordinary mechanic. The contrast with modern law is clear. Under the statutory nonobviousness standard, a technical advance is patentable if it is not *obvious* to the person of skill at the time of invention. If an advance requires months of effort to achieve, it may very well be held nonobvious even though the advance is attributable more to the persistent application of ordinary skills than to a greater level of skill.

Thus, while *Hotchkiss* gave birth to a general doctrine of "invention," the direct predecessor of the modern nonobviousness standard, the test established by the Court would prove troubling both because it was vague and because it could be interpreted to be unreasonably demanding. Justice Woodbury argued in dissent that the Court's holding "open to great looseness or uncertainty in practice,"[24] and his warning was prescient. *Hotchkiss* purported to demand *more* skill and ingenuity than that possessed by the ordinary mechanic, but it was unclear how much more skill and ingenuity was needed to sustain a patent.

Within a quarter century of *Hotchkiss*, the standard of invention already seemed to be moving quite high, with some Supreme Court cases describing the relevant distinction as being "between mechanical skill

---

[22] *Id.*

[23] 35 U.S.C. § 103(a).

[24] *Hotchkiss*, 52 U.S. at 270 (Woodbury, J., dissenting).

. . . and inventive genius."[25] But the Court was not consistent. Sometimes the Court interpreted the *Hotchkiss* standard in a manner seemingly more lax than modern law—holding that patentability could be presumed where, because of the inventor's efforts, "a machine has acquired new functions and useful properties."[26] Other times, the Court used language quite similar to the modern standard. In an 1880 case, for example, the Court described a patentable invention as "involv[ing] something more than what is obvious to persons skilled in the art to which it relates."[27] And in an 1883 case, the Court contrasted invention, "which adds to our knowledge and makes a step in advance in the useful arts," with an unpatentable "trifling device, every shadow of a shade of an idea, which would naturally and spontaneously occur to any skilled mechanic or operator in the ordinary progress of manufactures."[28] This formulation too is very close to the modern obviousness test because it makes unpatentable only things that would "naturally and spontaneously" occur to persons of skill in the art, and it recognizes that any "step in advance" should be patentable, even if the step was made merely by diligent efforts of ordinary ingenuity.

The various interpretations of the invention standard became infamous; they would lead Judge Learned Hand to despair that the "invention" standard "is as fugitive, impalpable, wayward, and vague a phantom as exits in the whole paraphernalia of legal concepts. . . . If there be an issue more troublesome, or more apt for litigation than this, we are not aware of it."[29]

But vagueness was only one possible failing of the *Hotchkiss* standard. The other was that the standard could be interpreted too stringently, and by the middle of the twentieth century, the Supreme Court seemed to doing just that. The 1941 decision in *Cuno Engineering Corp. v. Automatic Devices Corp.*[30] was seen as a particularly extreme example. The invention in *Cuno* was an automatic electric cigarette lighter for cars. Prior art car lighters had to be held in place while they heated. If the user did not hold the lighter in place long enough, it would not be hot enough to light a cigarette. If held in too long, the lighter could overheat and burn out. The inventor in *Cuno* succeeded in building a lighter with a thermostatic control so that the lighter would click off when it reached the correct temperature. As a bonus, the click would

---

[25] Reckendorfer v. Faber, 92 U.S. 347, 357 (1876).

[26] Smith v. Goodyear Dental Vulcanite Co., 93 U.S. 486, 496 (1877).

[27] Pearce v. Mulford, 102 U.S. 112 (1880).

[28] Atlantic Works v. Brady, 107 U.S. 192, 200 (1883).

[29] Harries v. Air King Products Co., 183 F.2d 158, 162 (2d Cir. 1950).

[30] 314 U.S. 84 (1941).

alert the user that the lighter was ready. The Court acknowledged that the invention showed "[i]ngenuity" but nonetheless held it unpatentable because the amount of ingenuity was "no more than that to be expected of a mechanic skilled in the art."[31] A patentable invention, the Court held, "must reveal the flash of creative genius, not merely the skill of the calling."[32]

Cuno's "flash of creative genius" test was not unprecedented; it flowed rather naturally from one strand of the decisions interpreting *Hotchkiss*. Nonetheless the clarity with which the *Cuno* Court stated the test had the potential to be catastrophic for the patent system. Many technical advances are made by rather ordinary engineers who have nothing more than the "skill of the calling"—with the calling being the engineering of improvements on existing technologies. These engineers may not have many flashes of "genius;" they are not in contention for Nobel prizes. But their hard work does push forward the useful arts. If, ex ante, the engineers are confronting difficult problems with uncertain prospects of finding a solution, then the solution—if and when it is found—should be patentable, without regard to whether the solution was found by genius or tenacious plodding.[33] Otherwise, firms may have inadequate incentives to underwrite this sort of work, and research into improvements in the useful arts could be severely curtailed.

Patent practitioners were generally not happy with the Court's increasingly stringent standard of invention. In fact, even some of the Justices themselves began to question whether they were going too far. In one particularly poignant passage, Justice Jackson lamented that the Court had developed such a "strong passion" for striking down patents under its increasingly stringent invention standard "that the only patent that is valid is one which this Court has not been able to get its hands on."[34] In sum, it seemed as if the Court was trying to resolve the vagueness of *Hotchkiss* by endorsing an impractically high standard.

In the midst of general unhappiness with the Court's invention standard—and just three years after Justice Jackson's famous lament—Congress stepped in and enacted section 103 of the 1952 Patent Act. The new statute provided that a new and useful advance would be viewed as unpatentable only if it "would have been obvious at the time the invention was made to a person having ordinary skill in the art to which

---

[31] *Id.* at 91–92.

[32] *Id.* at 91.

[33] *See* Robert P. Merges, *Uncertainty and the Standard of Patentability*, 7 High Tech. L.J. 1 (1993).

[34] Jungersen v. Ostby & Barton Co., 335 U.S. 560, 572 (1949).

said subject matter pertains."[35] This is not a ridiculously low standard of patentability; the standard still requires a fairly substantial contribution. But it was designed to end the Court's search for a distinction between ordinary and extraordinary ingenuity, and to focus the inquiry solely on obviousness. The statute also stated that "[p]atentability shall not be negatived by the manner in which the invention was made."[36] Though perhaps awkwardly phrased, this further provision was intended to clarify that the particular inventor's method and talents would be irrelevant to the inquiry. Thus, the inventor seized with a "flash of genius" would not be favored over an engineer with ordinary skill and ingenuity who worked diligently and ploddingly toward a useful advance.

The statute had one cloud hanging over it. In some of its cases, the Supreme Court had stated that the judicially-created standard for invention was dictated by the Constitution.[37] If this were true, then perhaps the congressional attempt to modify the Court's invention standard would be held unconstitutional! The possibility was real. In the Court's final "invention" decision prior to the enactment of section 103, two Justices (Douglas and Black) emphasized that "[t]he question of invention goes back to the constitutional standard in every case," and they warned, "[w]e speak with final authority on that constitutional issue as we do on many others."[38] It was against this background that the *Graham* case reached the Supreme Court. The patent bar waited eagerly (and perhaps nervously) to see whether the Court would follow the new statute. Meanwhile, William Graham just wanted to have his patent sustained. That history, interesting in its own right, comes next.

William Graham's Story

The most cited and celebrated case about the nonobviousness requirement of patent law had its origins in a very practical problem involving plows, clamps and rocks. The plow itself was an innovation that has been credited with saving the American Midwest from ecological disaster. The plow made William Graham a fortune, though he did not invent it. But Graham did invent clamps that saved the plow, and one of his clamp patents would bring Graham to the bar of the Supreme Court.

"The Plow to Save the Plains" and the Clamps to Save the Plow

In the early 1930s, decades of destructive farming practices coupled with drought turned large portions of the U.S. Midwest into a "Dust

---

[35] 35 U.S.C. § 103(a).

[36] *Id.*

[37] See, e.g., Thompson v. Boisselier, 114 U.S. 1, 11 (1885).

[38] Great Atlantic & Pacific Tea Co. v. Supermarket Equipment Corp., 340 U.S. 147, 156 (1950) (Douglas, J., concurring).

Bowl.'' The problem was that then-standard plowing techniques fueled severe wind erosion. The fertile topsoil was literally being blown away, destroying the value of the land and creating massive duststorms that plagued the region. In 1933, an Oklahoma farmer named Fred Hoeme (pronounced 'hm; rhymes with "gamey' ") set out to build a plow that would cause less ecological damage. Hoeme noticed that the heavy chisels on industrial scarifiers—large machines used for ripping up earth in preparation for road building—could dig deep toughs while still leaving the soil in large clods resistant to wind erosion.[39] He applied this insight to farming and, two years later in 1935, he and a co-inventor applied for patents on a chisel plow that would "dig[] out and throw[] up a moist and heavier sub-soil creating 'a ridged surface of a corrugated nature to avoid wind erosion.' "[40] (See Figure 1.) In 1936 (within twelve months of the application!), the Patent Office issued three patents on Hoeme's chisel plow and its components.[41]

Hoeme manufactured and marketed about 2000 of his chisel plows before 1939, when he sold the rights to his invention to William Graham for $38,000.[42] Graham started the Graham–Hoeme Plow Company (later renamed simply "Graham Plow") in Amarillo, Texas, and the company was soon selling thousands of the patented plow. Marketed as the "Plow

---

39 *See* Arland Schneider, USDA Conservation and Production Research Laboratory, *Conservation Landmark* . . . , Water Management Research Unit Newsletter vol. 1 no. 2, Nov. 1997, *at* http://www.cprl.ars.usda.gov/WettingFront/WF–Vol1–No2.pdf.

40 U.S. Patent No. 2,029,249 col.1 l.9–12 (issued Jan. 28, 1936).

41 The patents covered the basic structure of the plow frame, U.S. Patent No. 2,029,250 (issued Jan. 28, 1936); the clamps that attached the curved plow shanks to the I-beams of the plow frame, U.S. Patent No. 2,029,049 (issued Jan. 28, 1936); and the plow combined with a mechanism for raising and lowering the frame so that the plow chisels could be raised above the ground while the frame was being towed into and out of the fields, U.S. Patent No. 2,041,616 (issued May 19, 1936). The patents obtained by Hoeme were particularly broad and did not foreclose competitors from selling similar chisel plows. *See* Jeoffroy Mfg., Inc. v. Graham, 206 F.2d 772, 774 (5th Cir. 1953) (noting that since 1937 another company, Jeoffroy Manufacturing, had also "manufactured and sold a basic type chisel plow of 'H' or 'I' beam frame construction with curved spring steel shanks attached to the frame by various clamping means"); *see also* U.S. Patent No. 2,082,163 (issued June 1, 1937) (setting forth a patent to Jeoffroy on a similar I-beam framed, chisel plow); Hoeme v. Jeoffroy, 100 F.2d 225 (5th Cir. 1938) (denying Hoeme a preliminary injunction against Jeoffrey's manufacturing operations). (The last cited decision produced no further published opinions and, since Jeoffrey remained in the business of producing competing plows, it can be inferred that Hoeme either settled or abandoned the litigation.) Despite the limited patent rights protecting it, Hoeme's plow became very successful in the marketplace after William Graham purchased the rights to it.

42 Graham apparently offered Hoeme a royalty of $5 per plow, but Hoeme opted for the lump sum payment of $38,000. Within two years of the sale, Graham was selling 200 plows per day. *See* Interview by John A. Heldt with Andy Hoeme, Auburn, Wash. (Nov. 1989), *at* http://www.angelfire.com/fold/hoeme/earlydays2.html.

to Save the Plains," the Graham–Hoeme plow became famous.[43] Indeed, the American Society of Agricultural Engineers has since recognized the development of the Graham–Hoeme chisel plow as one of the most significant developments in agricultural engineering in the United States.[44]

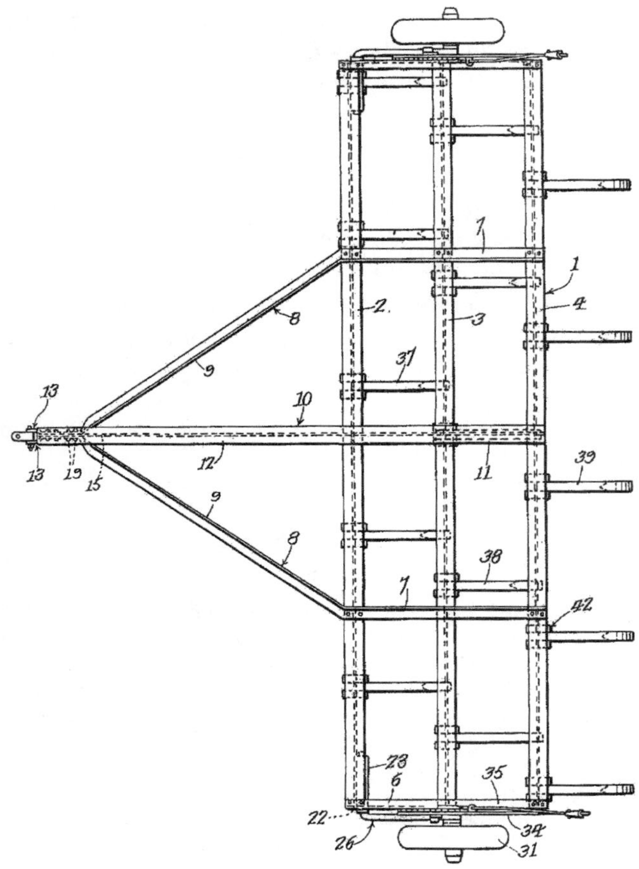

Figure 1: The Hoeme Cultivator (1935).

[43] The plow gained so much fame that it became a part of the vocabulary: farmers said that they "Hoemed" rather than plowed the land. *See* Kay Ledbetter, *Amber Waves: Savior of the soil*, AMARILLO GLOBE NEWS, Oct. 24, 2000, *at* http://www.amarillonet.com/storeis/102400/bus_amberwaves.shtml.

[44] *See ASAE Historic Events*, http://www.asae.org/awards/historic2/index.html (listing the development of the Graham–Hoeme plow as one of 44 significant events in agricultural engineering).

All this, however, is only the beginning of the story. So far it is only the story of a plow, and of how William Graham came to own the rights to it. The rest of the story involves the clamps on the plow, and what rocks in farming fields did to those clamps.

Among the first patents obtained by Hoeme was a patent covering the clamp that attached each plow shank to the metal "I"-shaped beams of the plow carriage. In Figure 2, this simple clamp is shown attaching a shank to the metal I beam. The clamp is nothing more than a metal clasp having a threaded hole and a bolt. By tightening the bolt, the shank would be secured against the I-beam.

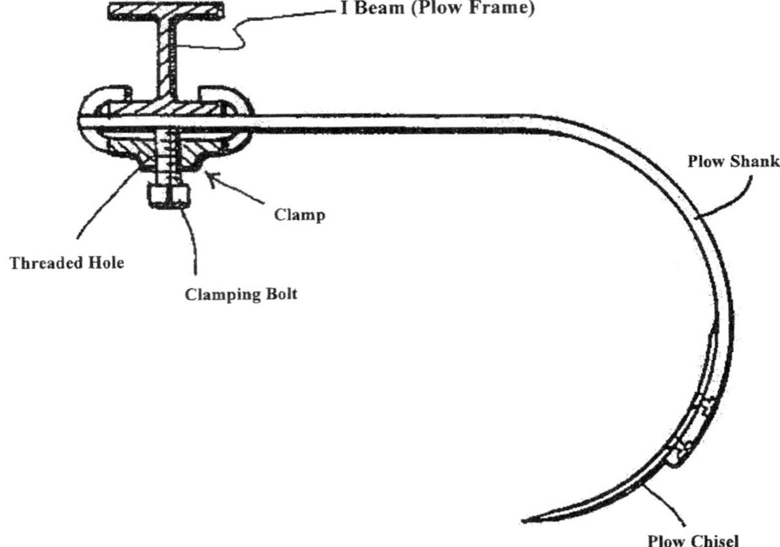

Figure 2: Hoeme's Original Clamp (1935).

These clamps worked fine for farming in the Great Plains of the American Midwest, where the soil is largely free of rocks. Beginning in the 1940s, however, Graham began selling the plows in the northern part of the Midwest—the Dakotas, Montana, Minnesota and Wyoming—where farm fields contain rocky remnants of the Ice Age glaciers that covered the area thousands of years ago. To put it mildly, the rocks caused some significant problems. When a chisel bit at the end of the plow shank struck a rock, the collision created forces strong enough not only to damage the plow bit, the shank and the clamp—all of which could be replaced—but also to bend the lower flange of the I-beam, which was an integral part of the whole plow frame. As Graham himself explained in his first patent addressing the problem, the Hoeme clamp transmitted "all of the forces developed by engagement of the ground working tool . . . to the lower flanges of the [I-beam]" so that "[i]n actual operation the flanges of the [I-beam] occasionally are distorted when excessive forces are encountered resulting in failure of the apparatus."[45] Though Graham tried to minimize the problem—saying only that the I-beams *occasionally* were distorted—he was almost certainly understating what one court would describe as a "considerable difficulty" with his company's plow.[46] Graham was candid about the consequences of a bent I-beam flange; it meant "failure of the apparatus"—i.e., the rocks could ruin the whole plow frame.

If the Graham–Hoeme Plow saved the Plains, patented Graham Clamps saved the plow. Graham's first attempt to solve the problem might be called a "brute-force" solution: he substituted a reinforced "brace clamp" that would distribute the forces of rock collisions across the entire I-beam. This clamp, which Graham invented no later than 1946 and patented in 1949, is shown in Figure 3.[47] Its key feature is a new brace (13) that distributes the forces from the plow shank (11) toward the upper portion of the I-beam (10) and thereby protects, to some extent, the lower flange of the I-beam (10a) from bending.

This first, simple solution had both a practical and a legal problem. The practical problem was that, while the new brace tended to prevent the lower flange of the I-beam from bending, it did nothing to protect the chisel and the shank. Indeed, because the new brace holds the shank more firmly, it increases the forces on the plow shank and chisel causing them to fail more frequently. Sacrificing the shank and chisel was better than bending the I-beams of the plow frame, but it was not an optimal solution.

The legal problem with Graham's brace clamp was that it was really quite simple—so simple that the courts quickly held the patent on it invalid for lack of invention. The case for invalidity of the brace clamp patent was straightforward. First, as the Fifth Circuit noted in invalidating the patent, "[t]he mere use of a brace to distribute stress and provide added strength and resistance in a structure . . . is one of the

---

[45] U.S. Patent No. 2,464,225 col.1 l.14–21 (filed July 1, 1946) (issued Mar. 15, 1949).

[46] *See also* Graham v. Jeoffroy Mfg., Inc., 206 F.2d 769, 770 (5th Cir. 1953) ("Beginning about 1940, considerable difficulty was experienced by a number of farmers in the northern and northwestern states from bending of the lower flanges of the H-beams on their plows, this bending being caused by the upward and rearward force exerted upon the shank from the operation of the plow.").

[47] *Id.* (noting that Graham testified that he built a model of his brace clamp as early as 1940 but that the patent application was not filed until July, 1946). *See also* U.S. Patent No. 2,464,225 (issued Mar. 15, 1949).

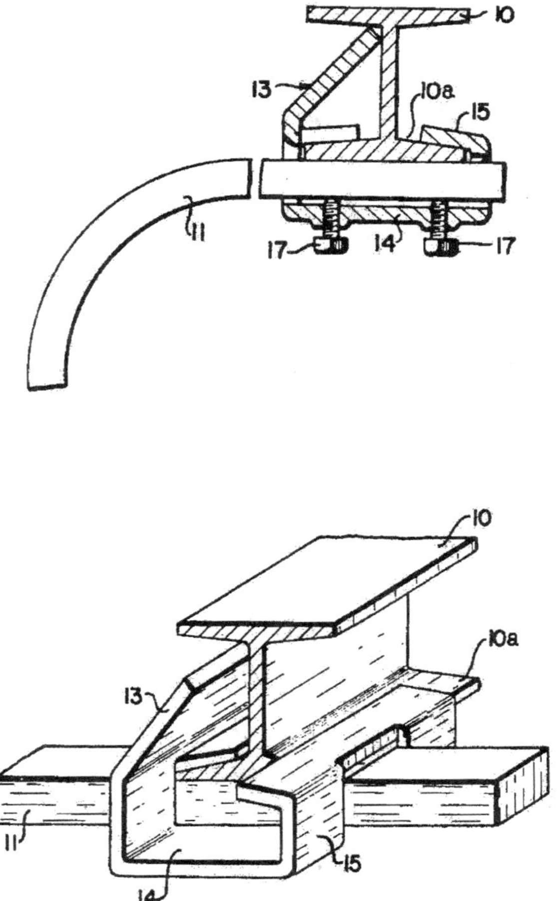

Figure 3: Graham's First Improved Clamp for the Hoeme Plow (1946). The added brace (13) distributes the forces from the plow shank (11) toward the upper portion of the I-beam (10) and thereby protects the lower flange of the I-beam (10a).

simplest and most commonly used mechanical expedients known."[48] Moreover, the clamp was nearly identical to clamps that had long been used in the railroad industry.[49] And finally, when the problem of bent I-

[48] Graham v. Jeoffroy Mfg., 206 F.2d at 771.

[49] *Id.* For example, *see* U.S. Patent No. 1,061,801 (issued May 13, 1913) (which discloses a railroad clamp or tie including a "brace or support" that extends diagonally from the base of the clamp to the top of the rail). Railroad clamps and ties are properly

beams arose, two other individuals also hit upon the idea of adding the same kind of brace to prevent bending of the lower portion of the I-beam. Though these two individuals probably developed their brace after Graham had developed his, the Fifth Circuit thought "these developments ... remain significant as tending to reveal spontaneous and independent solutions of the problem without any knowledge of the Graham device by ordinary unskilled farmers and laymen, and effectively refute appellants' claim that the Graham patent involved any invention, or anything beyond the skill of an ordinary workman or mechanic."[50]

Although the Fifth Circuit was applying the pre–1952 standard of invention, Graham's brace clamp almost certainly be unpatentable under the modern obviousness standard too. The situation also fits well with theory: as soon as the need arose—as soon as Graham's plow started to be sold in the rocky farming areas—multiple parties independently developed the same simple solution.

Graham's simple brace clamp was, however, only his first attempt at solving the problem created by rocky fields. His second attempt was much more elegant, and much more inventive. Rather than bracing his clamp so that it held the shank more rigidly, Graham took the opposite tack; he added a spring mounting so that the clamp would give way when the forces on the shank were too great (see Figure 4). This invention successfully "provide[d] a mounting for the ground working tools that reduces breaking and bending of the plow parts when operating in hard and rocky soils."[51] The spring mounting had another benefit too: it produced "a pronounced pumping or vibratory action of the ground working tools" which generated "alternating pockets and ridges" in the furrows dug by the plow.[52] These pockets were useful for "for collecting and storing small pools of moisture" that could help sustain crops during dry periods.[53] Graham applied for a patent on his spring clamp in 1947; the patent issued in January of 1950 as number 2,493,811.

Spring mounts for chisel-style plows were not novel. For example, Figure 5 shows a "spring tooth for cultivators" that was patented in 1893.[54] Thus, Graham was not entitled to a broad patent covering all

considered part of the prior art for evaluating the obviousness of Graham's brace clamp because they involve a similar sort of problem involving fastening or tying something to a metal rail or beam. Railroad clamps and plow clamps for are thus "analogous" arts.

50 Graham v. Jeoffroy Mfg., 206 F.2d at 771.

51 U.S. Patent No. 2,493,811 col.1 l.44–47 (issued Jan. 10, 1950).

52 *Id.* col.1 l.17–19 & 23–24.

53 *Id.* col.1 l.25.

54 U.S. Patent No. 503,288 (issued Aug. 15, 1893).

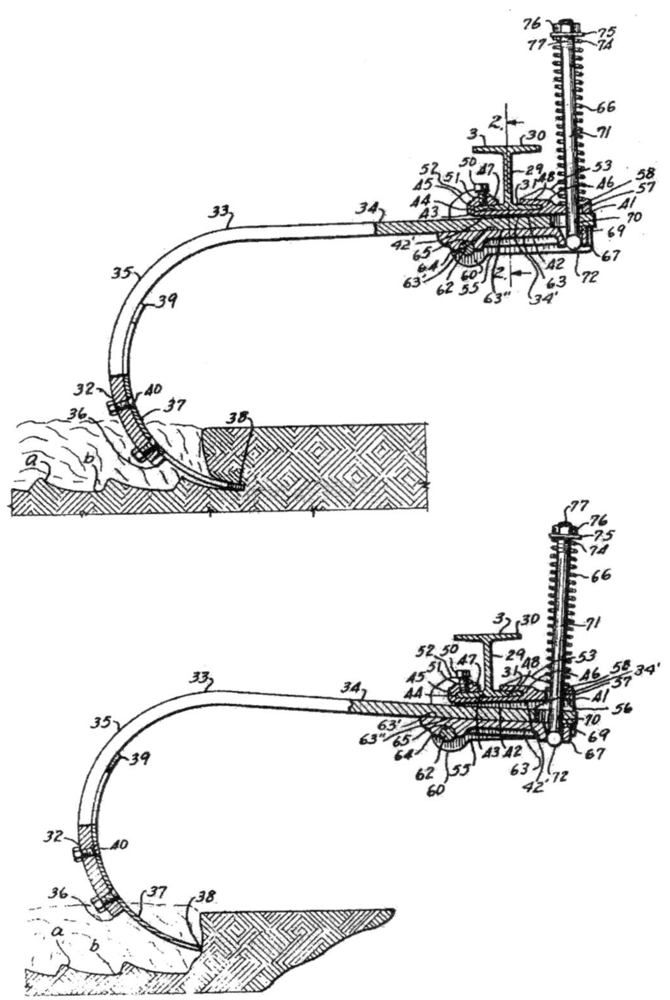

Figure 4: Graham '811 Spring Clamp (1947). In top image, the spring (66) at the front end of the clamp holds the plow shank flat against the I-beam frame. In the bottom, the shank is pivoting against the rear of the clamp and the pivoting compresses the spring.

types of spring mountings for chisel plows. Graham's new spring clamp was, as the Fifth Circuit Court of Appeals described it, "a meritorius [sic], yet not an outright pioneer invention."[55]

---

[55] Jeoffroy Mfg., Inc. v. Graham, 219 F.2d 511, 514 (5th Cir. 1955) (quoting, and agreeing with, the district court's assessment of Graham's patent).

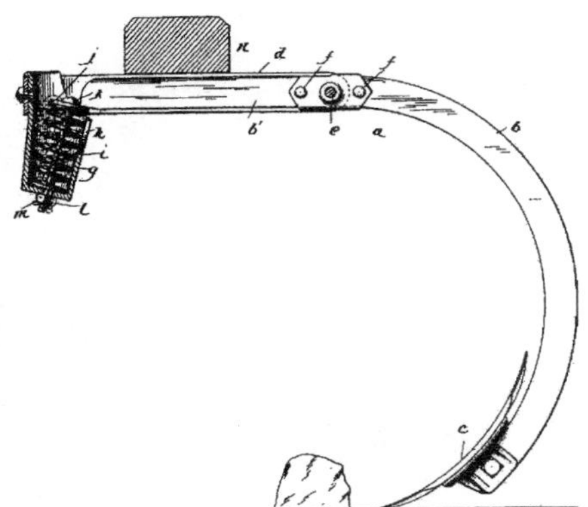

Figure 5: A Prior Art "Spring Tooth for Cultivators" (1893).

The '811 patent (as it was known in the *Graham v. John Deere* litigation) turned out to be a very successful clamp in the marketplace. Graham Plow began marketing the clamp according to the teachings of the '811 patent in the late 1940s or early 1950s and continued producing the design, with some modifications, for at least a decade and a half. Still, the '811 had certain flaws. First, as it pivoted, the shank would rub against the fixed upper plate of the clamp.[56] Wear on the upper plate was troublesome because the plate was connected directly to the frame of the plow and was therefore difficult to replace.[57] Another problem was that the plow shank was held within the clamp only by the spring rod, which passed through a hole in the shank. That hole could not be too confining because, as the shank pivoted, the spring rod needed enough room to pass through the shank at various angles. Thus, the hole in the shank was more of a slot in which the shank could move back and forth somewhat. See Figure 6 (slot marked 70). As it was pulled backward due to the force of hitting rocks, the shank would wear against, and damage, the spring rod.[58]

The wear against the upper plate and the spring rod provided the primary impetus for Graham to design and patent a new clamp. This third patent on plow clamps—Pat. No. 2,627,798 (Feb. 10, 1953)

---

[56] *Id.*

[57] Record Appendix at 690, Graham v. John Deere Co., 383 U.S. 1 (1966) (No. 11) (noting that the fixed upper plate is "larger and therefore is far more expensive to replace than the smaller pivoted part.").

[58] *See id.* at 242 (setting forth trial testimony of William Graham).

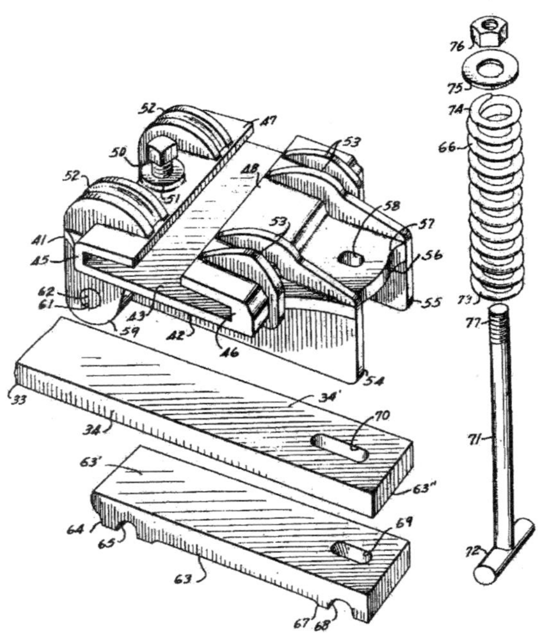

Figure 6: The Spring Clamp (unassembled) from Graham's '811 Patent. The spring rod (71) is passed through the slot (70) to hold the shank (33) in the clamp. The shank's motion causes wear on the spring rod and the underside of the clamp body above the pivot (61).

(the '798 patent)—was the one at issue in Graham's suit against John Deere. The design is shown in Figure 7. The major changes are:

(1) the hinge plate has been moved above the shank so that the shank does not come into contact with the fixed upper plate; and

(2) the shank is secured to the hinge plate by a nut and bolt arrangement at the forward end and a stirrup at the rear.

Graham conceived of this design in 1950 but did not file his patent application until August 27, 1951.

In prosecuting the patent application through the Patent Office, Graham stressed that the new arrangement eliminated wear against the fixed upper plate and secured the shank in a novel fashion. The examiner first rejected Graham's application as being not patentably distinct from the Graham § 811 patent because "[t]he expedient reversal of the relative positions of the [shank] and [hinge plate] of [the § 811 patent] and the mere provision of a fastening means between the forward ends of [the shank and hinge plate] are considered matters of design well within the expected skill of the art and devoid of invention."[59] The examiner concluded that "[c]learly *no new or unexpected result* is obtained by these expedient modifications"[60]

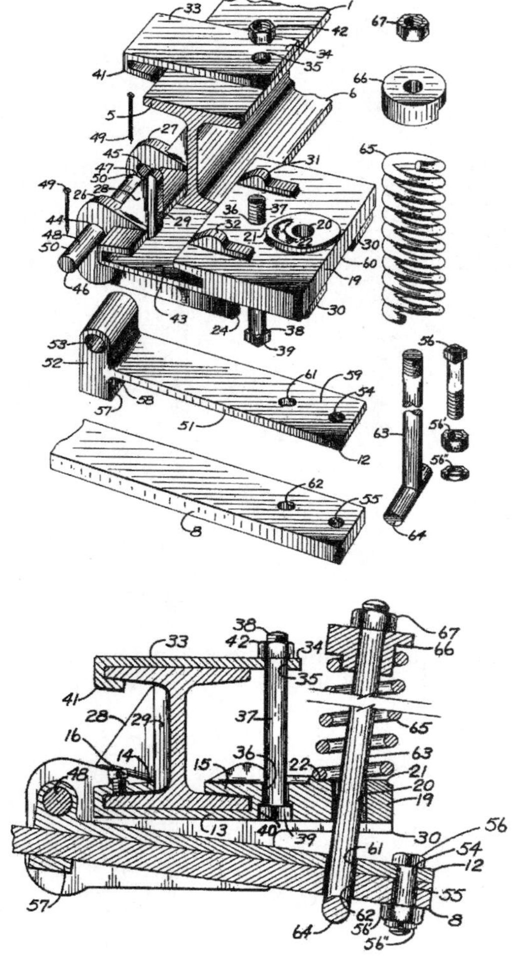

Figure 7: Unassembled and Assembled Views of the Spring Clamp from Graham's '798 Patent (August 1951). A bolt and two nuts (56, 56' and 56") and a stirrup (57) have been added to secure the shank (8) to the hinge plate (12). Also, the hinge plate is placed above the shank so that the shank does not come into contact with the fixed upper plate (13).

---

[59] *Id.* 685–86.

[60] *Id.* 686 (emphasis added).

That conclusion was, however, an invitation to come back with arguments as to why the new arrangement *did* produce at least a "new" (even if not unexpected) result. This was precisely the tactic Graham's attorneys took. They obtained an interview with the examiner, and in that interview, they "pointed out that the present construction avoided this wear [between the shank and upper plate] by inserting the moveable [hinge plate] between the plowing shank and the fixed [upper plate] and by locating the pivot to avoid rubbing contact of the [hinge plate] with the fixed [upper plate] of the clamp."[61] They also argued that the prior art did not disclose a means for "maintaining the upper face of the shank in constant continuous contact with the underface of the [hinge plate]" and, more specifically, that the prior art did not disclose combining the attachments at the forward end of the hinge plate with an "embracing means" (e.g., stirrup) at the opposite end.[62] Based on these arguments, the examiner allowed the patent to issue with two claims in February of 1953, less than eighteen months after the application had been filed.

The prosecution history of the '798 patent leaves a strong impression that the examiner was fairly generous to Graham. Graham distinguished the '811 patent merely by demonstrating that his new arrangement solved a real world problem—the problem of wear caused by the motion of the shank against the fixed upper plate. But the existence of that problem seems to do little to undermine the examiner's earlier conclusion that reversing the positions of the shank and hinge plate is "well within the expected skill of the art." The wear problem simply supplies the reason for making the obvious switch. Why then did the examiner allow the patent?

The best answer to this puzzle was supplied by Edmund Kitch. Writing soon after the *Graham* decision, Kitch noted that the Patent Office had historically applied an "inventive novelty" test, which made a development patentable provided that it was new, and "newness" could be demonstrated with a new result or function *even if that result or function were obvious*.[63] This historical point explains why the examiner's initial rejection of Graham's application used the disjunctive "or": Graham's new clamp, the examiner initially thought, did not produce a "new *or* unexpected result." Under modern obviousness law, *unexpected* results can be used to establish nonobviousness and thus patentability. But the examiner's rejection hints that if Graham could prove merely a new result—even an expected one—the new clamp might be patentable.

---

61 *Id.* 689.

62 *Id.* at 692, 693.

63 Edmund W. Kitch, Graham v. John Deere Co.*: New Standards for Patents*, 1966 S.Ct. Rev. 293, 344.

That approach to examining may not have been wildly inappropriate at the time when the examiner was acting. Though the Graham patent was not issued until early 1953, the examiner accepted the arguments of Graham's attorneys in June of 1952, one month prior to the enactment of the modern § 103 and more than six months prior to the new statute's effective date (January 1, 1953). As previously discussed, the law of "invention" was not entirely clear prior to the enactment of § 103. While cases like *Cuno Engineering* endorsed a seemingly more stringent test, other precedents supported the view that a new function or result could be considered sufficiently inventive to be patentable. The examiner seemed to be applying some of the pre–1952 precedents that suggested a standard of patentability even more lax than the nonobvious standard in § 103. Thus, the Graham '798 patent had, to put it mildly, a rickety foundation from the very beginning.

The Litigation with John Deere

As early as 1953, the John Deere Company was planning to compete with Graham in marketing spring action chisel plows. The company began by sending employees into the field to survey and to write reports on the competition. Those reports, along with copies of existing patents on farming technology, were maintained by Deere in libraries accessible by the company's engineers and patent attorneys. Thus, when Deere's engineers designed two spring clamps to compete with Graham's clamp, they had access to all of the Graham patents and to detailed field reports about the operation of the Graham clamps. Deere's own patent attorneys initially objected to the two new designs on the ground that both infringed Graham's '798 patent. The objections lead Deere's engineers to make "minor" changes in their initial designs, but the changes were not enough to avoid litigation.[64] Graham and his company had a history of aggressively enforcing their patents; the predictable infringement suit against Deere was filed on September 24, 1959.

The district court held Graham's '798 patent valid and infringed by two of John Deere's clamps. The appeal went to the Eighth Circuit, which was not bound by two prior Fifth Circuit decisions holding the patent valid (though not infringed).[65] In reversing the trial court, the Eighth Circuit held the '798 patent obvious and therefore invalid. That decision created a clean "circuit split" on the validity of the '798 patent. Circuit splits commonly attract certiorari from the Supreme Court, but the chances of further review in *Graham* were increased even more because the Eighth Circuit specifically noted that it was analyzing the

[64] Graham v. John Deere Co., 216 F. Supp. 272, 277 (W.D. Mo. 1963).

[65] Jeoffroy Mfg., Inc. v. Graham, 219 F.2d 511 (5th Cir. 1955); *Graham v. Cockshutt Farm Equipment, Inc.*, 256 F.2d 358 (5th Cir. 1958).

legal issue using a different standard than that applied in the Fifth Circuit.[66] The court of appeals opinion thus provided Graham's lawyers with the perfect opportunity to seek Supreme Court review.

Despite the direct split, the decision to grant certiorari was not unanimous. Justice Clark, who would ultimately author the *Graham* cases, does not seem to have supported certiorari. His law clerk during the 1964 Term, Michael Maupin, recommended against granting cert because "a decision in this case would be a foregone conclusion."[67] "Seems to me," Maupin wrote, "the Court should wait until a case that seems wrong comes up."[68] Clark appeared to be undecided. He wrote "Deny?"[69] on the law clerk's memo, and his conference sheet for the case does not record any vote for him on granting certiorari. On January 18, 1965, Graham's petition was granted with six votes, including the three most junior Justices, the two most senior (Black and Douglas) and Chief Justice Warren. Justices Harlan and Brennan voted to deny review despite the clean split.[70]

One month later, the U.S. Solicitor General (Archibald Cox) filed a petition in another case, *United States v. Adams*, that suggested consolidating *Graham*, *Adams* and a third case, *Calmar v. Cook Chemical,* in which a petition for certiorari was also pending. Reviewing a trio of cases, Cox argued, would allow the Court to rule on the patentability standard "in a variety of contexts and in broad perspective."[71] Moreover, Cox noted, the Court had not reviewed a case on the standard of patentability since 1950, even though it had reviewed a large number of cases on the issue between 1925 and 1949.[72] As Justice Clark's clerk described it, "[t]he SG really wants the Court to . . . have a sort of one

---

66 John Deere Co. v. Graham, 333 F.2d 529, 533–34 (8th Cir. 1964).

67 Memorandum from Michael W. Maupin re: *Graham v. John Deere Company of Kansas City*, at 5 (Dec. 17, 1964) (from the Papers of Justice Tom C. Clark, Tarlton Law Library, University of Texas School of Law, Box B208, Folder 5) (hereinafter Clark Papers).

68 *Id.*

69 *Id.* at 1 (handwritten note).

70 For the records of the vote, see Conference Sheet in No. 580, O.T. 1964, *Graham v. John Deere Co.* (from Clark Papers Box C81, Folder 5).

71 Pet. for Cert. at 16, in United States v. Adams, 383 U.S. 39 (1966) (No. 55).

72 *Id.* at 15 n.11. Cox's brief asserted that the Court had "reviewed the application of the standard of patentability in no less than one hundred cases" during the period. *Id.* This count, if accurate, must include companion cases and similar matters that did not produce full opinions from the Court. A more recent study of cases having full merits opinions shows that, during this period, the Court was deciding about one case per year on this issue. *See* John F. Duffy, *The Festo Decision and Return of the Supreme Court to the Bar of Patents*, 2002 S.Ct. Rev. 273, 295 n.81 (2003).

day orgy of patent arguments, to celebrate the end of a thirteen year dry spell.''[73] Counsel for Calmar, Abe Fortas (who would soon be on the Court and would have to recuse himself from the *Graham* cases), warmly endorsed the government's suggestion,[74] and five Justices (Black, Douglas, Clark, White and Goldberg) voted to grant certiorari in the two additional cases.[75] Thus, the Court was set to have its ''one day orgy of patent arguments,'' with *Graham* the lead case by which the consolidated appeals would be forever known.

The Court's Opinion in Graham: A Victory for Inventors in One Patentee's Defeat

The *Graham* trilogy of cases would give the Court its first opportunity to interpret the nonobviousness standard codified in 1952.[76] The patent community was hoping that the new statute would change the direction of the Court's increasingly stringent invention test. The results of three consolidated cases did not seem to be a promising beginning. The Court affirmed the invalidation of Graham's patent and also held obvious the patent at issue in *Cook Chemical*. True, the Court did sustain the patent in the *Adams* case, but that patent involved the chemical composition of batteries, not a mechanical invention. Even prior to the 1952 Act, the Court had been more willing to find ''invention'' in matters of chemistry than in mechanics. Indeed, three years after it announced the infamous ''flash of creative genius'' test, the Court had sustained a patent on an improved battery.[77] Thus sustaining Adams' battery patent in itself was not necessarily an indication that the Court had done anything to change its pre–1952 jurisprudence. Moreover, the *Graham* Court itself stated that the 1952 codification of obviousness ''was not intended by Congress to change the general level of patentable invention.''[78] On its surface, *Graham* appeared to dash any hope for improvement in the Court's patentability standard.

73 Memorandum from Michael W. Maupin re: *United States v. Adams*, at 8–9 (Mar. 12, 1965) (from Clark Papers Box B208, Folder 6).

74 Supp. Br. for Petitioner at 4, Calmar v. Cook Chemical, 383 U.S. 1 (1966) (No. 37).

75 *See* Conference Sheet in No. 778, O.T. 1964, *Calmar v. Cook Chemical* (from Clark Papers Box C81, Folder 6); Conference Sheet in No. 906, O.T. 1964, *United States v. Adams* (from Clark Papers Box C81, Folder 7).

76 Indeed, when the Court granted certiorari in *Graham*, the Court had not yet decided any cases involving patent validity since the enactment of the 1952 statute. The Court's involvement with patents dropped precipitously after the enactment of the 1952 Patent Act; the few patent cases heard by the Court between 1952–1965 generally involved issues on the periphery of patent law, such as issues of venue and patent-antitrust matters. *See* Duffy, *supra* note 72, at 294–96.

77 *See* Goodyear Tire & Rubber Co. v. Ray–O–Vac Co., 321 U.S. 275 (1944).

78 383 U.S. at 17.

Why then was *Graham* greeted so warmly by the patent community, as if it *had* changed the standard of patentability? One reason for this reaction was the Court's treatment of the "flash of creative genius" test. The Court forthrightly acknowledged that "Congress intended by the last sentence of § 103 to abolish the test it believed this Court announced in the controversial phrase 'flash of creative genius.' "[79] But the Court asserted that, if Congress "believed" the Court had announced a new test in *Cuno*, Congress was mistaken: the phrase "flash of creative genius" was merely a "rhetorical embellishment of language" that signified no change in the patentability standard.[80] The Court's opinion was an artful dodge: it avoided any possible constitutional question as to whether Congress could overrule *Cuno* by reinterpreting that decision. Similarly, while the Court said that Congress had intended § 103 "merely as a codification of judicial precedents embracing the *Hotchkiss* condition," it also acknowledged and agreed to follow the "congressional directions that inquiries into the obviousness ... are a prerequisite to patentability."[81] If there was a conflict between the new statute and the Court's precedents, the statute clearly won, but the Court denied that any conflict existed.

The early drafts of the *Graham* opinion and the internal correspondence between the Justices show that this artful dodge was a fierce compromise between two factions on the Court. Justice Black and, to a lesser extent, Justice Douglas pushed to change Clark's draft as much as possible to maintain the pre–1952 status quo. Justices Harlan and Stewart tried, gently as it so happens, to keep Justice Clark from giving away too much.

Clark's first draft opinion in *Graham* was circulated on December 8, 1965. It contained many of the points that have become famous in the final opinion, including (1) the assertion that "Congress intended by the last sentence [of § 103] to abolish the test it *erroneously* believed to be announced in 'flash of genius;' "[82] (2) the claim that § 103 "was not intended to change the general level of patentable invention;"[83] and (3) the conclusion "that the section was intended as a codification of judicial precedents embracing the *Hotchkiss* condition."[84] But the first draft of

---

[79] *Id.* at 15.

[80] *Id.* at 15 n7.

[81] *Id.* at 17.

[82] Draft of Dec. 8, 1965, at 14 (emphasis added) (Clark Papers Box A182, Folder 5). The emphasized word "erroneously" was later omitted. Perhaps Justice Clark thought it inappropriate to label as "erroneous[]" a belief attributed to Congress.

[83] *Id.* at 15.

[84] *Id.* Justice Clark later inserted the word "merely" after "intended" in response to Justice Black's objections to the opinion.

the opinion was also far more candid than the final opinion in recognizing that § 103 *did* authorize change. The draft overtly recognized that § 103 had made a "change" from "[t]he old 'invention' formulation" to "the nonobviousness condition."[85] Though the draft claimed the change to be "one of inquiry, not quality," it nonetheless celebrated the "positive advantages to be gained by testing for nonobviousness rather than for invention," including the possibility that § 103 would "add clarity to the 'invention' concept by directing the inquires along more practical channels, i.e., 'obviousness.' "[86] Clark's opinion openly disparaged the old invention test, which was called an "elusive concept." A subsequent draft circulated on January 3, 1966, used even stronger language, lauding § 103 as "permit[ting] a more practical test than the prior judicial formulation, couched as it was in so gossamer a concept as 'invention.' "[87]

Clark's candor drew a strident letter from Justice Black, who wrote:

> You say . . . that this Act shifts "patentability and validity inquiries from 'invention' to 'non-obviousness.' " This interpretation of the 1952 Act is repeated in your opinion a number of times and in fact seems to be its central theme. I do not believe that Congress did this, intended to do it, or could have done it consistently with its limited power granted by Section 8 of the Constitution. . . . In view of the language and history of the Constitution and the patent laws, I cannot treat the term "invention" as a "Gossamer" or "illustive" [sic, probably "elusive"] concept which Congress could ignore or repudiate at will.[88]

Black concluded with his own interpretation that § 103 "was intended to be an additional or supplemental test and not a substitute for the old novelty, utility and invention test."[89]

In response, Justice Clark edited out all of the candid language in the earlier drafts that suggested § 103 had made a change. He also excised the disparaging descriptions ("elusive" "gossamer") of the old invention test. He even went so far as to hint—very obliquely and ambiguously—that § 103 provided an "additional" test, as per Black's view. The hint was added by modifying the first sentence of Part V of the opinion, which in its final form reads: "Approached in this light, the

---

[85] *Id.* at 16.

[86] *Id.* at 16 & at 15.

[87] Draft of Jan. 3, 1966, at 15 (Clark Papers Box A183, Folder 1).

[88] Letter from Hugo Black to Tom Clark, Jan. 11, 1966, at 1 (Clark Papers Box A183, Folder 4).

[89] *Id.* at 2.

§ 103 additional condition, when followed realistically, will permit a more practical test of patentability."[90] Though the word "additional" was added to placate Justice Black, the meaning of the sentence remains ambiguous: it could mean that § 103 is intended to be either an addition to the invention test (as Black wanted), or an addition to the other statutory tests—novelty and utility—that Congress had previously codified. The rest of the sentence tends to support the latter reading, for it states that § 103 is "a more practical test of patentability." More practical than what? While the final opinion does not say "a more practical test than the prior judicial formulation [of] 'invention' " (as the corresponding sentence from the Jan. 3 draft did), that remains the natural implication of the sentence. Thus, while placating Justice Black, Clark successfully resisted giving any suggestion to lower courts that they should continue to apply the old "invention" test in addition to the new statutory standard.

Clark also received pressure on the other side. For example, Justice Harlan suggested eliminating "language which might indicate that the standard of patentability is a constitutional one."[91] Harlan made the suggestion, he explained, because "I feel pretty sure that you would agree that patentability in a particular case must be judged against the standards of the statute, there being no claim made in any of these cases about the statute's constitutionality."[92] Justice Stewart also lobbied for the deletion of a sentence that Clark had inserted at the request of Justice Douglas; the sentence included what could possibly be construed as a favorable reinterpretation of *Cuno*'s "flash of creative genius" test. Stewart wanted it out because the *Cuno* test had "much disturbed the lawyers and commentators, and I would much regret to see it now evicted through one door but re-admitted through another."[93] These suggestions were probably intended to stiffen Clark's resolve so that he didn't give too much away in accommodating Black and Douglas.

In the end, Clark was diplomatic. He took most of Harlan's suggestions, but he explained to Stewart why he could not remove the sentence about *Cuno*:

> I talked to WOD [William O. Douglas]—he was disturbed about my taking it out. I believe (after Hugo settles down) we can get it out. I will keep you advised.[94]

---

90 383 U.S. at 17.

91 Letter from John M. Harlan to Tom Clark, Feb. 11, 1966, at 1 (Clark Papers Box A183, Folder 4).

92 *Id.*

93 Letter from Potter Stewart to Tom Clark, Jan. 4, 1966, at 1 (Clark Papers Box A183, Folder 4).

94 Letter from Tom Clark to Potter Stewart, Jan. 20, 1966 (Clark Papers Box A183, Folder 4).

The sentence never came out. It remains the last sentence (plus citations) in footnote 7 of the Court's opinion.[95] It was Justice Douglas's only contribution to the opinion.

Despite the changes demanded by other Justices, Justice Clark remained firmly in control of the tone and methodology of the Court's opinion in applying the new obviousness test. And it is in this careful, painstaking methodology that the patent bar could find the most to celebrate.

Of the three patents at issue in the consolidated cases, Graham's was the first addressed in the Court's opinion. As previously discussed, the patent was weak. It had been invalidated in the court below. While two prior appellate courts had sustained the patent, they did so only by giving it a very narrow interpretation. And the prosecution history of the patent showed that the Patent Office seemed to have applied a very loose standard in granting the patent. If the Court had been applying its old "creative genius" test, Graham's patent could have been dealt with summarily. Indeed, that is how the Court often handled cases when applying its pre–1952 invention doctrine (*Cuno* itself was decided in an eight-page opinion). That's not what happened in *Graham*. Instead, the Court carefully articulated, and then followed, a detailed process for resolving nonobviousness issues. This process requires that:

> [T]he scope and content of the prior art are to be determined; differences between the prior art and the claims at issue are to be ascertained; and the level of ordinary skill in the pertinent art resolved. Against this background, the obviousness or nonobviousness of the subject matter is determined.[96]

What the Court found in following this process was not helpful to Mr. Graham. It was, however, helpful to the patent system that the Court took such care even in striking down a relatively weak patent.

While Graham's '798 patent had seemed doubtful even when it was prosecuted, three additional weaknesses in the patent had come to light by the time of the John Deere litigation. First, the Patent Office did not have all of the relevant prior art before it. Recall that although Graham conceived his invention in 1950, he did not constructively reduce it to practice (i.e., file his application) until August 27, 1951. In May of 1951, Elmer Rolf of the Glencoe Manufacturing Company reduced to practice and began selling a spring clamp that was highly similar to the Graham's '798 device. Since Graham could not prove diligence between 1950

---

[95] The sentence reads: "It was the device, not the invention, that had to reveal the 'flash of creative genius.' " 383 U.S. at 15 n.7.

[96] 383 U.S. at 17.

and August of 1951, he was stuck with his filing date as his date of the invention. Thus, the Glencoe clamp was prior art.[97]

The Glencoe clamp was a devastating piece of prior art against Graham. As the Supreme Court noted, Graham had stressed to the Patent Office that his '798 clamp was better because of "wear and repair" considerations. The older '811 patented clamp allowed the shank to wear against the fixed upper plate of the clamp, which was costly to repair. The '798 clamp solved this problem by (1) isolating the shank from the hard-to-replace upper plate; and (2) bolting the shank to the

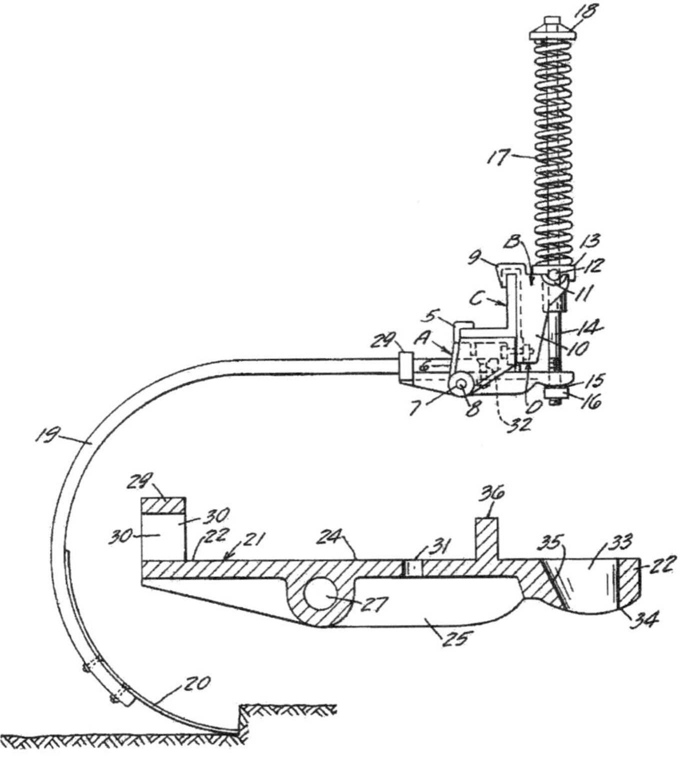

Figure 8: The Rolf/Glencoe Spring Clamp (May 1951). The hinge plate (inset) isolates the shank from the fixed upper plate of the clamp and also contains a stirrup (29) and bolt plus hole (32 & 31) for securing the shank to the hinge plate.

97 Rolf applied for a patent in April of 1952, but the Patent Office did not declare an interference between the two applications. Rolf's patent issued in 1956. *See* U.S. Patent No. 2,739,518 (issued Mar. 27, 1956).

hinge plate so that the shank moved less and thereby caused less wear. Yet the Glencoe clamp accomplished both of these objectives in a very similar fashion. See Figure 8.

Because the Glencoe device achieved the goals Graham touted before the Patent Office, Graham tried to develop a new theory to distinguish his clamp from Glencoe's. The new theory was that, within the confines of the hinge plate, the shank could flex more in Graham's '798 configuration than in Glencoe's clamp. In both structures, upward forces on the shank would tend to cause the shank to bow downward inside the hinge plate. However, because the hinge plate (excepting the stirrup) was above the shank in Graham's device, the shank was free to bow downward. In Glencoe's device, the hinge plate was below the shank and it therefore restricted any downward flexing.

This new "flexing" theory raised a second problem for Graham: the flexing property was nowhere disclosed in Graham's patent specification or in the prosecution history. If increased flexing was the key to his invention, Graham seemed utterly unaware of it prior to the litigation with Deere. This second problem did not escape the attention of the Court. The Court viewed the new theory as an "afterthought" not "hinted at in the specifications of the patent."[98] The Court believed that "[i]f this were so vital an element in the functioning of the apparatus it is strange that all mention of it was omitted."[99]

The third and final problem for Graham was that between the time that the patent issued and the Supreme Court's decision in 1966, Graham never produced or licensed the '798 invention.[100] Instead, Graham continued marketing the older '811 structure with modifications designed to reduce the wear and repair problems of the old configuration.[101] While the law is absolutely clear that American patent holders are not required to practice their inventions, Graham's failure to market the invention also meant that he could not rely on so-called secondary considerations, such as market success, to help sustain his patent. Moreover, Graham's nonuse of the invention also limited how strongly the flexing quality could be touted. Graham's expert had to admit that the flexing in the '798 structure was "[n]ot a great factor" in the

98 383 U.S. at 25.

99 *Id.*

100 As Graham admitted in trial testimony, the '798 clamp was never commercially manufactured and had never been produced at all prior to the construction of a test piece as an exhibit for the litigation with John Deere. S.Ct. Appendix at 252.

101 The key modification was that the shank was bolted to the hinge plate so that it would no longer rub against the spring rod.

functioning of the structure, and that the magnitude of the flex was "the same or substantially the same" as the flex achieved by the older '811 structure.[102] These quotes made their way into the Supreme Court's opinion. In sum, the Court did its homework carefully, and it discovered that the flexing benefits of the '798 clamp were, if they existed at all, certainly no part of what Graham had thought was his improvement at the time of invention.

The Companion Cases

On the same day that it decided *Graham*, the Court also decided two other patent disputes. It held one patent invalid and one valid. Neither case was particularly difficult.

Cook Chemical, the Scope of the (Secret) Prior Art, and the Supreme Court's Error

Calmar v. Cook Chemical involved a patent on a "hold down" cap for an insecticide sprayer; it was invented by Baxter Scoggin, an officer of the Cook Chemical Company. The purpose of the cap was to secure the pump sprayer in the down position and also to create a seal around the sprayer to prevent any liquid from leaking out of the cap. Scoggin's cap was supposedly better than the prior art in creating a good seal below the sprayer head and above the screw threads that attached the cap to the bottle. As in *Graham*, the basic technology was not new; the art of sealing caps for sprayers and other dispensing bottles was already a relatively crowded field. As in *Graham*, the Patent Office granted a very narrow patent based on very minor differences between the applicant's arrangement and prior art devices. And as in *Graham*, the Patent Office did not consider one of the most relevant pieces of prior art. However, the Supreme Court made a factual error that made the case appear much more difficult than it in fact was. With that error corrected, the result in the case reveals an important facet of nonobviousness analysis—the law sometimes assumes that the person of ordinary skill in the art possesses quite extraordinary knowledge.

In invalidating Cook Chemical's patent, the Court relied on three pieces of prior art: (1) 1938 patent to Lohse; (2) a 1952 patent to Mellon; and (3) the piece of prior art that the Court found most relevant, a patent to Livingstone that the Court cited as if it had been *issued* in 1953.[103] The Court was wrong about the last patent; it was *filed* in 1953 and did not issue until 1955. Technically, that error did not make a

---

[102] 383 U.S. at 24–25 nn. 12–13.

[103] *See* 363 U.S. at 32 (citing the Livingstone patent as a 1953 patent). In its citation of the other relevant patent, the Court correctly used the issue dates in citing the patents, *see id.* at 31–32.

difference in the outcome of the case because, under section 102(e) of the Patent Act, a United States patent application becomes part of the prior art as of its filing date provided that the application ultimately is issued as a patent. (In fact, the Court had clarified that very aspect of the law just one year prior to deciding *Graham*.)[104] But as a practical matter, the Court's factual mistake meant that Cook Chemical appeared to have a much stronger argument of "secondary considerations" to support the validity of its patent. To explain this point, we need to recount the facts of the case.

At the Patent Office, Cook Chemical had stressed (1) that Scoggin's new cap had a rib seal above the screw threads of the cap; and (2) that, when fully screwed down, the cap did not touch the shoulder of the container so that the shoulder would not interfere with screwing the cap down tightly onto the rib seal. Unfortunately for Cook Chemical, Livingstone's 1953 patent application (which the Patent Office had not considered in granting Cook its patent) disclosed a cap having both of these features, with the only slight difference being that Livingstone's cap used a more sophisticated seal—a "tongue-in-grove" seal—rather than a simple rib seal. To sustain its patent in light of the newly discovered prior art, Cook Chemical could not argue that the change from a tongue-in-grove seal to a rib seal was a patentable difference. The allegedly infringing product manufactured by Calmar actually *did* use a tongue-in-grove seal and, to prove infringement in the lower courts, Cook had successfully argued that the difference between tongue-in-grove and rib seals was not substantial.[105]

In trying to save the Scoggin patent, Cook Chemical advanced two arguments. First, Cook tried to have the Livingstone cap excluded from the obviousness analysis. The Livingstone cap was designed to be used on a bottle with a *pouring spout*, not with a *pump sprayer*. Under § 103, the obviousness inquiry proceeds from the perspective a person skill in "the art to which said subject matter [of the invention] pertains." If a prior art reference does not "pertain[]" to the relevant art, it is excluded for the inquiry, and Cook Chemical argued that the caps for pour spouts are not pertinent to the art of designing a cap for a pump sprayer. This was a weak argument. As the Court noted, the technical problems confronting Scoggin "were mechanical closure problems."[106] Scoggin's goal was to design a cap with a leak-proof seal so that it could contain whatever liquid might seep out of the bottle top (be it a spout or sprayer). As the Court concluded, "[c]losure devices in such a closely

104 *See* Hazeltine Research v. Brenner, 382 U.S. 252 (1965).

105 Calmar, Inc. v. Cook Chemical Co., 336 F.2d 110, 114–115 (8th Cir. 1964).

106 383 U.S. at 35.

related art as pouring spouts for liquid containers are at the very least pertinent references.''[107]

Cook Chemical's other argument is where the Court's error really hurt the opinion. Cook argued that the development of a practical hold-down cap for a sprayer had long eluded its competitors in the insecticide industry and that its cap, which Scoggin perfected in 1956, was widely adopted when it became available. Cook's argument links up well with the theory for determining whether a novel development should be considered nonobvious. If all of the relevant pieces of prior art were in place by 1953, then why did the entire insecticide industry for years miss this obvious adaptation of the existing art to solve a persistent problem?

There's a very good answer to this question: the entire insecticide industry did not have access to the key Livingstone patent in 1953. It did not become publicly available until it issued in August of 1955; prior to that, the Patent Office held the application in secret. Scoggin began his research into building a better cap in 1954, when the Livingstone application was still secret. The cap was perfected in 1956—just a matter of months after the Livingstone patent became public.

Because of its error, however, the Supreme Court did not have a good answer to Cook's argument.[108] To its credit, the Court noted that Cook's argument had significant weight. The Court recognized that ''secondary considerations''—including ''commercial success, long felt but unsolved needs, failure of others, etc.''—''focus attention on economic and motivational rather than technical issues and are, therefore, more susceptible of judicial treatment than are the highly technical facts often present in patent litigation.''[109] Such ''subtests'' of patentability could ''lend a helping hand to the judiciary which . . . is most ill-fitted to discharge the technological duties cast upon it by patent legislation.''[110]

---

107 *Id.*

108 The Court's error made the case seem harder than *Graham*. In fact, at the Supreme Court one Justice—Harlan—initially voted to sustain the patent. (The vote against Graham's patent was unanimous from the start.). After Clark's opinion was circulated, however, Justice Harlan joined in, saying: ''The only of the cases as to which I had any real doubt was Calmar, but you have convinced me on that score.'' Memorandum from Justice John M. Harlan *Re: Nos. 11, 37, and 43–Patent Cases* (Feb. 11, 1966) (Clark Papers Box A183, Folder 4). Justice Clark's law clerk, Charles Reed, also had a ''first impression . . . that the result reached by the Court [majority] was wrong.'' Undated Letter from Charles Reed to Justice Tom Clark, at 2 (Clark Papers Box A182, Folder 1). Reed changed his mind, however, in writing a first draft of the opinion and ultimately concluded that ''the arguments of long-felt but unsatisfied needs and commercial success'' were ''overbalanced'' by the ''direct evidence of the lack of unobvious differences in the prior art (viewing the invention as [Cook Chemical] did in the patent office).'' *Id.* at 203.

109 383 U.S. at 18 & 36.

110 *Id.* at 36.

Nonetheless, the subtests or secondary considerations could not, the Court held, "tip the scales of patentability" in Cook's favor.[111] The differences between Scoggin's cap and the prior art were, the Court believed, "rendered apparent in 1953 by the *appearance* of the Livingstone patent, and unsuccessful attempts to reach a solution . . . before that time became wholly irrelevant."[112] But Livingstone patent did not "appear" in 1953; that would not happen until the second half of 1955. The Court could have, and should have, discounted all of the failed efforts to find a solution prior to late 1955. Instead, the Court incorrectly believe that "no one [in the insecticide industry] apparently chose to avail himself of knowledge stored in the Patent Office and readily available by the simple expedient of conducting a patent search—a prudent and nowadays common preliminary to well organized research."[113] But such a search would not have found the Livingstone cap during most of the relevant period when Cook, and the rest of the industry, was looking for a solution.

The invalidation of Cook Chemical's patent shows one feature of the modern nonobviousness doctrine that has changed little since the time of *Graham*: while obviousness is tested from the perspective of the person of ordinary skill in the art, it is tested against *all* of the relevant prior art. As Judge Rich would describe it just a few months after *Graham* was decided, the § 103 test hypothesizes a person skilled in the art "working in his shop with the prior art references—which he is presumed to know—hanging on the walls around him."[114] If, given that complete tableau of references, the person would find the subject matter covered in the patent to be obvious, then the patent is not valid. The test is thus very stringent in terms of *knowledge*; the person of skill in the art is presumed to have perfect knowledge of the whole tableau of pertinent references. But, unlike some articulations of the pre–1952 standard, the test is somewhat more forgiving as to the standard of effort and creativity necessary to win a patent: if the person of ordinary skill in the art would not find the invention "obvious," then it is patentable even if the person of ordinary skill could have come up with the invention with persistence and hard work.

The obviousness doctrine's stringent approach to knowledge—considering *all* pertinent prior art including some pieces, like the Livingstone cap, that could not have been known to the patentee—is consistent with theory underlying the nonobviousness doctrine. Patent law employs

---

111 *Id.*

112 *Id.* (emphasis added).

113 *Id.*

114 *In re* Winslow, 365 F.2d 1017, 1020 (C.C.P.A. 1966).

such a demanding standard of creativity precisely because patent rights are such strong rights, with no defense of independent invention. Invalidating Cook's patent seems fair when one considers Livingstone's perspective. If the Cook patent had been held valid, then Cook could stop Livingstone from practicing an obvious variant of technology that he (Livingstone) developed years before Scoggin perfected his cap. The point here is familiar—with strong rights comes a strong standard of creativity. Thus, even where a person such as Scoggin has exercised a significant amount of creativity, he will lose out if an earlier inventor already arrived at the same or nearly the same result.

United States v. Adams: Finding for Nemo

Like *Graham* and *Cook Chemical*, the final case decided by the Court—*United States v. Adams*—was also not difficult, but in this case patentee had the easy time. Bert Nemo Adams was an inventor who was, as his own lawyers admitted, a "tyro" having "no scientific training or experience."[115] He made his contribution to battery design by hard work and testing rather than through the application of any superlative "genius." If the pre–1952 test of invention had been applied in the case, Adams' patent *might* have been invalidated. Under the statutory obviousness test, however, Adams would win, and win easily.

To understand the *Adams* case, one must appreciate the argument against patent validity. All batteries consist of three parts, two opposing electrodes and an electrolyte. Adams' new battery used magnesium and cuprous chloride as electrodes, and plain water as an electrolyte. Each of these three parts was old in the art of battery making. Magnesium and cuprous chloride were known to be possible electrodes, and some prior art batteries used water as an electrolyte. No prior art battery combined the three. Indeed, no operative battery seemed to have ever been made with magnesium and cuprous chloride electrodes, whatever the electrolyte.[116] In its briefs, the United States conceded that "[i]t is true that Adams put together elements not actually combined before and obtained more favorable results, for some purposes, than had prior combinations."[117] But the government's view was that Adams merely "put into

115 Respondent's Brief at 11; Brief in Opposition at 3, United States v. Adams, 383 U.S. 39 (1966) (No. 55).

116 An 1880 battery patent to Skrivanoff seemed to disclose a battery with magnesium and cuprous chloride electrodes, though with a different electrolyte. However, Adams' expert witness testified that, when he followed the 1880 patent's teachings for constructing this battery, he succeed only in creating an explosion. *See* 383 U.S. at 48.

117 Pet. for Cert. at 11. In its briefs filed after certiorari was granted, the government flip-flopped on this point and argued that Adams' battery was *not* novel. Adams' attorneys pointed out the inconsistency and easily argued that the government's earlier concession,

practice a battery composed of components which anyone 'skill[ed] in the art' would have listed as among the possible components of such a battery if asked to compile a list of the available materials [for making a battery]."[118] The U.S. quoted pre–1952 Supreme Court opinions to argue that although "Adams" achievement might be described as "progressive idea" or an exercise of "mechanical skill," it was not an "exercise of the inventive faculty' or 'inventive genius.' "[119]

In sum, the government tried to make the case appear to be quite similar to *Hotchkiss*—the patentee had merely made an obvious substitution from a range of possible materials. This argument's weakness—gaping hole might be a better description—was that the substitution of one substance for another in a chemical invention was not so easy as substituting clay for wood. As the Court would ultimately conclude, battery elements were known to have "an interdependent functional relationship."[120] Substituting one known battery element for another could, in any particular arrangement, lead to disaster. Thus, when one expert tried to modify a prior art battery to use magnesium and cuprous chloride electrodes (as the government had suggested), the combination exploded. The prior art also "taught away" from Adams' combination—it suggested that this particular set of ingredients would never be able to function in combination as a battery. Indeed, when Adams initially tried to sell his battery to the government, the government's experts were certain that the battery could not possibly work.

The Court's opinion details such a mountain of evidence demonstrating the inventiveness of Adams' battery that the case appears to be an obvious example of nonobviousness. But was the case really so easy? Two aspects of the case might suggest that the case was more difficult than the majority made it out to be. First, Justice White dissented. Second, the case was brought to the Court by the lawyers in the Office of the Solicitor General at the U.S. Department of Justice—a frequent litigator before the Court with strong institutional reasons not to squander its reputation for credibility by making frivolous arguments to the Court. Do these two factors suggest that the majority was hiding something, or that it was straining to sustain at least one of the three patents before it?

The short answer is no. Let us begin with Justice White. Though he chose not to publish an opinion, Justice White did draft a dissent in the

---

which was supported by the findings of the Trial Commissioner and the Court of Claims, was the only plausible view of the facts. Respondents Br. at 62–76.

118 Brief for the United States at 21.

119 Pet. for Cert. at 12 (citations omitted).

120 383 U.S. at 50.

case. On at least one important point, the dissent was simply factually incorrect: white concluded that Adams had failed to provide a "record to support the suggestion that those skilled in the art had been unsuccessfully searching to fill a long-felt need."[121] To prove that point, however, Justice White quoted the following exchange between Adams' counsel and Dr. Joseph White, whom the draft dissent incorrectly identifies as "Adams' expert"[122]:

> Q: Doctor, how is it that it took a man skilled in the art, I think you said, until 1938, to put the combination together, where all the components had been known in the art since 1888 for the last one? How do you explain the time lapse of 50 year or half century?
>
> A: I think this can't very well be answered. Maybe there was no need for it. Somebody has to have the need and the opportunity. I don't know.
>
> Q. You don't know?
>
> A. That is right.[123]

Dr. Joseph White was actually the *government's* expert; he was the Brand Head of the Electrochemistry Branch of the Chemistry Division at the United States Naval Research Laboratory.[124] Indeed, Adams had stressed this exchange in *his* briefs to show that even the government's experts had no good explanation for why such a valuable battery had not been produced if it had been obvious for half a century.[125] Also, Adams' briefs pointed out that the new battery had satisfied a number of different needs (supplying power for signal lights, motors, emergency radio equipment, etc.), all of which were very old and long pre-dated Adams' discovery.[126] It was just not true that Adams had failed to establish a long-felt need for the battery.

Justice White's mistake about the record may not have been crucial to his outcome. But the mistake does suggest that White may not have thoroughly understood the case. Thus, his dissent does not undermine the conclusion that the case was easy.

---

121 Unpublished Draft Dissent by Justice White at 6 (Feb. 11, 1966) (Clark Papers Box A187, Folder 55) [hereinafter White Dissent].

122 *Id.*

123 Record Appendix at 382, United States v. Adams, 383 U.S. 39 (1966) (No. 55) (quoted in White Dissent at 6–7).

124 Record Appendix at 343–44.

125 *See* Brief for Respondent at 75.

126 *See* Brief for Respondent at 54.

The complete record in the case also suggests that the Department of Justice lawyers came to realize their case was unwinable. Indeed, the government seemed pretty much to give up halfway through the case. The government's petition for certiorari showed real passion. It argued that the ruling in Adams' favor in the court below "sharply illustrates" the lower courts' "much laxer standard of invention" which "seriously impairs efforts to maintain a predominantly competitive economy by creating countless unnecessary and unwarranted monopolies."[127] The government stressed the "urgent need" for the Supreme Court "to assure that [the standard of invention] is not relaxed by years of unreviewed departures effectively changing . . . the established rule."[128] The issue was one of the "pressing problems relating to the administration of the patent laws" and, the government's petition emphasized, the Court's patent jurisprudence was designed "to curb, not to expand, monopolies."[129] Perhaps most significantly, the government repeatedly characterized the issue in the case as involving not merely the statutory but also the "constitutional" standard of patentability.[130]

Yet by the time the merits briefs were filed, this strident rhetoric had vanished. Instead, the government found it "doubtful that an attempt at verbal refinement of the [statutory nonobvious standard] would contribute substantially to the resolution of particular cases" and merely urges the Court to insure that the statutory standard is "rigorously and independently applied."[131] The brief disparages the *Cuno* "flash of creative genius" test, calling it "a relatively recent suggestion of uncertain validity" that the 1952 Act was intended to "change."[132] Gone is resort to a constitutional standard, and when the government brief discusses federal monopoly policy, it speaks approvingly of "the fact, explicitly recognized by the Framers, that limited monopolies may nonetheless be desirable in order adequately to reward invention."[133] The government's argument on the merits is shockingly slim: although the government's argument for granting certiorari had been over 10 pages long, the argument in the merits brief shrunk to only eight and a half pages, with more than half of that space devoted to the argument that the Adams battery was not novel—a position the government had conceded away in its petition! The obviousness analysis occupies only

---

127 Pet. for Cert. at 7.

128 *Id.* at 13.

129 *Id.* at 15–16 & 14.

130 *Id.* at 2, 13, 13–14.

131 Brief of the United States at 13 & 12.

132 *Id.* at 20.

133 *Id.* at 9–10.

four pages, only two of which attempt to apply the statutory standard to the facts of the case. It could not have escaped the attention of the Court that the government was unable to follow its own demand for "rigorous[]" application of § 103 with any detailed analysis of the facts in the case. Finally, at oral argument, the government attorney conceded that the trial court had found inoperable the main piece of prior art relied on to prove nonobviousness. Undaunted, the attorney argued that Adams' battery was nothing new even though his battery worked and the prior art battery didn't![134]

If the government harbored any illusions about the strength of its case, the Court's opinion concludes with a subtle rebuke that could not have escaped the attention of the government lawyers. At the very end of its opinion, the Court stated that "noted experts," who at first "expressed disbelief" that Adams' invention would work, later came to recognize the invention's significance and even to patent improvements. The Court cites "Fischbach et al., U.S. Patent No. 2,636,060 (1953)." What the Court does not say, but the parties certainly knew, was that Dr. Fischbach was employed by the U.S. Army Signal Corps Laboratory. He was one of the government officers to whom Adams had originally disclosed his technology, and the government itself was the assignee of Fischbach's 1953 patent! The Court's citation of this patent could only be viewed as a rebuke to the government's whole course of conduct with Adams: after all, Adams had disclosed his invention to the government's agents, who told him it could not work. Yet those very agents were soon patenting their own improvements to the supposedly worthless battery. The government itself now owned those patent rights and yet it was refusing to recognize the value of the discovery that had made those further advances possible. The Court was not favorably impressed.[135]

The full record shows that the government attorneys probably expected to lose by the time they filed their brief on the merits. They tried not to lose too much credibility before the Court by keeping their

[134] Transcript of Oral Argument, in United States v. Adams, at 5–6. The oral argument transcript also shows that Adams' attorney brought a working example of Adams' battery to the argument and used it to power a light during the argument. It has become part of the lore of patent law that the light bulb helped Adams to win victory at the Court, *see, e.g.,* Tom Arnold, *Side Bar: The Way the Law of Section 103 Was Made, in* Donald S. Chisum et al., Principles of Patent Law 571 n.11 (3rd ed. 2004), but such claims are almost certainly overstated. In addition to showing that Adams' attorney did light a light during argument, the transcript also shows that the Court asked few questions to the government—a good sign that the Justices had already made up their minds.

[135] Even Justice White was not happy with the government's positions. He acknowledged that the government may have "in effect taken inconsistent position in seeking to patent its own batteries and denying the patentability of Adams' battery,' " but he thought that inconsistency did "not justify sacrificing the public interest by issuing a patent to Adams." White Dissent at 7.

arguments as perfunctory as possible. The shift in position seems to have occurred as attorneys in the Solicitor General's Office became more familiar with the facts of the case in preparing their full merits briefing. The petition for certiorari was likely more influenced by trial attorneys who had handled the case below, but the merits briefs reflected a more considered position that took into account the larger interests of the government.

The significance of all this is that *Adams*—the only case in which the Supreme Court has ever sustained the nonobviousness of a patent—was an exceptionally easy case. The Court has yet to confront an even modestly difficult case and to sustain the patent.

Epilogues

William Graham and the Appropriate Rewards of the Patent System

William Graham continued in the plow making business for only four more years after the Supreme Court's decision; his firm went bankrupt in 1969. The firm was sold in bankruptcy to M.B. Graham, his first cousin, who sold the firm to another company in 1975. William Graham remained a prominent resident of Amarillo, Texas, living in a "magnificent house" until his death on March 20, 1980,[136] but his company had by then long since been absorbed into other firms.

Graham's story is not atypical in the annals of innovation. He and his predecessor, Fred Hoeme, made their major innovations in the 1930's and 1940's, and they had vigorously defended the firm's patent portfolio in litigation stretching from the 1930's through to the Supreme Court's decision in 1966. The loss at the Supreme Court was the last piece of patent litigation for Graham and his firm. Still the patent system functioned well in Graham's case. It had rewarded Graham and Hoeme for their true innovations but had refused to allow patenting the obvious.

A Fine and Flawed Opinion

The patent bar embraced *Graham* as a great victory, though this was partly because the patent bar desperately wanted to declare victory. Yet *Graham* was a great triumph for good patent policy because the decision adhered to the statutory obviousness standard, which clarified the patentability standard and ended the Court's search "genius" in inventors. In retrospect, however, we can also appreciate the flaws in the *Graham* opinion. Two have had the most lasting effects.

First, the Court touched upon but ultimately avoided saying much about a highly important issue in the *Graham* litigation—whether and to

[136] *Services Pending for Plow Developer*, Amarillo Globe-Times, March 20, 1980.

what extent inventors must identify the nonobvious characteristic of their inventions in their specifications or during the course of their prosecutions. The Court plainly counted as a strike against the patent that the supposedly advantageous flexing quality of Graham's '798 device were not "hinted at in the specifications of the patent" nor "raised in the Patent Office." The Court described the flexing function as an "afterthought" but did not say that such an afterthought could never support a holding of nonobviousness. Because of the way the Federal Circuit has structured the nonobviousness inquiry, the relationship between disclosure and nonobviousness has not been litigated much in the last two decades. Earlier decisions did, however, count it as a strike against nonobviousness if inventors failed to disclose in their specifications why those inventions would be viewed as nonobvious.[137] Yet the courts have never specified the weight to be given to nondisclosure, and the Federal Circuit has allowed applicants to supplement their claims to nonobviousness with additional evidence not contained or referenced in the patent specification.[138]

Second, and much more importantly, the *Graham* Court devoted only two sentences to articulating the policy of nonobviousness, and neither is very helpful. In the first sentence, the Court identifies "the underlying policy of the patent system" as being "that 'the things which are worth to the public the embarrassment of an exclusive patent,' as Jefferson put it, must outweigh the restrictive effect of the limited patent monopoly."[139] The key word in that sentence—"worth"—has greater potential to confuse than to clarify. As the Court itself held in *Cook Chemical*, even an obvious item could be worth a great deal to the public and enjoy commercial success. In other words, the worth or valuableness of the challenged patent is simply not a good measure of obviousness. In the other sentence, the Court declares that "[t]he inherent problem" of the nonobviousness doctrine is "to develop some means of weeding out those inventions which would not be disclosed or

137 *See In re* Vamco Mach. & Tool, 752 F.2d 1564, 1575 (Fed. Cir. 1985); Young Corp. v. Jenkins, 396 F.2d 893, 895–96 (9th Cir. 1968) (relying on *Graham* to hold a patent invalid because "the asserted difference in result" that was the "predicate" for the patentee's argument of nonobviousness was "an afterthought not to be ascertained from an examination of the patent itself"). *See also In re* Davies, 475 F.2d 667, 670 (C.C.P.A. 1973) (holding that, in determining nonobviousness, the Patent Office did not have to consider evidence of properties that were not disclosed in the application and that do not "inherently flow" from what was disclosed in the application).

138 *See In re* Chu, 66 F.3d 292, 298 (Fed. Cir. 1995) (holding that the PTO Board "erred in apparently requiring [the patent applicant's] evidence and arguments responsive to the obviousness rejection to be within his specification in order to be considered"); *In re* Piasecki, 745 F.2d 1468, 1471–72 (Fed. Cir. 1984) (permitting the applicant to submit additional evidence of nonobviousness by affidavit during the prosecution process).

139 383 U.S. at 10–11.

devised but for the inducement of a patent.''[140] This sentence identifies the correct problem, as some commentators have noted,[141] but gives no hint of the solution.

The *Graham* opinion would have been much stronger if it had provided some sense for when the problems of obviousness are likely to arise, and when they are not. As we discussed in Part I above, *change* is the key to understanding the nonobviousness doctrine. Changes in needs, conditions, or technology can give rise to new possibilities that might have great value but that also can be easily developed and exploited. In such circumstances, the nonobviousness doctrine serves a substantial function by denying patents to such easy-to-devise but nonetheless valuable novelties. Consider, for example, Jeff Bezos' patent on the ''one-click'' method of internet shopping—a patent with substantial commercial value that is almost certainly obvious.[142] Why was this novelty not created until Jeff Bezos ''invented'' it in 1997? The answer here is straightforward, and it has nothing to do with Jeff Bezos' inventive faculties. Prior to the mid–1990's, there was little internet shopping. Furthermore, computer connections were slow and what few websites existed were primitive. The need for a streamlined internet check-out mechanism simply did not exist. When the need arose, the problem of streamlining a internet checkout was easily solved; it required the production of no substantial new information but merely the obvious application of existing techniques to a new problem.

In other instances, the relevant change may be attributable to another person's development. Here too, the nonobviousness doctrine serves a valuable function, though it involves more the allocation of rights between competing inventors. This function can be seen clearly in the facts of both *Graham* and *Cook Chemical*. In both cases, the inventors of the patents in suit may very well have worked hard to solve a reasonably challenging technical problem. In both cases, however, conditions changed before they completed their inventions; other inven-

140 *Id.* at 11.

141 *See, e.g.*, Kitch, *supra* note 63, at 301 (identifying ''the basic principle on which the non-obviousness test is based: a patent should not be granted for an innovation unless the innovation would have been unlikely to have been developed absent the prospect of a patent''); Robert P. Merges, *Uncertainty and the Standard of Patentability*, 7 High Tech. L.J. 1, 3 (1993) (postulating that the nonobviousness doctrine helps to insure that ''society will reward only those who *require* a reward to do their work'').

142 See Amazon.com, Inc. v. Barnesandnoble.com, Inc., 73 F. Supp. 2d 1228, 1237 (W.D. Wash. 1999) (finding that Amazon.com's one-click patent has ''significant commercial value''); Amazon.com, Inc. v. Barnesandnoble.com, Inc., 239 F.3d 1343, 1363 (Fed. Cir. 2001) (vacating a preliminary injunction on the defendant's use of a one-click ordering system because the defendant succeeded in raising a ''substantial question of [the patent's] invalidity'' on grounds of obviousness).

tors had completed nearly identical work. In such cases, the nonobviousness doctrine protects the full scope of the earlier development and prevents the later inventor from obtaining rights to small variations of the other person's work. But in these situations too, nonobviousness gains its importance from the fact of change—the fact that society and technology is not static.

In contrast, where social needs and technology have remained relatively static, the problems of obviousness are unlikely to be a major concern because, if an inventor develops something new and valuable in such relatively static conditions, it is almost impossible to consider the development to be obvious. *Adams* provides a perfect example. The government's case in *Adams* was so weak precisely because of the undisputed facts (I) that all the components to built Adams' battery had been known for fifty years, and (ii) that the needs satisfied by Adams' battery (a good power sources for signal lights, military applications, etc.) had also existed for many decades. Under such static conditions, the only realistic way to explain Adams' development of a valuable new battery was to acknowledge that Adams was able to find something not obvious to anyone else in the field.

Focusing on the presence or absence of changing conditions provides good intuition for understanding and properly applying the nonobviousness doctrine. Unfortunately, this sort of reasoning never found its way into *Graham*.

Graham's Progeny

Both the Supreme Court and the lower courts have repeatedly cited and applied *Graham*. Yet precisely because it fails to explain the rationale for the nonobviousness doctrine, *Graham* has been applied in radically different ways. The Supreme Court has decided only three obviousness cases since *Graham*, and in each case it invalidated the patent.[143] The results in those cases are almost certainly correct, but as in *Graham*, the Court did not articulate strong theoretical underpinnings for the nonobviousness requirement. In all three cases, the Court cited pre–1952 decisions with approval, thus showing that the Court meant what it said in *Graham*: it was not interpreting the 1952 statute to be a radical break with the past. In two of the three cases, the Court seemed to endorse a requirement that a new combination of old components must show a "synergistic" effect in order for the combination to be patentable.[144] The Court, however, provided no practical guidance for

---

143 Anderson's-Black Rock, Inc. v. Pavement Salvage Co., 396 U.S. 57 (1969); Dann v. Johnson, 425 U.S. 219 (1976); Sakraida v. Ag Pro, Inc., 425 U.S. 273 (1976).

144 *See Anderson's-Black Rock*, 396 U.S. at 61; *Sakraida*, 425 U.S. at 282.

identifying "synergies" and no further policy rationale to help understand and apply the nonobviousness doctrine.

The results at the Federal Circuit are no better. That court has stressed only one theme—that courts applying the nonobviousness doctrine should avoid what the court has dubbed the "hindsight syndrome" where inventors' teachings are used against them to prove the obviousness of the development.[145] To guard against this syndrome, the court has fashioned a "suggestion test" which requires proof that the prior art explicitly or implicitly suggested the invention's combination of elements.[146]

The theme of avoiding hindsight reasoning is important; it identifies one problem that could potentially infect the decisionmaking process. *Graham* itself warned courts "to guard against slipping into use of hindsight."[147] But this theme provides no guidance into the circumstances in which valuable novelties should properly be held obvious and unpatentable. Moreover, the hindsight theme should not be stressed too much since the statute plainly requires a backward-looking inquiry into what *would have been obvious* at the time of invention. If courts become too concerned with avoiding hindsight, they will have a difficult time enforcing the statute.

Moreover, the Federal Circuit's doctrinal tool for avoiding hindsight—the "suggestion" test—either is too stringent or simply substitutes a different verbal formulation for the statutory obviousness inquiry. In some cases, the Federal Circuit has treated the suggestion test as requiring a "clear and particular" showing to combine prior art references.[148] This test is too stringent because social, economic or technical changes may make new applications of old knowledge highly valuable. In such circumstances, it is unlikely that references prior to the change could have or would have commented on the desirability of the new combination or new combination. In other cases, however, the Federal Circuit has stressed that a "suggestion" may be implicit rather than explicit.[149] But if this caveat is taken seriously, then the court has merely

---

145 *In re* Dembiczak, 175 F.3d 994, 999 (Fed. Cir. 1999).

146 *See, e.g., id.*

147 383 U.S. at 36 (quoting Monroe Auto Equipment Co. v. Heckethorn Mfg. & Sup. Co., 332 F.2d 406, 412 (6th Cir. 1964)).

148 *Dembiczak*, 175 F.3d at 999. *See also In re* Lee, 277 F.3d 1338 (Fed. Cir. 2002) (refusing to find obviousness based on "the common knowledge and common sense of a person of ordinary skill in the art").

149 *See, e.g.,* Ruiz v. Chance, 357 F.3d 1270, 1276 (Fed. Cir. 2004) (holding that an implicit suggestion or motivation to combine prior art references may be found "in the nature of the problem to be solved").

substituted a different verbal inquiry. When should the prior art be interpreted as "implicitly" teaching the combination? The appropriate answer would seem to be that an implicit teaching exists if a person skilled in the art would find it *obvious* to make the combination.[150] Thus the formulation merely leads back to the starting point.

In sum, the understanding of the nonobviousness doctrine has advanced little since the decision in *Graham*. The Supreme Court itself has not decided a case on the matter in over a quarter century, and its few decisions immediately following *Graham* did not provide much additional guidance. The Federal Circuit has been obsessed with avoiding hindsight to deny patents to meritorious inventions. While that instinct is noble, it has not advanced the understanding of situations in which the nonobviousness doctrine is most necessary.

Graham's Constitutional Legacy

Apart from its central place in the pantheon of Supreme Court decisions on patentability, *Graham*—or rather, certain language in it—has often been invoked in broader constitutional debates about Congress's power under the intellectual property clause of the Constitution. The most oft-cited language is from the following passage:

> The [constitutional intellectual property] clause is both a grant of power and a limitation. This qualified authority, unlike the power often exercised in the sixteenth and seventeenth centuries by the English Crown, is limited to the promotion of advances in the "useful arts." It was written against the backdrop of the practices—eventually curtailed by the Statute of Monopolies—of the Crown in granting monopolies to court favorites in goods or businesses which had long before been enjoyed by the public. The Congress in the exercise of the patent power may not overreach the restraints imposed by the stated constitutional purpose. Nor may it enlarge the patent monopoly without regard to the innovation, advancement or social benefit gained thereby. Moreover, Congress may not authorize the issuance of patents whose effects are to remove existent knowledge from the public domain, or to restrict free access to materials already available. Innovation, advancement, and things which add to the sum of useful knowledge are inherent requisites in a patent system which by constitutional command must "promote the Progress of . . . useful Arts." This is the standard expressed in the Constitution and it may not be

150 *See In re* Berg, 320 F.3d 1310, 1315 (Fed. Cir. 2003) (allowing the PTO to hold a claimed invention obvious based on "the meaning of prior art references to persons of ordinary skill in the art and the motivation those references would provide to such persons").

ignored. And it is in this light that patent validity "requires reference to a standard written into the Constitution."[151]

This passage must be read very carefully. Recall that Justice Clark was trying to build a compromise between the Justices who wanted to constitutionalize a specific standard of patentability (Black and Douglas) and more moderate Justices such as Harlan and Stewart (and probably Clark too) who did not want to suggest that Congress lacked power to change the standard of patentability. The compromise can be seen in the passage. Although the passage says that patent validity issues require reference to "a standard written into the Constitution" (so there is some constitutional requirement), the particular standard identified is not the invention concept as articulated in the Court's pre–1952 opinions, but only the constitutional command that the patent system must "promote the Progress of . . . useful Arts." That standard permits a goodly amount of congressional latitude in legislating on intellectual property.

Thus, the above-quoted passage was really part of effort to "de-constitutionalize" the standard of patentability. But it is the first sentence, with its "grant and . . . limitation" language, that is most often quoted by proponents of stringent Supreme Court review of federal intellectual property legislation. Unfortunately for advocates of this view, the passage above is only dictum in the context of the *Graham* opinion. Although it captures the Supreme Court's sense that Congress cannot under the constitution expand IP protection infinitely in all directions, *Graham* itself is not an exercise in defining these limits. It is, if anything, a statement that the then recently enacted § 103 did not come near such limits as might exist.

This dictum from *Graham* was not cited much until recent years, and even now the most expansive readings of it are confined to the scholarly literature and some prominent dissenting opinions. After a spate of citations in the immediate aftermath of the *Graham* opinion (in the context of standard patent infringement cases), this aspect of *Graham* was ignored. Even the recent cases that have picked up on the language show an understanding of its context. Recently, the Supreme Court in *Eldred v. Ashcroft* cited the "grants and limits" language from *Graham*, but then proceeded to hold that (1) "it is generally for Congress, not the courts, to decide how best to pursue the Copyright Clause's objectives"; and (2) that Congress' justifications for "enactment of the [Copyright Term Extension Act at issue in that case] . . . provide a rational basis for the conclusion that the [Act] 'promote[s] the Progress of Science.' "[152] Thus while the dissenters in *Eldred* gave major prominence to *Graham*'s "grants and limitations" language, the majority did

---

[151] 383 U.S. at 5–6.

[152] 537 U.S. 186, 212–13 (2003).

not. After quoting from several older federal cases affirming Congress' right to extend patent and copyright terms, the Supreme Court noted in a footnote in Eldred (referring to Justice Stevens' dissent):

> Justice STEVENS would sweep away these decisions, asserting that *Graham* ... "flatly contradicts" them.... Nothing but wishful thinking underpins that assertion. The controversy in *Graham* involved no patent extension. *Graham* addressed an invention's very eligibility for patent protection, and spent no words on Congress' power to enlarge a patent's duration.[153]

This quite clearly shuts the door on any attempt to inflate *Graham*'s "grants and limitations" language into an authorization for stringent constitutional review of intellectual property legislation. This is surely a disappointment for scholars who had hoped to use this language from *Graham* to support an active Supreme Court role in reviewing intellectual property legislation under the Constitution. But it is the more accurate interpretation of the *Graham*.

Conclusion

Graham is a famous case because touches on an issue—the standard of creativity needed to support intellectual property rights—that lies at the very heart of intellectual property policy. Creativity is what the field is all about. It is so fundamental to the law that it has a constitutional dimension: the intellectual property clause authorizes the creation of rights for creative work in writing and inventing, not for any class of labors that may happen to fuel progress. The issue has long and rich history, and a true scholar of intellectual property law finds the cases in that history inherently interesting because they delve so deeply into the process of human creativity—in all its intricacy and beauty, and with all of its human stories of challenge, disappointment and triumph.

All these elements are wrapped together in *Graham*, and its great riot of complexity is also its great attraction. The Court's opinion recognizes the constitutional dimension of the issue, but at the same time, it weaves a compromise leaving Congress with broad powers to craft standards of creativity for intellectual property. The case is also an enigmatic milestone in the historical emergence of patent law's creativity standard. While attentive to its century of precedents on the issue, the Court subtly rewrites some of that history so as to minimize the tension between the Court's past teachings and the directions Congress enacted in the new § 103. In addition to all the jurisprudential complexities, there are the innovation stories themselves. Thus, we read of William Graham and Baxter Scoggin, two very creative individuals who both lose their patent rights because of the creative efforts of others whose work

---

153 *Id.* at 202.

was just slightly earlier. But we read too of Bert Adams' stubborn and ultimately triumphant persistence in the face of skepticism and disbelief. In these stories, we can see the practical side of the patent nonobviousness standard, which not only must establish an appropriately high level of creativity but must also identify the right creative person to reward.

Finally, *Graham* shows how primitive the current understanding of the creativity standard really is. As the pace of social and technological change has increased in the last two centuries, the standard of creativity has become more and more important in patent law. A faster pace of change means that existing knowledge is applied more frequently in somewhat new situations. The nonobviousness requirement protects the public's right to continue using that common pool of knowledge to address new challenges. As the pace of technological change quickens, the nonobviousness requirement must also mediate the increasingly frequent conflicts between multiple individuals who seek rights over similar technological advances. Yet in *Graham* and in subsequent cases, we see very little recognition of the functions that the creativity standard does and should play, and as a result the legal doctrine remains, to borrow Judge Learned Hand's phrase, more "fugitive, impalpable, wayward, and vague" than it should be. We can only hope and expect that the creative project of building the legal doctrine in this area will continue, and that the future will bring a noble sequel to *Graham*.

3

Freedom of Ideas and of Competition

The Story of *Baker v. Selden*: Sharpening the Distinction Between Authorship and Invention

Pamela Samuelson*

The Selden and Baker Bookkeeping Systems

Eighteen sixty-five was a year of great hope and high expectations for Charles Selden, then chief accountant to the treasurer of Hamilton County, Ohio, in Cincinnati and author of six books on a condensed ledger system of bookkeeping.[1] In May of that year, Selden signed a lucrative contract with Hamilton County for use of his bookkeeping system.[2] He also believed he was about to sell a version of his system to the U.S. Department of the Treasury.[3] Selden planned to spend several weeks during the spring of 1865 in Washington D.C. making appropriate adaptations of his system for Treasury uses and conclude the deal.[4]

In March of 1865, he was so optimistic about his business prospects that he contemplated forming a joint stock company to cash in on "the right to introduce the system throughout one or more of the States of the Union, into all State, county and township offices, as well as into the

---

* Brian Carver and Sean Butler deserve thanks for their outstanding research assistance as do Jane Ginsburg and Rochelle Dreyfuss for excellent editing suggestions.

1 *See* Supreme Court Record at 91–94, Baker v. Selden, 101 U.S. 99 (1880) (hereinafter Record).

2 *Id.* at 111. The contract was for 12 years and a total of $6600.

3 *Id.* at 94. Salmon P. Chase reported meeting Charles Selden on August 2, 1862. 1 Salmon P. Chase, The Salmon P. Chase Papers 356 (John Niven, ed. 1993). Selden's meeting with Chase suggests that he had the requisite contacts in Washington to make his belief of a deal with the U.S. Treasury conceivable, even though Chase was no longer Secretary of the Treasury in 1865.

4 Record at 94.

municipal offices of cities and towns, and into the counting houses of all corporations whose offices are kept within the States aforesaid."[5]

Selden was confident that his system would attract customers because it was more efficient than the old-fashioned data-entry intensive bookkeeping system then used by Ohio officials. Under the old system, clerks first recorded information pertinent to each transaction (say, a disbursement from a fund for bridge construction) in a journal for that type of account. (If a county had twenty types of accounts, it would need twenty journals.) The same information would then be entered in a ledger where all transactions were logged in sequential order, and a cross-reference prepared so that one could trace the information back to the appropriate journal.[6] With double entry bookkeeping, each transaction would be logged as a credit and a debit in the appropriate columns of the ledger. Preparing a trial balance of the accounts could take several days because information was so distributed throughout these books and much work was required to synthesize the information and assess its correctness. Consequently it was done infrequently, making detection of errors or fraud slow and difficult.

Selden figured out a way to condense the journals and ledger into one book. Users of his system could record pertinent information about transactions and accounts on one page or two adjoining pages.[7] Depending on the user's needs, the transactions of a day, a week, or a month could be recorded on the Selden form. The condensation of the journal and ledger made it easier to create a trial balance and discern the amount to be carried forward to the next period. This allowed for quicker detection of errors or fraud. His books illustrated the system by showing forms with hypothetical entries for a sample jurisdiction. Selden thought that $800 a year was a reasonable price for use of his system because it would save an estimated $2850 a year in clerk salaries.[8]

Selden's sense of the magnitude of his achievement is evident from the preface to an 1859 edition of his book: "To greatly simplify the accounts of extensive establishments doing credit business, and embracing an almost infinite variety of transactions would be a masterly achievement, worthy to be classed among the greatest benefactions of the age."[9] The preface also indicates that "[i]n addition to the copyrights

[5] *Id.*

[6] *Id.* at 92, 106.

[7] *See* sample Selden form, p. 171.

[8] Record at 92.

[9] *Id.* at 21.

of this little book, he has applied for a patent right to cover the forms of the publication, and prevent their indiscriminate use by the public."[10]

By June of 1865, however, the bloom was off this optimistic rose. Although Selden still believed he could adapt his system for use by the U.S. Treasury Department,[11] he was not able to do so in the spring of 1865, or apparently thereafter. He went deeply into debt, mainly as a result of his decision to authorize, apparently at his own expense, the printing of a very substantial number of copies of his books in anticipation of sales that failed to materialize.[12]

Selden's commercial prospects dimmed further in 1867 when W.C.M. Baker, auditor of Greene County, Ohio, published his first book on the Baker bookkeeping system.[13] The Baker forms were similar to Selden's in some respects, for example, in enabling journal and ledger entries to be made on one page, in having columns for entering the date of a disbursement, its number, the recipient, the disburser, and by whose authorization, and in having space for balances to be carried forward.[14] The principal difference between the Baker and Selden forms was in how they treated accounts. Baker's form featured several blank columns so that bookkeepers could label and then keep track of receipts and disbursements for each type of account; it also had space at the foot of each account column so that bookkeepers could calculate a total period-to-date sum for each account at the foot of the form.[15] With Baker's forms, "you can enter your orders daily and tell just how your accounts stand."[16] With Selden's forms, there was no space for entering orders sequentially or for calculating interim totals. Selden's system contemplated entering totals for each account at the end of the relevant period, so it was "hard to tell how your accounts [stood] during the month."[17]

Baker had several advantages over Selden. Baker's forms were not only more useful for keeping track of specific accounts, but they were

---

10 *Id.*

11 *Id.* at 103.

12 *Id.* at 89–90. Only a few counties used Selden's system for longer than short trial periods. *Id.* at 14–19, 30–31, 48–52, 68–69, 72, 145.

13 Its title was BAKER'S REGISTER OF RECEIPTS AND DISBURSEMENTS WITH BALANCE SHEETS AND REPORTS FOR COUNTY AUDITORS AND TREASURER'S (1867). *See* Record at 43.

14 Compare the Baker and Selden forms at pp. 170–71.

15 Record at 59. Selden's form was also more classically double-entry, having debit and credit columns for each fund of the condensed ledger, while Baker's form was more synthetic and less redundant. Also different were numerous captions and the ruling of most of the columns. *See* Seldon and Baker forms at pp. 170–71.

16 Record at 66.

17 *Id.*

also, by most accounts, easier to use.[18] The State Auditor of Ohio had unconditionally endorsed the Baker system.[19] Baker offered a lower price than Selden.[20] And he was a good salesman; by the fall of 1871, he had persuaded more than 40 counties in Ohio and a number of private firms, to become his customers.[21]

On July 30, 1871, after a period of ill health, Charles Selden departed this world.[22] His legacy to his widow Elizabeth was many thousands of dollars of debt and apparently only the copyrights in his books as assets with which to pay off the creditors and provide financial support for his widow and their young daughter.[23]

Six weeks after Selden's death, the Cincinnati Daily Gazette published an article extolling the virtues of Baker's bookkeeping system:

> Under the old system, it is a great labor to compile the accounts from the multitude of books and even after it is done, in many cases there are omissions and all responsibility is put upon those that are from their high position guardians of the treasury. With [the] Baker system no such defalcations can possibly occur if the books are thoroughly examined by the responsible parties daily, for each day carries its own record faithfully and as ordinary books are wound up at the end of the year's business by Baker's system the business is completely wound up every day.[24]

These were the very same virtues that Selden had claimed for his bookkeeping system. By promoting the Baker system in Selden's home town and mentioning his many customers, Baker may have inadvertently planted in Selden's widow, friends, and creditors the seeds of an idea for a last chance to vindicate Selden's reputation and attain the fortune that had seemed so close to fruition in the spring of 1865.

The Lawsuit Against Baker

Elizabeth Selden was reportedly destitute in 1872,[25] so perhaps it was her husband's creditors who provided the funds to hire a prominent intellectual property attorney to prepare a lawsuit against Baker. The

---

18 *See, e.g., id.* at 59. Compare Seldon and Baker forms at pp. 170–71.

19 Record at 13–14.

20 *Id.* at 73–74.

21 *Id.* at 12–14.

22 *Id.* at 41–42.

23 *Id.* at 89–90.

24 *Id.* at 14.

25 *Id.* at 89–90.

lawyer was Samuel S. Fisher, a former Commissioner of Patents with more than fifty reported federal cases to his credit (mostly patent cases).[26] Fisher was ably assisted by William S. Scarborough, who had represented Hamilton County on a number of occasions.[27]

In July of 1872, Fisher filed a complaint in federal court in the Southern District of Ohio on behalf of Elizabeth Selden against W.C.M. Baker, alleging copyright infringement.[28] The complaint characterized Selden as "the inventor, designer, and author of Selden's condensed system of bookkeeping," alleging that no such system had been known prior to Selden's development of it.[29] It also alleged that Selden was "the inventor, designer, and author of a book entitled 'Selden's condensed ledger or bookkeeping simplified,' " and of several other similarly titled books.[30] It claimed that Selden had complied with the requisite copyright formalities and that his widow Elizabeth had inherited Selden's copyrights.[31] It charged Baker with substantially harming the market for Selden's work by pirating it and requested provisional and permanent injunctive relief against further publication and distribution of Baker's book.[32] Baker answered the complaint with a general denial of Selden's allegations.[33] He was represented at the trial court level by a young and inexperienced lawyer, Edward Colston.

The Selden case was tried not with live witnesses in court, but rather through a set of depositions taken before a neutral examiner,

---

26 *See* In Memoriam Samuel S. Fisher (Cincinnati, Clarke & Co. 1875).

27 *See, e.g.*, State ex rel. Mills & Co. v. Comm'rs of Hamilton County, 20 Ohio St. 425 (1870) (absolving Commissioners of a charge of misleading bidders as to a printing contract that Moore Wilstach & Baldwin won). Scarborough had also defended Hamilton County in a patent infringement suit brought by Fisher. *See* Jacobs v. Hamilton County, 13 F. Cas. 276 (S.D. Ohio 1862) (No. 7161).

28 Record at 1–4.

29 *Id.* at 1.

30 *Id.* at 1–3. The complaint's reference to Selden as an inventor is not as odd as a modern reader might think. The copyright statute then in force conferred exclusive rights on "[a]ny citizen of the United States, or resident therein, who shall be the author, inventor, designer or proprietor of any book, map, chart, dramatic or musical composition, engraving, cut, print, or photograph" and several other categories of works, who complied with statutory formalities. Rev. Stat., § 4952.

31 Record at 3–4. Under today's work for hire doctrine, the Commissioners of Hamilton County, rather than Selden, might have been the "author" of his books and hence the owner of copyrights in them, insofar as the books were created within the scope of his employment. *See* 17 U.S.C. § 101 (definition of "work made for hire"), 201(b) (employer is author of employee work within scope of employment).

32 Record at 4.

33 *Id.* at 6.

transcripts of which were made available to the trial judge. In mid-May of 1873, Selden's lawyer deposed four supportive witnesses.[34] Two were Hamilton County officials; one was a Selden customer from a nearby county; and the fourth operated a business school in Cincinnati. Selden's lawyer showed each witness a copy of Baker's book and asked what material differences there were between Baker's and Selden's books and systems. All four testified that the principle was the same in both.[35] John Gundry, the business school proprietor, for example, testified that he saw nothing new in Baker's book.[36] "It is an effort to obtain the same result as the Selden system by combining the same features."[37] Gundry offered several criticisms of Baker's book, including a characterization of it as "defective."[38] When asked whether differences in certain captions were material, Gundry responded "[t]he change in the names amounts to nothing."[39]

To counter this testimony, Baker's lawyer in mid-September 1873 deposed six witnesses who testified about substantial and material differences between the Baker and Selden systems and forms.[40] One was a salesman for Baker's system, four were Baker's customers, and one was an official for a county that had been Selden's customer before switching to another bookkeeping system.[41] The witnesses explained similarities in the Baker and Selden forms as due in part to requirements of state law and to commonalities among bookkeeping forms (e.g., columns for credits and debits).[42] Some witnesses praised Baker's system as easier to learn than Selden's system, easier to use, and more likely to detect errors.[43] Baker's system was not only different from Selden's, in their view, but was better. Baker himself was not deposed.

What may have tipped the evidentiary balance in Selden's favor was the deposition of Eleazer Baldwin, which was taken by a lawyer new to the case, on a Saturday, six months after the other pro-Selden deposi-

---

34 *See id.* at 10–40 for testimony of these witnesses.

35 *Id.* at 16.

36 *Id.* at 38–39.

37 *Id.* at 38.

38 *Id.*

39 *Id.* at 40.

40 *Id.* at 45–73 for testimony of these witnesses. *See especially id.* at 46, 49–51, 55, 65–66.

41 Fayette County switched to Miltonberger's System of Accounts. *Id.* at 52.

42 *See, e.g., id.* at 59.

43 *Id.* at 46, 52, 56, 59–60, 67.

tions and only a few days before the pro-Baker depositions.[44] Baker's lawyer did not appear at this deposition, and later objected to inclusion of this deposition in the record because he had not received notice of it.[45] Baldwin testified that during the summer of 1865, he traveled around Ohio and Indiana to sell the Selden system and books.[46] He visited the auditor's office in Greene County on August 21, 1865. He met Baker and gave him a detailed explanation of the Selden system, which, Baldwin said, was new to Baker ("he required a great deal of explanation in order to understand it").[47] At first, Baker recommended adopting the Selden system, and Baldwin left a copy of Selden's book with Baker while the decision was pending. Baldwin later learned that the Commissioners of Greene County had decided against this contract, saying that the price was too high.[48]

Baldwin's testimony substantially aided Selden's case. Thanks to it, Selden's lawyers could argue that Baker had access to and had copied Selden's system and forms. Baker may have changed some captions and rearranged some columns in an attempt to disguise his copying, but he pirated a material part of the Selden book, thereby destroying the market for Selden's work. Since Baker didn't offer an explanation about the origins of his system, Baldwin's testimony offered otherwise missing testimony of "piracy."

The Trial Court Ruling and Post–Trial Proceedings

In January of 1875, District Judge Philip Swing, after hearing oral argument and assessing the deposition testimony and exhibits, issued findings of fact and conclusions of law.[49] Baker's books, the court found,

> are, in large and material part identical with and infringements of the books of Selden system..., and especially in this, to wit, that the device, method and form of the defendant's books for entering all the items of all monies received and disbursed, item by item, each item to its proper fund, are, as to the five left-

---

[44] *Id.* at 10–14. Baldwin's testimony, although taken long after those of Selden's other witnesses, is the first deposition in the Record.

[45] *Id.* at 112.

[46] Baldwin had previously worked with the Hamilton County treasurer's office and had used the Selden system while so employed, so he was well qualified to explain it to prospective customers. *Id.* at 10.

[47] *Id.* at 11.

[48] *Id.* at 11.

[49] Fisher did not represent Mrs. Selden at this hearing, for on August 14, 1874, Fisher and his ten-year-old son tragically drowned in a canoeing accident when they were carried over the Conewago Falls. In Memoriam Samuel S. Fisher, *supra* note 26.

> hand columns employed by him, identical with and an infringement of the said Selden system; and that the device, method, and form of defendant's said book for aggregating these items with previous balances to their respective funds, and so as to show the condition and balance to the debt and credit of each of these funds, are as to the column of funds, the two columns of brought forwards, the two columns of "totals," and the two columns of "balances," so far as these respect the funds, identical with and an infringement of the books of the said Selden system.[50]

The court ordered Baker to "forever refrain and be perpetually restrained and prohibited" from publication, sale, or otherwise disposing of his book.[51]

No record was kept of the proceedings in the Selden case before Judge Swing, so it is impossible to know what legal arguments were made to him or what (if any) precedents the lawyers relied upon in pleading their cases. Nor did Judge Swing's decision cite precedents in support of his ruling. However, a copyright infringement ruling from the Southern District of Ohio, *Drury v. Ewing*,[52] may have influenced him. That decision characterized Drury as the "authoress and inventress" of a copyrighted chart that depicted her method for taking measurements and cutting garments for women.[53] Ewing had infringed this copyright, the court held, because notwithstanding numerous differences in details, Ewing's chart used "the same principle" as Drury's and contained "the essential parts of Mrs. Drury's system."[54] The court rejected Ewing's improvement defense because dressmakers testified that Ewing's chart produced the same result at Drury's.[55] Mrs. Drury had, in the court's view, the exclusive right to control uses of her copyrighted chart, as well as publication of it.[56]

The ruling in *Drury* is consistent with Judge Swing's decision in Selden's favor. In both cases, the trial courts did more than protect authors against verbatim copying of their works. The courts treated alternative implementations of the plaintiffs' systems and reuse of system principles as copyright infringement. At a time when neither

---

50 Record at 9.

51 *Id.* Baker's appeal did not object to the perpetual injunction.

52 7 F. Cas. 1113 (C.C. S.D. Ohio 1862) (No. 4095).

53 *Id.* at 1114.

54 *Id.* at 1114, 1117.

55 *Id.* at 1117.

56 *Id.* at 1113.

Congress nor the courts had articulated a general approach for determining how much control creators should have over adaptations of their works,[57] the trial court rulings in *Drury* and *Baker* offered expansive protection. The courts even seemed willing to protect the plaintiffs' systems against unauthorized uses.

In March of 1875, shortly after Baker's lawyer filed an appeal to the U.S. Supreme Court and posted a $1000 bond,[58] Baker published a circular to Ohio county commissioners, auditors and treasurers, expressing confidence that he would be vindicated on appeal. Even if the appeal failed, Baker made clear that he would replace previously purchased books with copies of his new and improved book.[59] He quoted several sections of the copyright statute to support his conclusion that users of his books needn't worry about being sued by Mrs. Selden because copyright aimed only to "prevent publishers interfering with each other's rights."[60]

A month later, Elizabeth Selden (now Mrs. Ross) and her husband Howard (now a co-plaintiff in the case) fought back with gusto. They moved to increase the bond to $25,000–30,000,[61] and charged that Baker's new book also infringed the Selden copyrights and was within the court's injunction.[62] They submitted several affidavits and exhibits in support of these allegations,[63] as well as several affidavits casting aspersions on Baker's character[64] and challenging his net worth.[65]

The Rosses also issued a counter-circular to Ohio public officials,[66] pointing out that a federal court had ruled that Selden's copyrights were

57 *See* Anthony Reese, The Story of *Folsom v. Marsh*: Distinguishing Between Infringing and Legitimate Uses, elsewhere in this Volume.

58 Record at 9–10.

59 *Id.* at 77–78.

60 *Id.* at 78. The circular also assured the officials that the two year statute of limitations would have run as to them in any event.

61 This was the amount of damages they claimed for two years of infringement.

62 The Record does not reveal any court ruling on the bond motion; but it appears from Baker's brief to the Supreme Court that the injunction covered both books. Record, Argument for Appellant, at 27.

63 Record at 73–75, 84–89.

64 *Id.* at 88–89, 112–13. They charged him with running a "pharoh house" (that is, a gambling house). "Pharoh" (aka "faro") is a card game that was widely played in the US in the nineteenth century. A history of the game and its rules can be found on the web at http://www.bcvc.net/faro/history.htm and http://www.bcvc.net/faro/rules.htm.

65 Record at 114–15.

66 *Id.* at 79–80. Howard L. Ross had been added as a co-plaintiff on December 4, 1874. *Id.* at 7.

valid and infringed. From this, "[i]t clearly follows that all county auditors and treasurers who are using or have at any time used the books of said Baker, or procured their use, are infringers of the Selden copyrights and personally liable to the undersigned."[67] Further use of Baker's books "must be abandoned forthwith."[68] The Rosses were willing to offer favorable terms to those counties willing to settle "her just claims of past infringement and [pay] for the right to use the books of the Selden system."[69] Counties not so disposed "will be held to pay."[70]

In opposition to the motion to increase the bond, more than thirty of Baker's customers filed affidavits that typically attested that they had compared Baker's and Selden's forms and books and concluded that the two systems were materially different. Even more different and noninfringing was Baker's new book. Many said they would never use the Selden system, even if forced to stop using Baker's.[71]

Baker also submitted an affidavit in opposition to the bond motion that explained how he developed his bookkeeping system.[72] It began by recounting his twelve years of experience as deputy auditor and then auditor of Greene County, Ohio. (He was, in other words, an expert at bookkeeping himself.) Baker explained the identity in the five left-hand columns of the Selden and Baker forms (captioned "date," "no.", "to," "for," and "by") as due to the requirements of Ohio law. They were not original to Selden, as the trial judge had concluded. Baker said he had been using the categories of his system since 1859, and denied copying them from Selden. He pointed out dissimilarities between his forms and Selden's, explained why the differences were significant, and challenged the originality of other parts of Selden's forms.[73] In essence, Baker was belatedly making an independent creation defense.[74]

Reassessing the Merits

Was Baker a "pirate," as Mrs. Selden alleged, an improver, as the pro-Baker deposition witnesses asserted, or an independent creator, as

[67] *Id.* at 80.

[68] *Id.*

[69] *Id.*

[70] *Id.*

[71] The pro-Baker affidavits can be found, *id.* at 144–165.

[72] *Id.* at 116–19.

[73] Selden's lawyers objected to references to this and other post-trial affidavits in their brief to the Supreme Court. Record, Argument for the Appellee at 2–3.

[74] Baker did not respond to the allegations about gambling, but denied having significant debt. His affidavit said nothing about whether he had ever met Selden or Eleazer Baldwin.

Baker himself believed? If one credits Baldwin's testimony and infers from Baker's initial silence that the Baldwin testimony was truthful, it is reasonable to conclude that Baker copied something significant—the principle of condensing journal and ledger entries onto one form—from Selden's book and system.[75]

Several factors, though, suggest that Baker was not a slavish imitator of Selden's system or forms, let alone of Selden's books. Baker had a dozen years of experience as a bookkeeper by the time he published his first book. Judging from the texts of his three later books,[76] Baker was an intellectually curious professional who enjoyed communicating what he knew to those who might benefit from his knowledge. Selden's books, by contrast, were minor variations on one another, with almost no explanatory material.[77] The Baker and Selden forms are, moreover, demonstrably different in several respects,[78] especially in their treatment of accounts.

---

75 *See, e.g.*, Record at 19.

76 Baker wrote at least four books on bookkeeping, all of which were distinct texts. Three are available in the Library of Congress, and each explains the principles of bookkeeping in a lively and intelligent way. The most substantial is BAKER'S LABOR SAVING SYSTEM OF ACCOUNTS (Ohio, Columbia 1876). More than 200 pages long, it explains bookkeeping in detail and illustrates various textual points with sample forms and entries. A 1986 bibliography of accounting books lists this book as among the noteworthy eighteenth and nineteenth century books on this subject. *See* WALTER HAUSDORFER, ACCOUNTING BIBLIOGRAPHY, HISTORICAL APPROACH (1986). (Selden's books are not so cited.) Baker's 1876 book remains available in the Harvard and Columbia University Libraries as well as the Library of Congress and the Boston Public Library. *See also* W.C.M. BAKER, BOOK-KEEPING POCKET CHART (Ohio 1881); W.C.M. BAKER, BAKER'S SELF-INSTRUCTIVE BOOK-KEEPING (Ohio 1874). The 1867 book which attracted the widow Selden's lawsuit is not in the Supreme Court Record, nor in the Library of Congress, although Baker's appellate counsel inserted a copy of the Baker and Selden forms in the initial appellate brief. Record, Arguments for Appellant at 6–7.

77 Selden's sixth book, which is available in the rare book section of the Library of Congress, is only about 25 pages long, all but three of which are forms. If one omits the words on the title page, the forms, and the intellectual property rights notice, Selden's text is only 650 words long. Most of these words puff the merits of his system, rather than explaining how to use it. Selden's six books appear to have been minor variants on one another, not six wholly different books. One was tailored to the requirements of Ohio law, another to Indiana law, and one to U.S. government accounts. Selden apparently made some improvements in the forms from one edition to the next. One book had a slightly longer introduction.

78 *See supra* notes 15–17 and accompanying text.

[BAKER'S FORM.]

AUDITOR'S REGISTER.

DISBURSEMENTS.

Date.	No.	To.	For.	By.	Country.	Poor.	Bridge.							Total.
			Total.											

ADDITIONAL DISBURSEMENTS.

Exhibit.	

LEFT HAND PAGE

AUDITOR'S REGISTER.

RECEIPTS.

Date.	No.	From.	For.	County.							Total.
			Total.								

BALANCE SHEET

FUNDS			Rec'd to 186	[Dist'd] to 186	To Rec. to 186	To Dis. to 186	Balance 186	Ov'r Pd. 186
County.								
Poor.								
Bridge.								
School.								
Township.								
Corporation.								
Redemption of Lands.								
Teachers' Institute.								
Show Licences.								
Peddlers' Licences.								
Volunteer Relief.								
Section 16.								
State Fund.								
Road Taxes.								
Building.								
Rail Road.								
Ministry.								
Soldiers' Pay.								
Bounty.								
Balance in Treasury.								
Total.								
County Treasurer-General Acct.								

ADDITIONAL RECEIPTS.

Floating Order.	

RIGHT HAND PAGE

[SELDEN'S FORM]

AUDITOR'S RECORD.

DISBURSEMENTS.						RECEIPTS.					
County Fund.											
Date.	No.	Amount.	To.	For.	Authority.	Date.	No.	Amount.	Of.	For.	Authority

LEFT HAND PAGE

CONDENSED LEDGER.

Bro'ght Forward.		Distri- bution.		Date: from . . . . . . to . . . . . . inclusive.				Total.		Balan- ces.	
					Sundries to Sundries. TREASURER.						
					Dr.	Cr.					
Dr.	Cr.	Dr.	Cr.	Dr.	$	$	Or.	Dr.	Cr.	Dr.	Cr.
					County Fund. Bridge Fund. County Infirmary. Building Fund. Internal Fund. Kind Fund. Sale Redemptions. Refunders. Redemptions. Tax Omissions. Forfeitures. Duplicate. Section 16. Section 29. Peddlers' License. Show License. State Fund. School Fund. Corporation Fund. Township Fund. Treasurer's Fees. State Relief Fund. Soldiers' Fund. Militia Fund. Bounty Fund. School Examiners' Fund. CARRIED FORWARD.						
Floating Order											

RIGHT HAND PAGE

Independent creation is plausible because a smart auditor like Baker might well have realized that the old data-intensive system was unsuitable for the increasingly complex commerce of the late nineteenth century. Condensing the ledger and journals into one form would have been an obvious way to do more efficient data entry and rapid analysis.

Baker's independent creation defense is also plausible if one discredits Baldwin's testimony either because of the procedural irregularity of the deposition being taken without adequate notice to Baker's lawyer or because his post-trial affidavit contradicts his deposition. The affidavit states that Baldwin first met Baker in 1860 when Baker came to Hamilton County to learn about how it kept books and that Baldwin and Selden spent a lot of time explaining the Selden system to Baker to whom it was then new.[79] Yet, when deposed a year and a half earlier, Baldwin said that the Selden system was new to Baker in August 1865.[80] Both statements cannot be true.

Consider also that if Selden thought Baker was an infringer, he could have, but didn't, sue Baker for infringement during his lifetime. Selden and his publisher must have been aware of Baker's book in 1867 or soon thereafter, given their efforts to sell the competing systems to the same county officials in Ohio.[81] One of Selden's witnesses testified that Baker showed his forms to officials in the Hamilton County auditor's office in about 1867.[82] Another testified that Selden himself had showed the witness Baker's forms and asked the witness which he liked better.[83] Selden may have lacked the financial resources to initiate a lawsuit against Baker, yet his widow managed to do so, even though she too was burdened by his debts.

Baker's Appeal

Because a great deal of money was riding on the success of Baker's appeal to the Supreme Court—not only for Baker, but also for Ohio[84]—it was time to call upon more experienced and eminent counsel to represent him. Baker's appellate team included Edward F. Noyes, Alphonso Taft, and Harlan P. Lloyd. Noyes was a former Governor of Ohio, a hero

---

79 *Id.* at 74–75.

80 *Id.* at 11.

81 Franklin County decided to drop its use of Selden's system in favor of Baker's in 1867. *Id.* at 145.

82 *Id.* at 34.

83 *Id.* at 17.

84 The Rosses claimed annual damages amounting to about $250,000 in today's dollars.

of the Civil War, and U.S. Ambassador to France during the late 1870's.[85] Taft was a senior and distinguished member of the Cincinnati bar, and a former Superior Court Judge, city council member, and gubernatorial candidate.[86] In 1877, Taft became a law partner of Lloyd, who was also a Civil War hero and a daring young lawyer who had appeared before Taft in 1871 in an important case that recognized the validity of slave marriages.[87] Lloyd handled the oral argument before the Supreme Court on behalf of Baker.[88] Selden's appellate team was Milton I. Southard and Charles W. Moulton, about whom comparatively little information is available.

Baker's initial brief to the Supreme Court focused heavily on the explainable differences defense[89] and relied on conventional copyright cases[90] and the newly published Drone copyright treatise.[91] Obliquely it raised a copyrightable subject matter challenge to Selden's claim in contending that Selden's system was not a "book" and that "ruled lines for blank books do not constitute authorship."[92]

The Selden brief mainly focused on the originality of Selden's selection and arrangement of information in the forms and the substan-

---

85 Noyes is not listed on the Supreme Court briefs, but the Lawyer's Edition of the case mentions him as one of Baker's counsel. *Baker*, 25 L.Ed. at 841. Coincidentally, the Commissioners of Hamilton County sued Noyes in 1874 for defrauding the county of $13,526 through an allegedly non-competitive contract. Alphonso Taft and Edward Colston represented Noyes in this lawsuit. The Ohio Supreme Court ruled in favor of Noyes in December 1878. *See Board of Comm'rs v. Noyes*, 35 Ohio St. 201 (1878).

86 During the late 1870's, Taft was briefly Secretary of War and then Attorney General of the United States. After the *Baker* case, he became the U.S. Ambassador first to Austria and then to Russia. Taft was also father of the future president William Howard Taft and a co-founder of Skull and Bones at Yale.

87 Price v. Slaughter, 13 Ohio Dec. Rep. 641.

88 The *Bench and Bar of Ohio* has a highly laudatory biographical sketch of Lloyd, which mentions Lloyd's role in arguing the *Baker v. Selden* case as one of his significant achievements. George Irving Reed, Bench and Bar of Ohio 142–43 (1897).

89 Record, Argument for Appellant, at 11–17.

90 Among the conventional cases relied upon were *Wheaton v. Peters*, 33 U.S. 591 (1834), (see Craig Joyce, The Story of *Wheaton v. Peters*: A Curious Chapter in the History of Judicature, elsewhere in this Volume); *Emerson v. Davies,* 8 F. Cas. 615 (C.C. D. Mass. 1845) (No. 4436) (competing book on arithmetic infringed); and *Sayre v. Moore*, 1 East 361 (1785) (map that consolidated information from other maps and corrected errors was noninfringing). *See* Record, Argument for Appellant at 13–14 (citing *Wheaton*), 19–20 (citing and quoting from *Sayre*), and 21–22 (citing and quoting from *Emerson*).

91 Eaton S. Drone, A Treatise on the Law of Property in Intellectual Productions (1879). Record, Argument for Appellant, at 18, 22–23 (quoting *Drone* treatise).

92 *Id.* at 5–8. It hinted at the possible patentability of Selden's system as a reason to deny the Selden claim. *Id.* at 9.

tial identity of Baker's and Selden's forms as a basis for affirming the trial court's ruling.[93] It pointed to many authorities that supported giving the term "book" a liberal construction in copyright cases, *Drury* among them.[94]

The main points made during oral argument before the Supreme Court can be discerned from a synopsis that appears in the *Lawyer's Edition* report of the case.[95] It indicates that Baker's lawyers had reframed his defense. The main argument now was that Selden's work was not a proper subject matter for copyright protection because it was a contribution to the useful arts, not to science.[96] Selden himself had recognized this in seeking, although apparently not obtaining, a patent for the bookkeeping system.[97] (A patent would have given Selden the exclusive right to make, use and sell his bookkeeping system for 14 years.[98] A patent examiner would have had to be convinced Selden's system was novel and inventive before issuing the patent.) Baker's lawyer now principally relied upon *Perris v. Hexamer*,[99] a year-old Supreme Court decision holding that a system of symbols for representing information on maps of city blocks was unprotectable by copyright, and *Page v. Wisden*[100] an 1869 English decision holding blank cricket scoring sheets to be uncopyrightable.

The *Lawyer's Edition* reports that Selden's lawyer countered Baker's subject matter challenge, saying that the copyright statute offered protection to books, as long as they were original contributions to useful

---

93 Record, Argument for Appellee, at 5–9. The Selden brief relied on many of the same conventional cases as the Baker brief and the Drone treatise.

94 Record, Argument for Appellee at 4. Baker's brief challenged *Drury*, saying that it had been criticized by bench and bar. Record, Argument for Appellant at 9.

95 *See* Baker v. Selden, 25 L.Ed. 841, 841–42 (synopsis of lawyer arguments) (1880).

96 *Id.* at 841. "Science" at that time was understood to mean "knowledge," not just the disciplines deemed to be science nowadays (e.g., chemistry, biology, and physics).

97 *Id.*

98 The patent term was fourteen years until 1861, when Congress increased it to seventeen years. *See* George Ticknor Curtis, A Treatise on the Law of Patents for Useful Inventions at 562, 584–85.

99 99 U.S. 674 (1879).

100 20 L.T.R. 435 (1869). *Page v. Wisden* had not been cited in Baker's initial brief to the Court. Also newly cited in the oral argument was *The Trade-Mark Cases,* 100 U.S. 82 (1879), which the Court had decided only three weeks before it heard Baker's appeal. These cases were arguably relevant because of the opinion's discussion of Congress' power to protect "authors" and "inventors" under the Intellectual Property Clause of the U.S. Constitution. But Baker's counsel may also have wanted to emphasize *The Trade-Mark Cases* because the decision unanimously overturned the very same judge who had ruled against Baker.

knowledge,[101] as Selden's was. The *Baker* opinion indicates that Selden's lawyer relied heavily on *Drury v. Ewing*,[102]

In a supplemental brief, filed after the oral argument, Baker's lawyers elaborated on the subject matter defense.[103] Five of the six points in this brief discuss the distinction between patent and copyright subject matters. Selden's application for a patent, it argued, should be conclusive against his copyright claim, for it showed that he conceived of his system as a useful art.[104] When Selden's lawyer described the state of the art when Selden invented his system and when he characterized the Selden system as " 'an artificial system for the art of bookkeeping,' " this "d[id] not refer to authorship, but solely to invention."[105] Even if Selden's innovation fell in a gap between patent and copyright subject matters, only Congress could legislatively fill this gap.[106]

From the written materials available, it is fair to infer that during the oral argument, at least one of the Justices—perhaps Joseph P. Bradley who wrote the Court's opinion—showed interest in Selden's patent application and perceived the case before the Court as an effort to misuse the copyrights in his books to get patent-like protection for the bookkeeping system. Faced with questions about Selden's patent application, a good lawyer for Baker would have adjusted his argument, agreeing with his Honor that if Selden applied for a patent, he must have thought of his system as an invention, while a good lawyer for Selden might well have scrapped his prepared remarks and made much of *Drury v. Ewing*, the most apt precedent involving copyright protection in an original functional design that had been found infringing by a substantially similar competing product.

The Supreme Court's Decision

The *Baker* opinion is unusual in the attention it gives to the distinction between copyrights and patents and the respective roles of these laws in the protection of the fruits of intellectual labor.[107] The

---

101 *Baker*, 25 L.Ed. at 842. They relied upon five decisions and two treatises for giving a broad construction to the word "book" in copyright law.

102 *Baker*, 101 U.S. at 107.

103 Record, Supplemental Brief for the Appellant.

104 *Id.* at 2.

105 *Id.*

106 *Id.* at 2–3.

107 In most copyright cases, it is neither necessary nor appropriate to discuss the patent/copyright distinction, but *Baker* was unusual in several respects: 1) Selden had applied for a patent for his bookkeeping system, and apparently had not gotten one; 2) the complaint characterized Selden as the author and inventor of the Selden system as well as

Court could not readily explain why an author could not get copyright protection for a bookkeeping system by applying the then-conventional framework for analyzing copyright claims. Such an inquiry typically proceeded by asking: Was the plaintiff's work a "book" or otherwise statutory subject matter qualifying for copyright protection? Was the work original? Had the defendant copied a substantial or material part of the plaintiff's work?[108] If the two works were not identical, had the defendant tried to disguise his piracy by making immaterial variations, or was the second work materially different and/or an improvement?[109] Was he, in modern parlance, a free-rider or a fair follower?

Selden had certainly published several books, and books were a canonical subject matter for copyright protection. The books were original to him. There was evidence in the record that Baker had copied a substantial part of Selden's work, and the trial judge had resolved the conflicting evidence about whether Baker was a slavish imitator or the author of a different and improved work by ruling in Selden's favor. Selden's lawyers could plausibly argue that key similarities between Selden's and Baker's works were not due to their being about the same subject, nor to drawing ideas and information from the same common sources, which the Drone treatise and prior cases had recognized as reasons why works might be very similar to one another without infringing.[110]

The *Baker* opinion introduced a new kind of inquiry to the framework for analyzing copyright claims. In essence, it directed courts to consider whether the defendant had copied the author's description, explanation, illustration, or depiction of a useful art (such as a bookkeeping system) or ideas, or had only copied the useful art or ideas them-

the author and inventor of several books; 3) the trial court decision accepted the characterization of Selden as the author and inventor of a bookkeeping system as well as of certain books; 4) the evidence offered in support of Selden's claim focused on similarities between the Selden and Baker systems, and not on similarities in explanatory materials in the books; 5) the complaint raised the issue of the novelty of Selden's system and lawyers for Selden argued its novelty to the Supreme Court; and 6) the widow Selden had announced her intent to sue all of Baker's customers for their infringing uses of the system if the Supreme Court affirmed the lower court ruling in her favor. The *Drury* decision supported Selden's claim that author/inventors could get exclusive rights to control uses of novel systems through copyright law, *see supra* notes 52–57 and accompanying text, and the *Drone* treatise had endorsed *Drury*. *See* Drone at 406.

108 *See* Drone, Chapters 2, 3 and 8. Drone believed that taking a material part of a copyrighted work was piracy. *Id.* at 385, 407–08, 413–14.

109 *Id.* at 407–08. Drone criticized improvement as a defense, *Id.* at 406, although the famous *Sayre v. Moore* decision had endorsed it. *See* Sayre v. Moore, 1 East 361 (1785).

110 Drone at 416–17; Emerson v. Davies, 8 F. Cas. 615, 618, (1845).

selves.[111] In the absence of a patent,[112] the useful art depicted in a work, along with its ideas, could be used and copied by anyone, even in directly competing works. Any necessary incidents to implementing the art (e.g., blank forms illustrating use of the system) could likewise be used and copied by second comers without fear of copyright liability.

Modern readers come to the *Baker* decision expecting to find in it a classic statement of the idea/expression distinction and/or of the idea/expression merger doctrine. (The latter holds that if there is only one or a very small number of ways to express an idea, courts should find the idea and its expression to be "merged," and refuse to protect such expression in order not to grant a monopoly on an idea.)[113] But the Court intended to convey a substantially different message.

To come afresh to the *Baker* decision and to discern how important the patent/copyright distinction was to the *Baker* ruling,[114] it is helpful to review core parts of the opinion. The Court perceived the key question to be "whether the exclusive property in a system of bookkeeping can be claimed, under the law of copyright, by means of a book in which that system is explained."[115] Selden claimed that "the ruled lines and headings, given to illustrate the system, are part of the book and, as such, are secured by the copyright; and that no one can make or use similar ruled lines and headings. . . without violating the copyright."[116] The Court did not doubt that a work on the subject of bookkeeping could be copyrighted, nor that such a work might be "a very valuable acquisition to the practical knowledge of the community."[117] But the Court perceived "a clear distinction between the book, as such, and the art which it is intended to illustrate."[118] Someone might copyright a treatise "on the composition and use of medicines, be they old or new; on the construction and use of ploughs or watches or churns; or on the mode of drawing lines to produce the effect of perspective . . . but no one would contend

---

111 The Supreme Court did not use the word "expression" in the *Baker* opinion.

112 The Court did not specifically mention utility patents. It spoke only of patents, but viewed in context, it seems to have meant utility patents. Following the Court in this respect, I use the term "patent" to mean "utility patent."

113 This concept is discussed *infra* notes 196–206 and accompanying text.

114 Five of the seven paragraphs of the *Baker* opinion which constitute the core of the Court's analysis mention the patent/copyright distinction. Most intellectual property casebooks edit out one or more, and sometimes all but a few, of the references in *Baker* to the patent/copyright distinction.

115 *Baker*, 101 U.S. at 101.

116 *Id.*

117 *Id.* at 102.

118 *Id.*

that the copyright of the treatise would give the exclusive right to the art or manufacture described therein."[119] The reason was simple: "To give the author of a book an exclusive property in the art described therein would be a surprise and fraud upon the public. That is the province of letters patent, not of copyright."[120] Exclusive rights to inventions can only be obtained by subjecting one's claims to Patent Office examination.[121]

To hammer home this lesson, the Court devoted one paragraph each to three examples: one on medicines, one on drawing perspective, and one on mathematical sciences. A book about medicines does not give the author an exclusive right to make and sell medicines described therein; to get such an exclusive right, one needs a patent. No matter how many drawings a book on perspective might contain to illustrate this concept, copyright in the book would not give the author an exclusive right to control the use of perspective.[122] Nor would a copyright in a work on mathematical sciences give an author an exclusive right "to the methods of operation which he propounds, or to the diagrams which he employs to explain them, so as to prevent an engineer from using them whenever occasion requires."[123]

Yet, the Court also made clear that these observations did not apply to "ornamental designs or pictorial illustrations addressed to the taste."[124] Of such works, "it may be said that their form is their essence and their object the production of pleasure in their contemplation."[125] Scientific and technical works were different because "their final end [is] in application and use."[126] The explanatory texts of such works can be protected by copyright, but not the scientific and technical content such works embody.

Returning to Selden's claim, the Court stated that while "no one has a right to print or publish his book, or any material part thereof, as a book intended to convey instruction in the art, any person may practice

119 *Id.*

120 *Id.*

121 *Id.*

122 *Id.* The Court indicated that it didn't matter if the author described the useful art or used drawings or diagrams to illustrate the art; the underlying principle was the same. *Id.*

123 *Id.* at 103.

124 *Id.*

125 *Id.* at 103–04.

126 *Id.* at 104.

and use the art itself which he has described and illustrated therein."[127] (In other words, Baker's customers were off the hook.) It went on to say that "[t]he copyright of a book on bookkeeping cannot secure the exclusive right to make, sell and use account books prepared upon the plan set forth in such a book."[128] (In other words, Baker was off the hook.) Because Selden's system was not patented, it was "open and free to the use of the public,"[129] as were the ruled lines and headings that implemented the system.

Perhaps the most interesting paragraph in the *Baker* opinion is the one that attributes the plausibility of Selden's claim as due to the "peculiar nature of the art described in [his] books" because "the illustrations and diagrams happen to correspond more closely than usual with the actual work performed by the operator who uses the art."[130] One who kept books by Selden's system would necessarily rule his account books with the same or very similar headings as the forms in Selden's book. Usually, the Court observed, useful arts "can only be represented in concrete forms of wood, metal, stone, or some other physical embodiment."[131] But the principle was the same regardless of whether the useful art was embodied in writing or in metal.[132]

Near the end of the *Baker* opinion, seemingly tacked on as an afterthought, is a set of six paragraphs discussing prior caselaw.[133] The Court agreed with *Page v. Wisden* that cricket scoring sheets were uncopyrightable: " 'To say that a particular mode of ruling a book constituted an object for a copyright is absurd.' "[134] It also questioned *Drury v. Ewing*: "Surely the exclusive right to this practical use [of patterns to make clothing] was not reserved to the publisher by his copyright of the chart."[135]

---

127 *Id.*

128 *Id.*

129 *Id.*

130 *Id.*

131 *Id.* at 105.

132 *Id.* The Court characterized the "object" of the copyrighted work as explanation and of a useful art as use, saying that exclusive rights in use were only available with a patent. *Id.*

133 The *Baker* opinion does not mention the conventional copyright cases discussed in the briefs, nor any copyright treatises. Justice Bradley, as a patent expert, may not have been as familiar with the copyright literature, or he may simply have not found it very helpful in analyzing the *Baker* case.

134 20 L.T.R. 435, *discussed in Baker*, 101 U.S. at 106–07.

135 *Id. Baker*'s concern that inventors should not be able to get patent-like protection from copyrights in their writings resonates with concerns Justice Bradley had expressed in

The *Baker* decision ends with the conclusion that "blank account-books are not the subject of copyright, and that the mere copyright of Selden's book did not confer upon him the exclusive right to make and use account-books, ruled and arranged as designated by him and described and illustrated in said book."[136] The Court thought that these conclusions followed from its agreement with *Page* about the uncopyrightability of blank forms and its doubts about *Drury*'s grant of patent-like protection over practical use of Drury's copyrighted clothing patterns. Viewed in context of the case as a whole, the Court appears to have held Selden's forms to be uncopyrightable not because they were blank (and hence lacking in authorship),[137] but because the Court viewed the forms as embodiments of Selden's system.

The Legacy of Baker

Baker v. Selden is one of the few nineteenth century copyright decisions to have had continuing significance in the copyright caselaw and literature. *Baker* contains potent statements of limiting principles of copyright law from which many subsequent courts and commentators have drawn guidance.[138] Virtually every intellectual property and copyright casebook contains an edited version of the case. Its principal holding—that copyright does not protect systems described in copyrighted works—is now codified in section 102(b) of the Copyright Act.[139] Also

---

some patent decisions. The public interest in free competition would be harmed if courts allowed patent applicants or patentees to game the patent system, for example, by seeking to broaden patent claims through reissue proceedings. *See, e.g.,* Carlton v. Bokee, 84 U.S. 463, 471–72 (1872); Smith v. Goodyear Dental Vulcanite, 93 U.S. 486, 502 (1877) (Bradley, J., dissenting). Bradley may have realized that upholding Selden's claim would significantly undermine incentives to use the patent system, for who would bother to go to the Patent Office and subject a claimed invention to examiner scrutiny if he could simply write an article about it and thereby get exclusive rights to its use? In patent law, publishing a description of an invention without seeking a patent within a reasonable time dedicates it to the public domain.

[136] *Baker*, 101 U.S. at 107.

[137] Most of the forms in Selden's books were not, in fact, blank, but contained sample entries to illustrate how to use the system. *See* Record at 22–29. Baker was not charged with copying these entries.

[138] A LexisNexis Shephard search for citations to *Baker v. Selden* as of August 13, 2004, yielded 272 cases, 549 law reviews, 1 secondary source, 1 statute, 47 treatises, and 6 American Law Reports/Lawyers' Edition Annotations, while a Westlaw search the same day produced 1,432 documents, consisting of 258 case cites, 1 administrative decision, 3 registers, 1047 secondary sources, 24 appellate filings, 82 appellate briefs, 5 trial motions and memoranda, 3 Australian cases, 3 Canadian cases, and 6 Canadian secondary sources.

[139] "In no case does copyright protection for an original work of authorship extend to any idea, procedure, process, system, method of operation, concept, principle, or discovery,

codified are three other emanations of *Baker*: the useful article limitation on the copyrightability of pictorial, sculptural, and graphic works;[140] the rule that copyright protection for drawings of useful articles does not extend to the useful articles depicted in the drawings;[141] and the rule that blank forms are uncopyrightable.[142] *Baker* has also been widely cited for other doctrines and principles.[143] The legacy of *Baker* is worthy of study in part because of its longevity and influence, but also because the propositions for which it has been cited have evolved over time.

The Uncopyrightability of Useful Arts

The *Baker* decision announced that innovative useful arts are not copyrightable subject matter.[144] Relatively few post-*Baker* cases have claimed copyright in original designs for useful articles, and no such case has been successful.[145] Prior to 1976, Copyright Office regulations distinguished between original designs of useful articles, which were unregistrable on subject matter grounds, and original works of artistic craftsmanship, such as jewelry, which could qualify for copyright protection.[146] In the Copyright Act of 1976, Congress sharpened the distinction between protectable works of artistic craftsmanship and unprotectable useful articles by providing that original works of artistic craftsmanship can be protected as pictorial, graphic, or sculptural works "insofar as their form but not their mechanical or utilitarian aspects are con-

---

regardless of the form in which it is described, explained, illustrated, or embodied in such work." 17 U.S.C. § 102(b).

140 *See* 17 U.S.C. § 101 (definitions of pictorial, graphic, and sculptural works and of useful article).

141 17 U.S.C. § 113(b).

142 Copyright Office Regulations, 37 C.F.R. § . 202.1(c).

143 This chapter will discuss four other copyright doctrines influenced by *Baker*: the patent/copyright distinction, the idea/expression distinction, the idea/expression merger principle, and the narrow scope of protection for functional writings. *Baker* has also been widely cited for other principles. *See, e.g.,* Feist Pub. Inc. v. Rural Telephone Service Co., 499 U.S. 340, 350 (1991) (freedom of ideas).

144 *Baker*, 101 U.S. at 102–03.

145 *See, e.g.,* Brandir Int'l v. Cascade Pac. Lumber Co., 834 F.2d 1142 (2d Cir. 1987) (design of bicycle rack held uncopyrightable). *Baker* was even influential on this point in England. In *Hollinrake v. Truswell*, 3 Chanc. D. 420 (1894), the plaintiff sued a competitor for selling similar cardboard patterns for making dress sleeves. The lower court followed *Drury v. Ewing* and enjoined the defendant's manufacture of a similar pattern. The appellate court reversed, citing *Baker* not only for the doubt it cast on the ruling in *Drury*, but also for the unprotectability of mechanical contrivances, such as the plaintiff's pattern, and the method of measuring that it enabled. *Id.* at 426–29.

146 *See* Mazer v. Stein, 347 U.S. 201, 211–13 (1954) (discussion of history of these regulations).

cerned.''[147] Designs of useful articles are protectable ''only if, and only to the extent that, [they] incorporate[] pictorial, graphic or sculptural features that can be identified separately from, and are capable of existing independently of, the utilitarian aspects of the article.''[148] The test for whether useful articles are disqualified from copyright is whether they have ''an intrinsic utilitarian function that is not merely to portray the appearance of the article or to convey information.''[149] Harley–Davidson motorcycle designs may be elegant enough to be displayed in the Guggenheim Museum, but art and utility are too intermingled for these designs to qualify for copyright protection.

Congress has created two exceptions to the general *Baker*-inspired rule against copyright for works that might otherwise be deemed unprotectable useful arts: first, when it decided to protect machine-executable computer programs by copyright,[150] and second, when it extended copyright protection to architectural works in 1991, as part of the U.S. accession to the Berne Convention.[151]

The Drawing/Useful Art Distinction

More common have been cases in which plaintiffs have sought to assert copyright protection in useful articles indirectly by claiming that defendants copied designs from copyrighted drawings. National Cloak, for example, was unsuccessful in its copyright infringement suit against a competitor insofar as it was based on copying of dress designs from National Cloak's drawings.[152] Also unsuccessful were claims of infringement based on copying of a parachute design, a bridge approach design, and a natural gas pipeline route from copyrighted drawings.[153] *Baker* is the primary precedent courts have relied upon in denying such claims. Extending copyright protection to useful designs depicted in drawings would be inconsistent with *Baker* because it would indirectly protect the

---

147 17 U.S.C. § 101 (definition of ''pictorial, graphic, and sculptural works'').

148 *Id.*

149 17 U.S.C. § 101 (definition of ''useful article'').

150 Pub. L. No. 96–517, § 10(a), 94 Stat. 3028 (1980). *See* discussion *infra* notes 202–17 and accompanying text.

151 Pub. L. No.101–650, § 706, 104 Stat. 5133 (1990). Prior to this statutory change, the copyright caselaw generally accepted that copying of architectural plans might infringe copyright, but not construction of a building depicted in copyrighted architectural drawings. *See* DeSilva Construction Corp. v. Herrald, 213 F.Supp. 184, 195–96 (M.D. Fla. 1962).

152 National Cloak & Suit Co. v. Standard Mail Order, 191 F. 528 (S.D.N.Y. 1911).

153 *See* Muller v. Triborough Bridge Authority, 43 F. Supp. 298 (S.D.N.Y. 1942) (bridge approach); Fulmer v. U.S., 103 F.Supp. 1021 (Ct. Cl. 1952) (parachute design); Kern River Gas Transmission Co. v. Coastal Corp., 899 F.2d 1458 (5th Cir. 1990) (pipeline design).

useful arts that *Baker* opined were uncopyrightable subject matter. This aspect of *Baker*'s legacy is codified in the Copyright Act of 1976.[154]

The System/Description Distinction

The Supreme Court distinguished in *Baker* between Selden's bookkeeping system, which copyright did not protect, and Selden's description or explanation of the system, which copyright law protected against improper appropriation.[155] Given the clarity of the Court's statement about the unprotectability of methods and systems, it is surprising how many plaintiffs have sought copyright protection for systems described or otherwise embodied in copyrighted works. This was especially common in the 1930's through early 1950's. Perhaps it was the Depression and World War II, when so little capital was available to start new ventures that caused so many to use brainpower to figure out new ways of making money. One developed a shorthand system,[156] another a system for teaching cornet playing,[157] a third devised a bridge game problem and solution,[158] a fourth invented a system for giving away prizes in theatres,[159] a fifth devised new roller skating races,[160] a sixth made up a system for aiding tax preparations,[161] while a seventh developed a system for reorganizing insolvent life insurance companies.[162] These creators (and others)[163] sought to use copyright law to protect their creations against competitive copying. Courts relied principally on *Baker* in ruling against these infringement claims.

In the early twentieth century, a few courts began to reframe *Baker* as an idea/expression case, moving away from the system/description distinction. Had the Second Circuit followed *Baker*'s analysis in *Guthrie v. Curlett*,[164] for example, it would have denied Guthrie's claim of copyright infringement because Curlett had copied Guthrie's system for

---

154 17 U.S.C. § 113(b).

155 *Baker*, 101 U.S. at 104. The Court regarded useful arts to be equally unprotectable whether they were depicted in drawings or texts. *Id.*

156 Brief English Systems v. Owen, 48 F.2d 555 (2d Cir. 1931).

157 Jackson v. C. G. Conn Ltd., 9 U.S.P.Q. (BNA) 225 (W.D. Okla. 1931).

158 Russell v. Northeastern Pub. Co., 7 F. Supp. 571 (D. Mass. 1934).

159 Affilated Ent., Inc. v. Gantz, 86 F.2d 597 (10th Cir. 1936).

160 Selzer v. Sunbrock, 22 F. Supp. 621 (S.D. Cal. 1938).

161 Aldrich v. Remington Rand, Inc., 52 F. Supp. 732 (N.D. Tex. 1942).

162 Crume v. Pacific Mutual Life Ins. Co., 140 F.2d 182 (7th Cir. 1944).

163 *See, e.g.*, Dunham v. General Mills, 116 F.Supp. 152 (D. Mass. 1953).

164 36 F.2d 694 (2d Cir. 1929).

consolidating freight tariff information, not his description or explanation of the system.[165] The Second Circuit instead reasoned that Curlett had not copied Guthrie's means of expression, citing *Baker* only once for the proposition that an author "must be protected in his choice of expression, and his copyright held to that."[166]

Baker's system/description distinction did not impress Learned Hand, then a district court judge, in *Reiss v. National Quotations*, which upheld the validity of a copyright in a code book of made-up words.[167] National Quotations probably argued that under *Baker*, the contents of the book embodied an unprotectable coding system and/or that the book's object was practical use, not explanation. Like Selden's form, the code book conveyed no thought and expressed no idea. Hand dismissed this defense, characterizing *Baker* as "too foreign to the case at bar to deserve comment."[168] This was the only time in his long and influential career that Hand ever cited *Baker*.

More than any other judge, Hand was responsible for refocusing copyright infringement analysis on the idea/expression distinction and on the patterns of abstraction that might be laid upon any work.[169] Under the patterns test, higher level abstractions became unprotectable ideas, while lower level abstractions tended to be considered "expression."[170] Hand developed and applied the patterns test in cases involving literary and dramatic works. However, some courts have applied the patterns test and idea/expression distinction in other kinds of cases, occasionally resulting in different outcomes than a *Baker*-inspired system/description test would have produced.[171]

---

[165] Guthrie had not only sought, but obtained, a patent on his method of compressing freight tariff information. His first lawsuit against Curlett was for patent infringement. The Second Circuit ruled that Guthrie's patent claimed unpatentable subject matter. *See* Guthrie v. Curlett, 10 F.2d 725 (2d Cir. 1926). The copyright decision makes no mention of Guthrie's patent, nor of the prior decision on the patent claim.

[166] *Id.* at 696. *See also* Nutt v. National Institute for the Improvement of Memory, 31 F.2d 236, 238 (2d Cir. 1929) (finding infringement of instructional materials, citing *Baker* for the idea/expression distinction).

[167] 276 F. 717 (S.D.N.Y. 1921). The book was intended to enable confidential transmissions of messages via telegraph between parties who agreed that certain made-up words would signify English words.

[168] *Id.* at 719. Hand did not explain why he thought *Baker* was "foreign" to the *Reiss* case.

[169] Among Hand's most influential decisions were: Peter Pan Fabrics, Inc. v. Martin Weiner Corp., 274 F.2d 487 (2d Cir. 1960); Sheldon v. Metro–Goldwyn Pictures Corp., 81 F.2d 49 (2d Cir. 1936); Nichols v. Universal Pictures, 45 F.2d 119 (2d Cir. 1930). *Nichols* articulates the "patterns" test. *Id.* at 121.

[170] *See, e.g.,* Sheldon v. Metro–Goldwyn Pictures Corp., 81 F.2d 49 (2d Cir. 1936) (detailed sequences of events within scenes held to be protectable expression).

[171] *See, e.g.,* Lotus Dev. Corp. v. Paperback Software Int'l, 740 F.Supp. 37 (D. Mass. 1990).

After enactment of the Copyright Act of 1976, which codified the unprotectability of systems and methods of operation embodied in copyrighted works, one might have expected courts to be more attentive to the system/description distinction. However, defense efforts to rely on *Baker* and section 102(b)'s exclusion of methods and systems have generally fallen on deaf ears in the past few decades.[172] No consensus exists in the post–1976 Act caselaw or commentary about what systems or methods are excluded under section 102(b) or how to test for their exclusion.

Uncopyrightability of Blank Forms

The concluding paragraph of the *Baker* decision states that "blank account-books are not the subject of copyright."[173] Courts have generalized this proposition from *Baker* and ruled that blank forms are uncopyrightable subject matter.[174] The U.S. Copyright Office has accordingly refused to register claims of copyrights in "blank forms, such as time cards, graph paper, account books, diaries, bank checks, scorecards, address books, report forms, order forms, and the like, which are designed for recording information and do not in themselves convey information."[175] Several cases in the 1970's challenged the "blank form" exclusionary rule after *Nimmer on Copyright*, an influential treatise, challenged it as unsound. If forms satisfied copyright's originality standard, Nimmer thought they should be protectable by copyright law.[176] A few plaintiffs in the 1970's persuaded courts to follow *Nimmer* and extend copyright protection to blank forms.[177] However, most decisions follow *Baker* in refusing copyright protection to blank forms, although it

---

172 *See, e.g.,* Toro Co. v. R & R Products Co., 787 F.2d 1208 (8th Cir. 1986) (numbering system for products and parts); *ADA v. Delta Dental Plans Ass'n*, 126 F.3d 977 (7th Cir. 1997) (system of abbreviating types of dental treatments); Kregos v. Associated Press, 937 F.2d 700 (2d Cir. 1991) (method for predicting outcomes of baseball games).

173 *Baker*, 101 U.S. at 107.

174 *See, e.g.,* Time–Saver Check, Inc. v. Deluxe Check Printers, Inc., 178 USPQ (BNA) 510 (N.D. Tex. 1973).

175 37 C.F.R. § 202.1(c).

176 *See* Melville Nimmer & David Nimmer, Nimmer on Copyright, §§ 2.08, 2.18 (2004) (criticizing *Baker* and arguing that original forms should be copyrightable). The *Nimmer* treatise acknowledges that the Copyright Office regulation follows *Baker*. *Id.* at n. 22.

177 *See* Norton Printing Co. v. Augustana Hospital, 155 USPQ (BNA) 133 (N.D. Ill. 1967); Harcourt, Brace & World, Inc. v. Graphics Controls Corp., 329 F. Supp. 517 (S.D.N.Y. 1971).

is not always clear whether this is due to a perceived lack of authorship in "blank" forms or instead to concerns that forms are embodiments of systems for organizing information that should not be privatized through copyright law.[178]

The Patent/Copyright Distinction

The patent/copyright distinction was central to the Court's analysis of the *Baker* case. The Court perceived Selden to be trying to get exclusive rights to control practical use of his bookkeeping system through the copyright suit against Baker. The Court opined that to get exclusive rights over practical use of a useful art, one needed to apply for and comply with requirements of patent law, not just publish a book about it.

The useful article exclusion from copyright protection and the drawing/useful art distinction discussed above derive from the Court's patent/copyright distinction.[179] Some blank form cases have also invoked the patent/copyright distinction from *Baker*. In *Brown Instrument Co. v. Warner*, for example, the court upheld the Copyright Office's refusal to register 83 charts that Brown had designed for use with various machines to record data.[180] The court explained:

> Both law and policy forbid monopolizing a machine except within the comparatively narrow limits of the patent system. In several patents on recording machines, the necessary printed chart is rightly claimed as one of the operative elements. Since the machines that cooperate with the charts in suit are useless without them, to copyright the charts would in effect continue the appellant's monopoly of its machines beyond the time authorized by the patent law.[181]

The court in *Brown* drew this principle from *Baker*.

Over time, *Baker*'s patent/copyright distinction has been questioned and qualified to some extent. The Court did not find this distinction useful, for example, in its 1954 *Mazer v. Stein* decision as applied to copyright and design patent subject matters.[182] Stein was the creator of

---

[178] *See, e.g.*, Bibbero Systems, Inc. v. Colwell Systems, Inc., 893 F.2d 1104 (9th Cir. 1990).

[179] *See, e.g.*, National Cloak & Suit Co. v. Standard Mail Order, 191 F. 528 (S.D.N.Y. 1911) ("a manufacturer of unpatented articles cannot practically monopolize their sale by copyrighting a catalog containing illustrations of them").

[180] 161 F.2d 910 (D.C. Cir. 1947). *See also* Taylor Instrument Co. v. Fawley Brost Co., 139 F.2d 98 (7th Cir. 1943).

[181] *Brown Instrument*, 161 F.2d at 911.

[182] 347 U.S. 201 (1954).

several statuettes, which he registered as original works of art. Thereafter, Stein mass-produced copies of the statuettes to serve as lamp bases. After competitors copied the lamps, Stein sued them for copyright infringement. The defendants challenged the validity of Stein's copyrights, arguing that the lamp bases were unprotectable utilitarian articles, not protectable works of art.[183] Because Stein could have, but had not, obtained design patent protection for the statuette-lamp bases, Mazer et al., argued the statuette-lamp bases were ineligible for copyright protection.[184]

The Supreme Court upheld the validity of Stein's copyrights. Neither the mass-production of the statuettes nor their use as lamp bases disqualified them from copyright protection.[185] The Court's response to Mazer's patent/copyright exclusivity argument was that "[n]either the Copyright Statute nor any other says that because a thing is patentable it may not be copyrighted."[186] While this statement is literally correct, the useful article limitation on copyright protection for pictorial, graphic and sculptural works has averted conflicts between patents and copyrights in such works.

Insofar as *Baker* posits an intellectual property universe in which some intellectual creations (original writings) are the subject matter of copyrights and others (inventive useful arts) are the subject matter of patents, it seems oversimplistic. This framework assumes that an intellectual creation is either a writing or a useful art (and can't be both at the same time), and that once its nature has been discerned, the innovation can be consigned to the appropriate legal regime.

Some intellectual creations, however, do not readily conform to this model.[187] Computer programs, for example, are "machine[s] whose medium of construction happens to be text."[188] Computer program code is routinely protected by copyright law as an original work of authorship. Although programmers do not generally seek patents for computer program code, the Court of Appeals for the Federal Circuit would almost

---

183 The defendants relied on *Baker* for this proposition. They also argued that the statuettes were not works of art because they had been mass-produced.

184 The defendants drew this principle from *Baker* as well.

185 The statuettes were not operational parts of the lamp, but rather ornamental features. *Baker* recognized that copyright was appropriate for ornamental designs that appealed to taste. *Baker*, 101 U.S. at 103.

186 *Mazer*, 347 U.S. at 217. Design patents are available for original and inventive ornamental designs for articles of manufacture. *See* 35 U.S.C. § 171.

187 Some innovations—for example, mathematical formulas and scientific methods—may fall outside both patent and copyright subject matters.

188 Pamela Samuelson, et al., *A Manifesto on the Legal Protection of Computer Programs*, 94 Colum. L. Rev. 2308, 2320 (1994).

certainly regard code as patentable subject matter.[189] Since the mid–1980's, many patents have issued for functional design elements of programs, such as efficient algorithms or data structures, yet some cases and commentators regard structural designs of programs as protectable by copyright law.[190] The practical effect of patents on functional designs in programs is to limit the ability of subsequent programmers to embody the patented functionality in independently written machine-executable code. Intellectual property lawyers differ in their views about the extent to which (if at all) there is overlap in what copyright and patent protect in computer programs and the consequences of overlap.[191]

The Idea/Expression Distinction

Copyright cases and treatises predating *Baker* recognized the protectability of authorial expression and the unprotectability of ideas.[192] So, the idea/expression distinction is not wholly original to *Baker*. *Baker* does, however, contain powerful statements of this distinction. After *Baker*, it became more common to inquire whether the defendant copied the plaintiff/author's expression or her ideas, rather than whether the defendant had copied a material part of the plaintiff's work.[193] Yet, citations to *Baker* for the idea/expression distinction were relatively infrequent prior to the Supreme Court's decision in *Mazer v. Stein*. The Court in *Mazer* characterized *Baker* as an idea/expression case, saying that it had held "that a copyrighted book on a peculiar system of bookkeeping was not infringed by a similar book using a similar plan which achieved similar results where the alleged infringer made a different arrangement of the columns and used different headings."[194]

---

189 *See, e.g.,* In re Beauregard, 53 F.3d 1583 (Fed. Cir. 1995) (software on floppy disk as patentable subject matter). *See also* Maureen A. O'Rourke, The Story of *Diamond v. Diehr*: Toward Patenting Software, elsewhere in this Volume.

190 *See, e.g.,* Whelan Associates v. Jaslow Dental Labs., 797 F.2d 1222 (3d Cir. 1986) (taking a broad view of copyright protection for program structure); *cf.* Lloyd Weinreb, *Copyright for Functional Expression*, 111 Harv. L. Rev. 1149 (1998) (arguing against copyright protection for program structure); *see also infra* notes 205–17 and accompanying text.

191 *See, e.g.,* Pamela Samuelson, *Survey on the Patent/Copyright Interface for Computer Programs*, 17 AIPLA Q.J. 256 (1989) (showing divergence of opinion on the roles that patent and copyright law should play in the protection of program innovations); Dennis S. Karjala, *Distinguishing Patent and Copyright Subject Matter,* 35 Conn. L. Rev. 439 (2003) (suggesting method for distinguishing patent and copyright subject matters).

192 The *Drone* treatise, which was published, the year before *Baker*, discusses caselaw concerning the unprotectability of ideas and the protectability of expression. Drone at 93, 385.

193 *See, e.g.,* Simms v. Stanton, 75 F. 6, 10 (C.C.N.D. Cal. 1896).

194 *Mazer*, 347 U.S. at 217.

The *Nimmer* treatise interpreted *Mazer* as having narrowed the ruling in *Baker* to its statement of the idea/expression distinction.[195] Perhaps owing to the influence of Nimmer's treatise, *Baker* is now best known as an idea/expression case.

Idea/Expression Merger

The idea/expression merger doctrine is sometimes attributed to *Baker*.[196] The *Baker* opinion arguably supports this proposition by saying that "where the art [a work] teaches cannot be used without employing the methods and diagrams used to illustrate the book, or such as are similar to them, such methods and diagrams are to be considered as necessary incidents to the art, and given therewith to the public."[197] However, the merger doctrine did not begin to emerge until the late 1950's and did not reach its apogee until 1983.[198]

Herbert Rosenthal Jewelry Corp. v. Kalpakian[199] was among the cases in this period that considered what copyright law should do when there was only one or a small number of ways to effectively express certain ideas. Rosenthal manufactured a line of gold pins in the shape of a bee encrusted with jewels. When Kalpakian began selling jeweled bees that were very similar to Rosenthal's, Rosenthal sued his competitor for copyright infringement. Kalpakian's main defense was that he drew his design from nature. The Ninth Circuit ruled that Rosenthal's copyrights were invalid because "[t]here is no greater similarity between the pins of plaintiffs and defendants than is inevitable from the use of jewel-encrusted bee forms in both."[200] When an idea and its expression "are thus inseparable, copying the 'expression' will not be barred since protecting the expression would confer a monopoly of the 'idea' upon the copyright owner free of the conditions and limitations imposed by patent law."[201]

---

195 NIMMER, *supra*, § 2.18 [D](1).

196 *See, e.g., Kern River*, 899 F.2d at 1463–64.

197 *Baker*, 101 U.S. at 103.

198 *See, e.g.*, Continental Casualty Co. v. Beardsley, 151 F.Supp. 28 (S.D.N.Y. 1957) (no infringement despite similarities in forms providing blanket indemnity for replacement of lost stock certificates); Morrissey v. Procter & Gamble Co., 379 F.2d 675, 678–79 (1st Cir. 1967) (sweepstakes contest rules uncopyrightable); Apple Computer, Inc. v. Franklin Computer, Inc., 714 F.2d 1240 (3d Cir. 1983).

199 446 F.2d 738 (9th Cir. 1971).

200 *Id.* at 742.

201 *Id.*

The merger doctrine, as such and so named, emerged in *Apple Computer, Inc. v. Franklin Computer Corp.*[202] in response to a *Baker*-inspired challenge to the copyrightability of machine-executable forms of Apple's operating system programs. Franklin argued that *Baker* forbade granting copyright protection to useful arts, such as machines and machine processes.[203] Apple's programs were, Franklin observed, virtual machines as well as machine processes.

The Third Circuit upheld the validity of Apple's copyrights and found them infringed by Franklin's exact copying of the Apple code. The court regarded Congress as having decided to protect machine-executable forms of programs by copyright law. It construed *Baker* as denying protection to machine-executable programs only when there was a merger of idea and expression so that it was impossible for firms such as Franklin to write independently created programs to perform the same functions as the Apple programs.[204]

The Third Circuit extended its merger-based analysis of computer program copyrights and its narrow interpretation of *Baker* in *Whelan Associates v. Jaslow Dental Labs*.[205] Whelan charged Jaslow with copying the structure, sequence and organization ("SSO") of her dental laboratory programs. Jaslow claimed that program SSO was not protectable by copyright law because it constituted methods and processes that were unprotectable under *Baker* and section 102(b) of U.S. copyright law. The Third Circuit disagreed, in part because it regarded computer programs as "literary works" under the statute. Since copyright law protects the SSO of other literary works, the court reasoned that program SSO should also be protected. It also endorsed a merger-based test for software copyright infringement, under which programmers would be liable for copyright infringement if they copied SSO from another program unless there was only one or a very small number of ways to structure a program of that sort.[206]

Limited Scope for Functional Writings

Since 1992, *Baker* has been reinvigorated by a series of decisions taking a much narrower view than *Whelan* of the scope of copyright

---

[202] 714 F.2d 1240 (3d Cir. 1983).

[203] The trial court found Franklin's *Baker*-inspired defense convincing. *See* Apple Computer, Inc. v. Franklin Computer Corp., 545 F.Supp. 812 (E.D. Pa. 1982).

[204] *Apple*, 714 F.2d at 1253. *See* also Apple Computer, Inc. v. Formula Int'l, Inc., 725 F.2d 521, 524 (9th Cir. 1984).

[205] 797 F.2d 1222 (3d Cir. 1986).

[206] *Id.* at 1234–45. The merger doctrine has also been applied in other kinds of copyright cases. *See, e.g., Kern River*, 899 F.2d at 1463–64 (gas pipeline map).

protection in functional writings, such as computer programs.[207] *Computer Associates Int'l v. Altai, Inc.* initiated this trend with its criticism of *Whelan* for its overbroad interpretation of the scope of protection for computer programs.[208] The Second Circuit cited *Baker* in holding that functional design elements of computer programs, such as program-to-program interfaces, were not protectable by copyright law.[209] It directed courts to assess whether elements of programs that defendants may have copied were constrained by external factors, dictated by efficiency, or were standard programming ideas. If so, these similarities were to be filtered out before courts made a determination as to whether the defendant's program infringed.[210] *Altai* has displaced *Whelan* as the standard framework of analysis of the proper scope of copyright protection for computer programs.[211]

Although *Altai* relied on *Baker* for key principles, it, like *Whelan*, did not attempt to give content to the *Baker*-inspired "process, procedure, system, method of operation" limitations in section 102(b). The most notable post-*Altai* case to apply these limitations was the First Circuit in *Lotus Dev. Corp. v. Borland Int'l.*[212] Lotus charged Borland with copyright infringement because it copied the command hierarchy of the Lotus 1–2–3 program in an emulation mode of its competing spreadsheet program. Borland argued that this hierarchy constituted an unprotectable functional system or method under *Baker* and section 102(b) because the hierarchy was indispensable to users' ability to construct compatible "macros" for commonly used sequences of operations. The First Circuit, invoking section 102(b) and *Baker*, decided that Lotus' command hierarchy was an unprotectable method of operating a computer to perform spreadsheet functions.[213]

---

207 The *Whelan* analysis was initially influential in other computer program cases. *See, e.g.*, Johnson Controls, Inc. v. Phoenix Control Sys., Inc., 886 F.2d 1173, 1175 (9th Cir. 1989); Lotus Dev. Corp. v. Paperback Software Int'l, 740 F. Supp. 37, 67 (D. Mass. 1990).

208 982 F.2d 693, 705–06 (2d Cir. 1992).

209 *Id.* at 703–04.

210 *Id.* at 707–11.

211 *See, e.g., Pamela Samuelson,* Brief Amicus Curiae of Copyright Law Professors in Lotus Development Corp. v. Borland Int'l, Inc., 3 J. Intell. Prop. L. 103, 121–24 (1995) (brief to U.S. Supreme Court discussing influence of *Altai*).

212 49 F.3d 807 (1st Cir. 1995).

213 *Borland*, 49 F.3d at 815–17. The Supreme Court accepted Lotus' petition for certiorari, but shortly after the oral argument, the Court affirmed the First Circuit's ruling by an equally divided vote. Lotus Dev. Corp. v. Borland Int'l, Inc., 516 U.S. 233 (1996). Thirty-four copyright professors argued to the Court that the Lotus command hierarchy was unprotectable under section 102(b) because it was a fundamental part of the functionality of the Lotus macro system. *See* Borland Brief, *supra* note 211, at 131 (relying on *Baker*).

Sega Enterprises Ltd. v. Accolade, Inc. sought to ensure that copyright law would not indirectly protect functional elements of programs.[214] Reverse engineering of program code for purposes such as getting access to functional design elements of programs, such as interfaces, was held to be fair use. The court observed that "[i]f disassembly of copyrighted object code is per se an unfair use, the owner of the copyright gains a de facto monopoly over the functional aspects of his work—aspects that were expressly denied copyright protection by Congress,"[215] citing section 102(b). The court went on to say that "to enjoy a lawful monopoly over the idea or functional principle underlying a work, the creator of the work must satisfy the more stringent standards imposed by the patent laws."[216] Although the Ninth Circuit did not cite *Baker* for this proposition, the statement resonates with the Court's decision in *Baker*. The Ninth Circuit also agreed with *Altai* that functional works such as computer programs and those describing bookkeeping systems were entitled, as *Baker* had long ago held, to only "thin" protection from copyright law.[217] Other cases have followed *Sega*, although some controversy still exists about the proper scope of copyright protection for computer programs and the extent to which *Baker* limits the scope of copyright for functional writings.[218]

Conclusion

Baker v. Selden was a watershed case in the history of American copyright law. Although the distinction between expression and ideas was long-standing in copyright law, the Court's decision in *Baker* affected how courts interpreted this rule thereafter because it directed courts to focus more precisely on what the defendant had actually copied from the plaintiff's work. Copying ideas or useful arts, even when embodied in copyrighted works, was fair game as a matter of copyright law, although copying an author's explanation or illustration of those ideas or useful arts was not. This rule applied even if the most valuable aspect of an author's work—such as Selden's bookkeeping system—was the useful art itself. The Court perceived in the lower court ruling in *Baker* and in *Drury v. Ewing* a deep confusion about the nature of copyright and of patent law and the respective roles of these laws in the protection of intellectual creations. It sought to dispel this confusion by making a sharp distinction between copyright and patent subject matters and

---

214 977 F.2d 1510, 1527–28 (9th Cir. 1992).

215 *Id.* at 1526.

216 *Id.*

217 *Id.* at 1524.

218 *See, e.g., Symposium, Toward a Third Intellectual Property Paradigm*, 94 COLUM. L. REV. 2307 (1994).

giving numerous examples to illustrate this distinction. Courts in subsequent cases have generally followed *Baker* in this and several other respects, as the review of *Baker*'s legacy has shown.

This Story of Baker and Selden illustrates why copyright law should allow second comers such as *Baker* to build upon a first author's work, or put another way, why authors of functional writings should not have too much control over subsequent adaptations of their work. Selden's forms may have been a substantial improvement over the old-fashioned bookkeeping system previously used in Ohio, but they represented only one stage in the evolving art of bookkeeping. Selden's death meant that any further innovation in this field would have to come from others. Baker advanced the state of the art when he realized that county officials wanted to keep closer track of accounts than Selden's forms permitted. Baker's forms accommodated this interest which is probably why Baker attracted more customers than Selden did. When Mrs. Selden challenged him as a pirate, Baker not only stood his ground, but also continued to improve his system and to write additional books explaining the principles of bookkeeping, thereby contributing to the growth of knowledge in this important field. Had Mrs. Selden prevailed, further improvements to the "art" of bookkeeping might well have been thwarted until Selden's copyrights expired. This outcome would have disserved both patent and copyright goals because it would have slowed progress in the useful art of bookkeeping and would even have impeded fellow bookkeepers from explaining better than Selden had how to use his eponymous system.

The Story of *Diamond v. Diehr*: Toward Patenting Software

Maureen A. O'Rourke[1]

Introduction

In balancing the costs and benefits of granting exclusive rights, intellectual property systems and those who create them inevitably face the question of how to define the subject matter eligible for protection. Patent law, which grants broad exclusive rights to inventors, has historically not considered basic truths patentable subject matter. Granting one person exclusive rights in fundamental truths imposes large costs on society by imposing a "tax" on all (likely many) who seek to use that truth. On the other hand, granting exclusive rights in an application of a basic truth in a particular context likely costs much less, and may even be necessary to induce innovation. But how do a general purpose statute and the administrative agency and courts interpreting it strike the appropriate balance?

In patent law, this question has bedeviled the Patent & Trademark Office (PTO) and the courts for years, particularly in the field of software. The Patent Act includes new, useful, and nonobvious processes within its scope. At first glance then, computer programs, as particular kinds of processes, appear to be patentable subject matter. Over the years, though, the PTO and the Supreme Court developed a line of reasoning that suggested they were not, in part because programs were considered algorithms: mathematical algorithms (as basic principles) fall outside the scope of the Patent Act because their protection, particularly under the broad exclusive rights of patent law, would simply be too costly to society, hewing perilously close to protecting basic truths.

Software also challenged the intellectual property system for another reason. Although certain items might qualify for protection under

---

[1] I owe thanks to James Diehr, the inventor of the process litigated in the case, for talking to me about the invention and his recollections, Andrew Heinz, Zara Kyasky, Michelle Park and Raquel Ortiz for research assistance, and Rochelle Cooper Dreyfuss and Jane Ginsburg for thoughtful comments and editing assistance. For an excellent article that summarizes the development of the law both pre-and post-*Diehr*, *see* Pamela Samuelson, *Benson Revisited: The Case Against Patent Protection for Algorithms and Other Computer Program–Related Inventions*, 39 Emory L.J. 1025 (1990).

both the copyright and patent laws, generally the subject matter provisions of the statutes channel protection of expressive works to copyright law and utilitarian works to patent law.[2] Software combines the expressive (the actual programming code) and the utilitarian (the function the code performs), making it difficult to identify the appropriate mode of protection. Yet because software requires a great deal of investment for its production and may be easily copied once released, it requires some incentive for its production. The debate over the appropriate scheme of protection to provide that incentive has continued through most of the industry's history.

As time passed and software assumed increasing economic importance, it was inevitable that cases would continue to arise until the Supreme Court had enunciated a set of principles for distinguishing patentable and unpatentable subject matter in the area. The case of *Diamond v. Diehr*,[3] although not a recent decision, represents the Court's last consideration of what constitutes patentable subject matter in the context of computer programs. Although the Court's decision could have been interpreted narrowly to permit patenting software as an element of a claim directed toward a traditional industrial process that transforms matter, the lower courts, most notably the Federal Circuit, have interpreted *Diehr* in a way that favors including software itself as patentable subject matter. The practical effect of the decision as interpreted, then, has had a major impact on intellectual property protection in the computer industry.

The Background

Software and its Challenges

Understanding how *Diehr*, a case about a process for curing rubber, became an important software patenting case requires first understanding both why software presented difficult challenges for the law and how both the law and the industry attempted to address those challenges.

Any function implemented in hardware (physical objects like microchips and circuit boards) can also be implemented in software (instructions stored electronically on a physical media that, when run, direct the action of the hardware) or firmware (software physically encoded on a memory chip), and vice versa.[4] "[S]oftware is a machine whose medium of construction happens to be text."[5] The less functionality in hardware

---

[2] *See* Pamela Samuelson, The Story of *Baker v. Selden*: Sharpening the Distinction Between Authorship and Invention, elsewhere in this Volume.

[3] 450 U.S. 175 (1981).

[4] For definitions, see http://www.webopedia.com (last visited Dec. 5, 2004).

[5] Pamela Samuelson et al., *A Manifesto Concerning the Legal Protection of Computer Programs*, 94 COLUM. L. REV. 2308, 2320 (1994).

or firmware, the more versatile the computer is because it can run different types of software to perform a variety of functions. Engineers and programmers decide how to implement functionality based on the state of technology as well as the relative costs of their design choices.

Software combines literal text and functionality in a particular way. Its value inheres not so much in the literal source code the programmer writes (or the object code the machine understands) as in the tasks it performs when the object code runs on a computer.[6] One programmer can implement the same functionality in the same way as another without copying either the original program's design or code.[7] Improvements in software tend to be incremental and cumulative in nature, and to function effectively, one program often needs information about another.[8] For example, anyone who would like to write a spreadsheet program that runs successfully on Microsoft's Windows operating system would need to know and utilize information about that operating system.

If, as stated above, functionality can be implemented in either hardware or software, and machines are clearly patentable subject matter, then it seems both logical and non-controversial that software would also be considered patentable subject matter. Indeed, in *In re Bernhart* in 1969, the Court of Customs and Patent Appeals (CCPA) adopted that view:

> [W]e say that if a machine is programmed in a certain new and unobvious way, it is physically different from the machine without that program; its memory elements are differently arranged. The fact that these physical changes are invisible to the eye should not tempt us to conclude that the machine has not been changed. If a new machine has not been invented, certainly a "new and useful improvement" of the unprogrammed machine has been, and Congress has said in 35 U.S.C. 101 that such improvements are statutory subject matter for a patent.[9]

The CCPA never made much use of this logic after *Bernhart*. The PTO and courts instead began to focus on both administrative concerns like a lack of qualified Examiners, and substantive ones as well. The PTO and courts worried at least implicitly that software patents would come too close to protecting basic truths or at least rudimentary building blocks necessary for further progress in the field. This could frustrate innovation immensely in an industry characterized by incremental, cumulative invention. Another, unstated but likely concern, was whether

---

[6] *Id.* at 2316–18.

[7] *See generally id.* at 2315–16.

[8] *See id.* at 2330–32.

[9] 417 F.2d 1395, 1400 (C.C.P.A. 1969).

patent had a place in protecting software in light of protection already or potentially available under trade secret and copyright law.

The Early History of Software Patenting in the PTO and CCPA

In the early 1960s, the PTO faced increasing numbers of complex applications in new technological areas and prior art that had become difficult to manage.[10] Against this backdrop, the 1965 President's Commission on the Patent System suggested that Congress amend the Act to exclude specifically computer programs from statutory subject matter whether an applicant claimed the program as an article, process, or machine.[11] The Commission expressed concern that the Office lacked an appropriate classification technique and prior art which would enable it effectively to process software applications, and also implied that the incentive of a patent was not needed to induce software innovation.[12]

Precedent also supported the proposition that software was not patentable subject matter. An early Supreme Court decision, *Cochrane v. Deener*, had construed the term "process" in the patent law context to mean "a mode of treatment of certain materials to produce a given result [, . . .] an act, or a series of acts, performed upon the subject-matter to be transformed and reduced to a different state or thing."[13] This definition emphasized a physical transformation of matter, which software does not implicate at least in a traditional sense.

Additionally, well before computer programs became a controversial area, the PTO Board of Appeals and the CCPA, which, prior to the establishment of the Federal Circuit, had authority to review PTO decisions, had developed the doctrine of "mental steps," which they used to evaluate process claims. The notion was that processes that could be performed in the mind were not patentable, and the doctrine as applied

---

10 President's Commission on the Patent System, "To Promote the Progress of. . . useful arts" in an age of exploding technology, Report to the Senate Judiciary Committee 2, S. Doc. No. 5, 90th Cong., 1st sess. (1967) (noting also that "a substantial number of applications have a period of pendency of five to ten years or more"). In 1964, the PTO Board of Appeals seemed at least somewhat receptive to considering software inventions that properly claimed novel subject matter patentable, indicating that it might consider a general purpose computer running a program to be patentable as, in effect, a special purpose computer. *Ex parte King*, 146 U.S.P.Q. 590, 591 (PTO Bd. App. 1965) ("[I]f the difference between a general purpose computer and the claims to a special purpose computer can be supplied by merely placing a suitable program in a general purpose machine then the examiner would deny a patent even thought the art contained no suggestion for the preparation of such a program. We do not agree."); Samuelson, *supra* note 1, at 1039 & n.42.

11 President's Commission on the Patent System, *supra* note 10, at 12.

12 *Id.* at 13.

13 94 U.S. 780, 788 (1876).

focused on refusing patent protection to claims directed to data collection and analysis.[14] The mental steps doctrine in part represented a fear that permitting the patenting of processes that could be performed in the mind would be too costly to society by effectively granting exclusive rights in basic truths.[15] In the 1960s, after much debate, the PTO adopted Guidelines that reflected the doctrine of mental steps, leading it generally to reject software applications as not drawn to statutory subject matter.[16]

The Guidelines were, however, short-lived, because the CCPA took a different tack. Generally, the CCPA was more receptive than the PTO to granting patents on inventions involving software. In part, this difference of opinion reflected concerns about resources. The PTO worried about an inability to cope with increasing numbers of applications and to determine novelty and non-obviousness reliably, all concerns it had raised with and that influenced the President's Commission. The CCPA was arguably more concerned with substantive issues than administrative problems.

Its decisions, however, were unclear and inconsistent. The CCPA did use the mental steps doctrine for a time, but limited it. It held that the doctrine permitted the patenting of claims limited to a machine implementation of a process, and also that the law did not require that a process transform matter as a condition of patentability.[17] As noted above, in *In re Bernhart*, the court stated that a programmed computer could be patentable as a machine or an improvement over the unprogrammed computer.[18] By 1970, the CCPA repudiated the mental steps doctrine, adopting a broad view of patentable subject matter: "We cannot agree ... that ... claims ... are directed to non-statutory processes merely because some or all the steps therein can also be carried out in ... the human mind.... All that is necessary ... is that [a process] be in the technological arts."[19]

---

[14] Samuelson, *supra* note 1, at 1034–36.

[15] *Id.* at 1036 & n.34 (noting also that other reasons for the mental steps doctrine might include, *inter alia*, that such inventions: (i) are not part of the "technological arts;" and (ii) do not need the incentive of a patent to induce their invention).

[16] The Guidelines provided that computer programs were not patentable unless combined in a novel and nonobvious way to produce a physical result. *Id.* at 1040.

[17] *See In re* Prater, 415 F.2d 1378 (C.C.P.A. 1968) (*Prater I*), *rev'd in part,* 415 F.2d 1393 (C.C.P.A. 1969) (*Prater II*). The PTO petitioned for rehearing because the *Prater I* decision was at odds with the PTO's view of the law. *Prater II* used less expansive language and essentially addressed a different issue (the adequacy of the disclosure) but did note that a patentable process need not operate "physically upon substances." *Prater II*, 415 F.2d at 1403.

[18] *In re* Bernhart, 417 F.2d 1395, 1400 (C.C.P.A. 1969).

[19] *In re* Musgrave, 431 F.2d 882, 893 (C.C.P.A. 1970).

One way to view the differing approaches of the PTO and CCPA is as an argument over the most appropriate way to avoid granting rights in basic principles or, at least, in processes the Office could not reliably verify as novel and/or non-obvious. The PTO's approach, consistent with a mindset directed toward limiting the expenses of the Office and to avoid granting patents in error, was to bar patentability at the outset by rejecting applications for lack of statutory subject matter. The CCPA's approach, in contrast, was to recognize programs as patentable subject matter so long as the claims were limited to particular machine implementations.

Developments in the Industry, and in Trade Secret and Copyright Law

While the PTO and CCPA were engaging in a tug of war over the contours of computer program patentability, the computer industry also debated the appropriate means of protection for software. In the early days of mainframe distribution, manufacturers relied primarily on contract and trade secrecy protection to safeguard their source code.[20] Transactions were relatively few, allowing firms to obtain signed written agreements with their customers that included provisions intended to ensure confidentiality.[21]

During the 1960s, hardware manufacturers viewed software primarily as a means to enhance the demand for and revenues associated with their hardware, rather than as a profit-making product in its own right. They provided their customers with tools to permit them to write application programs, and encouraged them to share their solutions with each other.[22] Companies devoted primarily to writing software eventually developed to meet the needs of those customers who did not have an in-house department devoted to programming.[23] In 1969, IBM announced it would "unbundle" its software from the hardware, charging separately

---

20 Samuelson, *A Manifesto, supra* note 5, at 2373 ("Initially, software was delivered physically with a mainframe machine during the installation and acceptance process. Given the high cost and relative infrequency of the transactions involved in buying a mainframe, traditional contract and trade secrecy law provided sufficient protection for innovation.").

21 *See id.*

22 W. Edward Steinmueller, *The U.S. Software Industry: An Analysis and Interpretive History* 21–23, *in* THE INTERNATIONAL COMPUTER SOFTWARE INDUSTRY (David C. Mowery ed. 1996); *see also* H.W.A.M. HANNEMAN, THE PATENTABILITY OF COMPUTER SOFTWARE 35–36 (Kluwer Law and Taxation Publishers 1985).

23 *See* Steinmuller, *supra* note 22, at 23 (noting that by 1965 the market for software and services totaled around $500 million, with much of that total going to " 'service bureaus,' companies that specialized in developing applications software such as payroll

for each.[24] This further opened the market for independent software vendors, allowing them to develop applications for IBM mainframes that would compete with those of IBM itself. The introduction of smaller computers in the mid–1970s also expanded market opportunities for software firms.

As software production and distribution grew, firms sought protection beyond that offered by contract and trade secrecy law. They began registering object code with the Copyright Office under the 1909 Copyright Act, refusing to register source code for fear of losing whatever trade secrets remained therein. The Copyright Office accepted the registrations under its "Rule of Doubt:" It would issue a registration certificate indicating the Office's inability to determine the existence of copyrightable authorship.[25]

In 1975, President Gerald Ford appointed a National Commission on New Technological Uses of Copyrighted Works (CONTU), charged, in part, with considering the applicability of copyright law to computer programs.[26] In its report, CONTU concluded that copyright protection of programs was appropriate, and recommended legislation that Congress adopted in 1980.[27] The Commission and legislation left open a number of questions regarding the scope of copyright protection, including, for example, the extent to which copyright would protect a program's design as distinct from the literal code.

The industry generally accepted and even applauded copyright protection for software.[28] It was, however, divided in its view of patent

systems and selling information processing services to other, usually small, companies"); *see also* HANNEMAN, *supra* note 22.

[24] Steinmueller, *supra* note 22, at 24–25 (identifying three events as key to the development of independent software vendors: (i) introduction of IBM's System/360 family, a range of hardware which used the same operating system, allowing users to migrate software from machine to machine as their needs changed; (ii) IBM's unbundling; and (iii) development of the mini-computer industry).

[25] U.S. Congress, Office of Technology Assessment, *Finding a Balance: Computer Software, Intellectual Property, and the Challenge of Technological Change, OTA–TCT–527 at 66* (Washington, D.C.: U.S. Government Printing Office, May 1992), *available at* http://www.wws.princeton.edu/cgi-bin/byteserv.prl/?ota/disk1/1992/9215/921501.PDF (last visited Sept. 27, 2004) [hereinafter OTA Rep.] (describing the rule of doubt procedure).

[26] 5 COPYRIGHT, CONGRESS AND TECHNOLOGY: THE PUBLIC RECORD–CONTU'S FINAL REPORT AND RECOMMENDATIONS 3–6 (Nicholas Henry ed., 1980) (detailing the history of the Commission's formation).

[27] *Id.* at 22–27 (setting forth recommendations). The statutory changes consisted of adding a definition of "computer program" to § 101 of the 1976 Act and replacing § 117. *Id.* at 23.

[28] *See* Martin Goetz, *Memoirs of a Software Pioneer: Part 2*, 24 IEEE ANNALS OF THE HISTORY OF COMPUTING 14, 22 (2002) (noting "[t]here was little controversy over the copyrighting of computer programs").

protection. At the time of *Diehr*, hardware manufacturers worried that if software were patented and thus less freely available, the demand for and revenues associated with their hardware could decline. Although some software developers likely welcomed the added protection, others were concerned that they could not afford to seek patent protection or compete with those who could, and that copyright and trade secret protection sufficed and did not restrict software availability and market competition in the same way that patent law might.

The Invention[29]

In 1970, Federal Mogul Corp. hired chemical engineer James Diehr as the plant chemist for its Van Wert, Ohio plant. Federal Mogul manufactured a number of products including synthetic rubber seals and O-rings. Around the time it hired Diehr, the company was also working with consultants charged with breaking down the rubber molding process into its component parts with the goal of establishing standards for each segment of the process.

Rubber must be processed before it can become a usable product. Charles Goodyear discovered—and patented—the process of vulcanization, also known as "cure," in which rubber latex and sulfur could be processed into a finished product.[30] Later research helped illuminate the chemical reactions involved in cure.[31] Before being molded, the mix is soft and elastic. It is comprised of chemical compounds called polymers, large chains of repeating molecules.[32] Curing uses an agent—often sulfur—to link these long chains, hardening the mixture. The degree of hardness and elasticity of the final rubber product depends on how far the polymers are allowed to react with the sulfur.[33]

A key step in the process is the molding of the rubber in a heated press for a period of time. This segment of the process was particularly troublesome in part because the sizes and shapes of the rubber as well as the temperature of the press varied, making it difficult to determine how long the rubber should remain in it. The general approach was to leave the rubber in the press for a time lengthy enough to cure the entire product. This resulted in a large number of defects, particularly over-

---

[29] Most of the information in this section derives from the author's conversation with James R. Diehr, the inventor of the process.

[30] Brief for Respondent at 8, Diamond v. Diehr, 450 U.S. 175 (1981) (No. 79–1112), 1980 WL 339342.

[31] *Id.*

[32] *Id.*

[33] *See generally id.*; *see also generally* Learnchem.net, *available at* http://www.learnchem.net/glossary/u.shtml (last visited Sept. 18, 2004) (defining vulcanization).

cured products. Additionally, the press would be in use longer than necessary for each cure, and also often occupied by the re-processing of defective products.

The consultants asked Diehr, then in his twenties, a sensible question: why does Federal Mogul cure all of its parts for the same length of time and at the same temperature when the parts vary widely in size? Diehr, still a relatively new employee, gave the honest answer—because the company's Materials group said to do so. Ted Lutton, Diehr's boss, thought that if the company could develop relationships among time, temperature, and thickness, it could improve its molding process substantially. He assigned this task to Diehr.

It took between six and nine months for Diehr to develop a concept and generate and test the relationships among the variables. He found that the relationship was governed by an equation first formulated by Svante Arrhenius in 1889. However, repetitive calculations were necessary because of the variable temperature in the mold, and Diehr found it impractical to monitor continually the cure time and operate the press manually.

Computerization of the calculation and constant monitoring of temperature was a logical next step. Additionally, automation would allow Diehr to build a database containing information associated with different formulations and batches of rubber. Diehr worked with a consultant from IBM and, using an IBM System 7 and a thermocouple,[34] automated the process, and installed it on four presses. Developing the computer solution took approximately one year. Later, he expanded the installation to 50–60 presses, and moved to Federal Mogul's group headquarters to help install the system in other plants.

According to Diehr as well as to Federal Mogul's filings in the litigation, the process gave Federal Mogul a significant competitive advantage. It allowed Federal Mogul to increase the productivity of its mold presses because it helped avoid over-curing errors, thus freeing the presses to do more work. The new process resulted in a 20% increase in productivity and a savings of at least $25,000,000 over a six year period.[35] Diehr received $1 which he claims he still has for his assignment of the patent that eventually issued to Federal Mogul. To the best of Diehr's recollection, the company never licensed the patent. It had no interest in assisting its direct competitors, and others, like some tire manufacturers, did not want to invest in a license.

---

[34] A thermocouple is a temperature sensor that operates by measuring the voltage produced at the junction of two metals. Two dissimilar metals produce a predictable voltage when joined.

[35] Brief for Respondent at 6, Diamond v. Diehr, 450 U.S. 175 (1981) (No. 79–1112), 1980 WL 339342.

The Case

When Diehr met with Federal Mogul's patent attorneys, they were somewhat leery about applying for a patent, expressing concern that the PTO might be hostile to the application as claiming software. Indeed, Diehr recalls that initially the PTO rejected the application for just that reason—a result that was not surprising in light of the law at the time.

Supreme Court Precedent—Benson and Flook

Gottschalk v. Benson and its aftermath

In fact, *Diehr* was not the first time the Supreme Court had faced the question of patents in the computer field. In 1972, in *Gottschalk v. Benson*,[36] the Court addressed the patentability of a process for converting numbers from one form into another for use on any general purpose computer. The Court was clearly concerned that permitting the patent would provide the patentee with broad rights over a basic formula. The process as claimed would "wholly pre-empt the mathematical formula and in practical effect would be a patent on the algorithm itself."[37] The Court defined an algorithm as "[a] procedure for solving a given type of mathematical problem."[38] Patenting an algorithm in the abstract would be the equivalent of patenting an idea, and would impose unacceptable costs on society. The Court described the "clue" to the patent eligibility of process claims not including particular machines as the "[t]ransformation and reduction of an article 'to a different state or thing.' "[39] It did not rely explicitly on the doctrine of mental steps that the CCPA had rejected earlier. The Court's reasoning, however, is consistent with the mental steps doctrine, and, indeed, it mentioned that "mental processes ... are not patentable, as they are the basic tools of scientific and technological work."[40]

The *Benson* decision's emphasis on the unpatentability of mathematical algorithms re-focused the debate at the PTO and CCPA levels. Before *Benson*, neither entity had made "more than an incidental use of the word 'algorithm' in discussing ... patentability issue[s]."[41] After *Benson*, the question whether a claim recited an algorithm often became the central issue. Unfortunately, the focus on algorithms, while reflecting the important underlying policy concern of not patenting basic

---

36 409 U.S. 63 (1972).

37 *Id.* at 72.

38 *Id.* at 65.

39 *Id.* at 70.

40 *Id.* at 67.

41 Samuelson, *supra* note 1, at 1043.

truths, raised difficult line-drawing problems. While the Court's focus in *Benson* seemed to be on mathematical algorithms, suggesting that some patentable non-mathematical algorithms existed, computer scientists would likely disagree: "All computer programs are mathematical in nature."[42]

In the aftermath of *Benson*, the PTO adopted a "point of novelty" test under which it rejected applications if the only novel part of the claim was an algorithm. Although the PTO derived its test from a post-*Benson* CCPA decision, eventually the CCPA rejected the point of novelty approach, contending that claims must be assessed as a whole rather than dissected.[43] In 1978, in *In re Freeman*, the court adopted a two part test for assessing patentability: (i) analyze the claim to determine whether it states a mathematical algorithm (which, to the CCPA, meant a mathematical equation); and (ii) if so, determine whether the claim wholly preempts others' use of the algorithm—if so, the claim would not be patentable.[44] In a nutshell, the PTO favored a broad reading of *Benson*; the CCPA a narrow one. After *Benson*, applicants avoided claims drawn solely to software and focused instead on claiming programs as elements of traditional machines or processes.[45] This approach was more likely to achieve a favorable result in the CCPA because such applications did not appear to claim basic truths or fundamental building blocks, but rather traditionally patentable subject matter.[46]

Parker v. Flook

The choice between the PTO's point of novelty test and CCPA's *Freeman* test reached the Supreme Court in *Parker v. Flook*.[47] There the Court addressed a " 'Method for Updating Alarm Limits,' " useful primarily with a computer, in which a number of variables relevant to the catalytic conversion process (e.g. temperature, pressure, and flow rates) were measured and an updated alarm-limit (used to signal an abnormali-

---

[42] *Id.* at 1063.

[43] *See id.* at 1065–70 (describing the PTO's and CCPA's approaches in the years after *Benson*, and noting that there was dissension in the CCPA immediately after the *Benson* decision). The CCPA adopted a point of novelty test in *In re Christensen*, 478 F.2d 1392 (C.C.P.A. 1973), *overruled by In re Taner*, 681 F.2d 787 (C.C.P.A. 1982).

[44] *In re* Freeman, 573 F.2d 1237, 1245 (C.C.P.A. 1978); Samuelson, *supra* note 1, at 1075–76.

[45] *See generally* Julie E. Cohen & Mark A. Lemley, *Patent Scope and Innovation in the Software Industry*, 89 CAL. L. REV. 1, 9 (2001).

[46] *See id.*

[47] 437 U.S. 584 (1978).

ty) calculated.[48] The patent examiner had rejected the application because the only point of novelty was a mathematical formula and the Board of Appeals had upheld the rejection.[49] The CCPA had reversed, "read[ing] Benson as applying only to claims that entirely pre-empt a mathematical formula or algorithm, and not[ing] that respondent was only claiming on the use of his method to update alarm limits in a process comprising the catalytic chemical conversion of hydrocarbons."[50]

In a 6–3 decision, the Court held the process unpatentable, even though the claims would not "wholly preempt" use of the formula, stating, "[O]ur holding today is that a claim for an improved method of calculation, even when tied to a specific end use, is unpatentable subject matter."[51] It also stated that "post-solution activity" like updating an alarm limit could not "transform an unpatentable principle into a patentable process [: Otherwise, a] competent draftsman could attach some form of post-solution activity to almost any mathematical formula" and evade the policy of forbidding patent protection on basic truths.[52] On the other hand, "an inventive application of [a] principle may be patented."[53]

Under the Court's analysis, the algorithm is assumed to be part of the prior art and if the application when considered as a whole reveals no patentable invention, it does not state patentable subject matter.[54] Although this analysis seemed to adopt the PTO's point of novelty test, the CCPA did not regard that issue as settled, opting to focus instead on the Court's statement that it was construing the *Flook* claims as a whole.

The disagreement between the PTO and CCPA over appropriate claim analysis stems at least in part from the difficulty of understanding the point of novelty approach when viewed against the Patent Act in its entirety. By treating an algorithm as part of the prior art and then evaluating the rest of the claim for novelty to decide the subject matter question, the PTO was arguably conflating two separate statutory constructs—subject matter and novelty—into one focused on subject matter. In *Flook*, the Supreme Court finessed this problem by agreeing with the PTO that the algorithm should be treated as part of the prior art, but

---

[48] *Id.* at 585–86.

[49] *Id.* at 587.

[50] *Id.*

[51] *Id.* at 595 n.18.

[52] *Id.* at 590.

[53] *Id.* at 594.

[54] *Id.* at 594.

also stating that "once the algorithm is assumed to be within the prior art, the [question is whether] the application, considered as a whole, contains [a] patentable invention." [55]One way to interpret this is to say that a court must ask the question whether the claim, construed as a whole, recites the type of invention the patent law is intended to protect. If *Cochrane v. Deener* still defined the set of processes considered patentable, then a process claim failing to recite a transformation of matter from one state to another would not be patentable.[56] This would not bode well for the patenting of software.

Like the *Benson* Court before it, the *Flook* Court took a cautious approach to the question of patenting software. It noted that its decision should not be construed as barring patent protection for computer programs but that the Court should "proceed cautiously when . . . asked to extend patent rights into areas wholly unforeseen by Congress," and which raise difficult policy questions better answered by Congress than the judiciary.[57]

From *Flook* to *Diehr*

After *Flook,* the PTO and CCPA continued to disagree on the appropriate interpretation of *Benson*. Of the nine program-related cases the CCPA decided between *Flook* and the Court's decision in *Diehr*, the CCPA overturned five subject matter rejections by the PTO and upheld four others.[58] Indeed, despite the *Flook* Court's rejection of the notion that the key to patentability was whether the claims would wholly preempt an algorithm, the CCPA continued to apply the *Freeman* test, at least until the Supreme Court granted the petition for certiorari in Diehr's case.[59] Shortly after the grant of certiorari, the CCPA modified the *Freeman* test, shifting its focus from analyzing whether the claims would wholly preempt use of the algorithm to assessing whether the "mathematical algorithm is implemented in a specific manner to define structural relationships between the physical elements of the claim (in

[55] *Id.* ("Our approach . . . is not at all inconsistent with the view that a patent claim must be considered as a whole. Respondent's process is unpatentable not because it contains a mathematical algorithm as one component, but because once that algorithm is assumed to be within the prior art, the application, considered as a whole, contains no patentable invention.").

[56] 94 U.S. 780 (1876).

[57] Parker v. Flook, 437 U.S. 584, 595–96 (1978); *see also* Gottschalk v. Benson, 409 U.S. 63, 72 (1972) (citing the findings of the President's Commission, *see supra* note 10 and accompanying text, and inviting Congress to use its powers of investigation to consider the "wide variety of views" and "technological problems" associated with the question of computer program patentability).

[58] Samuelson, *supra* note 1, at 1083.

[59] *Id.* at 1086–87.

apparatus claims) or to refine or limit claim steps (in process claims)."[60] Thus, the CCPA continued to address the issue not by barring protection at the subject matter stage, but rather by ensuring that the claims were appropriately circumscribed so as not, in fact, to afford patent protection to abstract ideas, particularly in the form of mathematical equations.

Diamond v. Diehr

Proceedings Below

The patent as litigated in Diehr's case contained eleven method claims, with the essence of the invention described as placing the uncured rubber in the mold press, heating the mold, using a computer to calculate repetitively the appropriate cure time, and opening the mold when the calculated cure time equaled the actual time the rubber had been in the press. The Board upheld the examiner's rejection, agreeing that the only new matter claimed was a computer program which was not patentable subject matter.[61]

Applying the unmodified *Freeman* test, the CCPA reversed.[62] It found that the claims did recite a mathematical algorithm (the Arrhenius equation), but were not directed to the equation itself but rather at a process that used the equation to accomplish a new and useful end—appropriately cured rubber. The CCPA distinguished *Flook*: "In Flook . . . the claims recited nothing but the calculations, coupled with the post-solution activity consisting only of updating an alarm limit to the newly-calculated value which is merely a new number. Here, the calculation is intimately entwined with the rubber molding process recited. Therefore, appellants are not claiming a process for merely generating a new number by a calculation."[63]

The Solicitor General petitioned the Supreme Court for certiorari, arguing that the CCPA had failed correctly to apply *Flook*. The Solicitor General phrased the question in *Diehr* as "[w]hether a computer program that regulates the curing time of rubber products in a mold is patentable subject matter . . ."[64]

---

60 *Id.* at 1087.

61 *In re* Diehr, 602 F.2d 982, 984 (C.C.P.A. 1979). The companion case was *In re Bradley* which involved an invention in firmware. 600 F.2d 807 (C.C.P.A. 1979). The Supreme Court upheld the CCPA's finding that the invention was patentable subject matter on a 4–4 vote. Diamond v. Bradley, 450 U.S. 381 (1980).

62 *Diehr,* 602 F.2d at 988–89.

63 *Id.* at 989.

64 Diamond v. Diehr, 602 F.2d 982 (C.C.P.A. 1979), *petition for cert. filed*, Jan. 16, 1980 (No. 79–1112), at 2.

The Briefs and Oral Argument

The Briefs

The government's brief focused on *Flook*, describing Diehr's case as "*Flook* revisited: ... There, as here, the application claimed the continuous measurement of a process variable, a programmed recomputation using a mathematical formula, and an adjustment based upon that recomputation."[65] Federal Mogul argued that the government had mistakenly stated the issue for decision, rephrasing it as whether "a claim to a novel physical and chemical process for molding precision synthetic rubber products ... become[s] unpatentable because some of the novel steps used to determine the time when cure is complete and to trigger the opening of the mold ... involve, *inter alia*, the use of a programmed computer."[66] It categorized *Flook* as involving the production of a number and claiming in effect a calculation, while *Diehr* claimed a process for curing rubber that incidentally used a computer to implement certain steps as rubber was transformed from a "useless" mass to a "precision product."[67]

The parties thus disagreed on the ultimate issue of what Federal Mogul sought to patent. The government argued that the firm claimed a principle and Federal Mogul contended it was claiming an application of a principle to a process that improved the curing of rubber. The parties also disagreed about the way in which the Court should interpret the claims, with the government arguing along the lines of the point of novelty test, and Federal Mogul advocating analysis of the claims as a whole.

In amicus briefs, Chevron, Applied Data Research (ADR) and Whitlow Computer Systems, Inc., and the Los Angeles Patent Law Association all argued that a programmed general purpose computer becomes, in effect, a new machine, a contention with which the CCPA had once agreed in the *Bernhart* case.[68] Chevron filed the brief because it was involved in litigation over its own patent related to the processing of seismic data to indicate the likelihood of the presence or absence of oil: the outcome in *Diehr* would control the fate of Chevron's patent.[69] ADR and Whitlow were both small software companies, and ADR claimed to

---

65 Brief for Petitioner at 7, 10, Diamond v. Diehr, 450 U.S. 175 (1981) (No. 79–1112), 1980 WL 339341.

66 Brief for Respondent at 21, Diamond v. Diehr, 450 U.S. 175 (1981) (No. 79–1112), 1980 WL 339342.

67 *Id.* at 16.

68 *See supra* n. 9 & accompanying text.

69 Brief of Amici Curiae Chevron Research Co. at 1–2, Diamond v. Diehr, 450 U.S. 175 (1981) (No. 79–1112), 1980 WL 339343.

have obtained the first software patent awarded by the PTO.[70] The LA Patent Law Association, like the American Patent Law Association that also filed an amicus brief, represented the interests of patent attorneys who generally regarded an expansion of patentable subject matter as good for business.

Only National Semiconductor, an integrated circuit manufacturer, filed an amicus brief arguing for reversal of the CCPA's decision. The company based its objections at least in part on a fear that patenting software would hamper its ability to implement the same functionality in hardware.[71]

It appears that National Semiconductor's problem was the opposite of Chevron's. According to Chevron, patents had long issued on special purpose computers designed for seismic exploration. As functionality migrated from hardware to software, patents had continued to issue. Chevron feared that an adverse decision in *Diehr* would jeopardize software patents related to seismic exploration. In contrast, National Semiconductor ostensibly was moving into the handheld calculator business where functionality was going in the opposite direction—from software to hardware. If software patents related to calculators were held by others, National Semiconductor might have to pay royalties to those patentees before implementing functionality in the hardware contained in a handheld calculator.

The Oral Argument

Not surprisingly, much of the oral argument was devoted to questioning regarding how *Diehr* differed from *Flook*. Another case, though, *Diamond v. Chakrabarty*,[72] was also in the Justices' minds. In *Chakrabarty*, decided the year before, in 1980, the Court, by a 5–4 vote, held that genetically engineered bacteria were patentable subject matter over the government's objections that it should precede slowly and err on the side of unpatentability in areas not envisioned by Congress. As described in Rebecca Eisenberg's Story, *Chakrabarty* arguably represented "a shift

70 Brief of Amici Curiae Applied Data Research, Inc. & Whitlow Computer Sys. Inc. at 2, Diamond v. Diehr, 450 U.S. 175 (1981) (No. 79–1112), 1990 WL 10022420 (citing patents for a sorting system and a system for building charts as examples of existing software patents).

71 Brief of Amici Curiae National Semiconductor Corp. at 3, Diamond v. Diehr, 450 U.S. 175 (1981) (No. 79–1112), 1980 WL 339251. The National Semiconductor brief also characterized the major hardware firms as aggressively seeking patent protection for software. *Id.* at 2. It is not at all clear that was the case and, indeed, ADR described this contention as a misstatement and hardware manufacturers as "consistently oppos[ing] patents for software-implemented inventions". Brief of Amici Curiae Applied Data Research & Whitlow Computer Sys., Inc., *supra* note 70, at 5.

72 447 U.S. 303 (1980).

in the default rules that apply in the face of Congressional inaction."[73] The government, perhaps recognizing this, focused most of its argument not on whether the invention was unpatentable *per se,* but rather on how to analyze the claims. It contended that *Flook* should be interpreted as using § 101's subject matter requirement to limit the availability of patent on the use of principles; a result that the government thought could be achieved through application of the point of novelty approach. Thus, it argued that Diehr's claims were not patentable because there was nothing new besides the program in either any other element of Diehr's claims or the combination of elements.

The Court seemed troubled by this reading of *Flook*, and its questioning revealed that it had become uncomfortable with the inherent tensions in the point of novelty approach. The prior art included two patents that essentially claimed the same process as Diehr—thus, the process itself was considered the type of invention the patent law was designed to protect. In effect, the government was arguing that the point of novelty approach made an otherwise patentable process unpatentable simply because it included a computer program. That seemed illogical—if the process had been considered patentable before, why would adding a program to it render it unpatentable? The prior art embodied in the earlier process patents might render the new process *obvious* or *not novel*, but addition of a program would not make the new process *nonstatutory*—one the patent laws were not designed to protect.

Federal Mogul's attorneys had a somewhat easier time in the oral argument. One of their best moves was to bring in uncured as well as cured rubber products, allowing the Court to see the transformation that occurred in the press monitored by the process Federal Mogul sought to patent. Federal Mogul also managed to keep its argument narrow: it cast its argument in terms of patentability of a traditional industrial process, rather than the patentability of software. Justices Stevens and Blackmun, part of the majority in *Flook,* asked the most pointed questions regarding how to distinguish *Flook* from *Diehr*. It seemed in their view that, at the end of the day, Diehr's process, like that in *Flook*, simply calculated a number.

The Decision

The Supreme Court split 5–4 in its decision in *Diamond v. Diehr*:[74] the three dissenters in *Flook* (Justices Burger, Stewart, and Rehnquist) plus two in the *Flook* majority (Justices Powell and White) comprised the

---

[73] *See* Rebecca S. Eisenberg, The Story of *Diamond v. Chakrabarty*: Technological Change and the Subject Matter Boundaries of the Patent System, elsewhere in this Volume.

[74] 450 U.S. 175 (1981).

five upholding the patent against the subject matter challenge. The majority framed the issue along the lines argued by Federal Mogul, and focused on the question of what the term "process" means, referring back to its statement in *Cochrane*, and repeated in *Benson*, regarding the importance of the transformation of an article from one state to another.[75] It noted that "a claim drawn to subject matter otherwise statutory does not become nonstatutory simply because it uses a mathematical formula, computer program, or digital computer.... It is ... commonplace that an *application* of ... a mathematical formula to a known structure or process may well be deserving of patent protection."[76] Although the Arrhenius equation was well-known and not "patentable in isolation, ... a process for curing rubber ... which incorporates it in a more efficient solution of the equation ... is at the very least not barred at the threshold by § 101."[77]

The Court also clarified claim analysis, stating:

> It is inappropriate to dissect the claims into old and new elements and then to ignore the presence of the old elements in the analysis. This is particularly true in a process claim because a new combination of steps in a process may be patentable even though all the constituents of the combination were well known.... The "novelty" of any element or steps in a process, or even of the process itself, is of no relevance in determining whether the subject matter of a claim falls within the § 101 categories of possibly patentable subject matter.[78]

Justice Stevens dissented vigorously, arguing that the claims were drawn to a new method of calculating curing time, and not, as the majority claimed, a method of measuring temperatures inside a molding press.[79] He also disagreed with the Court's method of interpreting claims,

---

[75] *Id.* at 177–84 ("We granted certiorari to determine whether a process for curing synthetic rubber which includes in several of its steps the use of a mathematical formula and a programmed digital computer is patentable subject matter under 35 U.S.C. § 101.").

[76] *Id.* at 187.

[77] *Id.* at 188.

[78] *Id.* at 188–89.

[79] *Id.* at 206–07. Justice Stevens gave three reasons for his rejection of the court's reading: (i) the patent application did not suggest "anything unusual about the temperature-reading devices used in th[e] process ..."; (ii) it was "difficult to believe that a patent application filed in 1975 was premised on the notion that a 'process of constantly measuring the actual temperature' had just been discovered;" and (iii) the PTO Board of Appeals had found " 'the only difference' " between the prior art and the claims were " 'steps of the claims which relate to the calculation incident to the solution of [a] mathematical problem or formula ...' ". *Id.* at 207–08.

arguing that the point of novelty test was appropriate.[80] In Stevens' view, *Diehr* could not be meaningfully distinguished from *Flook*.[81]

Indeed, it is quite difficult to construe *Flook* and *Diehr* consistently. *Chakrabarty* may, as Professor Eisenberg argues, have marked an attitude shift within the Court toward an increased willingness to expand the bounds of patentable subject matter, leaving the more nuanced novelty and non-obviousness inquiries as the primary mechanisms for filtering out non-patentable inventions. Or it may simply have been that the Court made a distinction between the production of a number (the natural output of a mathematical formula) in *Flook* and the manufacture of a tangible product—cured rubber—in *Diehr*. Indeed, that the Court took some pains to limit its holding suggests this distinction may have influenced it:

> We view the respondents' claims as nothing more than a process for molding rubber products and not as an attempt to patent a mathematical formula . . . [W]hen a claim containing a mathematical formula implements or applies that formula in a structure or process which, when considered as a whole, is performing a function which the patent laws were designed to protect (e.g., transforming or reducing an article to a different state or thing), then the claim satisfies the requirements of § 101. Because we do not view respondents' claims as an attempt to patent a mathematical formula, but rather to be drawn to an industrial process for the molding of rubber products, we affirm . . . [82]

The Aftermath

The Immediate Impact of Diehr

The *New York Times* described the decision as narrowing the scope of the Court's earlier opinions that seemed hostile to patenting software, but also noted that it "stop[ped] far short of bringing ordinary computer

---

[80] *Id.* at 211–16 (arguing that the subject matter inquiry requires treating the computer program as part of the prior art, and the rest of the application did not reveal any other "inventive concept").

[81] *Id.* at 209–10 ("The essence of the claimed discovery in both cases was an algorithm that could be programmed on a digital computer. In *Flook*, the algorithm made use of multiple process variables; in [*Diehr*], it makes use of only one. In *Flook*, the algorithm was expressed in a newly developed mathematical formula; in [*Diehr*], the algorithm makes use of a well-known mathematical formula. Manifestly, neither of these differences can explain today's holding in [*Diehr*].").

[82] *Id.* at 191–93 (noting also the Court's approval of *Benson* and *Flook* by indicating that nothing in *Diehr* contradicted the notions that a mathematical formula is not patentable in the abstract (*Benson*), and that neither limiting the claims to a formula to a particular environment nor claiming "insignificant post-solution activity" would render a formula patentable (*Flook*)).

programs within the patent laws."[83] Indeed, particularly given the restrictive language quoted above, one might summarize the decision as "a very limited one . . . It is limited in that it affirms only that patents can issue for traditionally patentable industrial processes which include a computer program as an element."[84]

The decision, though, did have a major effect on the PTO's attitude—essentially, the PTO viewed *Diehr* as adopting the CCPA's approach to evaluating whether an invention stating a program constituted statutory subject matter. With the PTO more receptive to software-related inventions, the number of appeals from rejections based on lack of statutory subject matter decreased materially.[85] Thus, despite the limited nature of its holding, *Diehr* did signal the start of an increase in software patents, both in absolute and relative terms: "The increase in software patents at [an] accelerated pace . . . reflects (1) the new approach to patentability heralded by *Diehr*, and also (2) the overwhelming increase in the use of computers in our society."[86]

In 1982, in *In re Abele*,[87] the CCPA further refined the *Freeman-Walter* test. The court explained that *Walter* did not require anything other than that the algorithm be applied to physical elements or process steps.[88] The mode of analysis ostensibly was to assess the claims without the algorithm, an approach at least facially at odds with *Diehr*'s emphasis on analyzing the claim as a whole.[89] The emphasis on applying the algorithm to physical elements or process steps, however, was consistent with avoiding patenting abstract principles.

The *Freeman-Walter–Abele* test, although perhaps not entirely consistent with *Diehr*, attempted to implement *Diehr's* statement that the inclusion of software in a claim drawn to otherwise statutory subject

---

83 Linda Greenhouse, *Court Backs Patent in Computer Process*, N.Y. TIMES, Mar. 3, 1981, at D6.

84 Samuelson, *supra* note 1, at 1029.

85 HANNEMAN, *supra* note 22, at 91.

86 John T. Soma & B.F. Smith, *Software Trends: Who's Getting How Many of What? 1978 to 1987*, 71 J. PAT. & TRADEMARK OFF. SOC'Y 415, 419–21 (1989) (stating that the average number of software patents granted between 1978–81 was ten per year, that an increase occurred after *Diehr*—"from 34 in 1984 to 66 in 1987", and noting a 470% increase in software patents from 1978–87 compared to a 37% increase in total patents); *see also* OTA Rep., *supra* note 25 (charting the number of software patents, with the number going over 100 for the first time in 1984 and generally trending upward (except in 1988) thereafter).

87 684 F.2d 902 (C.C.P.A. 1982).

88 *Id.* at 907 (noting also that if the claim would be statutory without the algorithm, "the claim presents statutory subject matter when the algorithm is included").

89 *See id.* at 908 (viewing the claim steps in the absence of the algorithm).

matter would not render the claim nonstatutory.[90] Applicants responded to the CCPA's implementation of *Diehr* by becoming even more skilled at claiming software as a machine.[91] This enhanced the likelihood a patent would issue because machines were certainly "otherwise statutory subject matter." "During the 1980s and early 1990s, knowledgeable patent attorneys ... claimed software inventions as hardware devices, pizza ovens, and other 'machines.' ... [T]he 'otherwise statutory process or apparatus' limitation was not much of a limit at all."[92]

The early years after *Diehr* were also characterized by a major shift in the industry. Personal computers became ubiquitous, opening a huge market for software vendors.[93] Trade secrecy protection became less likely to offer meaningful protection as producers marketed pre-packaged software to a large market. Software vendors increasingly relied on contract and copyright law to protect their products. Early copyright decisions indicated that its protection would extend broadly, encompassing not only the code but also the program's design.[94] This lessened the need to rely on patents as the primary legal protection for software.

The Continuing Importance of Diehr

The Federal Circuit, established in 1982 to hear all patent appeals, did not decide a software related case until 1989. Its panels then seemed to render somewhat inconsistent decisions applying the *Freeman-Walter–Abele* test.[95] In 1990, the Secretary of Commerce established an Advisory

---

90 Cohen & Lemley, *supra* note 45, at 9.

91 *Id.* ("The Diehr decision and its progeny created what might be termed 'the doctrine of the magic words.' Under this doctrine, software was patentable subject matter, but only if the applicant recited the magic words and pretended that she was patenting something else entirely.").

92 *Id.*

93 Steinmueller, *supra* note 22, at 34 (noting that although a number of products were introduced in the late 1970s, all were "overshadowed by IBM's introduction of its personal computer (PC) in August 1981.... The market for personal computers grew very rapidly during the 1980s.... The rapid growth in the installed base of personal computers provided a homogeneous market for operating systems and applications of unprecedented size").

94 *See* Whelan Assocs. v. Jaslow Dental Labs., 797 F.2d 1222 (3d Cir. 1986) (granting broad protection to the structure of a program). *See also* Pamela Samuelson, The Story of *Baker v. Selden*: Sharpening the Distinction Between Authorship and Invention, elsewhere in this Volume.

95 *Compare In re* Grams, 888 F.2d 835 (Fed. Cir. 1989) (Archer, Michel, and Cowen, JJ.) (holding data analysis software unpatentable subject matter) *with In re* Iwahashi, 888 F.2d 1370 (Fed. Cir. 1989) (Rich, Bissell, and Nichols, JJ.) (holding voice recognition apparatus patentable subject matter). *See* Gregory J. Maier & Robert C. Mattson, *State Street Bank in the Context of the Software Patent Saga*, 8 Geo. Mason L. Rev. 307, 324 (1999).

Commission to assess the functioning of the patent system. Some witnesses raised the same objections to patenting software that had led the 1965 President's Commission to recommend excluding software from patentable subject matter. The 1990 Commission, however, took a different approach. In its 1992 Report, the Commission took the patentability of software as a given, indicating that although opinions in the industry differed, "continu[ing]" availability of patent protection for software was appropriate, and software did not require the PTO or courts to use any "special" test for statutory subject matter.[96]

In 1994, the PTO held hearings on patent protection for software-related inventions. By this time, copyright law was beginning to change. In 1992, the Second Circuit had developed a new test for protection of program design that was significantly less protective than earlier ones.[97] Additionally, other courts began construing copyright law as permitting users to reverse engineer object code despite the inevitable copying involved.[98] These courts held that copyright law's fair use doctrine permitted users to reverse engineer programming code to obtain design and other elements unprotected by copyright law even when the reverse engineer marketed a new product as a result.[99]

Nevertheless, the industry remained split: some software companies advocated patent protection while others did not.[100] Those opposed to software patenting offered many of the same arguments raised years earlier. For example, some argued that the broad rights of patent could frustrate further innovation and were unnecessary given the availability of copyright and trade secret protection. They also contended that patents would disadvantage those who could not afford to seek them or defend against infringement claims. With the advantage of additional years of experience, those opposed to patents also argued that the industry had undergone rapid expansion in the absence of patent protection. Some firms, like IBM, had grown to appreciate software as a

---

96 The Advisory Commission on Patent Law Reform, *A Report to the Secretary of Commerce* 145–68 (1992), *available at* http://world.std.com/obi/USG/Patents/overview.

97 *See* Computer Assocs., Inc. v. Altai, Inc., 982 F.2d 693 (2d Cir. 1992); Pamela Samuelson, The Story of *Baker v. Selden*: Sharpening the Distinction Between Authorship and Invention, elsewhere in this Volume.

98 *See* Sega Enters. v. Accolade, Inc., 977 F.2d 1510 (9th Cir. 1992); Atari Games Corp. v. Nintendo of Am., Inc., 975 F.2d 832 (Fed. Cir. 1992); Pamela Samuelson, The Story of *Baker v. Selden*: Sharpening the Distinction Between Authorship and Invention, elsewhere in this Volume.

99 *See Sega*, 977 F.2d at 1520; *Atari*, 975 F.2d at 843.

100 *See generally* OTA Rep., *supra* note 25, at 8–9 (identifying the "stakeholders" in the software debate and indicating that the dispute was not between small and large firms but rather between entities with differing financial interests and capabilities).

valuable product in its own right rather than simply as a marketing tool to enhance sales of hardware. Over the years, IBM changed its position to favor patent protection for software. Most did agree that if software were patentable, the PTO would need to take a number of steps to improve the quality of issued patents.

Meanwhile, the Federal Circuit continued to construe *Diehr* broadly. In its 1994 decision, *In re Alappat*, it held an invention designed to create a continuous waveform display patentable.[101] The court seemed to discard the *Freeman-Walter–Abele* test, adopting instead an approach focusing on the whole of the claim: if the entire claim is drawn to nothing other than an algorithm, it is not patentable under *Diehr*.[102] But a programmed computer is, in effect, a new machine which may be patentable subject matter. Applicants could now define their claims as software implemented in a machine rather than claiming the machine itself.

After *In re Beauregard* in 1995, applicants did not even have to claim a machine implementation but could instead claim programs themselves as embodied in a medium like a floppy disk.[103] Prior to *Beauregard*, many thought that patent law's "printed matter" doctrine which barred patentability of, literally, printed matter, would deny patent protection to computer program code.[104] In *Beauregard*, IBM challenged the PTO's denial under the printed matter doctrine of its application drawn to a program embodied on a floppy disk. Before the Federal Circuit could hear the oral argument, the PTO withdrew its objection, and shortly thereafter revised its guidelines to instruct examiners to grant such claims. This tendency to disregard *Diehr's* limits, including that the algorithm be applied in a structure, continued in future decisions.

Indeed, by 1998, the Federal Circuit had removed any remaining obstacles to patenting software. In *State Street Bank & Trust Co. v.*

---

[101] 33 F.3d 1526 (Fed. Cir. 1994).

[102] *Id.* at 1544 ("[T]he proper inquiry in dealing with the so called mathematical subject matter exception to § 101 . . . is to see whether the claimed subject matter *as a whole* is a disembodied mathematical concept, whether categorized as a mathematical formula, mathematical equation, mathematical algorithm, or the like, which in essence represents nothing more than a 'law of nature,' 'natural phenomenon,' or 'abstract idea.' ") (emphasis in original).

[103] 53 F.3d 1583 (Fed. Cir. 1995) (dismissing appeal for lack of a case or controversy after the Commissioner of Patents and Trademarks dropped his opposition to patenting programs embodied in tangible media).

[104] The printed matter doctrine originated in CCPA decisions and reflected, in part, a concern that merely recording information was not the type of activity that the patent laws were designed to protect: protection, if appropriate, should come from the copyright laws.

Signature Financial Group, Inc., the court upheld the patentability of a machine claim for a data processing system implementing a hub and spoke mutual fund pricing system.[105] *State Street* confirmed what *Alappat* had implied: the *Freeman-Walter–Abele* test had little, if any, ongoing substantive force. According to *State Street*, all that is required for patentability is that "an algorithm ... be applied in a 'useful' way."[106] It found this consistent with *Diehr*, reading that decision as permitting the patenting of a claim involving inputting, calculating and outputting numbers so long as the end result was " 'useful, concrete and tangible.' "[107] The tangible result in *State Street* was "a final share price momentarily fixed for recording and reporting purposes"[108]—a result quite different from the processed rubber that Federal Mogul's attorneys had presented to the Supreme Court. Indeed, the result in *State Street* seems to stretch *Diehr* beyond its bounds and discard *Flook* entirely.

In 1999, in *AT & T Corp. v. Excel Communications, Inc.*, the Federal Circuit made clear that software could be claimed as a process and explained that *Diehr's* use of the term " 'physical transformation' " could be "misunderstood ... [I]t is not an invariable requirement, but merely one example of how a mathematical algorithm may bring about a useful application."[109] The *AT & T* case upheld the patentability of a process that applied Boolean algebraic concepts to data to determine a value that was then applied to create a signal for billing record purposes: it found the value a "useful, non-abstract result that facilities differential billing ... Because the claimed process applies the Boolean principle to produce a useful, concrete, tangible result without pre-empting other uses of the mathematical principle, on its face the claimed process comfortably fits within the scope of § 101."[110]

The *State Street* and *AT & T* cases removed any remaining doubts regarding the patentability of software. Since the extent of copyright law's protection for software had decreased over the years, resort to patent law became more important and more sought after.[111] Additionally, patents have proliferated in areas like e-commerce where business

---

105 149 F.3d 1368 (Fed. Cir. 1998).

106 *Id.* at 1373.

107 *Id.* at 1374.

108 *Id.* at 1373.

109 172 F.3d 1352, 1358 (Fed. Cir. 1999).

110 *Id.*

111 *See* John T. Aquino, *Patently Permissive*, 85–May A.B.A. J. 30 (1999) (noting that State Street "appear[ed] to ... set off a stampede to the patent office, which report[ed] a 45 percent increase in the number of data processing and computer-related patents issued during its 1998 fiscal year").

methods are routinely implemented in software. Besides taking a favorable view of patenting software, the *State Street* case had held that patent law's scope includes business methods.[112]

Concluding Thoughts

Diamond v. Diehr today stands, at least to some, as the Supreme Court's approval of software as patentable subject matter. This is not, however, an accurate characterization of the decision. It may be fair to say that *Diehr* signaled an end (or at least the beginning of the end) of the hostility toward patents in the computer field. This, as Professor Eisenberg argues,[113] was perhaps part of a larger trend of broadening the scope of patentable subject matter as new technologies evolved in areas like biotechnology. *Diehr*, however, was a quite limited decision. It was the Federal Circuit that loosened and eventually removed the Court's limits, paving the way for the patenting of software as a stand-alone product.

A particular confluence of factors likely accounts for the manner in which the law evolved. As time went on, it became increasingly clear that the software industry accounted for a good deal of progress and wealth and that copyright law might not offer adequate protection. Additionally, it appears that much of the PTO's hostility to patenting software was based on fears of an administrative nightmare—too many applications and too few Examiners to process them. The CCPA's judges simply did not accord the PTO's administrative concerns much substantive weight. As time passed, and additional resources were provided to the PTO, its attitude changed. At the same time, applying *Freeman-Walter–Abele* proved more difficult as non-manufacturing related software became increasingly popular. Furthermore, the Supreme Court does not take many patent cases. This left the Federal Circuit freer than it might otherwise have been to interpret cases like *Diehr* quite liberally. Now that investors have expectations of patentability for software, it is unlikely that the Supreme Court would reverse the Federal Circuit and its interpretation of *Diehr*.

The history of *Diehr* illustrates a number of conceptual difficulties. For example, the distinction between an unpatentable basic truth and a patentable application of it is not always clear. As the *Diehr* Court itself noted, all inventions rest on principles of nature yet some are patentable and some are not. One might argue that computer programs, like other

[112] 149 F.3d 1368, 1375–76 (Fed. Cir. 1998). Prior to the *State Street* case, most applicants likely believed that precedent forbade patents on business methods.

[113] *See* Rebecca S. Eisenberg, The Story of *Diamond v. Chakrabarty*: Technological Change and the Subject Matter Boundaries of the Patent System, elsewhere in this Volume.

inventions, are not—or, at least, are capable of not being—in and of themselves principles of nature. In other words, if non-programming inventions may apply basic principles in a useful setting without being barred from patentability, so too can computer programs.

The software patent saga also reflects the difficulties of applying a generally worded statute to new technologies. With Congress unable to consider whether each new technology should be within the patent incentive structure, the courts are often left to make such decisions without any of the economic analysis that would help guide them to appropriate results. Thus, they introduce terms like "algorithm" that do not necessarily advance the analysis but that do reflect the underlying policy concern of not affording exclusive rights in basic truths. Limiting the exclusive rights to narrowly defined applications is a less drastic solution than simply barring subject matter from protection. The question is always how narrowly defined the application must be to qualify as patentable subject matter. Over the years, the Federal Circuit removed the limits of *Diehr* in a way that favored patenting software. Thus did a case about curing rubber become known as the case that shaped intellectual property protection in an entire, almost unrelated industry!

Coda

James Diehr remembers being quite surprised to find that the Arrhenius equation governed the relationship among the variables involved in the cure process. Indeed, he described the invention as not so much about software, but rather about the application of the Arrhenius equation in a new context to calculate and recalculate continuously the cure time and control the presses to produce appropriately cured rubber: software was simply a means to an end. It seems clear, however, that the prior art, including issued patents, contained references to the Arrhenius equation in the context of curing rubber. If other scientists are like Diehr, it raises the question whether many of patent law's assumptions about the "person having ordinary skill in the art" are valid. In real life, scientists may not engage in detailed library research before doing their own experiments. Thus, the notice function of patents—and their value in preventing duplicative research—may be severely overstated.

To whom then are all of these doctrines relevant? Certainly, the lawyers involved in a patent case are quite interested in the statutory constructs. Patent law then, may, in actual operation, be more about what lawyers understand than what scientists do.

The Story of *Kellogg Co. v. National Biscuit Co.*: Breakfast with Brandeis

Graeme B. Dinwoodie*

Kellogg Co. v. National Biscuit Co.[1] may be the Supreme Court's most versatile and influential trademark decision. Justice Brandeis' ten-page opinion contained language that is now at the core of the statutory test for whether a term should be unprotected because consumers understand the term as the generic name for the product on which it is used. That same language guides courts seeking to determine whether a mark has acquired the degree of consumer understanding ("secondary meaning," or "acquired distinctiveness") necessary to support trademark protection. Plaintiffs seeking to establish trademark rights in a product shape must demonstrate that the shape in question is not "functional" according to a standard that has its roots in *Kellogg*. And defendants seeking to parry claims that the design of their product is confusingly similar to the design of a once-patented product habitually invoke *Kellogg* to support a competitor's right to copy the subject matter of an expired patent.

These issues cover the waterfront of modern trademark law. As a result, *Kellogg* had a direct impact on the structure of the Lanham Act, it has been cited in numerous recent Supreme Court trademark opinions, and is a routine starting point for analysis in trademark opinions of lower courts. The opinion is regularly invoked by scholars seeking to understand the theoretical underpinnings of intellectual property and to shape the development of trademark law. By any objective measure, the *Kellogg* opinion is a trademark classic.

The scope of *Kellogg*'s influence might, at first blush, seem surprising. The Court was confronted by a relatively narrow issue of trademark and unfair competition law, and to a large extent was revisiting an issue it had decided forty years earlier.[2] The Court's opinion, addressing

---

* Thanks to Scott Cole and Christopher Kaiser for research assistance, to Brian Havel and Mark Janis for comments on a draft version of this chapter, and to the editors and contributors to this book, whose lively critiques of my early thoughts on *Kellogg* both made the project hugely enjoyable and improved the end-product immensely.

1 305 U.S. 111 (1938).

2 *See* Singer Mfg. Co. v. June Mfg. Co., 163 U.S. 169 (1896).

whether the National Biscuit Company ("NBC" or "Nabisco") could, after the expiry or invalidation of its patents on the SHREDDED WHEAT biscuit, use trademark and unfair competition law to prevent a rival manufacturer (Kellogg) from selling goods of the same shape under the same name, was also quite short. To fully understand its significance, one must be aware of the full range of philosophical reasons that motivated Justice Brandeis, including opposition to broad intellectual property rights, a concern for competition, and support for a misrepresentation-based model of unfair competition law. But one must also delve into the intense commercial rivalry in the cereal industry—a rivalry conducted by an odd mix of evangelists armed with even odder theories about nutrition and health.

The Cereal Wars and Intellectual Property Law

Today, ready-to-eat breakfast cereals are a staple of the American diet. Dietary advice, dispensed by the government and lifestyle gurus alike, emphasizes the importance of healthy and sustaining morning meals. In a country where time is money and health is business, the delivery of matinal sustenance efficiently is highly-prized. In the mid-nineteenth century, the American breakfast was not radically different from the American dinner, heavy on meat and light on grains and fiber. The development of breakfast cereals as an alternative morning meal was in part driven by health concerns. More precisely, the origins of breakfast cereal lie in the efforts of nineteenth century evangelical crusaders.

The first cold breakfast cereal developed in the United States was Granula, which "consisted of heavy nuggets made from bran, the outer husk of a grain that is removed when making flour."[3] Granula was launched in 1863 by James C. Jackson. Jackson was a disciple of Sylvester Graham, who argued that most health problems could be traced to masturbation. Eventually, Jackson saw good diet (apparently involving ingestion of large quantities of whole grains) as a means of moderating sexual desire.[4] Although he was able to serve Granula to the captive residents at his sanitarium in Dansville, New York, Granula required overnight soaking in order to be edible. A market gap (even perhaps outside sanitariums) clearly existed for a tasty, nutritious product that was ready-to-eat.

Several entrepreneurs sought to fill that gap. One of the most notable was John Harvey Kellogg, a doctor and writer, who became

---

[3] *The History of Cereal*, http://www.fitnessandfreebies.com/health/cereal.html (last visited Jan. 19, 2005); *see also* GERALD CARSON, CORNFLAKE CRUSADE 66–67 (1957).

[4] *See* Carrie McLaren, *Porn Flakes: Kellogg, Graham and the Crusade for Moral Fiber*, http://www.stayfreemagazine.com/10/graham.htm (last visited Jul. 25, 2005).

superintendent and physician of the Battle Creek Sanitarium health resort in Michigan in 1876. The Sanitarium, previously the Western Health Reform Institute of Battle Creek, had been formed by the religious sect, the Seventh Day Adventist, in 1866. Like Jackson, Kellogg was heavily influenced by Graham. And like Jackson (and Kellogg's predecessor at the Institute, Ellen White),[5] he saw masturbation as a central health problem, which could be solved by proper attention to diet.[6]

Kellogg's first dietary product was a "mixture of oatmeal and corn meal, baked into biscuits, then ground into bits."[7] Initially, he called this concoction GRANULA (the name of the product developed by Jackson), but after the use of this term was challenged in a lawsuit, Kellogg changed the name of the product to GRANOLA.[8] Several years later, after Kellogg had experimented with various health-conscious products,[9] a friend showed him shredded wheat biscuits that she had been sent for digestive trouble.[10] Initially, Kellogg found them tasteless, commenting that they were like "eating a whisk broom."[11] However, this exposure sowed the seeds of the dispute that eventually made its way to the Supreme Court.

Another evangelical crusader-cum-budding cereal magnate was C.W. Post.[12] Post spent time at the Battle Creek sanitarium to cure his upset

---

5 The Institute was initially headed by Ellen White, who had visited Jackson's Danville institution. Mrs. White had written a book on the subject of masturbation in 1866. *See id.*

6 *See* JOHN HARVEY KELLOGG, PLAIN FACTS FOR OLD AND YOUNG: EMBRACING THE NATURAL HISTORY AND HYGIENE OF ORGANIC LIFE (Burlington, Iowa, 1891), *available at* http://etext.lib.virginia.edu/toc/modeng/public/KelPlai.html (Chapters 11–15, on "Treatment for Self–Abuse and its Effects": "A Chapter for Boys", "A Chapter for Young Men," a "Short Chapter for Old Men" and a "Chapter for Girls"). Among his "One Hundred Choice Health Thoughts," Kellogg warned against the influence of "quacks." *See id.* at 625 ("QUACKS thrive upon the ignorance and gullibility of the people. The only remedy for quackery lies in the education of the people in those medical facts and theories, which will lead them to see that there is a scientific foundation for rational medical practice").

7 McLaren, *supra* note 4.

8 *See id.*

9 These included TOASTED CORN FLAKES. *See* Kellogg Toasted Corn Flake Co. v. Quaker Oats Co., 235 F. 657 (6th Cir. 1916).

10 *See* CARSON, *supra* note 3, at 120.

11 *See* McLaren, *supra* note 4.

12 Ironically, the company that Post formed obtained ownership of the NABISCO SHREDDED WHEAT brand in 1993, exactly one hundred years after Henry Perky had introduced the original product. *See* Shredded Wheat History and Chronology, http://members.aol.com/_ht_a/jwalton971/history.htm (last visited Jan. 18, 2005). Post, which is now owned by Kraft, advertises its product as THE ORIGINAL SHREDDED WHEAT on its

stomach. While there he became a devotee of Christian Science. After leaving Battle Creek, he began work on cereals of his own, the most successful of which was GRAPE NUTS. Initially, this product was advertised as an alternative treatment for an inflamed appendix, and Post also claimed that it could cure malaria and loose teeth.[13] The advertising for GRAPE NUTS (and every other Post product) emphasized the positive health consequences of consuming the product, and this marketing strategy was mimicked by other producers; a "full-scale health craze was underway."[14] Post supplied every purchaser of GRAPE NUTS with a copy of his pamphlet *The Road to Wellville*, which espoused the power of positive thinking.[15]

Today, the leading breakfast cereals are differentiated from each other in a number of ways that reflect contemporary branding practices (facilitated by modern trademark and publicity rights law). Thus, many of the leading cereals can be identified by their licensed use of cartoon characters on the cereal boxes, or their endorsement by sporting heroes and celebrities. For those less susceptible to the allure of cartoon characters and celebrity, private label branding has provided alternatives, vouched for by mass-market house marks. In the late nineteenth century, claims and connotations of health drove the brand. To be sure, nutritional claims are extremely important in modern marketing, but in the late nineteenth century they represented *the* marketing strategy.[16]

The shredded wheat biscuit that John Kellogg had tasted, without satisfaction, had been manufactured and distributed by Henry Perky. Perky, who developed the process for making the biscuits, introduced the product to the market in 1893, and was issued utility patents two years

packaging. *See* http://products.peapod.com/1661.html (visited Jan. 24, 2005); *cf.* King-Seeley Thermos Co. v. Aladdin Indus., Inc., 321 F.2d 577, 581 (2d Cir. 1963). In 1994, Kraft applied to register the term THE ORIGINAL SHREDDED WHEAT (with the term "Shredded Wheat" disclaimed) with the U.S. Patent and Trademark Office, but the application was abandoned in 1997. *See* Trademark Application, Serial No. 74594623, filed Nov. 3, 1994.

13 *See* McLaren, *supra* note 4.

14 *Id.*

15 *See* Carson, *supra* note 3, at 154. The Battle Creek sanitarium was the setting for a novel (and movie) that highlighted Kellogg's practices. *See* T.C. Boyle, The Road to Wellville (1993); The Road to Wellville (Columbia Pictures 1994).

16 Claims of nutrition (and convenience) have always dominated the marketing of breakfast cereals, perhaps because of the roots of the product. *See, e.g.*, 1947 Packaging for Nabisco Shredded Wheat, *at* http://www.adclassix.com/ads/47nabisco.htm ("You Start the Day OK With This Bowl of Flavor and Hearty Wheat . . . Delicious, Ready to Serve, Yet as Nourishing as a Hot Cereal"); 1945 Packaging for Nabisco Shredded Wheat, http://pages.tias.com/11382/PictPage/1922235937.html ("They'll Hail This Hearty Breakfast").

later on both the product and the machinery involved in making the biscuits.[17] Initially, Perky intended to sell the machines, not the biscuits. Indeed, his first company was known as The Cereal Machine Company. However, he did sell the biscuits, which were first marketed under the name SHREDDED WHOLE WHEAT, and later SHREDDED WHEAT.[18]

Shredded wheat biscuits were composed of whole wheat that was subjected to a process of boiling, drying, pressing, shredding and baking. The biscuits produced by this process typically were pillow-shaped, bulging in the center and pressed to a thin point at either end.[19] The biscuits were normally consumed in the form in which they left the cereal box, without the need for cooking or preparation by the consumer, after being partially submerged in a bowl of milk. The pillow shape arguably facilitated the integrity of the biscuit in shipping,[20] and enabled the biscuit to be ready to eat (while absorbing an ideal amount of milk).[21]

Initially, consumers agreed with John Kellogg's skeptical assessment of the biscuit's taste: critics at the World Fair in Chicago in 1893 described the biscuits as "shredded doormat."[22] Eventually, however, the biscuits were commercially successful (for no immediately apparent reason). Although Perky died in 1908, the companies that he formed to

---

17 Perky also obtained a design patent on the pillow-shaped biscuit, although that was invalidated in 1908, one year before it would have expired. Design patents are available to protect the novel *ornamental* features of a useful product that are original and nonobvious; they are not available for design features that are dictated solely by functional considerations. *See* 35 U.S.C. § 171; *see also* Best Lock Corp. v. Ilco Unican Corp., 94 F.3d 1563, 1566 (Fed. Cir. 1996) (functionality bar).

18 The biscuits were probably sold under the name SHREDDED WHEAT starting around 1908. *See* Wayne Mattox, Antique Talk: Breakfast Cereal Collectibles, *at* http://www.antiquetalk.com/column318b.htm; *see also Kellogg*, 305 U.S. at 113 (noting that "For many years, there was no attempt to use the term 'Shredded Wheat' as a trade-mark" and that "in 1905 plaintiff's predecessor . . . applied for registration of the words 'Shredded Whole Wheat' as a trade-mark.").

19 Quaker Oats did at one time in the mid-twentieth century sell round shredded wheat biscuits, called MUFFETS. *See Shredded Wheat Boxes, at* http://thenostalgia-league.com/treasures/barber/barber40.html (last visited Jul. 25, 2005).

20 *See* Shredded Wheat Co. v. Humphrey Cornell Co., 250 F. 960, 967–68 (2d Cir. 1918) (Ward, J., dissenting) ("The form evidently tends to strengthen a product made out of such fragile material and the size is apparently the best fitted for use as a breakfast food on a saucer.").

21 *See id.* at 961 (patent stated that "in this form it is ready for food"); *see also* the exchange of email between modern-day consumers regarding the qualities and challenges of a slightly different product sold in the United Kingdom, WEETABIX, at http://schumann.cleveland.oh.us/weetabix.html (visited Jan. 21, 2005) (discussing "sogginess" and "avoiding crumbs"); *see also Re-constructable Shreddies* http://www.halfbakery.com/ idea/ Re-constructable_20Shreddies (discussing surface area needed to prevent sogginess).

22 ERIK LARSON, THE DEVIL IN THE WHITE CITY 247 (2003).

produce the biscuits (the Natural Food Company, which later became the Shredded Wheat Company) continued to be the exclusive manufacturers of the biscuits through the expiration of the utility patents in 1912.

In 1912, the Kellogg Company, which had become an established cereal manufacturer under the leadership of John Kellogg's brother (Will Keith Kellogg), entered the wheat biscuit market, as was contemplated by patent law. Upon the expiration of the patent, competitors were free to use the technology covered and information disclosed by the patent. This was the consideration that the public received in return for the patentee's period of market exclusivity. As it happened, although the biscuits that Kellogg produced were somewhat similar in form, they were manufactured by a different process. But, after the Shredded Wheat Company (the successor to Perky's company) objected to Kellogg's activities, Kellogg ceased manufacturing the biscuit in 1919 (though the cause of the delay in raising an objection, and the nature of the settlement, is not clear).

As might have been expected by Kellogg's immediate entry into the market upon expiry of the Perky patents in 1912 (and perhaps also by John Kellogg's earlier cavalier approach to appropriation of the GRANULA mark), it was not long before Kellogg and the Shredded Wheat Company came into further conflict. Kellogg resumed its manufacture of shredded wheat biscuits briefly in 1922, and more seriously in 1927, this time copying both the shape and the manufacturing process. It called its product a SHREDDED WHOLE WHEAT BISCUIT. This prompted another lawsuit by the Shredded Wheat Company alleging unfair competition. Again, that suit was settled, apparently on the basis that Kellogg would sell its biscuits instead under the mark KELLOGG'S WHOLE WHEAT BISCUITS. The Shredded Wheat Company was acquired by the National Biscuit Company in 1930, and two years later Nabisco brought yet another suit, which six years later would reach the Supreme Court.

The case that went to the Supreme Court was not the only part of the battle between Nabisco and Kellogg that proceeded to litigation. The contest was an early example of what is now increasingly common, namely a multinational dispute resolved by serial national adjudication. Thus, the parties litigated the same trademark and unfair competition dispute in Canada and the United States.[23] In addition, in 1934, while the suit that went to the Supreme Court was pending, Kellogg brought a civil antitrust claim against Nabisco, alleging among other things that the false assertion of a trademark infringement claim by Nabisco amounted to attempted monopolization of the business of selling shred-

---

[23] *See* Canadian Shredded Wheat Co., Ltd. v. Kellogg Co. Of Canada, 1 [1938] All E.R. 618 (Privy Council, Canada 1938); *see also* Canadian Shredded Wheat Co., Ltd. v. Kellogg Co. Of Canada, [1939] S.C.R. 129 (Sup. Ct. Canada 1939).

ded wheat biscuits.[24] The claim also alleged duress to change the shape of the biscuits, and slanderous statements made by Nabisco salesmen to dealers in the rival products.

Putting aside that a monopolization claim might have been hard to sustain because Kellogg was at the time the country's largest cereal manufacturer,[25] the Second Circuit held that the mere false assertion of an infringement claim was not a per se violation of the antitrust laws. The court noted that a different result might pertain if Nabisco knew its marks were invalid (presumably under some sort of sham exception to antitrust immunity) and thus, with some reluctance, permitted the case to go to trial. However, the Second Circuit noted that "unless much more can be established than the bringing of [an unfair competition suit by Nabisco] and that [such suit] is unlikely to succeed, it would seem that the plaintiff should try out its rights there and not burden the courts with an action that would, in any event, show no promise."[26] Kellogg took the hint, namely, that to maintain the climate of competition it had to defend the trademark and unfair competition cause of action that Nabisco had initiated.

The *Kellogg* Opinion

The Central Issues

The issues presented in *Kellogg* were framed by two prior opinions: *Shredded Wheat Co. v. Humphrey Cornell Co.*, handed down by the Second Circuit, and the Court's earlier opinion in *Singer Mfg. Co. v. June Mfg. Co.* Although *Cornell* is a lower court decision, it was authored by Judge Learned Hand, a respected authority in intellectual property law, and reveals a long-standing strategy of Nabisco (and its predecessor companies) to sue any rival (not just Kellogg) that distributed pillow-shaped wheat biscuits.[27] Although *Cornell* was decided twenty

---

[24] *See Kellogg Co. v. National Biscuit Co.*, 71 F.2d 662 (2d Cir. 1934). Retaliatory antitrust actions are not entirely unusual when a former patentee seeks to assert trade dress rights against a competitor after expiry of the patent. *See, e.g.*, TrafFix Devices, Inc. v. Marketing Displays, Inc., 532 U.S. 23 (2001).

[25] Ironically, thirty-four years later, the Federal Trade Commission sought to require compulsory licensing of Kellogg's trademark on antitrust grounds. Such relief is now prohibited by international law, *see* Agreement on Trade–Related Aspects of Intellectual Property (TRIPS), Apr. 15, 1994, 33 I.L.M. 1197, art. 21, and is a strategy that domestic law had in any event abandoned since the 1970s. *See In re* Borden, 92 FTC 669 (1978), *rev'd*, 92 FTC 807 (1978); Jack Walters & Sons Corp. v. Morton Bldg., Inc., 737 F.2d 698, 704 (7th Cir. 1984).

[26] *Kellogg*, 71 F.2d at 666.

[27] *See* Shredded Wheat Co. v. Humphrey Cornell Co., 250 F. 960 (2d Cir. 1918). Indeed, around this time, other leading players in the cereal industry were bringing complaints based on alleged rights in the relatively descriptive names by which they identified their

years prior to *Kellogg*, it arose after the expiry of Nabisco's patents, and thus Nabisco relied on trademark and unfair competition law to restrain Cornell's distribution.[28]

In the early twentieth-century, trademark rights were largely a creature of common law. Registration schemes did exist, both at the federal and state level. But Congress, perhaps chastened by the striking down of the federal trademark statute as unconstitutional in 1879,[29] had restricted the option of federal registration to what were called "technical trademarks," that is, "arbitrary" terms that bore no relation to the product they identified (e.g., IVORY for hand soap) or terms "coined" for the purpose of acting as a trademark (e.g., CLOROX for bleach). Words that merely described the qualities or characteristics of the product upon which they were used (e.g., EXTRA–STRONG for pain killers) could not be registered. In contrast to arbitrary or coined terms, such "descriptive" terms were thought unlikely to identify the source of a product (i.e., were unlikely to act as a trademark). And according rights in descriptive terms to a single producer ran the risk that competitors would be prevented from using language that accurately described their products, a risk thought minimal where the producer had coined the term or had chosen an arbitrary term semantically unconnected to the product upon which it was used.

Trademark law was, however, a species of the broader law of unfair competition.[30] Unfair competition law might provide redress against use of a confusingly similar mark where trademark law proper did not. As a result, descriptive terms could be protected under principles of unfair competition if they had acquired "secondary meaning," that is, if the producer were able to show that the consumer had in fact come to identify a product by the symbol in which rights were claimed. This approach, grounded in a misrepresentation-based notion of unfair competition, imposed stricter standards of proof of harm upon plaintiffs and left marks permanently open to the challenge of descriptiveness. Such an approach ensured protection against unfair competition in two senses. First, it prohibited acts of passing off that would deceive consumers and allow rivals to trade on the goodwill of competitors. But, second, it also

products. *See* Kellogg Toasted Corn Flake Co.v. Quaker Oats Co., 235 F. 657 (6th Cir. 1916) (rejecting claims of rights in TOASTED CORN FLAKES).

28 The Second Circuit opinion in *Cornell* did not address rights in the name SHREDDED WHEAT; only the appearance of the biscuits (shape, color, and size) were at issue. The use of the term figures more significantly in the opinion of the district court, which likewise found for the plaintiff. *See* Shredded Wheat Co. v. Humphrey Cornell, 244 F. 508 (D. Conn. 1917).

29 *See The Trade–Mark Cases*, 100 U.S. 82 (1879).

30 *See* Hanover Star Milling Co. v. Metcalf, 240 U.S. 403 (1916).

ensured that the putative mark owner did not receive an unfair competitive advantage by securing exclusive rights in terms that were needed by others to compete fairly in the marketplace. Unfair competition law looked both to prevent unfairness and to promote competition.

The shape or design of a product could be protected under similar principles of unfair competition law, again upon proof of secondary meaning. In the *Cornell* case, Nabisco succeeded in showing that the pillow-shape of the biscuits had acquired secondary meaning, based upon uncontradicted testimony from jobbers, retailers, and consumers.[31] This source identification triggered the concerns of trademark and unfair competition law. The plaintiff had established an interest that warranted protection. Ordinarily, this finding would have supported the award of an injunction against the defendant's continued distribution of any confusingly similar products. And witnesses testified at trial that they had served or been served Cornell's biscuit as "shredded wheat."

However, according exclusive rights to use the shape of a product raises difficult questions for trademark and unfair competition law because it may affect the capacity of competitors to make a rival product. This concern is less acute with word marks. A product's shape may be closely connected to its utility. Typically, there are fewer ways to make a product work than there are words by which to call the product.[32] Thus, the threat of adverse effects on competition made courts cautious before offering protection to product design, a concern reflected most directly (but not solely) in the doctrine of functionality.

In *Cornell*, Learned Hand acknowledged the functionality doctrine and thus searched for a remedy that did not take away the *defendant's right* to compete.[33] He stressed that "under the guise of protecting against unfair competition, we must be jealous not to create perpetual monopolies."[34] The Second Circuit methodically surveyed the effect that changes in the appearance of the biscuit would have on the ability of Cornell to compete in the marketplace for cereals.[35] A change in coloring

[31] *See Humphrey Cornell Co.*, 250 F. at 963 ("The plaintiff has at least shown that the public has become accustomed to regard its familiar wheat biscuit as emanating, if not from it by name, at least from a single, though anonymous, maker, and the second is as good for these purposes as the first"). It did not matter to Judge Hand that some of the association may have been as a result of the exercise of the patent rights. *See id.*

[32] *See* Graeme B. Dinwoodie, *The Death of Ontology: A Teleological Approach to Trademark Law*, 84 IOWA L. REV. 611, 624–45 (1999).

[33] Although the articulation of a default right to compete may not have seemed notable at the time, it did come only ten months before the Supreme Court endorsed a right against misappropriation in INS. *See infra* "Intellectual Property Theory."

[34] *Humphrey Cornell Co.*, 250 F. at 964.

[35] The most cursory analysis is offered of the option of changing the "form" of the biscuit, with the court relying upon the invalidated design patent to support its conclusion

would have made the biscuit taste repellant and "either terminate or hopelessly cripple any competition between the parties." Increasing the size of the biscuits would have affected how many biscuits would fit in a standard dish, and decreasing the size would raise the defendant's costs. Both options were "too onerous" to impose upon the defendant.

The court, in language that reflected the balancing of interests at the heart of its analysis, concluded that it did "not see any possible change in the appearance of the biscuit itself which would be of enough service to the plaintiff to justify imposition upon the defendant."As a result, the pillow shape was found to be functional and the court refused to enjoin Cornell from making pillow-shaped biscuits or to force Cornell to change the shape of its biscuits. The court recognized that, in the final analysis, if the "secondary meaning is bound up in elements of the appearance which cannot be changed without cutting off the defendant's substantial right to make and sell that kind of goods, the plaintiff must suffer the confusion."

In addition, however, the court considered the option of impressing a mark on the biscuit or wrapping the biscuits in ways that contained a legend of source. In assessing whether such relief would interfere with the defendant's right to compete freely, Judge Hand emphasized that "the question is always commercial." On the record before the court, the "commercial possibilities" of such marking or wrapping were not clear, despite the court spending time analyzing the effect of marking or wrapping on costs, and determining whether a pre-baking marking would survive the cooking process. However, a majority of the court placed the burden on the defendant to show that marking the biscuits would "impose upon him a commercial handicap which will practically take from him his free right to compete," and thus required that Cornell impress a distinguishing mark upon its biscuits.

Even in formulating this limited relief, the court was quite conscious that its remedy served, in effect, to regulate the competition in the cereal market. Judge Hand refused to impose an injunction with respect to direct consumer sales, because in that context the difference between the markings on the cartons of the respective parties' products was sufficient to offer differentiation. Only biscuits which Cornell sold to "hotels, restaurants, lunch rooms, and guest houses" had to be marked. Moreover, the court, taking into account that experience would be the surest evidence of commercial possibilities, went so far as to impose a probationary period during which the defendant would attempt to mark its

---

that the defendant should not be required to alter the "form" of the biscuit. Indeed, even any limited relief could not "affect the design dedicated by the design patent." *Id.* at 965. This is the full extent of Judge Hand's express reliance on expired or invalidated patents.

products distinctly, with an invitation to return to the court if this mandate proved commercially prohibitive.[36]

The facts and issues presented to the Court in *Kellogg* were very close to those considered by the Second Circuit twenty years earlier in *Cornell*. The complaint was filed by Nabisco in federal district court in Delaware and invoked the court's diversity jurisdiction. Nabisco complained about several discrete aspects of Kellogg's activities: (1) the use on the cereal box of a picture of a dish containing two pillow-shaped biscuits submerged in milk; (2) the manufacture of the biscuit in the same pillow shape as the Nabisco product; and (3) the use of the term SHREDDED WHEAT. Nabisco's efforts to restrain use of the picture were grounded in trademark law,[37] but the claims with respect to rights in the pillow shape of the manufactured biscuits or the term SHREDDED WHEAT were based upon an allegation of passing off in violation of common law principles of unfair competition, because neither the shape nor the term was federally registered. Nabisco had previously failed to obtain a federal registration for the somewhat similar term SHREDDED WHOLE WHEAT, separate and apart from any packaging graphic, because the Patent and Trademark Office had concluded that the term was descriptive.[38] Any efforts to register SHREDDED WHEAT would likely have met a similar response.

The central elements of the actions for trademark infringement and unfair competition were, however, quite similar (although the owner of a registered trademark would encounter less stringent evidentiary hurdles). Either action was predicated upon proof that the term or symbol

[36] *Id.* at 964. Judge Ward filed a dissenting opinion in *Cornell*, concluding that the Shredded Wheat Company was entitled to no relief whatsoever. He reached a different conclusion because, in his assessment of the competing interests of the parties, he gave little weight to the interests of the Shredded Wheat Company; he thought that it sustained close to no injury through Cornell's use. In essence, Judge Ward disagreed with Judge Hand concerning the magnitude of Cornell's interests.

[37] Nabisco owned a registered trademark on a picture of pillow-shaped biscuits submerged in milk in a dish.

[38] *See* Natural Food Co. v. Williams, 30 App. D.C. 348 (C. App. D.C. 1908). The Natural Foods Company applied to register the term SHREDDED WHOLE WHEAT for its biscuits under the so-called "ten-year clause" found in the Trademark Act of 1905. The application was opposed by Williams, who claimed that the term was descriptive and that the Natural Food Company had *not* been the exclusive user of that phrase for ten years prior to 1905, as required by the pertinent provision of the 1905 statute. In particular, the phrase had been used by Williams and others who manufactured and sold shredded whole wheat. The court sustained the opposition, and noted that the term was an accurate description of the shredded wheat food product made by Williams and others. Although no single sentence in the *Williams* opinion unequivocally stated that the term was descriptive of the products of The Natural Foods Company, that conclusion was clearly implied. And the *Kellogg* Court certainly proceeded on the basis that the term was descriptive of both Williams' and Nabisco's products. *See* 305 U.S. at 117.

for which protection was sought was distinctive, meaning that the term identified the source of the product upon which it was used and distinguished that product from those manufactured by others. Distinctiveness was central to trademark and unfair competition law because unless a symbol was distinctive of one producer its use by another would not give rise to the consumer confusion those causes of action targeted. Absent distinctiveness, there existed no reason grounded in U.S. trademark and unfair competition law to restrain competition by the defendant.

Modern case law, since *Kellogg*, has neatly articulated a spectrum of distinctiveness, according to which marks can usefully be classified. Marks that are coined, arbitrary, or suggestive are treated as inherently distinctive, and protectable without proof of secondary meaning.[39] Descriptive terms are protectable *only* upon proof of secondary meaning. Generic terms, which "refer, or ha[ve] come to be understood as referring, to the genus of which the particular product is a species,"[40] cannot be protected by trademark law.

Distinctiveness doctrine was somewhat similar at the time of the *Kellogg* litigation. However, descriptive marks could not be registered *in any event*, and secondary meaning only secured the producer protection under principles of unfair competition. As the action of the Patent and Trademark Office in response to the earlier trademark application for SHREDDED WHOLE WHEAT suggested, proving distinctiveness (both of the term SHREDDED WHEAT and the similarly unregistered pillow shape) would require Nabisco to show secondary meaning.

However, distinctiveness was by no means the only issue that the *Kellogg* litigation would raise. As seen in *Cornell*, when rights were claimed in product shapes under trademark or unfair competition law, a plaintiff faced additional hurdles. In particular, where protection of a shape might inhibit competition, the shape would be deemed "functional," and hence unprotectable. Although the concept of functionality has been more fully developed in modern law, early twentieth century courts had already recognized the enhanced risk to competition associated with

---

[39] Modern trademark law refers to these classes of mark as "inherently distinctive." The category of "suggestive" marks developed between the 1905 statute (which, with one minor exception, barred federal registration of descriptive terms, even with secondary meaning, prompting the creation of the "suggestive" category) and the Lanham Act in 1946 (which made the suggestive category less somewhat less significant, by permitting the registration of descriptive marks that had acquired secondary meaning). *See* Abercrombie & Fitch Co. v. Hunting World, Inc., 537 F.2d 4 (2d Cir. 1976). "A term is suggestive if it requires imagination, thought and perception to reach a conclusion as to the nature of the goods." Stix Prods., Inc. v. United Merchants & Manufacturers Inc., 295 F. Supp. 479, 488 (S.D.N.Y. 1968).

[40] Abercrombie & Fitch Co. v. Hunting World, Inc., 537 F.2d 4 (2d Cir. 1976).

protection of product designs, and the need to deny protection on this ground.

Judicial reluctance to protect product designs was especially emphatic where the product in question had been the subject of an expired utility patent. As the Supreme Court had declared in *Singer Mfg. Co.* v. *June Mfg. Co.* in 1896, "on the expiration of a patent . . . there passes to the public the right to make the machine in the form in which it was constructed during the patent."[41] This was part of the bargain between the public and the patentee. In *Singer*, the leading manufacturer of sewing machines sought to restrain a competitor from copying the shape of Singer sewing machines. Singer had at one time owned patents on various parts of its sewing machines, but those patents had expired. The Court refused to allow Singer effectively to extend the life of those patents by asserting rights in the shape of the manufactured product based on principles of unfair competition. This so-called "right to copy" the subject matter of an expired patent would, of course, be an additional issue for Nabisco to confront because Perky had obtained, and Nabisco's predecessors had exploited, utility patents on both the pillow-shaped biscuit and the machine that made the biscuit.

The Kellogg Opinion

The District Court dismissed Nabisco's suit on the grounds suggested by *Singer* and, to a lesser extent, *Cornell*. It held that the term SHREDDED WHEAT described the products of both the plaintiff and the defendant (i.e., that the term no longer pointed to a single source and thus had become generic), and that upon expiration of the patent the name of the product made by the patented invention passed, along with the product shape, into the public domain. The Court of Appeals for the Third Circuit reversed the lower court and remanded the case directing the lower court to enjoin the use of the photograph, the use of the name, or the use of the shape in the manufacture, distribution, or advertising of the product.

After procedural posturing by the parties to clarify the scope of the Third Circuit's instruction,[42] the Supreme Court granted certiorari. In a 7–2 opinion authored by Justice Brandeis, it then reversed the Third Circuit.[43] The Court refused to award Nabisco the relief that it sought

---

[41] 163 U.S. 169, 185 (1896).

[42] After the first appellate decision, the Supreme Court denied a petition for a writ of certiorari. *See* 302 U.S. at 733. It was only after the lower courts clarified the scope of relief that the Supreme Court intervened.

[43] The Supreme Court did not address whether the use of the "two biscuits in a dish" picture on the cereal box constituted trademark infringement because the Court read the Third Circuit's clarifying decree as enjoining the picture only in connection with an

either with respect to the shape of manufacture or the term SHREDDED WHEAT. The majority opinion was short (though not as short as the dissent) and its reasoning somewhat enigmatic. The (several) grounds upon which the Court based its opinion were not surprising: lack of distinctiveness, functionality, and the right to copy the subject matter of expired patents. But the centrality of each ground to the Court's conclusion, and their relationship to each other, was unclear.

Protection of the Shape

The Court decided that the shape was unprotectable on three different theories: that there was a right to copy it after the patent expired; that it was functional; and that it was not distinctive. The Court first held that Nabisco could not enjoin the manufacture of biscuits in the pillow-shape because to do so would interfere with the premise of patent law that once a patent has expired the public has the right to practice that invention. The Court explained that expiration of the patents meant that the pillow shape, upon which a patent had been granted, was dedicated to the public. This ground of decision was not wholly surprising in light of *Singer*'s recognition of the right to copy.

The *Singer* Court had, however, attached a caveat to the "public's right to copy," namely, that the competitor should label the machines so as to disclose the competitor as the source of manufacture. The *Kellogg* Court endorsed that caveat, noting that despite the right to copy the subject matter of the expired patent, there remained an "obligation resting upon Kellogg Company . . . to identify its own product lest it be mistaken for that of the plaintiff." Thus, the Court conducted an assessment of the manner in which the defendant was exercising its right to copy (*i.e.*, how the products were being packaged and labeled) to determine congruence with principles of unfair competition: the Court stressed that "the question remains whether [the defendant] in exercising its right to use the name 'Shredded Wheat' and the pillow-shaped biscuit, is doing so fairly. Fairness requires that it be done in a manner which reasonably distinguishes its product from that of plaintiff."

The Court's analysis of this question was unusually fact-intensive for a supreme court, and not hugely unlike that conducted by Learned Hand in *Cornell*. It compared the size, form and color of the cereal cartons in which each company sold its biscuits, and noted the use (and size and prominence) of a house mark by Kellogg to differentiate its product. Indeed, the Court went so far as to assess the post-sale market such as restaurants, in which (because the carton was not present) the size and appearance of the competing biscuits themselves were crucial.

---

injunction against manufacture in the pillow shape and use of the term SHREDDED WHEAT. Nabisco had not sought Supreme Court review of whether the use of the picture independently constituted infringement. *See Kellogg*, 305 U.S. at 122 n.6.

Kellogg's biscuit was only two thirds of the size of Nabisco's biscuit, and slightly different in appearance. Moreover, because only 2½% of the Kellogg biscuits were sold to hotels and restaurants (where the carton differentiation would be irrelevant), and *within that market* 98% were sold in a different "two-biscuit" carton that also bore the Kellogg name, the size of the market in which deception might occur was "negligible." In contrast to the *Cornell* court, Justice Brandeis (twenty years later) declared that marking individual biscuits was not "commercially possible." He emphasized that Kellogg's obligation was "not to insure that every purchaser will know it to be the maker but to use every reasonable means to prevent confusion." And, unlike the defendant in *Singer*, which had failed to comply with the unfair competition-grounded caveat and had thus been subject to an accounting of profits,[44] Kellogg had made "every reasonable effort to distinguish its product" from that of Nabisco.[45]

The court also denied protection for the pillow-shape on the ground that the shape was functional, in that the "cost of the biscuit would be increased and its high quality lessened if some other form were substituted for the pillow shape." Presumably, a different shape would have required alteration of the (formerly-) patented machine or made the manufacturing process far more expensive. Although Justice Brandeis never explained precisely which advantages of the shape of the biscuit were so useful to rivals, the effect that the shape had on the integrity of the biscuit in shipping, the rate at which a pillow-shaped biscuit absorbed milk, and the readiness of a biscuit of that shape for consumption without cooking, might all have been relevant advantages. In addition, because utility patents were granted only on aspects of products that are useful, the existence of the patent on the shape and the machine necessarily spoke to the functionality of the design. However, the Court did not expressly link the *existence* of the patent to its finding of functionality (let alone use the *contents* of the patent to support its conclusion).[46]

The Court's laconic attitude to articulating the reasons for its conclusion of functionality stood in stark contrast to the detailed nature of the inquiry previously undertaken by Judge Learned Hand in *Cornell*. However, like Brandeis in *Kellogg*, Hand never addressed the relevance of the utility patent to the assessment of effects on competition that

---

[44] *See* 163 U.S. at 200–04.

[45] The complete avoidance of any possible confusion would not be required given the right to use the term and the product shape. *See Kellogg,* 305 U.S. at 121.

[46] In the parallel Canadian litigation, the Privy Council reached the same conclusion as the Supreme Court, but toward the end of its opinion, the Privy Council explicitly noted that "the decision has been reached without basing it specifically upon the existence of patents which have expired." [1938] 1 All E.R. at 633.

underlay the functionality doctrine. His analysis reflected competitive concerns that sustained a conclusion of functionality quite apart from the existence of the utility patent.[47]

Finally, the Court also suggested that the pillow-shape had become generic, having become "primarily associated with the article rather than a particular producer." It did not act as a source-identifier and thus could not provide the basis for an injunction against Kellogg manufacturing biscuits of that shape. This conclusion did not, however, deprive Nabisco of all protection under broader principles of unfair competition law. Although Kellogg was "free to use the pillow-shaped form, [this right was] subject ... to the obligation to identify its product lest it be mistaken for that of the plaintiff." The Court concluded that Kellogg had marketed its product in ways that complied with this obligation, and thus had satisfied the conditions attaching to the right to copy the pillow-shaped form.[48]

The term SHREDDED WHEAT

The Court denied protection to the term on the grounds that the term was not distinctive and use of the term by Kellogg was essential if Kellogg was effectively to exercise its right to copy the shape. On the question of distinctiveness of the term, the Court held that the term was generic because it did not identify a single source for consumers.[49] It

---

[47] Judge Hand's opinion in *Cornell* differed from *Kellogg* in that he placed no weight on the *expiry* of the utility patents, and thus on the right to copy the subject matter of expired patents (the first ground upon which Brandeis denied protection for the pillow shape). Judge Hand appeared more concerned with effects of protection on competition rather than its effects on the right to copy. Indeed, he did not find it troublesome that whatever secondary meaning that had been established in the shape might have been attributable to the prior patent monopoly. To the extent that the patents *in any way* appeared to have influenced Judge Hand, it was *the invalidated design* patent that was of the greatest significance with respect to protection of the shape. *See* Shredded Wheat Co. v. Humphrey Cornell Co., 250 F. 960, 964 (2d Cir. 1918) (noting that "as to form, the plaintiff appears to us finally concluded by its own design patent.... [T]he plaintiff's formal dedication of the design is conclusive reason against any injunction based upon the exclusive right to that form."). Judge Ward's dissent based the right of Cornell to copy explicitly on both competitiveness-based functionality concerns *and* the expired "product and design patents." *Id.* at 967.

[48] *See Kellogg*, 305 U.S. at 120–21; *supra* text accompanying notes 44–45 (discussing right to copy). The section of the opinion in which the Court discussed the reasonableness of Kellogg's efforts to differentiate its product from that of Nabisco is not linked specifically to either the protection of shape or the term. It would appear to have been a combined analysis of the caveats attached to both the "right to copy" and the "generic mark" doctrines.

[49] *See id.* at 116 (noting that the term "Shredded Wheat" "is the generic term of the article, which describes it with a fair degree of accuracy; and is the term by which the biscuit in pillow-shaped form is generally known by the public.").

described a product type, rather than a single producer. In contrast, the Third Circuit opinion had stated that in 1923 there was "no dispute" that the term SHREDDED WHEAT identified the plaintiff's biscuit.[50] Indeed, twenty-seven states and several foreign countries had registered the term as a trademark.[51]

To be sure, there was evidence that supported the Court's conclusion: for years, the term had not been used as a trademark; federal registration of a very similar term had been denied on the basis that the term was descriptive; and, use of the term "shredded wheat" in various patent documents appeared to have been otherwise than as a mark. But the Court never really tackled these empirical questions in any detail. Nor did it explain why the Third Circuit's conclusion was incorrect. The Third Circuit had examined both whether the biscuit was comprised of shredded wheat (the Third Circuit declined to characterize the process of producing slivers of wheat prior to baking as "shredding") and whether alternative terms were available to competitors.

A finding that the term SHREDDED WHEAT was generic should, under one reading of trademark law, have terminated the Court's inquiry. Generic terms were unprotected, and free to be copied. As the Court noted, the existence of secondary meaning was beside the point once the term was classified as generic. No evidence of plentiful sales or extensive advertising, typical evidence pointing to secondary meaning, could alter the unprotectability of the term SHREDDED WHEAT. Yet, after concluding that the term was generic, the Court rebutted efforts by Nabisco to suggest that it had developed secondary meaning in the term SHREDDED WHEAT and thus should have been entitled to protection at common law. In rejecting the argument that the term SHREDDED WHEAT had acquired secondary meaning, the Court suggested that, to be protected, the source-identifying meaning must not be "subordinate." The Court accepted that "many people associate the product . . . with the plaintiff's factory," but this was insufficient to sustain an argument for protection. Instead, the plaintiff would have to have shown that the "primary significance of the term in the minds of the consuming public is not the product but the producer," which the Court concluded (without explanation) that Nabisco "ha[d] not done." This conclusion, albeit unsupported in the opinion, implicitly reflected the empirical reality of consumer association.

Perhaps the Court's venture into secondary meaning might have been better understood if the Court had prefaced its discussion with language to the effect that "even if the term SHREDDED WHEAT is thought to be descriptive rather than generic, it is unprotectable because Nabisco has failed to show secondary meaning." Perhaps the Court's

---

[50] *See* National Biscuit Co. v. Kellogg Co., 91 F.2d 150, 152 (3d Cir. 1937).

[51] *See id.* at 152–53.

discussion of the legal standard for proving secondary meaning was indeed an attempt to engage with the contrary empirical assessments of consumer association made by the Third Circuit.[52] Or perhaps this was the Court offering an alternative justification for placing the term SHREDDED WHEAT on the generic side of the descriptive/generic line.

Each of these conjectures is, however, refuted by the language of the opinion, and in particular the structure of the Court's analysis. In the opinion, the Court's discussion of secondary meaning was detached from its initial discussion of distinctiveness (i.e., whether the term was the generic name by which the public identified the product). An explanation of the second ground for denial of protection to the term was interposed between them. The Court thus appeared to treat the "secondary meaning" argument as a discrete basis upon which Nabisco sought relief, rather than a consideration integral to the Court's analysis of distinctiveness and its conclusion that the term SHREDDED WHEAT was generic.

Why did the Court offer a discrete analysis of secondary meaning? Perhaps the answer lies in the complexities of the concept of "distinctiveness."[53] While much of Brandeis' distinctiveness analysis is couched in language of consumer association, there is throughout the opinion a strong undercurrent of concern for competition. Yet, nominally, formulations of the concept of "distinctiveness" focus on consumer association: do consumers see the term as a designation that identifies goods of a single producer?[54] The *Kellogg* Court's discussion of secondary meaning was at one with this (empirical) perspective of distinctiveness as a measure of consumer association, focusing on "significance of the term in the minds of the consuming public."[55]

---

52 The Third Circuit had made some reference in its distinctiveness analysis to some policy considerations that were grounded in competition (e.g., available alternatives) as well as actual consumer association.

53 In addition, the lesser remedy—and, thus, this additional analysis of secondary meaning—was contemplated only because principles of unfair competition law might provide some relief in circumstances where trademark law afforded no (prohibitory injunctive) remedy. The Supreme Court had stressed in the early twentieth century that trademark law was a subset of the broader law of unfair competition. *See* Hanover Star Milling Co. v. Metcalf, 240 U.S. 403 (1916); *cf.* Two Pesos, Inc. v. Taco Cabana, Inc., 505 U.S. 763 (1992) (Stevens J., concurring).

54 *See, e.g.,* Restatement (Third) of Unfair Competition § 13 (1995) (definition of "distinctive"); *see also* 15 U.S.C. § 1127 (definition of "trademark"); 15 U.S.C. § 1064(3) ("the primary significance of the registered mark to the relevant public . . . shall be the test for determining whether the registered mark has become the generic name of goods or services on or in connection with which it has been used").

55 The Court's high standard for secondary meaning might, however, reflect a concern for competition (or even the sanctity of the right to copy, which might be imperiled by easy de facto patent protection through the trademark system).

However, in *classifying* a mark by the later-devised terms of "arbitrary," "coined," "suggestive," "descriptive," or "generic"—that is, in situating the mark on the spectrum of distinctiveness—judicial analysis is often conducted according to multiple metrics.[56] In particular, classification (which the *Kellogg* Court had earlier in its opinion cursorily performed, finding SHREDDED WHEAT to be generic) is often explicitly viewed through two lenses: consumer association, and effects on competition.[57] For example, if a mark is one which "competitors would be likely to need . . . in describing their products," it is likely to be regarded as descriptive.[58] If conferring trademark rights on a term would accord the mark owner a monopoly over a product market, that term will be found generic.[59]

It may be that, although competitive concerns warranted the Court classifying the term SHREDDED WHEAT as generic, the term SHREDDED WHEAT *was* in some sense distinctive if viewed empirically as a question of consumer association. Here, the opinion offered inconsistent clues. Despite little supporting analysis, the Court had expressly grounded its finding that SHREDDED WHEAT was generic on the fact that it was "the term by which the biscuit in pillow-shaped form is generally known by the public." Yet, the Court implicitly acknowledged that Nabisco had made *some* showing of protectable meaning by requiring "that the defendant use reasonable care to inform the public of the source of its product." Absent some distinctiveness *in fact* (what courts and commentators now call "de facto secondary meaning"), there would have been no reason under then-prevailing U.S. law to contemplate granting Nabisco *any* relief,[60] because no actionable confusion would as a

---

[56] Competition is not the only other policy that might be implicated. *See* Rochelle Cooper Dreyfuss, *Expressive Genericity: Trademarks as Language in the Pepsi Generation*, 65 Notre Dame L. Rev. 397, 418 (1990) (arguing that the expressive value of certain trademarks should also lead to a finding of genericity regardless of competition questions).

[57] *See* Graeme B. Dinwoodie, *Reconceptualizing the Inherent Distinctiveness of Product Design Trade Dress*, 75 N.C. L. Rev. 471, 503–04 (1997) (explaining the dual lenses through which distinctiveness is assessed).

[58] Zatarain's, Inc. v. Oak Grove Smokehouse, Inc., 698 F.2d 786 (5th Cir. 1983).

[59] *See, e.g.*, Filipino Yellow Pages, Inc. v. Asian Journal Pubs., Inc., 198 F.3d 1143 (9th Cir. 1999).

[60] If the United States had an unfair competition law that resembled that found in the civil law countries of Europe, relief might have been available without this harm being involved. Indeed, even under an expansive unfair competition law that is limited to acts of misrepresentation, causes of action might exist in circumstances other than those raising trademark-like issues (and hence not truly dependent upon distinctiveness). The false advertising provision of the Lanham Act can be viewed in these terms, and so too could the "false designation of origin" provision (although the Court's recent *Dastar* decision may have limited the extent to which that provision affords relief beyond trademark-proper

factual matter have been likely to ensue.[61] Thus, the Court's supposedly empirical conclusion of genericity is partially belied by its contemplation of some lesser relief.

As a result of this ambiguity, fully understanding the Court's discussion of secondary meaning is difficult. The Court's overall analysis of distinctiveness is stretched and conclusory because it was seeking to sustain as an empirical conclusion what was in truth a legal policy choice driven by concerns about competition. The opinion did not clearly explain whether the possibility of a lesser remedy under unfair competition principles is triggered by some meaning to consumers less than "primary significance" or instead simply by "primary significance" that the Court would not recognize *de iure* for other reasons. Of course, the Court neatly avoided the ambiguity *in the case before it* by finding that Kellogg had in any event fully met its obligation under unfair competition law. But the ambiguity remained.

The suggestion that the Court acted on a rationale other than actual consumer understanding of the term SHREDDED WHEAT was also reflected in the Court's alternative explanation of the unprotectability of the term, which could again be traced to *Singer*.[62] This explanation was explicitly rooted in broader intellectual property policy. Thus, the Court suggested that "as Kellogg had the right to make the article it also had the right to use the term by which the public knows it."[63] Protectablity of the term SHREDDED WHEAT thus appeared derivative, and intended to ensure the commercial effectiveness, of the right to practice the expired patent on the pillow shape.[64]

---

claims, Dastar Corp. v. Twentieth Century Fox Film Corp., 539 U.S. 23 (2003)). Whether such protection would have been available at the time under prevailing U.S. law may have depended upon whether the Court was applying state or federal law. *See infra* "Intellectual Property Theory."

61 *Cf.* Shredded Wheat Co. v. Humphrey Cornell Co., 250 F. 960, 963–64 (2d Cir. 1918) (explaining why no protection need be conferred on descriptive terms). It is possible that this obligation flowed from the de facto distinctiveness of the *shape*. However, the Court included the "reasonable efforts at differentiation" caveat separately in discussion of both the term's genericity, *see Kellogg*, 305 U.S. at 119, and the pillow-shape, *see id.* at 120, and the factual analysis is combined after discussion of the protection of both the shape and the term. *See id.* at 120–21.

62 *Kellogg*, 305 U.S. at 119 (holding that the expiration of the patent conferred on the public the right to use the "generic designation of the thing which has arisen during the monopoly in consequence of the designation having been acquiesced in by the owner, either tacitly, by accepting the benefits of the monopoly, or expressly by his having so connected the name with the machine as lend countenance to the resulting dedication.").

63 *See Kellogg*, 305 U.S. at 118 (citing *Singer*); *see also id.* (use of the name SHREDDED WHEAT "was essentially necessary to vest the public with the invention that became theirs on the expiry of the patent.").

64 The Court might, under this alternative rubric, have been articulating a rule of law that deems as "generic" a term identifying a product on which a patent has expired. It is of

After-Story: The Varied Use of *Kellogg*

As seen in Part II, although the *Kellogg* case involved a relatively narrow issue, and was in large part controlled by the Court's decision in *Singer*, Justice Brandeis' opinion implicated a number of central issues in trademark and unfair competition law. Most obviously, the opinion contained language addressing distinctiveness, functionality, and the right to copy the subject matter of expired patents. Less clearly, it spoke to the doctrine of "de facto secondary meaning" and, more speculatively, the relationship between trademark law and broader principles of unfair competition. But the perfunctory nature of some of the Court's analysis, and the failure to address the relationship between the different grounds of decision, left the opinion open to varied interpretation. As a result, *Kellogg* has been used by Congress, courts, and scholars in a number of different ways.

The Lanham Act

Kellogg had an immediate effect in Congress, and its hold over policymakers has continued in successive revisions of the Lanham Act. Trademark law was in a state of ferment in 1938, when *Kellogg* was decided. That year saw the publication of the first Restatement of Torts, which addressed important principles of trademark and unfair competition law. And, although the congressional gestation of the Trademark Act of 1946 can be traced back to 1924,[65] it was in 1938 that Congressman Fritz Lanham introduced the first of the bills[66] that would eventually lead to the enactment of the Lanham Act. An intense debate ensued, as reflected both in legislative hearings and in the pages of the leading trademark law journal, *The Trademark Reporter*.

The Department of Justice was an active participant in these debates. It was concerned that a strengthening of trademark rights, as contemplated by the early (pre-Fritz Lanham) versions of trademark reform legislation, would have dire anti-competitive consequences.[67] Ex-

---

course possible to reach a similar conclusion through conventional doctrinal devices, namely, by defining the relevant product market for distinctiveness purposes as the market covered by the patented product. Language added to section 14(3) of the Lanham Act in 1984 may make this hard to do as a matter of law.

[65] *See* S. 2679, 68th Cong., 1st Sess. (1924). The bar associations were also extremely active in these efforts, and stirrings in those bodies can be seen as early as 1920. *See* Edward S. Rogers, *The Lanham Act and the Social Function of Trade–Marks*, 14 LAW & CONTEMP. PROBS. 173, 177 (1949).

[66] *See* H.R. 9041, 75th Cong., 1st Sess. (1938).

[67] *See* Sigmund Timberg, *Trade-Marks, Monopoly, And the Restraint of Competition*, 14 LAW & CONTEMP. PROBS. 323, 360 (1949) (noting concerns about early versions of the Lanham Act). Several aspects of the bill prompted complaints by the Department of Justice

plicit codification of *Singer/Kellogg* was an important part of the Department's agenda to ensure competition.[68] In particular, these cases were part of the discussion regarding what at the time were known as the "patent clauses" of the pending legislation.[69] Although there had been numerous "patent expiry" trademark cases decided by lower courts since *Singer,* it may be that the decision of the Supreme Court in *Kellogg* brought the *Singer* issue to the forefront of legislative consideration.[70] The 1938 Lanham Bill, introduced prior to *Kellogg,* contained no provisions regarding products covered by expired patents.[71] Nor did legislative hearings on that bill address the topic. Yet, the 1939 bill included a provision (section 8) that would have caused a trademark registration of a term that was the "sole name of an article . . . having patent protection" to expire two years after the expiration of the patent, and this was the focus of some deliberation before Congress.[72]

During the evolution of the legislation, the patent expiry issue was dealt with instead by what became sections 14(3) and 15(4) of the Lanham Act, which specifically addressed the trademark law consequences of patent expiration by providing that a registration could be canceled "at any time if the registered mark becomes the [generic] name of an article *or substance on which the patent has expired*"[73] and that no

regarding the anticompetitive threats it posed. *See* Rogers, *supra* note 65, at 183 ("Whenever there was a hearing before any committee on the trademark bill, sooner or later there appeared zealous men from the Department of Justice who raised all sorts of objections"); *see also* Abraham S. Greenberg, *The "Patent" Clauses of the Lanham Act*, 38 TRADEMARK REP. 3, 17–18 (1948) (noting role of Justice Department).

68 *See* Greenberg, *supra* note 67, at 13–14 (discussing views of representatives of the Department of Justice, the Federal Trade Commission, and the Food and Drug Administration); Timberg, *supra* note 67, at 353 (author with Antitrust Division of the Department of Justice).

69 *See, e.g.,* Greenberg, *supra* note 67.

70 Edward S. Rogers, a leading practitioner and writer, was one of the driving forces behind the development of the Lanham Act, see Sara Stadler Nelson, *The Wages of Ubiquity in Trademark Law*, 88 IOWA L. REV. 731, 755 (2003) (describing Rogers as the "father of the Lanham Act"), and represented Kellogg in the Nabisco litigation. *See National Biscuit Co. v. Kellogg Co.*, 91 F.2d 150, 151 (3d Cir. 1937); 305 U.S. at 113 (on brief before the Supreme Court). Twenty years earlier, Rogers had represented Quaker Oats against Kellogg in litigation over trademark rights in TOASTED CORN FLAKES. *See* Kellogg Toasted Corn Flake Co. v. Quaker Oats Co., 235 F. 657 (6th Cir. 1916).

71 *See* Greenberg, *supra* note 67, at 4.

72 *Kellogg* is not the only possible explanation for the appearance and discussion of this proposal. The two-year grace period may have been inspired by a parallel provision in the British Trademark Act of 1938. *See id.* at 13 n.23.

73 *See* Pub. L. No. 79–489, 60 Stat. 427 (1946) (emphasis added).

incontestable right could be acquired in a term that was the generic name of an article that had been patented.[74]

In 1962, the italicized language in section 14(3) was deleted, transforming the *Kellogg*-specific provision into a general *genericness* provision.[75] And in 1984, the gloss of *Kellogg* on the genericness provision would be completed with the codification of *Kellogg's secondary meaning* language into the provision authorizing cancellation of registrations of marks that had become generic. That year, Congress enacted the Trademark Clarification Act in response to a decision of the Ninth Circuit in *Anti-Monopoly, Inc. v. General Mills Fun Group, Inc.*[76] The Ninth Circuit had emphasized consumer motivation in assessing whether the term MONOPOLY for a board game was generic, and thus held the term to be generic because a survey revealed that most purchasers wanted the game MONOPOLY but did not care who made it. In reaching this conclusion, the court had approvingly cited and adapted the *Kellogg* language to support the proposition that, to avoid classification as a generic term, it must be shown that the "primary significance of the term in the minds of the public is not the product but the producer."[77]

---

[74] Although the *Kellogg* Court found both the term SHREDDED WHEAT and the pillow shape of the biscuits to be generic and thus non-distinctive, the Court's opinion was initially most influential among policymakers in establishing the non-protectability of *terms* used in connection with a product upon which the patent had expired. One might speculate that this was because the right to copy the *shape* was securely established by the right to copy and the functionality doctrine. Although the Court's discussion of the protection of the shape included a brief analysis of whether the pillow shape was generic, the other grounds provided a more than adequate basis upon which to deny protection. In contrast, the ability to copy the term SHREDDED WHEAT was more heavily dependent upon the finding that the term was generic.

[75] *See* Pub. L. No. 87–772. Neither the courts nor policymakers at the time of the Lanham Act appear to have seen *Kellogg* as an opinion from which to extract a general test for determining whether a mark was generic (as opposed to whether a word might be unprotected in the specific context of where the product with which it was associated was covered by an expired patent). Yet, the seeds of that later development can perhaps be detected in contemporaneous discussion of how the *Singer/Kellogg* doctrine could best be reflected in the statutory scheme of the Lanham Act. In particular, the mutation of language from *Kellogg* into (eventually) the statutory standard for determining whether a mark is generic might be traced to debate in the 1942 hearings on whether the general definition of "abandonment" in the pending bill was sufficient to codify the "Shredded Wheat" case. Outside the context of products upon which a patent had expired, an attack on a mark on grounds of genericness would prior to 1962 have relied on the abandonment provision. *See* Statement of House Managers Regarding Conference Report on Lanham Trade–Mark Bill, *quoted in* Greenberg, *supra* note 67, at 21–22. Some scholars argued that it was not sufficient, and that a specific provision regarding such a mark becoming generic was required.

[76] 684 F.2d 1316 (9th Cir. 1982). *See* Trademark Clarification Act of 1984, Pub. L. No. 98–620, 98 Stat. 3335. The 1984 amendments were aimed primarily at rejecting reliance on consumer motivation as the determinant of whether a mark was generic, rather than at stressing the need for a mark to show its primary significance was source-identification.

[77] *See id.* at 1319 (quoting *Kellogg* language and citing passage in prior decision in the case that had cited *Kellogg*).

The 1984 legislation effectively over-ruled *Anti-Monopoly* and amended section 14(3) to provide that "the primary significance of the registered mark to the relevant public rather than purchaser motivation shall be the test for determining whether the registered mark has become the generic name of goods or services on or in connection with which it has been used."[78] Although Congress codified the "primary significance" language directly from *Kellogg*, it did not adopt the formulation that the association be with "the producer, not the product." That formulation, which possibly captured the particular inquiry that the Court was pursuing in *Kellogg*, actually mis-states broader trademark law, which does protect symbols that identify goods.[79] Indeed, Congress also added language to the same provision in 1984 to the effect that "a registered mark shall not be deemed to be the generic name of goods or services solely because such mark is also used as a name of or to identify a unique product or service." Thus, although the *Kellogg* language regarding secondary meaning has been partially codified by Congress, it has also been partially repudiated (at least when divorced from the specific context in which it arose).

The Courts

Secondary Meaning

The language of the *Kellogg* opinion was also, not surprisingly, immediately seized upon by lower courts as the prevailing legal standard for assessing secondary meaning.[80] However, many courts, replicating the mistakes of the Ninth Circuit in *Anti-Monopoly* rather than the care of Congress in 1984, stressed the formulation of the *Kellogg* opinion that secondary meaning existed only when the "primary significance of the term in the minds of the consuming public is not the product but the producer."[81] Indeed, in *Wal-Mart Stores, Inc. v. Samara Bros.*, the Supreme Court recently affirmed this language, originally from *Kellogg*,

---

[78] *See also* 15 U.S.C. § 1127 (definition of "abandoned").

[79] *See* 15 U.S.C. § 1127 (definition of trademark); *see also* Statement of Michael A. Grow, Chairman, Federal Legislation Committee, U.S. Trademark Association, Hearings Before the Subcomm. On Patents, Copyrights & Trademarks, of the Comm. on the Judiciary, S. Hrg. 98–901, Feb. 1, 1984, *reprinted in* Jerome Gilson, Trademark Protection and Practice, at 14–278 (2004)

[80] *See, e.g.,* Selchow & Righter Co. v. Western Printing & Lithographing Co., 142 F.2d 707, 709 (7th Cir. 1944); American Fork & Hoe Co. v. Stampit Corp., 125 F.2d 472, 476 (6th Cir. 1942).

[81] *Kellogg*, 305, U.S. at 118.

as the secondary meaning standard.[82] As Judge Helen Nies noted in her concurring opinion in *In re D.C. Comics*,[83] the "truism that a trademark functions to indicate the source of goods, not the goods themselves . . . cannot be applied as a mere legalism" but has to be applied with due attention to the purposes of trademark law. That is, a trademark is furthering the goals of trademark law (and should thus be protected) when it identifies one product and distinguishes it from another, even if the producer of the goods is unknown. The truism, like the "producer, not product" language from *Kellogg*, reflects efforts by courts to ensure that trademark law did not become a de facto product design law, protecting the shape of all goods. As demonstrated in the context of generic marks, however, the "producer, not the product" language that comprises the second half of the *Kellogg* test for secondary meaning can be, and has been, misunderstood by later courts.

This danger is perhaps most acute when the language is applied outside the context in which it arose in *Kellogg*. To be sure, *Samara* did involve product designs, namely, the design of children's seersucker clothing. Although the language still runs the risk of not perfectly capturing the concept of secondary meaning, it arguably serves as a rough proxy in that context. But the language of *Kellogg* came to drive distinctiveness analysis in cases well beyond the context of product designs or patented products. It is still cited, and used, by courts as the basis for the general standard for secondary meaning.[84] The danger is that, in these other contexts, it excludes marks that do identify and differentiate a product even if the producer is unknown.

Functionality

Although *Kellogg* involved rights claimed in a formerly patented shape, the Court's opinion has also been cited frequently in cases involving claims of rights in product designs that were *not* the subject of an expired patent. Product design cases have proliferated, especially under cover of section 43(a) of the Lanham Act. In these cases, *Kellogg* has played two roles: it has both provided a foundation for the doctrinal development of the functionality doctrine, and more broadly guided the

---

[82] 529 U.S. 205, 211 (2000) (secondary meaning is shown by establishing that "in the minds of the public, the primary significance of a [mark] is to identify the source of the product rather than the product itself.") (quoting Inwood Labs., Inc. v. Ives, 456 U.S. 844 (1982)).

[83] 689 F.2d 1042, 1053 (C.C.P.A. 1982) (Nies J., specially concurring).

[84] Although one of the primary innovations of the Lanham Act was the federal registration of descriptive terms that had acquired secondary meaning, *see* 15 U.S.C. § 1052(f), the discussion of secondary meaning in *Kellogg* does not appear to have generated much discussion either in the scholarly literature or congressional debate at the time.

development of the scope of protection of product design. In the early years after the opinion, courts were unlikely to cite *Kellogg* as the source of doctrinal functionality standards because the Restatement of Torts provided an adequate definition in section 742.[85] Instead, courts tended to rely on *Kellogg* for general support regarding the limited nature of the protection to be afforded product shapes, perhaps detecting within the opinion hints of overarching trademark policy as well as narrow doctrinal rules. These invocations of *Kellogg* were made not only to support a denial of blanket injunctions against the copying of shapes, but also to sustain arguments that some form of labeling or source-differentiation might be required of defendants copying the shape of the plaintiff's product.[86]

Over time, however, *Kellogg* has come to be cited as the foundation for the functionality doctrine, even though the finding of functionality was arguably not critical to the *Kellogg* opinion. The weight of the functionality ground in *Kellogg* was at best unclear, and the Court's treatment of the argument appeared almost incidental. However, the test for functionality endorsed by the current Supreme Court with increasing certitude in a series of cases (*Inwood*, *Qualitex*, and *TrafFix Devices*) purports, both by the Court's initial reference in *Inwood* and by the received wisdom of lower courts, to have its roots in *Kellogg*.[87] Although it is surely appropriate to include *Kellogg* as one of the cases where a court was dissuaded from protecting a shape by virtue of its functionality, it is almost impossible to determine from Brandeis' opin-

---

85 *See* Restatement of Torts § 742 (1938) ("A feature of goods is functional, . . . if it affects their purpose, action or performance, or the facility or economy of processing, handling or using them; it is non-functional if it does not have any of such effects.").

86 Some courts in this period appear to have read *Kellogg* as requiring the same level of secondary meaning to obtain an injunction or the limited relief of compelling a competitor to take affirmative steps to avoid confusion. *See, e.g.*, American Fork & Hoe Co. v. Stampit Corp., 125 F.2d 472, 475 (6th Cir. 1942).

87 The etymology is complicated. *See Inwood Labs., Inc. v. Ives*, 456 U.S. 844, 850 n.10 (1982) ("in general terms, a product feature is functional if it is essential to the use or purpose of the article or if its affects the cost or quality of the article") (citing *Kellogg* and *Sears*); Qualitex Co. v. Jacobson Prods., 514 U.S. 159, 165 (1995) (endorsing *Inwood* test but adding the elaboration on *Inwood*—a feature is functional "if exclusive use of the feature would put competitors at a significant non-reputation-related disadvantage"); *TrafFix Devices*, 532 U.S. at 32–33 (reaffirming *Inwood* and explaining that the elaboration from *Qualitex* would apply only if *Inwood* was not satisfied, and most likely only in cases of "aesthetic functionality"). *See also* Valu Engineering Inc. v. Rexnord Corp., 278 F.3d 1268, 1273 (Fed. Cir. 2002) (tracing functionality doctrine to *Kellogg*, and suggesting that that doctrine is grounded in concerns about end-runs on the patent system). The roots of the precise test may in fact lie in section 742 of the First Restatement of Torts. *Cf.* Margreth Barrett, *Consolidating the Diffuse Paths to Trade Dress Functionality: Encountering* TrafFix *on the Way to* Sears, 61 Wash. & Lee L. Rev. 79, 116 (2004) (suggesting that the *TrafFix* Court has brought functionality closest to the position in section 742).

ion *how* the pillow shape was "essential to the use or purpose of the article or . . . affect[ed] the cost or quality of the article," as the Court's current test would require.

The Right to Copy the Subject–Matter of Expired Patents

In the immediate aftermath of the case, scholars and policymakers primarily viewed the *Kellogg* decision as resting on the right to copy previously announced by the Court in *Singer*.[88] Although courts continue to cite *Kellogg* for the right to copy a shape that was the subject matter of an expired patent, *Kellogg* does not provide a comprehensive answer to the questions surrounding that right, because the *scope* of the right cannot readily be deduced from the Court's opinion. In particular, if a competitor has the "right to copy what is covered by an expired patent", what precisely does that right free for copying? Those parts of the product covered by the claims of the patent? Those parts referenced in the specification? Those parts of the product sold on the market during the term of the patent?[89] The *Kellogg* Court, like the *Singer* Court before it, included in its opinion several articulations of the right that might each suggest a different scope.[90] These different articulations were likely not intended to supply a rule of precise scope, and thus their significance is hard to gauge.

The *Kellogg* Court clearly recognized that the defendant's right to copy emanates from the expiry of the patent. But the dedication of an invention to the public upon patent expiry might be grounded in a "patent bargain" theory, in concerns about the integrity of the patent system, or in the concern that trademark protection for once-patented

[88] Objections to this view of *Kellogg* were voiced by a leading scholar. *See* Walter J. Derenberg, *Shredded Wheat—The Still–Born Trade–Mark,* 34 BULL. U.S. TRADEMARK ASS'N 68, Feb., 1939, cited in Greenberg, *supra* note 67, at 12 n.22 (suggesting that the application of the *Singer* doctrine in *Kellogg* was dicta because whatever exclusive use there had been up to 1912 had been due to the "patent monopoly rather than any trademark monopoly"). It is unlikely that Professor Derenberg's efforts to draw a distinction between the two cases would have been persuasive given that Singer's exclusivity had likewise owed some to its patent rights.

[89] Granting the defendant the right to make cereals in the pillow shape was necessary to effectuate the unquestioned right to practice the expired patents. The patented machines were designed to produce only the pillow-shaped biscuits, and thus the shape of the biscuits was dictated by the practicing of the expired patents. *See Kellogg*, 305 U.S. at 119; *see also* Singer Mfg. Co. v. June Mfg. Co., 163 U.S. 169, 179 (1896) (premising the right to make machines in Singer's distinctive configuration upon such configurations being the necessary result of practicing the expired patents on the component parts). It is not clear whether the Court intended this consideration to be a feature of any right to copy analysis, and the brevity of the Court's explanation for its conclusion left us without guidance.

[90] *See Kellogg*, 305 U.S. at 117 ("the product, the process, and the machinery employed in making it, had been dedicated to the public"); *id.* ("there passed to the public . . . the right to make the article as it was made during the patent period").

product designs might impair the competitive climate.[91] Each theory might generate a different answer to the question "what of the patented product is dedicated to the public"? The closest the *Kellogg* court came to articulating a precise theory behind the right to copy is to quote a passage from *Singer* that talked of the "conditions" under which a patent was granted, suggesting an attachment to (some) patent bargain theory.[92] But *Kellogg* cannot with any certainty be cited in support of any statement of the *scope* of the right to copy.

The Relationship Between Functionality and the Right to Copy

Claims of functionality often arise in tandem with invocations of the right to copy. In *Kellogg,* the Court limited the protection available to Nabisco based upon both the functionality doctrine and the right of Kellogg to copy the subject matter of Nabisco's expired patent. However, Justice Brandeis did not connect the existence or the expiry of the patent to the functionality analysis. Yet, modern articulations of the functionality doctrine often do just that, and frequently cite *Kellogg* in the process.

The *existence* and *content* of a utility patent are surely relevant to the functionality analysis. Likewise, the *expiry* of a patent might be pertinent. However, because of the *Kellogg* Court's failure to elaborate upon the theoretical relationship (if any) between its functionality determination and the right to copy, or to develop more fully a theory for the latter, the loose citation to *Kellogg* in modern explanations of functionality has served only to complicate and obscure our understanding of the scope of the right to copy and the relevance of patents (especially expired patents) in functionality doctrine.

More recent Supreme Court decisions have done nothing to help.

---

91 *See* Qualitex Co. v. Jacobson Prods., 514 U.S. 159 (1995); *see also* Barrett, *supra* note 87.

92 I say "some" patent bargain theory, because the detailed terms and conditions of the bargain might remain open to debate. But knowing that the right is grounded in the bargain would at least provide us with the relevant frame of reference in which to have the discussion about "terms and conditions." For example, it is unclear whether the right to copy should extend to designs covered by invalidated patents. Invalidation might be viewed as a breach of contract by the public in that the patentee is deprived of the benefit of its bargain. If the patentee entered into the bargain based upon the representation of the public's representative (the Patent Office) that exclusive rights would be available for the full term, the patentee might have a claim that the bargain should be rescinded. A bargain-based theory of the right to copy would require consideration of the reason for the invalidation. If caused by a misinterpretation of the law on the part of the Patent Office, it would seem unfair to hold the patentee to the bargain (particularly as she will have already dedicated information in the patent to the public, and foregone the potential benefit of trade secret rights). On the other hand, if the invalidation of the patent was due to the fault of the patentee, such as fraud on the Patent Office (or perhaps self-anticipation or delay by the patentee), then the right to copy might more equitably be recognized.

For example, in *Qualitex Co. v. Jacobson Prods.*,[93] the Court sought to explain the functionality doctrine in a case not involving an expired patent, but in which the functionality doctrine might have been relevant to satisfy competitiveness considerations (which were heightened by the possibility of registering colors per se). The Court did so, however, in a fashion that served only to muddy the waters, blending without elaboration *Kellogg*'s patent-based right to copy with competitiveness-based functionality doctrine:

> [T]he functionality doctrine prevents trademark law, which seeks to promote competition by protecting a firm's reputation, from instead inhibiting legitimate competition by allowing a producer to control a useful product feature. It is the province of patent law, not trademark law, to encourage invention by granting inventors a monopoly over new product designs or functions for a limited time, . . . after which competitors are free to use the innovation. If a product's functional features could be used as trademarks, however, a monopoly over such features could be obtained without regard to whether they qualify as patents and could be extended forever (because trademarks may be renewed in perpetuity). See *Kellogg Co. v. National Biscuit Co.*, 305 U.S. 111, 119–120 (1938) (Brandeis, J.); . . . . Functionality doctrine therefore would require, to take an imaginary example, that even if customers have come to identify the special illumination-enhancing shape of a new patented light bulb with a particular manufacturer, the manufacturer may not use that shape as a trademark, for doing so, after the patent had expired, would impede competition—not by protecting the reputation of the original bulb maker, but by frustrating competitors' legitimate efforts to produce an equivalent illumination-enhancing bulb. *See, e.g.*, *Kellogg Co.*, *supra*, 305 U.S., at 119–120.

This articulation grounded functionality doctrine in a number of different policies—ensuring free competition, the integrity or primacy of the (limited) patent system as the regime by which to protect useful features, and effectuation of the patent bargain upon expiry of the patent. *Kellogg* is cited twice, but for which proposition is unclear. (The pages of the *Kellogg* opinion that were cited contain Justice Brandeis' discussion of the right to copy; *Kellogg*'s functionality discussion appeared on page 122 of the opinion in U.S. Reports).

Subsequently, in *TrafFix Devices*, the Court should have been forced to confront directly the relationship between the right to copy an expired patent and functionality. In *TrafFix Devices*, the plaintiff sought to

[93] 514 U.S. 159 (1995).

protect the shape (in particular, the dual-spring design) of a road sign on which its utility patents had expired. The dual-spring design enabled the road sign to withstand the gusts that would often blow on the open road. When a rival copied the dual-spring design after the expiry of the plaintiff's patents, the plaintiff brought an action under trademark and unfair competition law. The status of the right to copy as a defense standing independently of competition-based functionality doctrine was placed front and center because the lower courts had held that rivals did not need to copy the dual-spring design to compete, there being adequate alternative designs that would perform the same function.

Formally, the Court took *TrafFix* to resolve the apparent split between the Tenth Circuit, which in *Vornado Air Circulation v. Duracraft* had held that "[w]here a product configuration is a significant inventive component of an invention covered by a utility patent ... it cannot receive trade dress protection," and all other circuits, which had held that trade dress protection was not foreclosed by the existence of a prior patent on the product design provided the trade dress was not functional. But again this issue also raised the relationship of the right to copy and the functionality doctrine because the Tenth Circuit in *Vornado* had found that the design of the product in that question (an electric fan) was both distinctive and non-functional.[94] Indeed, the *Vornado* opinion cited and relied on *Kellogg* (and other Supreme Court cases).[95]

It was not surprising, therefore, that *Kellogg* was cited in almost every brief filed by the parties and amici in *TrafFix Devices* and was the subject of discussion during oral argument. Yet, the Supreme Court never even cited *Kellogg* in its opinion and thus declined the opportunity to clarify the nature and scope of the right to copy.[96] Instead, the Court

---

94 Vornado Air Circulation v. Duracraft Corp., 58 F.3d 1498 (10th Cir. 1995). The Tenth Circuit would not permit the plaintiff to use trademark law to (in the court's mind) extend the patent on the product in question, *even* where the plaintiff could show distinctiveness. The Tenth Circuit thus confronted the question that the Supreme Court in *Kellogg* had finessed by its finding that the shape was generic.

95 Although the *Vornado* court acknowledged that *Kellogg* could be distinguished from the facts in the case before it (because the plaintiff in *Vornado* had demonstrated distinctiveness of its design), it acted on what it saw as the principle (or "trend") in *Kellogg* and other cases in favor of the right to copy.

96 *See* Transcript of Oral Argument in TrafFix Devices, Inc. v. Marketing Displays, Inc., *reprinted in* 91 TRADEMARK REP. 649, 653 (2002). To be fair to the Court, answers provided by counsel at oral argument might not have helped the Court determine whether the right to copy was a self-standing principle independent of competitiveness questions, or what the scope of any such right would be. For example, counsel for the petitioner (the defendant), John G. Roberts, later to become Chief Justice of the Supreme Court, offered this explanation: "I think Justice Brandeis' opinion in Kellogg answers that. Kellogg did not have to show that there was no way to make or sell shredded wheat other than in the

held merely that if a design feature is "essential to the use or purpose of the article in question or affects the cost or quality of the article" then that feature is functional, regardless of whether rivals need to copy the design in order to compete or whether alternative designs were available. Moreover, the Court declared that "[a] utility patent is strong evidence that the features therein claimed are functional." The Court did not offer any consistent explanation of why (or which part of) the *expired* patent contributed to a finding of functionality, such that we would know the scope of the right to copy and whether it existed apart from broader functionality analysis.

In one sense, the Court is to be commended. It resisted the faulty argument of defendant's counsel, oft-repeated in product design litigation, that *Kellogg* provided the definitive answer to the scope of the right to copy. By the same token, the holdings in *TrafFix* (together with the convoluted explanations of functionality in *Qualitex*) create even greater uncertainty and further obscure *Kellogg*. The Court has without any explanation intertwined the right to copy with the doctrine of functionality, in a way that Justice Brandeis (however consciously) avoided.[97] By failing to answer the question on which it granted the petition for writ of certiorari, the Court placed in doubt one of the more certain readings of *Kellogg*, namely, that there is some right (of admittedly uncertain scope)[98] to copy the subject matter of an expired patent that exists independently of competitiveness (or other) concerns.[99] Yet, at the same

---

pillow-shaped biscuit form that Nabisco had made famous when it had its patent." This appears to suggest a right to copy independent of competitive need. Counsel continued: "It was enough that that was the form in which Nabisco had practiced its patent." This spoke to the scope of the right, albeit without an explanation why this was the correct scope. But then both issues became less clear: "That's important precisely because of the purpose of the patent bargain to promote competition . . . It's the commercially proven version that the public has the right to copy. That is important to enhance competition. To require people, if they are going to make improvements, to design around the form that the public had become accustomed to, would inhibit competition.".

97 Notwithstanding the now-confused state of functionality doctrine, it might be possible and helpful to develop a single doctrine that accommodates both rationales. *See* Dinwoodie, *The Death of Ontology*, *supra* note 32.

98 The specific contours of the right to copy would be much clearer if the Court would—as it did not do in *Kellogg* and *Traffix*—clearly articulate the rationale for the right. *See* Graeme B. Dinwoodie, *The Seventh Annual Honorable Helen Wilson Nies Lecture in Intellectual Property Law*, 8 MARQ. INTELL. PROP. L. REV. 187, 202 (2004).

99 Ironically, the Court held that the freedom of the defendant to use the shape *by virtue of the functionality doctrine* did exist independently of competitiveness concerns. Although this created for functionality an identity different from that which it assumed in *Kellogg* and *Cornell*, it might move toward an independent right to copy when taken with the holding that "[a] utility patent is strong evidence that the features therein claimed are functional." Yet, it was unhelpful to answer a question left open by *Kellogg* by revising two

time, *TrafFix* unmoored functionality doctrine from questions of competitiveness, which apparently informed both *Kellogg* and *Cornell*.

Intellectual Property Theory

To what does *Kellogg* owe its broad influence? The *Kellogg* opinion contained language that canvassed numerous doctrines of trademark and unfair competition law, instantly creating potential influence in a great number of cases. And the opinion contained sufficient ambiguity (in both content and structure) that later courts and Congress could infuse it with further (perhaps incorrect) significance. However, the significance of the opinion might also be because the case was about more than trademark doctrine. To assess this possibility, we might consider the passions of Justice Brandeis himself.

Why focus on Justice Brandeis? In 1938, Justice Brandeis was at the end of a glorious career on the Supreme Court. He had offered to retire from the Court in 1937, but Chief Justice Hughes persuaded him to remain on the Court.[100] In fact, Brandeis wrote very few opinions during the 1937 and 1938 terms, and retired only three months after the *Kellogg* opinion was handed down, writing only two opinions after *Kellogg*. Around the time *Kellogg* was decided, he was engaged in what he deemed a far more significant activity, meeting privately with President Roosevelt to urge greater U.S. involvement to protect Jews in Europe.[101] Why, at this stage of his career, did he take an interest in the *Kellogg* case?

From the outset of the opinion, it was clear that it was drafted for broader effect. The case was decided only months after the Court decided *Erie R.R. Co. v. Tompkins*,[102] in which *Swift v. Tyson* was over-ruled and Justice Brandeis' majority opinion rejected the notion that federal courts exercising diversity jurisdiction had power to create federal common law. One might have thought, therefore, that the *Kellogg* case would be decided under Delaware law. For example, because Delaware had issued a state trademark registration on the term SHREDDED WHEAT, any doubts that the Court harbored regarding the existence of consumer association surely would have to be measured against that administrative assessment. Yet, in footnote 1 of the opinion, Justice Brandeis accepted without question the parties' assumption that the outcome would be the same under federal and state law. In glossing over the

of *Kellogg's* clearer holdings, and still leaves the question of the scope of the right uncertain.

100 *See* LEWIS J. PAPER, BRANDEIS 390 (1983).

101 *See id.* at 3–4.

102 304 U.S. 64 (1938).

important *Erie* question,[103] an issue about which Justice Brandeis campaigned hard on the Court for several years, the Justice may have sought to influence the evolution of trademark and unfair competition law both philosophically and doctrinally at the federal as well as at the state level.

At the philosophical level, *Kellogg* fed into a broader debate regarding the theoretical basis of trademark and unfair competition law that was playing out in the courts, Congress, and in scholarly literature at the time, and which is still sharply contested today. Brandeis' opinion can be seen as a repudiation of the philosophy of unfair competition law underlying the Court's decision twenty years earlier in *International News Service v. Associated Press (INS)*.[104] In *INS*, the Court's majority upheld a claim of unfair competition based upon the defendants' misappropriation of non-copyrighted news stories published by the plaintiff.[105] In expansive language that went beyond the narrow holding of the case, the majority noted that the defendant was "endeavoring to reap where it has not sown." The Court explained that actions in unfair competition law were not limited to misrepresentation, but extended to cover acts of misappropriation.

Significantly, Justice Brandeis dissented in *INS*, unwilling to acknowledge property rights absent explicit legislative instruction.[106] For him, unfair competition consisted of misrepresentation: "The fact that a product of the mind has cost its producer money and labor, and has a value for which others are willing to pay, is not sufficient to ensure to it this legal attribute of property." Unfair competition law required simply the restraint of conduct that would deceive the public into a mistaken belief regarding the source of the product, and he found no such conduct in *INS*.[107]

Brandeis' vision of unfair competition law as protection against misrepresentation and not misappropriation finally secured the upper hand in *Kellogg*. Although Brandeis did not cite his *INS* dissent in *Kellogg*, one could view *Kellogg* as vindication of the views that he expressed in *INS*. That Nabisco had invested in the shredded wheat

---

[103] *See* Bartholomew Diggins, *Federal and State Regulation of Trade–Marks*, 14 Law & Contemp. Probs. 200, 203–04 (1949) (discussing federal courts sitting in diversity jurisdiction in the early 1940s refusing to enforce *INS* and applying instead state law limiting unfair competition to passing off).

[104] 248 U.S. 215 (1918).

[105] *See generally* Douglas G. Baird, The Story of *INS v. AP*: Property, Natural Monopoly, and the Uneasy Legacy of a Concocted Controversy, elsewhere in this Volume.

[106] *See* 248 U.S. at 267 (Brandeis J., dissenting) (noting that courts were ill-equipped to determine the conditions for the grant of a new right of property).

[107] *See id.* at 258 (Brandeis J., dissenting). Justice Holmes, who also dissented in *INS*, would have required the crediting of Associated Press as the source of the news stories.

product did not give it control over the use of the pillow shape (or the term SHREDDED WHEAT); it had no property right against misappropriation of the shape after the expiry of the patents. Instead, Brandeis inquired whether Kellogg had engaged in any acts of misrepresentation. The dissent in *Kellogg* made only one very short point, and it was a view that Brandeis had unsuccessfully rebutted in *INS*: the cause of action should be sustained because "Kellogg ... is fraudulently seeking to *appropriate* to itself the benefits of a goodwill *built up at great cost* by the respondent and its predecessors."[108]

If *INS* was an iconic statement of the misappropriation model of unfair competition law, *Kellogg* could be seen as a quiet but powerful plea for the misrepresentation model and a respect for competition. As such, it was a significant marker in the broader theoretical debate about the role of trademarks, and inevitably had implications for the debate that took place in Congress from 1938–1946 and in the courts thereafter. It was the philosophy underlying Brandeis' opinion, as much as the doctrinal language, that has attracted policymakers, advocates, and courts.

This hushed statement of philosophy has had a surprisingly pervasive effect in doctrinal developments in a number of different fora. Brandeis' implicit vision of intellectual property law in *Kellogg* immediately attracted the attention of policymakers skeptical of broad misappropriation-based trademark rights and committed to aggressive regulation of the competitive environment. Brandeis was a natural ally.[109] He was an advocate of strong antitrust laws. He had helped to establish the Federal Trade Commission on behalf of the Wilson Administration, and was instrumental in the passage of the Sherman and Clayton Acts,

---

108 *Kellogg*, 305 U.S. at 123 (McReynolds J., dissenting) (emphasis added). The Court of Appeals for the Third Circuit had also made much of the expenditures of Nabisco in deciding to offer protection. *See* National Biscuit Co. v. Kellogg Co., 91 F.2d 150, 153 (3d Cir. 1937).

109 Brandeis was no fan of intellectual property rights. *See* Mark L. Wolf, *Thomas Jefferson, Abraham Lincoln, Louis Brandeis and the Mystery of the Universe*, 1 B.U. J. Sci. & Tech. L. 1, 25 (1995) (noting Brandeis' distaste of patent laws). He authored eight other opinions on intellectual property, and found for the plaintiff in only two. *See* General Talking Pictures Corp. v. Western Electric Co., 305 U.S. 124 (1938); Leitch Mfg. Co. v. Barber Co., 302 U.S. 458 (1938); Permutit Co. v. Graver Corp., 284 U.S. 52 (1931); Carbice Corp. of Am. v. American Patents Dev. Co., 283 U.S. 420 (1931); Carbice Corp. of Am. v. American Patents Dev. Co., 283 U.S. 27 (1931); Jewell–Salle Realty Co. v. Buck, 283 U.S. 202 (1931); Buck v. Jewell–La Salle Realty Co., 283 U.S. 191 (1931); International News Serv. v. Associated Press, 248 U.S. 215 (1918) (dissenting). But in both *INS* and *Kellogg* he articulated an affirmative concept of unfair competition that is rooted in misrepresentation. Indeed, in both cases he spent some time considering whether the defendant's conduct amounted to misrepresentation. He might have articulated a relatively narrow notion of what amounted to misrepresentation—witness the difference between Holmes and Brandeis in *INS*—but he did recognize the cause of action.

which remain pillars of U.S. antitrust law.[110] "He was greatly concerned about small competitors and the way they were treated in the marketplace."[111]

Although Kellogg hardly represented a "small competitor," Brandeis' basic concern about competition may well have been piqued by the ongoing dispute between Nabisco and Kellogg, especially as Washington debated the reform of trademark law. Certainly, pro-competition policymakers were alert to what was going on at the Court. Affirmation, by Brandeis of all people, of a misrepresentation model of trademark law in the midst of a growing legislative debate that implicated the basic philosophical choice inevitably would have been seized upon. Thus, representatives of the Department of Justice, seeking to curtail the expansion of protection in the Lanham Act as discussed above, later identified *Kellogg* as an example of "the more conservative school of trade-mark protection ... which considers the trade-mark's sole function to be that of indicating source of origin ... [rather] than those which would claim for the trade-mark a more far-reaching significance as the conservator of independent property rights ..."[112]

And the Brandeis-inspired Department of Justice did secure what they regarded as important gains in the final version of the Lanham Act.[113] For example, the 1938 Lanham bill proposed that descriptive marks could be federally registered upon proof of secondary meaning. Of course, descriptive marks were already protected in similar circum-

---

110 *See* Mary Murphy Schroeder, *The Brandeis Legacy*, 37 San Diego L. Rev. 711, 713–15 (2000).

111 *Id.* at 715.

112 Timberg, *supra* note 67, at 326. *Kellogg*'s commitment to a pro-competition metric internal to trademark law was insufficient in and of itself to make antitrust regulators entirely comfortable. *See id.* at 333 ("It may be most gratifying to find out that 'Shredded Wheat' has been in the public domain since 1912; but how many small businesses can take the necessary gamble of possible defeat and pay counsel and court fees from 1912 to 1938 when that determination was finally and authoritatively made?").

113 The conclusion of the Lanham Act did not end the debate about trademark law and competition. *See* Lawrence C. Kingsland, *The Future of the Trade-Mark System in the American Economy*, 38 Trademark Rep. 607 (1948); Milton Handler, *Trade-Marks and Anti-Trust Laws*, 38 Trademark Rep. 387 (1948). In the immediate wake of the Lanham Act, the assessment by the Department of the effect of the legislation on competition was cautious, but optimism about pro-competitive effects was again linked to *Kellogg* and Brandeis. It was, they suggested, "the hope of antitrust policy" that courts would adopt the narrow view of trademarks that they identified with *Kellogg*. *See* Timberg, *supra* note 67, at 360. If competition is to be adequately protected, sentimental notions that competitors are not entitled to a "free ride" must be carefully scrutinized. As Mr. Justice Brandeis has remarked, "Sharing in the goodwill of an article unprotected by patent or trade-mark is the exercise of a right possessed by all—and in the full exercise of which the consuming public is deeply interested." *Id.* at 361 (quoting *Kellogg*, 305 U.S. at 122).

stances under principles of unfair competition. However, the proposal also introduced the notion of incontestability, under which five years after registration, trademark owners could ensure quiet(er) title. In particular, marks covered by incontestable registrations could not be challenged on the ground that they were descriptive. These proposals to change the nature and scope of trademark rights were among the reasons that led the Department of Justice initially to oppose the Lanham Act's reforms on the grounds that they were anti-competitive.[114] The disagreement reflected in part a philosophical divide about the conceptual identity of trademark law. Although, in order to prevail in an infringement action, the owner of an incontestable mark would still be required to show a likelihood of confusion,[115] this was a first step toward a model of trademark law that appeared more "property-like" and contrary to the vision underlying Brandeis' opinion. The Department's concerns led to the inclusion in the Lanham Act of provisions creating an "antitrust defense" to incontestability,[116] and granting the Federal Trade Commission the power to petition for cancellation of a trademark registration.[117]

Brandeis' equivocation in footnote 1 regarding the application of state or federal law might also have been a more direct attempt to extend the doctrinal influence of *Kellogg* to the core of *INS*. *INS* was clearly a federal common law decision, and thus *Erie* alone effected its evisceration. But by suggesting that the same result would pertain in *Kellogg* under federal common law, Brandeis ensured that *Kellogg's* anti-misappropriation counter to *INS* might gain traction in the courts as something other than a mere statement of Delaware law. As a result, the approach of Brandeis in *Kellogg* has shaped (sometimes without explicit acknowledgment) protection available to data under state common law misappropriation doctrines developed by federal courts,[118] com-

---

114 *See* Timberg, *supra* note 67, at 347–48 (noting that the ability to register, inter alia, descriptive marks "shows a surface intention to let down the bars" against overbroad protection but suggesting that the "main impact of the Lanham Act on competition will be the new effectiveness ... given registration," including the restricted grounds of cancellation and the grant of incontestability after five years).

115 This was made explicit with changes to section 33(b) of the Lanham Act in 1988. *See* Trademark Law Revision Act of 1988. *See* Pub. L. No. 100–667, 102 Stat. 3935 (1988). Although most scholars believe that the same was true prior to 1988, the respondent in a case recently decided by the Supreme Court argued that prior to 1988, the owner of incontestable registrations would prevail without the need to prove likely confusion. *See* Brief of Respondent, KP Permanent Makeup v. Lasting Impression I, Inc., 2004 WL 1843966 at * 11 (Aug. 13, 2004).

116 *See* 15 U.S.C. § 1115(b)(7).

117 *See* 15 U.S.C. § 1064(5).

118 *See* National Basketball Association v. Motorola, Inc., 105 F.3d 841 (2d Cir. 1997) (discussing the continued viability of an *INS*-like "hot news" cause of action under state

mon law trade dress protection sought under the federal unfair competition provision of section 43(a),[119] and more conceptually ambiguous claims brought under the "false designation of origin" language of that statutory provision.[120] In 1938, the resuscitation of federal unfair competition law, let alone in the form endorsed in *INS*, may have seemed unlikely. But the force of Brandeis' philosophy, perhaps buttressed by his decision to characterize the case more broadly than an application of Delaware law, has ensured that *Kellogg*, at least, remains a vital marker in the development of modern trademark and unfair competition law.[121]

Conclusion

Kellogg is a somewhat rare Supreme Court opinion; its correctness has never really been questioned. But because a variety of rationales were offered by the Court for a conclusion upon which most would agree, the precise scope of the opinion has never been fully clear. This has allowed the opinion to achieve significance, both judicially and legislatively, well beyond the narrow context of the type of case the Court was deciding. But the (perhaps purposeful) ambiguities that remained might

---

law and articulating factors that seek to maintain competition while affording very limited property rights to the originator of the data).

119 *See, e.g.*, Qualitex Co. v. Jacobson Prods., 514 U.S. 159 (1995); *Home Builders Ass'n of Greater St. Louis v. L & L*, 226 F.3d 944 (8th Cir. 2000); *Landscape Forms, Inc. v. Columbia Cascade Co.*, 113 F.3d 373 (2d Cir. 1997). *Kellogg* has been cited by the Court in connection with the "right to copy" designs of products covered by expired patents. But many of the Court's cases upon which the right to copy jurisprudence is founded are explicitly based upon the Supremacy Clause, making it easy for later courts adjudicating claims of products design trade dress under a federal statute to distinguish this case law. To the extent *Kellogg* reflected a different (or less certain) source of limitation, it contained the potential (along with *Singer*) to prescribe limits that would apply in the modern setting of federal protection of product design trade dress. *See* Vornado Air Circulation v. Duracraft Corp., 58 F.3d 1498 (10th Cir. 1995).

120 *See* Dastar Corp. v. Twentieth Century Fox Film Corp., 539 U.S. 23 (2003).

121 Perhaps Justice Brandeis understood that the validation of the New Deal portended the onset of voluminous federal law (including a trademark law which was beginning to loom large in congressional deliberation in 1938). Indeed, *Erie* may have, to some extent, precipitated the Lanham Act because it made national enforcement of trademark rights less certain. *See* Diggins, *supra* note 103, at 204; *see also id.* at 219 ("The [Lanham] Act eliminates most of the effects of the *Erie* decision in trade-mark and unfair competition cases"). To be sure, the Lanham Act (enacted eight years later in 1946) was, with minor exceptions, not intended to alter the substantive principles of trademark law that existed at common law. Instead, the Lanham Act primarily sought to facilitate enforcement of rights on a national basis, by liberalizing the rules of federal registration and establishing a clear federal jurisdiction to adjudicate claims of unfair competition. But liberalization of registration and enforcement inevitably did affect substantive principles of trademark law, and caused the enlargement of federal law. *Cf.* Edward A. Purcell Jr., *The Story of Erie*, in CIVIL PROCEDURE STORIES 21, 73 (Clermont ed. 2004) (noting that *Erie* did not signal the end of federal power "as its author would have hoped.").

also have prevented the opinion contributing to the *clear* development of areas of law that were directly addressed by the *Kellogg* Court. This partially explains the irony that the current Supreme Court has cited *Kellogg* in a number of trademark cases for a series of different propositions (e.g., regarding secondary meaning, or functionality), but did not cite the case in the most recent effort to tackle the very question at issue in *Kellogg* (the scope of trademark protection for a product covered by an expired patent).

By the same token, however, Justice Brandeis' quiet efforts to supply a more fundamental (and long-term) statement about the philosophy of trademark and unfair competition law may have been far more influential than a narrow application of existing law might have been. And those efforts to articulate a philosophy for trademark and unfair competition law, which do not spring as obviously from the text of the *Kellogg* opinion, but instead are more readily apparent from historical context, may also be important in the years ahead as scholars and policymakers consider whether trademark law has inappropriately become a law against misappropriation.

*

4

Scope of Protection

The Story of *Folsom v. Marsh*: Distinguishing Between Infringing and Legitimate Uses

R. Anthony Reese*

Folsom v. Marsh[1] was decided by Supreme Court Justice Joseph Story, sitting as a circuit court judge in Massachusetts in 1841. It involved two books that drew on the letters and papers written by probably the most famous person in American history at the time, President George Washington. The two authors were figures of growing prominence: one was a history professor at Harvard, the other was a leading local minister about to launch upon a political career. The plaintiffs' work collected original documents important to understanding the American Revolution and the early development of the United States, making them available both to citizens and historians. The defendant's book appeared in a series designed to foster local school libraries, part of the larger educational reform movement of the time. The attorneys for each side were prominent in the Massachusetts bar and in its politics. Nearly everyone involved in the case was part of the Harvard-educated Boston elite, active in developing the new nation's literature or government (or both). By modern standards, the case would have been a celebrity lawsuit.

Today, though, copyright students know *Folsom* almost entirely second-hand, through the substantial tribute paid to the decision in the

---

* Many thanks are due the staffs of the Tarlton Law Library at The University of Texas at Austin (especially Beth Youngdale) and the Robert Crown Law Library at Stanford Law School for research assistance. I also thank Oren Bracha, Paul Goldstein, Christopher Leslie, Edith MacMullen, and the participants in the May 2004 conference at the Samuelson/Glushko Center, for comments on earlier drafts or for discussions on this subject.

1 9 F.Cas. 342 (C.C.D.Mass. 1841) (No. 4,901).

Supreme Court's 1994 *Campbell v. Acuff–Rose*[2] opinion, which considered whether Two Live Crew's rap version of the Roy Orbison song "Oh, Pretty Woman" constituted a fair use of the original song. A closer look at *Folsom* and its history shows that Justice Story confronted a number of important copyright issues, but most fundamentally the decision considered when copying from a copyrighted work reaches the level of infringement and held that it did so when the copying would harm the market for the copyrighted work. Justice Story's concern for protecting the copyright owner's market remains an important aspect of copyright law, though modern doctrine embodies the concern much differently. While Justice Story originally made the economic harm inquiry central to evaluating a copyright owner's prima facie claim of infringement, modern courts generally expressly consider harm to the copyright owner *only* in resolving a claim by the copier that her use of the copyrighted work is a fair use. So while today *Folsom* is often said to have delineated the scope of the fair use *limitation* on copyright protection, in 1841 it represented a significant expansion of the protection that copyright afforded an author's work.

Folsom and Copyright in the Early Republic

It is fitting that one of the most enduring early copyright cases involved a dispute over George Washington's letters, compiled and edited by a future Harvard history professor, and the later use of those letters in a biography of Washington written for school libraries. While those who hear the phrase "copyright law" today often associate it with art and entertainment, in the early days of the United States copyright was far more closely associated with education and national development.

The focus on education and nation-building appears in the title of the first federal copyright law in 1790—"An act for *the encouragement of learning*"—as well as in the types of works it protected—maps, charts (*i.e.,* marine maps), and books, in that order. As Professor Jane Ginsburg has noted, "The first framers of copyright laws . . . sought primarily to encourage the creation of and investment in the production of works furthering national social goals."[3] Early U.S. copyright law particularly sought to foster the development of works that would help educate the public.[4] The founders generally viewed an informed citizenry as a necessary condition for the successful establishment of the nation, and copyright was one means of promoting an educated populace. And by granting copyright only in works by citizens or residents of the U.S., early

---

[2] 510 U.S. 569 (1994).

[3] Jane C. Ginsburg, *A Tale of Two Copyrights: Literary Property in Revolutionary France and America*, 64 Tul. L. Rev. 991, 996 (1990).

[4] *Id.* at 1001.

copyright law sought to foster a distinctly American culture. The hope that copyright would stimulate the production of educational and informational works useful to the young country was not disappointed, as the extant records of early copyright registrations indicate "a preponderance of useful, instructional texts" over fictional or entertaining works.[5] Indeed, the few reported federal copyright cases decided before *Folsom* concern maps, charts, nonfiction books or periodicals, reports of court opinions, textbooks, and a historical print of the Declaration of Independence. Most of these works relate directly to the American experience, and none involves a work of fiction.

The books at issue in *Folsom* fit squarely within the early copyright goals of fostering an educated and virtuous citizenry, developing a national culture, and communicating the values of the new American republic to a burgeoning population. Both are works of U.S. history, and the defendants' book was targeted directly at schools and students. The promotional materials for, and introductions to, the plaintiff's work made clear the author's view of the importance of preserving and making available primary sources of U.S. history. And the authors of both works viewed Washington as a uniquely important American icon, from whom their readers could learn much about both U.S. history and good character. Both books were thus emblematic of the kinds of works that the drafters of early U.S. copyright laws were hoping to encourage.

Jared Sparks, Documentary Historian: *The Life and Writings of Washington*

The *Folsom* story begins with Jared Sparks.[6] Born in 1789, Sparks studied at Phillips Exeter Academy, and then went to Harvard. After graduating in 1815, he worked as an editor for the journal *North American Review* while pursuing graduate theology studies at Harvard. In 1819 he received his master's degree and became a Unitarian minister in Baltimore, where he continued his editorial pursuits, founding and editing the journal *Unitarian Miscellany*. He served briefly as the chaplain of the U.S. House of Representatives, the first Unitarian to do so, but in 1823 he left his ministry, returned to Boston, purchased the *North American Review*, and became its editor. Under his leadership, it became "the leading literary journal" in the nation.[7]

In March 1824, Charles Folsom, a friend of Sparks's from Phillips Exeter and Harvard, wrote to Sparks expressing interest in publishing a complete edition of George Washington's writings and seeking advice on

---

5 *Id.* at 1004.

6 The biographical material on Sparks comes from H.B. ADAMS, THE LIFE AND WRITINGS OF JARED SPARKS (1893) and Richard J. Cox, *Sparks, Jared, in* 20 AMERICAN NATIONAL BIOGRAPHY 420 (1999).

7 Cox, *supra* note 6, at 420.

where to find them. At the time, Folsom was Harvard's librarian and worked part time at the University Press, and presumably wrote Sparks in the latter capacity.[8] Folsom apparently quickly abandoned the Washington project, but Sparks pursued it, gathering information on where Washington's writings were available both in print and in archives and personal collections.[9] Within two years, Sparks had formulated a plan to collect and publish Washington's writings, including state papers and private and official letters.

When George Washington died in 1799, he left his voluminous papers to his nephew, U.S. Supreme Court Justice Bushrod Washington. In January 1826, Sparks wrote to Justice Washington about the proposed collection, seeking access to President Washington's papers in order to ensure the work's completeness. Justice Washington declined, noting that he and Chief Justice Marshall planned to publish a three-volume selection of his uncle's letters. (Marshall had written a five-volume biography of Washington 20 years earlier). Washington's rejection disappointed but did not deter Sparks. Access to President Washington's own papers would make the project easier and more complete, but Sparks felt he could obtain all the important materials from other sources, so he continued his efforts to locate Washington's writings. In September 1826, Sparks again wrote to Justices Washington and Marshall, explaining that he intended to publicly announce his plans to publish the writings, to solicit materials from the public, and to proceed with preparing the collection. Entreating the justices to reconsider his project, Sparks offered a deal. If Bushrod Washington would give Sparks access to the papers, Sparks would prepare the collected writings. Sparks on the one hand, and Washington and Marshall on the other, would then divide equally the copyright in Sparks's work and the profits made from it.[10] In January 1827 Washington and Marshall accepted the offer, and the three soon signed a contract on the terms Sparks had outlined.

The Washington manuscripts, including 40,000 letters, were shipped to Boston for Sparks to select and edit.[11] Though Sparks worked on the Washington collection from 1827 to 1837, it was far from his only project

---

[8] Kenneth E. Carpenter, *Folsom, Charles*, *in* 8 AMERICAN NATIONAL BIOGRAPHY 177, 177–178 (1999); Theophilus Parsons, *Memoir of Charles Folsom*, 11 PROC. MASS. HIST. SOC'Y, 26, 27 (APR. 1873).

[9] The story of the formulation of the plan of Sparks's work, and his early pursuit of it, is derived in large part from Sparks's correspondence on the matter published in 1 ADAMS, *supra* note 6, at 389–413; *see also* Michael Culver, *An Examination of the July 8, 1838 Letter From Harriet Martineau to United States Supreme Court Justice Joseph Story As It Pertains to United States Copyright Law*, 32 J. OF THE COPYRIGHT SOC'Y 38, 40 (1984).

[10] Chief Justice Marshall appears to have acquired an interest in the papers as part of his preparation of his biography of Washington.

[11] 2 ADAMS, *supra* note 6, at 274.

during that decade. He remained editor of *North American Review* until 1830, when he sold his interest in the journal to raise capital for other projects, including the Washington papers.[12] But much of Sparks's work during this period, like the Washington project, involved American history and biography. In 1832 Sparks conceived and began editing the *Library of American Biography* series. The first volume appeared in 1834 and included Sparks's biography of Ethan Allen, together with three biographies by other authors; by 1838, Sparks had edited ten volumes, and contributed two more biographies from his own pen.[13] Sparks combined his interest in biography with work collecting, preserving, and making available primary materials of American history,[14] particularly of the revolution and the founding of the U.S., then forty and fifty years in the past. Sparks and some contemporaries realized that these events were passing from living memory, and that the documentary record should be preserved before it disappeared, in order to help younger Americans to understand the nation's origins. Toward that end, in addition to the Washington collection, Sparks edited the 12-volume *Diplomatic Correspondence of the American Revolution*, published in 1829–30, and the papers of revolution-era leader Gouverneur Morris. He also collected Benjamin Franklin's writings: in 1833 he edited a volume of Franklin's unpublished personal letters, acquired from various sources, and between 1836 and 1840 he published a ten-volume edition of *The Works of Benjamin Franklin; with Notes and a Life of the Author.*

Jared Sparks, Businessman: *Publication of Life and Writings of Washington*

Sparks had written to Justice Washington that "although I doubt not the pecuniary results [of President Washington's collected writings] will be adequate to the expense of money, and perhaps of time and trouble, in carrying it on, yet this has been and is still a secondary consideration."[15] Despite these protestations, from an early stage of the project Sparks was clearly attentive to its commercial aspects and the value of copyright protection, as his contract with Washington and Marshall showed. (He paid similar attention to the financial aspects of his other historical publishing projects.)[16] Sparks also attended carefully to marketing the series to the public. In May 1827, various newspapers

---

[12] 1 ADAMS, *supra* note 6, at 364.

[13] Sparks edited 25 volumes of *The Library of American Biography* from 1833 to 1849. 2 ADAMS, *supra* note 6, at 207.

[14] *See* Jared Sparks, *Materials for American History*, 23 N. AM. REV. 275 (1826); Cox, *supra* note 6, at 420.

[15] 1 ADAMS, *supra* note 6, at 407.

[16] In 1828 he published a biography of John Ledyard, an early American explorer of foreign lands. Sparks sold the copyright for this book for $325, which he said was "all I

printed two open letters from Sparks describing in detail his plan to publish Washington's writings.[17] Sparks intended these letters as a marketing device—designed "to prepare the public mind for a suitable reception of the work."[18] In one letter, he wrote that the volumes would not collect *all* of Washington's writings, since "it would be quite inexpedient to print in detail such a mass of papers which the public can neither spare money to purchase nor time to read."[19] And he assured prospective buyers that "the style of printing shall be handsome, and worthy of the subject, but not so expensive as to impose an unreasonable tax on the purchasers."[20] Sparks also planned to publish occasional extracts of Washington's letters in the *North American Review* "to excite an interest in the papers and keep the project of publishing them . . .

---

expect to receive for the work," noting that it would hardly cover his expenses, much less his labor. 2 ADAMS, *supra* note 6, at 608.

Sparks understanding of the value of copyright ownership was apparent in negotiations for the *Diplomatic Correspondence*, as he initially proposed to undertake it almost entirely at his own expense, in return for ownership of the copyright in the work. 2 ADAMS, *supra* note 6, at 134. The government declined to give him a copyright in the work, instead paying him a fee for each volume he prepared and allowing him to publish and sell the series as he saw fit. 2 ADAMS, *supra* note 6, at 136–40.

For the first four volumes of the *Library of American Biography*, the publishers paid 70 cents per page to the author and 30 cents per page to Sparks for editing. The publishers were allowed to print only 2,000 copies, and Sparks owned the copyright in the works. 2 ADAMS, *supra* note 6, at 195–96. For volumes 5 through ten, the publishers were allowed to print 2,500 copies from the plates in return for paying Sparks $650 per volume. Sparks owned the copyright and the plates, and paid each author $1 per page. 2 ADAMS, *supra* note 6, at 196–97. In the first printing, Sparks apparently made money on some volumes and lost money on others, but the success of the series in its first printing allowed him to sell the copyright and the plates to a publisher for $2400. 2 ADAMS, *supra* note 6, at 199. He reported at one point that he earned an average of $900 per volume for the series, which he said was not enough to induce him to agree to edit a second series. 2 ADAMS, *supra* note 6, at 202. Sparks did eventually edit a second series of 15 volumes, published by Little & Brown between 1844 and 1848. He was paid $250 per volume as editor, with the authors paid $1 per page, and the copyright in the works belonged to the publishers. 2 ADAMS, *supra* note 6, at 204.

Sparks concluded essentially the same arrangement with Gouverneur Morris's widow for publication of his papers as he had with Washington and Marshall, but that work apparently did not succeed financially. Sparks apparently recovered his costs but nothing more, and relinquished his claim to compensation from the copyright when the publishing firm dissolved. 2 ADAMS, *supra* note 6, at 162–64, 170–71.

17 2 ADAMS, *supra* note 6, at 236, 266.

18 2 ADAMS, *supra* note 6, at 23.

19 2 ADAMS, *supra* note 6, at 249. *See also* 2 ADAMS, *supra* note 6, at 263 and 12.

20 2 ADAMS, *supra* note 6, at 263. Initially, Sparks offered the series by subscription, and although agents attracted about 1100 subscriptions, the subscription method was abandoned. 2 ADAMS, *supra* note 6, at 263, 278–79. Sparks's open letters served as the subscription prospectus.

before the readers" without "interfer[ing] with the future prosperity of the work."[21] In addition, as early as 1828, Sparks pursued arrangements for French and German translations; his initial agreement for a German edition promised him half the profits from the work's sales, though eventually he appears to have arranged for French and German versions without any financial compensation.[22]

Sparks himself also arranged for the work's production. Instead of turning his manuscript over to a publisher, he contracted directly with the University Press in Cambridge to make printing plates for the books so that he could control the typesetting quality. (Indeed, when the first volume was ready for typesetting, Sparks moved to Cambridge to be near the printing office in order to supervise.) The press, no longer formally affiliated with Harvard, was run in part by Sparks's old classmate Charles Folsom, and Sparks noted happily in his journal that "Mr. Folsom's scholarship, his skill and accuracy in correcting the press, and his high personal character are a pledge that the printing will be executed in the best manner."[23] Once the printing plates were prepared, Sparks agreed to allow the Boston publishers Hilliard, Gray & Co. to print 4,000 copies. Hilliard, Gray was to pay Sparks a royalty of somewhat less that 62.5 cents for each printed copy, for a total royalty of about $30,000 for the series.[24]

From 1834 to 1837 Sparks published eleven volumes of Washington's writings, including editorial changes, footnotes, several appendices, portraits, surveys, military plans, and an index.[25] The twelfth and final volume, which appeared in 1837, was actually volume one of the set, consisting of Spark's biography, *The Life of Washington*. Sparks's publisher, Hilliard, Gray & Co. apparently dissolved that same year,[26] and in 1838 Sparks granted the right to publish the series to Folsom, Wells &

---

21 2 ADAMS, *supra* note 6, at 15–16. Sparks's concern for the sale of the Washington volumes also appears in connection with a related project. While editing Washington's writings, Sparks proposed to Justice Washington printing a companion series composed of letters written *to* President Washington. 2 ADAMS, *supra* note 6, at 13–15. Later, as the first volumes of Washington's own writings appeared, Sparks's publishers convinced him that publishing a second series might confuse the public and hurt sales of the *Life and Writings*, so Sparks put aside the second project. 2 ADAMS, *supra* note 6, at 309.

22 ADAMS, *supra* note 6, at 87–88, 311–20.

23 2 ADAMS, *supra* note 6, at 277–78, 279; Max Hall, *Cambridge as Printer and Publisher: Fame, Oblivion, and Fame Again*, 44 PROC. CAMBRIDGE HIST. SOC'Y 63, 76 (1985).

24 2 ADAMS, *supra* note 6, at 277–78, 279. Sparks had published his biography of Ledyard with Hilliard's previous firm, 1 ADAMS, *supra* note 6, at 373, and contracted with the firm to publish the *Library of American Biography*.

25 2 ADAMS, *supra* note 6, at 278, 281–82.

26 JOHN W. TEBBEL, A HISTORY OF BOOK PUBLISHING IN THE UNITED STATES: THE CREATION OF AN INDUSTRY, 1630–1865 at 416; 2 ADAMS, *supra* note 6, at 279–80.

Thurston, a publishing firm that Folsom had formed with Thomas Wells and Lyman Thurston.[27] Overseas, Sparks's *Life*, together with an abridged selection of writings, appeared in a two-volume German translation in 1839 and a six-volume French translation in 1839–40.[28] Plans for a British edition were not realized, so copies were exported to Britain and sold there, but a two-volume unauthorized edition appeared in London in 1839 (and British law at the time offered no copyright protection to American authors such as Sparks).[29]

Sparks's work succeeded financially for the author. When all the volumes had appeared, Sparks fulfilled his contractual obligations to the heirs of Bushrod Washington and John Marshall.[30] Sparks incurred expenses of $15,356.37 in preparing and publishing the work, and after deducting that amount, $15,384.63 remained to be divided evenly between Sparks on the one hand and Washington's and Marshall's families on the other.[31] Initial critical review seems to have been favorable as well.[32] And the work likely added to Sparks's reputation as an historian: in 1838 Sparks was appointed the McLean Professor of Ancient and Modern History at Harvard.

Rev. Charles W. Upham, *The Life of Washington*, and the School Library

The next step toward the *Folsom* litigation was the publication of *The Life of Washington* by Reverend Charles W. Upham.[33] Upham had been born and raised in St. John, New Brunswick: his father, a Massachusetts-born, Harvard-educated lawyer, was a loyalist in the Revolution, so Massachusetts confiscated his property and exiled him, and he settled in New Brunswick and became a justice of the provincial Supreme Court. In 1816, Charles, aged 14, moved in with family in Boston.

---

27 2 ADAMS, *supra* note 6, at 280. The publishers were to pay a royalty of eighty-five cents a copy on Sparks's *Life of Washington* (volume 1) and fifty cents a copy on each of the volumes of the *Writings*.

28 2 ADAMS, *supra* note 6, at 311–330.

29 2 ADAMS, *supra* note 6, at 318–19.

30 Bushrod Washington had died in 1829, and John Marshall in 1835.

31 2 ADAMS, *supra* note 6, at 295 & n.1.

32 Chief Justice Marshall wrote Sparks in 1834 and 1835, praising Sparks's achievement, and a positive review of the series appeared in 1838 in *North American Review*. 2 ADAMS, *supra* note 6, at 285, 288. The reviewer wrote that "Mr. Sparks must not look for his reward to pecuniary compensation . . . for his ten years of unrelaxing and conscientious labor."

33 The biographical information on Upham is drawn from Dean J. DeFino *Upham, Charles Wentworth, in* 22 AMERICAN NATIONAL BIOGRAPHY 112 (1999), and George E. Ellis, *Memoir of Charles Wentworth Upham*, 15 PROC. MASS. HIST. SOC'Y, 182–221 (1876).

Like Sparks, he attended Harvard, graduating in 1821. (Classmates, including Ralph Waldo Emerson, later recalled Upham as the second-best student in the class.) Also like Sparks, Upham then studied divinity and became a Unitarian minister, and in 1824 he became associate pastor of the First Church in Salem.[34] And Upham shared Sparks's literary and historical interests. While pastor in Salem in the 1820s and 1830s, Upham published several theological, historical, and biographical works. Indeed, Sparks and Upham knew each other at least by 1835, when Upham wrote a biography of early Massachusetts governor Sir Henry Vane as part of Sparks's *Library of American Biography*, probably at Sparks's request.

The origins of Upham's *Life of Washington* are intertwined with efforts in Massachusetts to support public elementary education, part of a wider movement of reforming and extending education in the middle third of the nineteenth century. The movement, based in part on the view of universal educability, was part of a general "intellectual ferment" of the time, including trends such as increasing numbers of magazines and newspapers.[35] Among other initiatives, the educational movement of the time promoted school libraries, which, it was hoped, would have intellectual benefits of spreading knowledge and moral benefit as a means to "promote virtue" and "repress vice." As one source put it, such libraries would allow "the children of the Farmer, the Merchant, the Manufacturer, the Mechanic, the Laborer,—all to profit by the lights of science and literature, that they may be rendered the more virtuous and happy, and become more useful to themselves, to one another, to the community, and mankind at large."[36] In 1837, Massachusetts granted local authorities the power to impose a small tax to create and support libraries in local public schools.[37]

The idea of school libraries in Massachusetts also received support from the state Board of Education, established in 1837 as part of the educational reform movement, and composed of prominent politicians and educators (including, from 1838 to 1841, Jared Sparks).[38] The new

---

[34] In 1826, he married Ann Susan Holmes, the sister of Dr. Oliver Wendell Holmes (making Upham the uncle of the future Supreme Court Justice Oliver Wendell Holmes).

[35] Sidney Ditzion, *The District-School Library, 1835–55*, 10 LIBRARY QUARTERLY 545, 556 (1940).

[36] MASSACHUSETTS STATE BOARD OF EDUCATION, THIRD ANNUAL REPORT 25 (1840) (reproducing advertisement for Marsh, Capen, Lyon & Webb's School Library).

[37] Mass. Acts 1837, chap. 147 (Apr. 12, 1837). Massachusetts was following a similar program recently adopted in New York. Ditzion, *supra* note 35, at 552; Laws of New York, 58th Sess., ch. lxxx (Apr. 13, 1835).

[38] 2 ADAMS, *supra* note 6, at 366–67. The Board's secretary was Horace Mann, former Massachusetts senate president, whose Board work would make him a preeminent figure in the early development of American education.

Board enthusiastically encouraged school districts to establish libraries,[39] but few responded. The Board decided that one obstacle was the difficulty of selecting books, and the fear that the selection could become sectarian or partisan. So in 1838 the Board arranged with Boston publishers Marsh, Capen & Lyon to issue two series of books, one for younger readers and one for older ones, suitable for inclusion in school libraries. (Several similar "school library" projects began around the same time, including a particularly successful series published by Harper Brothers, the ancestor of today's Harper & Row publishing company.)[40]

For the Massachusetts series, the members of the Board of Education had to unanimously approve every book, a requirement designed to reassure local schools that the books were not "calculated to favor the tenets of any particular sect of Christians."[41] The Board emphasized that the "enterprise is to be entirely at the expense and risk of the publishers," and local school districts had no obligation to buy these volumes.[42] Board member Jared Sparks "took an active interest" in school libraries and prepared the Board's report on the subject.[43]

By 1840, Marsh, Capen & Lyon had published the first ten volumes, offered "to Schools, Academies, &c." for seventy-five cents each. The series published primarily the same kinds of works encouraged by early U.S. copyright law—informational works of a distinctly American character by American authors.[44] The publishers indicated that "preference [was] being given to works relating to our own country, and illustrative of the history, institutions, manners, customs, &c. of our own people." The initial ten volumes were factual works, including a three-volume *Lives of Eminent Individuals, Celebrated in American History*, which

---

[39] MASSACHUSETTS STATE BOARD OF EDUCATION, FIRST ANNUAL REPORT, Section 4 (1838).

[40] Ditzion, *supra* note 35, at 549, 565; LAWRENCE A. CREMIN, AMERICAN EDUCATION: THE NATIONAL EXPERIENCE 1783–1876 at 309 (1980).

[41] "It was felt, in view of the religious heterogeneity of the Board, that such a course would effectively eliminate sectarian views in the materials." LAWRENCE A. CREMIN, THE AMERICAN COMMON SCHOOL: AN HISTORIC CONCEPTION 194 n.452 (1951).

[42] MASSACHUSETTS STATE BOARD OF EDUCATION, SECOND ANNUAL REPORT (1839).

[43] 2 ADAMS, *supra* note 6, at 366–67. The School Library project soon encountered controversy. Frederick Packard of the American Sunday School Union (which published a similar series of books for Sunday school libraries) proposed a book for the Massachusetts series. Board of Education Secretary Horace Mann rejected the book because he felt it promoted the tenets of particular Christian denominations, and the rejection led Packard to publicly attack the School Library project, which in turn led to published defenses of the series. For discussions of the controversy, *see* JONATHAN MESSERLI, HORACE MANN: A BIOGRAPHY 309–315 (1972); CREMIN, THE AMERICAN COMMON SCHOOL, *supra* note 41, at 192–195. The controversy, however, did not derail the project.

[44] Many of the authors or proposed authors were faculty members at Yale, Harvard, Dartmouth, Brown, and the University of Virginia.

largely drew on Sparks's *Library of American Biography* (and included Sparks's biography of Ethan Allen and Upham's of Sir Henry Vane).[45] The "forthcoming" titles in 1840 were similarly heavily weighted to nonfiction works, primarily on science, agriculture, law, and biography (including a biography of Benjamin Franklin by Jared Sparks).[46]

The eleventh and twelfth volumes in the series were Upham's *Life of Washington*. Upham had initially declined the publishers' solicitation to write the book, primarily because "as Professor Sparks,—the Author of the Life, and Editor of the Writings, of Washington,—was himself one of the Board of Education, and was understood to have taken a leading part in getting up the Library, it was proper, on all accounts, that the 'Life of Washington' should be provided by him." Upham reports that the publishers declared that they had repeatedly solicited Sparks to write the volume but that "he had positively and decidedly declined," so eventually Upham agreed to do so.[47]

Upham's work was not a conventional biography. Rather, he extracted material from Washington's journals, speeches and letters, allowing Washington, as far as possible, to "relate his own history . . . from his own lips," with Upham providing the narrative connecting the various extracts.[48] Upham's preface acknowledged that his work "necessarily owes much of its materials to the very valuable collection of [Washington's] writings edited and published by Mr. Sparks," though he also stated that many of the letters and addresses he drew from had been published prior to Sparks's volume or had never previously been published.[49] In light of the subsequent litigation, some pre-emptive defensiveness might be read into Upham's statement that in the 1780s Washington himself wrote "that his memoirs could not be written, in a satisfactory or effectual manner, without a large selection from his papers; and that, so soon as Congress should see fit to open their archives to the historian, his own papers should, at the same time, be freely disclosed for examination and use."[50]

---

[45] MASSACHUSETTS STATE BOARD OF EDUCATION, THIRD ANNUAL REPORT 26–27 (1840). Horace Mann apparently had a hand in selecting the volumes, and Mann had reservations about the value of fiction for the school libraries, see MESSERLI, *supra* note 43, at 345–6, for reasons that echoed in part sentiments of Thomas Jefferson: "A great obstacle to good education is the inordinate passion prevalent for novels, and the time lost in that reading which should be instructively employed." 15 THOMAS JEFFERSON, THE WRITINGS OF THOMAS JEFFERSON 166 (1903). *See also* Ditzion, *supra* note 35, at 564–73.

[46] MASSACHUSETTS STATE BOARD OF EDUCATION, THIRD ANNUAL REPORT 27–31 (1840).

[47] REV. CHARLES W. UPHAM, THE LIFE OF WASHINGTON (1841).

[48] *Id. at* 4.

[49] *Id. at* 5.

[50] *Id.*

Upham's *Life* appeared in 1840. No evidence has been found about the publishing arrangements between Upham and the Marsh firm, and little information survives about the publishers. Bela Marsh had worked in the Boston book trade in various capacities, and in the mid–1820s, he entered a partnership with Nahum Capen. Gardner P. Lyon joined them in 1830, and Thomas H. Webb joined in 1839, shortly before Upham's book was issued. Capen, the best known of the four, was "an aggressive protagonist of the copyright laws, making appeals to Congress and writing letters on the subject to Daniel Webster and to Henry Clay," advocating copyright protection in the United States for works by foreign authors.[51] Capen spent a year abroad in 1835 to 1836, and upon his return, he became active in the cause of public education "and was largely instrumental in securing the establishment of the State Board of Education of Massachusetts,"[52] which may partly explain the Marsh firm's interest in publishing the School Library series.[53]

The Lawsuit

Each work in the School Library series was to be approved by the entire Board of Education. Sparks, as a Board member, had the opportunity to review Upham's book before publication, and apparently complained at the time to Upham and his publishers that the book infringed on Sparks's copyright.[54] But the book was published, and Folsom, Wells, Thurston and Sparks filed a bill of complaint against Upham and his publishers on August 8, 1840. They may have feared that Upham's *Life* would compete with an abridged edition of Sparks's *Life* (the first volume of his series), which Folsom, Wells, & Thurston contracted with Sparks in 1840 to publish, and which ultimately appeared in 1842, though the official record leaves no indication of this.[55]

The plaintiffs chose Phillips & Robins to represent them, and Willard Phillips was probably the lead attorney. The Harvard-educated Phillips had once represented Boston in the state legislature, and was appointed probate judge for Suffolk County in 1839, though he continued to practice law. Phillips also had a literary career: he edited, and contributed to, *North American Review* beginning in its early days,[56] and

[51] John F. Fulton, *Capen, Nahum*, *in* 2 DICTIONARY OF AMERICAN BIOGRAPHY, pt. 1, 481, 481 (1929); TEBBEL, *supra* note 26, at 559.

[52] Fulton, *supra* note 51, at 481.

[53] In addition to publishing, Capen organized and became secretary of the Boston Phrenological Society.

[54] Culver, *supra* note 9, at 44.

[55] 2 ADAMS, *supra* note 6, at 280 & n.1. The publishers were to pay Sparks a royalty of 25 cents per copy. *Id.*

[56] 1 ADAMS, *supra* note 6, at 366–71.

turned to legal writing in 1823 with an insurance-law treatise. In 1837 he published *The Inventor's Guide* and *The Law of Patents for Inventions*; at the time of *Folsom*, he also had some copyright experience, having successfully represented plaintiffs alleging copyright infringement in the case of *Gray v. Russell*[57] in 1839.

Rantoul & Kimball filed the defendants' answer, denying copyright infringement, three months after the complaint. The Harvard-educated Robert Rantoul, Jr., was probably the lead attorney. He was active in Democratic politics as a reformer, and in the 1830s served four years in the state legislature, where he was an early opponent of the death penalty (following in the footsteps of his father, a famous advocate for abolishing capital punishment.) While Phillips had some experience in copyright and patent law, Rantoul was, at the time of the *Folsom* case, apparently just beginning to develop a patent law practice.[58] Rantoul's interest in the case went beyond the usual lawyer-client relationship. As an original member (with Jared Sparks) of the state Board of Education, Rantoul enthusiastically supported the School Library series and wrote an essay in the first volume introducing the series.[59] Rantoul thus seems a natural choice to defend the School Library's publishers, and a contributor, against charges of copyright infringement.

Justice Joseph Story

The plaintiffs filed suit in the U.S. Circuit Court for the District of Massachusetts.[60] At the time, each circuit court sat periodically in each of the judicial districts within its compass, and consisted of the district judge for that district and the U.S. Supreme Court Justice assigned to that circuit. Joseph Story, the Supreme Court justice responsible for Massachusetts, heard the case.

---

57 10 F.Cas. 1035 (C.C.D.Mass. 1839) (No. 5,728).

58 *See* Robert Rantoul, Jr., Memoirs, Speeches and Writings of Robert Rantoul, Jr. 29–30 (Luther Hamilton, ed., 1854). Rantoul also contributed once to *North American Review*. 1 Adams, *supra* note 6, at 366–71.

59 *See* Robert Rantoul, *Remarks on Education*, North American Review (1839), *reprinted in* Rantoul, *supra* note 58, at 97–98. The first volume was a version of Washington Irving's biography of Columbus. The choice of Rantoul to write the introduction was apparently a last-minute one: "Mr. Rantoul was requested, on the spur of a sudden emergency . . . to prepare the 'Introductory Essay to the School Library,' a series of works sanctioned by the Board of Education." *Id.* at 71–72.

60 An 1819 statute granted the circuit courts original jurisdiction, in both law and equity, over any cases arising under the federal copyright or patent laws. 3 Stat. 481–82 (1819).

Born in 1779 in a well-off Massachusetts family,[61] Story graduated second in his class from Harvard in 1798. In 1801 he was admitted to the bar and opened an office in Salem. His early career included political posts: he represented Salem in the state legislature (1805–07), filled a vacancy in the U.S. House of Representatives (1808–09), then returned to the Massachusetts house, where he became Speaker in 1811. That year, President Madison appointed Story to the Supreme Court at age 32, the youngest person ever appointed, and Madison's fourth choice to fill the vacancy.

After nearly 20 years on the bench, Justice Story added other legal pursuits to his career. In 1829, he became Harvard's inaugural Dane Professor of Law. A pioneer of legal education at Harvard, his teaching proved a draw: while Harvard had only one law student in 1828, Story's affiliation helped attract 28 new students the next year, and by the mid–1840s over 150 students from 21 states were studying law at Harvard. In addition, Story was an important legal author. He had begun writing legal treatises and commentaries while a young lawyer, but in the early 1830s, in connection with his professorship, he began an extremely prolific career publishing legal treatises, producing nine separate (often multivolume) works in a little over a decade. This work not only added to his prominence in legal circles, but proved lucrative as well. By the end of his career in the mid–1840s, his annual publishing income was said to be $10,000, more than twice his judicial salary.

When the *Folsom* case reached Justice Story, he was familiar, outside the courtroom, with the books, and many of the people involved, and particularly with Jared Sparks and the *Washington* series. Sparks and Story were acquainted as early as the mid–1820s, as Justice Story sometimes contributed to *North American Review*.[62] Justice Story was an enthusiastic supporter of the Washington project from its early stages. When Sparks first formalized his proposal in January 1826, Story told Sparks that the project was "noble" and "deserving of universal encouragement,"[63] and wrote "I know not into whose hands the task could have better fallen."[64] Indeed, Story himself appears to have delivered Sparks's initial proposal to Justices Washington and Marshall, his Supreme Court

---

[61] The biographical information on Story comes from George E. Woodbine, *Story, Joseph*, *in* 9 DICTIONARY OF AMERICAN BIOGRAPHY pt. 2, 102 (1936), Paul Finkelman, *Story, Joseph*, *in* 20 NATIONAL AMERICAN BIOGRAPHY 889 (1999), and R. KENT NEWMYER, SUPREME COURT JUSTICE JOSEPH STORY: STATESMAN OF THE OLD REPUBLIC (1985).

[62] Story wrote six pieces for the *Review*, starting in 1817. In April 1825, Story wrote Sparks to return a payment he unexpectedly received for a contribution. 1 ADAMS, *supra* note 6, at 341. In his diary in January 1827, Sparks recorded that "Judge Story expresses the most lively interest in the prosperity of the 'North American Review,' and says he shall omit no opportunity to aid it in every way in his power." 2 ADAMS, *supra* note 6, at 3.

[63] 1 ADAMS, *supra* note 6, at 401.

[64] 1 ADAMS, *supra* note 6, at 402.

colleagues and best friends on the Court,[65] to have spoken with them on Sparks's behalf,[66] and to have consulted with Sparks during the negotiations with Justice Washington.[67] Indeed, the two open letters published in May 1827 to attract interest and solicit subscribers were letters written by Sparks *to* Justice Story.[68] Story wrote to Sparks of his "unmixed satisfaction" at the open letters. Story called Sparks's plan for the publication "the very best that could be devised" and concluded, "I rejoice exceedingly in your success in this enterprise. I am confident it will give you a permanent fame..."[69] Story wrote to Sparks with similar enthusiasm in 1833 after reviewing the manuscript for a "specimen" volume: "I . . . confess myself very greatly pleased with it in all respects. The paper and print are good; the letters themselves quite characteristic and interesting, and your own notes excellent for the illustration and connection of the matter. I do not see well how they could be improved."[70] And Sparks himself publicly acknowledged Story's long support in the preface to the *Life of Washington*: "My thanks are due to Mr. Justice Story for the lively interest he has manifested in my labors, and for the benefit I have often derived from his suggestions and advice."[71]

Story also had connections with the *Folsom* defendants, though his ties with them are less clearly documented. Story probably knew Upham from Salem:[72] given that Story was a Unitarian,[73] he was very likely

---

65 NEWMYER, *supra* note 61, at 158.

66 1 ADAMS, *supra* note 6, at 401. Story also advised Sparks on commercial aspects of the project: "I think the publication will have a great sale, and will secure a most extensive patronage. What do you mean to do as to England? You ought, if possible, to secure some of the profits of an edition there. On this subject we must talk when I have the pleasure of meeting you." 2 ADAMS, *supra* note 6, at 265. Story had previously urged Sparks to make "a vigorous effort" to sell the *Writings* in England. 2 ADAMS, *supra* note 6, at 8.

67 2 ADAMS, *supra* note 6, at 3. When the deal was concluded, Sparks wrote that Story "has taken an ardent interest in this work from the beginning, and has assisted me much in bringing the matter to its present issue." 2 ADAMS, *supra* note 6, at 8.

68 2 ADAMS, *supra* note 6, at 236.

69 2 ADAMS, *supra* note 6, at 265.

70 2 ADAMS, *supra* note 6, at 283. Story then proceeded to make detailed suggestions for improvement, mostly related to discussing the propriety of Sparks's editorial revision of Washington's writings. *See also* Culver, *supra* note 9, at 42.

71 JARED SPARKS, 1 THE WRITINGS OF GEORGE WASHINGTON at xi-xii (1837). Of the plaintiff publishers, Justice Story was probably acquainted with at least Folsom, who printed at least one volume of Story's opinions on the Circuit Court for the First Circuit. 1 SUMNER'S REPORTS (1836).

72 NEWMYER, *supra* note 61, at 44–45; Woodbine, *supra* note 61, at 109; 2 WILLIAM WETMORE STORY, LIFE AND LETTERS OF JOSEPH STORY 23 (1851).

73 Story appears to have converted to Unitarianism at Harvard. NEWMYER, *supra* note 61, at 28–29.

acquainted with Upham, Unitarian pastor at Salem's First Church during Story's last five years in town. Story's ties to the defendant publishers are clearer. In 1840, the year Upham's *Life* appeared, Marsh, Capen, Lyon & Webb published Story's book, *A Familiar Exposition of the Constitution of the United States* (a condensed version of his 1833 *Commentaries on the Constitution*) as volume 13 in its School Library series.[74] The financial arrangements between Story and the Marsh firm regarding publication of *Exposition* are unclear, but quite possibly the *Folsom* defendants were paying, or had recently paid, royalties to the judge hearing the case.

In addition to knowing many of the parties, Story was, not surprisingly, familiar with their lawyers. Phillips was counsel in several earlier cases before Justice Story, including the 1839 case *Gray v. Russell*, which involved copyright in compilations of preexisting material. Indeed, Justice Story's opinion in *Gray* referred to Phillips's insurance treatise as an example of a compilation, and one "to which the whole profession are so much indebted."[75] And in the preface to Phillips's 1837 patent treatise, Phillips wrote, "[I]t is no injustice to the other eminent jurists of the country to say, that this department of law has been more especially indebted to the learning and talents of Mr. Justice Story [and his] indefatigable research and luminous expositions ...."[76] Justice Story also knew Rantoul, at least from the Massachusetts debates over whether to codify state law.[77]

While Justice Story's relationships with parties on both sides of *Folsom* would today present a potential conflict of interest, Story decided several cases during his career in which he had relationships with those involved. In the Supreme Court's *Dartmouth College* case,[78] he apparent-

---

74 JOSEPH STORY, A FAMILIAR EXPOSITION OF THE CONSTITUTION OF THE UNITED STATES 5–6 (1840).

75 Phillips had also represented the defendant in a patent infringement case that Justice Story decided in the May 1839 term in favor of the plaintiff. Blanchard v. Sprague, 3 F.Cas. 648 (C.C.D.Mass. 1839) (No. 1,518). Phillips appears to have represented a client before Justice Story as early as 1822. Tappan v. Darling, 23 F.Cas. 688 (C.C.D.Mass. 1822) (No. 13,746).

76 WILLARD PHILLIPS, THE LAW OF PATENTS FOR INVENTIONS iii (1837).

77 Rantoul advocated codification over the common law process, and Story, as chair of a commission to consider codification, suggested that Rantoul be appointed to the commission "so as to avoid any possible suggestion of the scheme being a mere party measure." NEWMYER, *supra* note 61, at 278. Story, though, apparently changed his mind, afraid "that the radical character of [Rantoul's] opinions might embarrass the prudent execution of the Commission." *Id.* at 278–79. Rantoul may have appeared once before Justice Story prior to the argument in *Folsom*. Champney v. Bancroft, 5 F.Cas. 438 (C.C.D.Mass. 1841) (No. 2,587).

78 17 U.S. (4 Wheat.) 518 (1819).

ly advised Daniel Webster on legal strategy, and collaborated in deciding cognate cases on circuit so that they could be joined with the main case before the Supreme Court.[79] In 1837, Story dissented in the Court's decision in the *Charles River Bridge*[80] case, even though Harvard University was one of the largest stockholders in the plaintiff bridge company[81] and Story was a longtime member of Harvard's Board of Overseers and the Harvard Corporation, as well as a professor there. And in the Court's 1834 copyright case of *Wheaton v. Peters*,[82] the story of which is told in chapter 1, Story had encouraged the defendant Peters to publish the allegedly infringing *Condensed Reports* and "facilitated their sale once they were published."[83] Story's ties to parties in these cases, and in *Folsom*, apparently prompted no concerns at the time over possible conflicts of interest. Indeed, even much closer ties seem to have been seen as unproblematic: two years after *Folsom*, Story decided a case in favor of clients represented by his own son and his soon-to-be son-in-law.[84]

Reference to Master

Although the suit was filed in August 1840, the first activity toward resolving it occurred in May 1841, when the court referred the case to a master in chancery to compare the two works and determine to what extent Upham had copied from Sparks's work or had independently drawn on the same sources that Sparks had used. The master chosen was George S. Hillard, a 33–year old Harvard-educated lawyer. Like many connected to the case, he was involved in politics—he had served as a state representative—and literature—he was a regular contributor

---

79 Newmyer, *supra* note 61, at 131, 177.

80 36 U.S. (11 Pet.) 420 (1837).

81 Newmyer, *supra* note 61, at 225–26. Other stockholders were friends of Story's, and one of the lawyers arguing the case for the defendant company was Story's close friend and colleague as a law professor at Harvard. *Id.*

82 33 U.S. (8 Pet.) 591 (1834).

83 Newmyer, *supra* note 61, at 141, 143. In addition, in 1839 Justice Story decided on circuit *Gray v. Russell*, in which the plaintiff publishers were involved in the firm which published Story's own legal commentaries.

84 *In re* Brown, 4 F. Cas.342 (C.C.D.Mass. 1843) (No. 1,985). George Ticknor Curtis, who together with Justice Story's son William represented the winning party, married Justice Story's daughter Mary the following year. The case report was also prepared by the justice's son William, who was the reporter for the First Circuit from 1839 to 1845.

John Adams, the future president, encountered a similar situation in the preceding century in his first case as a lawyer. "The justice of the peace, before whom Adams would appear, and the lawyer for [the other party] were father and son ... a circumstance that obviously did not bode well for Adams and his client." Adams lost the case. David McCullough, John Adams 45 (2001).

to *North American Review*,[85] a founder and editor of two other periodicals, and the editor of a well-received 1839 five-volume edition of Edmund Spenser's poetry. Hillard also had ties to many of the participants in the case.[86] He was a favorite student of Justice Story at Harvard.[87] He knew Sparks as well: in 1834 he wrote a biography of Captain John Smith for Sparks's *Library of American Biography*. Hillard certainly knew Sparks's *Washington* series, as in 1840 he had translated into English the introduction to the French edition.[88] And he was no doubt familiar with the defendants' School Library series, as his biography of Smith had appeared in that Library's *Lives of Eminent Individuals*.[89]

Hillard filed his report on Oct. 2, 1841. He reported that Sparks's work filled 6,763 pages, including 158 index pages, in twelve volumes, while Upham's work filled 866 pages, including 76 glossary/index pages, in two volumes. (The pages of Upham's work were smaller than those of Sparks's and so contained less text.) Hillard concluded that 353 pages of Upham's work were identical to passages in Sparks's work, but all of the identical passages were from Washington's own writings and not from Sparks's original *Life of Washington*. This total of 353 pages consisted mostly of passages of two pages or less, though several longer passages were identical (including one of 29 pages). The pages in Upham's work cited in the report sometimes contain an entire letter or letters (often running only to a few lines), and sometimes contain excerpts from a letter or letters; in some cases, the pages counted by Hillard include letters written *to* Washington, rather than by him, though the report never notes that fact. Of the pages Hillard concluded were copied, he classified 83 pages as "official letters and documents" by Washington and the remaining 270 pages as Washington's private letters and papers.

---

85 He contributed 23 articles between 1831 and 1864. 1 ADAMS, *supra* note 6, at 366–71.

86 In addition to the ties noted below, Culver quotes an 1835 letter from Upham to Sparks in which Upham indicates he had some years before had "an angry and to him rather injurious correspondence" with the "Hillard" of "Hillard and Gray." Culver, *supra* note 9, at 43. It seems clear from the context, however, that Upham is referring to the publishing firm of Hilliard and Gray, and thus referring to the publisher William Hilliard, rather than to the lawyer George S. Hillard, who would later serve as master in the *Folsom* case.

87 NEWMYER, *supra* note 61, at 268–69. In 1831, Story described Hillard in a letter of introduction as "a scholar, a gentleman, a lover of the law, & a sound advocate of sound literature," and as "one of those who are destined to fulfill the best expectations of the public & of the profession by directing their genius to the noblest ends by the noblest means." Joseph Story, *Letter to James Kent* (Apr. 4, 1831) 14 PROC. MASS. HIST. SOC'Y (2d ser.) 421 (1901).

88 2 ADAMS, *supra* note 6, at 329 n.1.

89 MASSACHUSETTS STATE BOARD OF EDUCATION, THIRD ANNUAL REPORT 26 (1840).

Hillard further reported that 319 of these 353 identical pages contained writings that had not appeared in print before Sparks published them, and he thus concluded that Upham had copied this text from Sparks's work. As to the remaining 34 pages, the master concluded that similarities between Upham's and Sparks's versions of the material (and dissimilarities between Upham's versions and those published before Sparks's edition) indicated that this material, too, had been copied from Sparks's work, rather than from the earlier editions. In most instances, though, the report shows that the differences between the Upham and Sparks versions, on the one hand, and the previously published versions, on the other hand, usually involved no more than one or two words per line.

Argument and Decision

No details of the argument exist in the report or the original case file. What survives is the opinion, which Justice Story began by noting that "Patents and copyrights approach, nearer than any other class of cases belonging to forensic discussions, to what may be called the metaphysics of the law, where the distinctions are, or at least may be, very subtle and refined, and, sometimes, almost evanescent." Having noted that the case presented "one of those intricate and embarrassing questions . . . in which it is not, from the peculiar nature and character of the controversy, easy . . . to lay down any general principles applicable to all cases," Justice Story proceeded to address the two essential issues familiar in any modern copyright infringement litigation: Does the plaintiff actually own a valid copyright, and has the defendant done anything that infringes on the copyright owner's exclusive rights?

Story's Opinion: Validity of Plaintiffs' Copyright in Washington's Writings

Justice Story began with the validity of copyright in Washington's letters. At the time, two distinct bodies of law offered copyright protection. The common law protected the exclusive right to control the initial publication of an author's work, for as long as the work remained unpublished—potentially forever. Washington's writings that were unpublished when Sparks compiled them would have been protected by common law copyright. Once published, a work lost its common law protection and federal statutory copyright would protect the work for a limited term if certain notice, registration, and deposit formalities were complied with. The *Folsom* plaintiffs alleged such compliance and the case never discusses the statutory formalities further. In considering the copyrightability of Washington's letters, Justice Story seems to have been articulating general principles he viewed as applicable under both common law and statutory copyright regimes.

Story rejected several arguments that Washington's letters were not protected by copyright law.[90] A writer did not, he concluded, need to pen letters that qualified as "literary compositions," with an eye to future publication, in order for the letters to be copyrightable. Rather, Justice Story announced his view that "the author of any ... letters, ... whether they are literary compositions, or familiar letters, or letters of business, possess[es] the sole and exclusive copyright therein." Justice Story's approach to the standards for copyrightability harkens back to a 1741 British copyright decision regarding letters, *Pope v. Curl*,[91] and anticipates that taken decades later by Justice Holmes in the *Bleistein* case, the story of which is told in Chapter 2.

If letters were copyrightable, what effect did sending a letter have on its copyright? Justice Story ruled that unless a letter writer unequivocally dedicated his or her rights to the public (which he found had not happened in this case), the writer retained the copyright in the letter. Even the addressee could not publish a letter unless, for example, the writer publicly accused the addressee of improper conduct, making publication "necessary to vindicate [the addressee's] character and reputation, or free him from unjust obloquy and reproach." Story even suggested that a letter's author retains the "general property in the manuscripts" of the letters—that is, ownership of the tangible letters themselves, as well as the copyright in the contents of the letters.

Justice Story based his view the of copyrightability of letters in part on English precedent,[92] but more fundamentally on the need to provide exclusive rights in order to encourage creation and, in particular, publication, of letters:

> Indeed, if the doctrine were otherwise, ... it would operate as a great discouragement upon the collection and preservation [of letters]; and the materials of history would become far more scanty, than they otherwise would be. What descendant ... of the deceased author, would undertake to publish, at his own risk and expense, any such papers; and what editor would be

---

90 Plaintiffs clearly were not claiming infringement of copyright merely in Sparks's selection and arrangement of Washington's writings, or in Sparks's editorial enhancements, but rather in Washington's writings themselves, as Story's analysis focuses entirely on the protectability of those writings and whether Upham's copying of those writings themselves infringed.

91 26 Eng. Rep. 608 (Ch. 1741).

92 The reliance on English precedent was natural in light of the paucity of American opinions. By 1841, federal courts had decided only nine copyright cases in reported decisions, while state courts had decided only ten copyright-related cases in reported decisions. Justice Story was likely familiar with the federal precedents, as they had been decided during his Supreme Court tenure and all but one had been decided by the Supreme Court or by a Supreme Court justice sitting on circuit.

> willing to employ his own learning, and judgment, and researches, in illustrating such works, if, the moment they were successful, and possessed the substantial patronage of the public, a rival bookseller might republish them, either in the same, or in a cheaper form, and thus either share with him, or take from him the whole profits? It is the supposed exclusive copyright in such writings, which now encourages their publication thereof, from time to time, after the author has passed to the grave.[93]

While Justice Story offered this standard incentive rationale for copyright protection, he took no note of potential difficulties that copyright in historically important letters might pose for their collection and publication—difficulties that Jared Sparks himself had initially faced in the Washington project. Sparks was determined to publish Washington's writings even after the President's heir, Bushrod Washington, declined to approve the project. Sparks had written *to Justice Story* in March 1826 that "Washington's public letters and papers are the property of the nation. As such they ought to be before the nation..." But while Sparks was able to obtain copies of the writings from sources other than Bushrod Washington, had Sparks placed those letters before the nation (as he planned to do), he would have committed copyright infringement in Justice Story's view in *Folsom*. Story's conclusion in *Folsom* also raises questions about Sparks's inclusion in his volumes of letters written *to* Washington, since Sparks presumably needed permission from the authors of all those letters or their successors.[94] Thus, while Justice Story viewed copyright in letters as providing incentive for their collection and publication, Jared Sparks's own experience suggests that copyright in unpublished letters could also hinder such efforts at dissemination if finding the authors' successors, or getting permission from them, proved difficult—which might well be the case, given the common law's potentially perpetual protection of unpublished letters.

Of course, the letters in this case were not just any letters, they were letters written by George Washington. The defendants argued that they were free to republish letters written in Washington's capacity as a public official. Justice Story acknowledged that official letters might require different treatment: the government might license, or prohibit, their publication for public purposes, but Story was less certain that any private person would have the right to publish such official letters. He concluded that he need not resolve the question, because only about 20%

---

[93] *Folsom*, 9 F.Cas. at 346.

[94] Similarly, Sparks's edition of Benjamin Franklin's writings included numerous previously unpublished letters, and it is unclear whether Sparks had received permission from Franklin's heirs to publish the papers, so that Sparks's edition may itself have been infringing under Justice Story's decision in *Folsom*.

of the material that Hillard found to be copied constituted official, rather than private, letters.

Finally, the defendants argued that the U.S. government's 1834 purchase of George Washington's physical papers from his descendants made the letters public property free for anyone to use. Justice Story concluded, though, that the government had purchased the manuscripts subject to any copyright that Sparks had previously acquired in them, and thus the sale to the government did not impair the plaintiffs' copyright.

Story's Opinion: Infringement by Defendants of Sparks's Work

Having found the plaintiffs' copyright in Washington's letters valid, Justice Story came to the crux of the case: had Upham infringed on that copyright? Justice Story never mentions the specific rights actually conferred on the plaintiffs by the copyright statute, but the 1831 Act provided that the copyright owner of a book "shall have the sole right and liberty of printing, reprinting, publishing, and vending such book." The question, then, was whether the defendants had reprinted, published, and sold Sparks's book.

Justice Story had opened his opinion with a general statement of his view of copyright infringement or "piracy." He contrasted cases in which it was "exceedingly obvious, that the whole substance of one work has been copied from another" (with only "studied evasions" in an attempt to disguise the copying) to cases in which "the identity of the two works in substance, and the question of piracy, . . . depend on a nice balance of the comparative use made in one of the materials of the other; the nature, extent, and value of the materials thus used; the objects of each work; and the degree to which each writer" used the same sources. The difficulty was deciding cases in the latter category. Story explained that a reviewer who quotes "largely" from a reviewed work, or someone who abridges a copyrighted work, might, depending on the circumstances, be an infringer or be engaged only in "fair quotation" or "fair abridgment."

The *Folsom* defendants indeed appealed to the line of English cases that Story had cited and that held that an abridgment of a copyrighted work did not necessarily infringe the work's copyright. They argued that Upham's work was a fair abridgment, and that they had "a right to abridge and select, and use the materials which they have taken" in the preparation of "an original and new work." The abridgment cases generally held that whether a defendant's use was a noninfringing abridgment depended on all the circumstances of the case, and the judges in those cases had looked to whether the defendant's use prejudiced the sales of the plaintiff's work,[95] how much of the plaintiff's work

[95] Dodsley v. Kinnersley, Amb. 403 (1761).

the defendant had used,[96] and, perhaps most significantly, whether the defendant had invested mental effort to produce a new work. As one of Story's authorities put it, there was no infringement in "a real and fair abridgment [as] fair abridgments may with great propriety be called a new work, because ... the invention, learning, and judgment of the author is shewn in them, and in many cases are extremely useful."[97] Although the fair abridgment doctrine originated in England, it may also have made sense in the young United States as a way to make written works available more affordably in a nation seeking to spread education and literacy.

Story was well acquainted with the fair abridgment doctrine. He had discussed it in his 1836 *Commentaries on Equity Jurisprudence*[98] and in his 1839 *Gray v. Russell* opinion. He may not have liked the doctrine, though. In 1839, Chancellor James Kent had written to Story for advice on whether to prepare an abridgment of Kent's famous *Commentaries*, noting demand for a cheap and abridged version for "Western schools" and suggestions that if Kent did not prepare such a version, others would.[99] Justice Story advised Kent to prepare the abridgment, in language that indicates hostility to a third party's right to abridge an author's work: "I am sure that if you do not execute the task yourself, it will be undertaken by others, & I greatly fear that in such a case it will become a mere bookseller's job, & be a miserable piece of patchwork."[100] The Story–Kent exchange suggests that as new markets for abridged versions of published works emerged, some authors were unhappy to find third parties supplying unauthorized but legal abridgments that satisfied demand that the author might have met through his own abridgment and that may have presented the author's work in what he viewed as a distorted form.

While Story may have disliked the abridgment rule, in *Folsom* he "led no assault on the established English doctrine."[101] Instead, with little explanation and no citation to authority, he concluded the abridgment doctrine simply did not apply because "the defendants' work cannot properly be treated as an abridgment" of Sparks's work. Story cast Upham's work instead as a selection of particular letters, in their

---

96 Whittingham v. Wooler, 2 Swans. 428 (1817).

97 Gyles v. Wilcox, 2 Atk. 141, 143 (1740). *See also* Wilkins v. Aikin, 17 Ves. 422 (1810).

98 Section 939. Story published a revised second edition in 1839.

99 James Kent, *Letter to Joseph Story, May 29, 1839*, 14 PROC. MASS. HIST. SOC'Y (2d ser.) 418 (Jan. 1901).

100 Joseph Story, *Letter to James Kent, June 1, 1839*, 14 PROC. MASS. HIST. SOC'Y (2d ser.) 423 (Jan. 1901).

101 BENJAMIN KAPLAN, AN UNHURRIED VIEW OF COPYRIGHT 28 (1967).

entirety, from Sparks's volume.[102] Although Story gives no analysis of why such a selection was not an abridgment, his opening discussion of the fair abridgment doctrine may shed some light:

> It is clear, that a mere selection, or different arrangement of parts of the original work, so as to bring the work into a smaller compass, will not be held to be [a noninfringing] abridgment. There must be real, substantial condensation of the materials, and intellectual labor and judgment bestowed thereon; and not merely the facile use of the scissors; or extracts of the essential parts, constituting the chief value of the original work.[103]

Story acknowledged Upham's "intellectual labor and judgment" in selecting the letters for his book, writing that "[f]rom the known taste and ability of Mr. Upham, it cannot be doubted, that these letters are the most instructive, useful and interesting to be found in [Sparks's] large collection." But Story appears to have concluded that selection alone, even if it represented "intellectual labor," did not produce an abridgment. He seems to have understood "abridgment" as another Supreme Court justice did a few years later:

> To copy certain passages from a book, omitting others, is in no just sense an abridgment of it. It makes the work shorter, but it does not abridge it. The judgment is not exercised in condensing the views of the author. His language is copied, not condensed; and the views of the writer in this mode, can be but partially given. To abridge is to preserve the substance, the essence of the work, in language suited to such a purpose.[104]

Upham's work could not, of course, abridge Washington's individual letters in this way, as Upham's goal of telling Washington's story in Washington's own words required verbatim quotation, rather than condensation in Upham's own language.

---

[102] Hillard's report had identified only *passages* that were identical, and the number of pages they occupied, without indicating whether those passages took entire letters or only portions of them. An examination of the pages from Upham's book cited in the report indicates that in many cases those pages reprint entire letters, but that in other instances Upham reprinted only excerpts from a longer letter.

[103] *Folsom,* 9 F.Cas. at 345. As an author of his own works, Justice Story also distinguished between abridgment and mere selection. In 1833, he sent to an English correspondent his volume, *Commentaries on the Constitution*, and noted that "[i]t purports to be an abridgment of a large work in 3 volumes, which I published about two months since; but it is in reality a *selection* almost without alteration of the most important parts of the larger work without the accompanying illustrations & notes." Joseph Story, *Letter to James J. Wilkinson, May 27, 1833*, 15 PROC. MASS. HIST. SOC'Y (2d ser.) 217–18 (Oct. 1901).

[104] Story v. Holcombe, 23 F.Cas. 171 (C.C.D.Ohio 1847) (No. 13,497) (McLean, J.).

Having rejected a claim of abridgment, Justice Story instead framed the main question as whether what Upham had done was "a justifiable use of [Sparks's work], such as the law recognizes as no infringement of the copyright." Essentially, Story was considering how to tell whether a copyrighted work has been infringed when a defendant has not merely reprinted the work but has instead taken some part of the work, and added other original material to it. Story states unequivocally that "[i]t is certainly not necessary, to constitute an invasion of copyright, that the whole of a work should be copied, or even a large portion of it," noting that "it is no defence, that another person has appropriated a part, and not the whole, of any property." But Justice Story seems equally unprepared to conclude that *every* taking from a copyrighted work constitutes infringement, leaving the question of when less than complete, verbatim copying of a work is infringement. In other words, how much copying is too much?

For the first century of English copyright law, as Professor Benjamin Kaplan has explained, that question was answered "by looking not so much to what the defendant had taken as to what he had added or contributed."[105] In *Folsom*, however, Justice Story essentially reversed the inquiry: "If so much is taken, that the value of the original is sensibly diminished, or the labors of the original author are substantially to an injurious extent appropriated by another, that is sufficient . . . to constitute a piracy." Story's test for whether a defendant's work infringes focuses on whether the defendant has made a substantial injurious appropriation, not on whether the defendant has failed to use what he took from the plaintiff's work to produce an new and improved work by adding his own contribution.[106]

Justice Story then elaborated on this test for whether a taking is infringing:

> In short, we must often, in deciding questions of this sort, look to the nature and objects of the selections made, the quantity and value of the materials used, and the degree in which the use may prejudice the sale, or diminish the profits, or supersede the objects, of the original work.[107]

He gave examples to illustrate the application of this infringement test, and drew entirely from recently decided English cases that also moved away from the traditional approach of evaluating the defendant's contribution and toward the approach of asking whether the defendant's use

---

[105] KAPLAN, *supra* note 101, at 17.

[106] He makes clear that the measure of infringement is not merely quantitative, but that the value of the material taken must also be considered.

[107] *Folsom*, 9 F.Cas. at 348.

of the plaintiff's material would injure the plaintiff's interests.[108] For example, Story quoted an 1807 English decision that a book review could infringe the book's copyright if the review extracted so much that it "communicates the same knowledge" and would "serve as a substitute for the book reviewed."[109] The cases Justice Story cites and discusses had focused on two considerations: whether the defendant had used intellectual effort to create a new work, and whether the defendant's work would interfere with the market for the plaintiff's work. But Justice Story's discussion of the infringement inquiry strongly emphasized the latter issue, and paid little attention to the former. While the defendant's mental labor appears relevant in Justice Story's view, the dominant focus for determining infringement seems to be whether the defendant's use will harm the value of the plaintiff's work, even if the defendant has produced a new and valuable work.[110]

Having expounded his test for infringement, Story made quick work of applying it to the facts before him, indicating he had "no doubt whatever" that Upham's work infringed. First, he dismissed any notion that the taking was quantitatively too little to be infringing: "if the defendants may take three hundred and nineteen letters . . . there is no reason why another bookseller may not take other five hundred letters, and a third, one thousand letters, and so on, and thereby the plaintiffs' copyright be totally destroyed." (Of course, Hillard had not found that Upham took 319 *letters* from Sparks, but rather that 319 *pages* in Upham's book contained passages identical to text in Sparks's series of nearly 7,000 (larger-sized) pages—and that at most 270 of those pages contained private letters, to which Sparks's rights were unquestioned.)

Next, Story concluded that Upham's book was "mainly founded upon" the letters copied from Sparks, which constituted one-third of Upham's book and "impart[] to it its greatest, nay, its essential value." Indeed, he said that without the letters from Sparks, Upham's work "must fall to the ground." This conclusion is not based on the master's findings, which dealt only with the *amount* of copying and not the

108 *See, e.g.*, Mawman v. Tegg, 2 Russ. 385 (1826); Wilkins v. Aikin, 17 Ves. 422 (1810); Sweet v. Shaw, 3 Jur. 217 (1839); Saunders v. Smith, 3 My. & Cr. 711 (1838); Lewis v. Fullarton, 2 Beav. 6 (1839). Several of these cases used language that moved away from the traditional approach but principally *held* that taking a large portion, but not the whole, of a copyrighted work could be infringement.

109 Roworth v. Wilkes, 1 Camp. 94 (1807).

110 Justice Story's emphasis on whether the defendant had taken the "value" of the copyrighted works also permeated his discussion of the fair abridgment and fair quotation doctrines in the *Gray v. Russell* decision, but that discussion was purely dictum, as Justice Story confirmed the master's finding in that case that the defendant had used the substance of all of the plaintiff's copyrightable notes on a public domain textbook, so the case involved substantial verbatim copying, rather than any claim of partial appropriation allowed under the abridgment and quotation doctrines.

quality or importance of the material copied. Perhaps Story had himself read Upham's volume, though in the opinion he only supports his conclusion by stating that "every one must see" that this is so. While Upham's book clearly relies heavily on Washington's own writings (albeit with substantial amounts of original connecting narrative), no evidence suggests that the particular writings copied from Sparks's work, as opposed to any of the others, are "essential" to the value of Upham's biography. Upham may have copied close to one-third of his work from protected letters that appeared in Sparks's work, but he surely exercised intellectual effort in his selection and arrangement of material from Sparks and from other sources, as well as in his own narrative contributions, and Justice Story offered no real reason to think that the "essential value" of the book came from the copied letters rather than from Upham's efforts and *all* of Washington's writings in the book.

Finally, Story concluded that Upham has infringed because he had not taken just "abbreviated or select passages ... from particular letters" but instead he took entire letters, and he took "those of most interest and value to the public, as illustrating the life, the acts, and the character of Washington." Under Story's test, this final conclusion seems to be the key, indicating that Upham's copying was qualitatively, even if not quantitatively, significant. Again, however, the factual basis for this conclusion is unclear. Perhaps Justice Story based his conclusion on his own earlier statement that Upham's "known taste and ability" ensured that he would have chosen "the most instructive, useful and interesting" letters from Sparks's collection.

Despite the emphasis Justice Story's infringement *test* places on whether the defendant's work economically injures the plaintiff's work—superseding its objects or use, prejudicing its sale, or diminishing its profits—his opinion actually says very little about the extent to which Upham's work might so injure Sparks's. The books certainly seem unlikely to have competed directly with each other. Upham's work was directed specifically to fledgling school lending libraries with relatively small budgets, which seem unlikely to invest in a copy of Sparks's twelve-volume set of Washington's writings. And those interested in a relatively comprehensive selection of Washington's writings seem unlikely to have been satisfied with Upham's work, which ran to less than one-eighth the length of Sparks's. Perhaps Justice Story feared that Upham's work might injure the sales of Sparks's original biography of Washington (or the planned condensed biography), though of course Upham was not accused of having copied anything from that work. In modern terms, Upham's work could of course be seen as harming Sparks's potential market for creating (or licensing someone like Upham to create) a book with a much smaller selection of Washington's letters than in Sparks's full set, but Justice Story offered barely a hint that prejudice to the sales not of the plaintiff's work but of *potential* works that might be created based on the plaintiff's work is relevant in considering whether the defendant's copying constitutes substantial injurious appropriation. The existing conception of the copyright owner's statutory rights to print, reprint, and publish a copyrighted book certainly did not include potential new works that might be based on that book, and while *Folsom* marks an early point in a long trend of extending such rights to the copyright owner, the decision says nothing expressly about such extension. So while Justice Story concluded that Upham infringed under his test, he offered little analysis as to the injury Upham's use caused to the value of Sparks's work.

Having applied his infringement test, Justice Story enjoined the defendants' use of the 319 copied "letters" (ignoring the distinction between private and official letters)[111] and ordered an accounting of the defendants' profits to be paid to the plaintiffs. Perhaps because of his ties to the defendants, Story carefully softened the blow of his decision. He had "no doubt" that the defendants did not act maliciously but instead thought that they had made "a perfectly lawful and justifiable use of the plaintiffs' work." He expressed "some regret" at finding infringement, because the result "may interfere, in some measure, with the very meritorious labors of the defendants, in their great undertaking of a series of works adapted to school libraries." As a result, he expressed hope "that some means may be found, to produce an amicable settlement of this unhappy controversy."

No evidence has been discovered of any such settlement. The court decree states that the plaintiffs waived the accounting they originally requested, so they seem to have recovered no monetary remedy. By 1843 the Marsh, Lyon, Capen & Webb firm may no longer have been in business, and relatively few schools seem to have instituted libraries, so the plaintiffs may have found that the defendants had not made any profits that could be recovered. (The defendants' advertised price of seventy-five cents per volume may have hampered sales; in 1841, Harper & Brothers in New York were selling volumes in their School District Library series at thirty-eight cents each.)[112]

Folsom's Afterstory: How the Courts Have Used *Folsom* Since its Decision

As of mid–2004, approximately 114 reported decisions in U.S. courts have cited Justice Story's *Folsom* opinion. In the first 110 years after

---

[111] The actual entered decree enjoins the defendant with respect to all 353 pages identified by the master, including those that had been printed in other sources before Sparks published them and those identified as official, even though Justice Story had not decided on the validity of Sparks's copyright in the latter.

[112] Connecticut Common School Journal, Mar. 15, 1841.

Folsom was decided, it was cited only 44 times, while in the following forty years, from 1955 to 1994, when the Supreme Court decided *Campbell*, it was cited in 45 cases, almost three times as frequently as in the previous 110 years. And in the single decade after *Campbell*, it has been cited in 25 opinions, twice as often as in the preceding forty years. Courts today not only cite *Folsom* more frequently but also for different propositions than in earlier times: only in the 1950s does *Folsom* begin to be regularly cited in discussions of fair use, though today courts cite it almost wholly in that context.

The following sections consider the various propositions for which *Folsom* has been cited since its publication, but they no doubt understate somewhat the case's influence. Over time, some courts discussed or applied key principles from the decision as those principles had been explicated in previous cases, treatises, or encyclopedias, but cited only to the intervening source and not to the *Folsom* decision itself.[113] The following discussion of cases actually citing *Folsom* therefore gives a better picture of the relative magnitude of the areas of the law that the case has influenced than of the absolute magnitude of that influence.

Letters and Official Papers

Seventeen cases, most before the 1950s, cite *Folsom*'s holding that the author of an unpublished letter, rather than the recipient, can control the letter's publication. Modern U.S. copyright law follows Justice Story: the letter's author initially owns the copyright and sending the *letter* does not transfer that *copyright* to its addressee.[114] But while Justice Story suggested that the author retained ownership even of the physical letter, the modern view, consistent with § 202 of the 1976 Act, is that the recipient, rather than the author, generally owns the tangible object sent to her.[115]

---

[113] For example, a number of cases use Justice Story's basic test for determining infringement and cite not to *Folsom* but to *Lawrence v. Dana*, other intervening cases, or the encyclopedia *Corpus Juris*. *See, e.g.*, West Pub. Co. v. Lawyers' Co-op. Pub. Co., 79 F. 756 (C.C.A. 2d Cir. 1897); West Pub. Co. v. Edward Thompson Co., 169 F. 833 (C.C.E.D.N.Y. 1909); M. Witmark & Sons v. Pastime Amusement Co., 298 F. 470 (E.D.S.C. 1924); National Institute, Inc. v. Nutt, 28 F.2d 132 (D.Conn. 1928); Universal Pictures Co. v. Harold Lloyd Corp., 162 F.2d 354 (9th Cir. 1947). Similarly, at least three cases set forth Justice Story's factors as relevant to fair use analysis without citing *Folsom*. Mathews Conveyer Co. v. Palmer-Bee Co., 135 F.2d 73 (6th Cir. 1943); Karll v. Curtis Pub. Co., 39 F. Supp. 836 (E.D.Wis. 1941); New York Tribune, Inc. v. Otis & Co., 39 F. Supp. 67 (S.D.N.Y. 1941).

[114] Seven opinions, mostly by early twentieth century state courts, involve cases addressing what we would today consider rights of publicity and cite *Folsom*'s principle of a letter writer's right to control publication of her letters as an analogy in discussions of a person's right to control the use of her likeness by others.

[115] *See, e.g.*, Salinger v. Random House, Inc., 811 F.2d 90, 94–95 (2d Cir. 1987). *See also* Baker v. Libbie, 97 N.E. 109 (Mass. 1912).

Five cases—four involving disputes over former President Nixon's official papers (and recordings)—cited *Folsom* in connection with the ownership of a public officeholder's official papers. While modern copyright law does not govern ownership of the actual papers of government officials, Section 105 of the 1976 Act does expressly provide that no copyright exists in works created by federal government officers or employees as part of their official duties, contrary to Story's tentative views in *Folsom*.[116]

Fair Abridgments

One early case cited *Folsom* in elaborating the fair abridgment doctrine. *Story v. Holcombe*, decided just six years after *Folsom*, looked to Story's opinion in deciding a case in which the executors of Justice Story's own estate alleged infringement by the author of a much shorter work based on Story's *Commentaries on Equity Jurisprudence*. The defendant argued that his work was a fair abridgment. Justice McLean expressed strong disagreement with the doctrine that fair abridgments did not infringe, arguing that any abridgment would to some extent affect the sale of the abridged work and therefore should be restrained. But he acknowledged the precedents establishing the fair abridgment doctrine and proceeded to apply it.[117] In defining the general boundaries of fair abridgment he placed special emphasis (as Justice Story had) on whether the defendant's abridging use would substitute for the plaintiff's work. McLean concluded that only the last two-thirds of the defendant's book were a non-infringing fair abridgment. The decision follows Story's path in *Folsom* in shifting the inquiry in abridgment cases away from the substantiality of the abridger's intellectual effort and toward the potential economic effect of the defendant's abridgment on the plaintiff's work, though it shows that even under this view courts could find an unauthorized abridgment to be fair. But the entire fair abridgment doctrine formally ended in the 1909 Copyright Act, which granted owners of copyrights in literary works the exclusive right "to make any other version" of their work, which included an abridged version.

Determining Infringement

While modern courts treat *Folsom* as a fair use case, Justice Story's opinion does not articulate a fair use analysis, at least not as modern copyright law understands that concept. Today, if a defendant has copied from a copyrighted work, and if the copying amounts to improper

---

116 17 U.S.C. §§ 105, 101 ("work of the United States government").

117 In 1869, another Supreme Court justice noted similar skepticism about the fair abridgment rule in a case decided on circuit, but found the rule too settled and long-established not to follow it. Lawrence v. Dana, 15 F.Cas. 26 (C.C.D.Mass. 1869) (No. 8,136).

appropriation, the defendant ordinarily has infringed the copyright. But even if a defendant's copying constitutes improper appropriation, she has not infringed if her copying qualifies as fair use. That is, once a court determines that a defendant has done something ordinarily within the copyright owner's exclusive rights, the court proceeds to consider whether the defendant's activity is nonetheless permitted as fair use. In *Folsom*, however, Justice Story's analysis focuses entirely on the first question: whether a defendant's copying in fact amounts to improper appropriation—that is, whether the copyright owner has made out a prima facie case for infringement.

Justice Story essentially confronted the same question that Judge Learned Hand faced in 1930 in *Nichols v. Universal Pictures*, where Hand stated that "It is of course essential to any protection of literary property ... that the right cannot be limited literally to the text, else a plagiarist would escape by immaterial variations. That has never been the law, but, as soon as literal appropriation ceases to be the test, the whole matter is necessarily at large..."[118] In *Folsom*, Justice Story articulated a test for deciding when less than complete, literal appropriation is infringement: when the taking is substantial enough to injure the copyright owner. *Folsom* shifted copyright infringement analysis, minimizing consideration of the defendant's own intellectual contributions to her work and emphasizing instead the effect of the defendant's use on the plaintiff's market.[119]

In its first 110 years, courts in fact read *Folsom* primarily for guidance in determining infringement. Courts cited *Folsom* fifteen times—more than for any other proposition—as precedent for how to determine whether the defendant had in fact infringed the plaintiff's copyright, usually where the defendant had copied from the plaintiff's work but had taken only some part and not the whole of the work.

In the last fifty years, though, only seven cases cited *Folsom* in connection with the test for infringement. Courts today generally use a more modern formulation: to prove infringement, the owner of a valid copyright must show that a defendant actually copied from the copyrighted work and that the defendant's copying amounted to improper appropriation. In *Folsom*, Story primarily articulated an early version of the improper appropriation test: even where a defendant copied from the plaintiff's work, the copying is improper only if it "sensibly diminishes" the value of the plaintiff's work or takes from that work "to an injurious

---

[118] 45 F.2d 119 (2d Cir. 1930).

[119] This shift was consistent with a relatively contemporaneous trend in British copyright decisions away from finding that a defendant did not infringe if she made intellectual "improvements" to a copyrighted work. *See* KAPLAN, *supra* note 101, 17–25, 27–30.

extent." But Story's focus on economic harm by the defendant is now largely absent from analysis of a plaintiff's infringement case, except perhaps for a faint echo. As Professor Paul Goldstein explains in his copyright treatise, proving improper appropriation today involves, in part, showing that audiences will perceive substantial similarity between the copyrighted work and the defendant's work. This "audience test," Professor Goldstein says, "is a practical implementation of copyright law's traditional object: to secure to authors the exclusive market—audience—for their protected expression."[120] Noting the parallels with *Folsom*, Goldstein states that the policy underlying the test is whether, "[h]aving purchased, read, heard, or seen those parts of the defendant's work that were appropriated from the plaintiff's work, . . . members of the intended audience [would] be disinclined to purchase, read, hear, or see those same parts in the plaintiff's work."[121] But he explains that in applying the audience test, courts "tend simply to ask whether the ordinary lay observer would have detected similarities between plaintiff's and defendant's work" and *not* to ask expressly whether the defendant's appropriation from the plaintiff would reduce the latter's audience or otherwise injure her market. Thus, while *Folsom* shifted the infringement inquiry from asking whether the copying defendant had invested her own intellectual effort in creating her work to asking instead whether the defendant's work would interfere with the market for the plaintiff's work, courts today generally presume such interference whenever the factfinder decides that audiences would perceive substantial similarity of protected expression between the plaintiff's and the defendant's works. To the extent that courts deciding copyright infringement liability today inquire at all into the economic harm that the defendant's work causes to the plaintiff's, they generally do so only when considering a defendant's claim of fair use.

Fair Use

Though courts today principally cite *Folsom* for having established the fair use doctrine, in its first 110 years only two courts cited *Folsom* in deciding what we would today call fair use questions. *Lawrence v. Dana*, an 1869 case involving various editions of a treatise on international law, was apparently the first American case to use the phrase "fair use" to describe in general the extent to which a subsequent author may use a copyrighted work without the copyright owner's consent. Having concluded that the defendant's work did not qualify as a fair abridgment of the plaintiff's work, *Lawrence* considered whether the defendant's use infringed, and said that "[f]ew judges have devised safer rules upon the subject than Judge Story." The court quoted Story's test

---

[120] 2 PAUL GOLDSTEIN, GOLDSTEIN ON COPYRIGHT (3d. ed. 2005) at 9:33 to 9:34.

[121] *Id.*

that infringement required substantially injurious appropriation, which could be seen by considering "the nature and objects of the selections made, the quantity and value of the materials used, and the degree in which the use may prejudice the sale or diminish the profits, or supersede the objects of the original work." The only other citation to *Folsom* in a fair use case in this period was in 1941, when a district court in New York, denying summary judgment to a defendant claiming fair use in reprinting a newspaper's political editorial, cited *Folsom* as one of two authorities for the proposition that a evaluating a claim of fair use required considering all of the evidence in the case. The lack of citation of *Folsom* as a fair use precedent in its first 110 years was not due simply to an absence of fair use cases in those years. A 1936 copyright treatise included a 30–page chapter on fair use and quoted or cited about 25 American decisions involving the doctrine,[122] but while the treatise discussed *Folsom* as an important fair use case, the other opinions it discussed generally did not even cite *Folsom*.[123]

Courts came to cite *Folsom* as a fair use case between 1955 and 1994: 28 of 45 citations in this period related to the doctrine. These cases cited *Folsom* in several ways. Eleven merely referred to *Folsom* as the origin of the fair use doctrine, briefly mentioned it as part of a general overview of the doctrine, or offered it as a "see" cite in the fair use analysis. Three cases involved claims of fair use of letters and cited to *Folsom* as a factually analogous precedent. But fourteen cases actually made use of *Folsom* in their substantive analysis of fair use claims, and half of these cases rely on Story's language that a defendant's copying infringes if it supersedes the objects of the original work. Story was cited for the importance of considering harm to the market for the plaintiff's work, the focus of his *Folsom* test, only now the consideration came not in evaluating a plaintiff's claim of infringement but as part of a defendant's claim for fair use. Credit for the prominence of *Folsom* in fair use cases in this period belongs mostly to Second Circuit courts. Of the 28 fair use cases citing *Folsom*, 17 opinions were by either the Second Circuit or its district courts (principally the Southern District of New York), while no other circuit's courts made more than two citations.

This period also marks *Folsom*'s copyright debut in the Supreme Court.[124] In 1984, Justice Blackmun, dissenting in the *Sony* case[125]

122 Leon H. Amdur, Copyright Law and Practice (1936).

123 As noted above, *see* note 113 and accompanying text, merely counting citations understates *Folsom*'s influence, as some courts applied Justice Story's principles as explicated in cases or treatises discussing *Folsom*, but cited only to the intervening source and not to the *Folsom* decision itself.

124 In the late 1970s, the Court cited *Folsom* in a noncopyright dispute over ownership of President Nixon's papers. Nixon v. General Services Administration, 433 U.S. 425 (1977).

(whose story is told in chapter 5) quoted Justice Story's opinion in a footnote as an early expression of the fair use doctrine. The following year, *Folsom* moved from dissent to majority and from footnote to text in the *Harper & Row* case, in which the magazine *The Nation* had quoted 300 words about the Watergate crisis from President Gerald Ford's memoir shortly before the book was published. Justice O'Connor quoted *Folsom* as an illustration that fair use "has always precluded a use that 'supersede[s] the use of the original.' "[126]

The 1976 Copyright Act, the culmination of a decades-long project to revise the copyright statute, codified the fair use doctrine and for the first time provided express direction to courts as to how to evaluate fair use claims in the form of four detailed factors to be considered. Those who codified fair use did not expressly attach any particular significance to the *Folsom* opinion or draw directly on Story's work in formulating the statutory factors. An initial Copyright Office revision study of fair use listed what it called "the oft-quoted criteria [for fair use] set forth by Mr. Justice Story in *Folsom v. Marsh*," but did not extensively discuss the case or the test, or label it the origin of the fair use doctrine.[127] And the various reports by the Copyright Office and Congressional committees made no mention of *Folsom* as having guided the formulation of Section 107. Nevertheless, the four statutory criteria bear a strong resemblance to the factors Story listed in *Folsom*. While Justice Story's principles might have seemed more necessary before Congress provided express guidance on fair use, in fact courts have cited *Folsom* far more often in deciding fair use claims under the statute than they had under the common law.

How did *Folsom* come to be seen in the second half of the twentieth century as the origin of the fair use doctrine? Copyright law treatises from the 1870s on discussed *Folsom* in explaining fair use, but generally did not treat it as a seminal case. That view may trace in part to a 1954 University of Chicago Law Review comment, called *What is Fair Use?*, by Chief Judge Leon Yankwich of the Southern District of California. Yankwich stated that "the criteria evolved in the American cases [for defining fair use] stem from a statement by Mr. Justice Story" and quoted extensively from *Folsom*.[128] Five years later, Yankwich wrote the third opinion ever to firmly cite *Folsom* as a fair use precedent. Judge Yankwich may thus have planted the seed of the view that fair use in

[125] Sony Corp. v. Universal City Studios, Inc., 464 U.S. 417 (1984).

[126] Harper & Row Publishers v. Nation Enterprises, 471 U.S. 539, 550 (1985).

[127] The study did note that the law review essay by Judge Yankwich, discussed in the following paragraph, found Story's fair use criteria to be the basis of the doctrine in U.S. cases.

[128] 22 U. Chi. L. Rev. 203, 210.

America originated in *Folsom*. Another contributing factor may have been that two towering copyright scholars of the mid-twentieth century, Benjamin Kaplan of Harvard and Ralph Brown of Yale, included a 38–line excerpt and summary of *Folsom* in their *Copyright and Unfair Competition* casebook starting with the first edition in 1958, and stated that the case "first gave the [fair use] doctrine definition" in the U.S.

However *Folsom* first came to be viewed as originating fair use (rather than as describing the boundaries of a prima facie claim of infringement), that view has been cemented for the moment by the *Campbell* opinion. Justice Souter, in evaluating whether Two Live Crew's version of Roy Orbison's song "Oh, Pretty Woman" constituted fair use, cited *Folsom* as the key American fair use precedent. *Campbell* credited Justice Story with having "distilled the essence of law and methodology from the earlier cases" into the foundational fair use passage: "look to the nature and objects of the selections made, the quantity and value of the materials used, and the degree in which the use may prejudice the sale, or diminish the profits, or supersede the objects, of the original work." (Viewing this passage as the basic formulation of fair use is somewhat ironic, given Justice Story's opening statement in *Folsom* about the difficulty of "lay[ing] down any general principles applicable to all cases.")

The *Campbell* Court found Story's distillation of fair use principles "discernable" in Section 107's list of factors for fair use analysis and aligned each factor with language from Justice Story. The "purpose and character of the use" factor "draws on Justice Story's formulation, 'the nature and objects of the selections made,' " and, Justice Souter explained, has as its central purpose "to see, in Justice Story's words, whether the new work merely 'supersede[s] the objects' of the original creation . . . or instead adds something new, with a further purpose or different character, altering the first with new expression, meaning or message; . . . in other words, whether and to what extent the new work is transformative.' "[129] *Folsom*, of course, deemphasized the relevance to infringement analysis of a copying defendant's intellectual contribution—putting the older case in some tension with the importance that *Campbell* placed on transformativeness, which largely centers on the copier's investment of authorship into her own work. The Court also quoted *Folsom* to explicate the second factor ("the nature of the copyrighted work" used draws "on Justice Story's expression, the 'value of the materials used' ") and the third ("the amount and substantiality of the portion used" was, "in Justice Story's words, 'the quantity and value of the materials used' "). The final factor, "the effect of the use upon the potential market for or value of the copyrighted work," reflects Justice

---

129 Campbell v. Acuff–Rose Music, Inc., 510 U.S. 569, 578 (1994).

Story's central concern in *Folsom*—"the degree in which the use may prejudice the sale, or diminish the profits ... of the original work." But the Court surprisingly fails to quote Story here or to give *Folsom* a prominent place in its discussion of the modern statutory analog to what Story saw as the heart of the case.

The *Campbell* decision's substantial use of *Folsom* in elaborating fair use analysis has led to increasing citation by lower courts. In the first decade after *Campbell*, 25 reported cases have cited *Folsom*, and 21 did so in the fair use context. Some courts merely refer to *Folsom* as the origin of, or an important development in the history of, the fair use doctrine, or cite it in quotations from *Campbell*. But eleven cases cite or quote *Folsom* as part of the substantive analysis of the fair use claims before them, and in most instances the courts cite *Folsom* for the principle that a use that supersedes the use of the copyrighted work has a weak claim to fair use, while one that makes transformative use of the original has a stronger claim. For the moment, then, *Folsom* has a secure place in contemporary copyright law as a landmark of fair use, even though Justice Story's analysis focused on defining the scope not of fair abridgment, an early predecessor of fair use, but rather of a copyright owner's prima facie claim of infringement.

***Folsom's* Afterstory: Whatever Happened To ...?**

Justice Story and Master Hillard

Four years after *Folsom*, Justice Story made plans to resign from the Supreme Court after 33 years of service, and to become a full-time professor, but in September 1845, before announcing his retirement, he died at age 66. Hillard practiced law until the 1870s, representing clients such as Nathaniel Hawthorne and Henry W. Longfellow. His involvement in public affairs continued, including as a state senator, Boston's city solicitor, and U.S. Attorney for Massachusetts. His literary career continued as well. Among other works, Hillard published *Six Months in Italy* in 1853; it was later described as "probably the most popular book about Italy by an American."[130] In 1872, Hillard became the first dean of Boston University School of Law, though his health allowed him to serve for only one or two years. He died in 1879.

The Plaintiffs and the Life and Writings of Washington

Jared Sparks became president of Harvard from 1849 to 1852. He retired in 1853,[131] and for the rest of his life worked on a history of the

---

[130] Paul R. Baker, The Fortunate Pilgrims: Americans in Italy, 1800–1860 (1964).

[131] That year, Sparks published the four-volume *Correspondence of the American Revolution*, mostly letters written *to* George Washington, thereby largely fulfilling the plan he developed in 1827 while first examining Washington's papers at Mount Vernon. *See*

American Revolution, which remained unfinished when he died in 1866. The *Life and Writings of Washington* remained in print, though Sparks changed publishers frequently.[132] By 1852, over 7,000 sets of Washington's edited *Writings* had been sold, as well as 8,500 copies of Sparks's original *Life*. Sparks continued to divide earnings on the work with the Washington and Marshall families with periodic (though diminishing) payments through 1856.[133]

Sparks's historical work, including Washington's *Writings*, attracted criticism during his lifetime because he made sometimes significant editorial changes to the historical documents that he published, rather than presenting them exactly as written. That criticism has continued, with Sparks "vilified by professional historians as a documentary editor who freely rewrote and revised original texts as his mood determined."[134] Indeed, at least one modern Washington scholar has accused Sparks of suppressing a 73–page first draft, in Washington's hand, of his first inaugural address, and of cutting parts of that manuscript into fragments to distribute to autograph collectors.[135]

Charles Folsom's connection to the University Press apparently ended around 1842.[136] He ran a school for young women for several years, then returned to library work, serving as librarian of the Boston Athenaeum for eleven years. He died in 1872.

Willard Phillips, the plaintiffs' attorney, left law practice in 1845. In the early 1840s, he was a founder of the New England Mutual Life Insurance Company, and he later resigned as probate judge to become company president, a position he occupied for many years. He later received an honorary LL.D. from Harvard, and died in 1873.

The Defendants, the Life of Washington, *and the "School Library Series"*

Upham went on to a career in politics. He was mayor of Salem, a three-term state representative and three-term state senator, and he

---

note 21, *supra*. And Sparks, as he had originally proposed to Bushrod Washington, split the proceeds evenly with the Washington and Marshall families. 2 ADAMS, *supra* note 6, at 308–09.

[132] Tappan & Dennet of Boston had the exclusive publication rights for five years from October 1, 1841. In 1846, Harper & Brothers contracted to sell a cheap edition (the price not to exceed $1.50 per volume) and pay Sparks a 25 cent per volume royalty. In 1852 and 1854, Sparks and Little & Brown entered a contract for the series, with a royalty rate of $2.50 per set. 2 ADAMS, *supra* note 6, at 280 n.1.

[133] 2 ADAMS, *supra* note 6, at 295–96 n.1.

[134] Cox, *supra* note 6, at 421.

[135] JAMES T. FLEXNER, GEORGE WASHINGTON AND THE NEW NATION (1783–1793) at 162–63, 181 (1969).

[136] John Palfrey, *Tribute to Mr. Folsom*, 11 PROC. MASS. HIST. SOC'Y 308, 311 (1872).

served one term in the U.S. House of Representatives as a member of the new Republican party. His major literary endeavor after *Folsom* was a two-volume work entitled *Salem Witchcraft*.[137] Upham's *Life of Washington* reportedly appeared in London in 1852, presumably in an unauthorized printing.[138] Politics and literature may have merged in Upham's later life in connection with his friend, the author Nathaniel Hawthorne, who was the surveyor at the Salem Custom House. Hawthorne, a Democrat, was fired after Zachary Taylor, a Whig, won the White House in 1848. Upham, a Whig and Taylor supporter, apparently did nothing to prevent Hawthorne's firing and may have participated "in a newspaper slur campaign against Hawthorne" designed to disguise the political nature of the firing. Hawthorne reportedly forever thereafter regarded Upham as an enemy, and apparently caricatured him in *The House of the Seven Gables* (as Jaffrey Pyncheon).[139] Upham died in 1875.

Publisher Bela Marsh continued in the book trade in Boston, later specializing in publishing "spiritual and reform books," until he died in 1869. Nahum Capen served as postmaster of Boston from 1857 to 1861 and wrote several books, mainly history and political science, before his death in 1886.

Attorney Robert Rantoul continued his reform work in both law and politics. In the Supreme Judicial Court of Massachusetts in 1842, he successfully defended journeymen boot-makers charged with an unlawful conspiracy to force employers to recognize collective bargaining, an important early labor rights decision.[140] He later served as U.S. Attorney for Massachusetts. In 1851, he filled the unexpired U.S. Senate term of Daniel Webster, who had become Secretary of State, but served only 9 days. Elected to the House of Representatives in 1851, Rantoul was refused a seat in the 1852 Democratic convention, in part for opposition to the Fugitive Slave Law. He died suddenly in 1852 at age 47.[141]

As of 1842, the Board of Education reported that only about 300 sets of the School Library series had been sold.[142] By January 1843, Thomas H. Webb & Co. was publishing the series, presumably as successor to Marsh, Capen, Lyon & Webb. Despite an 1842 law providing state matching funds of $15 per year per district for the support of school

---

[137] *See generally* DeFino, *supra* note 33; Ellis, *supra* note 33. He also wrote three volumes in the *Life of Timothy Pickering*, the Revolutionary War figure, as well as the *Life, Explorations, and Public Service of John Charles Fremont*.

[138] Ellis, *supra* note 33, at 198–99.

[139] DeFino, *supra* note 33, at 112.

[140] Commonwealth v. Hunt, 45 Mass. 111 (1842).

[141] RANTOUL, *supra* note 58, at 848.

[142] MASSACHUSETTS STATE BOARD OF EDUCATION, FIFTH ANNUAL REPORT 79 (1842).

libraries, the school library enterprise apparently never really took off in the state, and by 1859, the Board of Education reported that the libraries "have generally failed to excite the interest necessary to keep them in existence."[143]

Conclusion

Folsom was very much a copyright case of its own time. It involved a conflict between early Republican authors and publishers fulfilling the goals of early copyright law by producing distinctly American informational works as part of a larger movement to develop a national culture and increase educational opportunity. The decision gave short shrift to the older copyright doctrine of the fair abridgment rule and started down the road of broader exclusive rights for copyright owners.

More than a century and a half after Justice Story wrote his opinion, courts cite *Folsom* more frequently than ever, but to very different ends than those at which he aimed. In 1841, Story sought to expand the concept of when a defendant's copying constituted copyright infringement by focusing on defining infringement as copying that would cause economic harm to the copyrighted work. Today, most courts do not cite *Folsom* for the principle that infringement consists of economically harmful copying, but rather as the origin of the fair use limitation on the greatly expanded rights of the copyright owner and the factors to be evaluated in determining the scope of that limitation. And where *Folsom* shifted the focus of infringement from a copier's own intellectual contributions to whether the copying caused economic harm, modern courts citing *Folsom* in fair use cases often bring the focus back to the copier's creative transformation of the work.

---

143 WILLIAM J. RHEES, MANUAL OF PUBLIC LIBRARIES, INSTITUTIONS, AND SOCIETIES, IN THE UNITED STATES AND BRITISH PROVINCES OF NORTH AMERICA 556 (1859) Rhees estimated that throughout the country, there were 18,000 district school libraries, with collections amounting to 2 million volumes (or about 110 volumes per library). *Id.* at xxviii.

The Story of *Graver Tank v. Linde*: Intellectual Property Infringement in Flux

John R. Thomas*

"An American has invented a new welding system that permits us to build ships many times faster."[1] The invention that Franklin Delano Roosevelt described to Winston Churchill during World War II is believed to be not of a single person, but actually of three free-lance experimenters—Lloyd Jones, Harry Kennedy, and Maynard Rotermund—who in 1932 were moonlighting on a San Francisco water pipeline project. Their revolutionary arc welding technique took the U.S. manufacturing industry by storm, quickly displacing earlier methods, streamlining production in a number of fields, and generating many millions of dollars in royalties.

The Jones–Kennedy–Rotermund invention would also have a significant impact upon U.S. intellectual property jurisprudence. Enforcement of their patent rights would ultimately spawn nine reported judicial opinions, including two from the Supreme Court and four from the Court of Appeals for the Seventh Circuit, spanning twenty years of litigation. The most significant of these, the 1950 Supreme Court opinion in *Graver Tank & Manufacturing Co. v. Linde Air Products Co.*,[2] has been identified as the most-cited patent case of our time.[3] *Graver Tank* endures because here, as in so many other cases, the courts have struggled to determine the appropriate right of control due to an

---

* Professor of Law, Georgetown University Law Center. I am grateful to the participants in the INTELLECTUAL PROPERTY STORIES workshop at the Samuelson/Glushko Center, and in particular volume editors Rochelle Dreyfuss and Jane Ginsburg, for their helpful and challenging comments and suggestions. I also thank Professor Paul Janicke, both for providing the two illustrations that appear below, and for publishing his exceptionally well-researched and thoughtful article on the *Graver Tank* case. Readers of this chapter are strongly encouraged to consult Professor Janicke's article, cited in footnote one below, for additional historical details and insightful observations.

1 *Quoted in* Paul M. Janicke, *Heat of Passion: What Really Happened in Graver Tank*, 24 AM. INTELL. PROP. L. ASS'N Q.J. 1, 4 (1996).

2 339 U.S. 605 (1950).

3 Janicke, *supra* note 1, at 4.

intellectual property owner. This chapter reviews the story of *Graver Tank* and explores the broader themes at play in that case.

The Invention

Jones, Kennedy, and Rotermund first joined forces at the South San Francisco facility of Western Pipe & Steel Co. in 1932. Kennedy, a free-lance inventor, received a bachelor's degree in electrical engineering from Berkeley in 1914 and remained in the Bay Area for many years thereafter. Jones was a Ph.D. physicist who had known Kennedy since 1927. Little record survives concerning Rotermund's background. Photographs of the period suggest that he was the "hands on" member of the group, likely being the one who physically formulated the welding fluxes and tested them in the field. The three inventors moonlighted from other jobs, arriving at the Western plant late in the day and, in an era that predated the Bay Bridge, either taking the last boat back to Oakland at night, or the first one back in the morning.[4]

The three inventors soon became involved in Western's major project of the day, the construction of a new water pipeline for the city of San Francisco. The effort involved an enormous amount of steel pipe–88 miles in total, with a thickness of 7/16 inch and a diameter of four feet.[5] Obtaining this quantity of pipe would prove a challenge. Steel mills do not produce pipe. Rather, they make and sell rectangular steel plates. Western was therefore left to form the plates into pipe segments itself. The most common way to do this is to bend two steel plates into two half-cylinders and place them side-by-side:[6]

4 Trial testimony of Lloyd T. Jones and Harry E. Kennedy, Trial Record at 26–35, 133–37.

5 Trial testimony of Harry E. Kennedy, Trial Record at 53.

6 Professor Paul Janicke courteously provided this illustration.

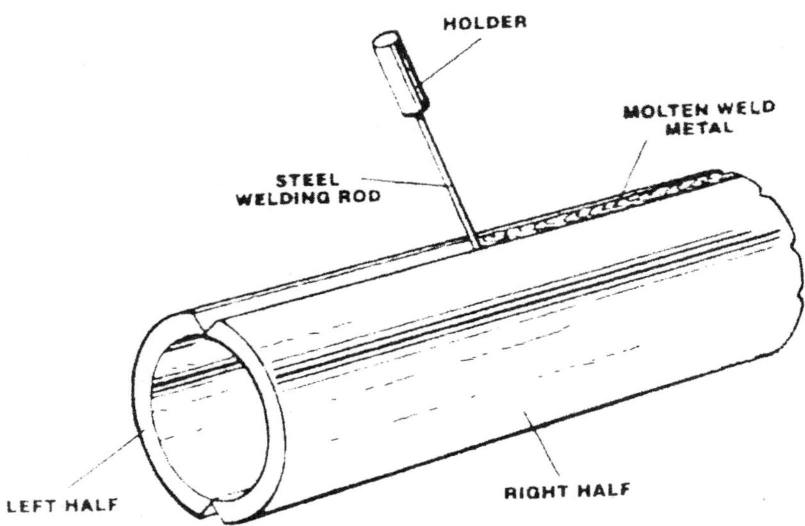

The next step is obviously to join the steel plates along the abutting beveled edges. Rivets or other mechanical means can do the job, but welding—a procedure for fusing two pieces of metal—produces stronger seams and is more reliable.

The steel industry knew of a number of welding techniques as of the 1930's. The most straightforward was gas welding. Here the welder simply applies a hot acetylene blowtorch to the edges of two steel plates. As the edges of the plates melt, the molten steel intermixes and the two plates are effectively fused upon cooling. Gas welders may also employ an additional metal, called a "filler material," that they place over the seam to be fused. Filler material strengthens the weld and prevents cracking.[7]

Another technique, arc welding, was the focus of the *Graver Tank* case. This method uses an electric arc to produce heat, which then melts and fuses the steel plates. Arc welding involves the complicated apparatus depicted below.[8]

---

[7] Department of the Army, Welding Theory and Application § 6–3, Training Circular No. 9–237 *available at* http://www.machinist.org/army_welding/Ch6.htm (May 7, 1993).

[8] I once more relied upon Professor Paul Janicke's generosity in providing this diagram.

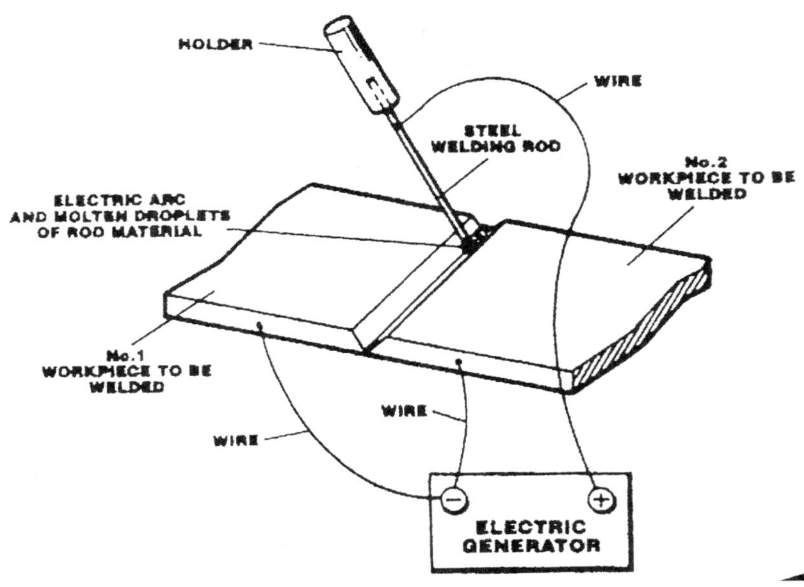

Arc welders commonly hold a steel rod near the joint to be welded. The rod is connected by a wire to one pole of an electric voltage generator. The two steel plates are then attached to the opposite pole of the voltage generator by two other wires.

The result of this arrangement is that the steel rod conducts electrical current that ionize, or charge, the air gases between the tip of the rod and the steel plates. The ions then flow in an electric arc between the rod and the plates. This arcing effect produces the very bright light seen in this type of welding. It also raises the temperature sufficiently to melt the rod's tip as well as the edges of the plates. Molten metal then drips from the rod into the joint that is to be welded. The mixture of metal from the plates and welding rod then cools and hardens, fusing the two plates.[9]

In the early 1930's, the state of the art in electric arc welding suffered from some difficulties. One of them was oxidation. Hot molten steel sitting in the open air undergoes a chemical reaction with oxygen, resulting in weaker welds. Welders responded by developing various protective materials to cover the steel welding rod and the seam. These so-called "fluxes" shield molten metal from the atmosphere and prevent oxidation.[10]

---

9 *See generally* Richard Finch, Welder's Handbook (1997).

10 *See generally* William H. Minnick, Flux Core Arc Welding Handbook (1994).

The selection of fluxes available in 1932 had their own share of problems, however. First, the fluxes known at that time were only effective at relatively low levels of electric current. Turning down the power meant that welds took longer to complete. In addition, arc welders sometimes discovered that the use of fluxes resulted in numerous pinholes in the completed weld. These "Swiss cheese" welds were probably due to gas that formed during the welding process and escaped into the atmosphere. In addition, the so-called "evolving gas" would sometimes cause small explosions that projected extremely hot flux particles through the air, to the obvious detriment of the welder and anyone else standing nearby.

Jones, Kennedy and Rotermund set out to solve the problems faced by electric arc welders. Rather than assuming the problem was the ineffective implementation of welding techniques, they chose to explore the fundamentals of flux chemistry. During their evenings and, sometimes, early mornings at the Western plant, the three conducted hundreds of tests involving a large number of potential fluxes.

Through a great deal of trial and error, the three inventors discovered that fluxes comprised primarily of eight different metal silicates—calcium, sodium, barium, manganese, cobalt, magnesium, nickel and aluminum—offered considerable advantages. These metal silicates eliminated the creation of pores during the welding process, resulting in much stronger welds. They additionally allowed arc welders to charge their apparatus with alternating current (AC) rather than direct current (DC). AC provided a much higher current at the same voltage, in turn increasing the amount of molten weld metal deposited per minute and dramatically improving the welding rate.[11]

Further experiments revealed an additional fact about the use of flux compounds for welding steel. Existing practice employed fluxes consisting of oxides that would react to the heat generated by the welding operation to produce silicates. These reactions contributed to the production of gas. To solve the problem, the inventors replaced the oxides with silicates. For example, they found that existing fluxes contained manganese dioxide, which reacted to form manganese silicate. Accordingly, they tried using manganese silicate as an original component of the flux. This approach did the trick. By incorporating so-called "fused fluxes" rather than unreacted compounds into the flux, the inventors eliminated the previously experienced explosions and airborne flux particles.

Jones, Kennedy and Rotermund quickly realized that they were on to something. Perhaps they recognized that their invention was the

[11] For more on the differences between AC and DC, consult Margaret Cheney, Tesla (2001).

breakthrough that would allow industry to make greater use of automation. Earlier inventors had developed automatic welding machines that featured a welding head that moved under power at a set rate. These machines required less skilled labor and diminished welding times dramatically. Given the unsatisfactory welds produced with prior art fluxes, however, hand welding by skilled manual workers remained the dominant practice. With these problems solved, the industry could at last turn to automatic welding methods, using a high level of current that completed a seam in a single pass. These two advantages would soon loom large for the United States. The Jones–Kennedy–Rotermund invention was among those that enabled the United States to expand its civilian manufacturing capabilities during the World War II, even though many skilled welders were then serving in the Armed Forces.[12]

The three inventors recognized that such a valuable invention should be protected through the intellectual property laws. Upon reviewing their options, they decided to pursue patent protection. Because chemists could readily determine what the composition of the flux once they had obtained a sample, trade secrecy was hardly an attractive alternative. Jones, Kennedy and Rotermund therefore sought the aid of counsel in preparing and filing an application at the Patent Office. They engaged the San Francisco law firm of Townsend & Loftus, which is known today as Townsend & Townsend & Crew, LLP. On February 21, 1933, Townsend & Loftus filed a patent application titled "Method of Electric Arc Welding and a Flux Therefor."

Jones, Kennedy and Rotermund contemporaneously sought out a commercial partner with sufficient resources to put their invention to good use. They ultimately agreed to assign their invention to Union Carbide & Carbon Research Laboratories, Inc., and its corporate affiliate Linde Air Products Co. Linde and the three inventors consummated their deal on November 28, 1933. The inventors assigned their patent rights in exchange for 15% of any flux sales over the next 17 years, along with 15% of any royalties obtained from licensing these patents. The agreement also called for minimum payments, starting at $5,000 in 1935 and increasing by $10,000 per year thereafter. This arrangement proved exceptionally profitable for Jones, Kennedy, and Rotermund, who would ultimately share over $2.6 million in royalties due to sales of their invention.[13]

Once it had been assigned the Jones–Kennedy–Rotermund invention, Linde assumed responsibility for the prosecution of their application at the Patent Office. The focus of this administrative process, as is

---

12 Frederic Chapin Lane, Ships for Victory 547, 560 (2001), discusses the use of the Jones–Kennedy–Rotermund welding process in World War II-era production facilities.

13 Plaintiff's Exhibit 9.

the case for most patent acquisition proceedings, was determining the precise language of the claims. In order to obtain the claim scope it preferred, Linde filed two additional applications and engaged in considerable dialogue with the Patent Office examiner.

On June 9, 1936, the Jones–Kennedy–Rotermund applications at last issued as U.S. Patent No. 2,043,960. The '960 patent incorporated 29 claims.[14] Claims 1–17 were written in process format, while claims 18–29 recited flux compositions. Claim 11 was the most concisely drafted of the process claims:

> 11. A process of electric welding which comprises the step of forming a conductive high-resistance melt, containing a major proportion of alkaline earth metal silicate and substantially free from uncombined iron oxide, on a metal part to be fused; and passing an electric current through a circuit comprising said melt and said metal part.

Several compositions claims are notable as well. Along with claim 26, claim 24 was a broadly worded composition claim that merely called for the use of a metallic silicate, without stipulating the relative proportions of the metallic silicate and the flux's other ingredients. As stated in the '960 patent:

> 24. A fluxing material for electric welding comprising metallic silicate and calcium fluoride.

In addition, claim 18 was one of four claims that recited a flux made primarily of an alkaline earth metal silicate:

> 18. A composition for electric welding containing a major proportion of alkaline earth metal silicate, and being substantially free from uncombined iron oxide and from substances capable of evolving gases under welding conditions.

Having drafted 29 patent claims, one might think that Linde had covered all its bases. However, Linde managers in fact labored under a misimpression that would become extremely significant in later litigation. A letter written by Linde Vice President R.E. "Gene" Cornwell, commenting upon the drafting decisions associated with the '960 patent, illustrates this misunderstanding:

> [D]ue to the fact that there should be no prior art on this particular type of material, it was felt that all materials having the necessary characteristics to produce a good weld could be covered in the claims and the claims have been directed to this protection. There are, however, specific claims directed to the

[14] Interested readers can read the entirety of U.S. Patent No. 2,043,960 at the website of the U.S. Patent & Trademark Office, http://www.uspto.gov.

> calcium silicates, calcium magnesium silicates and manganese silicates with the addition of calcium flouride.[15]

In fact, the '960 patent contained no "specific claims" to any of the substances identified in Mr. Cornwell's letter. Claims such as claim 18, which recited the entire class of alkaline earth metal silicates, were the most narrow within the '960 patent. But manganese is not an alkaline earth metal, so its silicates are not covered by claim 18. As we shall see, the absence of a claim specifically directed towards manganese silicate would prove to be a significant event within the history of U.S. patent law.

Lincoln Enters the Scene

With its patent rights secure, Linde commenced selling its "Unionmelt" brand of fluxes in early 1938. These products proved to be an immediate success. Over thirty licensees had signed up to use Linde's Unionmelt process by April 1, 1938. During the next decade, Linde would enlist over 700 licensees and generate over seven million dollars in royalty income. The U.S. Army and Navy, along with each of the Big Three Automakers, were among those that signed up. Together these licensees consumed 105 million pounds of weld metal. If used on one-half inch steel joints, this amount would produce a welding seam that would twice circle the equator.[16]

One price of Linde's marketplace success was that others copied its compounds, a development that spawned a great deal of litigation. Courtrooms across the country became familiar with the '960 patent as Linde both commenced and defended a variety of lawsuits. In addition to patent infringement litigation,[17] Linde also prevailed in one so-called "interference" proceeding brought at the Patent Office and settled another.[18] Linde additionally staved off, for the most part, antitrust charges leveled by the Justice Department against Linde's licensing practices. The district court rejected claims that Linde was attempting to

---

15 Letter from R.E. Cornwell, Vice President, Linde Air Products, to J.B. Hirst, Townsend & Loftus (Dec. 19, 1933), Plaintiff's Exhibit 158.

16 Testimony of Ross E. Cornwell, Trial Record at 224–26, 411–26.

17 *See* Notice from the Clerk of the District Court, Southern District of California, Los Angeles, R.S. Zimmerman, to the Commissioner of Patents, advising of final consent decree in Linde Air Products Co. v. Western Pipe & Steel Co. (Jan. 21, 1938); Prosecution History of U.S. Patent No. 2,043,960.

18 "Interference" proceedings are conducted by the U.S. Patent & Trademark Office when more than one person files a patent application that claims the same invention. The party who was first to invent the disputed subject matter ordinarily wins the interference and is awarded the patent. *See* 35 U.S.C. § 135 (2000). Filings related to both of Linde's interferences may be found in the prosecution history of U.S. Patent No. 2,043,960.

monopolize the market for welding rod used in the patented process. However, Linde was required to cease providing discounts to licensees who agreed to purchase all their requirements for welding rod from Linde.[19]

Linde also attracted a vigorous and legally sophisticated competitor in the Lincoln Electric Company. This Cleveland-based firm billed itself as "the largest manufacturer of arc welding equipment in the world."[20] Its engineering accomplishments included the welding of the lengthy Mokelumne pipeline in California during the 1920's.

Lincoln was also no stranger to the patent system. Its founder, John C. Lincoln, was named as the inventor of U.S. Patent No. 1,589,017. The Lincoln patent claimed an automatic electric arc welding machine that could be used with flux placed along the seam to be welded. Unlike Linde's '960 patent, the Lincoln patent did not identify silicates as a possible flux material. Due to its pioneering disclosure of automatic welding techniques, the Lincoln patent was nonetheless a precursor to Linde's '960 patent.

As early as 1934, Lincoln had obtained a sample of the Jones–Kennedy–Rotermund flux and subjected it to chemical analysis. Lincoln appeared to be toying with the idea of producing its own version of a Unionmelt flux until Linde's patent issued in 1936. Lincoln then sought to partner with Linde by marketing electric generators, a product that Linde did not sell, for use with the Unionmelt process. Linde's cool reception towards this proposal sent Lincoln back to the drawing board.[21]

By 1941, Lincoln made the decision to compete head-to-head with Linde. Lincoln considered various options that would allow it to market a high-current flux. First, Lincoln asked the Cleveland, Ohio patent law firm of Oberlin, Limbach & Day to evaluate whether the '960 patent could be invalidated. Second, Lincoln considered whether it would be able to bring a lawsuit against Linde for infringement of the Lincoln patent. Finally, Lincoln attempted to develop a flux that would not infringe the '960 patent.[22]

Following these preliminary considerations, Lincoln representatives began to negotiate with Linde. Lincoln initially proposed a cross-license, through which Linde would be licensed under the Lincoln patent in

---

[19] *See* United States v. Linde Air Prods. Co., 83 F. Supp. 978 (N.D. Ill. 1949).

[20] Report of the Special Master, Findings Paragraph 23, Record in Damages Proceeding at 1159.

[21] Letter from R.E. Cornwell, President, Linde Air Products, to J.F. Lincoln, President, Lincoln Electric (Feb. 7, 1939), Plaintiff's Exhibit 27 in Damages Proceeding.

[22] Janicke, *supra* note 1, at 60, 71–73.

exchange for the grant of a license under the '960 patent. As the president of Lincoln explained in an October 8, 1941, letter:

> We are advised by our attorneys that our flux and method of welding in no way conflicts with any issued patents. However, as I made clear to you, I do not want to spend a good deal of my future life, which is now drawing rapidly to a close, in fighting a silly patent suit which could be expensive, time-consuming, and utterly non-sensical.
>
> Therefore, I have requested our attorneys to draw up a simple form of cross-license, which if consummated would relieve us both of possibility of patent conflict. . . .[23]

Linde was not receptive to this approach. Before discussions could proceed further, however, the December 7, 1941, attack on Pearl Harbor led to the U.S. entry into World War II. A December 30, 1941, letter from Lincoln proposed to suspend patent discussions for the remainder of the war:

> [U]nder present wartime conditions and in view of the demands which our government's military preparations have placed on the welding industry in particular, we do not feel that this is the time to engage in patent litigation. . . .
>
> [I]t seems to us that the only proper course is for both our companies to bend every energy to the one great object—that of winning the war in which our nation is engaged, by furthering the production of essential equipment in every way within our power.[24]

Linde apparently acquiesced, with Lincoln later explaining that it was "leaving this entire matter in abeyance because of the present national emergency."[25]

Although there is no reason to doubt its patriotic sentiments, Lincoln did continue work on developing a non-infringing flux during the early days of World War II. Lincoln soon arrived at "Lincolnweld 660," which consisted of 80–90% manganese silicate. Lincoln ultimately sold over 4.6 million pounds of Lincolnweld 660 during the war. Such a quantity of flux obviously did not escape Linde's attention. But true to their word, the parties set aside their patent differences until after the

---

[23] Letter from J.F. Lincoln, President, Lincoln Electric, to R.E. Cornwell, President, Linde Air Products (Oct. 8, 1941), Plaintiff's Exhibit 31 in Damages Proceeding.

[24] Letter from J.F. Lincoln, President, Lincoln Electric, to R.E. Cornwell, President, Linde Air Products (Dec. 30, 1941), Plaintiff's Exhibit 31 in Damages Proceeding.

[25] Letter from J.F. Lincoln, President, Lincoln Electric, to R.E. Cornwell, President, Linde Air Products (Feb. 27, 1942), Plaintiff's Exhibit 31 in Damages Proceeding.

war had ended. At that time Linde would commence a campaign that would consume 20 years and ultimately result in one of the patent law's great cases.

Litigation Commences

World War II officially ended on September 2, 1945. On October 1, 1945, Linde brought its patent infringement suit against Lincoln. In filing infringement charges Linde faced an important preliminary decision. Linde realized that bringing suit in Lincoln's home town of Cleveland, Ohio, was not in its best interests. Rather than confront an established, popular employer on its home turf, Linde looked for a more neutral forum elsewhere.

Linde ultimately opted to bring suit against one of Lincoln's customers, Graver Tank & Manufacturing Co., in the federal district court of Hammond, Indiana. Graver Tank was a small firm with facilities in Indiana. This situation led to one of the ironies of this litigation, for Graver Tank was in fact a bit player in the famous case that bears its name. Linde's succinct complaint charged Graver Tank with using a process and flux composition claimed in the '960 patent. Lincoln faced similar charges, and was also alleged to have sold the patented composition to Graver Tank.

Lincoln quickly fired back. On October 8, 1945, it sued Linde in Cleveland, asserting that Linde infringed the Lincoln patent. As patent cases go, the Cleveland litigation ended rather quickly. The district court granted Linde's motion for summary judgment and, on July 9, 1947, held that the Lincoln patent was unenforceable under the doctrine of patent misuse.[26] The Sixth Circuit affirmed the next year, effectively ending Lincoln's affirmative case.[27]

In the meantime the Indiana litigation continued to march forward. The case was assigned to Judge Luther Swygert, a prominent jurist who was later elevated to the Court of Appeals for the Seventh Circuit. He presided over a bench trial that was far from garden variety. On the first day of trial, with inventor Harry Kennedy on the stand for cross-examination, Judge Swygert visited Linde's facilities in East Chicago, Indiana. The judge observed welding demonstrations, along with several X-rays of cut-open welds.

Back in the courtroom, the trial was also notable for its large number of distinguished witnesses. Two well-regarded chemistry profes-

[26] A patent owner commits misuse when he exploits a patent in such a manner as to exceed its lawful scope. Misuse cases often involve patentee licensing practices, such as tying, that the courts have disfavored. *See* Morton Salt Co. v. G.S. Suppiger Co., 314 U.S. 488 (1942).

[27] Lincoln Elec. Co. v. Linde Air Prods. Co., 171 F.2d 223 (6th Cir. 1948).

sors, Hobart Willard of the University of Michigan for Linde and Harold Booth of Western Reserve University for Lincoln, provided expert testimony. Linde also made a point of presenting numerous witnesses who lauded the benefits of the invention. A T.M. Jackson of Sun Shipbuilding & Drydock Company explained, for example, that the patented invention reduced the construction time of ships from 10–12 months to three months. Another witness, Leigh Sanford of the U.S. Maritime Commission, testified that the patented invention had allowed shipbuilders to overcome the war-induced shortage of skilled manual welders.

Following the close of trial, Judge Swygert issued his opinion on June 6, 1947. In it he invalidated most of the asserted claims of the '960 patent. Judge Swygert struck down a number of the patent's method claims as "too broad and indefinite." He reasoned that claims 1, 3–4, and 7–9 did not specify which specific flux composition should be employed, but rather stated that this composition should merely be made of "a fused nonmetallic material" or other general category of materials. Because the '960 patent stressed throughout that the choice of a particular kind of flux was extremely important for achieving the advantages of the invention, Judge Swygert reasoned that the claims were indefinite and thus invalid.[28]

Other method claims were struck down for another reason. Claims 5,6, and 11–17 each stipulated that during the welding process, electric current traveled directly between the rod tip and the flux. Based upon the technical evidence he had received during the trial, Judge Swygert concluded that such a direct transfer of current was scientifically impossible. Electric current must instead travel from the rod tip through a medium of vaporous flux and then into the flux. Believing that these claims were technically inaccurate as written, Judge Swygert held them invalid.[29]

Judge Swygert next turned to the '960 patent's broadly worded composition claims. Claims 24 and 26 called for the use of any metal silicate within the flux. As a result they literally read upon the Lincolnweld 660 flux, which was made mostly of manganese silicate. Judge Swygert struck down these claims as well, however. He relied upon the general patent law principle that when a claim is broadly drafted, covering many inoperative embodiments, the claim is invalid for lack of enablement. With experts for both Linde and Lincoln in agreement that

28 Linde Air Prods. Co. v. Graver Tank & Mfg. Co., 86 F. Supp. 191, 196–97 (N.D. Ind. 1947).

29 86 F. Supp. at 197. Judge Swygert also struck down composition claim 27, which employed similar wording, on the same grounds. Today these claims would face scrutiny under the definiteness standard of 35 U.S.C. § 112 ¶ 2 (2000).

many metal silicates simply did not function as welding fluxes, the claims were held invalid.[30]

Following Judge Swygert's rulings, the only asserted claims that had survived were the narrow composition claims. Claims 18, 20, 22, and 23 each required that "alkaline earth metal silicates" comprise the principal ingredient of the flux. Lincoln had not devoted much effort during the litigation towards arguing that these claims were invalid, presumably because it believed it did not infringe them. Lincolnweld 660 was made primarily of manganese, after all, and manganese is not an alkaline earth metal.

Judge Swygert nonetheless dealt Lincoln a surprise blow. Agreeing with Linde, he ruled that Lincolnweld 660 infringed the remaining claims of the '960 patent under the doctrine of equivalents. The doctrine of equivalents is a judicially created principle that allows courts to find infringement even though the defendant's product does not fall within the literal wording of a patent's claims. A leading Supreme Court case, *Sanitary Refrigerator Co. v. Winters*,[31] had articulated the well-known tripartite test of the doctrine of equivalents. When an accused product did not fall within a patent's claims, but yet performed "substantially the same function in substantially the same way to obtain the same result," an infringement occurred under the doctrine.

Explaining his reasoning for applying the doctrine of equivalents, Judge Swygert observed that Linde's Unionmelt 20 product was made mostly of magnesium silicate, a alkaline earth metal silicate, while Lincolnweld 660 was primarily made of manganese silicate. He also determined that the two compositions acted identically and produced the same kind of weld. Judge Swygert therefore concluded "that for all practical purposes, manganese silicate can be efficiently and effectually substituted for calcium and magnesium silicates as the major constituent of the welding composition." As a result, manganese was considered equivalent to the claimed "alkaline earth metal silicates" and judged an infringement.[32]

Many commentators have questioned Judge Swygert's ruling over the years. Some have doubted the conclusion that manganese and magnesium are equivalents as a matter of chemistry. Harold C. Wegner has observed that "manganese and magnesium are both metals and start with an 'm' and have at least three syllables, but otherwise are so different structurally that they are in different categories on the periodic

[30] 86 F. Supp. at 198.

[31] 280 U.S. 30, 42 (1929).

[32] 86 F. Supp. at 199–200.

table of elements."[33] On the other hand, a comparison of the atomic structure of manganese and magnesium reveals each element has two electrons in its outer shell.[34] This trait suggests that the two elements will share common chemical properties.

In any event, both Linde and Lincoln appealed first to the Seventh Circuit. The Court of Appeals sided with Linde's views in their entirety, reversing Judge Swygert's invalidity judgments while affirming his conclusion with regard to the doctrine of equivalents.[35] The Supreme Court agreed to hear the case in 1949 and issued the first, and less memorable, of its two *Graver Tank* opinions. Here the Court reversed the Seventh Circuit and in all respects reinstated Judge Swygert's judgment.[36]

Lincoln then sought rehearing at the Supreme Court. Lincoln chose to attack the infringement holding of the four flux claims left standing, asserting that promotion of the doctrine of equivalents would effectively "exclude the public from an additional penumbral area to which the patent holder in law has no title."[37] The Court agreed to rehear the case, leading to the *Graver Tank* decision destined to serve as a mainstay in intellectual property casebooks

The Supreme Court Decision

The Supreme Court responded to Lincoln's petition by issuing majority and dissenting opinions that continue to frame dialogue on the doctrine of equivalents today. The majority opinion, authored by Justice Jackson, affirmed that Linde had infringed the four valid flux claims of the '960 patent under the doctrine of equivalents. Justice Jackson observed that confining patent rights to cases of literal infringement would merely encourage competitors to make minor changes to the claimed invention, profiting from the teachings of the patent but avoiding the patent owner's proprietary rights. Such a hollow grant of rights would place inventors at the "mercy of verbalism" and discourage inventors from seeking patents in the first place. A cabined scope of proprietary rights would therefore thwart a principal purpose of the patent system, the disclosure of new inventions. In sum, the essence of the doctrine of equivalents was prevention of a "fraud on a patent."[38]

---

33 Harold C. Wegner, *Equitable Equivalents: Weighing the Equities to Determine Patent Infringement in Biotechnology and Other Emerging Technologies*, 18 Rutgers Computer & Tech. L.J. 1, 28–29 n.100 (1992).

34 Schematics of the shell structure for both manganese and magnesium can be found in many chemistry textbooks, as well as at http://www.webelements.com.

35 167 F.2d 531 (7th Cir. 1948).

36 336 U.S. 271 (1949).

37 Petition for Rehearing at 3.

38 339 U.S. at 608.

Justice Jackson next confirmed the familiar tripartite equivalency test of *Sanitary Refrigerator*.[39] Under that standard an accused infringement is equivalent to the claimed invention "if it performs substantially the same function in substantially the same way to obtain the same result." Here the Court lost an opportunity to clarify an equivalency standard that had long been criticized. Most often the three-part test collapsed merely into a question of whether the patented invention and the accused device perform in "same way." After all, if the accused technology did not perform the same function to achieve the same result, it ordinarily would not be the subject of a patent infringement suit at all. Of course, such a vague equivalency test as "substantially the same way" was of scant use in resolving actual cases. As Judge Learned Hand had observed two decades earlier:

> Each case is inevitably a matter of degree, as so often happens, and other decisions have little or no value. The usual ritual, which is so often repeated and which has so little meaning . . . does not help much in application; it is no more than a way of stating the problem.[40]

To the Court's credit, it did further clarify the test by specifying that the known interchangeability of the claimed and substituted ingredients was an important factor in an equivalency determination. Justice Jackson also stated that a finding of equivalence was a question of fact, provable through the use of experts, learned texts and the disclosures of the prior art.[41] All of this was rather light lifting, however, and subsequent courts did not find that *Graver Tank* had much clarified the equivalency standard in patent law.

Applying the few principles it had gathered to the facts at hand, the Court affirmed the finding of infringement under the doctrine of equivalents. According to Justice Jackson, chemists had testified that magnesium and manganese were substitutes in the welding art, and the trial court had properly found that the Lincolnweld and Unionmelt fluxes were in all respects the same. The Court also saw no evidence that the defendant had engaged in independent development of the Lincolnweld flux. Justice Jackson closed with the observation that "it is difficult to conceive of a case more appropriate for application of the doctrine of equivalents."[42]

---

[39] 280 U.S. 30, 42 (1929).

[40] Claude Neon Lights, Inc. v. E. Machlett & Son, 36 F.2d 574 (2d Cir.1929).

[41] 339 U.S. at 608–10.

[42] 339 U.S. at 612.

To appreciate just how remarkable the majority's sweeping view of the doctrine of equivalents was, it is important to place *Graver Tank* in the context of the other Supreme Court patent cases of the day. Only a year before he wrote the majority opinion in *Graver Tank*, Justice Jackson had quipped that "the only patent that is valid is one which this Court has not been able to get its hands on."[43] Six months later, the Supreme Court would release the infamous decision in *Great A & P Tea Co. v. Supermarket Equipment Corp.*, again authored by Justice Jackson.[44] Here the Court counseled that inventions must meet a "synergy" requirement to be patented, and that "combination patents" should be subject to special scrutiny—two pronouncements that cast a great deal of doubt on the validity of many issued patents. As is revealed elsewhere in these volume, neither of these principles remains valid patent law today.[45] Within its historical setting, however, the *Graver Tank* majority's sweeping view of the doctrine of equivalents was a notable event in an era where judicial antipathy to the patent regime was at an all-time high.

One possible explanation for this atypical ruling lies in the Court's desire to achieve a just result. Unquestionably Jones, Kennedy, and Rotermund had come up with a groundbreaking invention that industry had widely adopted. Indeed, it is not an exaggeration to assert that their advance may have had something to do with the success of the United States during World War II. Linde had done its part by broadly promoting the invention to U.S. industry. Yet had the upheld flux claims been confined to their literal wording, the three inventors and their assignee would have been left with patent rights so narrowly cabined that they would have effectively been worthless. As Professor Paul Janicke has remarked, surely that is not the way the patent system is supposed to work![46]

Dissenting opinions by Justices Black and Douglas suggested that other factors deserved consideration, however.[47] Justice Black principally urged that the Court should have pointed the plaintiff to the reissue statute rather than freely apply the doctrine of equivalents.[48] He reminded the majority that Congress had an enacted an express statutory

43 Jungersen v. Ostby & Barton Co., 335 U.S. 560, 572 (1949).

44 340 U.S. 147 (1950).

45 *See* John F. Duffy & Robert P. Merges, The Story of *Graham v. John Deere Company*: Patent Law's Evolving Standard of Creativity, elsewhere in this Volume.

46 Janicke, *supra* note 1, at 99.

47 Justice Minton, who had served on the Seventh Circuit panel adjudicating this case prior to being elevated to the Supreme Court, recused himself.

48 339 U.S. at 612–18.

procedure for amending patent claims. This so-called "reissue" proceeding allows patentees to return to the Patent Office in order to correct a defective patent.[49] Among the accepted grounds for pursuing a reissue is that a patent's claims read upon the prior art and are therefore too broad. Another is that a patent's claims are too narrow and therefore do not cover a competitor's product.

Although the Patent Act allows patent proprietors to broaden claims through reissue, Congress recognized that sudden changes to patents may upset the reliance interests of third parties. A third party may have begun marketing a new product, built new production facilities, or otherwise made significant investments based on the narrow claims of another's patent. If the PTO abruptly reissues the patent with broadened claims that the competitor now infringes, the competitor may be justly aggrieved.

Congress therefore limited the ability of patentees to broaden their claims during reissue. The statute requires patent holders to seek broadening reissues within two years of receiving the patent. In addition, infringers of reissued patents are in many circumstances able to claim "intervening rights." Intervening rights allow infringers to sell existing inventory without regard to the reissued patent. In some cases, courts may even allow the infringer to continue to practice the invention under terms established by the courts.[50]

Justice Black was very much concerned that judicial application of the doctrine of equivalents essentially ignored the statutory reissue proceedings. Rather than ask the courts for relief under the doctrine of equivalents, Justice Black counseled, patent proprietors should return to the Patent Office and seek reissue. The Court's conclusion in *Graver Tank,* Justice Black explained, left patentees with few incentives to seek reissue, and therefore deprived adjudicated infringers and other intervening users of the safeguards provided in the Patent Act.

Justice Douglas had other reasons to disagree. He observed that the asserted patent had originally included broad, generic claims that would have read upon the Lincolnweld flux. These claims had been struck down during infringement litigation due to lack of enablement. Justice Douglas urged that use of the doctrine of equivalents to resurrect claims that had been invalidated was particularly inappropriate.[51]

---

[49] 35 U.S.C. § 251 (2000).

[50] 35 U.S.C. § 252 (2000). Intervening rights may also apply to claims that are narrowed, as competitors may have based their decisions upon their belief that a patent's claims were overly broad and thus invalid. *See* Roger E. Schechter & John R. Thomas, PRINCIPLES OF PATENT LAW § 7.5.3.5 (2004).

[51] 339 U.S. at 618. Justice Douglas also observed that "manganese silicate had been covered by prior patents, now expired." *Graver Tank*, 339 U.S. at 618. Justice Douglas was

The Close and Aftermath of Litigation

After the Supreme Court's second encounter with this case, it might have seemed time for the parties to put this litigation behind them. The courtroom struggle between Linde and Lincoln was destined to march onward for another 15 years, however. The parties spent considerable effort towards determining the damages to be awarded to Linde for Lincoln's infringement. Following the appointment of a Special Master and two further trips to the Court of Appeals for the Seventh Circuit, Linde ended up with an award of only $687,000—likely a fraction of its legal fees through two decades of litigation.[52] On the other hand, Linde had obtained over seven million dollars of licensing revenue. And the award of an injunction in Linde's favor—which prevented Lincoln from selling its original Lincolnweld formulation, and discouraged others from marketing competing fluxes—was likely worth considerably more.

The parties also jostled over a new product that Lincoln developed shortly after the Supreme Court issued its second *Graver Tank* opinion. The "Lincolnweld 700" series consisted primarily of unreacted manganese oxide, although it did include some fully reacted manganese silicate. This composition did not mesh well with Linde's infringement position. Jones, Kennedy, and Rotermund had, after all, stressed the importance of using fused, rather than unreacted, ingredients in its fluxes. Linde nonetheless pursued contempt proceedings in which it asserted that Lincoln's 700-series fluxes infringed the '960 patent.

This time the Seventh Circuit was ultimately unsympathetic towards Linde. The Court of Appeals relied upon a patent law principle that is today known as "prosecution history estoppel" in order to reject Linde's arguments. Under this rule, if an applicant relinquished certain subject matter at the Patent Office in order to secure the allowance of her claims, she may not assert the doctrine of equivalents to recapture the renounced subject matter.[53] Applying this principle, the court observed that during prosecution at the Patent Office, Linde had faced a rejection over a prior art reference that taught the use of 20–33% silicate. Linde had responded by inserting into the language of the '960

---

referring in particular to U.S. Patent No. 1,754,566, which disclosed the use of a prefused manganese silicate flux. Traditional patent law doctrine establishes that patent proprietors cannot obtain a construction of their claims under the doctrine of equivalents that would cover technologies that have entered the public domain. Professor Janicke has forcefully argued that the *Graver Tank* case was wrongly decided because it extended the patent to cover technology disclosed in the prior art. *See* Janicke, *supra* note 1, at 126.

52 Union Carbide Corp. v. Graver Tank & Mfg. Co., 345 F.2d 409 (7th Cir. 1965).

53 *See* Festo Corp. v. Shoketsu Kinzoku Kogyo Kabushiki Co., 535 U.S. 722 (2002). Courts previously used the term "file wrapper estoppel" to describe the doctrine today known as "prosecution history estoppel."

patent claims the limitation that its fluxes consist in "major proportion" (more than 50%) of a silicate. The Seventh Circuit therefore concluded that Linde was estopped to claim rights over fluxes that were less than half silicate. Because the Lincolnweld 700–series fluxes consisted of 24–41% silicate, they could not infringe[54]

Linde had gotten all the mileage it could out of its four surviving patent claims. Future battles between Lincoln and Linde would occur not in the courtroom, but in the marketplace. In this arena Lincoln ultimately proved the victor. As this litigation was drawing to a close, Lincoln had become the leader in the arc welding industry, a position that it still maintains. In 2003, Lincoln achieved sales of $1.04 billion based on the output of 25 manufacturing facilities in 18 countries.[55] In contrast, Linde's flux business declined over the years. In 1984, Linde sold its entire welding and cutting business to a group of investors for $70 million.[56]

The Themes of *Graver Tank*

To this day *Graver Tank* remains among the few cases every patent attorney has studied. It is also one of the few patent cases that lawyers practicing in other fields have read. Why, in a legal discipline that must continually reinvent itself to address fast-paced fields like computer science, business methods, and biotechnology, are we still talking about a judicial opinion written in 1950?

The resilience of *Graver Tank* is ultimately due to the enduring nature of the issue with which the Supreme Court grappled. Determining the appropriate scope of control due to the rights holder remains of central interest to the intellectual property community today.[57] This litigation had the advantage of raising this issue crisply. Patent opinions have a deserved reputation for being difficult texts to parse, often due to

---

[54] Union Carbide & Carbon Corp. v. Graver Tank & Mfg. Co., 196 F.2d 103 (7th Cir. 1952).

[55] United Securities & Exchange Commission, Form 10–K, Lincoln Electric Holdings, Inc. (2003) *available at* http://content.lincolnelectric.com/pdfs/corporate/investor/ar/ar03/linc_ar_10K.pdf.

[56] Union Carbide Press Release, PR NEWSWIRE, Dec. 19, 1984.

[57] A more cynical view is that contemporary decisions continue to debate the meaning of *Graver Tank* is because the next Supreme Court decision on point, *Warner-Jenkinson Co. v. Hilton Davis Chemical Co.*, 520 U.S. 17 (1997), issued 47 years later. The *Graver Tank* framework for the doctrine of equivalents was therefore the only game in town for several generations of patent practitioners. Notably, much of the *Warner-Jenkinson* opinion occupies itself with identifying the holding of *Graver Tank*, and for the most part the Supreme Court confirmed what had been said earlier. Only the doctrine of prosecution history estoppel, a doctrine not addressed in *Graver Tank*, received much advancement in *Warner-Jenkinson*.

their exhaustive descriptions of contraptions so elaborate that they would make Rube Goldberg proud.[58] In contrast, the substitutions made among the fluxes here are easy to understand, providing an ideal vehicle for considering the breadth of rights that a patent owner should receive.

The majority and dissenting opinions in *Graver Tank* framed the scope of protection issue as involving a balancing of competing goals. On one hand, innovators should obtain a scope of protection consistent with the aspirations of an intellectual property rights regime. On the other, competitors should receive an appropriate degree of notice as to the scope of the proprietary interests of others. Reflection upon these competing views offers some insight as to assigning the appropriate scope of control due to an intellectual property owner.

The majority was sold on the argument that broad intellectual property rights, including liberal use of the doctrine of equivalents, would prevent cagey copyists from reaping rewards that more justly belong to the inventor. This rationale recognized that the system of claiming is an imperfect mechanism for defining a patent holder's rights. The limitations of language might cause the drafter to include claim elements that are easily evaded by trivial substitutes; future developments could result in insignificant substitute technologies that fall within the teachings of the patent, yet outside the literal wording of its claims; and patent attorneys may simply fail to fashion claims as broadly as the law allows.[59] The doctrine of equivalents provides courts with a mechanism for resolving these potential inequities on a case-by-case basis.

In addition to these fairness-based concerns, the doctrine of equivalents was also inspired by instrumental motivations. The patent system encourages investment in research and development by rewarding successful inventors with exclusive rights in their advancements. Under this view, the greater the award of proprietary rights, the greater the incentives to invent. Aware that the courts would make liberal use of the doctrine of equivalents to protect patented inventions, other potential innovators would devote their energies towards research and development as well.

The doctrine of equivalents also increases the dynamism of the innovation the patent system is said to promote. If a patentee's rivals were confident that courts would limit protection to literal infringement, they might content themselves with seeking incremental improvements just outside the wording of the claims. In a patent system with a doctrine

[58] For more on Rube Goldberg (1883–1970) and his drawings depicting convoluted mechanical devices, see http://www.rubegoldberg.com.

[59] *See* Festo Corp. v. Shoketsu Kinzoku Kogyo Kabushiki Co., 535 U.S. 722, 731 (2002).

of equivalents, however, innovative firms are aware that minor developments may be judged as equivalent infringements. The doctrine of equivalents therefore encourages innovative firms to "leapfrog" beyond the current teachings of the patent literature, rather than make more modest contributions to technological progress.

The *Graver Tank* majority was also of the view that broad intellectual property protection would encourage individuals to seek patent protection for their new inventions, rather than rely upon trade secrets. Justice Jackson recognized that a principal purpose of the patent law is the dissemination of knowledge. This goal is realized through the publication of patent instruments that fully disclose the protected invention.[60] In this respect the patent system exists in tension with the law of trade secrets, which protects valuable information only if it has been withheld from the public eye. A robust doctrine of equivalents was seen as one way to encourage inventors to avail themselves of the patent system, rather than secret their developments away.

Ironically, this rationale for the doctrine of equivalents was misplaced as to the case at hand. Chemists of the day were readily able to determine the composition of competitor's welding fluxes. Once they chose to employ their invention in the marketplace, Jones, Kennedy, and Rotermund effectively had two options: either procure a patent on the flux, or dedicate it to the public domain. Trade secrecy simply was not a possibility. Of course the concern that inventors will opt for trade secrets over patents has more relevance for inventions that can be simultaneously exploited and concealed, depending in part upon one's sense that inventors will find one regime more desirable than the other.[61]

Although these arguments in favor of the doctrine of equivalents were convincing to the *Graver Tank* majority, both fairness and efficiency arguments can be offered in favor of a narrow scope of intellectual property rights. Patent rights provide incentives to some, but they create limitations for everyone. Patent holders obtain the right to exclude others from practicing the patented invention, effective not only throughout the United States, but to some extent overseas as well.[62] Further, in comparison to other intellectual properties, few restraining doctrines cabin the scope of patents. The Patent Act offers no fair use privilege analogous to copyright or trademark, for example, and the courts have been disinclined to develop affirmative infringement defenses on their own.[63] Simple notions of fairness therefore dictate that patent

[60] 35 U.S.C.A. § 112 (2000).

[61] For discussion on this point, see *Kewanee Oil Co. v. Bicron Corp.*, 416 U.S. 470 (1974).

[62] 35 U.S.C. § 271 (2000).

[63] *See* Madey v. Duke University, 307 F.3d 1351 (Fed. Cir. 2002).

rights should be as well-defined and predictable as possible, so that members of the public can confidently determine whether their conduct is permissible or not. Under this view, expanding a patentee's property rights through the doctrine of equivalents defeats the public notice of patent claims and unfairly upsets the reliance interests of others.

Another fairness-based argument against liberal use of the doctrine of equivalent is that in comparison with the general public, inventors are also well-positioned to draft patent claims of the appropriate scope. Indeed, the Patent Act grants inventors the opportunity to choose the working of their own claims, and with a moderate level of funding they can obtain virtually as many claims as they wish. Patent holders may even return to the Patent and Trademark Office in order to correct and fine-tune their patents via reissue. Again, fundamental fairness suggests that the patent proprietor should bear responsibility for any shortfalls in the wording of her claims.

These arguments apply with full force to the *Graver Tank* case. The authors of the '960 patent apparently had no difficulty discussing the use of manganese in the specification. They should have been readily able to draft claims directed towards a manganese-based flux as well, and their failure to do so appears to have been a simple oversight.[64] As a result, use of the doctrine of equivalents in this case was not so much a matter of defeating a clever copyist, but rather correcting mistakes patent lawyers had made during their preparation of the application. Whether the doctrine of equivalents should be used to correct applicant errors—particularly given the availability of patent reissue procedures—remains a controversial point.[65]

Efficiency concerns also cast doubt upon a robust doctrine of equivalents. Imprecise patent boundaries may render accurate determinations of the scope and value of a patent quite elusive. These uncertainties may in turn increase the transaction costs of bargaining and make these assets more difficult to license or sell. For example, the record in the *Graver Tank* case suggests that Lincoln was unwilling to license the '960 patent because its attorneys believed any claims that literally read upon its Lincolnweld fluxes were invalid. Lincoln's attorneys were correct, but

[64] One explanation for Linde's failure to obtain claims explicitly reciting manganese silicate are Patent Office rules of the day. These rules apparently prevented applicants from claiming more than three species of a genus also claimed within a particular patent application. *See* Hilton Davis Chem. Co. v. Warner–Jenkinson Co., 62 F.3d 1512, 1575 n.28 (Fed. Cir. 1995) (*en banc*) (Nies, J., dissenting). However, as pointed out by Professor Janicke, this rule does not excuse Linde from procuring literal claim coverage of manganese silicate. Linde could have obtained *another patent* with claims specifically directed towards manganese silicate. Janicke, *surpra* note 1, at 120–21 n. 443.

[65] *See* Johnson & Johnston Assocs. Inc. v. R. E. Service Co., 285 F.3d 1046, 1059 (Fed. Cir. 2002) (*en banc*) (Rader, J., concurring).

they did not predict that the courts would find infringement under the doctrine of equivalents anyway. Lincoln's refusal to accept Linde's standard license lead to twenty years of expensive litigation—time and money that could conceivably have been directed towards further research and development. Ironically, then, liberal use of the doctrine of equivalents could actually reduce the effectiveness of the patent system as a means for promoting innovation.

A more narrow scope of intellectual property rights may also do a better job of promoting competition in the technology marketplace. Infringers of intellectual property rights may sometimes be lazy copyists, but often they are innovators themselves. Infringing goods may be directed towards new technological applications or new markets, and they not uncommonly improve upon, or simply work better than, the patented product. We can also generally expect that expanded consumer choice will lead to higher quality and lower costs[66]—an environment that arguably existed during World War II, when Linde refrained from asserting the '960 patent in order to promote the national welfare. Expansion of an intellectual property owner's right of control may therefore have significant consequences for second-comers that have made their own contributions to the state of the art.

Unfortunately, although each of these arguments has a varying degree of intuitive appeal, none has been empirically validated. No conclusive study tells us how to fine-tune the scope of control due to a rights holder in a manner that would best fulfill intellectual property policy. Likely there is not one right answer, with the optimal scope of control depending upon the pace of innovation within the relevant field, industrial concentration, the amenability of particular firms to licensing, and myriad other factors. The varying justifications for and against the doctrine of equivalents therefore remain open to challenge by those who are unpersuaded by their internal logic.

Roads Not Taken

A close reading of *Graver Tank* suggests a few roads not taken in the modern patent law. Justice Jackson used *Graver Tank* as an opportunity to speak of the so-called "reverse doctrine of equivalents":

> The wholesale realism of this doctrine is not always applied in favor of the patentee but is sometimes used against him. Thus, where a device is so far changed in principle from a patented article that it performs the same or a similar function in a substantially different way, but nevertheless falls within the literal words of the claim, the doctrine of equivalents may be

66 *See* Richard Posner, Economic Analysis of Law 37 (3d ed. 1986).

used to restrict the claim and defeat the patentee's action for infringement.[67]

Under this conception, the reverse doctrine of equivalents is a defense to literal infringement. Even though an accused product or process falls within the literal scope of the patent claims, if it is sufficiently "changed in principle" from the patented device a court could nonetheless dismiss the plaintiff's complaint.

The reverse doctrine might have been a noteworthy addition to a patent law that is not rich in infringement defenses. An accused infringer may assert that the patent is invalid or unenforceable under current law, of course, but other common law or statutory exceptions are few and narrowly constrained. The patent law lacks the "fair use" privilege that exists in other intellectual property disciplines, for example, and the compulsory licenses so commonly found in the Copyright Act have no analog in the patent regime.[68] Despite these notable absences, in over a half-century since *Graver Tank*, the reverse doctrine has been a nonstarter. The Federal Circuit has termed it an "anachronistic exception" and, in its twenty years of existence, not once squarely applied it.[69]

Perhaps the reverse doctrine never made it into the patent community's toolbox due to the Court's succinct discussion. Justice Jackson merely mentioned the reverse doctrine and abruptly moved on, offering no guidance on the class of cases to which it should be applied. In the years that followed the lower courts did not seize upon opportunities to invoke the reverse doctrine. In doing so they overlooked a potentially useful technique for furthering innovation policy.

The increasing speed of technological advancement may allow the courts more opportunities to think creatively about the reverse doctrine. For example, much criticism has surround recently issued patents on cDNA, ESTs and other biological compounds.[70] Some observers believe that these patents offer a broad scope of protection that is out of proportion with their relatively modest technical achievements. Although much work needs to be done to develop "downstream" technologies that put these inventions into practical use, these broad "upstream" patents

---

67 339 U.S. at 608–09.

68 *See* 17 U.S.C. §§ 107–122 (2000).

69 Tate Access Floors, Inc. v. Interface Arch. Res., Inc., 279 F.3d 1357, 1368 (Fed. Cir. 2002).

70 Complementary DNA ("cDNA") corresponds to proteins used by human cells. Expressed sequence tags ("ESTs") are DNA sequences that correspond to a small portion of each cDNA. *See* Linda J. Demaine & Aaron Xavier Fellmeth, *Reinventing the Double Helix: A Novel and Nonobvious Conception of the Biotechnology Patent*, 55 STAN. L. REV. 303 (2003).

may potentially discourage improvement inventors. Use of the reverse doctrine of equivalents—and the potential ability to exempt infringement when the relative importance of the improvement dramatically exceeds that of the initial invention—provides one avenue for resolving this policy dilemma.[71]

The fundamental disagreement between the majority and dissenters also suggests a path that the *Graver Tank* Court did not itself pursue. The conversation between Justices Jackson and Black can be characterized as another episode in the classic rules versus standards debate. Whether society is better served by a precise set of bright-line rules, or instead flexible standards that are more susceptible to judicial discretion, is a long-standing debate in many fields of law. Advocates of formally realized rules contend that they lead to more certain outcomes and provide private actors with the certainty necessary to order their affairs in an efficient fashion. On the other hand, bright-line rules may prevent the fine-tuning needed to reach individualized judgments and instead encourage behavior to the boundaries of prohibited conduct.[72]

Justice Jackson and Justice Black each employed rhetoric commonly found within this debate in order to support their conclusions. The majority opinion favored a standards-oriented doctrine of equivalents, while the dissenter advocating a rules-based approach that emphasized literal infringement and the reissue statute. Like much discourse over rules and standards, this exchange of views was not especially productive. The very structure of the discussion seemed to leave these jurists without a way to synthesize their views into a coherent legal principle.

Although the majority and dissent seemed locked into irreconcilable positions, not too much imagination is needed to identify a plausible middle ground. The Court might have approved of continued judicial application of the doctrine of equivalents—provided that adjudicated infringers under the doctrine were granted intervening rights commensurate with the reissue statute. The doctrine of equivalents arises in equity, of course, and the same equitable powers that allowed courts to find nonliteral infringement could also be employed to fashion an appropriate remedy in individual cases.

Under this concept of a "judicial reissue," the grant of an injunction could be made contingent upon allowing the defendant limited rights to employ the infringing product or process. Perhaps the nature of these rights could vary case-by-case, based upon such considerations as the degree of equivalence between the claimed invention and the adjudicated

---

[71] *See* Robert P. Merges & Richard R. Nelson, *On the Complex Economics of Patent Scope*, 90 COLUM. L. REV. 839 (1990).

[72] *See generally* Pierre Schlag, *Rules and Standards*, 33 UCLA L. REV. 379 (1985).

infringement, whether the patent proprietor learned of the accused infringement and failed to seek reissue within the two-year statutory period, and the extent to which the patent overlaps with an industry standard.[73] Whether the availability of the infringing product would improve social welfare due to its lower cost, technological advantages, tendency to promote competition, or other benefits could also play a role. A final factor, that proved to be of great practical importance in the flux marketplace following the Supreme Court's *Graver Tank* opinion, might be the ease with which the defendant can "design around" the patent in order to participate again in the relevant market.

The potential of a more flexible remedial scheme for equivalency cases would have been worthy of further exploration. This regime conceivably offers more sophisticated tools for working innovation policy than the blunt policy instrument wielded by the *Graver Tank* Court. Each opinion offered an all-or-nothing possibility: either the accused device is an equivalent infringement, subject to all the remedies available under the Patent Act, or it is not. Empowered to establish what are effectively degrees of infringement liability, courts might be better able to account for the unique circumstances of particular patent infringement cases.

Although the possibility of creating intervening rights when the doctrine of equivalents is used to expand the scope of the patent has been floated since the *Graver Tank* opinion issued,[74] Congress has never seized upon it. Indeed, the entire subject of the doctrine of equivalents remains without a statutory basis at all.[75] This state of affairs is actually a rather curious one. At the time the Supreme Court decided the *Graver Tank* case a team of legal experts was at work on a sweeping patent law reform project. Their efforts resulted in the 1952 Patent Act, which remains the governing U.S. patent legislation today. Even though this effort aimed in part at codifying judicially developed principles, Congress did not take this opportunity to further refine the doctrine of equivalents. This continued absence of statutory support provides mute testimony to the difficulty of articulating general factors that courts should consider when deciding doctrine of equivalents cases.

Finally, *Graver Tank* reminds us of a road from which we have diverged. At the time the Supreme Court decided this case, judicial practice was to subject patent claims to very strict scrutiny. However,

---

73 *See* Paul M. Janicke, *When Patents Are Broadened Midstream: A Compromise Solution to Protect Competitors and Existing Users*, 66 U. Cin. L. Rev. 7 (1997).

74 *See* Hilton Davis Chem. Co. v. Warner–Jenkinson Co., 62 F.3d 1512, 1560 (Fed. Cir. 1995) (*en banc*) (Nies, J., dissenting).

75 35 U.S.C. § 112 ¶ 6 (2000).

those claims that survived this withering gaze enjoyed broad protection.[76] Here, the courts invalidated those claims of the '960 patent that were of sufficient scope to cover manganese literally. The patent proprietor was awarded a scope of control well beyond the literal wording of the four extant flux claims, however. Through an infringement principle, the courts effectively compensated the patentee for a proprietary interest that had been lost through a validity doctrine.

Today the situation is exactly reversed. Patentability requirements such as claim definiteness, nonobviousness and statutory subject matter have become far more porous under the stewardship of the Federal Circuit. In the modern era few claims are struck down as being indefinite,[77] the showing needed to demonstrate that an invention would have been obvious has been elevated,[78] and inventions from virtually any area of endeavor can be patented.[79] Yet as the Court of Appeals has treated patent validity issues more leniently, it has also placed new obstacles upon use of the doctrine of equivalents. The Federal Circuit has constrained the doctrine through use of the prior art,[80] the "all elements rule",[81] the "public dedication doctrine,"[82] and, especially, through the concept of prosecution history estoppel.[83]

Applying modern patent law doctrine to the facts of *Graver Tank* is an revealing exercise. Most likely the issued judgment would likely be

---

[76] *See* Glynn S. Lunney, Jr., *Patent Law, the Federal Circuit, and the Supreme Court: A Quiet Revolution*, 11 SUP. CT. ECON. REV. 1 (2004).

[77] *See* Exxon Res. & Eng'g Co. v. United States, 265 F.3d 1371, 1375 (Fed. Cir. 2001).

[78] *See In re* Lee, 277 F.3d 1338 (Fed. Cir. 2002).

[79] *See* State Street Bank & Trust Co. v. Signature Fin. Group, Inc., 149 F.3d 1368 (Fed. Cir. 1998).

[80] The courts have reasoned that patentees should not be able to obtain a construction of their claims under the doctrine of equivalents that would reach technologies that would cover the prior art. *See* Wilson Sporting Goods Co. v. David Geoffrey & Assocs., 904 F.2d 677 (Fed. Cir. 1990).

[81] Under the "all elements rule," a finding of infringement may arise only if each element of a claim is expressed in the accused infringement, either literally or equivalently. *See* Corning Glass Works v. Sumitomo Elec. U.S.A., Inc., 868 F.2d 1251 (Fed. Cir. 1989).

[82] The Federal Circuit has ruled that subject matter that is disclosed in a patent's written description, but not claimed, may not be appropriated through the doctrine of equivalents. *See* Johnson & Johnston Assocs. Inc. v. R. E. Service Co., 285 F.3d 1046 (Fed. Cir. 2002) (*en banc*). Such unclaimed subject matter is considered to have been deliberately disclaimed and therefore dedicated to the public.

[83] The principle of prosecution history estoppel precludes a patentee from obtaining a claim construction before a court that would include subject matter surrendered at the PTO during patent acquisition procedures. *See* Festo Corp. v. Shoketsu Kinzoku Kogyo Kabushiki Co., 344 F.3d 1359 (Fed. Cir. 2003).

the same today as it was in 1950: Graver Tank and Lincoln would be judged infringers and owe damages to Linde. Important differences in reasoning would exist, however, between the actual *Graver Tank* opinion of 1950 and the hypothetical one of 2005. A modern court would likely uphold the broader method and composition claims of the '960 patent. As a result, this would be a case of literal rather than equivalent infringement.

These differences in reasoning would have held important consequences for the welding industry. Following the *Graver Tank* case, Lincoln was readily able to design around the four narrow flux claims of the '960 patent, even given their generous judicial interpretation.[84] This effort may have gone far less smoothly had the patent's more capacious method and composition claims remained extant. This comparison yields an important insight. Although the Federal Circuit currently speaks in much more somber tones about the doctrine of equivalents than did the majority in *Graver Tank*, viewed in its entirety, current law is generally much more favorable to patent proprietors than it was at the time of *Graver Tank*.

This doctrinal shift may hold even more significant consequences for the patent system as a whole. In effect, the judicial climate of *Graver Tank* allowed inventors to procure a small number of broadly construed patent claims. Modern inventors are instead invited to obtain a large number of more narrow ones. Unfortunately, the contemporary patent regime seems more susceptible to manipulation than its predecessor. Sophisticated inventors can potentially exploit this shift in judicial attitude by simply procuring more patents.

U.S. Patent & Trademark Office data comport with this account. In 1996, about the time of the Federal Circuit began to evidence more cabined views of the doctrine of equivalents, inventors presented 191,116 applications to the PTO. In 2003 they filed 333,452.[85] Surely other factors besides a narrowing doctrine of equivalents play a role in industry's increasing demand for patent protection. Commentators have nonetheless appreciated the point that in an era where the doctrine of equivalents is dwindling, more focus need be placed upon claim drafting during patent acquisition.[86] Whether society is better served by precision claiming in every patent, or the more flexible application of the doctrine

---

[84] *See supra* notes 49–51 and accompanying text.

[85] The U.S. Patent & Trademark Office provides statistics on patent filings at its website, http://www.uspto.gov. These figures include utility and plant patent applications, as well as reissues.

[86] *See, e.g.*, John R. Thomas, *Formalism at the Federal Circuit*, 52 Am. U. L. Rev. 771, 786 (2003).

of equivalents for those few patents enforced in infringement litigation, remains an open question.[87]

Conclusion

Although *Graver Tank* issued over half a century ago, the opinion still seems fresh. Some things haven't changed much since 1950. Lincolnweld and Unionmelt welding fluxes remain available for purchase in the twenty-first century. Patent litigation still takes a long time. And, despite the best efforts of inventors, Californians are still having trouble with their water supply.

Another constant has been discussion over the doctrine of equivalents itself. The dialogue between the majority and dissenters in *Graver Tank* continues to frame current debate over the scope of control due to a patent owner. Predictably, courts have continued to struggle in their efforts to identify when the use of the doctrine of equivalents is appropriate, and precisely what its contours should be. Perhaps it is time for the intellectual property community to move past the *Graver Tank* approach to the doctrine of equivalents and seek more sophisticated solutions for resolving cases of equivalent infringement. An understanding of the strengths, and the weaknesses, of this famous decision can help us to do just that.

---

[87] Professor Lemley has concluded that "at most only about two percent of all patents are ever litigated, and less than two-tenths of one percent of all issued patents actually go to court." Mark Lemley, *Rational Ignorance at the Patent Office*, 95 Nw. L. Rev. 1495, 1501 (2001).

5

Responses to Technological Change

The Story of *Diamond v. Chakrabarty*: Technological Change and the Subject Matter Boundaries of the Patent System

Rebecca S. Eisenberg*

Technological change often exposes unstated assumptions lurking in the law and makes them problematic, and patent law is no exception. Although the core mission of the patent system is to promote technological progress, path-breaking new technologies have not always been easily assimilated within its boundaries. The first wave of patent applications on advances in biotechnology in the 1970s illustrate some of the difficulties. Before that time, living organisms had generally been assumed to fall outside the range of patent-eligible subject matter under a time-honored exclusion for "products of nature."[1] But genetically engineered organisms, although derived from naturally occurring life forms, seemed to involve too much human intervention to be characterized as natural products. Were they eligible for patent protection? Should the default rule be protection or no protection? What are the roles of the courts, the Patent and Trademark Office (PTO), and the legislature in figuring it out?

The first stop for inventors seeking patent rights in new technologies, and thus the first institution to confront the legal issues that these technologies raise, is the PTO. In the 1970s, as Ananda Chakrabarty's patent application on a genetically modified, oil-eating bacterium worked its way through the system, the PTO was confronting growing numbers of patent applications in emerging "high technology" fields, notably

 I am grateful to Rochelle Dreyfuss, Jane Ginsburg, and Daniel Kevles for helpful comments on earlier versions of this paper.

[1] *See* Funk Bros. Seed v. Kalo Inoculant, 333 U.S. 127 (1948).

information technology and biotechnology, that strained the capacities of its existing corps of examiners. Examination of patent applications in new fields always presents special administrative challenges, including a lack of examiners with the appropriate technical training and a lack of readily accessible prior art in the form of previously issued patents.[2] These challenges were particularly daunting in the days before examiners had access to commercial databases of prior art or even to personal computers. In this environment, the PTO had a strong institutional incentive to exclude these fields categorically from patent eligibility pending explicit legislation providing for their protection. Categorical exclusions offer an efficient mechanism for filtering out patent applications at the threshold of the PTO, without the need for examiners to delve into the underlying technology and to compare the claimed inventions to the prior art. If Congress thought that patent protection was appropriate, it could address the resource needs of the PTO at the same time that it considered what additional legislation was necessary for these fields.

On its face, the Patent Act extends protection to "any new and useful process, machine, manufacture or composition of matter," without explicit subject matter exclusions.[3] But over the years the courts and the PTO have sometimes seemed to endorse exclusions from patent eligibility for certain categories of inventions, including architectural designs,[4] medical and surgical techniques,[5] plants,[6] agricultural methods,[7]

---

[2] *See generally* Bhaven N. Sampat, *Examining Patent Examination: An Analysis of Examiner and Applicant Generated Prior Art*, NBER Working Papers (Aug. 2004 draft) (concluding on basis of empirical examination of prior art references cited by examiners and applicants that examiners are far better at identifying prior art in U.S. patents than they are at searching non-patent prior art or foreign patents, and that examiners face particular challenges in identifying prior art in emerging technological fields).

[3] 35 U.S.C. § 101.

[4] *See, e.g.,* Jacobs v. Baker, 74 U.S. (7 Wall) 295 (1869) (suggesting that improvements in the construction of jails were not patent-eligible subject matter, although also noting that patents were properly invalidated for lack of novelty).

[5] Morton v. New York Eye Infirmary, 17 F. Cas. 879 (S.D.N.Y. 1862) (No. 9865) (holding ineligible for patent protection method of performing surgery by applying ether to render patient insensitive to pain); *Ex parte* Brinkerhoff, 24 Dec. Comm'n Pat. 349 (1883) (holding that "the methods or modes of treatment of physicians of certain diseases are not patentable."). *But cf.* Smith & Nephew v. Ethicon, 54 U.S.P.Q.2d (BNA) 1888, 1889 (D. Ore. 1999) (claiming "a method of attaching tissue to bone by using a resilient suture anchor which is pressed into a hole in the bone"); Catapano v. Wyeth Ayerst Pharmaceuticals, 88 F.Supp.2d 27, 28 (E.D.N.Y. 2000) (claiming a method of treating a human patient to effect the remission of AIDS).

[6] *Ex parte* Latimer, 1889 Comm'n Dec. 13 (1889) (holding ineligible for patent protection a claim to "cellular tissues of the Pinus australis" tree separated from "the silicious, resinous, and pulpy parts of the pine needles and subdivided into long, pliant filaments adapted to be spun and woven"). *But cf.* J.E.M. Ag Supply v. Pioneer Hi–Bred International, 534 U.S. 124 (2001) (holding plants eligible for patent protection).

[7] Wall v. Leck, 66 F. 552 (9th Cir. 1895) (invalidating patent on a process of fumigating citrus trees in the absence of light).

business methods,[8] mathematical algorithms,[9] and products and phenomena of nature.[10] These exclusions have been viewed skeptically by the Court of Appeals for the Federal Circuit (Federal Circuit) and by its predecessor, the Court of Customs and Patent Appeals (CCPA),[11] and by now most have been repudiated.[12] But thirty years ago the exclusions appeared far more robust. They retained vitality, despite skepticism from the CCPA, because they could claim authority from decisions of the U.S. Supreme Court.[13] This divergence of views between the CCPA on one hand, and the PTO and Supreme Court on the other, set the stage for repeated rejections, appeals, reversals, and further appeals, generating a confusing and inconsistent body of caselaw.[14]

---

[8] Hotel Security Checking Co. v. Lorraine Co., 160 F. 467 (2d Cir. 1908) (holding invalid a patent on a "method for cash-registering and account-checking designed to prevent frauds by waiters" while noting that "a system of transacting business disconnected from the means for carrying out the system is not . . . an art."). *But cf.* State St. Bank & Trust v. Signature Financial Group, 149 F.3d 1368 (Fed. Cir. 1998) (rejecting business method exception and stating that basis for *Hotel Security* decision was lack of novelty rather than lack of patent-eligible subject matter).

[9] Gottschalk v. Benson, 409 U.S. 63 (1972).

[10] Funk Bros. Seed v. Kalo Inoculant, 333 U.S. 127 (1948).

[11] Congress created the Court of Appeals for the Federal Circuit in 1982, consolidating intermediate appellate jurisdiction over patent law matters in a single court that would hear appeals from decisions of the PTO and decisions of the Federal District Courts in patent cases. Federal Courts Improvement Act of 1982, Pub. L. No. 97–164, 96 Stat. 25. An important goal was to bring about greater uniformity and consistency in interpretations of the patent laws.

[12] *E.g.*, State St. Bank & Trust v. Signature Financial Group, 149 F.3d 1368 (Fed. Cir. 1998), *cert. denied*, 525 U.S. 1093 (1999); AT & T Corp. v. Excel Communications, Inc., 172 F.3d 1352 (Fed.Cir.1999); Pioneer Hi–Bred Int'l v. J.E.M. Ag Supply, 200 F.3d 1374 (Fed. Cir. 2000), *aff'd sub nom.* J.E.M. Ag Supply v. Pioneer Hi–Bred Int'l, 534 U.S. 124, 130 (2001).

[13] *See, e.g.*, Funk Bros. Seed v. Kalo Inoculant, 333 U.S. 127 (1948); Gottschalk v. Benson, 409 U.S. 63 (1972).

[14] *See, e.g.*, In re Benson, 441 F.2d 682 (C.C.P.A. 1971) (reversing PTO rejection of claims to a computer-implemented method of converting numbers expressed in binary coded decimal to pure binary form), *rev'd sub nom.* Gottschalk v. Benson, 409 U.S. 63 (1972); *In re* Johnston, 502 F.2d 765 (C.C.P.A. 1974) (reversing PTO rejection of claims to a "machine system for automatic record-keeping of bank checks and deposits"), *rev'd sub nom.*, Dann v. Johnston, 425 U.S. 219 (1976); *In re* Flook, 559 F.2d 21 (C.C.P.A. 1977) (reversing PTO rejection of claims to a method of updating alarm limits in a catalytic conversion process through use of a novel mathematical formula), *rev'd sub nom.* Parker v.

Supreme Court review has long been something of a wild card in patent law adjudication. Although the U.S. Supreme Court has ultimate appellate jurisdiction over patent cases in the federal courts, patent law consumes relatively little of the Supreme Court's attention, whereas it is a central concern of the PTO and its reviewing court (the Federal Circuit today and the CCPA at the time of the *Chakrabarty* decision). Aggrieved litigants, including the PTO, have often sought Supreme Court review of Federal Circuit (and CCPA) decisions, and occasionally have persuaded the Court to reverse. But the Supreme Court's sporadic interventions in the field have sometimes seemed like rules laid down by a noncustodial parent during weekend visits with the kids—at best, sparingly enforced once everyday life resumes under the supervision of someone whose judgment differs.

A leading voice on the intermediate appellate court for limiting categorical exclusions and for making patent protection available to inventions in all fields was that of Judge Giles Rich, who served first on the CCPA and then on the Federal Circuit for a total of 43 years.[15] As he sometimes noted in his opinions and other writings,[16] Judge Rich played a major role in drafting the Patent Act of 1952 prior to his appointment to the bench in 1956. Judge Rich believed that the 1952 Act had overturned restrictions on the availability of patent protection set forth

---

Flook, 437 U.S. 584 (1978); *In re* Bergy, 563 F.2d 1031 (C.C.P.A.1977) (reversing PTO rejection of claims to a biologically pure culture of a microorganism), *vacated and remanded for further consideration in light of* Parker v. Flook *sub nom.* Parker v. Bergy, 438 U.S. 902 (1978), *on remand*, 596 F.2d 952 (C.C.P.A. 1979) (again reversing rejection of claims), *vacated and remanded with directions to dismiss as moot sub nom. Diamond v. Chakrabarty*, 444 U.S. 1028 (1980); *In re* Chakrabarty, 571 F.2d 40 (C.C.P.A. 1978) (reversing decision of PTO to reject claims to a bacterium that had been genetically engineered to degrade multiple components of crude oil), *cert. dismissed sub nom.* Banner v. Chakrabarty, 439 U.S. 801 (1978), *on rehearing*, *In re* Bergy, 596 F.2d 952 (C.C.P.A. 1979) (again reversing rejection of claims), *aff'd*, 447 U.S. 303 (1980); *In re* Diehr, 602 F.2d 982 (C.C.P.A. 1979) (reversing PTO rejection of claims to method of curing synthetic rubber which includes use of a mathematical formula and a programmed digital computer), *aff'd sub nom.* Diamond v. Diehr, 450 U.S. 175 (1981).

[15] *See* Paul R. Michel, *Recollections of Judge Giles S. Rich*, 14 Berkeley Tech. L.J. 3 (1999), *available at* http://www.law.berkeley.edu/journals/btlj/articles/vol14/Michel/html/reader.html.

[16] *E.g.*, Paulik v. Rizkalla, 760 F.2d 1270, 1276 (Fed. Cir. 1985) (Rich, J. concurring) ("I write in order to express some additional thoughts respecting 35 U.S.C. § 102(g) as a member of the group which drafted that section.... In my view, considering what I know to have been the intent of [§ 102(g) of the Patent Act], it has been thoroughly misapplied by the board and the dissent here ..."). *See generally* Giles S. Rich, *Congressional Intent—Or, Who Wrote the Patent Act of 1952?*, *in* Southwestern Legal Foundation, Patent Procurement and Exploitation: Protecting Intellectual Rights 61, 78 (1963) (quoting a member of Congress who said that Rich and the other drafters of the statute, "far more than any member of the House or Senate, knew and understood what was intended by the language used.").

in prior Supreme Court decisions, making the analysis and even the vocabulary of the older cases obsolete and irrelevant.[17]

A leading voice on the Supreme Court for restricting patent eligibility, both before and after passage of the 1952 Act, was that of Justice William O. Douglas, who, before his retirement in 1975, served almost as long on the Supreme Court as Judge Rich served on the intermediate appellate courts.[18] To Justice Douglas, the patent system was a limited exception to an overall preference, on the part of both Congress[19] and the framers of the Constitution,[20] for free competition in the U.S. economy. He believed that patent rights had to be administered parsimoniously to avoid extending monopolies beyond what Congress intended and the Constitution permits.[21] Justice Douglas therefore set high standards for getting a patent and endorsed broad exclusions from patent protection for fundamental building blocks of science and technology such as phenomena of nature[22] and mathematical formulae.[23] Although Justice Douglas was no longer on the Court when it decided *Diamond v. Chakrabarty*, his prior decisions in patent cases remained influential.

Against the backdrop of these competing judicial currents, science and technology moved forward, bringing new technologies before the PTO.

---

17 *E.g., In re* Bergy, 596 F.2d 952, 959 (C.C.P.A. 1979) (noting that pre–1952 cases used the terms "inventions," "inventive," and "invent" to convey meanings which the terms no longer have in the revised statute). A notable example of a vocabulary change brought about by the Patent Act of 1952 is the reframing of the Supreme Court's requirement, drawn from the language of the U.S. Constitution, that a patent could only be issued for an "invention," into the statutory requirement, set forth in 35 U.S.C. § 103, that in order to be patentable a claimed invention must be "nonobvious." *Cf.* Graham v. John Deere, 383 U.S. 1 (1966) (noting that the limitation of patent protection to "inventions" is required by the Constitution, that the Court interprets the statutory standard of "nonobviousness" to be consistent with the Constitutional limitation, and that if Congress were in fact to diminish the standard for protection below that required by the Constitution, the Court would be compelled to hold the statute invalid).

18 Justice Douglas was appointed to the Supreme Court in 1939 and retired in 1975, for a total term of 36 1/2 years. Oyez U.S. Supreme Court Multimedia, *William O. Douglas,* http://www.oyez.org/oyez/resource/legal_entity/79/ (last visited Jul. 25, 2005).

19 Kewanee Oil v. Bicron, 416 U.S. 470, 495 (1974) (Douglas, J., dissenting) ("Congress in the patent laws decided that where no patent existed, free competition should prevail. . . .").

20 A & P Tea v. Supermarket Corp., 340 U.S. 147, 154 (1950) (Douglas, J., concurring) ("The Congress does not have free rein . . . to decide that patents should be easily or freely given. . . . The Framers plainly did not want those monopolies freely granted.").

21 *Id.*

22 Funk Bros. Seed v. Kalo Inoculant, 333 U.S. 127 (1948).

23 Gottschalk v. Benson, 409 U.S. 63 (1972).

Chakrabarty's Invention

Ananda Chakrabarty is a Distinguished Professor of Microbiology and Immunology at the University of Illinois who has accumulated a long list of scientific publications over a career spanning four decades.[24] But in legal circles, he is better known as the patent applicant who litigated the issue of the patentability of living organisms in the landmark Supreme Court case of *Diamond v. Chakrabarty.*[25]

After completing his Ph.D. at the University of Calcutta in 1965, Chakrabarty went to the University of Illinois at Urbana as a postdoctoral associate, where he studied the ability of *Pseudomonas* bacteria to utilize a wide variety of organic compounds as nutrition. In the course of this work, he discovered that the genes that allowed the bacteria to digest compounds such as camphor and octane did not reside on the bacterial chromosome, but rather on separate DNA elements called plasmids that are more readily transmissible from one bacterium to another. Chakrabarty's research demonstrated the potential of *Pseudomonas* bacteria to transfer between organisms plasmids containing the genes that permit assimilation of these compounds, thereby enhancing their nutritional versatility.[26]

In 1971 Chakrabarty left the University of Illinois for a position in the Research and Development Center of General Electric, where he was assigned to work on the nutritionally frugal (if unappetizing) problem of converting cow manure into cattle feed.[27] But he retained an interest in basic research, and soon found a persuasive commercial justification for continuing his prior research on *Pseudomonas*. In the early 1970s, in some parts of the world, oil was cheap, but protein sources were

---

24 A list of Chakrabarty's scientific publications is posted at http://www.uic.edu/depts/mcmi/faculty/chakrabarty.html (last visited Oct. 4, 2004).

25 447 U.S. 303 (1980). This decision was the focus of extensive law review commentary. *See, e.g.*, Peter B. Maggs, *New Life for Patents: Chakrabarty and Rohm & Haas Co.*, 1980 Sup. Ct. Rev. 57 (1980); Note, *The Patentability of Living Matter: Hey Waiter, What's Chakrabarty's* Pseudomonas *Bacterium Doing Back in the Supreme Court's Soup?*, 37 Wash. & Lee L. Rev. 183 (1980); Note, *Live, Human-made Bacteria As Patentable Subject Matter Under 35 U.S.C. § 101: Diamond v. Chakrabarty*, 1980 BYU L. Rev. 705 (1980); Note, *Diamond v. Chakrabarty: Living Things as Statutory Subject Matter*, 1 N. Ill. U. L. Rev. 119 (1980); Note, *Patentability of Living Microorganisms: Diamond v. Chakrabarty*, 94 Harv. L. Rev.261 (1980); Note, *Diamond v. Chakrabarty: Oil Eaters: Alive and Patentable*, 8 Pepp. L. Rev. 747 (1981); Note, *Building a Better Bacterium: Genetic Engineering and the Patent Law After Diamond v. Chakrabarty*, 81 Colum. L. Rev. 159 (1981).

26 Ananda M. Chakrabarty, *Patenting of Life–Forms From a Concept to Reality*, *in* D. Magnus et al., Who Owns Life? (2002). The definitive historical account of the *Chakrabarty* case is Daniel J. Kevles, *Ananda Chakrabarty wins a patent: Biotechnology, law, and society, 1972–1980*, 25 Hist. Stud. in the Physical and Biological Sciences 111 (1994).

27 Kevles, *supra* note 26, at 114.

expensive. These relative values made it commercially attractive to develop a process for converting crude oil to bacterial biomass (which would ultimately provide nutrition higher up in the food chain).[28] It occurred to Chakrabarty that *Pseudomonas* bacteria could be put to use in this bioconversion task, since he knew they could derive nutrition from various components of crude oil. But crude oil is a mixture of many different hydrocarbons, of which known *Pseudomonas* strains could only degrade a limited number. A mixed culture of strains could potentially digest more components, but some strains inevitably dominated others in mixed cultures, limiting the extent of degradation (and therefore limiting the generation of biomass). Knowing from his prior work that the genes for degrading the separate components were borne on plasmids that could be transferred from one bacterium to another, Chakrabarty hit upon the idea of constructing a single *Pseudomonas* strain with multiple plasmids. He worked on the problem after-hours and on weekends, and eventually succeeded.[29] While his research proceeded, the price of crude oil rose substantially in world markets, calling into question the value of the strain as a means of converting petroleum to biomass. But his colleagues at GE decided that an oil-eating bacterium might nonetheless be useful for another purpose—cleaning up oil spills—and on June 7, 1972, GE filed a patent application on Charkrabarty's invention.[30]

The PTO's Response

Patents on technologies involving the use of microorganisms were by this point familiar subject matter for the patent system. The pharmaceutical industry had been securing patents on methods of producing antibiotics from microbial strains for decades,[31] and patents on microbial processes for waste treatment were older still.[32] What made Chakrabarty's application unusual was that he claimed not only methods of using his bacterial strains, but also the bacteria themselves.

The patent examiner allowed Chakrabarty's process claims, but rejected the product claims to the bacteria on two grounds: (1) that the claimed microorganisms are "products of nature"; and (2) that as "live organisms" they are not eligible for patent protection.[33] Chakrabarty

[28] Chakrabarty, *supra* note 26, at 18.

[29] *Id.* at 19.

[30] *Id.* at 19–20.

[31] *E.g., In re* Mancy, 499 F.2d 1289 (C.C.P.A. 1974) (upholding patent claims to process of making antibiotic by cultivating strain of bacteria).

[32] *E.g.,* City of Milwaukee v. Activated Sludge, 69 F.2d 577 (7th Cir. 1934) (patent on method of treating raw sewage).

[33] *In re* Chakrabarty, 571 F.2d 40, 42 (C.C.P.A. 1978).

appealed the rejection to the PTO Board of Appeals (the Board). The Board set aside the examiner's holding that the bacteria were products of nature, agreeing with Chakrabarty that his multi-plasmid *Pseudomonas* bacteria were not naturally occurring, but nonetheless affirmed the rejection on the ground that living organisms may not be patented.[34]

Meanwhile, in *Ex parte Bergy*,[35] a different Board panel applied a similar analysis to an appeal from a rejection of a claim to a "biologically pure culture" of an antibiotic-producing microorganism. Bergy's organism had not been genetically altered, and thus might have been more readily characterized as a "product of nature" than Chakrabarty's multi-plasmid bacterium. (Indeed, the sole basis for the examiner's rejection of Bergy's claim was that it constituted an unpatentable product of nature.)[36] But the Board declined to consider whether the biologically pure culture was a product of nature, and instead affirmed the rejection on the different ground that it was living, and thus was not a patentable "manufacture" or "composition of matter" within the meaning of § 101 of the Patent Act.[37]

In both cases, the Board thus set aside the "products of nature" ground for rejections and focused instead on the fact that the claims were drawn to living subject matter. In retrospect, this choice seems both puzzling and fateful. Although patent applications on living organisms had been rejected in the past,[38] there was no precedent explicitly stating that living things are *ipso facto* ineligible for patent protection. Instead, the stated ground for exclusion had been that they were unpatentable products of nature. Under the circumstances, one might expect that the PTO would retain on appeal the tried-and true ground for rejection rather than resting solely on an argument that the courts had never considered.

To be sure, the products of nature argument was problematic in the facts of both *Chakrabarty* and *Bergy*. A series of cases had previously upheld patents on purified versions of products that exist in nature only in an impure state, reasoning that the purified products were the result of human intervention, and that in a purified state they were suitable for purposes that the impure versions could not serve.[39] Similar arguments

---

34 571 F.2d at 42.

35 197 U.S.P.Q. (BNA) 78 (U.S. P.T.O. Bd. App. & Interf., 1976), *rev'd sub nom. In re* Bergy, 563 F.2d 1031 (C.C.P.A. 1977).

36 *In re* Bergy, 563 F.2d at 1032–33.

37 197 U.S.P.Q. (BNA) at 79–80; 563 F.2d at 1033.

38 *E.g., Ex parte* Latimer, 1889 Comm'n Dec. 13 (1889).

39 *E.g.,* Parke–Davis & Co. v. H.K. Mulford & Co., 189 F. 95 (S.D.N.Y. 1911) (purified adrenaline); Kuehmsted v. Farbenfabriken, 179 F. 701 (7th Cir. 1910), *cert. denied*, 220

could be made for the organisms claimed by both Chakrabarty and Bergy. But none of the "purified substances" cases had been affirmed by the Supreme Court.

Indeed, the Supreme Court had seemed to endorse a more expansive exclusion in its 1948 decision in *Funk Brothers Seed Company v. Kalo Inoculant*,[40] a case with notable similarities to *Chakrabarty*. The patent at issue in that case claimed a mixed culture of naturally occurring strains of bacteria of the genus *Rhizobium*, useful as an inoculant to permit plants to fix nitrogen from the environment. In the past, different species of *Rhizobium* had been used to inoculate the roots of different plants, but when multiple strains were combined, they had inhibited each other's effectiveness. The inventor, Bond, identified strains that did not have this mutually inhibitive effect and combined them in a single product that could be used to inoculate multiple crops. The PTO issued the patent and, in a subsequent infringement action, the Court of Appeals upheld the validity of Bond's claim to the mixed culture, characterizing it as a new composition of matter that contributed utility and economy to the manufacture and distribution of commercial inoculants. The Supreme Court reversed. In an opinion by Justice Douglas, the Court elaborated upon the exclusion of the work of nature from patent protection:

> Bond does not create a state of inhibition or of non-inhibition in the bacteria. Their qualities are the work of nature. Those qualities are of course not patentable. For patents cannot issue for the discovery of the phenomena of nature. The qualities of these bacteria, like the heat of the sun, electricity, or the qualities of metals, are part of the storehouse of knowledge of all men. They are manifestations of laws of nature, free to all men and reserved exclusively to none. He who discovers a hitherto unknown phenomenon of nature has no claim to a monopoly of it which the law recognizes. If there is to be invention from such a discovery, it must come from the application of the law of nature to a new and useful end.[41]

Justice Douglas conceded that Bond had indeed applied his discovery of the noninhibitive qualities of the bacterial strains to a new and useful end by combining them into a new product—the mixed culture of his claim.[42] He nonetheless concluded that the product was not patentable, in language that sometimes suggested a categorical exclusion and some-

U.S. 622 (1911) (purified prostaglandins); Merck & Co. v. Olin Mathieson Corp., 253 F.2d 156 (4th Cir. 1958) (purified vitamin B12).

[40] 333 U.S. 127 (1948).

[41] *Id.* at 130.

[42] *Id.* at 131–32.

times suggested a failure to meet the patent law standard for "invention":

> But we think that that aggregation of species fell short of invention within the meaning of the patent statutes. Discovery of the fact that certain strains of each species of these bacteria can be mixed without harmful effect to the properties of either is a discovery of their qualities of non-inhibition. It is no more than the discovery of some of the handiwork of nature and hence is not patentable.... [H]owever ingenious the discovery of the natural principle may have been, the application of it is hardly more than an advance in the packaging of the inoculants.... The combination of species produces no new bacteria, no change in the six species of bacteria, and no enlargement of the range of their utility. Each species has the same effect it always had. The bacteria perform in their natural way. Their use in combination does not improve in any way their natural functioning. They serve the ends nature originally provided and act quite independently of any effort of the patentee.[43]

One could, by analogy, have argued that Chakrabarty had also discovered some of the handiwork of nature—naturally occurring plasmids that could be transferred from one microbial host to another, each permitting its host to degrade a different component of crude oil—and combined them in a single host organism. As Chakrabarty himself explained in a 1980 interview with *People*, "I simply shuffled genes, changing bacteria that already existed."[44] In Chakrabarty's combination, as in Bond's, each of the subunits (Chakrabarty's plasmids, Bond's species) continued to perform in its natural way. If Chakrabarty's aggregation of multiple selected plasmids in a single organism required more ingenuity than Bond's aggregation of selected species in a mixed culture inoculant, this distinction would seem to be a matter of nonobviousness, or "invention" in the vernacular of pre–1952 Act decisions, rather than a matter of patent eligibility.

The distinction between the threshold question of patent eligibility and the more fine-grained question of patent-worthiness was easy to miss in the pre–1952 cases, when the single term "invention" might be used to describe what was lacking in both situations.[45] The 1952 Act

[43] *Id.* at 131.

[44] PEOPLE, July 14, 1980, at 38 (as cited in Kevles, *supra* note 26, at 116).

[45] *Compare* Mackay Radio & Telegraph Co. v. Radio Corp. of America, 306 U.S. 86, at 96 n.4 (1939) ("While a scientific truth, or the mathematical expression of it, is not patentable *invention*, a novel and useful structure created with the aid of knowledge of scientific truth may be." (emphasis added)) *with* Great Atlantic & Pacific Tea Co. v. Supermarket Equipment Corp., 340 U.S. 147, 149 (1950) ("Courts should scrutinize

codified the requirement of "invention" in the latter sense and gave it a new name, "nonobviousness,"[46] but *Funk v. Kalo* was decided before that time and explained in language that left a lingering ambiguity about whether Bond's invention was categorically ineligible for patent protection or was merely unworthy of patent protection because it was trivial. This ambiguity may have made *Funk v. Kalo* questionable as authority for rejecting the claims of Chakrabarty and Bergy.

But *Funk v. Kalo* was not the last word from the Supreme Court on this subject. Even after passage of the 1952 Act, in the years leading up to its decision in *Diamond v. Chakrabarty* the Supreme Court had relied on *Funk v. Kalo* in two more cases, each involving rejections of claims to computer-implemented inventions.[47] Although the precedential value of a case about a mixed culture of bacteria for resolving cases about computer-implemented inventions might not be not self-evident, Justice Douglas, writing for the Court, not only cited *Funk v. Kalo* with approval but seemed to rely upon it:

> Phenomena of nature, though just discovered, mental processes, and abstract intellectual concepts are not patentable, as they are the basic tools of scientific and technological work. As we stated in *Funk Bros. Seed Co. v. Kalo Co.*, "He who discovers a hitherto unknown phenomenon of nature has no claim to a monopoly of it which the law recognizes. If there is to be invention from such a discovery, it must come from the application of the law of nature to a new and useful end." We dealt there with a "product" claim, while the present case deals with a "process" claim. But we think the same principle applies.[48]

Categorical exclusions from patent eligibility for "products of nature" thus retained considerable vitality in the Supreme Court in the 1970s, making it all the more puzzling that the PTO would set aside this ground for rejecting the Charkrabarty and Bergy claims while resting

---

combination patent claims with a care proportioned to the difficulty and improbability of finding *invention* in an assembly of old elements." (emphasis added)).

[46] 35 U.S.C. § 103; Graham v. John Deere, 383 U.S. 1 (1966).

[47] In the first of these cases, *Gottschalk v. Benson*, 409 U.S. 63 (1972), a unanimous Court overturned the CCPA and reinstated the PTO's rejection of a claim to a method of converting binary-coded decimal numerals into pure binary numerals. The Court again invoked the "products of nature" cases in its 6–3 decision in Parker v. Flook to overturn the C.C.P.A. and reinstate the PTO's rejection of a claim to a computer-implemented method for updating an alarm limit in the startup of a catalytic conversion plant. 437 U.S. 584 (1978). This 1978 decision had not yet come down when the PTO Board decided the *Chakrabarty* and *Bergy* cases. *See infra* notes 72 to 79 and accompanying text. For a fuller discussion of of *Gottschalk v. Benson* and and *Parker v. Flook*, see Maureen A. O'Rourke, The Story of *Diamond v. Diehr*: Toward Patenting Software, elsewhere in this Volume.

[48] 409 U.S. at 67–68 (citation omitted).

solely on an unprecedented categorical exclusion for living things. It is generally easier to persuade courts to adjust the boundaries of existing legal categories to accommodate new facts than it is to persuade them to create new categories.

Lacking explicit precedent for the principle that living things may not be patented, the PTO was left to make a complex, and ultimately unpersuasive, argument for an inference about Congressional intent (or assumptions) concerning the patentability of living things from the fact that Congress had passed special legislation to provide intellectual property protection for plants. The argument went as follows: Congress twice acted to provide intellectual property rights in plants: first, in the Plant Patent Act of 1930, which conferred patent rights in asexually reproduced plants;[49] and second, in the Plant Variety Protection Act of 1970, which conferred more limited protection under the auspices of the Department of Agriculture for sexually reproduced varieties.[50] Since Congress went to the trouble of passing special legislation to provide protection for plants, Congress must have believed that, absent such legislation, plants would not be eligible for ordinary utility patent protection under the general patent statute. Congress must therefore have believed that plants did not fit within the existing patentable subject matter categories of "manufacture" or "composition of matter." The reason Congress thought that plants were excluded from those statutory categories must have been that plants are living, and therefore Congress must have believed that the statutory categories of patentable subject matter excluded not only plants, but also all other living things. From legislation that made it easier to get protection for plants, the PTO thus drew an inference that Congress intended as a general rule to exclude all living things from patent eligibility.

To recite this syllogism is to draw a roadmap for its rebuttal. The relevant statutory language was, at the time, almost 200 years old, and the actions of later Congresses is a questionable source for understanding the meaning of language used by an earlier Congress. Quite apart from this difficulty, it is easy to come up with competing explanations that are equally compelling. Perhaps, rather than believing that plants were categorically excluded from the patent system on subject matter grounds, Congress believed that plants could not satisfy the usual standards for getting a patent (such as "invention"/nonobviousness and written description) and wished to provide a source of protection that avoided these obstacles. (Indeed, both the Plant Patent Act and the Plant Variety Protection Act provided relief from some of the more

[49] 46 Stat. 376, codified as amended at 35 U.S.C. §§ 161 et seq.

[50] 84 Stat. 1547, codified as amended at 7 U.S.C. §§ 2402 et seq.

stringent requirements of patent law for plants.)[51] Perhaps Congress believed that plants were ineligible for patent protection not because they were living, but because they were products of nature. Perhaps Congress focused narrowly on the problems of plant breeders because that was the issue before them, and gave no thought to the patenting of other living things.

However narrowly Congress may have focused its attention in 1930 and in 1970, it is hardly possible that the PTO and the courts were oblivious to public controversy over biotechnology as they contemplated the issues before them in *Chakrabarty* and *Bergy*. The invention in the early 1970s of recombinant DNA techniques, which permitted scientists to create new organisms by splicing together genes from different species, had provoked profound anxiety among scientists as well as the general public.[52] While most scientists soon concluded that initial worries about the hazards of gene-splicing had been overstated,[53] popular interest and anxiety continued, taking on a new dimension with the advent of commercial biotechnology in the latter half of the1970s.[54] Although neither Chakrabarty nor Bergy had used recombinant DNA technology in making their inventions, it was surely apparent to those considering their cases that their decisions would have important implications for future inventions in this controversial new field.[55]

---

51 *See* 35 U.S.C. § 162 ("No plant patent shall be declared invalid for noncompliance with section 112 of this title [regarding description and disclosure] if the description is as complete as is reasonably possible."). The Plant Variety Protection Act has no counterpart to the nonobviousness requirement and has disclosure requirements that are easier to meet than those for an ordinary utility patent. For a comparison of the two schemes, see Mark D. Janis & Jay P. Kesan, *U.S. Plant Variety Protection: Sound and Fury . . . ?*, 39 Hous. L. Rev. 727, 745–78 (2002).

52 Concerns within the scientific community led to a historic conference of molecular biologists at the Asilomar conference center in Pacific Grove, California to discuss the hazards associated with recombinant DNA research in early 1975. Much has been written about these events. A useful synthesis may be found in Judith P. Swazey, James R. Sorenson, & Cynthia B. Wong, *Risks and Benefits, Rights and Responsibilities: A History of the Recombinant DNA Research Controversy*, 51 So. Cal. L. Rev. 1019–78 (1978). For an interesting retrospective on the controversy within the scientific community from the perspective of the NIH Director at the time, see Donald S. Fredrickson, *Asilomar and Recombinant DNA: The End of the Beginning*, in Institute of Medicine, Biomedical Politics (1991). For a more critical perspective, see Sheldon Krimsky, Genetic Alchemy: The Social History of the Recombinant DNA Controversy (1982).

53 Kevles, *supra* note 26, at 121.

54 *See* Martin Kenney, Biotechnology: The University-Industrial Complex 90–106, 132–75 (1986); David Dickson, The New Politics of Science 56–106 (1984).

55 *Cf.* Kevles, *supra* note 26, at 121 (suggesting that "considerations of political economy of biotechnology" did not figure in the PTO's analysis until after its decision had been reversed by the C.C.P.A., when it had to decide whether to appeal to the Supreme

Perhaps awareness of contemporary social discourse best accounts for the PTO's focus on "living things" rather than "products of nature" as the basis for rejecting the claims. In the rhetoric of the "products of nature" cases, it was nature that had done the heavy lifting, creating products and phenomena with awesome capabilities. The value-added of human inventors was relatively trivial, consisting primarily of figuring out what nature had done and then making minor adaptations without really changing much. In the anxious rhetoric surrounding genetic engineering in the 1970s, the relationship between nature and human inventors was pictured quite differently. Human interventions in this setting did not seem trivial, but profound and unsettling. Rather than merely copying from nature, humans seemed to be altering nature's plans in unprecedented (and, to some, alarming) ways. Neither proponents nor adversaries of the new technology saw it as the work of nature. The concerns and intuitions that had persuaded previous courts to leave natural products and natural phenomena as part of an unpatented "storehouse of knowledge ... free to all men and reserved exclusively to none" may thus have seemed inapposite in that particular historical moment.[56]

Even if the products of nature doctrine could serve to exclude the relatively "low-tech" inventions of Chakrabarty and Bergy, it was unlikely to stretch far enough to exclude the results of "high-tech" genetic engineering from the patent system. The essence of public anxiety about genetic engineering was not that it was natural, but rather that it was *un*natural, that it amounted to audacious human tampering with life. An argument for excluding living things from patent protection, although lacking explicit support in precedent, may have resonated more closely with this sentiment than the time-honored argument for excluding products of nature.

The CCPA Reverses

Chakrabarty and Bergy each appealed the rejections of their claims to the CCPA, which reversed in each case by a vote of 3–2.[57] Both

Court). But even prior to that time, as the PTO was deciding the *Chakrabarty* and *Bergy* appeals in the first instance, PTO personnel were surely aware of extensive coverage of controversy over recombinant DNA research in both the scientific press, *e.g.*, Davis, *Genetic Engineering: How Great Is the Danger?*, 186 SCIENCE 309 (1974); Erwin Chargaff, *A Slap at the Bishops of Asilomar*, 190 SCIENCE 135 (1975), and the popular press, *e.g.*, Horace F. Judson, *Fearful of Science: after Copernicus, after Darwin, after Freud comes molecular biology. Is nothing sacred?*, 250 HARPER'S 1498 (1975); Bennett & Guerin, *Science That Frightens Scientists,* ATLANTIC MONTHLY, Feb. 1977, at 49.

56 Concerns about patents on natural phenomena impeding future scientific work resurfaced much later in controversies over the patenting of DNA sequences as the Human Genome Project got under way in the 1990s. *See* Rebecca S. Eisenberg, *Why the Gene Patenting Controversy Persists*, 77 ACADEMIC MEDICINE 1381 (2002).

57 *In re* Bergy, 563 F.2d 1031 (C.C.P.A. 1977); *In re* Chakrabarty, 571 F.2d 40 (C.C.P.A. 1978).

majority opinions were authored by Judge Rich, who took care to isolate the issue for decision as narrowly as possible. He began each opinion by stating that the PTO had not questioned that the inventions satisfied the statutory criteria for patentability apart from the issue of statutory subject matter.[58] He then reviewed the proceedings in the PTO, noting in each case that, although the examiners had rejected the claimed inventions as "products of nature," the Board had affirmed instead on the different ground that statutory subject matter does not extend to "living subject matter."[59] Having thus pared each case down to the single issue of whether living subject matter may be patented, he had little trouble concluding that it could be. The *Bergy* case, although filed after Chakrabarty's, was the first to reach the CCPA. The court therefore addressed the issue at greater length in *Bergy* than in *Chakrabarty*, concluding in *Chakrabarty* that the two cases raised exactly the same issue and therefore the former decision controlled.

Judge Rich observed in *Bergy* that, although the PTO had only addressed the single issue of whether living organisms are eligible for patent protection, Bergy had also argued on appeal "the product of nature question sidetracked by the Board."[60] Characterizing as "incontrovertible" Bergy's evidence that the biologically pure culture does not occur in nature, Judge Rich surmised that "the board went in search of another reason to support the rejection because it realized the examiner's position was untenable," and concluded: "The biologically pure culture of claim 5 clearly does not exist in, is not found in, and is not a product of 'nature.' "[61]

Turning to the PTO's argument that living organisms are unpatentable, he began with the "clarifying observation" that "we are not deciding whether living things in general, or, at most, whether any living things other than microorganisms, are within § 101. These questions must be decided on a case-by-case basis. . . ." He then considered a series of decisions cited by the PTO in which the claims at issue had been drawn to processes of using microorganisms, and the courts had suggest-

---

58 *In re* Bergy, 563 F.2d at 1032 ("No references have been cited against claim 5 because the novelty and unobviousness of the biologically pure culture claimed are not questioned. Neither has utility been questioned."); *In re* Chakrabarty, 571 F.2d at 42 ("The PTO . . . has not questioned that appellant has invented and adequately disclosed strains of bacteria . . . which are new, useful, and unobvious.").

59 *In re* Bergy, 563 F.2d at 1033; *In re* Chakrabarty, 571 F.2d at 42.

60 563 F.2d at 1035.

61 *Id.*

ed in *dicta* that the microorganisms themselves would not have been patentable.[62] Turning the PTO's analysis of these cases on its head, Judge Rich observed that "processes, one of the categories of patentable subject matter specified in § 101, are uniformly and consistently considered to be statutory subject matter notwithstanding the employment therein of living organisms and their life processes."[63] It would be "illogical," he concluded, to insist that "the existence of life in a manufacture or composition of matter" renders such products unpatentable, while "the functioning of a living organism and the utilization of its life functions in processes does not affect their status under § 101."[64] To Judge Rich, Bergy's culture was "an industrial product used in an industrial process—a useful or technological art if there ever was one."[65] Characterizing the organisms and their uses as "much more akin to inanimate chemical compositions such as reactants, reagents, and catalysts than they are to horses and honeybees or raspberries and roses," he concluded that the PTO's fears that their patenting would make "all new, useful, and unobvious species of plants, animals, and insects created by man patentable" was "far-fetched."[66] Having thus resolved that microorganisms are not categorically excluded from patent eligibility, he concluded that the rejection in *Chakrabarty* must also be reversed when that case came before him five months later.[67]

By this point the advent of commercial biotechnology had raised the stakes of the controversy over patentability of microorganisms. The day after the CCPA's decision in *Chakrabarty*, a front-page story in *The Washington Post* reported that the decision "represents a potential gold mine for corporations involved in genetic engineering research."[68] Among scientists, anxiety about the hazards of genetic engineering had begun to subside, leading the National Institutes of Health (NIH) to relax previously imposed safety restrictions on use of the technology by its grantees.[69] But controversy continued among the general public, with

---

[62] *Id.* at 1035–37.

[63] *Id.* at 1037.

[64] *Id.*

[65] *Id.* at 1038.

[66] *Id.* at 1038–39. The two dissenters characterized Judge Rich's distinction between microorganisms and other living things as "purely gratuitous and clearly erroneous," noting that the majority had failed to "advance any rationale for distinguishing between different types of living things. . . ."

[67] *In re* Chakrabarty, 571 F.2d 40, 43 (C.C.P.A. 1978).

[68] Austin Scott, *Court Rules GE Can Patent Life Created in Lab*, WASH. POST, Mar. 3, 1978, at A1. *See also, Oil–Eating Bacterium Can Be Patented by G.E., Court Rules in 3–2 Vote*, N.Y. TIMES, Mar. 3, 1978, at A26.

[69] 43 F.R. 60080 (Dec. 22, 1978).

some local governments considering their own restrictions on biotechnology research as federally-imposed restrictions were relaxed.[70]

While the government pondered its options, the PTO was aware of the precarious force of Judge Rich's decisions in the face of continuing public controversy.[71] At the time, intermediate appellate jurisdiction over patent matters was divided between the CCPA, which heard appeals from decisions of the PTO, and the regional circuit courts of appeal, which heard appeals from decisions of the federal district courts in patent infringement cases. These other courts might not share Judge Rich's picture of industrial biotechnology as merely an efficient way to do chemistry, and might declare patents on life forms invalid when they came before them for enforcement. The PTO ultimately urged the Solicitor General to appeal the issue to the U.S. Supreme Court, figuring that the issue would eventually be resolved by Congress.[72]

Remand and Reconsideration

While the government's petitions for review in *Bergy* and *Chakrabarty* were pending, the Supreme Court reversed the CCPA in another case involving patent eligibility, *Parker v. Flook*.[73] The invention in that case was a computer-implemented method for updating alarm limits during catalytic conversion processes through use of a novel mathematical formula. Justice Stevens's opinion for the majority took a strikingly different approach to the issue of patent eligibility than that expressed by Judge Rich. He began by noting that the Court's decision six years earlier in *Gottschalk v. Benson*[74] was inconsistent with a literal interpretation of § 101 of the Patent Act, notwithstanding the apparently unqualified language of the statute:

> The plain language of 101 does not answer the question. It is true, as respondent argues, that his method is a "process" in the ordinary sense of the work. But that was also true of the algorithm . . . that was involved in *Gottschalk v. Benson*. The holding that the discovery of that method could not be patented as a "process" forecloses a purely literal reading of 101.[75]

---

[70] *See* Donald S. Fredrickson, *The Recombinant DNA Controversy: A Memoir: Science, Politics & the Public Interest* 1974–1981 (2001), *available at* National Library of Medicine, http://profiles.nlm.nih.gov/FF/Views/Exhibit/documents/rdna.

[71] Kevles, *supra* note 26, at 122–123.

[72] *Id.*

[73] 437 U.S. 584 (1978).

[74] 409 U.S. 63 (1972).

[75] Parker v. Flook, 437 U.S. at 589–90.

Echoing Justice Douglas's analogy between mathematical algorithms and laws of nature in *Gottschalk v. Benson*, the majority concluded that the Court's earlier decision in *Funk v. Kalo* indicated the proper analysis:

> Whether the algorithm was in fact known or unknown at the time of the claimed invention, as one of the "basic tools of scientific and technological work," it is treated as though it were a familiar part of the prior art. . . .[76]

The Court rejected the argument that this approach confuses the determination of patent eligibility under § 101 with the determinations of novelty and "inventiveness" under §§ 102 and 103. In language reminiscent of Justice Douglas's opinion in *Funk v. Kalo*, Justice Stevens elaborated:

> The rule that the discovery of a law of nature cannot be patented rests, not on the notion that natural phenomena are not processes, but rather on the more fundamental understanding that they are not the kind of "discoveries" that the statute was enacted to protect. The obligation to determine what type of discovery is sought to be patented must precede the determination of whether that discovery is, in fact, new or obvious. . . . Respondent's process is unpatentable under 101, not because it contains a mathematical algorithm as one component, but because once that algorithm is assumed to be within the prior art, the application, considered as a whole, contains no patentable invention.[77]

Yet there were signs that the Supreme Court was softening in its approach to patent eligibility. The Court acknowledged that its reasoning was "derived from opinions written before the modern business of developing programs for computers was conceived,"[78] and that its decision should not be interpreted "as reflecting a judgment that patent protection of certain novel and useful computer programs will not promote the progress of science and the useful arts, or that such protection is undesirable as a matter of policy."[79] Rather, the Court saw the issue before it as raising "difficult questions of policy" that could better be answered by Congress, and concluded that "we must proceed cautiously when we are asked to extend patent rights into areas wholly unforeseen by Congress."[80]

---

[76] *Id.* at 591–92.

[77] *Id.* at 593–94.

[78] *Id.* at 595.

[79] *Id.*

[80] *Id.* at 596, *citing* Deepsouth Packing Co. v. Laitram Corp., 406 U.S. 518, 531 (1972). Perhaps the most conspicuous harbinger of the Court's imminent liberalization of its

A few days later, the Supreme Court vacated the decision of the CCPA in *Bergy* and remanded for reconsideration in light of *Parker v. Flook*.[81] The CCPA granted the PTO's petition to vacate its own decision in *Chakrabarty* and set the two cases for hearing together, asking the parties to file supplementary briefs on the effect, "if any," of *Parker v. Flook* on its prior decisions.[82]

Judge Rich again wrote for the majority on reconsideration, again reversing the rejections in both cases. He was conspicuously unimpressed by the *Flook* decision and visibly irritated at the government for having taken the cases up to the Supreme Court. He began with a back-to-basics review of the anatomy of the patent statute, purportedly for the benefit of the Supreme Court, which he felt had exposed some confusion about the statute in its *Flook* opinion:

> The reason for our consideration of the statutory scheme . . . is that . . . we find in *Flook* an unfortunate and apparently unconscious, though clear, commingling of distinct statutory provisions which are conceptually unrelated, namely, those pertaining to the categories of inventions in § 101 which may be patentable and to the conditions for patentability demanded by the statute for inventions within the statutory categories, particularly the nonobviousness condition of § 103. . . . The problem of accurate unambiguous expression is exacerbated by the fact that prior to the Patent Act of 1952 the words "invention," "inventive," and "invent" had distinct legal implications related to the concept of patentability which they have not had for the past quarter century. . . . Statements in the older cases must be handled with care lest the terms used in their reasoning clash with the reformed terminology of the present statute; lack of meticulous care may lead to distorted legal conclusions.[83]

He offered an analogy to three doors that a patent applicant must open and pass through in order to get a patent, corresponding to §§ 101, 102,

interpretation of § 101 was the fact that three justices dissented, taking the position that the majority was confusing the issue of subject-matter patentability under § 101 with the criteria of novelty and inventiveness under §§ 102 and 103. Parker v. Flook, 437 U.S. at 598, 600 (Stewart, J. dissenting, joined by Burger, C.J., and Rehnquist, J.).

81 Parker v. Bergy, 438 U.S. 902 (1978).

82 *In re* Bergy, 596 F.2d 952, 956–58 (C.C.P.A. 1979).

83 *Id.* at 959. The unmistakable condescension toward the Supreme Court in Judge Rich's opinion led amicus University of California to distance itself from the opinion of the CCPA in its Supreme Court brief, even as it asked the Supreme Court to affirm the decision, noting that the CCPA "tends toward legal error and has long waged war against this Court's venerable and unvaried interpretations of the patent laws." Brief Amicus Curiae of the University of California at 24 (filed Jan. 28, 1980) (Westlaw Supreme Court Briefs file).

and 103 of the Patent Act. To get through the first door, the invention need not satisfy any "qualitative conditions," so long as it fits within the "broad and general" categories of "any ... process, machine, manufacture, or composition of matter, or any ... improvement thereof." Judge Rich's ellipses omitted the statutory language "new and useful," which appears twice in § 101. As he explained, "the invention is not examined under that statute for novelty because that is not the statutory scheme of things or the long-established administrative practice." Instead, the invention, whether new or old, passes through the first door, to be examined for novelty at the second door under the standards set forth in § 102. To reject a claim for lack of novelty under § 101 rather than § 102 "is confusing and therefore bad law."[84] In contrast to his tone of gentle condescension toward the Supreme Court for confusing the issues of patent-eligibility and patent-worthiness in *Parker v. Flook*, Judge Rich excoriated the Solicitor General for having done the same thing in its briefs, "badly and with a seeming sense of purpose."[85]

Turning to the assigned task on remand of determining what light the Supreme Court's opinion in *Parker v. Flook* shed on the issue in *Bergy* and *Chakrabarty*, Judge Rich concluded that the only thing the three cases had in common is that they all involved § 101. He noted that:

> *Flook* was about the patentability of computer programs as "processes," not about the patentability of living subject matter as "manufactures" or "compositions of matter." Nor did the Court's review of "hornbook law" concerning the nonpatentability of "principles, laws of nature, mental processes, intellectual concepts, ideas, natural phenomena, mathematical formulae, methods of calculation, fundamental truths, original causes, motives, the Pythagorean theorem, and ... computer-implementable method claims ..." have any application to the *Bergy* and *Chakrabarty* appeals, which "do not involve an attempt to patent any of these things."[86]

On two final points, Judge Rich was not content to simply distinguish *Flook* from the cases before him, but felt the need to set the Supreme Court straight. First was the statement in *Flook*, relying on the authority of *Funk v. Kalo*, that a mathematical formula, like a law of nature, must be deemed to be "a familiar part of the prior art"—"even when it was not familiar, was not prior, was discovered by the applicant

---

[84] *Bergy* at 961.

[85] *Id.* Judge Rich characterized as "subversive nonsense" the Solicitor General's argument that the opening phrase, "Whoever invents or discovers ..." continues in effect the prior judicial standard of "invention" as a requirement of § 101. *Id.* at 963.

[86] *Id.* at 965.

for patent, was novel at the time he discovered it, and was useful."[87] Although insisting that "the foregoing novel principle has no applicability whatever" to the appeals before him, Judge Rich also warned that the Supreme Court's approach "gives to the term 'prior art,' which is a very important term of art in patent law, . . . an entirely new dimension with consequences of unforeseeable magnitude."[88] Second was Justice Stevens's concluding observation, relying on the authority of *Deepsouth Packing Co. v. Laitram Corp.*,[89] that the courts should proceed cautiously when "asked to extend patent rights into areas wholly unforeseen by Congress."[90] Peering behind the *Flook* opinion to the *Deepsouth* case, Judge Rich thought that what had made it appropriate for the Court in *Deepsouth* to await further guidance from Congress was that it was asked to overturn a long line of prior decisions. By contrast, Judge Rich observed that the *Bergy* and *Chakrabarty* cases raised an issue of first impression, which the courts could resolve on their own without awaiting any signal from Congress.[91] He returned to this theme at the end of the opinion, turning the charge of unauthorized lawmaking back on the PTO:

> Faced with the necessity of rendering a decision one way or the other on whether these inventions are encompassed by § 101, there being no prior decisions to guide us, we merely carry out our normal judicial function in deciding to say yes rather than no. . . . Rather, it seems to us, it is the PTO, not this court, that is attempting to legislate. It may have reasons for not wanting to examine the appealed claims for patentability under §§ 102 and 103, but if so, it has not revealed them . . . For whatever reason, it decided to reject, first on one ground and then on another, and then set out, lawyer-like, to devise unduly exaggerated justifications spiced with bits and pieces from wholly unrelated plant patent legislation from nearly half a century ago. . . . "We should not read into the patent laws limitations and conditions which the legislature has not expressed."[92]

---

87 *Id.* at 965–66 ("This gives to the term 'prior art,' which is a very important term of art in patent law, particularly in the application of § 103, an entirely new dimension with consequences of unforeseeable magnitude. . . . The potential for great harm to the incentives of the patent system is apparent.' ").

88 *Id.*

89 406 U.S. 518 (1972).

90 Parker v. Flook, 437 U.S. 584, 596 (1978).

91 596 F.2d at 966–67.

92 *Id.* at 987–88 (quoting from U.S. v. Dubilier Condenser Corp., 289 U.S. 178, 199 (1933)).

Judge Rich's opinion on remand offered substantially the same analysis as his original opinions for the CCPA in *Bergy* and *Chakrabarty*. But the decision on remand picked up an additional vote from Judge Baldwin, who had dissented the first time around in both cases.[93] He wrote a separate concurring opinion disagreeing with Judge Rich's conclusion that *Parker v. Flook* had no bearing on these appeals, and then offered a painstaking analysis of Supreme Court precedents that had excluded certain categories of subject matter from patent protection notwithstanding that they fell within "the dictionary definitions of process, manufacture or composition of matter:"

> The common thread throughout these cases is that claims which directly or indirectly preempt natural laws or phenomena are proscribed, whereas claims which merely utilize natural phenomena via explicitly recited manufactures, compositions of matter or processes to accomplish new and useful end results define statutory inventions.[94]

Because he concluded that the claims before the court "do not reach out to encompass natural phenomena . . . but rather recite only non-naturally occurring compositions of matter that are but single tools for utilizing natural phenomena in producing new and useful end results," he voted with the majority to reverse the rejections.[95] The sole remaining dissenter was Judge Miller, who chastised the majority for concentrating on "literal statements" in *Parker v. Flook* while ignoring the thrust of the Court's admonition to await a clear signal from Congress when there is a basis for substantial doubt as to its intent.[96]

Back to the Supreme Court

By this point the scientific and commercial significance of the controversy over patenting life was manifest. As concerns about the hazards of gene-splicing were subsiding among scientists,[97] researchers had successfully used recombinant DNA technology to clone medically

---

[93] 596 F.2d 952, 988 (Baldwin, J. concurring).

[94] *Id.*

[95] *Id.* at 997. Judge Baldwin also dismissed the argument that the decision would inevitably lead to the patenting of higher life forms with the prediction that inventors would find it too difficult to comply with the disclosure requirements of § 112 of the Patent Act for higher organisms. *Id.* at n.7.

[96] 596 F.2d 952, 999 (Miller, J., dissenting).

[97] After initially imposing stringent guidelines on the use of government funds in recombinant DNA research, 41 Fed. Reg. 27902 (Jul. 7, 1976), the National Institutes of Health relaxed the restrictions considerably 2 ½ years later after preliminary experience produced no evidence of illness or other harm. 43 Fed. Reg. 60080 (Dec. 22, 1978).

important genes in microorganisms.[98] New companies were forming to develop promising therapies out of these discoveries, raising capital from investors who hoped to earn a return on their investments.[99] Both private firms and universities engaged in biotechnology research looked to patents as a means of capturing the value of the new technology, and took note of the *Chakrabarty* and *Bergy* cases.

While the cases were before the CCPA on remand from the Supreme Court, the University of California, the American Patent Law Association, and Genentech filed amicus briefs on behalf of the patent applicants.[100] By the time the cases reached the Supreme Court again, these amici were joined by the New York Patent Law Association, the Pharmaceutical Manufacturers Association, the American Society for Microbiology, the American Society of Biological Chemists, the Association of American Medical Colleges, the American Council on Education, and the California Institute of Technology, as well as several eminent scientists, all arguing in favor of patent protection. Indeed, according to historian Daniel Kevles, by this point many people within the PTO favored patent protection for living organisms, including the new Commissioner, Donald Banner, who thought the CCPA decision was correct and was not inclined to seek Supreme Court review.[101] Others within the PTO favored taking the case to the Supreme Court in the hope of getting an affirmance that would give biotechnology investors greater assurance of the validity of their patents, while the Solicitor General of the United States favored reversal.[102] The government filed for *certiorari* in both cases, but after the petition was granted, the patent applicant in *Bergy* voluntarily canceled its claims to the purified microorganism, leading the Supreme Court to remand with instructions to dismiss *Bergy* as moot.[103] As a consequence (indeed, perhaps by design),[104] the Supreme Court was left

---

98 *See, e.g.*, K. Itakura et al., *Expression in* Escherichia coli *of a chemically synthesized gene for the hormone somatostatin*; 198 SCIENCE 1056–63 (1977); D. Goeddel et al., *Expression in* Escherichia coli *of chemically synthesized genes for human insulin*, 76 PROC. NATL. ACAD. SCI. 106–110 (1979); D. Goeddel et al., *Direct expression in* Escherichia coli *of a DNA sequence coding for human growth hormone*, 281 NATURE 544–48 (1979).

99 *See, e.g.*, R. Reinhold, *There's Gold in Them Thar Recombinant Genetic Bits*, N.Y. TIMES, June 22, 1980, sec. 4, p.8, col. 3; *Where genetic engineering will change industry*, BUS. WK., Oct. 22, 1979, at 160.

100 *In re* Bergy, 596 F.2d at 957.

101 Kevles, *supra* note 26, at 126.

102 *Id.* at 123, 126–27.

103 Diamond v. Chakrabarty, 444 U.S. 1028 (1980) (vacating judgment in *In re Bergy* and remanding with directions to dismiss as moot).

104 According to Professor Kevles, Bergy's lawyer believed that Chakrabarty had a stronger case, and thought it more likely that the Supreme Court would uphold the

to consider the patentability of life forms only in the more compelling context of the human-modified organism claimed in *Chakrabarty*.

If the PTO Commissioner was an ambivalent petitioner before the Supreme Court, the Petitioner's Brief did not betray it.[105] Characterizing the question presented as whether a living organism is patentable subject matter, the brief cited venerable Supreme Court precedent requiring that "the patent laws . . . be strictly construed in light of the basic national economic policy against monopoly, and in order to preserve to Congress decisions concerning extension of the patent laws into new areas."[106] According to the petitioner, "it was generally assumed by the legal profession, writers on the subject, and Congress" that living organisms are not patentable, and Congress had acted on that assumption in passing the Plant Patent Act in1930 and the Plant Variety Protection Act in 1970.[107] Congress, but not the courts, could adapt the terms of protection to suit the attributes of living subject matter, as it had done in those prior acts, and could decide what weight to attach to perceptions of ethical problems and public health risks associated with genetic engineering.[108] The brief made no mention of *Funk v. Kalo* or the products of nature doctrine.

Chakrabarty disputed that allowance of his claim would extend the patent laws into new areas,[109] counting over sixty issued U.S. patents claiming living subject matter and identifying official PTO classes and subclasses to deal with such patents.[110] Highlighting a passage from the legislative history of the Patent Act, Chakrabarty urged that a patentable manufacture "may include anything under the sun that is made by man,"[111] and went on to distinguish his engineered organism from the relatively unchanged living materials that had been denied patent protection in past judicial decisions. He concluded that "[i]f the Government

---

patentability of living subject matter if the only case before it were *Chakrabarty* than if it were deciding both cases together. Kevles, *supra* note 26, at 127.

[105] *See* Brief for Petitioner on Writ of Certiorari to the United States Court of Customs and Patent Appeals, Diamond v. Chakrabarty (filed Jan. 4, 1980) (available from Lexis–Nexis).

[106] *Id.*, text preceding note 9.

[107] *Id.*, text at note 9.

[108] *Id.*, text at notes 14–23.

[109] *See* Brief for Respondent On Writ of Certiorari to the United States Court of Customs and Patent Appeals, Diamond v. Chakrabarty (filed Jan. 29, 1980) (available from Lexis–Nexis).

[110] *Id.* text at notes 9–10.

[111] *Id.* at note 22 (quoting H.R. Rep. No. 1923, 82d Cong., 2d Sess. (1952), p.6; S. Rep. No. 1979 (1952), U.S. Code, Cong. and Admin. News, p. 2399).

wishes to reverse its policy, it should address its desires to the Congress, which can legislate an exclusion, if that is found to be required by the public interest."

Chakrabarty's numerous *amici*, including elite scientists, universities, and scientific societies, explained to the Court the sophisticated human intervention involved in the new biotechnology and argued that a *per se* rule excluding living things from patentability would discourage the commercial development of important scientific advances.[112] Some of the briefs urged that a distinction between living and nonliving subject matter was not only unprecedented as a matter of patent law, but unworkable and meaningless from a scientific perspective.[113]

Only one *amicus curiae* filed a brief in support of the government opposing patent protection for living subject matter on the merits—the Peoples Business Commission, a non-profit educational foundation formed by genetic engineering critic Jeremy Rifkin. That brief paradoxically echoed the arguments in favor of patent protection for living organisms, noting that such patents "would significantly contribute to the profit potential of the genetic industry, thus generating a greater momentum in research and development of genetic engineering technologies" leading to a "rapid proliferation of genetic techniques . . . in many other aspects of the nation's economic life."[114] Reading these arguments today, it takes some imagination to reconstruct the prevailing anxiety about genetic engineering that would lead the authors to expect these incentive effects to be counted as a reason to *exclude* living subject matter from patent protection.

The Supreme Court ultimately affirmed the CCPA by a 5–4 vote, revealing a significant shift in the balance of views on the Court since the 6–3 decision just two years earlier in *Parker v. Flook*. The *Chakrabarty* majority included Justice Stevens, who had authored the majority

---

112 The arguments advanced in the briefs are summarized in Kevles, *supra* note 26 at 127–31.

113 *See, e.g.*, Brief on Behalf of Dr. Leroy E. Hood, Dr. Thomas P. Maniatis, Dr. David S. Eisenberg, The American Society Of Biological Chemists, The Association Of American Medical Colleges, The California Institute of Technology, The American Council On Education As Amici Curiae at 12 (filed Jan. 26, 1980) (Westlaw Supreme Court Briefs file) ("There is no distinct line between life and non-life. The prevailing view among scientists is that the essential characteristic of 'living' subject matter is nothing more than its complexity."); Brief of Dr. George Pieczenik as Amicus Curiae at 3 (filed Jan. 29, 1980) (Westlaw Supreme Court Briefs file) ("The distinction between living and non-living matter has no real meaning in relation to this technology. . . . To attempt to separate patentable and unpatentable subject matter on the basis of such a concept is to invite confusion in the art, to ignore existing law and to ignore scientific reality.").

114 Brief on Behalf of the People's Business Commission, Amicus Curiae at 3 (filed Dec. 13, 1979) (Westlaw Supreme Court Briefs file).

opinion denying patent protection in *Flook*, and Justice Blackmun, who had joined in that opinion, as well as the three *Flook* dissenters, Justices Stewart and Rehnquist and Chief Justice Burger. Justice Stevens's opinion for the *Flook* majority and Chief Justice Burger's opinion for the *Chakrabarty* majority took strikingly different approaches to the proper construction of section 101 of the Patent Act. Whereas the *Flook* majority had insisted that the "plain language" of section 101 did not answer the question of what kind of "discoveries" the statute was enacted to protect,[115] the *Chakrabarty* majority rested heavily on the plain language of the statute, proclaiming that "courts 'should not read into the patent laws limitations and conditions which the legislature has not expressed.' "[116] The *Flook* majority had warned that "we must proceed cautiously when we are asked to extend patent rights into areas wholly unforeseen by Congress."[117] Two years later, the *Chakrabarty* majority balked at applying this principle to preclude patenting of living subject matter, quipping that "[a] rule that unanticipated inventions are without protection would conflict with the core concept of the patent law that anticipation undermines patentability" and insisting that "Congress employed broad general language in drafting § 101 precisely because such inventions are often unforeseeable."[118] Both opinions acknowledged that it was up to Congress, and not the courts, to set the boundaries of patent eligibility. But the *Flook* majority thought the PTO and the courts should await further clarification from Congress before allowing patent protection for computer-implemented inventions of the sort at issue in that case, while the *Chakrabarty* majority, believing that Congress had already broadly authorized patent protection for "anything under the sun that is made by man," thought that until Congress saw fit to amend the statute, "this Court must construe the language of § 101 as it is."[119]

---

115 Parker v. Flook, 437 U.S. at 588, 593.

116 Diamond v. Chakrabarty, 447 U.S. at 308.

117 437 U.S. at 596.

118 Diamond v. Chakrabarty, 447 U.S. at 315–16.

119 *Id.* at 318. One could reconcile the two decisions as a formal matter on the ground that in *Chakrabarty* the government was proposing a new limitation on patent eligibility (an exclusion for living subject matter) that had never previously been articulated in the case law, while in *Flook* it was relying upon a longstanding limitation (an exclusion for mathematical algorithms) that was well established in prior cases. If one imagines that Congress scrutinizes judicial opinions and enacts new legislation when it is unhappy with the directions of the case law, perhaps it makes sense for the Court to await guidance from Congress before creating a new judicial limitation (as it did in *Chakrabarty*), while retaining in effect time-honored judicial limitations that Congress has had plenty of time to correct (such as the limitation at issue in *Flook*). Indeed, perhaps this explains why Justice Stevens was willing to join the expansive majority opinion in *Chakrabarty*, although he had

The phrase "anything under the sun that is made by man" has been much quoted in subsequent judicial decisions as supporting an expansive interpretation of the scope of § 101.[120] But the expansive words "anything under the sun" are qualified by the restrictive condition "that is made by man." For the *Chakrabarty* majority, this restrictive condition captured the difference between Chakrabarty's microorganism and the kinds of discoveries that had previously been excluded from patent protection as "laws of nature, physical phenomena, and abstract ideas."[121] The Court saw the same distinction lurking in the legislative history of the Plant Patent Act:

> Congress ... recognized that the relevant distinction was not between living and inanimate things, but between products of nature, whether living or not, and human-made inventions.[122]

Although the government never argued that Chakrabarty's organism was a product of nature, Justice Burger nonetheless explained at some length why it was not, suggesting that the government's concession on this point made the outcome of the case a foregone conclusion. The very first sentence of the opinion characterized the issue before the court as "whether a live, *human-made* micro-organism is patentable subject matter under 35 U.S.C. § 101."[123] Later, the majority emphatically distinguished Chakrabarty's microorganism from the unpatentable discovery in *Funk v. Kalo:*

> There, the patentee had discovered that there existed in nature certain species of root-nodule bacteria which did not exert a mutually inhibitive effect on each other. He used that discovery to produce a mixed culture capable of inoculating the seeds of leguminous plants.... Here, by contrast, the patentee has produced a new bacterium with markedly different characteristics from any found in nature and one having the potential for significant utility. His discovery is not nature's handiwork, but his own; accordingly it is patentable subject matter under § 101.[124]

---

opposed patent protection for computer-implemented inventions just two years earlier when he authored the majority in Parker v. Flook and did so again one year later when he authored the dissent in Diamond v. Diehr.

[120] Diamond v. Diehr, 450 U.S. 175, 182 (1981); J.E.M. Ag Supply v. Pioneer Hi–Bred, 534 U.S. 124, 130 (2001); State St. Bank & Trust v. Signature Financial Group, 149 F.3d 1368, 1373 (Fed. Cir. 1998), *cert. denied*, 525 U.S. 1093 (1999).

[121] Diamond v. Chakrabarty, 447 U.S. at 309.

[122] *Id.* at 313.

[123] *Id.* at 305 (emphasis added).

[124] *Id.* at 310.

In other words, once it was conceded that the microorganism was not a product of nature, the invention had passed the test of § 101.

Beyond Chakrabarty

Although the Supreme Court recognized in *Chakrabarty*, as it had in prior decisions, that Congress has the authority to set the rules for determining what may be patented, *Chakrabarty* nonetheless seemed to represent a shift in the default rules that apply in the face of Congressional inaction.[125] Whereas *Flook*, by denying protection, had placed the burden of inertia on those who seek protection for new fields of technology to approach Congress, *Chakrabarty*, by granting protection, placed the burden of inertia on those who opposed it. This shift has had a number of important consequences.

First, it immediately stemmed the flow of cases involving the scope of § 101 into the courts. The decision in *Chakrabarty* signaled to the PTO that the Supreme Court was unlikely to back them up in future disputes with the CCPA (and, later, the Federal Circuit) over interpretation of the scope of patent eligible subject matter. The PTO promptly became less skeptical about the patent eligibility of new categories subject matter, holding, for example, that plants[126] and animals[127] were eligible for protection under § 101 and thereby avoiding the occasion for judicial review of the soundness of its § 101 rejections. When the PTO rejects patent claims, applicants may appeal their decisions immediately, but when the PTO allows claims, the courts have no occasion to consider the correctness of the allowances until an infringement defendant challenges the validity of an issued patent. A defendant may avoid infringement liability by proving that a patent is invalid by clear and convincing evidence,[128] and occasionally defendants have argued that an issued patent is invalid under § 101.[129] But because infringement defendants are typically commercial competitors of the plaintiffs who hold patents of

---

[125] The Supreme Court had once before authorized protection, over a vigorous dissent, for subject matter that Congress had thus far declined to protect in the case of *International News Service v. Associated Press*, 248 U.S. 215 (1918), affirming a lower court remedy for common law "misappropriation" of news stories that the parties conceded could not be protected under federal copyright law.

[126] *In re* Hibberd, 227 U.S.P.Q. (BNA) 443 (Bd. Pat. App. & Int.1985) (reversing examiner's rejection for lack of eligible subject matter of patent claims to seeds and plants in reliance on Diamond v. Chakrabarty).

[127] *Ex parte* Allen, 2 U.S.P.Q.2d (BNA) 1425 (Bd. Pat. App. & Int. 1987) (reversing examiner's rejection for lack of eligible subject matter of patent claims to oysters).

[128] *See* Cardinal Chemical Co. v. Morton Int'l, Inc., 508 U.S. 83 (1993).

[129] *E.g.,* State St. Bank & Trust v. Signature Financial Group, 149 F.3d 1368, 1373 (Fed. Cir. 1998), *cert. denied*, 525 U.S. 1093 (1999); J.E.M. Ag Supply v. Pioneer Hi–Bred, 534 U.S. 124, 130 (2001).

their own on similar subject matter, they are more likely to challenge the patents on grounds that are specific to the particular patents in suit (such as anticipation or obviousness in light of the prior art) rather than on broader grounds (such as lack of patentable subject matter) that might categorically invalidate the patents that they own along with the patents that they are charged with infringing. Even when infringement defendants are willing to challenge the patent eligibility of an invention, the issue is unlikely to come before the courts in this context until years after the patent was first issued. Meanwhile, as the PTO continues to issue patents in a field, the expectation interest of firms in the continuing availability of patents for their inventions grows, making it harder for courts to upset those interests by announcing a categorical exclusion from patent eligibility.

Second, although the Court purported to address only a narrow issue of statutory interpretation concerning whether Chakrabarty's microorganism was eligible for patent protection, it ultimately embraced a very broad rule of patentability for "everything under the sun that is made by man," leaving little room to distinguish *Chakrabarty* in subsequent cases. For this reason, *Chakrabarty* has become a standard citation for the patentability of subject matter ranging from computer-implemented algorithms[130] and business methods[131] to plants.[132] Those who believe the patent system should exclude any categories of human innovation from its reach have little hope of prevailing in the courts, even if they get sued for patent infringement,[133] but must make their case before Congress. The result has been a stunning expansion in the kinds of innovations that are brought before the PTO, including new sports moves, games, cooking recipes, and even the technology of legal practice.[134]

Third, the burden of persuading Congress to change the patent laws has proven to be a heavy one, especially in industries where patent holders have a strong interest in maintaining the status quo and are thus well motivated to outmaneuver and outspend their anti-patent adversaries. For example, although religious groups and others opposed

---

130 AT & T v. Excel Communications, 172 F.3d 1352, 1355 (Fed. Cir.), *cert. denied*, 528 U.S. 946 (1999).

131 State St. Bank & Trust v. Signature Financial Group, 149 F.3d 1368, 1373 (Fed. Cir. 1998), *cert. denied*, 525 U.S. 1093 (1999).

132 J.E.M. Ag Supply v. Pioneer Hi–Bred, 534 U.S. 124, 130 (2001).

133 Those who wish to challenge the issuance of patents that they are not infringing face the additional burden of persuading the courts that they have standing to litigate the issue. *See, e.g.*, Animal Legal Defense Fund v. Quigg, 932 F.2d 920 (Fed. Cir. 1991) (dismissing challenge to issuance of patents on animals for lack of standing).

134 Recent examples may be found in Robert P. Merges & John F. Duffy, Patent Law & Policy: Cases and Materials at 206–08 (3d ed. 2002).

to the patenting of animals as a matter of principle were able to get some members of Congress to hold hearings on the topic,[135] they ultimately failed to get any legislation passed. Opposition to patents on DNA sequences has followed a similar course in the legislative arena.[136]

In 1980, the Supreme Court assumed that Congress was "free to amend § 101 so as to exclude from patent protection organisms produced by genetic engineering" or "to craft a statute specifically designed for such living things."[137] Even at the time, such legislative action may have been improbable.[138] Twenty-five years later, the only special rules that Congress has enacted for biotechnology patents have been provisions that the biotechnology industry has favored.[139]

Conclusion

The decision of the Supreme Court in *Diamond v. Chakrabarty* was a watershed moment not just for the biotechnology industry, but also for

---

135 *E.g.*, Patents and the Constitution: Transgenic Animals: Hearings Before the Subcomm. on Courts, Civil Liberties and the Administration of Justice of the House Comm. on the Judiciary, 100th Cong., 1st Sess. (1987).

136 *E.g.*, Gene Patents and Other Genomic Inventions: Hearing Before the Subcomm. on Courts and Intell. Prop. of the House Comm. on the Judiciary, 106th Cong. (2000).

On the other hand, the American Medical Association effectively lobbied Congress for relief from remedies for infringement of patents on medical and surgical methods. P.L. No. 104–208, Div. A, Title I, § 101(a), codified at 35 U.S.C. § 287(c). For an account of the legislative process by which this provision was enacted, see Chris J. Katopis, *Patients v. Patents?: Policy Implications of Recent Patent Legislation*, 71 St. John's L. Rev. 329, 331–38 (1997).

More recently, following the decision of the Federal Circuit to allow patents on business methods in *State St. Bank*, Congress passed legislation protecting prior users of subsequently patented business methods from infringement liability. P.L. No. 106–113, Div. B, § 1000(a)(9), 113 Stat. 1536, codified at 35 U.S.C. § 273.

Neither of these legislative initiatives altered the range of subject matter eligible for patent protection under § 101.

137 Diamond v. Chakrabarty, 447 U.S. at 318.

138 Today, it might well place the U.S. in violation of its treaty obligations. The GATT–TRIPS agreement, to which the U.S. acceded in 1995, prohibits members from discriminating in the provision of patent protection on the basis of field of technology. In fact, although the U.S. patent system generally applies a unitary set of rules to inventions in all fields, the Patent Act has some field-specific provisions, some of which Congress has enacted since the TRIPS agreement took effect.

139 *See, e.g.*, 35 U.S.C. § 103(b) (permitting the patenting of a biotechnological process using or resulting in a composition of matter that is novel and nonobvious, notwithstanding that the process might not otherwise be deemed nonobvious). *See also*, 35 U.S.C. § 271(g) (defining as patent infringement the importation into the U.S. of a product made abroad by a U.S.-patented process, a change in the law favored by the biotechnology industry).

the ongoing struggle between champions of an expansive patent system on the CCPA and the skeptics on the Supreme Court. As predicted by both proponents and opponents of patents on living organisms, investment in biotechnology R & D has flourished in the wake of *Diamond v. Chakrabarty*. But the full consequences of the expansive approach to patent eligibility endorsed by the *Chakrabarty* majority continue to be felt far beyond the biotechnology industry. Five years after the departure from the Supreme Court of Justice Douglas, the *Chakrabarty* decision marked the beginning of the end of the Court's skeptical period. Thereafter, it would be up to the CCPA and the Federal Circuit, absent explicit restrictions from Congress, to decide just how expansive the subject matter boundaries of the patent system are. By the time of Judge Rich's death nearly twenty years later, the Federal Circuit had not only refrained from adopting new judge-made limitations on patent eligibility, but had retreated from limitations announced in prior caselaw.[140] The Supreme Court has not seen fit to reverse, and Congress has not seen fit to intervene. A quarter century ago it was unclear whether the subject matter boundaries of the patent system were expansive enough to embrace biotechnology and information technology. Today, it is not clear whether the patent system has any subject matter boundaries at all.

---

[140] *E.g., In re* Lowry, 32 F.3d 1579 (Fed. Cir. 1994) (overturning "printed matter" rejection); State St. Bank & Trust v. Signature Financial Group, 149 F.3d 1368 (Fed. Cir. 1998), *cert. denied*, 525 U.S. 1093 (1999) (reversing holding of invalidity based on exclusions for mathematical algorithms and business methods); AT & T v. Excel Communications, 172 F.3d 1352 (Fed. Cir.), *cert. denied*, 528 U.S. 946 (1999) (reversing holding of invalidity based on exclusions of mathematical algorithms and intangible processes).

The Story of *Sony v. Universal Studios*: Mary Poppins Meets the Boston Strangler

Jessica Litman*

Respondents argue that an abstract theoretician's view of the copyright monopoly allows them to control the way William Griffiths watches television. In the name of that abstract vision, they ask the federal courts to establish a bureaucracy more complex than anything Congress has established in the field of copyright to date, in order that they may levy an excise tax on a burgeoning new industry.

- *First draft of Justice John Paul Stevens's dissenting opinion in Sony v. Universal Studios*[1]

Sony v. Universal Studios[2] may be the most famous of all copyright cases. People who know nothing about copyright know that the *Sony-Betamax* case held that home videotaping of television programs is fair use. Paradoxically, although the Supreme Court granted certiorari in the case to decide whether the copyright law permitted consumers to engage in private home copying of television programs, the majority ended up crafting its analysis to avoid answering that question definitively. Instead, it ruled that even if consumers sometimes violated the copyright law when they taped television programs off the air, that violation did not make the manufacturer and seller of the copying equipment they used liable for copyright infringement. That was so, the Court ruled, because some of the time, home videotaping was authorized by the programs' copyright owners, and some of the time, home videotaping qualified as fair use. Since videotape recorders could be used for legitimate as well as infringing copying, making and selling the devices did not subject the Sony Corporation to liability.

---

* I'm grateful to Jon Weinberg, Cory Streisinger and Fred Von Lohmann, whose comments greatly improved this chapter, and to Chris Bloodworth and Georgia Clark of the Wayne State University Law Library, who helped me to get my hands on copies of several obscure documents.

[1] Justice John Paul Stevens, first draft, Memorandum in *Sony v. Universal Studios*, No. 81–1687 (circulated June 13, 1983), at 22.

[2] Sony Corp. of America v. Universal City Studios, Inc., 464 U.S. 417 (1984).

When the Justices initially met to discuss the case, only one of them was persuaded that consumer home videotaping was permissible under the Copyright Act. Justice Stevens argued that Congress had never intended to regulate a consumer's making a single, noncommercial copy. What became the majority opinion in *Sony* evolved as an effort by Justice Stevens to recruit four additional votes to a decision in Sony's favor.

Background

In the fall of 1975, when the first Sony Betamax appeared in stores, the American public had already become used to personal copying technology. The photocopy machine, invented in 1937 and sold commercially since 1950, was a common piece of equipment in business offices and libraries.[3] Copyshops had sprung up in the mid-1960s. Consumer audiocassette recorders, first marketed in 1963, had become ubiquitous. The telephone answering machine, introduced by Phonemate in 1971, had become increasingly familiar, and telefacsimile machines were making inroads in the U.S. market. Before the Sony Betamax, several manufacturers had introduced consumer home video devices, but all of them had flopped.[4]

A number of U.S. companies expected that the next big thing would be laser disc video playback-only devices. MCA, owner of Universal Studios, had invested heavily in a format it called DiscoVision. RCA (then-owner of NBC) was working on its own laser disc system, named SelectaVision. Magnavox was trying to perfect Magnavision. None of these systems was ready for the market, and none of them was compatible with the others. The appearance of a home video tape recorder threatened the potential market for laser disc devices: would consumers purchase playback-only machines if they could instead buy machines that could both play and record?

The first Betamax introduced in the U.S. was a combination television-video tape recorder that cost more than two thousand dollars. Several months later, Sony introduced the Betamax SL–7300, a stand-alone video tape recorder with a list price of $1300 (about $4400 in today's dollars). By the time of trial, the price of a Sony Betamax had dropped to $875, equivalent to about $2500 in 2005 dollars. Notwith-

---

[3] In *Williams & Wilkins Co. v. U.S.*, 487 F.2d 1345 (Ct.Cl.1973), *aff'd by an equally divided Court*, 420 U.S. 376 (1975), medical publishers sued the National Library of Medicine for massive photocopying of medical journal articles for the benefit of medical researchers. Justice Blackmun recused himself from the case because of his earlier relationship with the Mayo Clinic, and the remaining Justices divided 4 to 4 on whether the photocopying was fair use or copyright infringement.

[4] *See* James Lardner, Fast Forward 60–81 (2002); Nick Lyons, The Sony Vision 202–15 (1976).

standing the steep price, people bought it. Sony supported its product launch with a series of commercials and print ads touting the opportunity to watch two shows that were being broadcast at the same time. "We've all been in the situation where there are two TV programs on opposite each other and we'd give any thing to be able to see both of them. Well now you *can* see both of them," began one ad.[5] "Sony Betamax videocassette recorder, destined to be a superstar in your home entertainment scene: even if you're not there, it records TV programs you don't want to miss, builds a priceless videotape library in no time," claimed another.[6]

Journalist James Lardner, the author of *Fast Forward*, the definitive book on the history of the *Sony* case, begins his book with the story of an ad that Sony's ad agency conceived and sent to Universal Studios for its approval. "Now you don't have to miss Kojak because you're watching Columbo (or vice versa)." *Kojak* and *Columbo* were two of Universal's most popular shows, and the ad agency figured that the studio would be delighted that American audiences would be able to watch both of them. Sidney Sheinberg, the president of Universal, wasn't delighted. Indeed, Lardner reports, Sheinberg believed such a device usurped movie studio prerogatives; he didn't think that a home video tape recorder should be marketed at all. He consulted Universal's lawyers, who agreed that marketing a device that copied television programs seemed to violate Universal's exclusive right to reproduce its works under section 106(1) of the 1976 Copyright Act. In a meeting the following week between Sheinberg and Akio Morita, the chairman of Sony, to discuss the possibility that Sony would manufacture DiscoVision players for MCA, Sheinberg insisted that Sony withdraw the Betamax from the market or face a copyright infringement suit.

Universal's lawyers sent a private investigator to consumer electronics stores to pose as a customer and catch sales clerks making recordings of Universal programs. Meanwhile, they recruited one of their other clients, William Griffiths, to be a nominal individual defendant. They were concerned that a court might refuse to impose liability on Sony unless they were able to show that a Betamax owner had used the device to make infringing copies. Griffiths owned a Betamax. Universal's lawyers asked him to agree to be sued; Universal would promise, they explained, to seek no damages from him in the event it prevailed in the lawsuit. Meanwhile, Universal spoke with other studios in search of co-plaintiffs. Disney agreed to join the suit. Warner Brothers didn't want to be a named plaintiff, but was willing to contribute money towards legal costs.

---

[5] Sony Betamax display ad, N.Y. TIMES, Nov. 5, 1975, at 19.

[6] Macy's Sony Betamax display ad, N.Y. TIMES, March 30, 1976, at 13.

Display Ad 44 -- No Title
New York Times (1857-Current file); Mar 30, 1976; ProQuest Historical Newspapers The New York Times
pg. 13

Announcing: a new TV recording star!

SONY

Sony Betamax videocassette recorder, destined to be a superstar in your home entertainment scene: even if you're not there, it records TV programs you don't want to miss, builds a priceless videotape library in no time, $1300.

If you've ever felt you'd give a million to see one of those glorious old Sid Caesar *Show of Shows* routines again. . . If you've ever longed to have the incomparable Lord Olivier tear you apart just once more with his senior Tyrone in *Long Day's Journey*. . . If you've ever ached to see or re-see any of the marvelous moments television has given us over the last 20 years, then you know the Sony Betamax could be the best home entertainment investment you ever made.

Using it is easy. You don't need a speck of electronic know-how. Just plug the Betamax into your TV set (it works with both color and black-and-white). Snap a cassette into the tape deck. Pick the channel you want, and press "record." That's it. The Betamax records a full hour or any part of an hour. Then it's yours for good. To see on your TV set for free. Any time you want to study Connors' backhand or remind yourself that Ella and Ellington combine into a sound that's pure heaven.

It turns your living room into a private projection room. But there's more to Betamax than just record and play. Listen to this: It records at your command, whether you're there or not. Just set the Clock Watcher. It's a digital timer that automatically turns on both your set and the Betamax system to the program you've pre-selected, then turns it off. Your program then awaits you and your next leisure hour. (If you don't like the program, you erase it just as you erase sound tapes—by re-recording right over it.)

Think of the National Conventions coming up. Think of the great classic World Series games you can record. Think of having your very own permanent tapes of Nureyev or Streisand or Shirley MacLaine. Or (ah, bliss!) W. C. Fields. You may never want to go out to a movie again. So what in the world are you waiting for? Come check the Betamax out. It could make life a lot more fun.

We regret, no mail or phone. Add 3.50 delivery charge. TV Center (Dept. 223) Fifth Floor, Macy's Herald Square. Also at Queens, Kings Plaza, Roosevelt Field, Huntington, White Plains, Bay Shore, New Rochelle, Parkchester, Smith Haven, Massapequa, and Staten Island.

On November 11, 1976, Universal and Disney filed suit against the Sony Corporation, Sony's American subsidiary, Sony's advertising agency, five dealers in consumer electronics, and Mr. Griffiths. Griffiths would later testify that he had purchased his Betamax planning to create a library of taped TV shows, but that the expense of blank tapes had persuaded him that it made more sense to watch taped programs and then tape over them.

Sony in the Lower Courts

The trial began in January of 1979 and lasted for five weeks. The studios presented evidence tending to show that consumers were recording programs to keep in their video libraries. When *Gone with the Wind* was broadcast, one witness testified, stores across the U.S. sold out of blank videocassettes. The chairman of Walt Disney testified that the company had declined lucrative contracts to broadcast *Mary Poppins* and *The Jungle Book* on television because they feared that consumers might tape the movies. Sony's lawyer countered with evidence demonstrating that some copyright owners had no objection to home taping. The studios sought, unsuccessfully, to present evidence that Sony could have redesigned the Betamax by installing a jammer to prevent recording unless the copyright holder assented, at a cost of about $15 per machine.[7]

Judge Ferguson's opinion, handed down on October 2, absolved Sony of liability. The copyright law, Judge Ferguson held, did not give copyright holders "a monopoly over an individual's off-the-air copying in his home for private non-commercial use."[8] First, the court concluded, Congress could not have meant the courts to interpret absolutely literally the statutory language giving copyright owners the exclusive right to reproduce their works. Although legislative history accompanying the addition of sound recordings to the list of works entitled to copyright demonstrated that Congress had not intended to prohibit non-commercial home audio-taping, the statute contained no language expressly exempting it. By the same token, the judge concluded, Congress had not intended to give copyright owners the right to prohibit home video recording. "Congress did not find that protection of copyright holders' rights over reproduction of their works was worth the privacy and enforcement problems which restraint of home-use recording would create."[9] Even if home video recording were deemed an infringement of copyright, it was sheltered by the fair use privilege. Most consumers, the

---

[7] *See* Lardner, *supra* note 4, at 97–106.

[8] Universal City Studios v. Sony, 480 F. Supp. 429, 432 (C.D. Cal. 1979), *rev'd*, 659 F.2d 963 (9th Cir. 1981), *rev'd*, 464 U.S. 417 (1984).

[9] *Id.* at 446.

judge found, used their videotape recorders to "time-shift" programming—to tape a show in order to watch it at a more convenient time and then record over the tape.

> Betamax owners use plaintiffs' works noncommercially and privately. This use increases the owners' access to material voluntarily broadcast to them free of charge over public airwaves. Because the use occurs within private homes, enforcement of a prohibition would be highly intrusive and practically impossible. Such intrusion is particularly unwarranted when plaintiffs themselves choose to beam their programs into these homes.[10]

Further, even if the Copyright Act prohibited home copying, the defendants should not be liable for the copies made by consumers. Judge Ferguson drew an analogy from patent law, where manufacturers of staple articles of commerce were not held liable for infringement merely because they supplied devices that could be used in infringing ways.[11] Video tape recorders, like audio tape recorders, cameras, typewriters, and photocopy machines, were staple articles of commerce with infringing as well as noninfringing uses. Expanding the boundaries of liability to extend to manufacturers of staple articles would put an intolerable burden on commerce.[12] Judge Ferguson noted more than once that plaintiffs conceded that they had not yet suffered harm from the Betamax, and that they had failed to show that they would likely suffer harm in the future.

> The new technology of videotape recording does bring uncertainty and change which, quite naturally, induce fear. History, however, shows that this fear may be misplaced.... Television production by plaintiffs today is more profitable than it has ever been, and, in five weeks of trial, there was no concrete evidence to suggest that the Betamax will change the studios' financial picture.[13]

Universal appealed to the Ninth Circuit, and a unanimous panel reversed.[14] The court rejected Judge Ferguson's conclusion that Congress might have meant to protect consumers from liability for home taping but had failed to say so explicitly.

---

[10] *Id.* at 454.

[11] *See* 35 U.S.C. § 271(c) ("staple article or commodity of commerce suitable for substantial noninfringing use").

[12] 480 F. Supp. at 461.

[13] *Id.* at 469.

[14] Universal City Studios v. Sony, 659 F.2d 963 (9th Cir. 1981), *rev'd*, 464 U.S. 417 (1984).

> The statutory framework is unambiguous; the grant of exclusive rights is only limited by the statutory exceptions. Elementary principles of statutory construction would indicate that the judiciary should not disturb this carefully constructed statutory scheme in the absence of compelling reasons to do so. That is, we should not, absent a clear direction from Congress, disrupt this framework by carving out exceptions to the broad grant of rights apart from those in the statute itself.[15]

The court held that consumers who copied television programs off the air for private noncommercial use infringed the copyrights in those programs, and that Sony, its U.S. subsidiary, its advertising agency, and the retail store defendants were liable as contributory infringers. Judge Kilkenny's opinion dismissed the lower court's staple article of commerce theory as "inappropriate."[16] Videotape recorders were not staple articles because they were not suitable for noninfringing use:

> Appellees' analogy of videotape records to cameras or photocopying machines may have substantial benefit for some purposes, but does not even remotely raise copyright problems. Videotape recorders are manufactured, advertised, and sold for the primary purpose of reproducing television programming. Virtually all television programming is copyrighted material. Therefore, videotape recorders are not "suitable for substantial noninfringing use." That some copyright owners choose, for one reason or another, not to enforce their rights does not preclude those who legitimately choose to do so from protecting theirs.[17]

The Ninth Circuit remanded the case to the district court to fashion a suitable remedy, noting:

> The relief question is exceedingly complex, and the difficulty in fashioning relief may well have influenced the district court's evaluation of the liability issue. The difficulty of fashioning relief cannot, however, dissuade the federal courts from affording appropriate relief to those whose rights have been infringed. . . .
>
> In fashioning relief, the district court should not be overly concerned with the prospective harm to appellees. A defendant has no right to expect a return on investment from activities which violate the copyright laws. Once a determination has been made that an infringement is involved, the continued profitability of appellees' businesses is of secondary concern.

[15] *Id.* at 966.

[16] *Id.* at 975.

[17] *Id.* (citation omitted).

The following day, members of Congress introduced legislation in both the House and the Senate to legalize home video recording.[18] Other legislators weighed in with variant bills, and on April 12, 1982, the House Committee on the Judiciary held a special hearing in Los Angeles to consider the six different bills before it. The motion picture industry's chief lobbyist, Jack Valenti, was the first witness. He appeared armed with a 49 page legal memorandum authored by Harvard law professor Larry Tribe, which argued that any law that exempted home videotaping from liability for copyright infringement would be an unconstitutional taking of private property in violation of the Fifth Amendment.[19] Moreover, the memo continued, such an exemption would "endanger, and might indeed impermissibly abridge, First Amendment rights" because "motion picture and television producers will speak less often if the reward for their efforts is greatly reduced."[20] Valenti's testimony was nothing if not colorful:

> Now, we cannot live in a marketplace, Mr. Chairman—you simply cannot live in a marketplace, where there is one unleashed animal in that marketplace, unlicensed. It would no longer be a marketplace; it would be a kind of a jungle, where this one unlicensed instrument is capable of devouring all that people had invested in and labored over and brought forth as a film or a television program, and, in short, laying waste to the orderly distribution of this product. . . . .I say to you that the VCR is to the American film producer and the American public as the Boston strangler is to the woman home alone.[21]

By the spring of 1982, when the House convened its Los Angeles hearings, more than three million people had purchased home video cassette recorders, and videotape rental stores had sprung up across the U.S. The motion picture industry emphasized that studios did "not intend to file any actions against homeowners now or in the future."[22]

---

18 H.R. 4783, 97th Cong. (1981); H.R. 4794, 97th Cong. (1981); S. 1758, 97th Cong. (1981). *See Home Recording of Copyrighted Works: Hearings on H.R. 4783, H.R. 4794 H.R. 4808, H.R. 5250, H.R. 5488, and H.R. 5705 before The Subcomm. on Courts, Civil Liberties, and The Administration Of Justice of the House Comm. on the Judiciary*, 97th Cong. 1–3 (1982) (opening statement of Rep. Kastenmeier).

19 Laurence H. Tribe, *Memorandum of Constitutional Law on Copyright Compensation Issues Raised by the Proposed Congressional Reversal of the Ninth Circuit's Betamax Ruling* (Dec. 5, 1981), *reprinted in Copyright Infringements (Audio and Video Recorders): Hearings on S. 1758 Before the Senate Comm. on the Judiciary*, 97th Cong. 78 (1982). *See also Home Recording of Copyrighted Works*, *supra* note 18, at 4–16, 67–115 (testimony of Jack Valenti, MPAA).

20 Tribe, *supra* note 19, at 126.

21 *Home Recording of Copyrighted Works*, *supra* note 18.

22 *See id.* (testimony of Jack Valenti, MPAA).

Indeed, the industry had thought better of its demand that video tape recorders be outlawed. Instead, motion picture studios had agreed to support a bill that subjected video recorders to a compulsory license, levied royalties on the sale of video tape recorders and blank cassettes, and required copyright owners' permission for rental or lease of videotapes.[23] The recording industry began to lobby to expand the legislation to impose like royalties on the sales of audio tape recorders and blank audiotapes.[24] The House and Senate held more hearings. Video recorder dealers organized grass roots opposition to the legislation. On June 14, 1982, the Supreme Court agreed to hear the *Sony* case, and members of Congress sat back to wait and see what the Court would do.

Sony in the Supreme Court

By the day of oral argument, more than five million consumers had purchased Betamax videocassette recorders. Dean Dunlavey, counsel for Sony, began his argument by noting that the studios had not yet sought a remedy against any of the five million Betamax owners, but that the decision below put all of them at risk for an award of statutory damages for each of the programs they recorded at home for their own private viewing. The gist of Dunlavey's argument was that the majority of copyright owners had no objection to consumer home videotaping, and it would make no sense to let a small minority use copyright litigation to force a useful and popular device with significant legitimate uses from the market.

Stephen Kroft, arguing on behalf of the studios, assured the Justices that affirming the Ninth Circuit's decision did not mean that the Betamax would be banned. As he had urged in his brief, the Court could instead impose a royalty on the sale of Betamax recorders. Several Justices asked Kroft to speak to the staple article of commerce doctrine applied by the trial court. Kroft vigorously disputed that the staple article of commerce doctrine was appropriate. The doctrine arose in patent law, which, he said, was unlike copyright law. In any event, he insisted, the Betamax wouldn't qualify as a staple article of commerce because it was not suitable for any legitimate uses—it was designed and marketed to make unauthorized copies of entire television programs without compensation to the copyright owner. Kroft suggested that the Court instead apply a standard it had articulated the previous term in a trademark case. In *Inwood Laboratories v. Ives Laboratories*, a case involving the copying of drug capsule colors, Kroft claimed, the Court had remarked that selling a product with the implication that it could be used to infringe a trademark might give rise to liability for contributory

---

[23] *See* H.R. 5488, 97th Cong. (1982); S. Amdt. 1242 to S. 1758, 97th Cong. (1981).

[24] *See* H.R. 5705, 97th Cong. (1982); S. Amdt. 1333 to S. 1758, 97th Cong. (1982).

trademark infringement. Kroft argued that the same standard should apply in copyright cases. Justice Stevens then asked Kroft to address fair use. Kroft denied that the fair use doctrine would apply to home videotaping. When pressed on the issue of harm, Kroft complained that the district court had misallocated the burden of proof, wrongly expecting plaintiffs to prove harm rather than requiring defendants to disprove it. [25]

The papers of Supreme Court Justice Harry A Blackmun indicate that when the Justices met in conference to discuss the case, three days after oral argument, a majority of them were disposed to affirm the Ninth Circuit opinion, at least in part.[26] Justices Blackmun, Marshall and Rehnquist were comfortable with the conclusion that consumer home videotaping taping was illegal infringement, and voted to affirm. Justice Powell felt that home use should be deemed fair use, but saw no way to draw a workable distinction between fair and infringing uses, and he, too, voted to affirm. Justice O'Connor was also disposed to affirm: if she were a legislator, she said, she would vote to exempt home use, but Congress had not done so in the 1976 Copyright Act.[27] Justices Brennan, White and Burger argued that time-shifting was fair use, but building a videotape library was infringement.[28] They were inclined to remand for additional fact-finding on the issue of Sony's liability, given that the Betamax was used for both infringing and non-infringing purposes. Only

---

[25] Transcript of Oral Argument, *Sony* (No. 81–1687), Jan. 18, 1983, *available at* 1983 U.S. TRANS LEXIS 89 (citing Inwood Labs. v. Ives Labs., 456 U.S. 844, 851 (1982)). *Inwood Labs* involved an appeal from a lower court decision finding contributory trademark infringement; the Court reversed the judgment on an unrelated ground. Kroft's reading of the *Inwood* opinion was something of a stretch. The passage Kroft cited merely repeated the standard applied by the lower court. Elsewhere in the opinion, the Court had insisted that contributory trademark infringement required proof defendant intentionally induced infringement or continued to supply its products to retailers knowing that the retailers were using them to infringe trademarks.

[26] The Library of Congress Manuscript Reading Room houses the Supreme Court papers of Justices Harry A. Blackmun, William J. Brennan, and Thurgood Marshall, Jr. Those papers include handwritten and dictated notes, drafts of opinions, memoranda from law clerks and letters and memoranda sent by the Justices to one another. For a different, detailed analysis of the genesis of the *Sony* opinions drawn from the papers of Justice Thurgood Marshall, see Jonathan Band & Andrew J. McLaughlin, *The Marshall Papers: A Peek Behind the Scenes at the Making of Sony v. Universal*, 17 COLUM.-VLA J.L. & ARTS 427 (1994).

[27] Handwritten Notes of Justice Harry A. Blackmun, (Jan. 21, 1983).

[28] *Id. See also* undated file memo in the papers of Justice William A. Brennan. The memo appears to have been written or dictated between the January 18, 1983 oral argument and the January 21, 1983 conference. In it, Justice Brennan expresses his view that time-shifting is fair use but library building is not, that Sony might well be liable for statutory damages or profits as a contributory infringer, and that a flat ban on the sale of Betamaxes would be improper.

Justice Stevens insisted that the copyright statute did not prohibit consumers from making single copies of copyrighted works for their own private use.[29] Since consumers' use of the Betamax did not infringe plaintiffs' copyrights, Stevens argued, Sony could not be held liable as a contributory infringer.

As the senior Justice voting with the majority to affirm the Ninth Circuit decision, Justice Thurgood Marshall assigned the majority opinion to Harry Blackmun. Justice Stevens announced that he would be writing a dissent. He sent a note to Justice Blackmun, with copies to the other seven Justices, arguing that the copyright law permitted the making of a single copy for private noncommercial use. A review of the 1976 Copyright Act's legislative history, he urged, indicated that Congress never directly confronted the issue of private copying, but a variety of sources documented a widely-shared understanding that it was not illegal for individuals to make single copies for their own use. Moreover, the fact that the statute entitled copyright owners to seek statutory damages even from innocent infringers potentially subjected both consumers and the manufacturers of copying equipment to "truly staggering liability."[30] Justice Powell responded in a memo to Blackmun indicating that, while he had voted with Blackmun initially, Stevens's "single copy" argument was giving him pause, and he would wait to read drafts of the majority and dissenting opinions before deciding.[31]

On June 13, Justice Blackmun circulated the first draft of his opinion for the Court. The draft began with a rejection of Stevens's argument that a single copy made for noncommercial purposes did not infringe: "Although the word 'copies' appears in the plural in § 106(1), it is clear that the making of even a single unauthorized copy is prohibited."[32] Examining the 1976 Act, Blackmun listed a variety of detailed

---

[29] *See* Memorandum to the File from Justice John Paul Stevens (Jan. 20, 1983).

[30] Letter from Justice John Paul Stevens to Justice Harry A. Blackmun (Jan. 24, 1983).

[31] Letter from Justice Lewis F. Powell to Justice Harry A. Blackmun (Feb. 3, 1983).

[32] 1st Draft, Opinion in *Sony* (No. 81–1687) (circulated by Justice Blackmun, June 13, 1983), at 7. Justice Blackmun quoted House and Senate Report statements that the reproduction right "means the right to produce a material object in which the work is duplicated, transcribed, imitated, or simulated in a fixed form from which it can be 'perceived, reproduced or otherwise communicated, either directly or with the aid of a machine or device.' " *Id.* at 8 (quoting S. Rep. No. 94–473, at 58 (1975); H.R. Rep. No. 94–1476 at 61 (1976)).

> The making of even a single videotape recording at home falls within this definition; the VTR user produces a material object from which the copyrighted work later can be perceived. Unless Congress intended a special exemption for the making of a single copy for personal use, we must conclude that VTR recording is contrary to the exclusive rights granted by § 106(1).

Id. at 8.

exemptions that permitted the making of a single copy. When Congress intended to excuse the making of a single copy, it had said so, and articulated the circumstances under which that copy might be made in great detail. Congress had, moreover, shown no difficulty expressly providing special treatment for private use when it concluded it was warranted: the 1976 Act limited the copyright owner's performance right to public performances, and the library photocopying provisions include privileges limited to researchers engaged in "private study, scholarship or research."[33] If the law incorporated an implicit exemption for private copies, Blackmun concluded, these provisions would be completely unnecessary.

Justice Blackmun then rejected the argument that home copying could be excused under the fair use doctrine. The fair use doctrine, he explained, acts as a subsidy, at the copyright owners' expense, to permit subsequent authors to make limited use of copyrighted works for the public good. Fair uses were always productive uses, "reflecting some benefit to the public beyond that produced by the first author's work." Home taping was not such a use, so there was no need to subsidize it at the author's expense. Unproductive uses might in some circumstances escape liability because they caused little or no harm. Where a use was unproductive, however, courts should not deem it fair if the copyright owner produced evidence of a potential for harm. In that case, the use would be found infringing "unless the user can demonstrate affirmatively that permitting the use would have no tendency to harm the market for or the value of the copyrighted work."[34] Thus, unproductive uses could qualify for fair use only when they had no potential to harm the copyright owner's market. The introduction of evidence of potential harm from an unproductive use would shift the burden of proof to the defendant to disprove potential harm.

As for Sony's liability for consumers' use of its recorders, Blackmun wrote that contributory liability required neither direct involvement with individual infringers nor actual knowledge of particular instances of infringement. "It is sufficient that the defendant have reason to know that infringement is taking place."[35] By advertising the Betamax as suitable for the recording of "favorite shows" and "classic movies," Sony had induced copyright infringement by Betamax owners.[36] Blackmun conceded that some consumers might have used Sony's recorders for non-infringing as well as infringing uses, but "the existence of nonin-

[33] *Id.* at 12–13.

[34] *Id.* at 22, 26.

[35] *Id.* at 30–31.

[36] *Id.* at 32–33.

fringing uses does not absolve the manufacturer of a product whose 'most conspicuous purpose' is to infringe.''[37] Since copyright infringement was the Betamax's primary use, Sony was liable as a contributory infringer.

Even before Justice Blackmun completed the first draft of the opinion, Justice Stevens had prepared his alternative, and he circulated it on the same day. Justice Stevens, apparently hoping to pry a fifth vote loose from Blackmun's majority, styled his draft as a ''Memorandum'' rather than a dissent. Stevens argued that Sony could not be held liable for making and selling Betamax recorders unless the primary use of the Betamax were an infringing one; he concluded that it was not. Until the Court of Appeals decision below, Stevens began, no court had ever held that purely private noncommercial copying infringed the reproduction right, and the copyright law had never been understood to prohibit it. While the language of the 1909 Copyright Act appeared to give copyright owners control over the making of even a single copy, courts had not applied it so literally.[38] Litigation challenging the massive photocopying of scientific articles by the National Library of Medicine had proceeded on the express assumption that individual scholars acted lawfully when they made single copies for their own use.[39] When Congress extended copyright protection to sound recordings in 1971, it had repeatedly affirmed that the Copyright Act did not then reach consumer home taping of music, and would not reach it as amended.[40] Stevens found it unlikely that Congress could possibly have intended the 1976 Act to prohibit private home videotaping. Nothing in the language or legislative history of the 1976 Act supported a conclusion that Congress intended home video taping to be treated differently from home audio taping.[41] Stevens suggested that Congress would not lightly have elected intrusive regulation of noncommercial conduct within the home. ''It would plainly be unconstitutional,'' he suggested, ''to prohibit a person from singing a copyrighted song in the shower or jotting down a copyrighted poem he hears on the radio.''[42] Moreover, he rejected the argument that Congress might have intended to prohibit home taping on the understanding that

---

[37] *Id.* at 35.

[38] First draft, Memorandum of Justice Stevens, *Sony* (No.81–1687) (circulated June 13, 1983) at 16.

[39] *Id.* at 5 (*citing Williams & Wilkins v. U.S.*, 487 F.2d 1345 (Ct.Cl. 1973), *aff'd by an equally divided Court*, 420 U.S. 376 (1975)).

[40] *Id.* at 9–11.

[41] *Id.* at 12, 14.

[42] *Id.* at 17–18.

the prohibition would never be enforced against individual consumers, like defendant William Griffiths.

> It is significant that the Act does not purport to create "safe" violations. It plainly provides that every act of infringement—even if performed in complete good faith—gives rise to a minimum statutory liability of $100. That command cannot simply be transformed into a matter of indifference because the copyright owners do not intend to collect the heavy tribute that is their due.[43]

Finally, Stevens argued that even if the Court concluded that home taping infringed Universal Studio's copyrights, and that that infringement entitled them to some remedy against Sony, it was difficult to imagine a remedy properly within the competence of the courts.

> In their complaint, respondents pray for an injunction against the further manufacture or sale of video cassette records. They do so despite the fact that they have suffered no tangible harm. They claim the injunction is required by the potential future impact of this innovation. Surely that impact can be more precisely gauged by legislators than by this Court, on this record.[44]

Justice Stevens supplemented his draft with a memo noting the areas of agreement and disagreement between his memorandum and Justice Blackmun's opinion, and criticizing Blackmun's formulation of fair use; Blackmun responded with a memo of his own suggesting that Stevens had misread the legislative history of the Copyright Act. The legislative history, Blackmun argued, indicated that Congress had designed the 1976 Act to cover new and unexpected technologies as well as known ones, freeing Congress from the obligation to revisit the law each time a new use arose. Justice Brennan then circulated a memo seeking to put a third alternative on the table. Brennan disputed Stevens's conclusion that Congress had implicitly exempted private, non-commercial copying from liability, but thought that that was a point the Court need not address:

> As Harry explains, Sony can be liable for contributory infringement only if the Betamax's "most conspicuous purpose" or "primary use" is an infringing use.... I, however, think that a good deal of timeshifting is fair use.... I question whether the "ordinary"/"productive" distinction can be used to shift the burden of proving or disproving economic harm in a broad class of cases.... In my view, the Studios' allegations of potential

43 *Id.* at 19 (footnote omitted).

44 *Id.* at 20 (footnote omitted).

harm ... are simply empty when applied to most timeshifting. Unless the burden is shifted, there is no need for a remand to determine that a substantial amount of timeshifting is fair use. And if that is true, then I cannot agree that the Betamax's "primary use" is infringement or that Sony's advertisements evince a purpose to profit from infringement.[45]

The following day, Blackmun circulated a revised second draft, containing additional discussion of the private use and contributory infringement issues, and an expanded treatment of how the lower court might address the remedy for Sony's infringement.[46] Justices Rehnquist and Marshall agreed to join that opinion.

Justice O'Connor, who had been part of the initial majority voting to affirm the Ninth Circuit opinion, had reservations. She wrote to Blackmun, noting her agreement with the draft's conclusions that Sony violated the studio's reproduction right and that the fair use doctrine did not apply. "However," she continued, "I have considerable difficulty in rejecting the District Court's view that the respondents suffered no harm, actual or potential, as a result of Sony's use." O'Connor also expressed concern about Blackmun's fair use formulation, indicating that she was not persuaded that the burden of proof on the issue of harm should be shifted to Sony; wherever the burden of proof lay, however, she read Judge Ferguson's opinion as finding no harm, actual or potential.[47]

Justice Blackmun responded with a suggestion that the Court remand the case for new fact finding on the issue of harm. He was unwilling to adopt a standard requiring copyright plaintiffs to prove potential harm, but suggested language that clarified that the copyright owner's burden of production was a substantial one, requiring more than mere speculation.[48] O'Connor responded, questioning whether a remand on the issue of harm would be fruitful; it seemed clear that Judge Ferguson had concluded that there was no concrete evidence that the Betamax would harm the studios.[49] In the absence of any harm, O'Con-

[45] Memorandum from Justice William A. Brennan (June 14, 1983).

[46] Second Draft, Opinion in *Sony* (No. 81–1687) (circulated by Justice Blackmun, June 15, 1983).

[47] Letter from Justice Sandra Day O'Connor to Justice Harry A. Blackmun (June 16, 1983).

[48] Letter from Justice Harry A. Blackmun to Justice Sandra Day O'Connor (June 16, 1983).

[49] Letter from Justice Sandra Day O'Connor to Justice Harry A. Blackmun (June 18, 1983).

nor preferred the finding of liability against Sony to be reversed outright.

If there were to be a remand, Justice O'Connor continued, it was essential that the opinion acknowledge that fair use encompassed unproductive uses as well as productive ones. She felt strongly that the burden of proof on the issue of harm should stay with the copyright owner rather than shifting to the alleged infringer. Finally, O'Connor questioned Blackmun's rejection of the "staple article of commerce" doctrine:

> I had thought that the "staple article" doctrine developed in order to limit the patent holder from depriving society of the good that comes from the existence of other enterprises that nevertheless frustrate the patent holder's monopoly to some degree. I see no reason why we should not be similarly concerned with what the copyright holder does with his monopoly. If the videorecorder has substantial noninfringing uses, we should be reluctant to find vicarious liability. In addition, I think the focus of the inquiry should not be whether virtually all of the copied material is copyrighted, but rather, whether virtually all of the copying amounts to an infringement. Even if you do not wish to import the "staple article" doctrine directly to the copyright area, I fail to see why the same standard—whether the item is capable of substantial noninfringing use—should not be used.[50]

Justice Powell sent Blackmun a memo indicating that he was troubled by some of the same points Justice O'Connor had raised.[51] Blackmun circulated a revised draft seeking to meet their concerns,[52] reformulating the fair use analysis in an attempt to reach a compromise on the burden of proof. For Blackmun, what was crucial was that the law not requires copyright owners to prove actual harm when a new technology was at issue, because that would require them to wait to seek relief until too late. The legislative history of the statute, he insisted, "makes clear that copyright owners are not to be deprived of protection simply because the effects of a new technology are unknown."[53] In order to accommodate O'Connor's concerns, Blackmun revised the language in his draft to put the burden of proof of harm on the plaintiffs, but require

---

50 *Id.* at 2–3.

51 Letter from Justice Lewis F. Powell to Justice Harry A. Blackmun (June 20, 1983).

52 Third Draft, Opinion in *Sony,* (No. 81–1687) (circulated by Justice Blackmun, June 21, 1983).

53 Letter from Justice Harry A. Blackmun to Justices Lewis F. Powell and Sandra Day O'Connor (June 21, 1983).

them to show only "a reasonable possibility of harm."[54] Seeking to find middle ground on the staple article of commerce, Blackmun adopted a phrase from Justice O'Connor's letter: the focus of a contributory infringement inquiry should be "whether virtually all of the copying amounts to infringement."

Justice O'Connor wrote back the same day, requesting additional changes.[55] She continued to be dissatisfied with the treatment of the burden of proof on harm. Justice Blackmun's "reasonable possibility of harm" struck her as allowing copyright plaintiffs to prove too little. She proposed that the opinion instead describe the burden of proof using the statutory language, and require plaintiffs to prove "harm to the potential market for or value of the copyrighted work."[56] She objected to language implying that the studios had already met that burden in the lower court, since Judge Ferguson's findings indicated that no harm had been shown. Finally, O'Connor wrote, she "remained convinced that the standard for contributory infringement should be the one I articulated in my letter of June 18: is the VTR *capable* of substantial non-infringing uses."[57] If Blackmun incorporated her suggestions into a fourth draft, O'Connor continued, she would join that opinion.

Justice Blackmun replied that he was reluctantly willing to accept Justice O'Connor's formulation for the standard for contributory infringement, but would not yield further on the question of the burden of proof in fair use:

> The statutory language to which you refer comes into play when a *productive* use is found. Under your proposal, the copyright owner would have to prove actual harm to the value of the copyright or to a potential market even for unproductive uses. The problem with this, as I have tried to point out, is that copyright owners would be deprived of protection when the technology is a new one and when predictions of harm are necessarily imprecise. I strongly feel that the standard articulated in the opinion—that the copyright owner must show a "reasonable possibility of harm"—is the correct one.[58]

---

[54] Third Draft, Opinion in *Sony*, (No. 81–1687) (circulated by Justice Blackmun, June 21, 1983) at 26.

[55] Letter from Justice Sandra Day O'Connor to Justice Harry A. Blackmun (June 21, 1983).

[56] *Id.* at 2.

[57] *Id.* at 3–4.

[58] Letter from Justice Harry A. Blackmun to Justice Sandra Day O'Connor (June 23, 1983).

Meanwhile, Justice White proposed that Justices Brennan and Stevens try to assemble a majority for an opinion that took a position between the views that Brennan and Stevens had expressed following the oral argument. White suggested that such an opinion could reverse the judgment against Sony as a contributory infringer on the ground that the studios had failed to prove injury or damages, and leave the question of consumer liability unresolved.[59]

Justice Stevens circulated some new language on June 23.[60] The exchange of letters between O'Connor and Blackmun had been distributed to all nine Justices, and Justice Stevens's new draft seemed designed to attract O'Connor's vote by adopting the proposals Blackmun had rejected. Thus, while the draft nominally followed the model proposed in Justice Brennan's June 14 memo, concluding that because time-shifting caused the studios no harm, there was no basis for imposing contributory liability on Sony, the draft also incorporated the suggestions that O'Connor had been trying unsuccessfully to persuade Blackmun to include in his opinion. In particular, after emphasizing both the studios' failure to show any harm from the Betamax, and the trial court's finding that copyright owners other than the studios encouraged consumers to time-shift their programs, the draft imported the staple article of commerce doctrine from patent law and placed the burden of proof on the question of potential harm in a fair use analysis squarely on the plaintiff. O'Connor sent a note to Blackmun noting her agreement with Stevens's treatment of the burden of proof, and suggesting that Blackmun incorporate a modified version of it into his opinion.[61] "This issue," she wrote, "is significant, because the burden will likely determine the outcome of not only this case but most others in the future. I recognize the delicate balance we must make between protection of the copyright owner and encouragement of new technology."

Three days later, Justice Blackmun wrote back, refusing to make additional changes:

> I have endeavored of the past several days to accommodate your many concerns. My letter of June 23 to you represents the limit of what I am willing to do. Five votes are not that important to me when I feel that proper legal principles are involved.[62]

---

59 Letter from Justice Byron R. White to Justice William J. Brennan (June 17, 1983).

60 Memorandum from Justice John Paul Stevens to the Conference (June 23, 1983).

61 Letter from Justice Sandra Day O'Connor to Justice Harry A. Blackmun (June 25, 1983).

62 Letter from Justice Harry A. Blackmun to Justice Sandra Day O'Connor (June 28, 1983).

Justice Stevens, meanwhile, had circulated his completed draft, which combined the Brennan distinction between time-shifting and library building with the O'Connor formulations of the burden of proof and staple article of commerce doctrine, all while purporting to decide only the contributory infringement issue and leave the question of consumer liability for home taping for another day.[63] The draft noted that the Court had granted certiorari to address whether home videotaping was copyright infringement and, if so, whether the manufacturers of videotape recorders were liable for advertising and selling them, and whether a judicially imposed royalty was a permissible form of relief. Because the district court's factual findings were dispositive on the contributory infringement issue, the Court need decide only that question:

> In brief, the critical facts are these: the principal use of the video tape recorder is to enable its owner to view a program he would otherwise miss; this practice, known as "time-shifting," enlarges the television viewing audience. For that reason, a significant number of producers of television programs have no objection to the copying of their program for private home viewing. For the same reason, even the two respondents in this case, who do object to time shifting, were unable to prove that the practice has caused them any harm or creates any likelihood of future harm.[64]

The draft then discussed the doctrine of contributory copyright infringement, and expressly adopted patent law's staple article of commerce doctrine. As framed by Justice Stevens, the staple article of commerce doctrine applied to any article that was "widely used for legitimate, unobjectionable purposes. Indeed, if we apply the patent law rule, it need merely be capable of significant noninfringing uses."[65]

"The question," Stevens continued, "is thus whether the Betamax is capable of commercially significant noninfringing uses." Noncommercial private time-shifting was such a use both because much of it was authorized and because even unauthorized time-shifting qualified as fair use:

> Three different factors lead to the conclusion that under a "rule of reason" analysis, the respondents failed to carry their burden of proving in this case that home time shifting is not fair use. Those factors are (A) their complete failure to show that home

[63] Second Draft, Memorandum of Justice Stevens in *Sony*, (No. 81–1687) (circulated by Justice Stevens, June 27, 1983).

[64] *Id.* at 2.

[65] *Id.* at 24.

> time shifting would harm the potential market for, or value of, any identifiable copyrighted material, (B) the legislative history tending to show that Congress understood such activity to be fair use, and (C) the profoundly disturbing policy implications of finding that home time shifting is not fair use.[66]

The draft proceeded to a discussion of the four factors enumerated in section 107. It addressed only the final factor, the "effect of the use upon the market for or value of the copyrighted work." If a use has no effect on the potential market for a work, Stevens explained, it has no effect on the author's incentives to create. Prohibiting it would simply hinder access to the work without any countervailing benefit.

> Of course, every commercial use of copyrighted material is presumptively an exploitation of the monopoly privilege that belongs to the owner of the copyright. But noncommercial uses are a different matter. Any plaintiff seeking to challenge the non-commercial use of a copyrighted work should, as a threshold matter, prove either that the particular use is harmful or that if it should become widespread, it would be more likely than not that *some* non-minimal damage would result to the potential market for, or the value of, his particular copyrighted work. Actual present harm need not be shown; such a requirement would leave the copyright holder with no defense against predictable damage. Nor is it necessary to show with certainty that future harm will result. What is necessary is a showing by a preponderance of the evidence that *some* meaningful likelihood of future harm exists. If the intended use is for commercial gain, that likelihood may be presumed. But if it is for purely private purposes, however, it must be demonstrated.[67]

This formulation combined Stevens's initial conclusion that noncommercial private copying should be treated differently from commercial copying with O'Connor's insistence that the burden of proof on the issue of harm should be assigned to the plaintiff.

The end of June is a busy time at the Supreme Court: the Court adjourns each summer in early July, and by tradition disposes of all of the cases on its calendar before adjournment, so by late June the Court is hurrying to finish its work on all remaining decisions. Justice Brennan sent around a memo that did not offer to join Stevens's most recent opinion, but noted that the draft "came closer to expressing" Brennan's views. Justice Byron White sent a note to Chief Justice Burger suggesting that the Court set the case for reargument the following term: "If

---

[66] *Id.* at 31.

[67] *Id.* at 32.

this case is to come down this term, I prefer John's submission to any others. I would much rather, however, have the case reargued. It is important, and I would feel more comfortable if we could give the case more attention than time will now allow."[68] Justice O'Connor chimed in, noting that she also preferred Justice Stevens's most recent draft to the alternative, but would probably agree to set the case for reargument.[69] Justice Rehnquist also expressed support for reargument.[70] Justice Stevens remained hopeful of resolving the case that term rather than holding it over, and he circulated a further draft of his opinion. This draft incorporated extensive discussion of the testimony of copyright owners who welcomed consumer home taping as a method of expanding their audience, and an expanded discussion of the district court's findings on the studios' failure to show any harm.[71] It otherwise tracked the earlier draft. Stevens believed that the draft reflected a consensus of the views of Justices Brennan, Burger, White and O'Connor as well as himself. The Court decided, however, to set the case for reargument.

On July 6, the final day of the 1982 term, copyright lobbyists and journalists assembled at the Court to be the first to read the Betamax decision. There was no Betamax decision to read. The Court issued an order restoring the case to the argument calendar. It asked for no new briefs and identified no new issues it wanted counsel to address.[72]

Sony was reargued on October 3, 1983. Dean Dunlavey argued first for Sony, and noted that by the end of the year 9½ million households, or roughly 10% of the television viewing audience, would own videotape recorders. Home taping, he argued, was clearly fair use. Justice O'Connor asked whether the Court needed to resolve the fair use issue. Could the Justices not resolve the contributory infringement question without deciding whether home taping was fair use? Dunlavey agreed that the Court could indeed take that approach: "There are two roads to Rome." He then returned to his discussion of fair use. Justice White interrupted: "I'm wondering," he asked, "do we have to reach the questions you've been discussing if we agreed with you that this is a staple article of commerce and that there's no contributory infringement?" "If you agreed with me," responded Dunlavey, "you would think this case would

[68] Letter from Justice Byron R. White to Chief Justice Warren Burger (June 28, 1983).

[69] Letter from Justice Sandra Day O'Connor to Chief Justice Warren Burger (June 28, 1983).

[70] Memorandum from Justice William H. Rehnquist to the Conference (June 28, 1983).

[71] Third Draft, Memorandum of Justice Stevens in *Sony*, (No. 81–1687) (circulated by Justice Stevens, June 28, 1983) at 24–26, 30–34.

[72] Sony v. Universal, 463 U.S. 1226 (1983). *See* Mark Bomnster & Susan March, *Betamax Ruling Put on Hold*, 57 Retailing Home Furnishings, July 11, 1983 at 53.

be over.'' Justice White persisted: "Well we wouldn't have to talk about fair use at all, would we, if we agreed with you that this is a staple article of commerce?'' Dunlavey conceded that that was the case.

Stephen Kroft stood up to argue for the studios. "Underneath all the legal arguments and legal labels that we've thrown around in this case, the case is really very simple and straightforward,'' he began. "Petitioners have created a billion dollar industry based entirely on the taking of someone else's property. . . .''[73]Justices White and Stevens had a number of questions about the staple article of commerce test; Kroft insisted that it had no application to the case. Justice O'Connor noted that the district court had found no harm, and Kroft responded that under the copyright statute, plaintiffs were not required to prove harm. Rather, Kroft argued, a finding of infringement lead to a presumption of harm, shifting the burden to defendants to prove there would not be any harm. Justice Stevens asked for an example of harm that time-shifting might cause, and Kroft responded that homemade tapes could compete with prerecorded cassettes.[74] "Fair use,'' Kroft continued, "was a very narrow doctrine designed for very limited application, for use in the creation of scholarly or research works or works for contemporary comment or news reporting purposes, and only when a small amount was taken. Off the air recording for home entertainment purposes doesn't even come anywhere close to fitting that definition.''[75]

At the conference following the reargument, according to Justice Blackmun's handwritten notes, only Justices Marshall and Blackmun voted to affirm the Ninth Circuit decision. Justices Powell and Rehnquist favored affirming the portion of the court of appeals decision holding that consumer home videotaping infringed the studios' copyrights, but wanted to remand on the issue of contributory infringement. Justices Burger, Brennan, White, O'Connor and Stevens voted to reverse the decision outright. Justice Stevens undertook to write the opinion for the Court; Justice Blackmun agreed to write the dissent.

The Supreme Court Decision

Justice Stevens's opinion for the Court characterized the lawsuit as an "unprecedented attempt to impose copyright liability upon the distributors of copying equipment,'' and rejected "[s]uch an expansion of

---

[73] Transcript of Oral Argument, *Sony* (No. 81–1687) (Oct. 3, 1983), *available at* 1983 U.S. TRANS LEXIS 10.

[74] At the time of trial, neither Universal nor Disney had released any programs on prerecorded cassettes, although, beginning in late 1977, several other studios had released older material on videocassette. Video rental stores started springing up shortly thereafter. *See* LARDNER, *supra* note 4, at 154–88.

[75] Transcript of Oral Argument, *supra* note 73.

the copyright privilege" as "beyond the limits of the grants authorized by Congress."[76] Stevens's analysis essentially tracked the arguments made in his June 28 draft, combining his own solicitude for private noncommercial copying with Justice Brennan's distinction between time-shifting and library building, and Justice O'Connor's preference for the staple article of commerce doctrine and conviction that the burden of proof on the issue of harm to the copyright owner in a fair use determination should rest on the plaintiff. Stitching those positions together into a coherent opinion was not easy, and while the result the opinion reached was immediately clear, the reasoning it relied on was, at best, oblique.

Justice Stevens began by explaining that the courts had been and should be reluctant to expand copyright protection in response to new technology rather than allowing Congress to craft appropriate solutions. There was no precedent in copyright law for imposing liability for selling a product that enabled users to make infringing copies. The closest analogy to such a theory of liability was found in patent law, which imposed liability for contributory infringement but also exempted the sale of staple articles of commerce from liability. Although the Court recognized substantial differences between patent and copyright law, both sought to strike a balance between the interest in effective protection and the rights of others to engage freely in unrelated areas of commerce. "Accordingly," the opinion continued, "the sale of copying equipment, like the sale of other articles of commerce, does not constitute contributory infringement if the product is widely used for legitimate, unobjectionable purposes. Indeed, it need merely be capable of substantial noninfringing uses."[77]

As in his earlier draft, Stevens answered the question whether the Betamax was capable of commercially significant noninfringing uses by identifying private, noncommercial time-shifting as one use that satisfied that standard. He reviewed the testimony of copyright owners who welcomed time-shifting. The representative of one PBS station had testified that his station published a program guide inviting viewers to tape more than half of the programs on its schedule. Fred Rogers had testified that he had absolutely no objection to families' taping episodes of *Mr. Rogers' Neighborhood.*

> Of course, the fact that other copyright holders may welcome the practice of time-shifting does not mean that respondents should be deemed to have granted a license to copy their programs. Third-party conduct would be wholly irrelevant in an action for direct infringement of respondents' copyrights. But in

[76] Sony v. Universal Studios, 464 U.S. 417, 421 (1984).

[77] *Id.* at 442.

> an action for *contributory* infringement against the seller of copying equipment, the copyright holder may not prevail unless the relief that he seeks affects only his programs, or unless he speaks for virtually all copyright holders with an interest in the outcome. In this case, the record makes it perfectly clear that there are many important producers of national and local television programs who find nothing objectionable about the enlargement in the size of the television audience that results from the practice of time-shifting for private home use.[78]

Stevens then turned to unauthorized time-shifting, and concluded that it qualified as fair use. Justice Stevens rejected the Ninth Circuit's position that only productive uses could be deemed fair.[79] He focused instead on the distinction between commercial uses and non-commercial ones. "If the Betamax were used to make copies for a commercial or profit-making purpose," he explained, "such use would presumptively be unfair. The contrary presumption is appropriate here, however, because the District Court's findings plainly establish that time-shifting for private home use must be characterized as a noncommercial, nonprofit activity."[80]

> Even copying for noncommercial purposes may impair the copyright holder's ability to obtain the rewards that Congress intended him to have. But a use that has no demonstrable effect upon the potential market for, or the value of, the copyrighted work need not be prohibited in order to protect the author's incentive to create. The prohibition of such noncommercial uses would merely inhibit access to ideas without any countervailing benefit.[81]

Thus, while every commercial use should be deemed presumptively unfair, a challenge to a noncommercial use required proof of present or potential harm. The studios had failed to satisfy that burden.[82] The

---

[78] *Id.* at 446.

[79] *Id.* at 445 n.40.

[80] *Id.* at 449.

[81] *Id.* at 450–51.

[82] *Id.*:

> Thus, although every commercial use of copyrighted material is presumptively an unfair exploitation of the monopoly privilege that belongs to the owner of the copyright, noncommercial uses are a different matter. A challenge to a noncommercial use of a copyrighted work requires proof either that the particular use is harmful, or that if it should become widespread, it would adversely affect the potential market for the copyrighted work. Actual present harm need not be shown; such a requirement would leave the copyright holder with no defense against predictable damage. Nor is it necessary to show with certainty that future harm will result. What is necessary is a showing by a preponderance of the

Betamax videotape recorder was therefore capable of substantial non-infringing uses, and Sony's sale of it did not constitute contributory infringement.[83]

Justice Blackmun's dissent, joined by Justices Marshall, Powell and Rehnquist, repeated the arguments he had made the previous spring: the fair use defense was appropriate only when a productive use merited a subsidy at the copyright owner's expense or when the use had no potential to affect the author's incentive to create. Time-shifting, Blackmun argued, was an ordinary use rather than a productive one, and had a substantial adverse effect on the potential market for copyrighted television programs. By focusing on the potential harm to plaintiffs' current markets, Blackmun argued, the majority had failed to give appropriate weight to the likelihood of harm to the potential markets created by defendants' technology. The videotape recorder deprived copyright owners of the opportunity to exploit the market of potential viewers who found it inconvenient to watch television programs at the time they are broadcast. Accordingly, even time-shifting should not be deemed a fair use.[84]

The Immediate Impact of *Sony*

The *Sony* decision was reported widely, and approvingly, in the popular press as holding that consumers do not violate the law when they tape television programs off the air.[85] The decision was less popular

---

evidence that *some* meaningful likelihood of future harm exists. If the intended use is for commercial gain, that likelihood may be presumed. But if it is for a noncommercial purpose, the likelihood must be demonstrated.

In this case, respondents failed to carry their burden with regard to home time-shifting.

[83] *Id.* at 456.

[84] *See id.* at 457–93 (Blackmun, J., dissenting).

[85] *See, e.g.*, Fred Barbash, *Supreme Court Chooses Not to Stem the Tide of High Technology*, WASH. POST, January 22, 1983, at A5; Nathaniel C. Nash, *Sony Prevails in the Betamax Case*, *N.Y. TIMES*, January 22, 1984, § 3, at 16, col. 3. The *Washington Post*'s entertainment critic, Tom Shales, put it this way:

> There won't be dancing in the streets. There'll be taping in the living rooms. But if there were dancing in the streets and it was shown on television, you could tape it in the living room and not have to worry about some trench-coated specter from the FBI breaking down the door to your condominium.
>
> One small step for man, one giant kick in Big Brother's pants.
>
> Yesterday the Supreme Court ruled, by a frighteningly narrow 5–to–4 majority, that the home taping of TV programs and movies broadcast on the air is not illegal. Five million VCR users breathed an enormous "whew." Imagine. No more stuffing the Betamax machine under the bed at every unexpected ring of the doorbell. No more disguising tapes as pornographic magazines. No more covert tapings of "Remington Steele" with the shades drawn and the windows locked.

with the copyright bar.[86] To copyright lawyers, the Court's opinion seemed like a sharp break with longstanding precedent; from the copyright lawyer's standpoint, Justice Blackmun's dissenting opinion was grounded in long copyright tradition, while Justice Stevens's opinion for the Court had no real historical foundation. The majority's adoption of the staple article of commerce doctrine seemed unnecessary and ill-reasoned, and its presumption-mediated treatment of the burden of proof in fair use cases seemed ill-advised.[87] To people outside of the copyright bar, the case came immediately to stand for the proposition that private noncommercial copying was fair use. To many members of the copyright bar, that represented an unwarranted expansion of what they had believed to be a fairly confined privilege.[88] The motion picture industry vowed to overturn the decision in Congress, but found little enthusiasm in the Senate and House for imposing a copyright tax on videocassette recorders or blank tapes.

The Sony Betamax itself was soon superseded by a videorecorder using the different, and incompatible, VHS format. In 1988, Sony began phasing out the Betamax video tape recorder. Meanwhile, the motion picture industry grew to rely on the pre-recorded videocassette market as a significant source of its income.[89] Revenues from prerecorded videocassettes (and, later, DVDs) came to outstrip revenues from domestic theatrical ticket sales. The consumer electronics and computer industries introduced a variety of devices—digital audio recorders, digital cameras, computers, MP3 players, and peer-to-peer file sharing software—capable of infringing as well as legitimate uses.

No more midnight meetings of Time–Shifters Anonymous.

No more worrying if industry lobbyist Jack Valenti and his SWAT team are about to surround the house, shine in the big blinding spotlights, and order you by bullhorn to come out with your hands, and your recording heads, up. Citizens! Hear me! We are free! Free to tape as we choose! To tape as we see fit. To tape till the cows come home.

To tape "Till the Clouds Roll By," that dopey old MGM musical, the next time a TV station shows it.

1984 has been marked down to . . . yes! . . . 1776!

Tom Shales, I'll Tape Tomorrow, And So Will You, Thanks to the Court, WASH. POST, January 18, 1984, at B1.

86 *See, e.g.*, WILLIAM F. PATRY, THE FAIR USE PRIVILEGE IN COPYRIGHT LAW 205–10 (1985).

87 *See, e.g., id.* at 363–65; Ralph Oman, *The 1976 Copyright Act Revisited: "Lector, si momumentum requires, circumspice*," 34 J. COPYRIGHT SOC'Y 29, 32–33 (1986).

88 *See, e.g.*, Jack C. Goldstein, AIPLA BULLETIN, December 1984 at 635, 636–37.

89 *See* Ross Johnson, *Getting a Piece of the DVD Windfall*, N.Y. TIMES, Dec. 13, 2004, at C1.

The year after *Sony*, the Supreme Court decided its second fair use case, *Harper & Row v. Nation Enterprises*.[90] The case involved an unauthorized pre-publication excerpt from former President Gerald Ford's memoirs published by *The Nation*, a small political commentary magazine. The excerpt comprised 300 words from a 400–page book. The Court held, 6–3, that *The Nation* was not entitled to the shelter of the fair use privilege, in part because the news reporting and political commentary it engaged in had a commercial purpose rather than a non-profit one. Justice O'Connor authored the opinion. "The fact that a publication was commercial as opposed to nonprofit is a separate factor that tends to weigh against a finding of fair use," she wrote, " '[Every] commercial use of copyrighted material is presumptively an unfair exploitation of the monopoly privilege that belongs to the owner of the copyright.' "[91]

The *Harper & Row* decision represented the high point of *Sony*'s influence on the law of fair use. The presumption against commercial fair use quickly proved unworkable, making fair use unavailable to biographers,[92] parodists,[93] and news organizations[94] because they published their works for commercial gain. Ten years after *Sony*, in *Campbell v. Acuff–Rose Music*,[95] the Court finally abandoned the presumption, along with its twin, the presumption favoring non-commercial fair use. But before it was abandoned, the presumption favoring non-commercial fair use had persuaded the owners of copyrights in musical works and recordings to lobby Congress to enact a law that levied a royalty on the

---

[90] 471 U.S. 539 (1985).

[91] 471 U.S. at 562 (quoting Sony Corp. of America v. Universal City Studios, Inc., 464 U.S., at 451) (alteration in original).

[92] *See* New Era Publications Int'l v. Henry Holt & Co., 873 F.2d 576, 583–84 (2d Cir. 1989).

[93] *See* Rogers v. Koons, 960 F.2d 301 (2d Cir. 1992); Tin Pan Apple v. Miller Brewing Co., 737 F. Supp. 826 (S.D.N.Y. 1990); Original Appalachian Artworks v. Topps Chewing Gum, 642 F. Supp. 1031 (N.D.Ga. 1986).

[94] *See* Hi–Tech Video Productions, Inc. v. Capital Cities/ABC, Inc., 804 F. Supp. 950 (W.D. Mich. 1992).

[95] 510 U.S. 569, 584–85 (1994):

> *Sony* itself called for no hard evidentiary presumption. There, we emphasized the need for a "sensitive balancing of interests," 464 U.S. at 455, n.40, noted that Congress had "eschewed a rigid, bright-line approach to fair use," *id.*, at 449, n.31, and stated that the commercial or nonprofit educational character of a work is "not conclusive," *id.*, at 448–449, but rather a fact to be "weighed along with other[s] in fair use decisions," *id.*, at 449, n.32 (quoting House Report, p. 66). The Court of Appeals's elevation of one sentence from *Sony* to a *per se* rule thus runs as much counter to *Sony* itself as to the long common-law tradition of fair use adjudication.

sale of digital audio recorders and blank digital media, while requiring manufacturers of recording devices to incorporate copy protection technology that permitted multiple first-generation copies but prevented the devices from copying copies. One part of that bargain included a prohibition on bringing copyright infringement suits against consumers who engaged in non-commercial copying of recorded music,[96] a concession that seemed cheap when the governing test for fair use favored noncommercial copying.

The same case that discarded the presumption against commercial fair use also reversed course on the issue that had lost Justice Blackmun his majority: the placement of the burden of proof. In *Campbell v. Acuff–Rose Music*, Justice Souter held that fair use is an affirmative defense, and that the burden of proof on the issue of potential harm lies with the defendant.[97] Finally, in *Campbell*, the Court acknowledged the importance to the fair use inquiry of a distinction between productive and unproductive uses. Citing Blackmun's *Sony* dissent, Justice Souter wrote that "the goal of copyright, to promote science and the arts, is generally furthered by the creation of transformative works. Such works thus lie at the heart of the fair use doctrine's guarantee of breathing space within the confines of copyright. . ., and the more transformative the new work, the less will be the significance of other factors, like commercialism, that may weigh against a finding of fair use."[98] Thus, the fair use principles for which the *Sony* case is known have largely been abandoned, and the real estate it takes up in the fair use chapters of copyright casebooks has dwindled accordingly. Fair use law today is much closer to something Justice Blackmun might have recognized with approval.

The Court's holding on liability for contributory infringement, in contrast, is still with us. Networked digital technology has supplied myriad new ways for consumers to make unauthorized copies, and whether and under what circumstances the purveyors of technology that makes infringement easier should be held liable is one of the most important questions facing the copyright law. The producers of computers, CD and DVD recorders, digital video recorders and MP3 players, the

---

[96] Audio Home Recording Act, Pub. Law. No. 102–563, 106 Stat. 4237, codified at 17 U.S.C. §§ 1001–1010 (2000).

[97] *See* 510 U.S. at 591–92. Professor Glynn Lunney attributes the reversal of course to poor lawyering on the part of Campbell's counsel, who conceded that he bore the burden of proof without even mentioning that *Sony* had held that the burden should be born by plaintiff. *See* Glynn S. Lunney, *Fair Use and Market Failure: Sony Revisited*, 82 B.U.L. Rev. 975, 989 & n.70 (2002). Professor Lunney suggests that because the burden of proof issue was not contested, *Campbell*'s characterization of fair use as an affirmative defense was nonbinding dicta. *Id.*

[98] 510 U.S. at 515–16.

providers of Internet services and the designers of peer-to-peer file sharing software supply products and services that both facilitate copyright infringement and have substantial legitimate uses. Copyright lawyers have argued bitterly about whether and how *Sony* applied to the distribution of technology that facilitated digital copyright infringement. Two decades after the *Sony* decision, the Supreme Court agreed to take a second look at the question of contributory copyright liability in a case involving consumer copying over digital networks using peer-to-peer file sharing software.

The Continuing Importance of *Sony* Today

Peer-to-peer file sharing poses issues that are startlingly reminiscent of the record in *Sony*. Consumers use peer-to-peer file sharing networks to make unauthorized copies in their homes for their own personal, consumptive use. If making those copies violates the copyright law, then enforcing the law implicates the same privacy concerns that Justice Stevens raised in arguing that Congress had not intended to prohibit home videotaping. The copying is non-commercial in the same sense that home Betamax recordings were non-commercial.[99] As was true in *Sony*, there already is an enormous installed base of ordinary consumers using the technology. By the time the *Sony* case was first argued in the Supreme Court, Sony claimed to have sold 5 million Betamax recorders to American consumers. Current estimates of the number of peer-to-peer file sharers within the United States range from 40 to 60 million American consumers. A number of copyright owners have authorized the exchange of material they own over peer-to-peer networks. Some peer-to-peer file sharing is probably fair use, although the proportion of fair to infringing uses is the subject of passionate dispute. Other material transmitted over peer-to-peer is in the public domain. Studies attempting to measure whether and how much harm peer-to-peer file sharing causes to both actual and potential markets for recorded music have reached equivocal and conflicting results.[100] The owners of music copyrights have recently begun to release digital copies of their works in a variety of different copy-protected formats, none of them compatible with one another, and see peer-to-peer file trading as a threat to plans to

---

[99] *But see A & M v. Napster*, 114 F. Supp. 2d 896, 912 (N.D. Cal. 2000) (finding Napster use commercial because "Napster users get for free something they would ordinarily have to buy"), *aff'd in part, rev'd in part,* 239 F.3d 1004 (9th Cir. 2001).

[100] *Compare* Felix Oberholzer & Koleman Strumpf, *The Effect of File Sharing on Record Sales: An Empirical Analysis* (March 2004), *available at* http://www.unc.edu/?cigar/papers/FileSharing_March2004.pdf (concluding that file sharing does not reduce and may increase sales), *with* Stan J. Liebowitz, *Pitfalls in Measuring the Impact of File Sharing* (Oct. 13, 2004) *available at* http://papers.ssrn.com/sol3/papers.cfm?abstract_id=583484 (concluding that file sharing harms the sound recording industry), *See also* LAWRENCE LESSIG, FREE CULTURE 68–73 (2004).

persuade the public to invest in copy-protected digital music, much as the videocassette recorder appeared to threaten the market for laser discs.

Of course, there are also significant differences. It would be difficult to characterize the transmission of files among 40 to 60 million consumers as "private," and little of the material consumers exchange is programming they have been invited to view free of charge. Further, the economics of data storage suggest that consumers retain unauthorized peer-to-peer copies more often than they overwrite them. Most consumers engaged in peer-to-peer file sharing are probably building libraries rather than time-shifting. It is nonetheless clear that peer-to-peer file sharing software is capable of substantial non-infringing uses, and that at least one of those uses—authorized peer-to-peer distribution—is commercially significant. Under the *Sony* standard, then, even if the overwhelming majority of peer-to-peer file sharing in fact infringes copyright, holding the purveyors of the technology contributorily liable for individual consumers' infringement, solely on the basis of their dissemination of a technology with substantial non-infringing uses, is deeply problematic.

In *MGM v. Grokster*, the Court of Appeals for the Ninth Circuit read *Sony* to preclude the imposition of contributory liability on a distributor of peer-to-peer file sharing software where the defendant could not prevent specific incidents of infringement at the time it learned about them. Because the software had substantial non-infringing uses, and the distributor had no control over the uses consumers made of the software once they installed it, the court ruled, defendants could not be held liable merely on the basis of their design and distribution of software with both infringing and non-infringing applications.[101] Imposing liability in such a case, the court noted, would expand the reach of contributory and vicarious copyright liability "exponentially," and would alter general copyright law "in profound ways."[102] The court expressed the view that such a change in the law would be unwise:

> The introduction of new technology is always disruptive to old markets, and particularly to those copyright owners whose works are sold through well established distribution mechanisms. Yet, history has shown that time and market forces often provide equilibrium in balancing interests, whether the new technology be a player piano, a copier, a tape recorder, a video recorder, a personal computer, a karaoke machine, or an MP3

---

[101] MGM v. Grokster, 380 F.3d 1154 (9th Cir 2004), *aff'g* 259 F. Supp. 2d 1029 (C.D. Cal. 2003), *rev'd*, No. 04–480, 125 S.Ct. 2764 (2005). The court noted the record evidence of commercially significant authorized distribution through peer-to-peer file sharing and held that that distribution constituted substantial non-infringing use under the *Sony* standard.

[102] 380 F.3d at 1166.

> player. Thus, it is prudent for courts to exercise caution before restructuring liability theories for the purpose of addressing specific market abuses, despite their apparent present magnitude.[103]

Disappointed motion picture studios and record labels petitioned the Supreme Court to grant certiorari, arguing that "the Ninth Circuit's decision threatens the very foundations of our copyright system in a digital era."[104] When the Supreme Court agreed to hear the case, consumer electronics and high technology interests reacted with alarm: the *Sony* decision, they maintained, had for two decades protected innovators from overreaching copyright owners. The motion picture and record industries, they believed, had never liked the decision and would use this opportunity to try to persuade the Court to overrule it or severely limit its scope. They showered the Court with amicus briefs; supporters of the studios filed almost as many.

Many of the claims made in the *Grokster* briefs seemed eerily similar to claims that were raised and rejected in the course of the *Sony* litigation.[105] In *Sony*, the studios had argued unsuccessfully that Sony

---

[103] *Id.* at 1167.

[104] Petition for Certioriari at 3, *MGM v. Grokster*, No. 04–480, 125 S.Ct. 2764 (2005). Meanwhile, the recording industry had begun to pursue a different strategy: in the summer of 2003, the Recording Industry Association of America launched a wave of lawsuits against individual consumers engaged in peer-to-peer file trading. *See* Press Release, Recording Industry Association of America, Recording Industry Begins Suing P2P File Sharers Who Illegally Offer Copyrighted Music Online (Sept.8, 2003) *at* http://www.riaa.com/news/newsletter/090803.asp. A year later, motion picture studios followed the recording industry's example. *See infra* note 128.

[105] In *Sony*, for example, the motion picture studios' summary of argument explained:

> Even if it were proper in a copyright case to analogize to the staple article doctrine, that doctrine would not absolve petitioners of liability here. The staple article theory shields the seller of a staple article from contributory infringement liability only if (a) the seller does not actively cause, urge, encourage or aid purchasers to use the article for infringing purposes, and (b) the article is suitable and actually used for *substantial* non-infringing uses. The uncontroverted evidence and the district court's findings establish both that petitioners cause, urge, encourage and aid infringing VTR copying and that VTRs do not have actual, substantial non-infringing uses.

Brief of Respondents Universal City Studios and Walt Disney Production, *Sony*, at 20. The motion picture studios' brief in *Grokster* summarized its argument thus:

> Although *Sony-Betamax* provides a defense to contributory infringement where the defendant sells a staple article of commerce that may be used to infringe but also has commercially significant noninfringing uses, 464 U.S. at 442, Grokster and StreamCast cannot avail themselves of that defense, for two independent reasons.
>
> *First*, *Sony-Betamax* provides no safe harbor where, as here, a defendant engages in conduct that encourages or assists infringement, or intends to facilitate it.

should be required to incorporate a jammer into the Betamax to prevent unauthorized recording.[106] In *Grokster*, plaintiffs argued that designers and distributors of peer to peer file sharing software should be held liable because they declined to design their software to block unauthorized file sharing.[107] The studios in *Sony* had argued that Sony had built its business around the theft of copyrighted material;[108] the plaintiffs in *Grokster* made the same argument.[109] In *Sony,* the studios had pointed to Betamax ads, brochures and instruction manuals that they claimed encouraged consumers to infringe their copyrights;[110] in *Grokster*, the recording and motion picture industry claimed that the distributors of peer to peer file sharing software had "actively encouraged and assisted" millions of people to commit copyright infringement through the design of their software and the promotional materials that accompanied it.[111] In *Sony*, the plaintiffs had argued that less than 9% of home video recording involved programs of the type that might be copied without their owner's objecting.[112] In *Grokster*, plaintiffs insisted that only a miniscule fraction of the copying taking place was authorized.[113] In *Sony*, the studios had insisted "there would be little, if any, market for VTRs if they could not be used for infringing purposes."[114] In *Grokster*, plaintiffs argued that peer to peer file sharing software would not be commercially viable if it didn't facilitate massive copyright infringement.[115]

> Immunizing such conduct would be impossible to square with fundamental principles of copyright and patent law on which the Court relied in Sony–Betamax. . . . *Second*, and in all events, the Grokster and StreamCast services lack "commercially significant noninfringing uses."

Brief of Motion Picture Studio and Recording Industry Petitioners, MGM v. Grokster, No. 04–480, 125 S.Ct. 2764 (2005) (filed Jan. 24, 2005), at 18.

106 *See supra* note and accompanying text; Brief of *Sony* Respondents, *supra* note 105, at 12 n.4.

107 *See* Brief of *Grokster* Petitioners, *supra* note 105, at 32–33; Brief for Songwriter and Music Publisher Petitioners, MGM v. Grokster, No. 04–480, 125 S.Ct. 2764 (2005) (filed Jan. 24, 2005) at 15–16.

108 *See* Brief of *Sony* Respondents, *supra* note 105, at 40.

109 *See, e.g.*, Brief of *Grokster* Petitioners, *supra* note 105, at 43–44; Brief for Songwriter and Music Publisher Petitioners, *supra* note 107, at 10–13.

110 *See* Brief of *Sony* Respondents, *supra* note 105, at 20.

111 *See* Brief of *Grokster* Petitioners, *supra* note 105, at 27–29, 31.

112 *See* Brief of *Sony* Respondents, *supra* note 105, at 48 n.113.

113 *See* Brief of *Grokster* Petitioners, *supra* note 105, at 36–37.

114 *See* Brief of *Sony* Respondents, *supra* note 105, at 50.

115 *See* Brief of *Grokster* Petitioners, *supra* note 105, at 30–36.

Of the Justices who had decided *Sony* 21 years earlier, only three remained by the time *Grokster* reached the Court: Chief Justice Rehnquist, who had joined Justice Blackmun's dissenting opinion, Justices Stevens, who had authored the majority opinion, and Justice O'Connor, who had provided much of the majority's reasoning. Defendants Grokster and Streamcast had made the strategic decision not to contest MGM's assertion that consumers' use of peer-to-peer file sharing software infringed MGM's copyrights,[116] so the private copying issue that had been so vexing two decades earlier was not before the Court.

Plaintiffs sought to distinguish *Sony*, arguing that the Betamax, unlike peer-to-peer file sharing software, had been a legitimate product with predominantly legal uses (conveniently forgetting that the studios in *Sony* had not seen it that way).[117] They urged the Court that *Sony*'s staple article of commerce doctrine should shield defendants only when a product's principal use was non-infringing. Indeed, Petitioners urged, *Sony* should not protect producers of products or services whose commercially viability depended on infringement. Moreover, they argued, *Sony* should have no application to cases in which defendants actively encouraged infringing uses. [118]

Grokster and Streamcast emphasized the benefits of peer-to-peer software and the importance of *Sony* in protecting innovation. *Sony*, they insisted, precluded contributory liability for distributing any product that was capable of non-infringing uses. Any weakening of that rule would undermine the careful balance that the Court had struck. They urged the Court to leave any revision of the *Sony* standard to Congress.[119] The Solicitor General of the United States weighed in, arguing that *Sony* required the courts to compare the relative significance of the infringing and non-infringing uses.[120] More than fifty *amici curiae* filed briefs. The majority of them urged the Court to retain the *Sony* standard, but differed sharply on just what that standard provided.

Toward the end of the term, newspapers, copyright lawyers, and members of the entertainment, information and electronics industries waited nervously for the *Grokster* decision. The Court held it back until the final day of the term and then announced a unanimous decision,

---

116 *See* MGM v. Grokster, No. 04–480, 125 S.Ct. 2764 (2005), slip op. at 5, *available at* http:// www.supremecourtus. gov/opinions/04pdf /04–480.pdf.

117 *See* Brief of *Grokster* Petitioners, *supra* note 105, at 18–19, 30–31.

118 *See id.* at 26–32.

119 *See* Brief for Respondents, MGM v. Grokster, No. 04–480, 125 S.Ct. 2764 (2005) (filed March 1, 2005), at 6–7, 24–25, 40–50.

120 *See* Brief for the United States as Amicus Curiae Supporting Petitioners, MGM v. Grokster, No. 04–480, 125 S.Ct. 2764, 2770 (2005) (filed Jan. 24, 2005), at 14–20.

reversing the Court of Appeals for the Ninth Circuit, but leaving *Sony*—at least officially—undisturbed.

> The question is under what circumstances the distributor of a product capable of both lawful and unlawful use is liable for acts of copyright infringement by third parties using the product. We hold that one who distributes a device with the object of promoting its use to infringe copyright, as shown by clear expression or other affirmative steps taken to foster infringement, is liable for the resulting acts of infringement by third parties.[121]

Justice Souter's opinion for the Court explained that *Sony* had set the standard for imposing contributory liability for the design, production or sale of a product that was suitable for both infringing and non-infringing uses,[122] but that the case didn't displace older lines of authority imposing contributory liability for intentionally inducing third parties to commit infringement.[123] Congress had codified the principle of contributory liability for intentional inducement in the patent statute, and for the same reasons it made sense in *Sony* to adopt patent law's staple article of commerce doctrine, it made sense here to import patent's intentional inducement rule into copyright law.[124] Since the record in *Grokster* revealed ample evidence of "purposeful, culpable expression and conduct," designed to cause others to infringe plaintiffs' copyrights, *Sony* did not shield defendants from liability.[125]

> Because *Sony* did not displace other theories of secondary liability, and because we find below that it was error to grant summary judgment to the companies on MGM's inducement claim, we do not revisit *Sony* further, as MGM requests, to add

---

121 MGM v. Grokster, No. 04–480, 125 S.Ct. 2764, 2770 (2005), slip op. at 1.

122 *See id.* at 2777–78 slip op. at 15. Justice Souter explained that the doctrine announced in *Sony*

> absolves the equivocal conduct of selling an item with substantial lawful as well as unlawful uses, and limits liability to instances of more acute fault than the mere understanding that some of one's products will be misused. It leaves breathing room for innovation and a vigorous commerce.

123 *See id.* at 2779, slip op. at 17:

> *Sony's* rule limits imputing culpable intent as a matter of law from the characteristics or uses of a distributed product. But nothing in *Sony* requires courts to ignore evidence of intent if there is such evidence, and the case was never meant to foreclose rules of fault-based liability derived from the common law.

124 *Id.* at 2780, slip op. at 19.

125 Justice Souter cited evidence that, he said, revealed an unmistakable purpose to encourage users to use defendants' software in infringing rather than non-infringing ways. *See id.* at 2780–82, slip op. at 20–23.

a more quantified description of the point of balance between protection and commerce when liability rests solely on distribution with knowledge that unlawful use will occur. It is enough to note that the Ninth Circuit's judgment rested on an erroneous understanding of *Sony* and to leave further consideration of the *Sony* rule for a day when that may be required.[126]

Only the concurring opinions betrayed the dispute among the Justices as to what *Sony* had held and how that holding should apply to the case before it. Justice Ginsburg's concurrence (joined by Rehnquist, who had voted with Blackmun, as well as by Justice Kennedy) argued that Grokster and Streamcast had failed to show that their software was capable of "substantial" non-infringing use under *Sony*, because infringing uses dwarfed non-infringing ones. Justice Breyer's concurrence (joined by Stevens and O'Connor), in contrast, criticized Justice Ginsburg's opinion as an effort to narrow *Sony*. In Breyer's view, Grokster and Streamcast had indeed proved their software capable of substantial non-infringing use. Nor did he believe the standard should be changed: "*Sony*'s rule, as I interpret it, has provided entrepreneurs with needed assurance that they will be shielded from copyright liability as they bring valuable new technologies to market."[127] The two concurrences reflected the persistent split about *Sony*'s meaning among members of the copyright bar. Justice Ginsburg's narrowing interpretation followed the stingy reading of *Sony* long favored by lawyers for businesses in the entertainment industry, while Justice Breyer's more generous interpretation echoed the broader reading advanced by lawyers for high technology, library and consumer interests. The opinion for the Court avoided the issue entirely, inviting an inference that the Justices were able to agree on a unanimous opinion only by avoiding the invitation to narrow, broaden, clarify or apply the *Sony* rule—whatever that rule might be.

Justice Souter's articulation of the inducement basis for liability seems designed to catch only the most egregious contributory infringers. Some observers, though, have expressed alarm that the test invites extensive discovery about the intent and business models of copyright defendants. This, they fear, will make it easier for disgruntled copyright owners to bankrupt developers of innovative technology by subjecting them to ruinously expensive litigation. It remains to be seen how lower courts will apply it. Meanwhile, at least officially, the *Sony* standard shields other defendants from liability for technology capable of substantial non-infringing use. It will likely be years before we will get a peek at Supreme Court papers and learn what went on inside the Court in *Grokster*, but the opinions themselves suggest that the Justices found

---

[126] *Id.* at 2778–79, slip op. at 17.

[127] *Id.* at 2791 (Breyer, J. concurring), slip op. at 9.

themselves no more able to clarify what *Sony* should mean than the litigants before them, and were able to issue a unanimous opinion only by agreeing to leave the meaning of *Sony* unmodified and unclear.

Conclusion

The initial drafts of Justice Blackmun's majority opinion and Justice Stevens's dissent in *Sony* were elegantly written, tightly reasoned, and clear. The Supreme Court decision, in contrast, is an awkward amalgamation of different arguments and rationales, while the dissent reads like a compilation of passages rescued from a draft opinion for the Court, interspersed with pot shots at each of the majority's conclusions. Reviewing the history of the opinions within the Court reveals that Justice Stevens cobbled together points advanced by other Justices in order to build a majority, and Justice Blackmun turned his original majority opinion into a dissent. It makes for an interesting tale, if one is a Court-watcher or a copyright nerd, but does it tell us anything important about the meaning of *Sony* twenty years later?

Although the Supreme Court voted to hear the Betamax case to decide whether consumer home videotaping violated the copyright statute, the majority of the Justices came to conclude that fashioning the appropriate test for contributory infringement was as important as resolving the legality of home copying. As the Justices struggled to apply the statute to consumer home copying and to draw the lines of secondary liability for purveyors of new copying devices, it became clear that the Court's decision would affect future cases whenever copyright law clashed with new technology. Justice O'Connor in particular appreciated that the task of interpreting the copyright law required attention not only to the protection of authors and copyright owners but also to the encouragement of new technology. In her view, and ultimately in the view of the majority, that concern required the Court to adopt a test that limited contributory liability so that it would not make it illegal to distribute products that were capable of substantial non-infringing uses.

Sony v. Universal Studios is famous for its treatment of fair use. Its fair use analysis, however, proved to be neither workable nor particularly long-lived. Two decades after the *Sony* decision, copyright law still has not resolved how it should treat consumer home copying. Justice Stevens's specter of massive invasions of consumer privacy by the copyright police attempting to enforce the copyright statute against millions of 21st Century William Griffithses has become a real danger. In November of 2004, twenty-eight years after the first suit filed against William Griffiths, motion picture studios did what Jack Valenti had promised they would not do: they filed lawsuits against individual consumers.[128]

---

[128] *See, e.g.*, Twentieth Century Fox v. Doe, 2004 WL 3241669 (N.D. Cal. filed Nov. 16, 2004); Universal City Studios v. Doe, No. 1:2004cv03343 (N.D. Ga. filed Nov. 15, 2004); Metro Goldwyn Mayer Pictures v. Doe, No. 1:2004cv02006 (D. D.C. filed Nov. 15, 2004).

Sony's analysis of secondary liability, in contrast, proved to be as important as Justice O'Connor suspected that it might. More than two decades later, though, the standard the Court adopted continues to be the subject of dispute. Perhaps the *Sony* standard is unclear at least in part because, in an effort to attract and hold five votes, Justice Stevens incorporated multiple rationales into the majority opinion. Perhaps it is unclear in part because the case was tried when the technology was still in its infancy, and its potential to harm or enhance the copyright owner's market was not yet clear. In either case, it seems that the passage of time has not made it easier to identify the appropriate balance. In *Grokster*, the Supreme Court had an opportunity to clarify the *Sony* standard, but was unable to do so. Writing for a unanimous Court, Justice Souter observed: "The more artistic protection is favored, the more technological innovation may be discouraged; the administration of copyright law is an exercise in managing the trade-off."[129] Precisely how copyright law manages the trade-off remains to be seen.

---

[129] *See Grokster*, No. 04–480, 125 S.Ct. 2764, 2775 (2005), slip op. at 10.

6

International Dimensions of Protection

The Story of *Steele v. Bulova*: Trademarks on the Line

Graeme W. Austin*

One of the busiest international borders in the world, the border between Mexico and the United States stretches some 2,000 miles across continental North America. The border is enforced by high walls, barbed wire, and federal agents, and long stretches are demarcated by the Rio Grande valley. However intimidating these symbols of the political divisions between Mexico and the United States might seem, connections between the two nations exist at many levels of the economy: over a decade of lowered trade barriers facilitated by NAFTA, vast waves of migrant workers, established borderland businesses, and a burgeoning small business sector of "borderland entrepreneurs."[1] And, as residents of places such as Tijuana/San Diego, Nogales, and El Paso/Ciudad Juárez well know, culture also crosses the border, and penetrates deep into both countries. On the American side, as one writer has put it, "there is no Customs station for customs—for ideas and tastes, stories and songs, values, instincts, attitudes, and none of that stops in El Paso or San Diego anymore."[2] Fences, guards and guns may be the brutal signs of separated nations; but commerce and culture are persistent catalysts of integration.

* The author thanks Mark Hummels and Isabel Koprowicz, James E. Rogers College of Law, University of Arizona, for their excellent research assistance, and Professors Jane Korn and Bill Atkin and the faculty at Victoria University of Wellington Law School for their insightful comments.

1 David Spencer & Bryan R. Roberts, *Small Business, Social Capital and Economic Integration: Small Business on the Texas–Mexico Border*, *in* The U.S.-Mexico Border, Transcending Divisions, Contesting Identities 83 (David Spencer & Kathleen Staudt eds., 1998).

2 Nancy Griggs, *A Whole New World: Along the U.S.-Mexican border, where hearts and minds and money and culture merge, the Century of the Americas is born*, available at, http://www.time.com/time/covers/1101010611/opener.html.

Trademarks are part of a nation's commerce and its culture.[3] They are also difficult to confine within a nation's borders. The 1952 Supreme Court case of *Steele v. Bulova*[4] concerns the somewhat technical legal issue of the extraterritorial reach of the trademark laws of the United States. It also illustrates some of the tensions that exist between different understandings of the political, cultural and economic divisions achieved by geopolitical borders and different national legal systems in the trademark law context. Conventionally, trademark rights are territorial. Trademark rights do not stretch across international borders.[5] But in *Bulova*, the Supreme Court held that a U.S. district court has jurisdiction over—and that U.S. law could apply to—allegations of infringement of the famous "Bulova" trademark that occurred, at least in part, within Mexico. This affront to orthodox principles of trademark territoriality is one of the reasons the case remains important and controversial.

The physical setting for the district court trial—Bulova filed its case against Sidney Steele in the District Court for the Western District of Texas in San Antonio—is a palpable reminder of the international character of the case. San Antonio is located some 130 miles from the U.S.-Mexico border. With a large Mexican population and a substantial military presence, San Antonio is, and has been for much of its modern history, a city of migrants. The demographics of San Antonio in the late 1940s help us appreciate a key tension that is at the heart of *Bulova* and subsequent cases that have concerned the extraterritorial application of U.S. trademark law: the tension between the territoriality of trademark rights and the reality that trademark rights depend upon what goes on in consumers' minds. We are in an era when consumers frequently travel across international borders, picking up impressions of trademarks and branding strategies along the way. Moreover, the information that consumers receive about trademarked goods and services also travels internationally, flowing across borders in magazines, radio and television frequencies, and now, of course, through the international reach of the Internet. Despite its unpropitious beginnings—a suit filed against a small trader located in the dusty streets of 1940s San Antonio who recognized a possible business opportunity arising from the Bulova Watch Company's failure to register its trademarks in Mexico—the Supreme Court's decision in *Steele v. Bulova* will for some time to come remain an important source for legal principles as courts and policy

---

[3] *See generally* ROSEMARY COOMBE, THE CULTURAL LIFE OF INTELLECTUAL PROPERTIES: AUTHORSHIP, APPROPRIATION AND THE LAW (1998).

[4] 344 U.S. 280 (1952).

[5] A. Bourjois & Co. v. Katzel, 260 U.S. 689, 692 (1923).

makers continue to struggle with how to apply domestic trademark laws in increasingly globalized markets.

The Parties

In 1875, Joseph Bulova, a 23 year old immigrant from Bohemia, opened a small jewelry store in Maiden Lane, in New York City.[6] His business began with the marketing of desk clocks and pocket watches. Joseph Bulova's business was boosted by World War I, when it became the practice to issue wristwatches to military personal. During the War, a wristwatch became a vital item in battle.[7] Perhaps because the War was not fought on U.S. soil, American watch companies were initially quite slow to embrace the new wristwatch technology, initially leaving the field open to Swiss firms.[8]

Bulova marketed the first full line of men's jeweled wristwatches in 1919. A women's line of wristwatches soon followed. Initially, some consumers resisted moving from pocket watches to wristwatches.[9] Despite the widespread use of wristwatches by the military, many men apparently saw them as effeminate. Wristwatches were also not as accurate as pocket watches, whose larger size enabled more robust parts to be used in the watch mechanisms. Changes in women's fashions after the War made wristwatches an ideal accessory. Women's clothing was becoming more form-fitting, and the rising influence of French haute couture made smaller, more elegant wristwatches a more suitable fashion accessory than the bulkier pocket watch.[10] Eventually, men also took to the wristwatch trend, and Bulova was quick to take advantage of these new marketing opportunities.

Bulova's success continued through the 20th century. In 1920, it moved to a Fifth Avenue New York address, and built the first observatory located on a skyscraper, which measured "sidereal" time, which is based on the movement of distant planets and stars. Through the 1920s, the Bulova Watch Company, Inc., as Joseph Buolva's business was named in 1923, developed other manufacturing innovations, including the standardization of watch parts, which revolutionized watch servicing.

---

[6] Details in this section are sourced from information provided by the Bulova Watch Company, Inc. at its website, http://www.bulova.com.

[7] AMY K. GLASMEIER, MANUFACTURING TIME: GLOBAL COMPETITION IN THE WATCH INDUSTRY, 1795–2000 at 141 (2000).

[8] *Id.* at 142–43.

[9] A. Gohl, *The Wristwatch*, BULLETIN OF THE NATIONAL ASSOCIATION OF WATCH AND CLOCK COLLECTORS, Dec. 1977, at 587; D. SAUER, TIME FOR AMERICA: HAMILTON WATCH, 1892–1992 (1992).

[10] GLASTMEIER, *supra* note 7, at 142.

In 1928, Bulova introduced the world's first clock radio. A year later, it secured a patent for automobile clocks, and, in 1931, Bulova began manufacturing the first electric clocks.

After Joseph Bulova's death in 1935, his son Ardé continued to build the company. To compete with Swiss watchmakers, Ardé expanded mass production methods and standardization of watch parts.[11] Another of Bulova's notable corporate innovations was to establish in 1945 the "Bulova School of Watchmaking" in Woodside, Long Island, where severely disabled veterans could learn a new trade.[12] In the late 1940s, the company began work on a "Phototimer," a combination of photo-finish camera and timekeeper, and in the early 1950s it began work on another breakthrough technology, the "Accutron" electronic watch, which Bulova claimed kept time within two seconds a day. At the time of the Bulova litigation, it was, as the Supreme Court described it in 1952, "one of the largest watch manufacturers in the world."[13]

Bulova supported and encouraged its growth in the retail market with extensive media advertising, a point that was heavily emphasized by Bulova in the evidence it produced in the course of its proceedings against Sidney Steele. In the 1920s, Bulova was already taking out full-page color advertisements in publications such as the *Saturday Evening Post*. A 1925 advertisement touted that "Bulova Watches have long been known as the 'blue bloods' of the watch industry—probably because of their regal beauty, their princely precision, their nobility of purpose."[14] By the 1940s Bulova was famous for its advertising slogan, "America Runs on Bulova Time."[15]

Much less is known about Sidney Steele.[16] We do know that, like Joseph Bulova, Steele was also an immigrant. He arrived in the United States around 1921 from Austria, then with the name, "Simon Still." By the date of the litigation, Steele was living in San Antonio, Texas, within the jurisdiction of the United States District Court for the Western District of Texas, where Bulova initiated its Lanham Act proceeding. In the early 1920s, Steele had worked for the United Jewelry Company at a

---

11 *5 Billion Time Signals*, TIME, Dec. 28, 1953, at 48 (a profile article about Ardé Bulova).

12 *School Days at Bulova*, NEWSWEEK, Oct. 22, 1945, at 76; Martha E. Schaaf, *Watchmakers Don't Always Read About Watches*, LIBRARY JOURNAL, Feb. 1, 1946, at 155.

13 344 U.S. at 284.

14 SATURDAY EVENING POST, June 6, 1925.

15 *See, e.g.*, advertising in the December 1948 issue of FORTUNE MAGAZINE.

16 Information about Sidney Steele's life and business is taken from his testimony before the United States District Court for the Western District of Texas, which appears at pp. 78–133 of the Supreme Court Record [hereinafter S.C. Record].

store on Houston Street, a street close to the center of San Antonio that crosses the Alamo River and runs along the northern perimeter of "Alamo Plaza," one of the most famous historical sites in Texas.[17] Steele went into the watch making business on his own behalf in Mexico City around 1933. By the date of the litigation, however, Steele was splitting his time evenly between the United States and Mexico.

From the Record before the Supreme Court, we are able to ascertain a few details about the way Steele operated his watch making business. Doing business as the Sidney Steele Watch Company, Steele imported watches and watch parts into Mexico from Switzerland. The imported watches were branded with a variety of marks, including "Steele" and "Seeland." Others were blank. Steele would remove the original branding on some of the watches and affix the "Bulova" trademark.

During cross-examination, Steele acknowledged that he would change the branding on any of the watches he had imported to "Bulova" depending on the orders he had received.[18] It seems that Steele purchased around four or five thousand watches each year from his Swiss supplier, though it is unclear exactly how many he then sold with the "Bulova" mark attached. Steele admitted selling around two hundred and fifty "Bulova" watches in 1949. Much was made in the proceedings of the fact that Steele also sourced some of the parts he used to assemble his watches, including dials and case, from suppliers in the United States, a fact that was also mentioned in the Supreme Court's opinion.[19] As we shall see, this fact also was relevant to some of the judicial analysis in the case. All of Steele's direct sales, however, were within Mexico, a point that particularly concerned the district judge who first heard the case.

The U.S. District Court Proceedings

On June 13, 1949, Bulova filed a complaint in federal district court against Sidney Steele, his wife, Sofia Steele, and also S. Steele y Compania, S.A., Steele's Mexican business, whose principal office was in Mexico City.[20] Bulova alleged that its products were "extremely well known" throughout the world, including, of course, in the United States and Mexico, and that its products were generally known by the "Bulova"

[17] *See* San Antonio Conservation Society, San Antonio: An Authoritative Guide to the City and Its Environs 48 (1938) (map showing Alamo Fortress Area, in relation to street and plaza lines of 1938).

[18] S.C. Record, at 149–50.

[19] 344 U.S. at 285.

[20] Steele's wife, who never gave evidence, was joined to the proceedings because of her community interest under Texas law. 344 U.S. at 281 n.1.

brand.[21] It sought damages, an injunction restraining the Steele defendants from using the Bulova mark "in any part of the world," and an account of profits. Steele was represented by Wilbur L. Matthews, a prominent San Antonio attorney, who had just a year earlier represented Coke Stevenson in a dispute involving allegations of vote rigging in the primary for a U.S. Senate race that Lyndon B. Johnson eventually won.

Bulova had secured registration of the Bulova mark in the United States in 1927 for "watches, watch movements and watch cases," but, for reasons that never seem to have been addressed in the proceedings, it had failed to register equivalent marks in Mexico. One of the key difficulties for Bulova, and for the lower courts that considered the case, was that in 1933 Steele had himself registered the "Bulova" trademark in Mexico under Mexican trademark law.[22] Predictably, Bulova also applied for an order directing the defendants to obtain a cancellation of the Mexican "Bulova" trademarks, an application that was eventually rendered moot because of parallel Mexican proceedings between the parties.

Though the Bulova Watch Company was the first to adopt and use the mark in the United States and in numerous foreign markets, Steele was apparently the first to register the mark and market watches under it in Mexico. This situation is possible because of the territoriality of trademark rights. Steele was not, however, the first to engage in advertising of the Bulova mark in Mexico. Some of Bulova's own advertising—on U.S. border-town radio stations, for instance—had reached into Mexico. Armed with his Mexican trademark registration, however, Steele argued that, notwithstanding Bulova's advertising expenditure, his marketing of "Bulova" watches in Mexico was entirely lawful.

The district judge, the Hon. Ben H. Rice Jr., was troubled from the outset by the question of the court's jurisdiction in a case involving activity that occurred almost entirely in Mexico, and in which the defendant's principal defense relied on trademark rights secured under Mexican trademark law. On the morning of April 17, 1950, the first day of the proceedings, after hearing the opening statements, Judge Rice closely questioned Bulova's counsel about the jurisdictional issue:

Q: Where are these acts of unfair competition alleged to have occurred, in Mexico alone or entirely outside of the United States?

A: Not entirely outside of the United States, but even if outside entirely of the United States—

[21] S.C. Record, at 2.

[22] In the District Court proceedings Steele defendants exhibited a copy of *Titulo de la Marca, #33802*, the Mexican Trademark registration as an attachment to their answer to Bulova's complaint. S.C. Record, at 16A–16C.

Q: That is not answering my question [. . .].What are your allegations as to the acts?

A: Our allegations say that they reached beyond the United States.

Q: Well, do you expect to prove unfair competition in the United States?

A: We expect to prove that there is unfair competition with our products in the United States and outside of the United States.

Q: You mean to say that you charge the Defendants, and expect to prove that the Defendants committed acts within the United States which resulted in unfair competition?

A: Yes sir.

Q: Affirmative acts done in the United States?

A: Affirmative acts, yes, sir [. . .].

Q: Well, is it merely the fact that he is purchasing some watches and cases within the United States?

A: Yes, sir.

Q: But not any acts done within the United States with respect to sale of those watches?

A: Well, he has sold to United States citizens, who have come back to the United States, and who have brought their watches to [Bulova].

Q: Well, they were acts done or committed in Mexico, were they not?

A: Well, the actua[l] sales took place in Mexico.

Judge Rice then asked counsel to provide authority for the proposition that the district court had jurisdiction in the light of these facts. After further discussion between counsel and the court, during which no clear understanding of the relevant legal issues emerged, Judge Rice concluded that he "had better hear the case and pass on the question of jurisdiction later."[23]

Extensive oral testimony followed, first from Bulova's witnesses, who attested to the usual factual matters we see in a typical palming off or trademark infringement case: the length of time Bulova had been in business, Bulova's significant investment in developing its goodwill, and the extent and scope of advertising and public relations activities. Because of the international character of the case against Steele, the evidence also focused on the Bulova Watch Company's global branding strategies. Bulova's witnesses attested to Bulova's "general effort to make registrations in all the countries of the world."[24] A number of

---

[23] S.C. Record, 38–39.

[24] *Id.* at 63.

Bulova's witnesses emphasized the extent of sales in Latin America, advertising in Spanish-language newspapers, and advertising on radio stations with signals that reached across the U.S.-Mexico border. Through the late 1920s and early '30s, Bulova had advertised its watches on U.S. radio stations in at least twelve border towns, including San Antonio,[25] and one of Bulova's key witnesses attested that the signal from a radio station in San Antonio would "go many many hundreds of miles deep into Mexico, beyond question."[26] Witnesses and counsel were careful to emphasize the extent of Bulova's promotion of the Bulova mark as of 1933, which is around the time that Steele traveled to Mexico to begin the Mexican side of his business.

Steele's theory of the case emphasized the territoriality of trademarks. In the technical jargon of trademark law, his evidence attempted to characterize him as a "good faith geographically remote junior user."[27] The Bulova Watch Company might have been the first in the world to adopt and use the trademark, but, as the first adopter and user in Mexico, Steele argued that he had superior rights in that country. Accordingly, Steele's testimony emphasized that he operated his business only in Mexico, and never sold his watches elsewhere.[28] He introduced into evidence the certificate of his *Mexican* "Bulova" trademark as confirmation of his superior rights in Mexico.[29]

Counsel for Bulova attempted to impugn Steele's claim that he had adopted the "Bulova" mark in good faith. As we shall see, the issue of Steele's good faith was critical in the parallel Mexican proceedings and, eventually, to the Supreme Court's analysis. The questions focused on Steele's practice of removing the trademarks from the watches he bought from Switzerland that were branded with marks such as "Seeland" and "Sidney" and replacing them with "Bulova." But Steele had a ready answer, claiming that through the mid 1940s, his Swiss supplier had sent him watches branded wrongly, *necessitating* the otherwise suspicious-looking behavior of replacing the original brands with "Bulova."

[25] *Id.* at 48.

[26] *Id.* at 52.

[27] *See, e.g.,* United Drug Co. v. Theodore Rectanus Co., 248 U.S. 90 (1918). The Supreme Court held that a good faith geographically remote junior user is not liable for trademark infringement against the first to adopt and use the mark for the same goods within the United States.

[28] S.C. Record, at 162–63.

[29] That some of the evidence was to be given in Spanish challenged even a district court located in a border town. The Record discloses that one of the witnesses apparently spoke "Mexican." S.C. Record, at 133.

He also claimed that the cost of customs duties meant that he could not afford to send the wrongly branded watches back to Switzerland.[30]

Bulova's counsel also sought to establish the extent of Steele's knowledge of the plaintiff's Bulova brand while he was working in the watch business in the United States during the mid 1920s, before establishing his business in Mexico City, and the motivations behind his adopting and registering the Bulova trademark under Mexican law.[31] When asked why he adopted the Bulova mark, Steele continued to assert his good faith, and denied any attempt to take unfair advantage of the reputation that the plaintiff's Bulova brand enjoyed in Mexico:

Q: You put on the name Bulova in Mexico City?

A: That's right. [. . .]

Q: When did you do that?

A: In 1933.

Q: Why did you do that?

A: Because it was open, and I applied for registration.

Q:. . . what did you mean by open?

A: It was open: wasn't registered, so I applied for the registration and got it.

Q: You knew that Bulova Watch Company made Bulova watches, and you had heard about them, and you did that because it was a profitable name. Is that correct?

A: Not in Mexico.

Q: Well, why did you do it?

A: Because I was working with watches right there.

Q: You were what?

A: I was selling watches in Mexico.

Q: You thought that that would be a good name to take advantage of?

A: No: after I had worked hard in it: that's what I why I was trying to bring it up, something in Mexico.

Q: You had no idea, for instance, that the advertising of the International name of Bulova would do you any good?

A: Nobody heard in Mexico about it.

Q: Nobody ever heard of Bulova?

---

30 *Id.* at 148–49.

31 *Id.* at 84–87.

A: No sir, not at that time.

Q: Well, why didn't you take the name of some other name then?

A: Well, I took several different names I registered on watches also at the same time. . . .

And so on. Perhaps the most damaging evidence in the oral testimony, evidence the Court of Appeals for the Fifth Circuit regarded as particularly significant, came from one of the plaintiff's witnesses who had bought a watch from Steele. When the witness complained to Steele of the high price, Steele was alleged to have replied, "[n]ot for a Bulova." The court of appeals suggested that this was evidence from which Steele's bad faith could have been inferred.[32]

The district court did not, however, reach the merits of the case. Before the defendants had presented all of their evidence, Judge Rice announced that he did not believe that the court had jurisdiction over Bulova's claims. Urgent discussion between counsel and the court followed. Counsel for Bulova was concerned to ensure that the court had heard enough evidence, in case the court did have jurisdiction and could determine the case on the merits after all. In the end, however, the court heard no further evidence.

Judge Rice appeared to base his conclusions on the fact that none of Bulova's material allegations concerned acts committed in the United States. He ruled that Steele's actions were beyond the jurisdiction and control of the U.S. government and of U.S. law.[33] Sourcing some of the watch parts in the United States did not constitute use of Bulova's trademark in a way that infringed Bulova's rights. As a matter of law, therefore, Bulova's claims could not succeed. The court dismissed Bulova's case against Sidney Steele with prejudice.

Bulova Appeals to the Fifth Circuit

Bulova fared better in the U.S. Court of Appeals for the Fifth Circuit, which, in a split decision, held that the federal court did have jurisdiction, and remanded the case for further consideration consistent with its holding. Bulova hired more attorneys for the appeal, who, according to Steele's attorney, "pulled out all the stops in attacking Sidney Steele."[34] In his memoir, Steele's attorney recalled that they constantly referred to Steele as "Sidney the Steal." As a tactical legal matter, they also emphasized that some of Steele's "Bulova" branded

---

[32] 194 F.2d 567, 571 (5th Cir. 1952), *aff'd*, 344 U.S. 280 (1952).

[33] *Id.* at 568, n.2.

[34] Wilber L. Matthews, San Antonio Lawyer: Memoranda of Cases and Clients 123 (1983).

watches found their way into the United States, and that this was affecting Bulova's U.S. sales.[35]

The court of appeals based its analysis on a number of theories about the territorial reach of the Lanham Act. First, the court relied on the legislative history of the Act, which suggested that the intended reach of the Act was far broader than previous iterations of U.S. trademark law. As defined in the Act, "commerce" meant all commerce which may lawfully be regulated by Congress,[36] which, of course, is delineated by the grant in the Commerce Clause of the Constitution. The text of the Commerce Clause vests Congress with the power to regulate commerce with foreign nations. That power has been interpreted to include regulation of commerce with citizens or subjects of the foreign power.[37] From this history, the court of appeals concluded that with the enactment in 1946 of the Lanham Act, Congress intended to regulate interstate and foreign commerce to the fullest extent of the constitutional powers.

This did not provide the court with a complete answer to whether those constitutional powers reached conduct in Mexico. The court of appeals drew on a theory that might be described as a "supervisory power" over parties *domiciled* within its jurisdiction. The court reasoned that where a court has personal jurisdiction over parties domiciled in the forum, the court's jurisdiction was limited only where its exercise would involve violation of the law or public policy of the relevant foreign state. The court reiterated the orthodox conflict of laws principle that it had *in personam* jurisdiction over citizens domiciled in its jurisdiction to require them to obey the laws of the United States "even when doing acts beyond its territorial limits."[38] Because Steele was under no *affirmative duty* under Mexican law to exercise his trademark rights, the court reasoned that the exercise of federal jurisdiction "would not conflict with the sovereignty of the Republic of Mexico."[39] Accordingly, in the light of the congressional intention to extend the reach of the Lanham Act as far as the Constitution allows, there was no reason for a court to refuse to exercise jurisdiction over Steele's actions in Mexico.

The court derived its second theory supporting its conclusion that the district court had jurisdiction over acts in Mexico from the special character of trademark rights. To understand the circuit court's analy-

---

[35] *Id.*

[36] 15 U.S.C. § 1125.

[37] *See, e.g., The Trade-Mark Cases*, 100 U.S. 82 (1879).

[38] 194 F.2d at 572.

[39] *Id.* at 571.

sis, it is necessary to outline a few traditional principles of trademark law.

Conventionally, a trademark symbolizes a firm's goodwill. Because a trademark is not a "right in gross," it extends only where the trademark owner uses the trademark to derive custom.[40] Usually this means that, at common law, when the party who first adopts and uses a trademark seeks to expand the geographical area of its business, it may find that its trademark rights are subject to the rights of another party who, in good faith, had previous adopted and used the mark in a remote geographical area. But some courts have held that a second party cannot adopt and use a mark in an area that is within the first party's natural zone of expansion. Part of the significance of the Fifth Circuit's decision in *Bulova* is the court's willingness to apply this principle across international borders. Focusing on the Bulova Watch Company's extensive Spanish language advertising that had reached into Mexico, the court appeared to regard Mexico, or at least parts of it, as being within Bulova's natural zone of expansion. It reasoned: "Bulova Watch Company, at vast expense has built up an asset of good will in the use of its trade mark or trade name 'Bulova', that extends into if not throughout Mexico. If its watches are not actually being sold in that country now, Mexico may reasonably be expected to be within the normal expansion of its business."[41] Though the court of appeals did not make the connection between this principle and the issue of jurisdiction, it seemed to assume that Bulova's potential Mexican market was among the bundle of property rights attaching to its U.S. "Bulova" trademark, disputes over which a U.S. court was competent to adjudicate.

The court of appeal's third theory supporting jurisdiction was that Steele's conduct affected United States commerce. Again, the legislative history of the Lanham Act supported the view that its reach included activity that affected domestic trademark rights.[42] The court of appeals understood Steele's foreign conduct as causing injury to Bulova "within the United States."[43] Evidence of that injury included purchases of Steele's "Bulova" branded watches in border towns. Also, Bulova's Texan representative testified to receiving complaints from purchasers and retailers about Steele's watches, suggesting that Bulova's U.S. goodwill was being damaged by Steele's activities in Mexico. Based on these theories, the court of appeals ordered a rehearing.

---

[40] *See, e.g.,* Hanover Star Milling v. Metcalf, 240 U.S. 403 (1916); United Drug Co. v. Rectanus Co., 248 U.S. 90 (1918).

[41] 194 F.2d at 571.

[42] *See id.* at 571–72.

[43] *Id.*

This reasoning provoked a strenuous dissent from Judge Russell, who considered that the majority had given the Lanham Act an "extraterritorial force wholly unauthorized by the statute."[44] The majority's error was compounded, in Judge Russell's view, because a decision on Bulova's claims would involve a district court in adjudicating the "propriety, validity and legal effect" of the administrative and judicial determinations of Mexican officials.

Judge Russell's concerns went to the heart of the theoretical difficulty of the majority's approach: the overreaching character of the extraterritorial application of the Lanham Act. He regarded the Lanham Act as completely lacking any indication of an intention to "prescribe a standard of fair competition for the Nations of the world."[45] He was also unconvinced by the majority's "supervisory" theory, observing that the Lanham Act does not "so compellingly permeate the being, or saturate the conscience, of an American resident, doing business in a foreign country, as to impose a guilty stain upon his acts there done in accordance with authority granted by such country's laws."[46]

Judge Russell's dissent also emphasized the territorial quality of trademark rights, noting that a trademark has only such validity and protection in a foreign country as the foreign law accords it. Because Steele held a valid Mexican trademark, and none of the conduct for which he might be liable occurred in the United States, Judge Russell would have affirmed the district court's holding that a U.S. court had no jurisdiction over Bulova's complaint.

The Supreme Court's Decision

Noting that the appeal did not require it to reach the merits of Bulova's claims against Steele, the Supreme Court confirmed the remand, holding that there would be no impediment to the district court's jurisdiction to grant an injunction, if that were warranted after hearing all the relevant evidence. The Court emphasized that Congress could regulate conduct by American citizens abroad. Noting that the Court has held that congressional legislation will not extend beyond the boundaries of the United States unless a contrary intention were apparent, the Court saw the issue as being whether such an intention could be found in the Lanham Act.

Like the court of appeals, the Supreme Court emphasized that the Lanham Act reaches all commerce Congress can regulate under the

---

[44] *Id.* at 572.

[45] *Id.*

[46] *Id.*

Constitution.[47] The Court also emphasized that Steele had located parts for his watches in the United States, an activity the Court characterized as involving "essential steps in the course of business consummated abroad."[48] Acts that are legal in themselves, the Court reasoned, "lose that character when they become part of an unlawful scheme."[49]

In one critical respect, the Supreme Court's task was easier than that of either of the courts below. By the date of the Supreme Court proceedings, the Supreme Court of Mexico had upheld an administrative proceeding in Mexico, which is discussed in more detail below, in which Steele's Mexican registration of the "Bulova" mark had been canceled. Accordingly, for the Supreme Court, the issue was confined to whether the Lanham Act could be interpreted as reaching activities that occurred in Mexico, without the added complication of potentially trespassing on the administrative or judicial decisions of a foreign sovereign.

This reasoning did not, however, persuade two dissenters, Justices Reed and Douglas. They saw the issue simply as one of statutory construction: whether Congress intended the Lanham Act to apply to conduct in a foreign territory. There were some areas, such as prohibitions against foreign criminal activity, where an express intention to apply the legislation extraterritorially was not required. Foreign trademark infringement was not among them.[50] The final paragraph of the dissenting opinion adverted to the critical conceptual problem with the Court's approach: extraterritorial application of U.S. law would bring congressional legislation into conflict with the laws and practices of foreign nations. For the dissenting Justices, more explicit language was required before the Court should construe the Lanham Act in a way that would lead to this result.

The Mexican Proceedings

Bulova and Steele were involved in parallel proceedings in Mexico. On November 22, 1950, Sidney Steele received notice that the Secretariat of the National Economy of Mexico had initiated a proceeding to declare null Steele's Mexican registration of the Bulova trademark. The Secretariat's action stemmed from an earlier dispute, apparently[51] initi-

---

[47] 344 U.S. at 286.

[48] *Id.* at 287.

[49] *Id.*

[50] *See* U.S. v. Bowman, 260 U.S. 94, 98 (1922) (no express expression of statutory intention required where the government is exercising its right to defend itself against fraud committed by its own citizens).

[51] The record does not clearly explain the nature of the previous dispute. It appears that Steele requested the Secretariat of Economy in Mexico to declare Bulova's use of the mark illegal because the mark was already being used by Steele in Mexico.

ated by Steele trying to block Bulova's use of the Bulova trademark in Mexico, in which Steele relied on his Mexican registrations. That previous dispute remained pending when the Secretariat initiated action to nullify Steele's registration of the mark.

In the nullification proceeding, the Secretariat of the Economy received evidence that Steele had registered the Mexican Bulova mark in bad faith. Apparently, the source of that evidence was the transcript of the proceedings in Judge Rice's district court. Other evidence of "bad faith" noted by the Secretariat included two copies of contracts for radio advertising of "Bulova" in Ciudad Juarez in 1931, and declarations by several unnamed jewelers in Mexico that the Bulova mark was already known in Mexico before 1933.

Steele then sought review in *amparo,* asking a federal court to block the action proposed by the Secretary of the Economy. The *amparo* action is a federal suit brought by an individual for an alleged violation of an individual's constitutional rights.[52] However, early in 1951, the Secretariat declared that the Bulova mark registered by Steele in Mexico was void because it had been registered in bad faith. Steele then filed a petition to the Second Court of the Supreme Court in Mexico, claiming that the Secretariat's action violated articles 14 and 15 of the Mexican Constitution for failing to provide the reasons and legal basis for the nullification action, for failing to follow proper evidentiary rules, and for failing to provide a hearing on the proposed action. The Court eventually resolved, on a 3–1 vote, that the courts of Mexico would not protect or defend Steele against the nullification of the mark.

Some commentators have criticized the U.S. Supreme Court's decision in *Bulova* for being an imperialistic application of U.S. law to foreign conduct.[53] Had the Court reached the same decision with Steele's Mexican registrations intact, the result would have been a much more overt challenge to Mexico's foreign sovereignty interest in regulating Mexican trademarks. As we shall see, this is an issue that has engaged lower courts deciding cross-border infringement cases after *Bulova.* Courts applying the rule in *Bulova* have been ready to distinguish the case where the defendant in a trademark infringement suit *does* have a valid trademark under a foreign legal system. Moreover, when we take into account the contemporaneous Mexican proceedings, the case perhaps seems somewhat less "extraterritorial." The Bulova Watch Compa-

---

[52] Francisco A. Avalos, The Mexican Legal System 12 (2000); Jorge A. Vargas, Mexican Law: A Treatise for Legal Practitioners and International Investors 60 (1998).

[53] *See, e.g.,* Pamela E. Kraver & Robert E. Purcell, *Application of the Lanham Act to Extraterritorial Activities: Trend Toward Universality or Imperialism?*, 77 J. Pat. & Trademark Off. Soc'y 115, 131–32 (1995) (arguing that U.S. courts should have applied Mexican, rather than American, law to the dispute).

ny was using the legal systems of *both* jurisdictions to ensure that it was able to expand its existing American goodwill in the Bulova brand into Mexico. It might not have been able to secure the finding of bad faith that led to the cancellation of the Mexican trademark were it not for the evidentiary record it established in the U.S. district court proceedings. On the other hand, were it not for the cancellation of the Mexican trademark, it is possible that the Supreme Court might have been less ready to hold that a U.S. district court had jurisdiction over the case.

The Counterfeiting Context

The commercial motivations for Bulova's decision to bring the case are a key part of the *Steele v. Bulova* story. To appreciate what those motivations might have been, it is useful to have a sense of what was happening in relevant consumer markets around the time of the litigation. Bulova would likely have had at least two motivations for suing Sidney Steele. First, like all owners of U.S. trademarks, Bulova sought to protect its U.S. goodwill. The Supreme Court emphasized this aspect of Bulova's claim, noting that "Bulova Watch Company's sales staff received numerous complaints from retail jewelers in the Mexican border area whose customers brought in for repair defective 'Bulovas' which upon inspection often turned out not to be products of that company."[54] This part of the record helped the Court develop the theory underlying its conclusions about the reach of the Lanham Act. From a commercial perspective, unwanted association with inferior products, whatever their source, is a legitimate concern for any trademark proprietor. Through its extensive advertising efforts, Bulova had an established reputation in the United States that it alleged was being damaged by Steele's "spurious Bulovas" coming into the United States.

Around the time that the *Bulova* case came before the Supreme Court, counterfeiting of branded products was being recognized as a significant problem—a "nationwide abuse," as the *Saturday Evening Post* characterized the phenomenon some three years later.[55] Like other manufacturers of prestigious watch brands, Bulova had long been the target of counterfeiters. A *New York Times* article from 1932 noted that since the beginning of the 1930s counterfeit Bulova watches had been turning up in several Atlantic and mid-Western cities.[56] By 1932, however, sales of spurious watches had reached "great proportions." The article discussed the arrest of an organized syndicate of counterfeiters

---

[54] 344 U.S. at 284.

[55] Stanley Frank, *Do You Know What You are Buying?,* Saturday Evening Post, July 9, 1955, at 29.

[56] *Fake Watch Racket Halted by Arrests: Police Seize 6 Men and 50,000 Dials Counterfeiting Those of High–Grade Makers*, N.Y. Times, Sept. 14, 1932, at 44.

and the seizure of around 50,000 fake watches. Bulova continued to fight the trade in counterfeited watches during the following decades. Counterfeiting seems to have been stimulated by the same conditions that gave rise to black markets at this time. A large pent-up demand for consumer goods combined with continuing shortages led, as the *Saturday Evening Post* characterized it, to the "unloading of all sorts of trash, a lot of it under bogus trade-marks which brought higher prices than unbranded merchandise."[57] After the *Bulova* case, counterfeiting continued. Two years later, in 1954, the Illinois Attorney–General's Office uncovered a "national, and possibly international, ring" of counterfeiters that specialized in the imitation of Buolva watches. The Office estimated that 200,000 counterfeit watches had been peddled by the ring. An important target for these sales were military personnel to whom the watches had been represented as new models or factory rejects.[58]

The Bulova Watch Company might well have viewed Steele's activities as yet another instance of this general counterfeiting problem, which, even by 1949, it was well used to fighting through civil and criminal courts. The niceties of the territoriality of trademark law, and the idea that Steele's Bulova's might have been genuine "in Mexico," would likely have been of little concern to Bulova. Bulova would have simply wanted sources of "fake" Bulova watches shut down, whether foreign or domestic.[59]

Secondly, of course, and as the record makes plain, Bulova wanted to continue expanding its goodwill into Latin America. Bulova wanted all the *world* to run on Bulova time. As the Mexican side of the case indicates, Steele was thwarting Bulova's expansion into Mexico by attempting to use his Mexican trademark registration to prevent Bulova's entering the Mexican market. Had Steele been successful, Bulova might have needed to rebrand for the market just south of the Mexican–U.S. border—or pay Steele a significant sum to "buy out" his Mexican trademarks.

Territoriality and Trademarks—The Legacy of *Bulova*

Legal protection of trademarks has long been considered to serve two purposes. First, trademarks help avoid consumer confusion by

---

57 On post-World War II consumer markets, see generally LIZABETH COHEN, A CONSUMERS' REPUBLIC: THE POLITICS OF MASS CONSUMPTION IN POSTWAR AMERICA (2003).

58 *Illinois Uncovers Ring of Counterfeiters Faking Bulova Watches on National Scale*, N.Y. TIMES, Nov. 30, 1954.

59 In 1953, *Advertising Agency* ran a story describing the foreign manufacture of trademarked goods that found their way into U.S. retail streams. Don Wharton, *Made in USA or Somewhere*, ADVERTISING AGENCY, Oct. 1953, *reprinted in condensed form in* READER'S DIGEST, Nov. 1953, at 141.

ensuring that trademarks provide consumers with accurate information about the source of products—albeit often a single anonymous source. Secondly, trademark law protects the value that firms have built up in the goodwill that is symbolized by the mark against free-riding by others.

Both the Fifth Circuit and the Supreme Court saw the issue as essentially one of statutory interpretation: assuming Congress has the power to legislate to control some types of foreign conduct, is the Lanham Act a statute where Congress did that? Viewed in the light of the two purposes of trademark protection, it might seem obvious that Steele's activities should be shut down. First, "spurious" "Bulovas" were finding their way back to the United States, and some purchasers were clearly harmed by mistaken purchases of inferior products. Secondly, if Steele adopted the mark in bad faith, seeking to trade on the fact that Bulova's reputation had reached Mexico before it secured registered trademarks, he would seem to be unfairly "free riding" on the goodwill that Bulova had established. So, what was it about the context of the case that might have prompted Justices Douglas and Reed to resist an interpretation of the Lanham Act that would appear to be consistent with the principal purposes of trademark law?

The answer is the territoriality of trademarks, a concept that circuit courts of appeal have confirmed is "basic to trademark law."[60] Referring to the Court's decision, Justices Reed wrote, "Such extensions of power bring our legislation into conflict with the laws and practices of other nations, fully capable of punishing infractions of their own laws, and should require specific words to reach acts done within the territorial limits of other sovereignties."[61]

To appreciate the dissenting Justices' point, it is helpful to consider some key principles of U.S. trademark law. In the United States, federal registration provides a number of important incidents to trademark rights, such as national priority, notice, and, of course, recourse to federal courts in infringement actions. But federal trademark law is *not* the principal legal source of the property rights in the trademark. Underlying domestic trademark rights is a theory of the territoriality of state law property principles. The federal scheme merely confirms and further protects property that arises under state law. In *United Drug Co. v. Theodore Rectanus Co.,* Justice Pitney reasoned that, "[p]roperty in

---

[60] *See, e.g.,* KOS Pharmaceuticals, Inc. v. Andrx Corp., 369 F.3d 700, 714 (3d Cir. 2004); Barcelona.com, Inc. v. Excelentisimo Ayuntamiento De Barcelona, 330 F.3d 617, 628 (4th Cir. 2003); Pearson's Co. v. Christman, 900 F.2d 1565, 1568–69 (Fed. Cir. 1990). *See generally* Graeme B. Dinwoodie, *Trademarks and Territoriality: Detaching Trademark Law from the Nation–State*, 41 Hous. L. Rev. 885 (2004).

[61] 344 U.S. at 292.

trade-marks and the right to their exclusive use rest upon the laws of the several states, and depend upon them for security and protection."[62] Two years earlier, in a concurring opinion in the equally important decision, *Hanover Star Milling Co. v. Metcalf,* Justice Holmes also emphasized that trademark rights, while recognized under federal law, "are conferred by the sovereignty of the state in which they are acquired."[63] For Justice Holmes, that each state's laws provided the mark with legal protection (as the goodwill of a firm expanded) had implications for the territoriality issue. He reasoned:

> As the common law of the several states has the same origin for the most part, and as their law concerning trademarks and unfair competition is the same in its general features, it is natural and very generally correct to say that trademarks acknowledge no territorial limits. But it never should be forgotten... that when a trademark started in one state is recognized in another it is by authority of a new sovereignty that gives its sanction to the right. The new sovereignty is not a passive figurehead. It creates the right within its jurisdiction, and what it creates it may condition, as by requiring the mark to be recorded, or it may deny.[64]

For Justice Holmes, then, *legal* protection of a trademark was not the same as the *factual* expansion of the goodwill or reputation represented by the mark. Imagine bands of traveling sales personnel spreading out across the United States selling their wares. As the reputation and goodwill in the mark expands geographically through promotion of the brand and sales of goods, the legal systems of more and more states become involved in protecting the trademark. The proprietor of a national brand ends up with a bundle of property rights under each of the several states, which, taken together, protect the brand's expanding national reputation and goodwill.

The role of each state's laws in the national protection of trademarks has become largely theoretical as a result of the passage of the Lanham Act in 1946 and the jurisprudence it has generated. The federal trademark system protects registered and unregistered trademarks more-or-less alike, and is largely unconcerned with the role individual states' laws might play in giving legal life to the property right in "goodwill." Nevertheless, it may be illuminating to consider the facts in *Bulova* through the lens of these earlier analyses. Applying Justice Holmes' approach, (and putting aside for a moment the idea that Steele's

---

[62] 248 U.S. 90, 98 (1918).

[63] 240 U.S. 403, 425 (1916).

[64] *Id.*

actions also did harm *in* the United States), we might want to say that, when Bulova's goodwill expands into other nations, there may *in fact* be a single goodwill attached to Bulova's brand; but, according to the orthodox legal *theory*, the trademark is protected under the legal systems of all the nations where Bulova seeks to have its trademark protected. Accordingly, Mexican law would "creat[e] the right within its jurisdiction." This implies that Bulova, and the district court, should have looked to Mexican law, including *its* rules on priority, good faith registrations, and so on, to determine the rights of the two principal parties in the case to use the trademark *in* Mexico.

None of the U.S. courts approached the case in this way. The district court based its conclusion on the theory that U.S. law did not apply to the activities in Mexico. It was not asked by Bulova to consider the *content* of the relevant Mexican law or to apply it. Had the court of appeals been asked whether Holmes' territoriality theory operated in the international context, it probably would have responded that it did not apply: either Congress had vested the court with jurisdiction under the Lanham Act, or,—and this would represent the clearest rejection in the international context of the relevance of Holmes' approach,—the goodwill in the mark is a single entity, which may be protected in U.S. courts under a single body of (U.S.) law. Likewise, there is little indication in the Supreme Court's analysis that the international expansion of an American firm's goodwill needs any more protection than U.S. law affords, at least when they bring infringement actions in U.S. courts. The Supreme Court's approach in *Bulova* was really the opposite of that of Justice Holmes: Mexican law was not what protected Bulova's trademark in Mexico; rather, by emphasizing the cancellation of Steele's Mexican trademark under Mexican law, the Supreme Court implied that the role of the foreign law was, at its highest, to *preclude* the application of U.S. law.

The concept of territoriality continues to influence lower courts that have decided cross-border trademark infringement cases. Lower courts have never seen *Bulova* as an invitation to apply the Lanham Act extraterritorially in every cross-border infringement action. Indeed, there are echoes of the concerns of Justices Reed and Douglas in some lower courts' approach to the application of the Lanham Act to activities conducted abroad.

The Second Circuit was the first court of appeals to interpret and apply *Bulova*. Four years after the *Bulova* decision, in *Vanity Fair Mills v. Eaton Co.*, the Second Circuit distilled from the Supreme Court's opinion a three-step test to determine when a court could apply the Lanham Act to conduct occurring in foreign jurisdictions. The Second Circuit's analysis seems to limit the scope for application of the Lanham Act abroad. Before the Act applies to foreign conduct, the *Vanity Fair* approach requires the defendant's conduct to have a "substantial effect" on United States commerce. (Interestingly, the Supreme Court itself did not discuss the degree of effect on U.S. commerce required, which, as we shall see below, is a point that the Ninth Circuit has recognized.)[65] Secondly, the defendant needed to be a U.S. citizen. Thirdly, the Second Circuit reasoned that *Bulova* required a determination of whether the extraterritorial application of the Lanham Act would conflict with trademark rights established under foreign law.

The Second Circuit reasoned that the second two parts of the test were more important than the first, and that extraterritorial application of the Lanham Act might be precluded if one of the factors were not satisfied. Absence of two factors might be fatal. This is illustrated by the facts of *Vanity Fair* itself, where two of three factors were absent. The plaintiff was a U.S. corporation that sought to enjoin a Canadian corporation from using the "Vanity Fair" mark in Canada. The defendant held a trademark registered under Canadian law. The Second Circuit refused to grant relief under the Lanham act where a foreign defendant owned valid trademark rights under a foreign legal system.

Much subsequent case law responds to the Second Circuit's analysis in *Vanity Fair*, rather than to that of the *Bulova* Court. The relatively strict *Vanity Fair* test has been constantly refined, both in the second and in other circuits. The Second Circuit itself warned against an "unrefined" application of the Vanity Fair factors in *Sterling Drug v. Bayer AG*.[66] Bayer AG had lost its U.S. rights to the Bayer mark during World War I, when Bayer's U.S. subsidiary, the Bayer Company, Inc., was expropriated by the US government. It retained its rights in other countries. Sterling purchased the trademark rights from the U.S. Alien Property Custodian. The district court had enjoined Bayer AG from using its trademark in the United States and abroad where such use might find its way back to the American public. Bayer appealed. In the court of appeal case, the German government appeared as amicus curiae, contending that the extraterritorial reach of the lower court's decision failed to respect its sovereignty interests sufficiently.

Because two of the *Vanity Fair* factors were absent, this should have been a case precluding extraterritorial application of the Lanham Act: the defendant was German, and held valid trademark rights under foreign laws. Nevertheless, the Second Circuit reasoned that the *Vanity Fair* test might be "unnecessarily demanding" when a plaintiff was pursuing the "more modest goal of limiting foreign uses [of the trademark] that reach the United States,"[67] rather than seeking to stop all

---

[65] Wells Fargo & Co. v. Wells Fargo Express Co., 556 F.2d 406 (9th Cir. 1977).

[66] 14 F.3d 733 (2d Cir. 1994).

[67] *Id.* at 746.

uses of the mark in foreign commerce. The court was concerned that the original injunction might have been too broad, given that it had the potential to reach a great deal of Bayer AG's conduct—even conduct engaged in abroad. It remanded the injunction to the district court for reconsideration. The court of appeals recognized that the *Vanity Fair* test needed to be refined in a case where the U.S. trademark proprietor is not seeking a blanket prohibition against all foreign uses of the mark, but seeks to enjoin only those foreign uses that might find their way back into the United States. The court of appeals left open the difficulty in such cases of determining the significance for trademark rights of uses of marks in foreign media that reach a U.S. audience, such as the numerous copies of the German newspaper *Der Spiegel* that are purchased and read in the United States.

Courts within other circuits have also eschewed rigid application of the *Vanity Fair* three-step test, and have adopted a more flexible approach.[68] The Ninth Circuit, for example, has rejected the three-step test, and instead has adopted a more flexible "rule of reason,"[69] which it borrowed from case law concerning the extraterritorial application of U.S. antitrust law.[70] First, the Ninth Circuit requires only that there be "some" effect upon U.S. commerce, rather than the Second Circuit's more demanding "substantial" effects test. Here, the Ninth Circuit returned to the Supreme Court's analysis in *Bulova*, and noted that *Bulova* did not specify the extent of the effect of the defendant's conduct on U.S. commerce. Secondly, the Ninth Circuit required a balancing of a range of factors to determine whether the impact on American commerce is sufficiently strong in relation to that on foreign nations to justify the extraterritorial application of U.S. law. The factors include: the degree of conflict with foreign law or policy; the nationalities of the parties and the location of the principal places of business; the extent to which application of the laws of either the U.S. or some other relevant foreign nation might be expected to achieve compliance; the relative significance of effects on the United States compared with other nations; whether the defendant intended to harm or affect U.S. commerce; and the relative importance of the violations in the U.S. as compared with the conduct abroad.

---

[68] *See, e.g.,* American Rice, Inc. v. Arkansas Rice Growers Co-op. Ass'n, 701 F.2d 408 (5th Cir. 1983) (some, rather than "substantial" effect on U.S. commerce may suffice); Nintendo of America, Inc. v. Aeropower Co., 34 F.3d 246, 251 (4th Cir. 1994) (adopting a balancing test that assesses the extent of the effect on U.S. interests in the light of concerns for international comity).

[69] *See, e.g.,* Wells Fargo & Co. v. Wells Fargo Express Co., 556 F.2d 406, 428–29 (9th Cir. 1977); Star–Kist Foods, Inc. v. P.J. Rhodes & Co., 769 F.2d 1393 (9th Cir. 1985).

[70] Timberlane Lumber Co. v. Bank of America National Trust & Savings Ass'n, 549 F.2d 597 (9th Cir.1976).

In *McBee v. Delica,*[71] the First Circuit recently decided not to follow *Vanity Fair* in a case involving Lanham Act proceedings brought by an American jazz musician against a Japanese firm that was marketing an "adolescent teenage clothing line" within Japan under a mark that was identical to the musician's name, "Cecil McBee." The Japanese clothing retailer also operated an internationally-accessible website—http://www.cecilmcbee.net—that advertised its products. Its website was created and hosted in Japan, and was written almost entirely in Japanese. Mr. McBee, a serious musician with a long an distinguished career, found the defendant's use of his name, "undignified, highly offensive and repugnant," and testified that American friends and fellow musicians had seen the product line while touring Japan, and had "become confused as to whether McBee had some relationship with a clothing line."

Responding to the plaintiff's claim for damages against the Japanese firm under the Lanham Act, the court contrasted the case before it from cases in which the defendant is an American citizen: in the latter class of case, "the domestic effect of the international activities may be of lesser importance and a lesser showing of domestic effects may be all that is needed."[72] This is consistent with the "supervisory" principle that was invoked by the Fifth Circuit in *Bulova.* In cases involving foreign defendants, the court built on the *Bulova* test, drawing from doctrine that has been developed in cases that have concerned the extraterritorial application of U.S. antitrust law.[73] It reasoned that "the Lanham Act grants subject matter jurisdiction over extraterritorial conduct by foreign defendants only where the conduct has a substantial effect on United States commerce."[74] The substantial effects test "requires that there be evidence of impacts within the United States, and that these impacts must be of a sufficient character and magnitude to give the United States a reasonably strong interest in the litigation."[75] Unlike the Second Circuit in *Vanity Fair*, the First Circuit did not consider that further consideration of comity issues to be relevant to the extraterritorial reach of the Lanham Act, including whether the interests of the United States were sufficiently strong in relation to those of other nations so as to justify the extraterritorial application of U.S. law.

The court in *McBee* characterized application of the Lanham Act to a foreign firm's website that was established abroad and that did not

---

71 McBee v. Delica Co., 417 F.3d 107 (1st Cir. 2005).

72 *Id.* at 118.

73 *See, e.g.,* Hartford Fire Ins. Co. v. California, 509 U.S. 764 (1993).

74 McBee v. Delica, 417 F.3d at 120.

75 *Id.*

purport to sell to Americans as an "extraterritorial" application. In this instance, application of the Lanham Act would not be appropriate, given the paucity of effects of the website on United States commerce. As for the claim for damages for the defendant's Japanese sales, the First Circuit recognized that, in some instances, such activity might "cu[t] very close to the core purposes of the Lanham Act,"[76] on the basis that a Lanham Act defendant's foreign sales might eventually confuse domestic consumers, "thus costing the mark holder sales domestically as well as abroad."[77] In some cases, the court recognized, domestic confusion can often—though not always—be inferred "from the fact that American consumers have been exposed to the infringing mark."[78] In the case before it, however, there was an insufficient factual basis to establish that use of the "Cecil McBee" mark in Japan had led to American consumers even seeing the defendant's products. Nor was there any support for the conclusion that the defendant's activity had caused a substantial effect on U.S. commerce, as might occur, for instance, when substantial quantities of a foreign defendant's goods find their way into the United States.[79]

Flexible approaches that do not insist on strict territoriality may perhaps seem more acceptable to some U.S. courts because of the special character of United States trademark law. In general, the U.S. trademark system bases trademark rights on use.[80] This can sometimes mean that the dividing line between established goodwill and reputation is sometimes quite blurry. In registration systems, property rights in marks arise as a result of official action. One can perhaps see why U.S. courts, viewing cross-border issues through the lens of use-based rights, may not be overly troubled by expanding the scope of the Lanham Act to prevent free-riding on a trademark proprietor's reputation in foreign territories, even in cases in which the plaintiff's reputation is unaccompanied by goodwill in the traditional sense of an ongoing business. Those who are familiar with registration-based systems, where the grant of trademark rights comes more directly and obviously from state agencies, may be more so.

---

[76] *Id.* at 125.

[77] *Id.*

[78] *Id.*

[79] *Id.*

[80] Under the "intent to use" system established by the Trademark Law Revision Act of 1988, Pub. L. No. 100–667, 102 Stat. 3935 (codified as amended at 15 U.S.C. §§ 1051–1127), trademark proprietors can achieve priority based on an application claiming a bona fide intention to use a mark in commerce. Rights are perfected on a filing showing actual use. Lanham Act § 1, 15 U.S.C. § 1051(a)(2) (2000).

Recently, the Court of Appeals for the Ninth Circuit has addressed the opposite kind of fact pattern to that in *Bulova*. That is, under what circumstances will a foreign firm's reputation be protected under U.S. trademark law? In *Grupo Gigante v. Dallo*[81] a Mexican supermarket chain using the name "Gigante" brought an action for trademark infringement against a U.S. supermarket company which used substantially the same name for its Southern Californian stores. The U.S. firm was the first to use the mark in the United States, but the Mexican firm based its trademark claim principally on its prior Mexican use, including in Tijuana, a city that is separated from San Diego only by the U.S.-Mexico border. The court of appeals held that the Mexican company could establish priority of rights in the United States, based on the "famous marks" doctrine.[82] In the first federal appellate decision to apply the famous marks doctrine,[83] the Ninth Circuit reasoned that a foreign trader could establish priority if "a *substantial* percentage of consumers in the relevant American market is familiar with the foreign mark."[84] The territoriality principle prompted the court to adopt a standard that was higher than the "secondary meaning" standard that is applied when the scope of a firm's domestic goodwill is at issue. The court reasoned that to adopt a lower standard would eviscerate the territoriality principle altogether, "by eliminating any effect of international borders on protectability."[85]

[81] 391 F.3d 1088 (9th Cir. 2004). The case was complicated by the application of the laches doctrine. *See id.* 1101–05.

[82] In *Empresa Cubana del Tabaca v. Culbro Corp.*, 70 U.S.P.Q.2d 1650, at *3–27 (S.D.N.Y. 2004), the U.S. District Court for the Southern District of New York upheld the trademark rights in the "Cohiba" mark for Cuban cigars, even where the cigars could not be sold in the United States due to trade embargos, recognizing rights in the United States, applying a "well-known marks" standard. However, on appeal, the Second Circuit declined to reach the issue of whether rights in the U.S. arose under the famous marks doctrine, holding that the Cuban embargo regulations precluded recognition of any acquisition of property rights in the U.S. based on this doctrine. *See* 399 F.3d 462 (2d Cir. 2005) (applying 31 C.F.R. § 515.201).

[83] *International Bancorp, LLC v. Societe des Bains de Mer*, 329 F.3d 359, 362–63 (4th Cir. 2003), *cert. denied*, 540 U.S. 1106 (2004), adopted a "secondary meaning" standard to determine the rights of a foreign trader to invoke the Lanham Act to protect against a defendant that had registered various domain names for websites offering gambling services using variations on the "Casino de Monte Carlo" mark. The plaintiff ran the famous Casino de Monte Carlo and had registered relevant trademarks in Monaco, but not in the United States. Though the plaintiff did not carry on a gambling business in the United States, it had a New York office which offered travel services, which, the Fourth Circuit Court of Appeals reasoned, provided a sufficient constitutional foundation for application of the Lanham Act. The court then applied a "secondary meaning" standard to determine whether the plaintiff's mark merited protection under the Lanham Act.

[84] 391 F.3d at 1098.

[85] *Id.* at 1097.

Sociological and Psychological Challenges to Territoriality

Cases such as *Bulova* and *Grupo Gigante* negotiate a key tension in trademark law, one that is increasingly exposed as trademark issues arise in cross-border contexts: the tension between territoriality as a legal theory and the reality of the way goodwill in a brand gets to be created and expanded. Modern U.S. trademark law sees the source of the legal protection of trademarks as being discrete legal systems, but then uses consumers' impressions of the mark to determine the scope of trademark proprietors' rights. The Ninth Circuit observed: "Commerce crosses borders. In this nation of immigrants so do people. Trademark is, at its core, about protecting against consumer confusion and 'palming off.' There can be no justification for using trademark law to fool immigrants into thinking that they are buying from the store they liked back home."[86]

By adopting a higher standard than is applied in the purely domestic context, the Ninth Circuit appears to be adopting a compromise position between formal recognition of the territoriality principle and a functional approach to the fact that consumers *do* recognize trademarks, even when they are used within foreign territories. The idea that foreign brands might be recognized in the U.S. and that consumers might be confused by unauthorized junior use within the United States perhaps seems plausible when the uses are in contiguous locations, such as Tijuana and Southern California. But the ability of the Internet to disseminate information about brands instantly and globally has prompted legal scholars and policy makers to consider the issue of territoriality with new urgency. Just as tourists and workers flow across the Tijuana–San Diego border, picking up impressions of trademarks on their journeys, web surfers take virtual trips, and are exposed to branding messages from firms in geographically remote locations.

To understand this tension between legal territoriality and the possibility that consumers' minds may no longer be tethered within territorial confines, it might be helpful to return to the setting for the U.S. District Court proceedings that were under appeal in *Bulova*, the city of San Antonio. An "urban bridge that links Anglo and Latin America,"[87] San Antonio is located two hours' drive from Mexico, and many U.S. offices of Mexican firms are located there. The city we know today was built up around the Mission San Antonio de Valero (at a site known now as the "Alamo"), which was founded in 1718. It has been part of seven different jurisdictions during its long history. Before Texas became part of the United States, the Native American Nation, Mexico,

---

[86] *Id.* at 1088.

[87] James F. Petersen, *San Antonio, An Environmental Crossroads on the Texas Spring Line*, *in* ON THE BORDER: AN ENVIRONMENTAL HISTORY OF SAN ANTONIO 17 (Char Miller ed., 2001).

Spain, France, the Republic of Texas, the Confederate States of America all claimed sovereignty over the town.[88]

During the period leading up to the *Bulova* litigation, San Antonio had a highly mobile population. The city was growing rapidly. During the 1940s, the time of the *Bulova* litigation, the Mexican population increased from 25 to 46 percent.[89] In the mid–1940s, some 30,000 Mexicans came to San Antonio each year.[90] In 1947, it was reported that San Antonio sought to become the foremost U.S.-Mexican trading post.[91] Also relevant is that for much of San Antonio's history, the U.S. military has been "omnipresent."[92] City leaders in the 1930s and 1940s embraced the idea that the U.S. military would be the linchpin for the local economy,[93] and Randolph Field, which opened in 1930, became the "West Point of the Air."[94] During World War II, San Antonio was a "uniformed city."[95] After that War, federal military contracts and employment at San Antonio's five bases became the single most important segment of the local economy.[96]

The relevance of the San Antonio demographics to the development of modern trademark theory becomes apparent when we consider the characteristics of the property in a trademark. Property students all know that property rights are as much about relationships between people as about tangible things. But trademarks are perhaps even more abstract, in that the scope of the property rights depends on the mental impressions of the trademarks held by "ordinarily prudent consumers." Through branding strategies and advertising, firms seek literally to alter our minds, by creating a series of mental impressions associated with trademarks: recognition, favorable impressions, and a whole collection of images and ideas associated with the brand. As Judge Kosinski has put

---

88 *See generally* LEWIS F. FISHER, SAVING SAN ANTONIO: THE PRECARIOUS PRESERVATION OF A HERITAGE 13 (1996) (discussing the early history of San Antonio).

89 David R. Johnson, Derral Cheatwood, & Benjamin Bradshaw, *The Landscape of Death: Homicide as a Health Problem, in* ON THE BORDER, *supra* note 87, at 103 (2001); John Hutton, *Elusive Balance: Landscape, Architecture and the Social Matrix, in* ON THE BORDER, *supra* note 87, at 228.

90 *Foreign Trade, The Best of Everything*, TIME, July 21, 1947.

91 *Id.* at 88.

92 *See* Stephanie J. Shaw & Craig E. Cohen, *Battlefields: The Military and the Environment, in* ON THE BORDER, *supra* note 87, at 121.

93 *Id.* at 124–5.

94 Mason Sutherland, *Carnival in San Antonio*, NATIONAL GEOGRAPHIC MAGAZINE, Dec. 1947, at 825.

95 *Id.* at 816.

96 Johnson, et al., *supra* note 89, at 109.

it, advertising of branded products are "well-orchestrated campaigns intended to burn [brands] into our collective consciousness."[97]

Even by the 1940s, the minds of ordinarily prudent consumers who were resident in the San Antonio area were unlikely to be tethered within territorial confines. Instead, we might expect the collective "consumer consciousness" to be a conglomeration of impressions of branded products, impressions that would have come from experiences both within the United States and elsewhere. Now consider the ten million or so people who today live in the U.S.-Mexican border area,[98] many of whom are likely to cross the border regularly.[99] They do not discard the mental impressions and attitudes they have of brands on one side of the border, substituting them with new ones on the other side. They carry their impressions with them, in a decidedly *non*-territorial way. When we think about territoriality of trademarks from an individual consumer's perspective, the concept becomes even more murky: even if consumers don't themselves move across borders, information about brands can come to them through a diverse range of international sources—television signals, satellite footprints, print sources, and, of course, the Internet, all have the potential to cross political borders and reach into the consciousness of consumers situated far away from the geographical source of the information.

International Solutions

The conceptual struggle that underlies *Steele v. Bulova* is not likely to get any easier to resolve as methods of global communication such as the Internet become more widespread. Public international laws offer some solutions. The most venerable treaty regulating trademarks is the Paris Convention for the Protection of Industrial Property Law of 1883, which establishes an international Union for the protection of industrial property, such as patents and trademarks.[100] In some respects, the Paris Convention reinforces the principle of territoriality, by expressly providing that "a mark duly registered in a country of the Union shall be regarded as independent of marks registered in other countries of the

---

97 Alex Kozinski, *Trademarks Unplugged*, 68 N.Y.U. L. REV. 960, 975 (1993).

98 *See* Migration Information Source, *The US–Mexico Border* (July 1, 2002), *at* http://www.migrationinformation.org/Usfocus/display.cfm?ID=32.

99 The Bureau of Transportation Statistics recorded around 800,000 daily border crossings from Mexico to the Untied States in 2000. *See* Bureau of Transportation Statistics, *North American Trade and Travel Trends* (2001) http://www.bts.gov/publications/north_american_trade_and_travel_trends/.

100 Mexico has been a member of the Paris Union since 1903; the United States has been a member since 1887.

Union, including the country of origin."[101] In other ways, however, the Paris Convention impacts on the traditional territoriality of trademark rights. For instance, the Convention gives foreign applicants a right of priority to register trademarks within six months of filing an application in another country of the Union.[102] This allows a period of six months during which entry to markets cannot be blocked by local traders adopting the mark before a foreign applicant has had the opportunity to establish trademark rights in those markets.[103] There are also a number of other international law initiatives meant to streamline the trademark application process.[104] Perhaps most pertinent to the *Bulova* case, the Paris Convention requires member countries to protect "well known marks." For a defined time period, a proprietor of a well known trademark can request the cancellation of the same or a similar mark owned by another party that is used for the same or similar goods. The Paris Convention also provides that marks not be registered if they are the same as or similar to marks categorized as marks that are "well known" in the countries where the new registration or cancellation is sought. The Agreement on Trade Related Aspects of Intellectual Property has adopted the protections for famous marks, and has extended them to services.[105] These protections for well-known marks certainly enhance the prospects of international marketing of goods, and limits the extent to which local traders can take advantage of fame that has been achieved in foreign markets.[106]

---

101 Paris Convention for the Protection of Industrial Property, Mar. 20, 1883, art. 6(3), as last revised at the Stockholm Revision Conference, July 14, 1967, 21 U.S.T. 1538, 828 U.N.T.S. 305.

102 *Id.*, art. 4.

103 Because the United States had traditionally adopted a "use based" approach to trademarks, the U.S. legislation giving effect to the Paris Convention obligation actually put domestic U.S. firms at a disadvantage. Local firms might go through the expense of establishing goodwill in a mark, only to have their nascent goodwill "trumped" by a foreign trader taking advantage of an international priority. Congress addressed this issue with the Trademark Law Revision Act of 1988, Pub. L. No. 100–667, 102 Stat. 3935 (codified as amended at 15 U.S.C. §§ 1051–1127), which enacted an "intent to use" system for registration.

104 *See, e.g.*, the Madrid Agreement Concerning the International Registration of Marks, Apr. 14, 1891, 828 U.N.T.S. 389; Protocol Relating to the Madrid Agreement Concerning the International Registration of Marks, June 27, 1989, S. TREATY DOC. NO. 106–41 (1989).

105 Agreement on Trade–Related Aspects of Intellectual Property Rights (TRIPs Agreement), Apr. 15, 1994, 33 I.L.M. 1125, art. 16(2).

106 It is not clear, however, that this would have helped the Bulova Watch Company: some of its cross-border advertising might have meant that the mark was known in Mexico, but it might not have been "well known." At the time of writing, the Mexican Senate had passed legislation that would make it easier for foreign proprietors to establish trademark

So far, however, public international law initiatives have not addressed some key issues for international intellectual property laws that remain unresolved after *Bulova*. For instance, should domestic courts be more prepared to ascertain and apply foreign trademark laws? In the copyright context, some U.S. courts of appeal have said that trial courts should do exactly this, even if it means dealing with a large number of potentially applicable copyright laws of different nations.[107] In the trademark context, some courts might do more to clarify when application of *foreign* trademark laws by domestic courts would be more appropriate than application of U.S. law, such as might be the case when the plaintiff's real complaint is the defendant's use of a contested mark in a *foreign* marketplace. As we have seen, however, the most recent interpretation of *Bulova* by the First Circuit in *McBee v. Delica* seems largely to reject the relevance of the sovereignty interests a foreign state might have in application of its own trademark laws to conduct within its own territory.

Policy makers are also concerned that traders that put up websites featuring trademarks whose use is perfectly lawful in the country where the trader operates its business are not exposed to trademark infringement litigation merely because the use of the trademark conflicts with rights arising under the law of some other nation where Internet users can access the website.[108] Addressing this question requires policy makers to ensure use of the Internet is not chilled by a risk of trademark liability, while according existing trademarks appropriate protections.

The agenda of the next wave of international initiatives may be to address issues that concern the *interrelationship* between different domestic legal systems. In the trademarks context, an important initiative is the World Intellectual Property Organization and Paris Union *Joint Recommendation Concerning Provisions on the Protection for Marks, and Other Industrial Property Rights in Signs on the Internet*.[109] The *Joint Recommendation* provides a detailed set of principles for determining, in

---

rights within Mexico based on "well-known mark" status. Amending articles 6 and 90 of the Industrial Property Law (Ley de Propiedad Industrial), the new provision would enable marks to be recognized as famous or well-known through administrative action by the Mexican Patent and Trademark Office, rather than through the more expensive and time-consuming judicial proceedings. *See* Senado de la Repúblíca, 108 GACETA PARLAMENTARIA, April 19, 2005, *at* http://www.senado.gob.mx/sgsp/gaceta/?sesion=2005/04/19/1 & documento=28.

107 Boosey & Hawkes Music Publishers, Ltd. v. Walt Disney, 145 F.3d 481 (2d Cir. 1998).

108 On this issue, see Playboy Enterprises, Inc. v. Chuckleberry Pub. Inc., 939 F.Supp. 1032 (S.D.N.Y. 1996).

109 For discussion, *see* Graeme W. Austin, *Trademarks On-Line: The WIPO and Paris Union on the Protection of Marks on the Internet*, 8 N.Z. BUS. L. Q. 92 (2002).

the context of Internet use, what constitutes infringing "use" of a trademark in a particular jurisdiction. Another is the American Law Institute Project on *Intellectual Property: Principles Governing Jurisdiction, Choice of law, and Judgments in transnational Disputes*. Like the Joint Recommendation, the ALI project aims to provide judges and legislators with a set of principles that they might be encouraged to adopt to help govern cross-border intellectual property disputes, and it is hoped these principles will facilitate more streamlined, and internationally-accepted, procedures for intellectual property litigation that involves more than one nation.

Conclusion

In the meantime, without fully-realized solutions of this kind, U.S. courts will need to continue developing common law principles in the shadow of the *Bulova* case. Though *Bulova* is now over fifty years old, the case continues to speak to one of the key paradoxes arising from the property right known as "trademarks." Basic to trademark law, the territoriality principle regards trademark rights as owing their legal existence to the sovereign power of individual nations; but consumers' impressions animate trademark rights, and neither the worldview of consumers, nor the sensory information that influences how these worldviews get formed, is confined within those nations' borders.

For Steele's counsel, the story of *Steele v. Bulova* also distilled a tension between morals and legal principle. In his memoir, Wilber Matthews referred to the "obvious unfairness of Steele's position in appropriating the Bulova name which, even in 1949, was known throughout the world," an unfairness that initially made him hesitant to accept employment in the case. On the other hand, he said, "the contention that a court of the United States could control Steele's business conduct in Mexico permitted under Mexican law and cancel a trademark granted by the Republic of Mexico violated my ideas of logic and the law."[110]

---

[110] MATTHEWS, SAN ANTONIO LAWYER, *supra* note 34, at 122–2.

*

Biographies of *Intellectual Property Stories* Contributors

Graeme W. Austin

Graeme W. Austin is the J. Byron McCormick Professor of Law at the University of Arizona, James E. Rogers College of Law. A native of New Zealand, Professor Austin's teaching, scholarly and research interests include intellectual property, family law, and torts. His publications include *International Intellectual Property and the Common Law World* (co-ed. with C. Rickett), and *Children: Stories the Law Tells*. An advisor to the American Law Institute Project on Intellectual Property: Principles Governing Jurisdiction, Choice of Law and Judgments in Transnational Disputes, he has written and taught extensively on the intersection between conflict of laws and intellectual property. His recent teaching has also included a seminar on Human Rights and Intellectual Property.

Douglas Baird

Douglas Baird is the Harry A. Bigelow Distinguished Service Professor at the University of Chicago Law School. He joined its faculty in 1980 and was its Dean from 1994 to 1999. He is a Fellow of the American Academy of Arts and Sciences, and his research interests include contracts, corporate reorganizations, and intellectual property.

Graeme B. Dinwoodie

Graeme B. Dinwoodie is a Professor of Law, Associate Dean, and Director of the Program in Intellectual Property Law, at Chicago–Kent College of Law. Professor Dinwoodie has also taught at the University of Cincinnati College of Law and the University of Pennsylvania School of Law, and he has taught courses in international and EU intellectual property law at law schools in Poland and Germany. Professor Dinwoodie is the co-author of leading casebooks on Trademarks and Unfair Competition, International Intellectual Property Law, and International and Comparative Patent Law, and has written numerous articles on different aspects of intellectual property law. He holds a First Class Honors LL.B. degree from the University of Glasgow, an LL.M. from Harvard Law School (where he was a John F. Kennedy Scholar), and a J.S.D. from Columbia Law School (where he was a Burton Fellow).

Rochelle Cooper Dreyfuss

Rochelle Cooper Dreyfuss is the Pauline Newman Professor of Law at New York University School of Law. Her research and teaching interests include intellectual property, civil procedure, privacy, and the relationship between science and law. She holds B.A. and M.S. degrees in Chemistry and spent several years as a research chemist before entering Columbia University School of Law, where she served as Articles and Book Review Editor of the Law Review. After graduating, she was a law clerk to Chief Judge Wilfred Feinberg of the U.S. Court of Appeals for the Second Circuit and to Chief Justice Warren E. Burger of the U.S. Supreme Court. At NYU, she served as the director of the Engelberg Center on Innovation Law and Policy. She was also a consultant to the Federal Courts Study Committee, to the Presidential Commission on Catastrophic Nuclear Accidents, and to the Federal Trade Commission. She is a past chair of the Intellectual Property Committee of the American Association of Law Schools.

Professor Dreyfuss is currently a member of National Academies of Science Committee on Intellectual Property in Genomic and Protein Research and Innovation, having previously served on its Committee on Intellectual Property Rights in the Knowledge–Based Economy. She is also a Reporter for the American Law Institute project on INTELLECTUAL PROPERTY: PRINCIPLES GOVERNING JURISDICTION, CHOICE OF LAW AND JUDGMENTS IN TRANSNATIONAL DISPUTES. She has visited at the University of Chicago Law School, University of Washington Law School, and Santa Clara School of Law. In addition to articles in her specialty areas, she has co-authored casebooks on civil procedure and intellectual property law.

John F. Duffy

John F. Duffy is a Professor of Law at the George Washington University Law School. Professor Duffy received an A.B. in physics from Harvard College in 1985 and a J.D. from the University of Chicago in 1989. He was awarded an Olin Fellowship in Law and Economics at the University of Chicago and served as Articles Editor on the University of Chicago Law Review. Prior to entering academics, Professor Duffy clerked for Stephen Williams on the United States Court of Appeals for the D.C. Circuit and for Justice Scalia on the United States Supreme Court, served as an Attorney–Advisor in the Department of Justice's Office of Legal Counsel, and practiced law with the Washington firm of Covington & Burling. Professor Duffy has taught at the Cardozo School of Law (1996–2000), the William & Mary Law School (2000–2003), the

University of Chicago Law School (visiting, winter and spring of 2003), and the New York University School of Law (visiting, spring 2005).

Professor Duffy teaches patent law and is the co-author of a casebook on the subject, Patent Law and Policy (3rd ed. 2002) (with Robert Patrick Merges). He has published articles on regulatory law and intellectual property in the Texas Law Review, the Columbia Law Review, Supreme Court Review, the Berkeley Journal of Law and Technology, and the University of Chicago Law Review.

Rebecca S. Eisenberg

Rebecca S. Eisenberg is the Robert and Barbara Luciano Professor of Law at the University of Michigan Law School. She has written and lectured extensively about biotechnology patent law and the role of intellectual property in research science and has played an active role in policy debates concerning intellectual property in biomedical research. Professor Eisenberg currently teaches patent law, trademark law, and FDA law and has taught courses on torts, legal regulation of science and legal issues in biomedical research. She serves on the Panel on Science, Technology and Law of the National Academies of Science and is a member of the Committee on Intellectual Property in Genomic and Protein Research and Innovation of the National Research Council.

Jane C. Ginsburg

Jane C. Ginsburg is the Morton L. Janklow Professor of Literary and Artistic Property Law at Columbia University School of Law, and Co–Director of its Kernochan Center for Law, Media and the Arts. She teaches Legal Methods, Copyright Law, and Trademarks Law, and is the author or co-author of Foundation Press casebooks in all three subjects, as well as, with Professor Robert P. Merges, of FOUNDATIONS OF INTELLECTUAL PROPERTY. With Professor Rochelle Dreyfuss, she is a Co–Reporter for the American Law Institute project on INTELLECTUAL PROPERTY: PRINCIPLES GOVERNING JURISDICTION, CHOICE OF LAW AND JUDGMENTS IN TRANSNATIONAL DISPUTES.

Professor Ginsburg has taught French and U.S. copyright law and U.S. legal methods and contracts law at the University of Paris and other French universities. In 2004–05 she held the Arthur L. Goodhart Visiting Chair of Legal Science at the law faculty of the University of Cambridge, UK. A graduate of the University of Chicago (BA 1976, MA 1977), she received a JD in 1980 from Harvard, and a Diplôme d'études approfondies in 1985 and a Doctorate of Law in 1995 from the University of Paris II.

Craig Joyce

Craig Joyce, B.A., Dartmouth College; M.A., Oxford University; J.D., Stanford University. Joyce is Andrews Kurth Law Center Professor of

Law, and Co–Director, Institute for Intellectual Property & Information Law, at the University of Houston Law Center, where he teaches copyright, advanced copyright seminar, American legal history, and torts. He is a member of the American Law Institute and the International Association for the Advancement of Teaching and Research in Intellectual Property, a member of the boards of the Journal of the Copyright Society of the U.S.A., the Journal of Supreme Court History, and H-Law (the Humanities Social Sciences Online Discussion Network of the American Society for Legal History), and the lead co-author of a well-known casebook on the law of copyright.

Jessica Litman

Jessica Litman teaches copyright law, Internet law, and trademarks and unfair competition law at Wayne State University Law School in Detroit. She is the author of DIGITAL COPYRIGHT (Prometheus 2001) and the coauthor with Jane Ginsburg and Mary Lou Kevlin of TRADEMARKS AND UNFAIR COMPETITION LAW: CASES AND MATERIALS (Foundation 2001). She has published many articles on intellectual property topics, including *Breakfast with Batman: The Public Interest in the Advertising Age*, 108 YALE L.J. 1717 (1999), *Information Privacy/Information Property*, 52 STANFORD L. REV. 1283 (2000), and *The Public Domain*, 39 EMORY L.J. 965 (1990).

Robert P. Merges

Professor Merges is Wilson Sonsini Goodrich & Rosati Professor of Law and Technology at U.C. Berkeley (Boalt Hall) School of Law, and a co-Director of the Berkeley Center for Law and Technology, centerpiece of the top-rated Intellectual Property program among U.S. law schools. He is the co-author of leading casebooks on patent law and intellectual property, and has written numerous articles on the economics of intellectual property, in particular patent law. Professor Merges has worked with government agencies such as the Department of Justice and the Federal Trade Commission on IP-related policy issues. He has also consulted with leading law firms and companies. He received his B.S. from Carnegie–Mellon University, a J.D. from Yale Law School, and LL.M. and JSD degrees from Columbia Law School.

Maureen A. O'Rourke

On July 1, 2004, Professor Maureen O'Rourke was appointed Dean ad interim of the Boston University School of Law. She joined the faculty of the School of Law in 1993 after working at IBM Corporation, where she handled a variety of issues surrounding software licensing. The intersection of intellectual property law and other fields, such as contract law and antitrust, has long been her primary interest. In addition to teaching courses in commercial law and intellectual property law, Dean O'Rourke helps supervise the student-run Journal of Science and Technology Law. In May 2000, she became the School's sixth recipient of the Metcalf Award, the University's highest teaching honor. Dean O'Rourke graduated from Marist College with a B.S., summa cum laude, and received her J.D. with honors in all courses, from Yale Law School. She has published articles in the law reviews of Columbia, Duke, Iowa, and Minnesota, the technology journals of Berkeley, Harvard, and Boston University and other publications including the Journal of the Copyright Society. She also co-authored the casebook Copyright in a Global Information Economy.

R. Anthony Reese

R. Anthony Reese is Thomas W. Gregory Professor of Law at The University of Texas at Austin. He teaches courses on intellectual property, copyright, trademark, intellectual property theory and intellectual property in cyberspace, and regularly teaches in the Masters of Business Law program of the University of St. Gallen (Switzerland) and the Joint International IP Law Summer Program. He has written extensively on copyright and the Internet. Before entering academics, he served as a law clerk to the Honorable Betty B. Fletcher of the United States Court of Appeals for the Ninth Circuit, practiced law, and was a Research Fellow for the Program in Law, Science and Technology at Stanford Law School. Prof. Reese is also Special Counsel to the law firm of Morrison & Foerster LLP. He received his B.A. degree in Russian Language and Literature from Yale University and earned his J.D. degree from Stanford University.

Pamela Samuelson

Pamela Samuelson is a Chancellor's Professor of Information Management and of Law at the University of California at Berkeley, as well as a Director of the Berkeley Center for Law & Technology and an advisor to the Samuelson High Technology Law & Public Policy Clinic at Boalt Hall. She teaches courses on intellectual property, cyberlaw and information policy. She has written and spoken extensively about the challenges that new information technologies pose for traditional legal regimes, especially for intellectual property law. She is a Fellow of the Association for Computing Machinery (ACM), a Contributing Editor of Communications of the ACM, a past Fellow of the John D. & Catherine T. MacArthur Foundation, and an Honorary Professor of the University of Amsterdam. She is a member of the Board of Directors of the Electronic Frontier Foundation and of the Open Source Application Foundation, as well as a member of the Advisory Board for the Electronic Privacy Information Center.

A 1971 graduate of the University of Hawaii and a 1976 graduate of Yale Law School, Samuelson practiced law as a litigation associate with the New York law firm Willkie Farr & Gallagher before turning to academic pursuits. From 1981 through June 1996 she was a member of the faculty at the University of Pittsburgh Law School, from which she visited at Columbia, Cornell, and Emory Law Schools. She has been a member of the Berkeley faculty since 1996.

John R. Thomas

Jay Thomas is Professor of Law at Georgetown University in Washington, DC. He recently received a grant from the John D. and Catherine T. MacArthur Foundation in order to continue his work as Visiting Scholar at the Congressional Research Service. In addition to journal articles concerning intellectual property law, his publications include a hornbook on intellectual property, a treatise on pharmaceutical patents, and both a textbook and casebook on patent law. He previously served as law clerk to Chief Judge Helen W. Nies of the U.S. Court of Appeals for the Federal Circuit. Professor Thomas holds a B.S. in Computer Engineering from Carnegie Mellon, a J.D. *magna cum laude* from the University of Michigan, and an LL.M. with highest honors from George Washington University.

Diane Leenheer Zimmerman

Diane Leenheer Zimmerman is Samuel Tilden Professor of Law at New York University School of Law. She graduated magna cum laude from Beaver College in Pennsylvania, studied English and Comparative Literature at the Graduate Faculty of Columbia University, and worked at Newsweek Magazine and the New York Daily News as a journalist before attending law school. Professor Zimmerman received her J.D. with honors from Columbia University in 1976, and went on to clerk for the Honorable Jack B. Weinstein in the United States District Court, Eastern District of New York, before joining the NYU faculty. Professor Zimmerman is a Trustee of the Copyright Society of the U.S.A. and a member of the editorial board of its journal. She writes and lectures extensively on intellectual property, the first amendment, and on gender issues. Professor Zimmerman served as the Reporter on Gender for the Second Circuit Task Force on Gender, Racial and Ethnic Fairness. She co-edited "Expanding the Bounds of Intellectual Property" (Oxford University Press) with Rochelle Dreyfuss and Harry First. Professor Zimmerman was the inaugural Hosier Distinguished Visiting Professor in Intellectual Property at DePaul University College of Law and has served as the Distinguished Lee Visiting Professorship at the College of William & Mary. In 2004, she delivered the 17th annual Horace S. Manges Lecture on copyright at Columbia.

†